International Food Law

Energy and Environmental Law and Policy Series

VOLUME 40

Editor

General Editor: Professor Kurt Deketelaere, Professor of Law, University of Leuven, Belgium; Honorary Professor of Law, University of Dundee, UK; Honorary Chief of Staff, Flemish Government; Secretary-General, League of European Research Universities (LERU), Belgium. Kurt's CV – see www.kurtdeketelaere/en/kurt.

Introduction

Environmental protection and energy efficiency/security are important societal challenges. In order to tackle them, policy and legal frameworks are developed at national, regional and global level. Through study and best practices development, the challenges will prove to be solvable.

Contents/Subjects

Environment/Nature/Energy/Climate.

Objective

The aim of this series is to publish works of excellent quality that focus on the study of energy and environmental policy. Through this series the editors:

- contribute to the improvement of the quality of energy/environmental law and policy in general and environmental quality and energy efficiency in particular; increase the access to environmental and energy information for academics, non-governmental organizations, government institutions, and business; and
- facilitate cooperation between academic and non-academic communities in the field of energy and environmental law and policy throughout the world.

Readership

Academics and practitioners in environmental and energy matters.

The titles published in this series are listed at the end of this volume.

International Food Law

How Food Law Can Balance Health, Environment and Animal Welfare

Edited by

Cinzia Caporale
Ilja Richard Pavone
Maria Pia Ragionieri

Wolters Kluwer

Published by:
Kluwer Law International B.V.
PO Box 316
2400 AH Alphen aan den Rijn
The Netherlands
E-mail: international-sales@wolterskluwer.com
Website: lrus.wolterskluwer.com

Sold and distributed by:
Wolters Kluwer Legal & Regulatory U.S.
7201 McKinney Circle
Frederick, MD 21704
United States of America
Email: customer.service@wolterskluwer.com

ISBN 978-94-035-1761-2

e-Book: ISBN 978-94-035-1812-1
web-PDF: ISBN 978-94-035-1860-2

Editors

Cinzia Caporale is head of the Interdepartmental Center for Research Ethics and Integrity at the National Research Council of Italy (CNR). She is also the coordinator of the CNR Research Ethics and Bioethics Committee and represents CNR on these topics at the international level. She is Adjunct Professor of Bioethics at Sapienza University of Rome and since 2002 she has been a member of the Italian Bioethics Committee (appointed by the President of the Council of Ministers). She is the President of the Ethics Committee of L. Spallanzani National Institute for Infectious Diseases (Institute of Hospitalization and Care with a scientific character) and of the Italian Ethics Committee for COVID-19 studies and clinical trials; she is also a member of the government's Technical-Scientific Committee on the pandemic emergency (advisory board). She is a member of the Scientific Committee of the Courtyard of the Gentiles (Pontifical Council for Culture, Vatican), of the Italian Veterinary and Agri-Food Bioethics Committee, of the Research Integrity Committees of Sapienza University of Rome and of the University of Bologna, and Honorary President of the Umberto Veronesi Foundation Ethics Committee. She has been the Chairperson of UNESCO's Intergovernmental Bioethics Committee for two mandates. Under her presidency, the Universal Declaration on Bioethics and Human Rights was elaborated and adopted. She is the founder and Co-Director of the scientific journal *The Future of Science and Ethics* (ISSN 2421-3039) and a member of the Editorial Advisory Board of the *Journal of Medicine and Philosophy* (ISSN 0360-5310) and of *BioLaw Journal – Rivista di BioDiritto* (ISSN 2284-4503). She was the Scientific Editor of the volume *Europe and Scientific Research* edited by Treccani (2018).

Ilja Richard Pavone National Research Council of Italy, Researcher at the Interdepartmental Center for Research Ethics and Integrity, Rome, and Professor of European Law and Biotechnologies, Catholic University of the Sacred Hearth, Rome.

Ilja Richard Pavone gained his PhD in International Law and Human Rights at Sapienza University of Rome. He is a researcher of International Law at the National

Research Council of Italy, Rome, where he coordinates the research unit in International, European and National Biolaw. He is a member of the Bioethics Veterinary and Agri-Food Bioethics Committee. He is also a member of the Coordinating Committees of the European Society of International Law (ESIL) Interest Groups on Peace & Security and International Bio Law. In the past, he has taught at the universities the Sapienza University of Rome, Venice (Venice International University), Macerata, Siena and Viterbo. He has been a visiting professor at Queensland University, Bochum University and Max Planck Institute for Comparative Public Law and International Law (Heidelberg). He is the author of over fifty publications, essays and articles in International Law and European Union Law, with a particular focus on Bioethics, Human Rights, Animal Law, International Health Law and Environmental Protection. He is also a member of the Scientific Board of the journal *The Future of Science and Ethics*, published by the Fondazione Umberto Veronesi, and a member of the Editorial Team of *Biolaw Journal – Rivista di Biodiritto*.

Maria Pia Ragionieri is Full Professor of Environmental Law at University La Tuscia, Viterbo; Adjunct Professor of Food and Agricultural Law at LUISS University; Director of the LLM in Food Law, LUISS; European Professor J Monnet.

Maria Pia Ragionieri holds a degree in Law, Sapienza University of Rome, 1978, with final mark 110/110 cum laude; she was Solicitor at the Appeal Court in Rome, 1981 and Lawyer since 1987 registered in the Registry of Lawyers of Roma, qualified to practise in the Supreme Court of Cassation. She has a PhD in Italian and Comparative Agrarian Law, 1989. She is the winner of the European competition for the assignment of the Jean Monnet teaching posts in 2004, holder of the European Jean Monnet teaching post in 'European law of biotechnology', Università della Tuscia, Viterbo. She has been the first level full professor (professore straordinario) in Agrarian Law at Università degli Studi della Tuscia since 2006, Confirmed Full Professor (professore ordinario) in Agrarian Law at Università degli Studi della Tuscia since 2010. She also teaches agri-food law at LUISS School of Law (Rome) and she is co-director of the LLM in Food Law, LUISS School of Law.

Contributors

Francesco Alicino is Professor of Constitutional Law, Public Comparative Law, Ecclesiastical Law and Canon Law at the University of LUM 'Jean Monnet', Casamassima, Bari, Italy. He is also Professor at the MISLAM (Academic Master) of the School of Government (LUISS 'Guido Carli', Rome). He is a member of the academic staff of the Institute of S. Pio V., Rome. In 2008 he took his PhD at the 'école doctorale en droit', University Aix-Marseille III, Paul Cézanne, France. In 2008, he took his degree in 'formation doctorale européenne en droit canonique et droit des relations religions Etats', University of Paris-Sud 11 and Catholic Institute of Paris, France. In 2004 he obtained a post in a PhD course in Institutions and Comparative Politics at the University of Bari, Italy, resulting first in the relating competitive examination. He is a reviewer for international journals and has been involved in several international conferences and in international and national research projects. He is the author of several books and articles in English, Italian and French.

Francesca Allocco is a lawyer based in Italy. She earned a Master's in Environmental and Land Law from Ca' Foscari University in Venice. She is an associate of Ambientalex, an Italian law firm providing legal advice in environmental law.

Francesca counsels on environmental litigation, environmental compliance, including authorization procedures, focusing on agriculture and food.

Daria Boklan works at National Research University Higher School of Economics, Moscow, Russia, at International Public and Private Law Department, Faculty of Law and teaches Environmental Law, World Trade Organization (WTO) Law, Law of the Eurasian Economic Union and General International Law. She is part-time Professor at MGIMO University (Moscow State University of International Relations) teaching WTO Law. She has previously taught WTO Law and General International Law at Russian Foreign Trade Academy, International Economic Law at Moscow State University, Moscow and WTO Law at Russian State University of Justice. Professor Boklan is an expert in WTO law, international environmental law and law of the Eurasian Economic

Union (EAEU) with a special focus on interaction of international trade law and international environmental law.

Margherita Brunori is a post-doctoral research fellow at the Department of Sociology and Social Research at the University of Trento, Italy. She is a specialist in agri-food law and policy, and she worked on equitable access to natural resources, corporate responsibility and economic, cultural and social rights. She is the operational focal point of the working group on food of the Italian University Network for Sustainability.

Daniela Corona is currently a lecturer at the LUISS School of Law in Rome where she is also the scientific coordinator of LLM in Food Law. Before joining the LUISS School of Law, she was a senior lecturer at the College of Europe in Bruges. A former researcher of the Robert Schuman Center at the European University Institute in Florence, where she completed her PhD in Law in 2011, she also worked as a legal adviser at the European Parliament. She is the author of articles and contributions dealing with European institutions and policies, and she teaches as visiting professor in Italian and European Universities.

Justo Corti Varela is a faculty member of the Public International Law Department at Spanish National Open University (Universidad Nacional de Educacion a Distancia). He holds the official accreditation as Associate Professor by the Ministry Agency. He was a post-doctoral research fellow at the Centre National de la Recherche Scientifique (2008), a visiting scholar at University College London (2007), a visiting professor at Université de Nanterre - Paris X (2013-2016), and a visiting scholar at Scoula Superiore Sant'Anna - Pisa (2016). He is a member of the Editorial Board of the Journal *Revista de Derecho Comunitario Europeo* (Social Sciences Citation Index) and of the Review 'Ius et Scientia', and a member of the board of the Interest Group on International Bio Law at the ESIL.

Dr Khaled Eltaweel is an Egyptian diplomat and the former chair of the United Nations Committee on Food Security (CFS) Open Ended Group on Nutrition. During his chairmanship (2015-2018), he led the negotiations for the development of the CFS Policy on Nutrition, the CFS contribution to the UN Decade of Action on Nutrition as well as the Terms of Reference for the Policy convergence work on Nutrition and Food Systems. Dr Eltaweel has been elected for several positions in the UN organizations, including chairing Committee on Commodity Problems (CCP) (2016-2018) and being elected as Vice-President of the group of G77 and China in 2017. He has a PhD in International Law from the University of Pretoria, South Africa and a Master's in International Business Administration from ESLSCA Business school in Paris.

Luchino Ferraris graduated from the University of Milan, School of Law, Italy, in 2014 with a dissertation on the Relationship Between Human Rights and the Environment. He holds an LLM in 'Global Environment and Climate Change Law' at the University of Edinburgh, School of Law, United Kingdom. After several collaborations with law firms and NGOs in the field of food and agricultural law, particularly from a European legal perspective, he obtained a PhD at the Sant'Anna School of Advanced Studies of Pisa with a dissertation on sustainable agriculture in European Union free trade agreements in 2020. He is also Legal Officer at the Directorate General 'Agriculture and Rural Development' (DG AGRI) of the European Commission. He has made many publications in the field of European and national agriculture, food and environmental law.

Alberto Germanò is a Former Judge of the Court of Cassation (Chief Prosecutor at Minors Court in Florence) and Former Full Professor of Comparative Agricultural Law at Sapienza University of Rome. He was a member of: the Government Commission on milk quotas; the milk quota guarantee Commission; the administrative enquiry Commission to verify the correctness of the milk-fat estimation method. He was also a member of: the ministerial study group on reorganization and simplification of agricultural legal regulation; ministerial working group for the modification of the 2001 national decrees on agricultural farming; the ministerial working group on the implementation of national rules on Common Agricultural Policy medium-term reform. He was a ministerial coordinator for drawing up schemes on: a complete (ten books) 'Agricultural Code' (2004); the rearrangement of the agricultural farming discipline (2010); a short (134 articles) 'Agricultural Code' (2009-2011). He was also a legal advisor to the Department of Agriculture of the Tuscany Region for the drafting of a proposal for the reorganization and simplification of the rules for a new Agricultural Code (2017). He was Secretary General of the International and Comparative Agricultural Institute of Florence (IDAIC) from 7 March 1998 to 2 March 2017.

Pier Filippo Giuggioli is Associate Professor of Private Comparative Law at the University of Milan, Italy, specialized in consumer protection, Responsible for the assignation of the UNESCO Chair on 'Food: Access and Law' at the University of Milan, Director of the Specialization course on 'Nutrition: Health, Law and Market' at the University of Milan, Editor-in-chief of the Series 'Comparative Commercial Law' edited by CEDAM.

Tom Heilandt is a UN Diplomat with twenty-four years of experience in different fields of international legislation. He is now responsible for the UN organization dealing with food standards: Codex Alimentarius and skilled in leading a team of highly skilled senior professionals; facilitating international meetings and negotiating solutions for international food trade. He is experienced in building international networks of government and private sector representatives to work on common goals.

Dr Jill E. Hobbs is Professor in the Department of Agricultural and Resource Economics at the University of Saskatchewan, Canada. Her research focuses on food policy, consumer behaviour, and supply chain economics. Her work has examined a range of issues, including the regulation of healthy foods, consumer trust, food safety and quality, and traceability in agri-food supply chains. She is a co-author of the book *Regulating Health Foods: Policy Challenges and Consumer Conundrums* (Edward Elgar Publishing Ltd.) and has authored a number of papers on various aspects of food regulation, including labelling, biotechnology, food safety, and traceability. Professor

Hobbs is a former president of the Canadian Agricultural Economics Society. She served as co-editor of the *Canadian Journal of Agricultural Economics* from 2013 to 2016 and currently serves on the board of directors of several academic journals. She was appointed to an honorary chair in the School of Business and Management at Aberystwyth University (2014-2019) and became a Fellow of the Canadian Agricultural Economics Society in 2017. Dr Hobbs holds a PhD in Agricultural Economics from the University of Aberdeen in Scotland.

Gijs A. Kleter has been with Wageningen Food Safety Research since 1999. This institute is part of Wageningen University & Research Centre in the Netherlands. His particular field of expertise within food safety science is the safety of genetically modified food and feed. Besides advising national authorities on the safety of genetic modification applied to foods and animal feed, he has served, for example, on the European Food Safety Authority's Expert Panel on Genetically Modified Organisms (EFSA GMO Panel) as a member and vice-chair. Other committee and extension activities include work on the biosafety of GMOs within organizations such as the Organisation for Economic Co-operation and Development (OECD) and the United Nations Industrial Development Organization (UNIDO). He also leads and takes part in various projects on safety of biotechnology applied to food production, such as for the International Union for Pure and Applied Chemistry (IUPAC).

Harry A. Kuiper is a retired principal scientist and former department head at Wageningen Food Safety Research, part of Wageningen University & Research Centre in the Netherlands. Following an MSc in Food Science, he completed a PhD in biochemistry in 1976, and subsequently pursued a post-doctoral fellowship in Rome, before continuing his career at the Dutch Ministry of Agriculture and Wageningen Food Safety Research, from which he retired in 2006. This way he was able to build strong and wide-ranging background expertise in food toxicology, biochemistry, molecular biology, and food and feed safety assessment, among others, and he has led various large national and EU-funded research projects on food safety and chaired various international expert consultations. He served on the EU Scientific Committee on Plants for six years before moving over the European Food Safety Authority's Panel of Experts on Genetically Modified Organisms in 2003, which he chaired for three consecutive terms, until 2012. As such, he has built ample experience with the safety assessment of biotechnology and its regulatory and policy context.

Dr Stavroula Malla is Associate Professor in the Department of Economics at the University of Lethbridge, Canada. She holds a PhD in Agricultural Economics from the University of Saskatchewan, Canada. Her work has won several published research awards, including awards from the Canadian Agricultural Economics Society for outstanding PhD dissertation and outstanding journal articles. Her research interests include: the economics of health foods; regulations and health claims; public policy in agriculture and health; economics of R&D and technical change/innovation; economics of biotechnology; and agricultural productivity growth.

Alexia Brunet Marks joined the University of Colorado Law Faculty as Associate Professor of Law in the fall of 2009, after serving as Visiting Assistant Professor of Law at Northwestern Law School. She teaches and writes about food law and policy, international business transactions, international trade law and torts. Her approach is often empirical. Her articles have appeared in the *Journal of Empirical Legal Studies, the North Carolina Law Review, the Harvard Journal on Regulation*, among others, and she has presented globally and received numerous awards for her research.

A graduate of Northwestern Law School (cum laude), Brunet Marks also holds a PhD and an MS in Agricultural Economics from Purdue University, Indiana and a BA from Colgate University, New York. She has received competitive fellowships from the U.S. Department of Agriculture and the National Science Foundation, and the American Bar Foundation. In 2018, Professor Brunet Marks was a fellow at the University of Copenhagen, Center of Excellence for International Courts, iCourts. Prior to teaching, Professor Brunet Marks worked as a risk analyst for the U.S. Department of Homeland Security and Argonne National Laboratory and as a founding partner in an international trade venture. She has experience working in Japan, Guinea, Poland and Denmark. Professor Brunet Marks is a member of the American Bar Association, the Society for Empirical Legal Studies, the American and European Societies of International Law, and a founding member of the Academy of Food Law and Policy.

Uché Ewelukwa Ofodile is the E.J. Ball Professor of Law at the University of Arkansas School of Law. She was previously the Arkansas Bar Foundation Professor (2014-2016) at the Law School. Professor Ewelukwa Ofodile's expertise is in the areas of international economic law, food law and intellectual property law. Professor Uché Ewelukwa Ofodile has authored numerous book chapters and more than one-hundred articles and essays. Professor Uché Ewelukwa Ofodile has served as visiting professor/guest lecturer at numerous universities around the world, including Columbia University, the University of Oklahoma Law Center (Crowe and Dunlevy Visiting International Law Professor), University of Puerto Rico School of Law, Tufts University, the University of Armenia Faculty of Law, and the Nigerian Institute of Advanced Legal Studies. Professor Uché Ewelukwa Ofodile is the recipient of numerous fellowships and awards, including a fellowship award from the Carnegie Council on Ethics and International Affairs. Professor Uche Ewelukwa has law degrees from Harvard Law School, the University College London, and the University of Nigeria Nsukka.

Dr Domenico Pignone is presently the Scientific Director of the Veterinary and Agri-Food Bioethics Institute. He has been working for more than forty years in plant genetics at the Italian National Research Council. He has long been engaged in managing and exploiting plant genetic resources, especially of main Mediterranean crops. During his career he has often worked on pioneering research areas of plant genetic diversity assessment and exploitation, from molecular cytogenetics approaches for crop improvement, to the present use of high throughput plant phenotyping to identify wheat genotypes resilient to drought. He has coordinated many research projects in the agri-food sector and has been representing the National Research Council in national and international committees and organizations. He also acts with the expert role in supporting the Italian Ministry of Agriculture in the plant genetic resources management area. He has had a leading and expert role in international cooperation projects in Mediterranean and Sub-Saharan Africa. He has also served as director of two institutes of the National Research Council and as departmental director of the Agri-food Department of the same CNR.

Denise Prévost, PhD, is Associate Professor of International Economic Law at Maastricht University, the Netherlands. She was the Academic Coordinator of the Institute for Globalisation and International Regulation (IGIR) until 1 August 2009, when she was appointed as Deputy Academic Director of IGIR until 2011. Denise is the associate editor of the *Journal of World Trade* and is on the Editorial Boards of the *Netherlands Yearbook of International Law*, the *International Journal of Law and Public Policy*, the *Journal of the Colombian Institutes of Tax Law and Customs Law*, the *Maastricht Law Series* and the *Maastricht Law Faculty Working Paper Series*. Previously (2004-2007), she worked as Assistant Professor of International Economic Law at Utrecht University, the Netherlands, where she coordinated and lectured courses in this field on Bachelor's and Master's level and conducted research on WTO law issues. From 1998 to 2004, she worked as a research associate in the Department of International and European Law at Maastricht University. Her doctoral thesis is entitled: Balancing Trade and Health in the SPS Agreement: The Development Dimension (2009, Wolf Legal Publishers). In 2001, Denise interned at the Legal Affairs Division of the Secretariat of the WTO. She has also done consulting and capacity building work for various international organizations, the European Commission and Parliament, national bodies and industry groups, and has been a visiting lecturer in several international programmes, including the China Europe School of Law in Beijing, China; the Institut des Hautes Études Internationales at the University of Paris II, France; the International Trade and Investment course at the University of Padova, Italy; and the Joint CWS-WTI Academy in New Delhi, India. Denise studied Law at the University of Pretoria, South Africa (BLC cum laude 1992, LLB cum laude, 1994), the University of South Africa (LLM, 2001) and Maastricht University (LLM summa cum laude, 1998; PhD 2009). She was admitted as an advocate of the High Court of South Africa in December 1996.

Eva Rook Basile is Former Full Professor of Agricultural Law, Faculty of Law, University of Siena, Italy; Former Director of the department of 'Private-law Science', University of Siena; Former Secretary General of the International and Comparative Agricultural Law Institute of Florence (IDAIC) (ICALI) from 1985 to 1998 and Former Representative of the MiUR in board of IDAIC from 1998 to 2003, date of IDAIC unification in CNR. She was a member of the Committee for solicitor examination in Florence district in 1991/1992, Director of postgraduate course for experts on Environmental Law at Chamber of Commerce of Siena (1999-2012) and Director of the professional refresher course in agro-food fulfilment (food safety, traceability, quality labels, voluntary certifications for export). She is a member of the Scientific Committee of the journal *Agricultural, Food and Environmental Law and Jurisprudence* and *Sienese Studies*, editing board of the *Journal of Agricultural Law*.

David Röttgen is the founding partner of Ambientalex law firm. Prior to setting up Ambientalex in 2008, David worked with Freshfields Bruckhaus Deringer (Milan). Subsequently he held a managerial role in a leading Italian multinational company (Pirelli Group).

David is specialized in environmental law, providing extrajudicial assistance to multinational companies and trade associations as well as to other law firms.

He is a member of the Commission for Integrated Environmental Authorisation (IPPC) within the Italian Ministry for Environment. Furthermore, he is a representative within the Permanent Observatory relating to ILVA-Steel-Works, set up according to DPCM 29 September 2017. David has been a member of the ministerial expert commission nominated for the transposition, into Italian law, of the circular economy package, adopted by the EU in 2018.

In 2012/2013, he was part of the Minister for Environment's Technical Secretariat.

David is the author of many articles and publications on his specialized topics and frequently takes part as a speaker in conferences, workshops and training courses on environmental law.

May T. Yeung is a Professional Affiliate with the University of Saskatchewan's Johnson Shoyama Graduate School of Public Policy. She has an MBA focusing on International Marketing from the University of Wales and a BA in Economics from the University of Calgary. In her twenty-five-plus years of experience in research, study and writing about international trade, she has worked extensively on issues affecting international trade, including marketing environment, global trade policy, technical regulations affecting agri-food trade, global food safety trends, international food labelling regulations, and geographic indications. Much of her work has been in the agricultural and agri-food sector and involved the development of practical marketing and business development within these contexts.

Summary of Contents

Editors v

Contributors vii

Foreword xxix

Preface xxxi

Part I
Setting the Scene: International Food Law 1

Chapter 1
International Food Law: History and Evolution
Uché Ewelukwa Ofodile 3

Chapter 2
Right to Food in International Law
Margherita Brunori & Pier Filippo Giuggioli 41

Chapter 3
The UN Decade of Action on Nutrition: Opportunities and Challenges in a Time of a Pandemic
Khaled Eltaweel 57

Chapter 4
The International Treaty on Plant Genetic Resources for Food and Agriculture and the 2050 Food Challenge
Domenico Pignone 81

CHAPTER 5
Codex Alimentarius: Safe, Good Food for Everyone
Tom Heilandt 91

CHAPTER 6
Food Safety under WTO Law
Daria Boklan 113

CHAPTER 7
Checking Compliance with Food Law: Control, Inspection and Approval Procedures under the WTO SPS Agreement
Denise Prévost 125

CHAPTER 8
Food Production and Animal Welfare: An International Law Perspective
Ilja Richard Pavone 147

Part II
Selected Cases and Legislations and European Food Law 167

CHAPTER 9
Right to Food and Food Security: A Comparative Perspective
Francesco Alicino 169

CHAPTER 10
Regulating Health Claims: An International Comparison
Jill E. Hobbs, Stavroula Malla & May T. Yeung 187

CHAPTER 11
Food Safety in the United States
Alexia Brunet Marks 213

CHAPTER 12
CAFOs: Climate Change, Livestock Production and the Law
Justo Corti Varela 233

CHAPTER 13
An Overview of EU Food Law
Luchino Ferraris 253

CHAPTER 14
EU Agricultural Law and the Common Agricultural Policy
Alberto Germanò & Eva Rook Basile 263

Chapter 15
Food Safety System in the EU
Maria Pia Ragionieri 295

Chapter 16
Food Waste in EU Food Law
David Röttgen & Francesca Allocco 305

Chapter 17
The EU Policy to Protect Bees: The Restrictions onto the Use of Neonicotinoids and the Emergency Authorizations Granted by MS – In Search of a Long-Term Strategy on Pesticides
Daniela Corona 339

Chapter 18
Biotechnology and Food and Feed Safety Assessment
Gijs A. Kleter & Harry A. Kuiper 353

Index 367

Table of Contents

Editors v

Contributors vii

Foreword xxix

Preface xxxi

Part I
Setting the Scene: International Food Law 1

CHAPTER 1
International Food Law: History and Evolution
Uché Ewelukwa Ofodile 3

§1.01 Introduction 4
§1.02 Food Insecurity: Past and Present 5
[A] Introduction 5
[B] Global Food Security: Normative Developments 6
[C] Global Food Security: Institutional Developments 8
[D] Global Food Security: Progress and Challenges 10
§1.03 International Law's Fragmented and Incoherent Approach to Global Food Security 11
[A] Food Insecurity and International Trade Law 11
[1] Normative Developments 11
[2] Institutional Developments 13
[3] Progress and Challenges 15
[B] Food Security and International Human Rights Law 17
[1] Introduction 17
[2] Normative Developments 17
[3] Institutional Developments 20

[4] Progress and Challenges 21
[C] Food Security and International Investment Law 21
[1] Introduction 21
[2] Normative Developments 23
[a] Bilateral Investment Treaties 24
[b] Principles of Responsible Investments 25
[3] Institutional Developments 27
[4] Problems and Challenges 28
§1.04 The Global Food System and International Law: The Past, The Present, The Road Ahead 29
[A] An Impressive Legal Landscape 30
[B] Persisting Debates 30
[C] Persisting Challenges 32
[1] Sovereignty Concerns 32
[2] Democratic Deficit 33
[3] Monitoring and Enforcement Challenges 34
[4] Fragmentation and Lack of Coordination 35
§1.05 Conclusions 36

CHAPTER 2
Right to Food in International Law
Margherita Brunori & Pier Filippo Giuggioli 41
§2.01 Introduction 41
§2.02 Affirming the Rights to Food: Travaux Preparatoires 42
§2.03 The Successive Interpretation of the Right to Food 46
§2.04 Links Between Food and Health in International Law 48
§2.05 Expansion of the Right to Food 50
§2.06 Present and Future Challenges for the Right to Food: The COVID-19 Pandemic 52
§2.07 Conclusions 55

CHAPTER 3
The UN Decade of Action on Nutrition: Opportunities and Challenges in a Time of a Pandemic
Khaled Eltaweel 57
§3.01 Introduction 57
§3.02 Nutrition: A Global Priority 58
§3.03 Nutrition: The Key Players 59
§3.04 Different Forms of Malnutrition 60
[A] Undernutrition 60
[B] Overweight 61
[C] Micronutrient Deficiencies 61
§3.05 A Recent Deterioration of the World Nutrition Status 61
§3.06 COVID-19 and Nutrition 63

[A] The Supply-Side Impacts 64
[B] The Demand-Side Impacts 65
§3.07 The Multi-Sectorial Nature of Nutrition 66
[A] Nutrition and Food Systems 66
[B] Nutrition and Health Systems 68
[C] Nutrition and Social Protection 69
[D] Nutrition and International Trade 69
[E] Nutrition and Supportive Environment 71
[F] Nutrition and Governance 71
§3.08 Nutrition Across Agenda 2030 72
[A] Nutrition and Infrastructure 72
[B] Nutrition, Equity, Gender Equality and Inclusion 72
[C] Nutrition, Peace and Stability 74
[D] Nutrition, Poverty and the Economy 74
[E] Nutrition and Climate Change 75
[F] Nutrition and Education 76
§3.09 Stocktaking of the Implementation of the Decade of Action on Nutrition 76
§3.10 Dealing with the Dual Challenge of Malnutrition and COVID-19 78
§3.11 Conclusions 80

CHAPTER 4
The International Treaty on Plant Genetic Resources for Food and Agriculture and the 2050 Food Challenge
Domenico Pignone 81
§4.01 Introduction 82
§4.02 How Did We Get to This Point 82
§4.03 The 'Genetic Resources Movement' 83
§4.04 Towards a New Consciousness 84
§4.05 The Convention of Biological Diversity 85
§4.06 The International Treaty on Plant Genetic Resources for Food and Agriculture 86
§4.07 A Sight to the Future 89

CHAPTER 5
Codex Alimentarius: Safe, Good Food for Everyone
Tom Heilandt 91
§5.01 Food Is a Commodity Like No Other 92
[A] We All Need Food 92
[B] Food Is Fragile 92
§5.02 History of Standards and Codes 93
[A] From Prehistory to the Greek 93
[B] Codex Austriacus 93
[C] Joint Expert Committee on Contaminants and Food Additives 93
[D] The Codex Alimentarius Commission 94

[1] The Mandate 94
[2] The Status of Codex Standards 94
§5.03 Structure and Work Methods 95
[A] An Open Forum: Achievement Through Cooperation 95
[B] Committee Structure 95
[C] Work Process and Scientific Basis 96
[D] Based on Science: Adopted by Consensus 97
[E] Achievements: A World Full of Standards 98
[1] An Impressive Score Card 98
[2] Expectations Require Continued Work 98
[3] From Farm to Fork: HACCP – A Codex Signature Achievement 99
§5.04 SDGs and Codex Strategic Plan 2020-2025 100
[A] Codex and SDGs 100
[B] Codex Strategic Plan 2020-2025 102
§5.05 Food and Trade 102
[A] Vision of Harmonization and Challenges to Implementation 102
[B] Codex Standards Facilitating Trade 103
[C] Not Only for Food Safety: What Is a Sardine? 104
§5.06 The Future 104
[A] A Lot Has Been Done 104
[B] Overcoming Issues 105
[C] Past and Present Challenges 105
[D] Kava: An Important Food for Small Islands 106
[E] Makgeolli and the Challenge of Dealing with Alcoholic Beverages 106
[F] Challenges to Consensus 107
[G] Change Is a Thing We Can Count On 108
[1] From Farm to Fork: Opportunities for Fraud 108
[2] A Never-Ending Task 109
§5.07 Conclusions 109
§5.08 Afterword 110

CHAPTER 6
Food Safety under WTO Law
Daria Boklan 113
§6.01 Introduction 113
§6.02 Scope of the Agreement on Sanitary and Phytosanitary Measures 116
§6.03 Scientific Basis 118
§6.04 International Standards 120
§6.05 Risk Assessment and Appropriate Level of Sanitary and Phytosanitary Protection 121
§6.06 Conclusions 122

CHAPTER 7
Checking Compliance with Food Law: Control, Inspection and Approval Procedures under the WTO SPS Agreement
Denise Prévost 125
§7.01 Introduction 126
§7.02 Legal Framework for Control, Inspection and Approval Procedures 128
§7.03 Scope of Application 129
§7.04 Rules on Control, Inspection and Approval Procedures 130
[A] Undue Delay 131
[B] Non-discrimination 133
[C] Equitable Fees 139
[D] Systems of Prior Approval and Tolerance Determination for Food or Feed 140
§7.05 Conclusions 145

CHAPTER 8
Food Production and Animal Welfare: An International Law Perspective
Ilja Richard Pavone 147
§8.01 Introduction 147
§8.02 Animal Protection and the Legal Gap 150
§8.03 The Current Legal Framework 153
§8.04 Looking for International Standards 156
§8.05 In Search of International Standards 158
§8.06 The Terrestrial Code and the Welfare of Farmed Animals 162
§8.07 Conclusions 164

Part II
Selected Cases and Legislations and European Food Law 167

CHAPTER 9
Right to Food and Food Security: A Comparative Perspective
Francesco Alicino 169
§9.01 Introduction 169
§9.02 The International Human Rights to Food 171
§9.03 The Sectorial, Regional and Constitutional Rights to Food 174
§9.04 Framework Laws and Monitoring Mechanisms 176
§9.05 The Judiciary 179
§9.06 Conclusions 184

CHAPTER 10
Regulating Health Claims: An International Comparison
Jill E. Hobbs, Stavroula Malla & May T. Yeung 187
§10.01 Introduction 187
§10.02 Regulatory Objectives and Pitfalls 189
§10.03 Regulation of Health Claims in Selected Countries 191

[A] United States 191
[B] Canada 195
[C] The European Union 198
[D] Japan 200
[E] Australia (and New Zealand) 202
§10.04 Conclusions 207
§10.05 Appendix 209

CHAPTER 11
Food Safety in the United States
Alexia Brunet Marks 213
§11.01 Introduction 213
§11.02 A Cooperative New Governance Approach to Regulating Food Safety 214
§11.03 Direct Regulation 216
[A] Federal Regulation: Agencies and Legislation 216
[1] Challenges with Food-Borne Illness 218
[2] Challenges with International Trade 220
[3] New Legislation to Address These Challenges 222
[B] State and Local Agencies 223
§11.04 Indirect Regulation: Legal Liability 223
§11.05 Private Regulation 225
[A] Examples of a Modern, Co-regulation, New Governance Approach 229
§11.06 Examining Future Challenges and Conclusions 231

CHAPTER 12
CAFOs: Climate Change, Livestock Production and the Law
Justo Corti Varela 233
§12.01 Introduction 234
§12.02 Direct Impacts of an Animal Protein Diet 235
[A] On the Environment 236
[1] GHG Emissions 237
[2] Intensity in the Use of Land and Water 238
[3] Waste and Biodiversity Loss 238
[B] On Health 239
[1] Carcinogenic Impact 239
[2] Chemicals in Meat Production 240
[3] Fat and Obesity 241
[4] Zoonotic Infections 241
§12.03 The Hidden Side: Feedstuffs Trade 242
[A] Protein Deficit 242
[B] On the Environment 243
[1] Delocalization of Environmental Costs 243
[2] International Transport Costs 243
[C] On Health 244

[1] Lack of Controls on Herbicides and Pesticides: Impact on Consumers and Foreign Farmers 244
[2] No Traceability of Imported Foodstuffs 245
§12.04 Climate Change and International Trade Law: Limitations and Obstacles 246
[A] Process and Production Methods and Likeness under GATT/WTO Law 246
[B] Labelling and Other Consumer Information Measures 247
§12.05 Towards an Integration of Environmental and Health Targets in a Common Climate Change Strategy? 248
[A] Equalize Animal Protein Consumption Through Feed Carbon-Pricing 249
[B] Empowering Consumers on Health and Environmental Costs of Animal Protein 250
§12.06 Conclusions 250

Chapter 13
An Overview of EU Food Law
Luchino Ferraris 253
§13.01 EU Food Law: Origin and Definition of a Policy Domain 253
§13.02 The Sources and Coverage of EU Food Law 255
§13.03 The Search for an Essence of EU Food Law 257
§13.04 Looking Backwards and Forwards: COVID-19 Pandemic Crisis as an Earthquake for EU Food Law? 259

Chapter 14
EU Agricultural Law and the Common Agricultural Policy
Alberto Germanò & Eva Rook Basile 263
§14.01 European Agriculture in the CAP and Non-exclusive Areas of Union Competence 263
§14.02 Objectives of the CAP 265
§14.03 On 'Shared Competence' Regarding Agriculture and Nutrition 266
§14.04 The Definition of Agriculture in EU Law 269
§14.05 Annex I of the Treaty 270
§14.06 The Special Features of EU Agricultural Law 272
[A] Competition Law: General Rules 273
[B] Competition Law: The Agricultural Derogation 275
[C] The Prohibition of Public Aid: General European Legislation 277
[D] The Prohibition of Public Aid: The Agricultural Derogation 279
§14.07 The CAP: Premise 280
[A] Price Policy 280
[B] Structure Policy 283
§14.08 Trends in Agricultural Law in the EU in the Last Years 290

Chapter 15
Food Safety System in the EU
Maria Pia Ragionieri 295

Chapter 16
Food Waste in EU Food Law
David Röttgen & Francesca Allocco 305
§16.01 General Overview 305
§16.02 Monitoring: Quantitative Estimates 307
§16.03 The First (Soft) Regulatory Actions in Europe 310
§16.04 WFD 2008/98/EC and 'Green Paper' 311
§16.05 'Sustainable Development Goals' and 'Circular Economy Package' 315
§16.06 Legally Defining Food Waste: First Attempts 317
§16.07 The 'Circular Economy Package' 321
§16.08 Measures Taken after 2018/851 Directive 325
§16.09 The European Green Deal 328
§16.10 Food Waste and BAT Conclusions 330
§16.11 Most Significant Legal Developments in Member States 331
§16.12 The Pandemic's Effects on Food Waste Production and Management 334
§16.13 Concluding Remarks 336

Chapter 17
The EU Policy to Protect Bees: The Restrictions on the Use of Neonicotinoids and the Emergency Authorizations Granted by MS – In Search of a Long-Term Strategy on Pesticides
Daniela Corona 339
§17.01 Introduction 340
§17.02 The EU Actions to Combat the Loss of Honeybee Populations 342
§17.03 The Restrictions on the Use of Neonicotinoids in the EU 344
§17.04 The Emergency Authorizations Granted by MS 347
§17.05 Concluding Remarks 349

Chapter 18
Biotechnology and Food and Feed Safety Assessment
Gijs A. Kleter & Harry A. Kuiper 353
§18.01 Introduction 353
[A] Background 353
§18.02 Safety Assessment 355
[A] Food and Feed Safety in General 355
[B] Safety Assessment of Biotechnology 356
§18.03 Implications of New Developments for the Safety Assessment 363
[A] Specific Safety Features of RNA Interference 363

[B] Specific Safety Features of Gene Editing 365
§18.04 Concluding Remarks 366

Index 367

Foreword

The phenomenon of globalization together with the growth of the world population has implied a significant increase in the demand for food products. It entails new challenges under the profile of international and European law as to the necessity to harmonize rules and standards on animal welfare, environmental protection and food safety, especially in the optics of the crucial debate on the long-term sustainability of food production.

The volume *International Food Law* edited by Cinzia Caporale, Ilja Richard Pavone and Maria Pia Ragionieri examines the global and European landscape of food governance. Empirically, this book investigates the main legal issues related to food regulation in a global context. The underlying idea behind this book is that food law must be global (both in its transnational and multi-level dimension) in order to meet the challenges related to the process of globalization. In current times, all aspects of the food chain (from processing, distribution to consumer purchase and consumer use) have a transboundary dimension. Food has become, therefore, a global good that requires common and agreed standards ensuring at the same time food safety and sustainable production.

In detail, this book will evaluate whether the current legal landscape is able to guarantee high standards of protection to human health, environment and animal welfare, or whether further reforms are requested. As witnessed by the COVID-19 pandemic and its probable transmission within the Wuhan wet market, environmental law, health law and food law need probably to be more interconnected through a holistic approach built around the One Health Approach.

Indeed, it seems obvious that higher animal welfare standards imply food safety and a minor risk of zoonosis. But, at the same time, environmental law should be reformed in order to embrace an ecosystemic approach that attaches particular attention to the potential sources of threats to human health (such as deforestation and habitat destruction and their impact on the food chain and human health).

Importantly, the book also explores the public policy responses to the main challenging issues related to the food chain under the international and European perspective.

Against this empirical backdrop, the contributors provide insights into broader analytical issues.

This comprehensive book will be of great value to those interested in gaining an interdisciplinary understanding of the empirical area of food governance and the analytical issues of regulatory governance.

The book in addition deals with traditional issues such as food security and food safety, right to food, free trade, GMOs, organic food, animal welfare and food naming and labelling.

International Food Law gathers essays from the world's leading scholars in the field of food and environmental law to explore emerging legal issues linked to food production. It, thus, focuses on the current challenges of global food law from a transnational perspective. A global food law is the response to yet an almost exclusively domestic food production-related legislation on the one hand, and the global dimension of food production on the other hand.

The volume is divided into two parts. Part I ('Setting the Scene') is devoted to a reconstruction of international norms addressing various aspects of the food chain.

It begins with a reconstruction of the history and evolution of food law (Chapter 1) and then continues with a deep analysis of the efforts by the main intergovernmental organizations (United Nations, Food and Agricultural Organization, World Organization for Animal Health, World Trade Organization) to promote the right to food, food safety and food security, and sustainable development.

It finally focuses on the main legal issues related to meat production, with a focus on its impact on the environment and climate change and on animal welfare.

Part II is then addressed on the European Union (EU) legal framework on food production. Indeed, the EU has the highest world standard concerning food safety, food security, animal welfare. The highest attainable level of health protection is the main goal of the EU legislation that covers animal welfare, agriculture and the entire food chain production, as well as goods imported from third countries.

Against this backdrop, the problem arises in understanding whether the current 'global food law' is fit for the purpose to answer the new challenges related to COVID-19, to the over-population, to habitat destruction and to the necessity to guarantee a sustainable food production.

This is definitively the central issue posed by different contributors who have participated in this volume and whose task is to provide an answer to these core topics.

Marco Valletta
International Policy Officer
Former member of Cabinet of the Health and Food Safety Commissioner
European Commission

Preface

By 2050, the world's population is expected to reach 9.7 billion. In light of this steady population growth and the urbanization process, the demand for food will continue to soar, putting under pressure natural habitats, the environment, human health and animal welfare. Despite the huge production of food (intensive agriculture, farmed animals, fishing), a large segment of the population in developing countries – especially children – do not yet have access to adequate nutrition.

As clearly stated by Goal 2 of the 2030 UN Agenda on Sustainable Development, states should engage themselves towards the objective of ending hunger, achieving food security and improved nutrition and promoting sustainable agriculture. To this aim, a more equitable and sustainable food system is necessary and global food law should address this need.

This task has acquired a new sense of urgency due to the COVID-19 pandemic. Even though COVID-19 is not a food-borne disease, it has significantly impacted the production and access to food, adding new challenges for the food system and the promotion of the right to food.

In particular, the pandemic has shown how a health crisis may quickly turn into a food crisis, and thus have an impact on the right to food. The FAO has underscored that the COVID-19 pandemic has struck at the time when global hunger and malnourishment were already on the rise. As a consequence of the economic recession following the pandemic, in the incoming years, millions of people are expected to face new hurdles in accessing quality and nutritious food. At the same time, the pandemic has also directly contributed to increased food waste.

Furthermore, the effects of the COVID-19 pandemic have had, and will have, the greatest impact on these population that are already carrying a significant burden of health and socio-economical inequalities, increasing their food insecurity.

On a different scale, the COVID-19 crisis has also highlighted the need to rethink the model through which our food is currently produced. In this respect, the necessity of avoiding and controlling for future zoonoses has shown the entanglement between the right to food for humans and the need to enhance the welfare of animals as well as to protect the environment. The pandemic has therefore taught us that respecting the welfare of animals within the food system and preserving ecosystems are two essential pre-conditions for respecting human health and wellbeing.

Against this backdrop, the time has come to enrich the global literature on international and European law with an in-depth scholarly analysis of these most pressing challenges related to the topics 'food', 'nutrition', 'animals', 'health' and 'environment'.

This is precisely the purpose of this volume, which offers the opportunity to consider that the way we produce food has a deep impact in terms of environmental degradation.

The collection of essays presented as chapters in this volume, all written by eminent scholars and leading experts at FAO, offers an original and insightful analysis of the main challenges of modern food law.

In this framework, the volume will address the interplay between different layers of regulation and the main principles of international and European food law.

The authors - from different legal backgrounds and countries - address the common core issue that is how international and European law can address the impact of COVID-19 on global food systems.

This volume has been conceived and prepared by the Interdepartmental Center for Research Ethics and Integrity of the National Research Council (CNR) in collaboration with the Tuscia University of Viterbo, with the participation of Rifosal (Consortium on Research and Education on Food Safety), bringing together international scholars with specific expertise in the main ethical and legal issues of food and nutrition. This volume could have not been published without the staff support of CNR colleagues Paola Grisanti (who coordinated all the activities), Ludovica Durst, Emiliano Liberatori and Marco Arizza, as well as Mariangela Barletta and Valentina Tafuni as student assistants, and Rifosal of Paolo Felice and Marcello Di Francesco Torregrossa.

Cinzia Caporale, Ilja Richard Pavone & Maria Pia Ragionieri

Part I Setting the Scene: International Food Law

CHAPTER 1

International Food Law: History and Evolution

Uché Ewelukwa Ofodile

In the past two decades, food law has emerged and has taken hold in the consciousness of lawyers. In many countries, food law is seeing exponential growth characterized by new statutes, new judicial and administrative decisions, practical business impact, and the growing number of law firms that focus on food law. Not surprisingly, international food law is also seeing an explosive growth characterized by a growing number of treaties and soft law instruments pertaining to food and agricultural products, a proliferation of global organizations and bodies addressing agriculture and food-related issues, and a growing number of decisions emanating from international judicial and quasi-judicial dispute settlement mechanisms. The chapter 'International Food Law: History and Evolution' attempts to situate international law, including some of its specialized fields, in the evolving global food and agricultural system. As food and agricultural policy implicates a broad range of pressing humanitarian, public health, economic, and environmental challenges, the chapter explores how three fields of international law – international trade law, international human rights law, and international investment law – respond to the problem of food insecurity. Several questions are raised and answered. For example, what is the role of international law in constituting and managing global food and agricultural relations in general and food insecurity in particular? Has international law's role been positive or negative? What are the present and future challenges to effectively managing the global food and agricultural system using international legal instruments and mechanisms? The past five decades have witnessed not only the emergence of food insecurity as an issue in the problem of global proportion but also the development of international norms and global governance mechanisms designed to respond to the problem. Sadly, although international legal instruments that purport to address global food security challenges has proliferated and the number of international institutions and mechanisms designed to respond to the problem has multiplied, the number of hungry and malnourished people in the world remains at astronomical levels.

§1.01 INTRODUCTION

Food systems are as old as mankind and emerged with the dawn of civilization and with the onset of agriculture. The global food system is also as old as civilization and can be traced back to the Iron Age and the Roman Empire when the desire for agricultural products from distant lands, coupled with advances in food storage and new modes of transportation and development of extensive trading networks, made trade in agricultural commodities like salt, spices, and tea.[1] The global food system has evolved and continues to evolve as a result of political forces (e.g., the slave trade, colonization, and war), technological changes (e.g., development of transport technology and new production and processing technology), demographic changes (e.g., urbanization and population growth), and other changes. Today, the global food system is extensive, diverse, complex, and is still evolving. The global food system involves most countries and regions of the world, accommodates a wide range of actors from subsistence farmers to huge multinational food companies, and involves a wide range of activities from food production, food processing and food trade to food distributorship.

Given the challenges confronting the global food system today and future risks and challenges that are predicted, the role that international law has played, can play, and will play in the evolution of the system deserves close study. Using food insecurity as the organizing framework, the chapter examines the contribution of international law to the functioning (or malfunctioning) of the world's food and agricultural system. Specifically, the chapter examines the role that international law has played and is playing in creating and sustaining the global norms and institutions designed to respond to the problem of food insecurity. International law's encounter with domestic and global food and agricultural systems is not new but became more prominent and institutionalized in the twentieth century. The issue is not simply whether the international law is embracing and addressing the challenges in the global food and agricultural system, but whether international legal instruments are playing a useful role in the evolution of the system. Are international law's normative tools and governance mechanisms capable of effectively managing the world's diverse, complex, and evolving food system? section §1.02 of the chapter introduces the concept of food insecurity and analyses the legal and institutional evolution of this concept from about the middle of the twentieth century to the present. Section §1.03 offers an examination of international law's response to food and nutrition insecurity through the framework of three fields of international law: international human rights law, international trade law, and international investment law. Section §1.04 offers an assessment of the numerous interactions between the global food system and international law as the

1. K.D. White, *Roman Farming* (Cornell University Press 1970).

world struggled and continues to struggle to address hunger and malnutrition. Concluding thoughts are offered in section §1.05.

§1.02 FOOD INSECURITY: PAST AND PRESENT

[A] Introduction

Hunger and the eradication of hunger has been a preoccupation of the global community for a long time. In the wake of the food crisis of the early 1930s and the world food movement that quickly emerged, the Health Division of the League of Nations commissioned a study that focused on the health and nutrition of the unemployed and their families in the depressed areas of a number of countries. In 1936, the International Labour Organization published a report on the importance of adequate nutrition for the well-being of workers.[2] Food insecurity concerns also informed the creation of the Food and Agricultural Organization (FAO) in 1945, the establishment of the World Food Program (WFP) in 1961, the creation of the Committee on World Food Security (CWFS) in 1975, as well as the establishment of the International Funds for Agriculture and Development in 1977.

Despite efforts to address global hunger, the number of people in the world facing chronic food deprivation continues to rise. According to the *State of Food Security in the World 2020*:

- nearly 690 million people are hungry, or 8.9% of the world population up by 10 million people in one year and by nearly 60 million in five years;
- the number of people affected by severe food insecurity continues to show an upward trend. In 2019, close to 750 million – or nearly one in ten people in the world – were exposed to severe levels of food insecurity;
- considering the total affected by moderate or severe levels of food insecurity, an estimated 2 billion people in the world did not have regular access to safe, nutritious and sufficient food in 2019; and
- gender gap in accessing food increased from 2018 to 2019. At the global level, the prevalence of food insecurity at moderate or severe level, and severe level only, is higher among women than men.

The projection is that if recent trends continue, the number of people affected by hunger will surpass 840 million by 2030, or 9.8% of the population. The outlook is also grim when malnutrition is considered. According to estimates, the Prevalence of Undernutrition in the world in 2019 was 8.9% of the global population, up from 8.6% in 2014.[3] In terms of the absolute number of undernourished, the situation, in the past ten years, appears to be getting worse and not better. In 2019, 687.8 million people in

2. Workers' Nutrition and Social Policy, International Labour Office (Studies and Reports, Ser. B (Social and Economic Conditions), No. 23) 249. Paper.
3. *Ibid.*, 9.

the world were classified as undernourished, up from 678.1 in 2018, 653.2 in 2017, 657.6 in 2016, 653.3 in 2015, and 668.2 in 2010.

The COVID-19 pandemic has already complicated the global landscape and will complicate it even further. According to the Global Report of Food Crisis 2020, in 2019, about 135 million people experienced crisis (Integrated Food Security Phase Classification/Cadre Harmonisé Phase 3) and worse levels of acute food insecurity, the highest in the four years of the Global Report of Food Crisis' existence. In March 2021, the WFP executive director David Beasely told the United Nations Security Council that 272 million people face acute hunger today (up from 135 million last year).[4] On 11 March 2011, António Guterres, Secretary-General of the United Nations, warned the Security Council that the world is facing multiple conflict-driven famines, aggravated by climate change and the COVID-19 pandemic, and that without immediate action, millions of people – from the Sahel to Afghanistan – could well find themselves on the brink of extreme hunger and death this year.[5]

[B] Global Food Security: Normative Developments

International legal instruments have played an important role in shaping global debates about food security, in defining and refining the concept of food insecurity, and in creating global institutions and mechanisms tasked with addressing the problem. As far back as 1943, delegates at the United Nations (UN) Conference on Food and Agriculture in Hot Springs, Virginia, United States ('1943 Conference'), boldly affirmed that the goal of freedom from want can be achieved, and called on participating governments to declare to their citizens and to one another their intention to secure more and better food for the people. Adopted in 1948, the Universal Declaration of Human Rights, in Article 25, declares the right of everyone to a standard of living adequate for the health and well-being of himself and of his family, including food. In October 1960, against the backdrop of the decolonization process in the Global South, the UN General Assembly (General Assembly) adopted Resolution 1496 (XV) on 'the provision of food surpluses to food-deficit people through the United Nations Systems'.[6]

Food security concerns have inspired notable world food conferences, convened at the behest of key intergovernmental organizations, including the World Food Conference of 1974, the World Food Summit of 1996, the *World Food Summit + 5* of 2002, and the World Summit on Food Security of 2009. In 1992, the FAO and the World Health Organization convened the International Conference on Nutrition which was the first global conference devoted solely to addressing the world's nutrition problems. Following the 1992 conference, the International Conference on Nutrition2 was convened in 2014. The world food conferences are important not only for bringing world leaders together around the problem of hunger and malnutrition but also for

4. WFP chief calls for urgent funds to avert famine. 11 March 2021: https://www.wfp.org/news/wfp-chief-calls-urgent-funds-avert-famine.
5. SC/14463. 11 March 2021: https://www.un.org/press/en/2021/sc14463.doc.htm.
6. https://undocs.org/en/A/RES/1496(XV).

their contribution to the development of the legal and institutional architecture responsive to the problem of food insecurity. In its Resolution 3180 (XXVIII) of 17 December 1973, the General Assembly recognized 'that the principal task of a world food conference consisted in developing ways and means whereby the international community as a whole could take specific action to resolve the world food problem within the broader context of development and international economic co-operation'. Significantly, since the 1970s, every global conference on food and nutrition has ended with a notable declaration and a plan of action designed to spur action at both domestic and global levels. Since the 1970s, the General Assembly has endorsed the outcome of virtually all global conferences relating to food insecurity and malnutrition including:

- the *Universal Declaration on the Eradication of Hunger and Malnutrition* (1974) – adopted at the conclusion of the World Food Conference;[7]
- the *World Declaration on Nutrition and Plan of Action for Nutrition* – adopted at the conclusion of the International Conference on Nutrition of 1992;
- the *Rome Declaration on World Food Security* (1996) – adopted at the 1996 World Food Summit;[8]
- the *World Food Summit Action Plan* (1996) – adopted at the 1996 World Food Summit;[9]
- the *Declaration of the World Food Summit: five years later (2002)* – adopted at the World Food Summit in Rome;[10] and
- the *Declaration of the World Summit on Food Security (2009)* – adopted at the 2009 World Summit on Food Security.

In the *International Covenant on Economic, Social and Cultural Right* (ICESCR) adopted in 1966, global leaders recognized, for the first time in a binding international legal instrument, 'the fundamental right of everyone to be free from hunger', and promised international cooperation in the fight against hunger. To be sure, food security is not explicitly mentioned in the ICESCR. However, Article 11, paragraph 2, states that States Parties 'shall take, individually and through international co-operation, the measures, including specific programmes, which are needed: (a) To improve methods of production, conservation and distribution of food by making full use of technical and scientific knowledge, by disseminating knowledge of the principles of nutrition and by developing or reforming agrarian systems in such a way as to achieve the most efficient development and utilization of natural resources'. In the ICESCR, State Parties also agreed to '[t]ak[e] into account the problems of both

7. Adopted on 16 November 1974 by the World Food Conference convened under General Assembly resolution 3180 (XXVIII) of 17 December 1973; and endorsed by General Assembly resolution 3348 (XXIX) of 17 December 1974. *See*: https://www.ohchr.org/EN/ProfessionalInterest/Pages/EradicationOfHungerAndMalnutrition.aspx; The UN General Assembly subsequently endorsed this declaration. UN General Assembly, *World Food Conference*, 17 December 1974, A/RES/3348, available at: https://www.refworld.org/docid/3b00f1c434.html, accessed 12 September 2020.
8. Food and Agriculture Organization of the United Nations, *Report of the World Food Summit*, 13-17 November 1996 (WFS 96/REP), part one, appendix.
9. *Ibid.*
10. Food and Agriculture Organization of the United Nations, *Report of the World Food Summit: Five Years Later*, 10-13 June 2002, part one, appendix; *see also* A/57/499, annex.

food-importing and food-exporting countries, to ensure an equitable distribution of world food supplies in relation to need'.

International legal instruments have played and continue to play a significant role in the effort to clarify and refine the concept of food insecurity. A significant milestone was achieved in 1996 with the adoption of the *World Food Summit Plan of Action* which offers a definition of food security that is still widely accepted today. According to paragraph 1 of the *World Summit Plan of Action*, '[f]ood security exists when all people, at all times, have physical and economic access to sufficient, safe and nutritious food to meet their dietary needs and food preferences for an active and healthy life'.[11] First conceptualized as a problem of food availability, the *World Food Summit Plan of Action* helped broaden the concept of food insecurity to include notions of adequacy, accessibility, utilization, stability, and sustainability.

International legal instruments, mostly soft law instruments, have also been used, effectively, to set global food and nutrition security targets. Most recently, in 2015, UN Member States set very ambitious global targets with the adoption of Resolution A/RES/70/1 on *Transforming Our World: The 2030 Agenda for Sustainable Development* (SDG 2030 Agenda). In the SDG 2030 Agenda, UN Member States mapped out 17 sustainable development goals (SDGs) and 169 related targets. The SDG 2030 Agenda addresses both hunger and malnutrition and set global targets in respect to both in SDG 2 Targets 2.1 and 2.2. Under Target 2.1, UN Member States pledged to '[b]y 2030, end hunger and ensure access by all people, in particular the poor and people in vulnerable situations, including infants, to safe, nutritious and sufficient food all year round'. Under Target 2.2, they further pledged to '[b]y 2030, end all forms of malnutrition, including achieving, by 2025, the internationally agreed targets on stunting and wasting in children under 5 years of age, and address the nutritional needs of adolescent girls, pregnant and lactating women and older persons'. The SDG 2030 Agenda is not binding but has the potential to be transformational in effect. The SDG 2030 Agenda has built-in follow-up and review processes that is supposed to be informed by country-led evaluations and data.

[C] Global Food Security: Institutional Developments

International legal instruments have been used repeatedly to erect the institutional framework for addressing global food insecurity and for erecting the institutional architecture of the global food and agricultural system more generally. The 1943 Conference recommended the establishment of an interim commission to explore the possibility of establishing a permanent global organization in the field of food and agriculture. As recommended by the 1943 Conference, an Interim Commission was established among other things to formulate and recommend 'a specific plan for

11. World Food Summit Plan of Action, para. 1, available in Food and Agriculture Organization of the United Nations, *Report of the World Food Summit*, 13-17 November 1996 (WFS 96/REP), part one, appendix.

permanent organization in the field of food and agriculture'.[12] The work of the Interim Commission culminated in the establishment of the FAO in 1945. According to the FAO Constitution of 1945, the FAO was established to further the purpose of 'raising levels of nutrition and standards of living of the peoples under their respective jurisdictions'; 'securing improvements in the efficiency of the production and distribution of all food and agricultural products;' 'bettering the condition of rural populations'; and generally 'contributing towards an expanding world economy and ensuring humanity's freedom from hunger'.[13] Upon its establishment, one of the first tasks of the FAO was to launch the World Food Survey and to organize a 'Special Meeting on Urgent Food Problems'.[14] The FAO has since its inception continued to inspire and direct global action on issues relating to food and agriculture.

International legal instruments were deployed in the creation of the WFP which today is one of the leading and possibly the largest humanitarian organization that delivers food assistance in emergencies and works with communities to improve nutrition and build resilience. In 1961, against the decolonization processes in the Global South, the General Assembly through Resolution A/RES/1714 of 19 December 1961 created the WFP 'as an experiment to provide food aid through the UN system'.[15] According to its mission statement, the core strategies behind WFP activities are to provide food aid in order to: (1) save lives in refugee and other emergency situations; (2) improve the nutrition and quality of life of the most vulnerable people at critical times in their lives; and (3) help build assets and promote the self-reliance of poor people and communities, particularly through labour-intensive work programmes.[16]

International law's role in putting in place the institutional framework for food security is evident in the *Universal Declaration on the Eradication of Hunger and Malnutrition* ('Universal Declaration on Hunger') adopted at the conclusion of the World Food Conference of 1974. Among other things, the Universal Declaration on Hunger called for the creation of three institutional mechanisms – the CWFS, the World Food Council,[17] and the International Fund for Agricultural Development (IFAD).[18] Through its Resolution 3348 (XXIX) of 17 December 1974, the General Assembly endorsed the declarations and resolutions of the 1974 World Food Conference and called on governments 'to take urgent action to implement the resolutions adopted at

12. United Nations Conference on Food and Agriculture: Summation of the Work of the Conference by the Secretary General in United Nations Conference on Food and Agriculture: Hot Springs, Virginia, 18 May-3 June 1943: final act and section report, at 1. *See also* United Nations Conference on Food and Agriculture, *Nature* 152, 67-69 (1943): https://doi.org/10.1038/15206 7a0.
13. FAO Constitution, in Basic Texts of the Food and Agricultural Organization of the United Nations, Vols 1 and II (2017 ed.): http://www.fao.org/3/K8024E/K8024E.pdf.
14. UN General Assembly, World Food Conference, 17 December 1974, A/RES/3348, available at: https://www.refworld.org/docid/3b00f1c434.html, accessed 12 September 2020.
15. History: https://www.wfp.org/history.
16. Report on the World Food Program by the Executive Director. Rome, United Nations, 1965.
17. Resolution 3348 (XXIX) of 17 December 1974: https://webapps.ifad.org/members/wgg/docs/GA-Resolution-3348.pdf.
18. E/CONF.65/20 (United Nations publication, Sales No. E.75.Il.A.3).

the conference'.[19] Resolution 3348 (XXIX) established the World Food Council at the ministerial or plenipotentiary level to function as an organ of the UN; this body functioned in this capacity until 1993 when it was suspended. The CWFS was created in 1975 as a standing committee of the FAO.[20] The original mandate of the CWFS 'was to assist developing countries to implement national food reserves and coordinate the management of these reserves across developed and developing countries and other market'. The Agreement Establishing the International Funds for Agricultural Development (IFAD Agreement) was adopted on 13 June 1976, and entered into force on 30 November 1977. IFAD was subsequently established in 1977 as an international financial institution through UN Assembly Resolution 32/107 (30 December 1977). Annexed to Resolution 32/107 is the *Agreement between the United Nations and the International Fund for Agricultural Development* which recognizes the IFAD as a specialized agency of the UN (Article 1). According to Article 2 of the IFAD Agreement, the primary objective of IFAD is to mobilize additional resources to be made available on concessional terms for agricultural development in developing Member States.

[D] Global Food Security: Progress and Challenges

Over the past forty years, hard and soft international legal instruments have been used to shape and change the global conception of food security and to entrench food insecurity as a problem that deserves global attention. International legal instruments have also been used to refine and clarify the contours of food security, establish schemes (Food Security Assistance Scheme), set important global targets (e.g., the SDG Agenda 2030), and establish global institutions tasked with addressing problems relating to food insecurity (e.g., the World Food Council and the IFAD). Underscoring the importance of international legal instruments, including soft law instruments, in the global food security architecture, in 2014, the FAO acknowledged that the 1974 Universal Declaration on the Eradication of Hunger and Malnutrition was one of the key non-binding human rights instruments in relation to the right to food.[21]

Although international legal instruments have helped to highlight the problem of hunger and malnutrition in the world, they have been used to galvanized global action in response to the problem, and have been effectively used to create global institutions tasked with addressing global hunger, they have ultimately been weak and ineffective in actually ending hunger and malnutrition in the world or in resolving some of the fundamental tensions and challenges that plague the global food system. Many of the pressing issues that impact global hunger and malnutrition, including, social and economic inequality, powerlessness, climate change, gender discrimination, the plight

19. UN General Assembly, *World Food Conference*, 17 December 1974, A/RES/3348, available at: https://www.refworld.org/docid/3b00f1c434.html, accessed 12 September 2020.
20. FAO, Resolution 21/75 on the Establishment of a Committee on World Food Security (FAO 1975).
21. Food and Agriculture Organization, The Right to Food Within the International Framework of Human Rights and Country Constitutions: http://www.fao.org/3/a-i3448e.pdf (2014).

of peasants, agricultural workers and small producers, and inequities in the global trade and investment regime remain largely unresolved.

§1.03 INTERNATIONAL LAW'S FRAGMENTED AND INCOHERENT APPROACH TO GLOBAL FOOD SECURITY

This section examines international law's response to food and nutrition security through the lens of three fields of international law: international trade law, international human rights law, and international investment law.

[A] Food Insecurity and International Trade Law

Trade has always played a crucial role in delivering food and agricultural products to different parts of the globe. The twentieth century witnessed significant changes in the global food and agricultural markets - increase in global agricultural production, deeper integration of the world's food systems, growth in agro-food trade in terms of numbers and geographical reach, greater participation of emerging economies and other developing countries in the food and agricultural trade, and a widening of the agriculture and food value chain. The growth and expansion of agro-food trade is occurring at the same time that food insecurity is rising in many parts of the world and small producers are disappearing in many parts of the world. The relationship between global trade rules and food insecurity was and remains a matter of intense debate. To critics, expansion in agro-food trade and the global trade rules that bolster this expansion primarily benefit agribusiness and food manufacturing companies and come at a significant cost to consumers, small producers, agricultural workers, and the environment. Critics also argue that global trade rules significantly erode the power of governments to adopt policies that protect local farmers' livelihoods, protect biodiversity, address climate change, and help countries maintain food self-sufficiency

[1] Normative Developments

In the immediate aftermath of World War II, reducing tariff and non-tariff barriers to global trade and facilitating the export of commodities to feed the world was a priority for many countries. The proffered solution was successive trade liberalization. Signed on 30 October 1947, the *General Agreement on Tariff and Trade* of 1947 (GATT 1947) did not address food insecurity nor did it address agricultural trade in any meaningful or coherent fashion.[22] By signing GATT 1947, Contracting States entered into reciprocal arrangements 'directed to the substantial reduction of tariffs and other barriers to trade and to the elimination of discriminatory treatment in international commerce'. Although GATT 1947 did apply to agricultural trade, the agreement contained many troubling loopholes. Essentially, because of the widespread view of agricultural

22. General Agreement on Tariffs and Trade, 30 October 1947, 61 Stat. A-11, 55 U.N.T.S. 194 (GATT).

exceptionalism, for a long time, the multilateral trade rules did not impose strict disciplines on agricultural trade. Under the agreement, members could still use non-tariff measures such as quantitative restrictions (e.g., import quotas) and subsidies. The result of the regime of agricultural exceptionalism was a highly distorted global trade in food and agricultural products and a regime that was not really structured and could not be adapted to address emerging global problems such as those relating to food insecurity, environmental pollution, and climate change. Between 1947 and 1995, distortions in global food and agricultural trade ruled, thanks to protectionist measures in key markets and trade-distorting domestic agricultural policies in many developed countries. To be sure, GATT 1947 provided some flexibility for developing countries in the form of special and differential treatment and special safeguards. However, in practice, the flexibilities that were afforded to developing countries under GATT 1947 were weak, controversial, unenforceable, and ineffective as far as addressing the deep structural issues that impede fair trade and affect poor farmers around the world.

The Uruguay Round of multilateral trade talks ('Uruguay Round') which lasted from 1986 to 1994 produced the Agreement Establishing the World Trade Organization (WTO Agreement) and ushered in the first multilateral agreement dedicated to the agricultural sector – the Agreement on Agriculture (AoA).[23] The WTO Agreement did not address food insecurity explicitly. However, the preamble recognizes that trade relations should be conducted with a view to 'raising standards of living', 'expanding the production of and trade in goods and services, while allowing for the optimal use of the world's resources in accordance with the objective of sustainable development', and 'seeking both to protect and preserve the environment'. To some, the AoA is an important step towards reforming agricultural trade to the extent that it established an elaborate framework of rules to govern global agricultural trade. To be sure, the AoA addressed tariff and non-tariff barriers to agricultural trade. However, although the AoA took tentative steps towards addressing distorting agricultural policies, it failed to fully address agricultural subsidies. Very similar to GATT 1947, the AoA did not directly or explicitly address food security. Critics assert that rather than advance trade policy to promote development and human rights, the AoA 'has privileged those States and corporations that already have access to resources, infrastructure, credit and foreign markets'.[24]

The good news is that under Article 22 of the AoA, Member States of the World Trade Organization (WTO) are committed to continue reforming agricultural trade rules through new negotiations. The bad news is that subsequent trade rounds of multilateral trade talks have produced very limited results; within the WTO, deadlocks over agricultural trade issues remain the norm. Launched in 2001, the Doha Round of multilateral trade negotiations ('Doha Development Agenda' or 'Doha Round') lasted several years but did not produce many tangible results as far as advancing the goal of establishing a fair agricultural trading system is concerned, although some important

23. Agreement on Agriculture, 15 April 1994, Marrakesh Agreement Establishing the World Trade Organization, Annex 1A, 1867 U.N.T.S. 410. (Not reproduced in I.L.M.).
24. A/75/219, para. 28.

decisions were adopted.[25] One thorny issue is the issue of public stockpiling. Governments, particularly poor developing countries, use public stockholding programmes to purchase, stockpile and distribute food to people in need as part of a broader food security strategy. Controversies arise because '[w]hile food security is a legitimate policy objective, some stockholding programmes are considered to distort trade when they involve purchases from farmers at prices fixed by the governments, known as "supported" or "administered" prices'.[26] In 2013, at the Ninth Ministerial Conference, WTO Member States adopted the 'Bali Package' which *inter alia* addressed public stockpiling. In the 'Public Stockholding for Food Security Purposes, Ministerial Decision', WTO Member States agreed to find a permanent solution to the issue of public stockholding for food security purposes. Until a permanent solution was found, Member States agreed to refrain from challenging, through the WTO Dispute Settlement Mechanism, public stockholding programmes in a developing country even if the country's agreed limits for trade-distorting domestic support were breached. At the WTO's Tenth Ministerial Conference in Nairobi ('2015 Nairobi Ministerial Conference'), WTO Member States adopted the 'Decision on Public Stockholding for Food Security Purposes' ('Stockpiling Decision').[27] The Stockpiling Decision reaffirmed the commitments made in 2013 and encouraged WTO members to engage constructively in finding a permanent solution to the issue of public stocking.[28] To date, no permanent solution has been found. At the 2015 Nairobi Ministerial Conference, WTO Members States adopted two additional decisions as part of the 'Nairobi Package': the Ministerial Decision on Export Competition[29] and the Decision on the Special Safeguard Mechanism (SSM) for Developing Countries (Decision on SSM).[30] Under the Ministerial Decision on Export Competition WTO Members have committed to eliminate export subsidies. The Decision on SSM allows developing countries to temporarily increase tariffs on agriculture products in cases of import surges or price declines. The implementation of the Bali and Nairobi outcomes have been extremely slow.

[2] Institutional Developments

As conceived, the GATT was a framework for regulating international trade rather than an institution designed to manage global trade in all its complexities. Although some developing countries were among the founder members of GATT, GATT was founded principally by developed countries and was never really designed to address food insecurity or broader development issues and challenges. Between 1947 and 1995, the GATT was governed by 'provisional' and 'interim' measures, and essentially remained

25. Bill Pritchard, *The Long Hangover from the Second Food Regime: A World-Historical Interpretation of the Collapse of the WTO Doha Round*, 26 Agriculture and Human Values 297, 299 (2009).
26. WTO, Food Security: https://www.wto.org/english/tratop_e/agric_e/food_security_e.htm.
27. WT/MIN(15)/44.
28. Ministerial Decision of 19 December 2015 (WT/MIN(15)/44 and WT/L/979). The Decision noted the Ministerial Decision of 7 December 2013 (WT/MIN(13)/38 and WT/L/913) and reaffirmed the General Council Decision of 27 November 2014 (WT/L/939).
29. WT/MIN(15)/45.
30. WT/MIN(15)/43.

an agreement without a formal organization to enforce it. Although, in the preamble of GATT 1947, Contracting Parties recognized that trade and economic relations should be conducted with a view to 'raising standards of living', 'developing the full use of the resources of the world' and 'expanding the production and exchange of goods', the agreement, at its inception, contained no explicit provisions regarding developing countries or food insecurity and fundamentally stressed the importance of substantially reducing tariffs and other barriers to trade and eliminating discriminatory treatment in international commerce. Between 1947 and 1980, provisions (e.g., changes to Article XVIII) were adopted to address the needs of developing countries as these countries began to raise concerns and identify special challenges that they faced in international trade. Unfortunately, the changes that were introduced were piecemeal and limited. For example, in 1956, GATT Contracting Parties adopted a joint resolution on 'Particular Difficulties Connected with Trade in Primary Commodities'. In 1961, the GATT adopted the declaration on the 'Promotion of Trade of Less developed Countries'. In 1964, the GATT introduced Part IV which dealt specifically with Trade and Development and containing three new Articles, XXXVI, XXXVII, and XXXVIII.

Established in 1995, the primary focus of the WTO is trade liberalization.[31] Although WTO agreements contain provisions that explicitly address the rights and obligations of developing and least developed countries, the primary task of the WTO, as specified in Article II(1) of the WTO Agreement, is to provide the common institutional framework for the conduct of trade relations among Member States in matters related to the Marrakesh Agreement and associated legal instruments. That said, although the WTO is not tasked with addressing global food insecurity, it has addressed issues that are related to food insecurity such as the issue of public stockpiling. Furthermore, since 2008, the WTO has been part of the UN Secretary General's High Level Task Force on the Global Food Security Crisis.[32] In partnership with eight other international organizations, the WTO contributes to the functioning of the Agricultural Market Information System (AMIS), a system used to detect abnormal market conditions that would affect food security.[33] AMIS is described as 'an inter-agency platform to enhance food market transparency and policy response for food security'.[34] The Group of Twenty (G20) Ministers of Agriculture launched AMIS in 2011 following the global food price hikes in 2007/2008 and 2010. AMIS is composed of G20 members plus Spain and seven additional major exporting and importing countries of

31. Marrakesh Agreement Establishing the World Trade Organization, 15 April 1994, 1867 U.N.T.S. 154 (hereinafter Marrakesh Agreement). *See also* P. van den Bossche, *The Origins of the WTO: The Law and Policy of the World Trade Organization: Text, Cases and Materials* (Cambridge University Press 2005). *See also* John H. Jackson, *Managing the Trading System: The World Trade Organization and the Post-Uruguay Round GATT Agenda*. In *Managing the World Economy: Fifty Years after Bretton Woods* (Peter B. Kenen ed., Institute for International Economics 1994): https://archive.org/details/managingworldeco0000kene.
32. https://www.un.org/en/issues/food/taskforce/.
33. http://www.amis-outlook.org/.
34. About AMIS: http://www.amis-outlook.org/amis-about/en/.

agricultural commodities.[35] The initial focus of AMIS is on four grains: wheat, maize, rice, and soybeans.

[3] Progress and Challenges

The goal of the Uruguay Round was *inter alia* 'to establish a fair and market-oriented agricultural trading system'. Its long-term objective was 'to provide for substantial progressive reductions in agricultural support and protection sustained over an agreed period of time, resulting in correcting and preventing restrictions and distortions in world agricultural markets'. To critics, neither the Uruguay Round nor the Doha Development Round succeeded in effectively addressing some of the persisting problems in global agricultural trade. Although agriculture has been progressively incorporated into the multilateral trading system, the system suffers many weaknesses and challenges. *First*, in general, the global trading system is far from achieving the stated goal of establishing a fair agricultural trading system or effectively addressing the problems associated with agricultural subsidies, agricultural dumping and other protectionisms in global trade in food and agriculture. *Second*, global agricultural trade rules were incorporated into a multilateral trading system that is built around the logic of trade liberalization which was and remains largely contested today. *Third*, international trade rules do not address a host of issues at the intersection of trade and sustainable development including food insecurity, environmental pollution, and climate change.[36] *Fourth*, the multilateral trading system does not appear to be ready or equipped to address supply-side and demand-side threats to global trade in food and agriculture.

The logic of free trade that underpin the multilateral trading system remains a controversial and contested norm.[37] While proponents argue that free trade will ultimately increase the availability and accessibility of food, critics firmly believe that liberalization of agricultural trade has never and is not likely to ever work for the benefits of poor countries and poor farmers in these countries. Critics also believe that WTO rules constrain domestic policy options, undermine rural development, and expose developing countries to volatile international market. Anne Orford has argued that contemporary international trade law 'continues and perpetuates a colonial paradigm that encouraged the unidirectional flow of food from the "periphery" to the "centre"'.[38] To Orford, '[s]omething in the routine operation of international economic life, organised around global value chains, free trade, and open markets, produces a

35. The seven countries are: Egypt, Kazakhstan, Nigeria, the Philippines, Thailand, Ukraine, and Vietnam.
36. Elisabeth Caesens & Maritere Padilla Rodriguez, *Climate Change and the Right to Food: A Comprehensive Study*, 8 Heinrich Boll Stiftung Publication Series on Ecology (2009).
37. Immanuel Wallerstein, *The Modern World System I: Capitalist Agriculture and the Origins of the European World-Economy in the Sixteenth Century* (University of California Press 1974); Immanuel Wallerstein, *A World: System Perspective on the Social Sciences*, 61 The British Journal of Sociology 167 (2010).
38. Anne Orford, *Food Security, Free Trade, and the Battle for the State*, 2 Journal of International Law and International Relations 11, 19 (2015).

system of compulsion such that food is exported to foreign lands while the people who grow it are undernourished'. Hilal Elver, former UN Special Rapporteur on the Right to Food, is of the view that '[g]lobalization and financialization of food systems has enabled big agricultural firms to dominate the market, unilaterally deciding what and how much to produce' and that the resulting power imbalances 'leaves small and medium enterprises without food sovereignty and with almost no alternative but to accept the rules set by big agriculture'.[39]

International trade is important to meeting global food demand and is clearly essential for food security in many food-importing countries. Since 2000, agricultural trade has increased significantly in value terms. Today the global food trade is estimated at USD 1.7 trillion and is instrumental for food reaching millions around the globe. To a great extent, expansion in global food trade in the past five decades is a cause for celebration. There is a great cause for concern as well. The normative and institutional landscape of global agricultural trade is in great disarray. Part of the problem is rooted in the changing consensus on the international trade policies that are conducive to development and a refusal to accept that international trade in agricultural products, unless carefully managed, can undermine domestic food security strategies. International trade rules have not been effective at addressing or eliminating the trade-distorting measures that developed countries use to protect their food and agricultural sector or the devastating impact of agricultural dumping on poor countries.[40] New issues such as the impact of expanded trade in agricultural products on climate change are arising and deserve urgent attention.[41] 'We need trade, as all countries, with no exception, need to exchange products to feed their population. The question is what kind of exchange', FAO Director General Graziano da Silva said at the launch of the 2018 Global Food Policy Report.[42] That food insecurity and global trade are inextricably linked is reflected in the SDG 2030 Agenda. SDG Goal 2 (Target 2.B) addresses trade issues explicitly and directly and commits UN Member States to '[c]orrect and prevent trade restrictions and distortions in world agricultural markets, including through the parallel elimination of all forms of agricultural export subsidies and all export measures with equivalent effect, in accordance with the mandate of the Doha Development Round'.

When it comes to the relationship between global trade rules and food security, many questions remain unanswered. Where do WTO rules fit in the global food security agenda? Are global trade rules compatible with global food security goals and action plans? Has the WTO succeeded in its goal 'to establish a fairer trading system that will increase market access and improve the livelihoods of farmers around the

39. A/HRC/43/44, para. 14.
40. *See* Dumping: the Beginning of the End?, Oxfam Briefing Paper (June 2004); *See also* Dumping Without Borders: How US agricultural policies are destroying the livelihoods of Mexican corn farmers, Oxfam Briefing Papers (2003); Institute for Agriculture and Trade Policy, United States Dumping on World Agricultural Markets, Minnesota (IATP 2002); Public Citizen, NAFTA's Seven-Years War on Farmers and Ranchers in the US, Canada and México (Washington, Public Citizen 2001).
41. Alejandro Nadal, *The Environmental and Social Impacts of Economic Liberalization on Corn Production in Mexico* (WWF and Oxfam 2002).
42. http://www.fao.org/news/story/en/item/1128223/icode/.

world?'[43] Are all countries reaping the gains from trade in the agro-food sector? Are global trade rules able to deal with new uncertainties in world agricultural markets? These questions are difficult to answer and are likely to elicit vastly different answers from different constituencies. Unfortunately, the hope of finding acceptable global solutions grows ever dimmer as more and more states turn to regional and bilateral trade arrangements. In the past two decades, and against the backdrop of lack of success in the WTO, bilateralism and regionalism has emerged as an alternative pathway to trade regulation.[44] Underscoring the crisis in the international trade regime, there are growing calls for a new structure of governance to replace the WTO.[45]

[B] Food Security and International Human Rights Law

[1] Introduction

The concept of the right to food is not new but gained momentum in the past two decades. In 1941, US President Franklin D. Roosevelt, in his 'State of the Union' address, identified 'freedom from want' as one of 'Four Freedoms' that was important in life. Right to food became an international law concept when it was enshrined in the Universal Declaration of Human Rights. Since 1948, various international law instruments have been used to gradually refine and define the right to food. Food security is a narrower concept than the right to food. While right to food creates legal obligation on states, food security does not. The concept of the right to food advances the goals of food security by imposing explicit obligations on states and by casting freedom from hunger in the language of legal entitlements that are justiciable and remediable when violated. In sum, '[a] human rights-based approach reminds States to focus on the most marginalized, excluded or discriminated-against segments of the population and to account for power imbalances that undermine governance'.[46]

[2] Normative Developments

Article 25(1) of the Universal Declaration of Human Rights declares that '[e]veryone has the right to a standard of living adequate for the health and well-being of himself and of his family, including food, clothing, housing and medical care and necessary

---

43. WTO, Agriculture: https://www.wto.org/english/tratop_e/agric_e/agric_e.htm.
44. Scott L. Baier & Jeffrey H. Bergstrand, *Do Free Trade Agreements Actually Increase Members' International Trade?*, 1 Journal of International Economics 71, 72, 95 (2007); Jason H. Grant & Dayton M. Lambert, *Do Regional Trade Agreements Increase Members Agricultural Trade?*, 90(3) American Journal of Agricultural Economics 765, 782 (August 2008); Richard E. Baldwin & Anthony Venables, *Regional Economic Integration*. In *Handbook of International Economics*, Vol. III, 1597-1644 (Gene M. Grossman & Kenneth Rogoff eds, Amsterdam, Elsevier Science Publishing 1995); Jo-Ann Crawford & Roberto V. Fiorentino, *The Changing Landscape of Regional Trade Agreements*, WTO Discussion Paper No. 8 (World Trade Organization 2005).
45. Wanki Moon, Won W. Koo & Chang-Gil Kim, *New Global Governance for Agriculture, Climate Change, Sustainability, and Food Security*, 34(2) Journal of Rural Agriculture 45-73 (2011).
46. A/HRC/43/44, para. 64.

social services'.[47] In 1966, the right to food reached a major milestone and assumed new significance when it was enshrined in a binding treaty – the ICESCR.[48] The ICESCR refined the concept of the right to food in at least two ways. *First*, the ICESCR introduced the concept of 'adequate food' instead of 'food' found in the Universal Declaration of Human Rights (UDHR). In Article 11 of the ICESCR, State Parties commit to 'recognize the right of everyone to an adequate standard of living for himself and his family, including adequate food ...'. *Second*, the ICESCR clarified that it is 'the fundamental right of everyone to be free from hunger'. In Article 11(2) of the ICESCR, State Parties 'recognize[ed] the fundamental right of everyone to be free from hunger'. *Third*, the ICESCR elaborated on the duty of states as regards the right to food. State Parties pledged to 'take appropriate steps to ensure the realization of this right' (Article 11(1)) and made a commitment to take necessary measures '[t]o improve methods of production, conservation and distribution of food' (Article 11(2)(b)). States Parties also committed to '[take] into account the problems of both food-importing and food-exporting countries, to ensure an equitable distribution of world food supplies in relation to need'. Furthermore, pursuant to Article 2(1) of the ICESCR, each State Party to the ICESCR 'undertakes to take steps, individually and through international assistance and co-operation ... to the maximum of its available resources, with a view to achieving progressively the full realization of the rights recognized in the ... Covenant by all appropriate means, including particularly the adoption of legislative measures'.

Beyond the ICESCR, the right to food has been recognized in numerous other binding as well as non-binding international legal instruments. Binding international legal instruments that recognize the right to food include: the Convention on the Elimination of All Forms of Discrimination Against Women (1979), the Convention on the Rights of the Child (1989), and the Convention on the Rights of Persons with Disabilities (2006). The number of non-binding instruments that recognize the right to food also continues to grow. Paragraph 1 of the *Universal Declaration on the Eradication of Hunger and Malnutrition* (1974) declares that 'Every man, woman and child has the inalienable right to be free from hunger and malnutrition in order to develop fully and maintain their physical and mental faculties.' In the *Rome Declaration on World Food Security* (1996), participating states 'reaffirm[ed] the right of everyone to have access to safe and nutritious food, consistent with the right to adequate food and the fundamental right of everyone to be free from hunger'. In the 2002 *World Food Summit Declaration* (2002), participating states 'reaffirm[ed] the need to assure gender equality and to support empowerment of women' (paragraph 11).

International legal instruments, particularly soft law instruments, have been used to deepen global understanding on the meaning and scope of the right to food. In the World Food Summit Plan of Action (1996), UN Member States resolved to 'implement, monitor, and follow-up this Plan of Action at all levels in cooperation with the

47. UN General Assembly, Universal Declaration of Human Rights (UDHR) (10 December 1948). GA Res. 217 A(III),10 December 1948.
48. UN General Assembly Resolution 2200A, International Covenant on Economic, Social and Cultural Rights (ICESCR) (3 January 1976).

international community'. Specifically, Objective 7.4 was '[t]o clarify the content of the right to adequate food and the fundamental right of everyone to be free from hunger, as stated in the International Covenant on Economic, Social and Cultural Rights and other relevant international and regional instruments, and to give particular attention to implementation and full and progressive realization of this right as a means of achieving food security for all'. The right to food achieved significant milestones in 2004 with the release of the Voluntary Guidelines to support the progressive realization of the right to adequate food in the context of national food security (VGRF)[49] and, in 2012, with the publication of the *CESCR General Comment No. 12: The Right to Adequate Food (Article 11)* (GC 12).[50]

The Committee on Economic, Social and Cultural Rights (CESCR), the body tasked with implementing the ICESCR, released GC 12 in 2012 to contribute to global understanding on the meaning and contours of the right to food. According to GC 12, '[t]he right to adequate food is realized when every man, woman and child, alone or in community with others, have physical and economic access at all times to adequate food or means for its procurement'. GC 12 affirms that the right to adequate food 'is indivisibly linked to the inherent dignity of the human person and is indispensable for the fulfilment of other human rights enshrined in the International Bill of Human Rights'.[51] GC 12 reiterates the understanding that the right to adequate food is inseparable from social justice and 'require[es] the adoption of appropriate economic, environmental and social policies, at both the national and international levels, oriented to the eradication of poverty and the fulfilment of all human rights for all' (paragraph 4). GC 12 also cautions against a narrow or restrictive interpretation of the right to food - one which simply equates it with a minimum package of calories, proteins and other specific nutrients (paragraph 6). The right to food is multidimensional and includes notions of availability, accessibility, adequacy, sustainability, cultural appropriateness. The core content of the right to food implies '[t]he availability of food in a quantity and quality sufficient to satisfy the dietary needs of individuals, free from adverse substances, and acceptable within a given culture' as well as '[t]he accessibility of such food in ways that are sustainable and that do not interfere with the enjoyment of other human rights' (paragraph 8).

While acknowledging that the right to adequate food 'will have to be realized progressively', GC 12 introduces the notion of 'core obligation'. At its core, State Parties are obliged 'to ensure the satisfaction of, at the very least, the minimum essential level required to be free from hunger'. States Parties have an obligation to take the necessary action to mitigate and alleviate hunger even in times of natural or other disasters. Furthermore, the right to food prohibits any discrimination in access to food, as well as to means and entitlements for its procurement. Significantly, GC 12 clarifies the nature

49. *See* Food and Agriculture Organization of the United Nations, Report of the Council of the Food and Agriculture Organization of the United Nations, One Hundred and Twenty-seventh Session, Rome, 22-27 November 2004 (CL 127/REP), appendix D; *see also* E/CN.4/2005/131, annex.
50. UN Econ. & Soc. Council, Committee on Econ. Soc. & Cultural Rights (CESCR), General Comment No. 12: The Right to Adequate Food (Article 11), para. 6, UN Doc. E/C.12/1999/5 (12 May 1999) (hereinafter General Comment No. 12).
51. Doc. E/C.12/1999/5 of 12 May 1999.

of state obligation in relation to the right to food and explains how the obligations to *respect*, to *protect* and to *fulfil* apply to the right to food. According to paragraph 15 of GC 12:

> 15. The right to adequate food, like any other human right, imposes three types or levels of obligations on States parties: the obligations to respect, to protect and to fulfil. In turn, the obligation to fulfil incorporates both an obligation to facilitate and an obligation to provide. The obligation to respect existing access to adequate food requires States parties not to take any measures that result in preventing such access. The obligation to protect requires measures by the State to ensure that enterprises or individuals do not deprive individuals of their access to adequate food. The obligation to fulfil (facilitate) means the State must proactively engage in activities intended to strengthen people's access to and utilization of resources and means to ensure their livelihood, including food security. Finally, whenever an individual or group is unable, for reasons beyond their control, to enjoy the right to adequate food by the means at their disposal, States have the obligation to fulfil (provide) that right directly. This obligation also applies for persons who are victims of natural or other disasters.

[3] Institutional Developments

The task of monitoring and implementing global standards relating to the right to food falls on a number of intergovernmental bodies, chief among which are the CESCR, the UN Special Rapporteur on the Right to Food ('Special Rapporteur'), and the CWFS. Significantly, none of these three bodies has the power to actually enforce the right to food against states and non-state actors.

The CESCR was established in 1985 and is tasked with monitoring the implementation of the ICESCR (ECOSOC Resolution 1985/17 of 28 May 1985). The CESCR was established primarily to consider the reports of State Parties to the ICESCR. Although the mandate of the CESCR has been expanded over the years, it still lacks the power to compel State Parties to fulfil their treaty obligations. The Optional Protocol to the ICESCR (Optional Protocol) entered into force in May 2013 and mandates the CESCR to receive and consider communications from individuals claiming that their rights under the ICESCR have been violated. Essentially, the Optional Protocol creates an optional procedure meaning that no communication can be received by the CESCR against a State Party to the ICESCR that has not ratified the Optional Protocol.

The mandate of the Special Rapporteur was originally established in April 2000 by the UN Commission on Human Rights, the predecessor to the UN Human Rights Council ('Human Rights Council' or 'HRC'), pursuant to Resolution 2000/10. In 2006, the Human Rights Council endorsed and extended the mandate of the Special Rapporteur through Resolution 6/2 of 27 September 2007. In its Resolution 6/2, the Human Rights Council '[r]ecogniz[ed] that the problems of hunger and food insecurity have global dimensions and that they are likely to persist and even increase dramatically in some regions of the world unless urgent, determined and concerted action is taken'. The Special Rapporteur has broad promotional functions but no enforcement powers. The Special Rapporteur implements its mandate through different means and activities, including monitoring the situation of the right to food throughout the world, undertaking country visits, and promoting the realization of the right to food through dialogue with relevant actors and stakeholders.

The CWFS was created in 1975 as a standing committee of the FAO.[52] The original mandate of the CWFS 'was to assist developing countries to implement national food reserves and coordinate the management of these reserves across developed and developing countries and other market'. The CWFS drafted the VGRF which the General Council of the FAO adopted in 2004. In its Resolution 6/2, the Human Rights Council acknowledged that the VGRF 'represent a practical tool to promote the realization of the right to food for all, contribute to the achievement of food security and thus provide an additional instrument in the attainment of internationally agreed development goals, including those contained in the Millennium Declaration'.

[4] Progress and Challenges

The good news is that numerous international legal instruments now affirm the importance of full respect for the right to adequate food. A significant majority of states (about 170) have ratified the ICESCR. A growing number of states have enshrined the right to food in their national constitutions, are adopting framework laws on the right to food, and rolling out national strategies to implement the right to food. The bad news is that not all states have ratified the ICESCR; only about twenty-four states have ratified the Optional Protocol which allows individuals and groups file complaints alleging a violation of their treaty rights. Of the states that have ratified the ICESCR, not enough countries are taking steps to fully realize the rights recognized in the treaty using all appropriate means, including particularly the adoption of legislative measures. Human rights defenders, particularly those fighting for land rights and environmental conservation, are facing increased attacks in almost every part of the world (E/2019/68). Despite its growing popularity, the right to food framework lacks a strong and credible enforcement and accountability mechanism. In sum, although the concept of the right to food has transformative potential, how to make the right to food effective for the millions in the world experiencing hunger and malnutrition remains a major challenge.[53]

[C] Food Security and International Investment Law

[1] Introduction

With a view to boosting agricultural productivity and developing the agri-food sector in developing countries, the past few years have witnessed significant efforts by states

52. FAO, Resolution 21/75 on the Establishment of a Committee on World Food Security (FAO 1975).

53. *See also* Olivier De Schutter (Special Rapporteur on the Right to Food), Final Report: The Transformative Potential of the Right to Food, para. 2, UN Doc. A/HRC/25/57, 3 (24 January 2014).

and intergovernmental bodies to encourage private sector investment in agriculture.[54] Across the globe, particularly in developing countries, increased private sector investment in agriculture has been reported.[55] Large-scale industrial farming for commodities such as palm oil, sugar cane, and cocoa are springing up and are expanding at a phenomenal rate in some countries in Africa and Asia.[56] The past two decades have also witnessed significant increases in investment in agricultural lands.[57] Renewed interest in private sector investment in agriculture in developing countries is attracting a wide range of actors, including corporations, sovereign wealth funds, and institutional investors, to the food and agricultural ecosystem in many countries.[58]

International financial institutions are at the forefront of efforts to promote private sector investment in agriculture and industrial agricultural model more broadly. International development banks such as the World Bank Group play a pivotal role in promoting large-scale acquisition of agricultural land through the use of direct and indirect financing and advisory services. The International Finance Corporation (IFC) believes that 'a strong and engaged private sector is indispensable to ending extreme poverty and boosting shared prosperity' and has, since 1956, 'leveraged USD 2.6 billion in capital to deliver more than USD 285 billion in financing for businesses in developing countries'.[59] The IFC invests across the agribusiness supply chain – from farm to retail and identifies agribusiness and forestry as one of its areas of expertise and has made this sector one of its priorities.

Private sector investment in agriculture, particularly in poor countries, is very controversial.[60] Non-governmental organizations, trade unions, farmers' organizations, consumer and environmental groups are generally very critical of the push for increased private sector investment in agriculture. *First*, critics believe that the push for increased private sector investment in agriculture reflects a misdiagnosis of the true cause of hunger and malnutrition in the world and reflects a preoccupation with increasing food production rather than a focus on accessibility and empowerment. *Second*, critics question whether increased private sector investment in agriculture can really contribute to sustainable development and worry that enough attention is not being paid to the legal environment in which such investments operate. *Finally*, critics believe that unless properly regulated, the cost of private sector investment in agriculture in developing countries completely outweighs the promised benefits of such investment. Large-scale industrial farming is increasingly associated with environmental destruction, displacement of communities, and human rights abuses. In

54. FAO, The State of Food and Agriculture: Investing in Agriculture for a Better Future (Rome, Food and Agriculture Organization of the United Nations 2012).
55. FAO, Trends in Foreign Direct Investment in Food, Beverages and Tobacco (2017).
56. *See* World Bank, *New World Bank Report Sees Growing Global Demand for Farmland* (Washington DC, 7 September 2010): http://farmlandgrab.org/post/view/15309.
57. Klaus Deininger et al., *Rising Global Interest in Farmland: Can It Yield Sustainable and Equitable Benefits?* By Agricultural and Rural Development Department (World Bank 2011).
58. *See* High Quest Partners, *Private Financial Sector Investment in Farmland and Agricultural Infrastructure* (Paris, OECD August 2010): http://farmlandgrab.org/post/view/16060.
59. https://www.ifc.org/wps/wcm/connect/corp_ext_content/ifc_external_corporate_site/home.
60. *See* Timothy A. Wise, *Seeds of Resistance, Harvests of Hope: Farmers Halt a Land Grab in Mozambique* (GRAIN 30 October 2018).

many countries, particularly in Africa, the promised gains from increased private sector involvement such as job creation, rural development, contribution to the local and national economies, and increased food security have failed to materialize.[61] Large-scale agricultural investment is also synonymous with commercial inputs to increase yield and typically focuses on cash crops for export rather than stable food that can contribute to food security. Instead of large-scale agricultural investment, critics call for investment in smallholder agriculture.[62] The argument is that smallholder agriculture contributes more to food security than large-scale agricultural investments.[63]

In sum, increased private sector investment in agriculture in poor countries is sparking a lot of debates. The relationship between foreign direct investment (FDI) in agriculture and food insecurity is highly contested. Proponents believe that large-scale foreign investment in the agricultural sector in low-income countries can promote agro-industrialization, increase agricultural productivity, bring about an increase in value-added in the agri-food chain, and produce spill-overs in the form of employment creation, technology transfer and rural development. Critics disagree this.[64] To critics, the current industrial/corporate agricultural model has serious disadvantages as it 'generates food loss and waste, mistreats animals, emits greenhouse gases, pollutes ecosystems, displaces and abuses agricultural and fishery workers, and disrupts traditional farming communities'.[65]

[2] Normative Developments

There is presently no comprehensive multilateral investment treaty that addresses the rights and responsibilities of host states or host communities vis-à-vis foreign investors. In place of a multilateral investment treaty, today's international investment law is made up of over 3,000 international investment agreements (IIAs), including some 2,901 bilateral investment treaties (BITs) and 389 treaties with investment provisions. IIAs deserve close scrutiny because of their geographical reach (virtually every country in the world has concluded at least one BIT), because of the broad rights they grant foreign investors, and because of their potential to encroach impermissibly on domestic regulatory space.

---

61. Oakland Institute, *Country Report 'Understanding Land Investment Deals in Africa: Sierra Leone'* (2011): http://www.oaklandinstitute.org/understanding-land-investment-deals-africa-sierra-leone.
62. HLPE, Investing in smallholder agriculture for food security. A report by the High-Level Panel of Experts on Food Security and Nutrition of the Committee on World Food Security, Rome (Rome, Committee on World Food Security 2013).
63. IFAD & UNEP, *Smallholders, Food Security and the Environment* (Rome, International Fund for Agricultural Development 2013).
64. Cecilie Friis & Anette Reenberg, *Land Grab in Africa: Emerging Land System Drivers in a Teleconnected World*, GLP Report No. 1 (The Global Land Project Denmark, August 2010): http://farmlandgrab.org/post/view/14816, respectively.
65. Critical perspective on food systems, food crises and the future of the right to food Report of the Special Rapporteur on the right to food. A/HRC/43/44 of 21 January 2020.

[a] Bilateral Investment Treaties

BITs are designed primarily to protect investors.[66] In general, BITs provide investors with at least seven core rights/guarantees. *First*, the BITs require that investors and their 'covered investments' (i.e., investments of a national or company of one BIT party in the territory of the other party) be treated as favourably as the host party treats its own investors and their investments (National Treatment). *Second*, BITs require that investors and their 'covered investments' be treated as favourably as the host party treats investors and investments from any third country (Most Favoured Nation Treatment). *Third*, most BITs guarantee investors absolute standard of treatment, including 'fair and equitable treatment', 'full protection and security', and protection against unreasonable or discriminatory measures. *Fourth*, most BITs provide safeguards against expropriation by establishing clear limits on the expropriation of investments and providing for payment of prompt, adequate, and effective compensation when expropriation takes place. *Fifth*, most BITs provide for the transferability of investment-related funds into and out of a host country without delay and using a market rate of exchange. *Sixth*, most BITs guarantee investors and their investment most favoured nation treatment in the event of loss due to war. *Seventh*, and perhaps most important, most BITs give investors the right to submit an investment dispute with a host state to international arbitration and do not generally require that investors use host country's domestic courts.

Although agro-FDI is growing and is generating a lot of contentious issues, international investment law does not provide a lot of answers to these issues. The current legal framework that rests on thousands of BITs is problematic for several reasons. *First*, most IIAs focus primarily on the rights of investors and the responsibilities of host states rather than investor obligation.[67] An overwhelming majority of existing BITs do not address economic, social or governance issues and do not impose direct obligations on investors.[68] Although a growing number of recent BITs include provisions on environment, labour and corporate social responsibility, most do not impose binding obligations on investors and most do not address issues such as food security, sustainability or the right of smallholder farmers.[69] *Second*, critics argue that

66. Office of the United States Trade Representative, Bilateral Investment Treaties, available at: http://www.ustr.gov/trade-agreements/bilateral-investment-treaties (discussing the six core benefits BITs provide to investors).
67. Emma Aisbett et al., *Rethinking International Investment Governance: Principles for the 21st Century* (2018).
68. *See* United National Conference on Trade and Development, Investment Policy Framework for Sustainable Development (2015). *See* generally Patrick Dumberry & Gabrielle Dumas-Aubin, *How to Impose Human Rights Obligations on Corporations under Investment Treaties?*, 4 Yearbook on International Investment Law and Policy 569-600 (2011-2012); Megan Wells Sheffer, *Bilateral Investment Treaties: A Friend or Foe to Human Rights*, 39 Denver Journal of International Law and Policy 483 (2011); Jose E. Alvarez, *Empire, Contemporary Foreign Investment Law: An 'Empire of Law' or the 'Law of Empire'?*, 60 Alabama Law Review 943, 957-959 (2009).
69. Uche Ewelukwa Ofodile, *Foreign Investment in Land and the Clash of Regimes: Mapping the Role of International Investment Law and International Human Rights Law*, 7(1) Human Rights & International Legal Discourse (2013).

BITs unduly constrain the policy space of host states and make it extremely difficult for host states to regulate in the public interest. *Third*, most BITs grant investors the right to initiate a claim against host states before international tribunals but do not grant corresponding rights to individuals and communities affected by the activities of foreign investors. The past decade has witnessed a growing backlash against the international investment law regime in general and investment arbitration in particular.

[b] Principles of Responsible Investments

In the wake of massive growth in private sector investment in agriculture and growing criticisms of these investments, the concept of 'responsible agricultural investment' has emerged in international food policy circles and targets a host of issues at the intersection of agribusiness and human rights, agribusiness and the environment, as well as agribusiness and sustainable development. Soft law instruments that offer guidelines on responsible investment are beginning to emerge. The *Principles for Responsible Agricultural Investment that respects rights, livelihoods and resources (PRAI)* was launched in 2010.[70] PRAI was jointly developed by the Food and Agriculture Organization (FAO) of the UN, IFAD, UN Conference on Trade and Development, and the World Bank. Other related legal instruments, include the *United Nations Guiding Principles on Business and Human Rights* (2011), the *Voluntary Guidelines on the Responsible Governance on Tenure of Land, Fisheries and Forests in the Context of National Food Security* (2012), the *Voluntary Guidelines for Securing Sustainable Small-Scale Fisheries in the Context of Food Security and Poverty Eradication* (2014), and the *Principles for Responsible Investment in Agriculture and Food Systems* (Principles for Responsible Investment) published in 2014.

PRAI is a set of seven principles that cover a range of issues arising from investment in agriculture. The seven PRAI principles are as follows:

- Principle 1: Existing rights to land and associated natural resources are recognized and respected.
- Principle 2: Investments do not jeopardize food security but rather strengthen it.
- Principle 3: Processes relating to investment in agriculture are transparent, monitored, and ensure accountability by all stakeholders, within a proper business, legal, and regulatory environment.
- Principle 4: All those materially affected are consulted, and agreements from consultations are recorded and enforced.
- Principle 5: Investors ensure that projects respect the rule of law, reflect industry best practice, are viable economically, and result in durable shared value.

70. http://www.fao.org/fileadmin/templates/est/INTERNATIONAL-TRADE/FDIs/RAI_Principles_Synoptic.pdf.

- Principle 6: Investments generate desirable social and distributional impacts and do not increase vulnerability.
- Principle 7: Environmental impacts of a project are quantified and measures are taken to encourage sustainable resource use, while minimizing the risk/magnitude of negative impacts and mitigating them.

With respect to food security, PRAI's Principle 2 obliges states and businesses to ensure that agro-investments do not have an adverse effect on food security. Whenever there are potential adverse effects on any aspect of food security, policymakers are required to 'make provisions for the local or directly affected populations such that: (i) continuing access to food is assured; (ii) opportunities for outgrower involvement and off-farm employment are expanded to protect livelihoods and raise incomes; (iii) dietary preferences are taken into account if the mix of products grown may change; and (iv) strategies to reduce potential instability of supply are adopted'. Principle 5 addresses investors directly and declares that investors 'have a special responsibility to apply high standards in the design and execution of their projects'. In addition to conducting due diligence and project analysis, investors are expected to '(i) comply with laws, regulations, and policies applicable in the host country (and ideally with all relevant international treaties and conventions); (ii) adhere to global best practices for transparency, accountability and corporate responsibility in all sensitive areas; and (iii) strive not only to increase shareholder value but also to generate significant and tangible benefits for the project area, affected communities, and the host country'.

Endorsed in 2014 by the CWFS, the objective of the Principles for Responsible Investment is 'to promote responsible investment in agriculture and food systems that contribute to food security and nutrition, thus supporting the progressive realization of the right to adequate food in the context of national food security'.[71] Ten principles make up the Principles for Responsible Investment, as follows:

Principles for Responsible Investment in Agriculture and Food Systems:

- Principle 1: Contribute to food security and nutrition.
- Principle 2: Contribute to sustainable and inclusive economic development and the eradication of poverty.
- Principle 3: Foster gender equality and women's empowerment.
- Principle 4: Engage and empower youth.
- Principle 5: Respect tenure of land, fisheries, and forests, and access to water.
- Principle 6: Conserve and sustainably manage natural resources, increase resilience, and reduce disaster risks.
- Principle 7: Respect cultural heritage and traditional knowledge, and support diversity and innovation.
- Principle 8: Promote safe and healthy agriculture and food systems.
- Principle 9: Incorporate inclusive and transparent governance structures, processes, and grievance mechanisms.
- Principle 10: Assess and address impacts and promote accountability.

71. http://www.fao.org/3/a-au866e.pdf, para. 10.

Thus far, the legal instruments that advocate for responsible investment in agriculture are completely voluntary and are not binding on states and businesses. In the Principles for Responsible Investment, the CWFS states explicitly that '[n]othing in the Principles should be read as limiting or undermining any legal obligations to which a State may be subject under international law'.[72] The aim of most of the relevant instruments is not to create rights for individuals and groups affected by agro-investment, to impose binding obligations on investors, or to create mechanisms that can monitor investment-related violations. The CWFS has stated that the Principles for Responsible Investment only seek to: (a) address the core elements of what makes investment in agriculture and food systems responsible; (b) identify who the key stakeholders are, and their respective roles and responsibilities with respect to responsible investment in agriculture and food systems; and (c) serve as a framework to guide the actions of all stakeholders engaged in agriculture and food systems.

[3] Institutional Developments

There is presently no multilateral intergovernmental organization tasked with supervising FDIs in the agricultural sector, supervising the implementation of the thousands of BITs in existence today, or more generally monitoring the activities of foreign investors. For the most part, IIAs are interpreted and applied by institutional and ad hoc arbitral tribunals.[73] It is up to each state to regulate and monitor the activities of foreign investors operating within their jurisdiction. Despite its relatively broad mandate, the FAO lacks the power to monitor and/or supervise the activities of agribusinesses and agricultural investors. However, over the past two decades the FAO has published numerous guidelines including, the *FAO Code of Conduct for Responsible Fisheries* (1995),[74] and the FAO *Voluntary Guidelines for the Responsible Management of Planted Forests* (2006).[75]

Existing international human rights treaties, including the ICESCR, do not address the duties and responsibilities of businesses. Occasionally, human rights bodies address the activities of businesses but they do not have the mandate to monitor the behaviour of business and the power to compel corporate responsibility and/or accountability. For example, in its GC 12, the CESCR declares that while only states are parties to the ICESCR and are ultimately accountable for compliance with it, all members of society, including the private business sector have responsibilities in the realization of the right to adequate food. According to the CESCR, '[t]he private business sector – national and transnational – should pursue its activities within the framework of a code of conduct conducive to respect of the right to adequate food, agreed upon jointly with the Government and civil society'. In its GC No. 24 (2017) on *State Obligations under the International Covenant on Economic, Social and Cultural*

72. *Ibid.*, 5.
73. Emma Aisbett et al., *Rethinking International Investment Governance: Principles for the 21st Century* (2018).
74. http://www.fao.org/3/a-v9878e.pdf.
75. http://www.fao.org/3/j9256e/j9256e00.htm.

Rights in the Context of Business Activities (GC 17), the CESCR further elaborated on the legal and social responsibilities of businesses but stopped short of imposing any direct obligations on business enterprises.[76] Paragraph 13 of GC 24 draws attention to the potential risks investment treaties pose for human rights but does not prohibit such investments. According to paragraph 13:

> 13. States parties should identify any potential conflict between their obligations under the Covenant and under trade or investment treaties, and refrain from entering into such treaties where such conflicts are found to exist, as required under the principle of the binding character of treaties. The conclusion of such treaties should therefore be preceded by human rights impact assessments ... . Such impacts on human rights of the implementation of the agreements should be regularly assessed, to allow for the adoption of any corrective measures that may be required. The interpretation of trade and investment treaties currently in force should take into account the human rights obligations of the State ... . They are encouraged to insert, in future treaties, a provision explicitly referring to their human rights obligations, and to ensure that mechanisms for the settlement of investor-State disputes take human rights into account in the interpretation of investment treaties or of investment chapters in trade agreements.

[4] Problems and Challenges

To the extent that agro-FDI increases investment in the food and agricultural sector, that can be celebrated. For a long time policymakers have called for increased investment in the agricultural sector in poor countries. One of the targets of the SDGs is to '[i]ncrease investment ... in rural infrastructure, agricultural research and extension services, technology development and plant and livestock gene banks in order to enhance agricultural productive capacity in developing countries, in particular least developed countries'. In the Rome Declaration (Commitment Six), world leaders made a commitment to 'promote optimal allocation and use of public and private investments to foster human resources, sustainable food, agriculture, fisheries and forestry systems, and rural development, in high and low potential areas'. The critical question today is not whether private investment in agriculture is desirable but whether such investments produce win-win outcomes and whether they advance the SDG 2030 Agenda. Regarding food security, the critical question is whether private investments in food and agriculture, particularly in poor countries, promote or undermine food security objectives, and whether there are rules in place to ensure that such investments would benefit the local communities and that investors are held accountable if and when they violate human rights. Although reforms are underway in a growing number of countries, reform is slow and haphazard. Historically, BITs have been primarily used to protect foreign investors, facilitate investment entry and operation, and liberalize the economies of host states. Although a growing number of countries are reviewing and revising their BITs, most BITs in existence today still do

---

76. E/C.12/GC/24 of 10 August 2017.

not address corporate social responsibility, investor accountability or the rights of host states and host communities.

The good news is that the idea of responsible investment in agriculture is gaining traction. The bad news is that the concept of 'responsible investment' has generated and is still generating considerable criticism. *First*, the concept of 'responsible investment' is controversial and is questioned in many circles.[77] *Second*, the concept of 'responsible investment' currently lacks clarity and is not backed by any enforceable treaty. *Third*, the concept of responsible investment is not backed up by any credible compliance, monitoring or enforcement mechanism. *Fourth*, critics are also concerned about the top-down approach in which many of the new principles and guidelines have come about. *Finally*, there are widespread concerns that most of the international legal instruments that purport to promote responsible investment are actually designed to legitimize corporate-led agriculture in poor countries and corporate (foreign and domestic) takeover of rural people's farmlands in these countries. Thus, although welcomed by intergovernmental organizations and economic blocs such as the Group of Twenty (G20),[78] civil society organizations have denounced the PRAI.[79] To critics, responsible agricultural investment 'is not about facilitating investment in agriculture' but 'is about creating an illusion that by following a set of standards, large-scale land acquisitions can proceed without disastrous consequences to peoples, communities, ecosystems and the climate'.[80]

§1.04 THE GLOBAL FOOD SYSTEM AND INTERNATIONAL LAW: THE PAST, THE PRESENT, THE ROAD AHEAD

Is international law supportive of a well-functioning global food system? Has international law helped to establish global institutional mechanisms that are supportive of sustainable agricultural development and food and nutrition security in the world? The good news is that international legal instruments purporting to address food security concerns have proliferated and are still proliferating. The good news also is that there is today no shortage of international organizations committed to promoting a world of zero hunger and malnutrition in their mandates (A/HRC/43/44, paragraph 71). Nevertheless, the landscape of the global governance of the world food and agricultural system reveals fragmentation, policy incoherence, and major shortcomings in the normative and institutional response to food insecurity.

---

77. H. Mirza, W. Speller, G. Dixie & Z. Goodman, *The Practice of Responsible Investment Principles in Larger Scale Agricultural Investments* (Washington D.C. and Geneva, World Bank Group and United Nations Conference on Trade and Development 2014).
78. Annex II of the G20 Seoul Summit Leaders' Declaration, on the Multi-Year Action Plan on Development (November 2010).
79. Stop land grabbing now! Say NO to the principles on responsible agro-enterprise investment promoted by the World Bank, available online at: http://www.landaction.org/spip/spip.php?article553; *See also*: Responsibly destroying the world's peasantry by Olivier de Schutter, Brussels, 4 June 2010: http://www.project-syndicate.org/commentary/deschutter1/English.
80. *Why So-Called 'Responsible Agricultural Investment' Must Be Stopped*: https://www.tni.org/en/article/why-so-called-responsible-agricultural-investment-must-be-stopped.

[A] An Impressive Legal Landscape

Over the past several decades, tentative action within the framework of the League of Nations morphed into more sustained action within the framework of the UN, the FAO, and other intergovernmental organizations. Hopes were very high in the 1960s and many of the important foundations of the global food security regime were laid in that decade. A 1961 report of the Director General of the FAO entitled *Development Through Food: A Strategy for Surplus Utilization* made a case for utilizing the food surpluses in certain countries for the development of certain underdeveloped regions of the world.[81] Another 1961 report of the UN Secretary General entitled 'The role of the United Nations and the appropriate specialized agencies in facilitating the best possible use of food surpluses for the economic development of the less developed countries' suggested that global action in response to food insecurity in various parts of the globe was possible.[82] For over seventy years, going back to the establishment of the FAO in 1945, international legal instruments have played a role in shaping the broad contours of the international food security regime, creating key international institutions and mechanisms, deepening relevant concepts, and galvanizing concerted global action around food insecurity.

Today, food security is broadly conceived as both a domestic issue and as a global problem requiring concerted action of the global community. There is broad consensus that food security is a global problem that requires international attention, cooperation, and action. With advances in the understanding of the causes of hunger, there has also been a broad consensus about the multifaceted root of food insecurity and broad agreement that food insecurity is not simply a problem of availability but also a problem of accessibility. Thanks to international soft law instruments, there has been, since 1996, a consensus definition of food insecurity. New targets are still being set. 'By 2030, ensure sustainable food production systems and implement resilient agricultural practices that increase productivity and production, that help maintain ecosystems, that strengthen capacity for adaptation to climate change, extreme weather, drought, flooding and other disasters and that progressively improve land and soil quality' (Target 2.4), world leaders boldly declare in the SDG Agenda 2030.[83]

[B] Persisting Debates

The drivers of global food insecurity are diverse and complex. Not surprisingly, there is a lack of agreement on the main drivers of food insecurity and wide disagreement on what causes hunger and malnutrition in the world.[84] Whether food insecurity is primarily attributable to productivity gap and thus a problem that can be addressed

81. Food and Agriculture Organization of the United Nations, Rome, 1961.
82. Official Records of the Economic and Social Council, Thirty-second Session, Annexes, agenda item 8, document E/3509.
83. A/RES/70/1 of 21 October 2015.
84. World Food Programme, *What Causes Hunger?*: http://www.wfp.org/HUNGER/CAUSES (last visited 30 September 2020).

through mechanization, irrigation, and massive infusion of industrial inputs or whether food insecurity is primarily attributable to powerlessness is a matter of serious and continuing debate. While one group believe that global hunger is because there is not enough food to go around, the other believes that hunger is largely a result of poverty and lack of access to available food.[85] This disagreement is serious as it affects the solutions that are advanced to address food insecurity. One group believes that the solution lies in part in spurring private sector investment in agriculture; the other group believes that the solution lies not in increasing corporate agricultural investments but in empowering smallholder farmers and encouraging smallholder agriculture. The 1996 Rome Declaration on World Food Security embraces both approaches by stating that '[t]o feed a world population expected to surpass 9 billion in 2050, it is estimated that agricultural output will have to increase by 70 percent between now and then' and adding that '[c]oncomitantly, measures have to be taken to ensure access - physical, social and economic - by all people to sufficient, safe and nutritious food with particular attention to full access by women and children'.

Tensions in the global food and agricultural system run very deep. The vision of the proponents of food sovereignty is vastly at odds with the vision of those that advocate for increased globalization and financialization of the global food and agricultural system. According to the 2007 Nyéléni meeting:

> Food sovereignty suggests that in order to explore how food is produced, traded and consumed, we need to question the whole fabric of global economics and society:
>
> - resource-intensive industrial production of crops, livestock and seafood;
> - the emergence of dangerous technologies, such as genetically modified organisms and nanotechnology;
> - the paradigm of global trade peddled by institutions like the World Trade Organization and manifested in Free Trade Agreements;
> - food aid as an extension of the North dumping on the South;
> - the patenting of traditional knowledge, and;
> - the overarching increased consolidation of corporate control of food production, distribution and trade.

The 2007 meeting in the village of Nyéléni in Mali brought together more than five-hundred representatives from more than eighty countries, of organizations of peasants/family farmers, artisanal fisher-folk, indigenous peoples, landless peoples, rural workers, migrants, pastoralists, forest communities, women, youth, consumers, environmental and urban movements, gathered to strengthen a global movement for food sovereignty. The meeting essentially called on the global community to rethink many of the notions, concepts and practices that underpin the current food and agricultural system.

85. *See* generally A. Sen, *Poverty and Famines: An Essay on Entitlement and Deprivation* (Oxford University Press 1981).

[C] Persisting Challenges

[1] Sovereignty Concerns

With the globalization of food and agriculture, decisions that were once localized and anchored around local, national, and regional networks are increasingly made by international institutions and by powerful global actors, including transnational corporations, private investors, and foundations. Agricultural policies in some of the world's richest economies threaten the livelihoods of millions in poor countries and yet are beyond the reach of global trade rules.[86] For the most part, the concept of food sovereignty is yet to be embraced by most of the powerful actors that currently shape the global food and agricultural system. As laid out in the *Declaration of Nyéléni* (2007):

> Food sovereignty is the right of peoples to healthy and culturally appropriate food produced through ecologically sound and sustainable methods, and their right to define their own food and agriculture systems. It puts those who produce, distribute and consume food at the heart of food systems and policies rather than the demands of markets and corporations. It defends the interests and inclusion of the next generation. It offers a strategy to resist and dismantle the current corporate trade and food regime, and directions for food, farming, pastoral and fisheries systems determined by local producers. Food sovereignty prioritises local and national economies and markets and empowers peasant and family farmer-driven agriculture, artisanal % fishing, pastoralist-led grazing, and food production, distribution and consumption based on environmental, social and economic sustainability. Food sovereignty promotes transparent trade that guarantees just income to all peoples and the rights of consumers to control their food and nutrition.[87]

The deteriorating fate of the world's small-scale farmers is a matter of considerable concern. According to *The State of Food Insecurity in the World 2015*, '[m]ore than 90 percent of the 570 million farms worldwide are managed by an individual or a family, relying predominately on family labour', and the farms produce more than 80% of the world's food, in terms of value. Although more than half of the world's food is produced by small-scale farmers, a majority of the world's farmers experience food insecurity. Across the globe, farmers are bombarded by a host of problems and challenges, including dwindling resources, lagging farm economy, fluctuations in commodity prices, land degradations, climate change problems, as well as missing or inefficient markets. In December 2018, the General Assembly, through its Resolution 73/165 of 17 December 2018, adopted *the United Nations Declaration on the Rights of Peasants and Other People Working in Rural Areas* (UNDROP).[88] The good news is that

86. Keith E. Sealing, *Attack of the Balloon People: How America's Food Culture and Agricultural Policies Threaten the Food Security of the Poor, Farmers, and Indigenous Peoples of the World*, 40 Vanderbilt Journal of Transnational Law 1015, 1035 (2007) (citing Michael Pollan, *The Vegetable-Industrial Complex*, N.Y. Times Mag., at 17 (15 October 2006)), available at: http://www.nytimes.com/2006/10/15/magazine/15wwln_1ede.html.
87. https://nyeleni.org/DOWNLOADS/Nyelni_EN.pdf.
88. Available at: https://www.geneva-academy.ch/joomlatools-files/docman-files/UN%20Declaration%20on%20the%20rights%20of%20peasants.pdf.

UNDROP is the first-ever international legal instrument to explicitly recognize the rights of peasants. The good news also is that UNDROP addresses issues important to farmers such as the right to save, exchange and sell farm-saved seeds and access to land. The bad news is that UNDROP, adopted with 119 votes in favour, 7 against, and 49 abstentions, is a controversial legal instrument and is not binding on states and other actors that operate in the global food and agricultural space.

[2] Democratic Deficit

Critics point to democratic deficit in international's laws response to food insecurity. The argument is that international law relating to food has evolved in a top-down fashion and has not always reflected the voices of peasant and small farmers, fisherfolks, pastoralists, and other vulnerable groups and communities.[89] Issues of concern to the poor such as issues relating to food sovereignty are not reflected in current legal instruments.[90] The role of civil society organizations in the development of global trade rules or international investment law remains very limited despite increased calls for a participatory approach to global food governance. Many believe that the global food governance has been hijacked by private companies and other powerful actors. To be sure, world leaders do mention their commitment to the world's peasants and smallholder farmers. In Target 2.3 of the SDG 2030 Agenda, world leaders commit, by 2030, to 'double the agricultural productivity and incomes of small-scale food producers, in particular women, indigenous peoples, family farmers, pastoralists and fishers, including through secure and equal access to land, other productive resources and inputs, knowledge, financial services, markets and opportunities for value addition and non-farm employment'. In the Rome Declaration on World Food Security (Commitment Three), world leaders made commitments to 'pursue participatory and sustainable food, agriculture, fisheries, forestry and rural development policies and practices'. More than twenty years after the adoption of the Rome Declaration, the world's smallholder farmers and fisherfolks, particularly women, are still fighting for a seat at the table.

Deserving closer scrutiny is the effect of agricultural consolidation in rich countries on food security and livelihoods in poor countries.[91] The past two decades have witnessed increased cross-border and multijurisdictional mergers and acquisitions (M&A), joint ventures, and strategic alliances in the food and agricultural sector.[92] In a 31 May 2016 letter to the Principal Deputy Assistant Attorney General in the United States, the American Antitrust Institute (AAI), Food & Water Watch and National Farmers Union urged the U.S. Department of Justice Antitrust Division to

89. La Via Campesina, *The International Peasant's Voice*, available at: viacampesina.org/en/international-peasants-voice.
90. Ray Patel, *Food Sovereignty*, 36(3) The Journal of Peasant Studies 663 (2009).
91. *See* Agriculture and Antitrust Enforcement Issues in Our 21st Century Economy, U.S. Dept of Justice: http://www.justice.gov/atr/public/workshops/ag2010/index.html.
92. *See* generally, Uche Ewelukwa Ofodile, *Agribusiness Consolidation, Food Security and the Challenges of Global Governance*, JURIST & Academic Commentary (13 February 2017): http://jurist.org/forum/2017/02/Uche-Ofodile-agribusiness.php.

challenge the proposed merger of Dow Chemical Co. and DuPont Co. The letter identified three major areas of concern: eliminating head-to-head competition in the corn and soybean markets, reducing vital innovation competition, and creating a large, integrated 'platform' of traits, seeds, and chemicals that would make it harder for smaller biotechnology rivals to compete. Although concentrations in seeds and other agricultural inputs require careful antitrust scrutiny and enforcement where appropriate, most developing countries lack effective competition policies and do not have strong regulatory bodies able to adequately scrutinize consolidation in the agricultural sector.[93]

[3] Monitoring and Enforcement Challenges

The global food governance is based on voluntary legal instruments rather than binding treaties. Even when binding rules are at play, the agreements frequently lack effective monitoring and enforcement mechanism. Consequently, although global targets have been set on issues relating to hunger and poverty, these goals are not enshrined in binding instruments. There is also no mechanism to ensure that goals that have been formulated are integrated into every area of international policymaking. For example, although the SDGs are frequently mentioned, it is not clear how or where the SDGs fit in international investment law instruments or in the multilateral trade agreements.

To be sure, the rights of farmers are addressed in the *International Treaty on Plant Genetic Resources for Food and Agriculture* (International Seed Treaty). Although a binding instrument that has been ratified by over 140 countries, the International Seed Treaty lacks a strong monitoring and enforcement mechanism. In the International Seed Treaty, Contracting States 'recognize the enormous contribution that the local and indigenous communities and farmers of all regions of the world ... have made and will continue to make for the conservation and development of plant genetic resources which constitute the basis of food and agriculture production throughout the world' (Article 9.1) and 'agree that the responsibility for realizing Farmers's Rights, as they relate to plant genetic resources for food and agriculture, rests with national governments' (Article 9.2). Each Contracting Party undertakes '[i]n accordance with their needs and priorities', and 'as appropriate, and subject to its national legislation', to take measures to protect and promote Farmers's Rights, including: '(a) protection of traditional knowledge relevant to plant genetic resources for food and agriculture; (b) the right to equitably participate in sharing benefits arising from the utilization of plant genetic resources for food and agriculture; and (c) the right to participate in making decisions, at the national level, on matters related to the conservation and sustainable use of plant genetic resources for food and agriculture'. Article 9.3 declares that 'Nothing in this Article shall be interpreted to limit any rights that farmers have to save, use, exchange and sell farm-saved seed/propagating material, subject to national law and as appropriate.' The International Seed Treaty is silent on the issue of recourse or

93. *Ibid.*

remedy for farmers whose rights are violated. Article 22 is titled 'Settlement of Disputes', but only addresses potential disputes between Contracting Parties.

[4] *Fragmentation and Lack of Coordination*

Fragmentation and lack of policy coherence is a major and noticeable flaw in the post-war global governance framework for addressing global food insecurity.[94] Although food insecurity implicates a host of pressing issues at the meeting point between agriculture, the environment, human rights, global trade, international investment, and global security, there is little or no synergy among these sectors. Food and agriculture governance is under the mandate of at least three international bodies with vastly different agendas – the FAO, the WTO, and the CESCR.

The concept of food security is developed separately from and outside of the international rules that regulate global food and agricultural trade. Whether multilateral trade rules are in alignment with the objective of ensuring adequate food for all is a matter of considerable debate today. While there is agreement that trade rules have consequences for world food security, there is little or no agreement on whether their impact is negative or positive. What is clear is that human rights bodies are increasingly very critical of the rules governing global trade in agriculture. Human rights bodies have also expressed concern about the 'supermarketization' of food systems as well as the globalization and financialization of food systems.[95] According to a January 2020 report, the '[g]lobalization and financialization of food systems has enabled big agricultural firms to dominate the market, unilaterally deciding what and how much to produce' and the resulting power imbalance 'leaves small and medium enterprises without food sovereignty and with almost no alternative but to accept the rules set by big agriculture'.[96] Underscoring deep divisions among the main institutions that drive the global food and agricultural agenda, the current UN Special Rapporteur on the Right to Food, Michael Fakhri, in his first report, called for the WTO's AoA to be wound down and, in its place, for states to build new food and agriculture agreements on the foundation of human rights principles.[97]

There is broad acceptance on the need to reform the global governance of food security. Policymakers agree that there is a need to enhance cooperation and coordination among the key players in the food and agricultural sector, particularly among the agencies in the UN System, the Bretton Wood's institutions, regional organizations, economic blocs and states. As far back as 1972, the *World Declaration on Nutrition* and *Plan of Action for Nutrition* (1992) urged all concerned agencies and organs of the UN system 'to strengthen their collaborative and cooperative mechanisms in order to fully participate at international, regional, national and local levels in the achievement of the

94. United Nations General Assembly, *Fragmentation of International Law: Difficulties Derived from the Diversification and Expansion of International Law*, Report from the Work Group of the Commission for International Law, A/CN.4/L.702, 18 July 2006.
95. A/HRC/43/44: https://undocs.org/en/A/HRC/43/44.
96. *Ibid.*, para. 14.
97. A/75/2019, 22 July 2020: https://undocs.org/A/75/219.

objectives of the Plan of Action'. In 2009, the science and policy-based High-Level Panel of Experts on Food Security and Nutrition (HLPE) was created 'as an essential element of the CFS reform'. The HLPE aims to facilitate policy debates and inform policymaking 'by providing independent, comprehensive and evidence-based analysis and advice at the request of CFS'.[98] Sadly, after many years of reform and talking about reform, fragmentation and lack of policy coherence remain a major problem in the system.

§1.05 CONCLUSIONS

The relationship between international law and food security is contested, complicated, and even confusing. Over the past century, using both hard and soft international legal instruments, world leaders have successfully placed food and nutrition security on the global policy agenda and created institutions to drive this agenda. The good news is that from every indication, global food security is now seen as a global public.[99] After years of lack of global attention to food and agriculture, the agricultural sector is now prioritized in global and regional policymaking. There are growing commitments to increase support for agriculture, rural development, and food security at national, regional, and international levels. The world has also set measurable targets on issues relating to food security as demonstrated by SDG 2. In 2016, through its Resolution 70/259, the General Assembly proclaimed 2016-2025 as the UN Decade of Action on Nutrition. In 2017, through its Resolution 72/239, the General Assembly proclaimed 2019-2028 the UN Decade of Family Farming. Most importantly, new governance mechanisms directed at tackling perceived problems have emerged and there are fresh attempts at coordination of efforts.[100] Overall, on issues such as right to food, responsible agricultural investment, and international trade, rules are emerging on key issues and mechanisms are increasingly created to coordinate action.

The fight against global hunger and malnutrition continues unabated even in the middle of a global pandemic, thanks to the work of numerous intergovernmental organizations and institutions. Significantly, the Nobel Peace Prize for 2020 went to the WFP for its efforts to combat hunger and for acting as a driving force in efforts to prevent the use of hunger as a weapon of war and conflict. Back in 1961, the General Assembly, through Resolution A/RES/1714, created the WFP as an experiment to provide food aid through the UN system. Today, the WFP is the world's largest humanitarian organization addressing hunger and promoting food security. In 2019, the WFP provided assistance to about 97 million people in 88 countries who were victims of acute food insecurity and hunger. In June 2020, the WFP announced a massive rise in the number of hungry people it plans to assist around the world, as the COVID-19 pandemic pushes millions of more people into food insecurity in low- and

98. http://www.fao.org/cfs/cfs-hlpe/en/.
99. *See* UN, Key Conference Outcomes on Food, available at www.un.org/en/development/devagenda/food.shtml.
100. CFS, Reform of the Committee on World Food Security (CFS), Thirty-fifth Session, 14, 15 and 17 October 2009, Committee on World Food Security, FAO, Rome (2009).

middle-income countries; in 2020, the organization plans to assist up to 138 million, up from a record of 97 million in 2019.

Although international legal instruments have been used effectively to create numerous global institutions and mechanisms that address food security, they cannot and do not have the magic solution to the problem of hunger and malnutrition. Despite decades of action stretching back to at least the 1940s, in 2016, the General Assembly bemoaned the fact that 'nearly 800 million people remain chronically undernourished and 159 million children under 5 years of age are stunted, approximately 50 million children under 5 years of age are wasted, over 2 billion people suffer from micronutrient deficiencies and a rapidly increasing number of people are affected by obesity in all regions, with more than 1.9 billion overweight adults, of whom over 600 million are obese' (A/RES/70/259).

Normative and institutional fragmentation is a major problem in the global governance for food and agriculture.[101] Although '[t]here is no shortage of international organizations committed to promoting a world of zero hunger and malnutrition in their mandates' 'there is generally a disconnect and lack of coordination between them', Hilal Elver lamented in a January 2020 report.[102] Today, there is no comprehensive and coherent governance system for international policy action in the area of food and agriculture. With multiple governance mechanisms and structures, tensions, overlaps, and conflicts inevitably arise. Although the FAO is recognized as the primary international organization responsible for food and agriculture, many important issues that affect food security, such as trade in food and agricultural products, climate change, corporate accountability, and foreign investment, are outside the control of the organization. Institutions such as the WTO and the World Bank that shape global trade and investment rules, while not antagonistic to human rights principles, do not embrace and fully implement the human rights approach to assessing food insecurity that most human rights bodies call for.[103] In its Resolution 61/163 of 21 February 2007, the General Assembly recognized 'the need for a successful conclusion of the Doha Development Round negotiations of the World Trade Organization as a contribution for creating international conditions that permit the realization of the right to food'.

The challenge today is how to ensure effective coordination among international bodies with varying views on the causes of hunger and malnutrition in the world and the solution to the problem. While some international bodies conceive food insecurity as a problem primarily attributable to productivity gap, some attribute it to lack of legal, economic, and social access to food and productive resources. While some mechanisms are focused on advancing the interest of small-scale farmers, pastoralists, fisher-folk, women, indigenous people, and other marginalized groups, some are designed to advance the interest of agribusiness corporations. Furthermore, while

101. Matias E. Margulis, *The Regime Complex for Food Security: Implications for the Global Hunger Challenge*, 19 Global Governance 53 (2012).
102. A/HRC/43/44, para. 71.
103. *Ibid.*, para. 72.

some mechanisms prioritize market-led and even market-only solutions, others prioritize bottom-up, local solutions.[104] In short, the diversity of actors in the global food and agricultural space means a lack of coherence among policies, programmes and projects at the various levels (local, national, regional and continental).

Furthermore, despite the proliferation of international legal instruments designed to address the problem of hunger and malnutrition, there are still noticeable gaps in international law's response to the problem. For example, although market concentration in the global input sector has risen significantly in the past three decades and affect growers and consumers the world over, these processes and activities are outside the existing global legal framework for food and agriculture. There is no global competition watchdog even though cross-border and multijurisdictional mergers and acquisitions are on the increase and have wide-ranging regulatory and public interest implications. In the past fifty years many actors and organizational mechanisms – both public and private – have emerged and are addressing a wide range of issues relating to food and agriculture. According to a 2019 UN report, 'the global landscape for Sustainable Development Goal implementation has generally deteriorated since 2015' and 'the commitment to multilateral cooperation, so central to implementing major global agreements, is now under pressure' (E/2019/68, paragraph 12).

Globalization of food and agricultural systems, admittedly, has the potential to support greater availability and access to food. Unfortunately, as von Braun and Birner rightly note, 'globalization of agriculture and its dynamics and complexities have outpaced the capabilities of the organizations that have evolved over time to deal with the global dimensions of agricultural and food systems changes'. International legal instruments do not adequately account for all the old and emerging actors in the global food and agricultural space, including specialized global organizations, development organizations, international financial organizations, UN specialized agencies, private governance mechanisms, private foundations, and civil society organizations.

In GC 12, the CESCR rightly noted that '[d]espite the fact that the international community has frequently reaffirmed the importance of full respect for the right to adequate food, a disturbing gap still exists between the standards set in article 11 of the Covenant and the situation prevailing in many parts of the world'. After decades of action, the UN reports that hunger is on the rise again globally and undernutrition continues to affect millions of children (E/2019/68, paragraph 23). Although the decline of global poverty continues, it had slowed and the projection is that the world is not on track to achieve the target of less than 3% of the world living in extreme poverty by 2030 (E/2019/68, paragraph 22). The conclusion reached is that despite noticeable progress, international law is not fully ready to address a global food system that is increasingly diverse, complex, and very dynamic. International law is not

104. *See* Carmen Gonzales, *International Economic Law and the Right to Food.* In *Rethinking Food Systems* (Nadia C.S. Lambek et al. eds, Springer 2014).

presently structured to manage the numerous challenges facing the global food and agricultural system and is ill prepared to respond to future risks and uncertainties.[105] Overall, there is a growing gap between rhetoric and action as far as eradicating poverty and addressing food insecurity is concerned.

105. John Thompson & Ian Scoones, *Addressing the Dynamics of Agri-Food Systems: An Emerging Agenda for Social Science Research*, 12(4) Environmental Science & Policy 386-397 (2009).

CHAPTER 2

Right to Food in International Law

Margherita Brunori & Pier Filippo Giuggioli

The chapter illustrates the drafting history of the right to food together with the progressive elaboration of its contents. The study collocates the development of the content of the right within the broader evolution of international policies of food and nutrition. It then lingers on the synergies of the right to food with the right to health through the component of adequate nutrition, and finally illustrates how the right to food should be operationalized in the face of current and future global challenges.

§2.01 INTRODUCTION

At present, the number of people suffering from severe food insecurity (hunger) and moderate food insecurity (irregular access to nutritious and sufficient food) amounts to 2 billion.[1] Severe and moderate food insecurity causes malnutrition, which hinders physical and intellectual development and causes diseases and premature death. Besides, unbalanced diets, as well as unsafe food environments and consumption, can have adverse impacts on health and therefore on human development. As affirmed during the First International Conference on Nutrition, in 1992: 'optimal health cannot be achieved in the absence of adequate nutrition' and 'adequate nutrition can only be achieved through ensuring adequacy of food supplies at the household level'.[2] Health

1. FAO, IFAD, UNICEF, WFP and WHO, *The State of Food Security and Nutrition in the World 2019. Safeguarding against economic slowdowns and downturns* (FAO 2019) xvii. In 2017, the FAO annual report *The state of food security and nutrition* (SOFI), which since 1990 informs about the state of food insecurity globally, has officially included nutrition in its focus, and it saw for the first time the joint collaboration of WHO and UNICEF and the Rome agencies FAO, IFAD and WFP for its redaction. This reform was made to align the SOFI Report with the monitoring of Agenda 2030 Sustainable Development Goals of ending hunger and ensuring access to food by all (SDG Target 2.1) and of eliminating all forms of malnutrition (SDG Target 2.2).
2. Nutrition and development – a global assessment, written by FAO and WHO for the International Conference on Nutrition, 1992.

and food are therefore intimately connected. Under the human rights perspective, food and health are recognized as two self-standing rights (yet being indivisible, interdependent and interrelated as all human rights).[3] This is due to the different needs laying behind food and health as well as different sets of actions required for enabling their realization. This chapter illustrates the drafting history of the right to food together with its progressive elaboration. The study collocates the development of the content of the right within the broader evolution of international policies of food and nutrition. It then lingers on the synergies of the right to food with the right to health through the component of adequate nutrition, and finally illustrates how the right to food should be operationalized in the face of current and future global challenges.

The journey of the right to food can be portrayed in five stages. At its origins, it is conceived as a second generation right, connected to human dignity and therefore to the basic conditions for living a decent life.[4] After the adoption of the International Covenant on Economic, Social and Cultural Rights (ICESCR), the right to food and freedom from hunger becomes connected with agrarian policies, and then with international food security, covering mainly international trade. The 1990s elaborations on human development refocus the attention on the individual dimension and entitlements that people have with regards to states, and in this time, the right to food content is spelled out by the Committee on Economic, Social and Cultural Rights (CESCR). Finally, the elaboration of the right to nutrition enters not only into the personal dimension, but also in the intergenerational dimension, and illustrates the need to focus on urban environments and therefore food systems. At present, the right to food has acquired an additional dimension: by incorporating participation, access, control and choice (which go under the concept of 'food sovereignty') to its core meaning, the right to food has entered a social dimension.

§2.02 AFFIRMING THE RIGHTS TO FOOD: TRAVAUX PREPARATOIRES

Since the beginning of the negotiations of an International Bill of Rights, the right to food figured among the fundamental rights.[5] Article 25 of the Universal Declaration on Human Rights recognizes it as a component of the right to a standard of living adequate for the health of each person and family:

3. UN General Assembly, Vienna Declaration and Programme of Action, 12 July 1993, A/CONF.157/23, para. 5; For the meaning of this principle in the promotion of respect for human rights in the context of development activities carried on by international agencies, *see*: UN Committee on Economic, Social and Cultural Rights (CESCR), General Comment No. 2: International technical assistance measures (Article 22 of the Covenant), 2 February 1990, E/1990/23, para. 6.
4. In the famous Four Freedom Speech, delivered by D. Roosvelt on 6 January 1941, food belongs to the 'freedom from want'.
5. The Economic and Social Council, by Resolution 5(i) of 16 February 1946, established a Commission on Human Rights and instructed it to submit proposals, recommendations and reports regarding, *inter alia*, an International Bill of Human Rights. It was subsequently agreed to work on a general Declaration and a subsequent covenant with more details of the rights recognized thereof. The Universal Declaration on Human Rights was adopted by the General Assembly on the 10 December 1948.

> Everyone has the right to a standard of living adequate for the health of himself and of his family, including food, clothing, housing and medical care and necessary social services.[6]

After the adoption of the Universal Declaration on Human Rights by the United Nations (UN) General Assembly, the negotiations prosecuted for the elaboration and adoption of a binding Covenant on Human Rights. Following the request of some states, the economic, cultural and social rights were included in the draft, and eventually it was agreed to work on the formulation of those rights in close collaboration with relevant international organizations and agencies such as Food and Agricultural Organization (FAO), the World Health Organization (WHO), International Labor Organization (ILO) and United Nations Educational, Scientific and Cultural Organization (UNESCO).[7]

In the 1951 draft Covenant, food did not figure as a distinguished right,[8] and it was rather considered as implicitly recognized by the right to adequate standards of living and the right to health, which encompassed the need to improve nutrition.[9] As negotiations progressed, Chinese delegates issued the fact that, besides the right to

---

6. UN General Assembly, Universal Declaration of Human Rights, 10 December 1948, 217 A (III), Article 25.
7. In 1949, the Draft Covenant presented twenty-six articles on civil and political rights and several 'proposed additional articles on economic, social and cultural rights'. E/1371, E/CN.4/350, p. 47 (9-20 June 1949).
8. E/1992, E/CN.4/640, p. 23 (16 April-19 May 1951), Article 19:

   > The States Parties to the present Covenant,
   > 1. Bearing in mind the link between the rights and liberties recognized and denned above, and the economic, social and cultural rights proclaimed in the Universal Declaration of Human Rights;
   > 2. Resolved to combat the scourges, such as famine, disease, poverty, the feeling of insecurity and ignorance, which take toll of or degrade men, and prevent the free development of their personality;
   > 3. Resolved to strive to ensure that every human being shall obtain the food, clothing, shelter essential for his livelihood and well-being, and shall achieve an adequate standard of living and a continuous improvement of his material and spiritual living conditions;
   > 4. Undertake to take steps, individually and through international co-operation, to the maximum of their available resources with a view to achieving progressively the full realization of the rights recognized in this Part of the present Covenant.

9. In the same draft, the right to health, as a result of a negotiation which saw the proposal of an article based on the WHO Constitution, then modified by several amendments, read as follows:

   > Article 25
   >
   > The States Parties to the Covenant recognize the right of everyone to the enjoyment of the highest standard of health obtainable. With a view to implementing and safeguarding this right each State Party hereto undertakes to provide legislative measures to promote and protect health and, in particular:
   >
   > (a) To reduce infant mortality and provide for healthy development of the child;
   > (b) To improve nutrition, housing, sanitation, recreation, economic and working conditions and other aspects of environmental hygiene;
   > (c) To control epidemic, endemic and other diseases;
   > (d) To provide conditions which would assure the right of all to medical service and medical attention in the event of sickness.

adequate conditions of work, the right to adequate standard of living and the right to highest standard of health, an explicit mention to the right to housing and food, would be necessary, as housing was a compelling need for the urban dwellers and food for the rural population.[10] A separate article on the right to adequate food, clothing and housing was therefore added before the right to adequate standards of living and the right to health.[11] The right to health, at the time, contained the definition of health given by the WHO, as well as a second part adding details on 'the steps to be taken'.[12] In 1955, those rights looked as follows:

> Article 11 Right to adequate food, clothing and housing
>
> The States Parties to the Covenant recognize the right of everyone to adequate food, clothing and housing.
>
> Article 12 Right to an adequate standard of living
>
> The States Parties to the Covenant recognize the right of everyone to an adequate standard of living and the continuous improvement of living conditions.
>
> Article 13 Right to health
> 1. The States Parties to the Covenant, realizing that health is a state of complete physical, mental and social well-being, and not merely the absence of disease or infirmity, recognize the right of everyone to the enjoyment of the highest attainable standard of health.
> 2. The steps to be taken by the States Parties to the Covenant to achieve the full realization of this right shall include those necessary for:
>   (a) The reduction of infant mortality and the provision for healthy development of the child;
>   (b) The improvement of nutrition, housing, sanitation, recreation, economic and working conditions and other aspects of environmental hygiene;
>   (c) The prevention, treatment and control of epidemic, endemic and other diseases;

During one of those meeting, FAO pointed out that the current draft did not adequately protect the rights of cultivators, even though it expressed the doubt on whether the Covenant would be the right place to recognize them. Observations submitted by specialized agencies on the proposed Covenant on Economic, Social and Cultural Rights in pursuance to Resolution 543(VI) of the General Assembly/Food and Agriculture Organisation of the United Nations, E/CN.4/655/Add.31952.

10. E/CN.4/294, 1953.
11. A/2929 1 July 1955, UN General Assembly Draft International Covenants on Human Rights, Annotation, by the Secretary General.
12. A/2929 1955, p. 320. This detailed explanation of the right, much longer than the rest, was recommended by the WHO. Later, it was decided to remove from the article the definition of health because it did not mirror the structure of other articles of the draft covenant, that did not have definitions. Tobin explains that the elaboration of the right to heath was carried on in two complementary approaches: the individualist and the collectivist approach; the normative and the instrumental approach. To the individualist and the normative approaches, enjoying the highest levels of attainable health is a fundamental human right and therefore the state has the obligation to protect it. This vision found, at the time, the support of many Latin American Countries that already recognized in their Constitution the rights to health together with the right to food and housing. The collectivist and the instrumental approaches conceive health as an essential means for international well-being, peace and security. The aim and objective of the WHO is carved in both these spirits, as the WHO Constitution recognizes the right to health and calls for strong cooperation among States. J. Tobin, *The Right to Health in International Law* (OUP 2012) 14-43.

(d) The creation of conditions which would assure to all medical service and medical attention in the event of sickness.

After more than ten years of negotiations on the Human Rights Covenants, the Third Committee reported to the UN General Assembly the discussion held on the opportunity to add a provision on the right to freedom from hunger. In particular, it said that the new Director General of FAO, B.R. Sen, drew attention on the fact that after the adoption of the Universal Declaration on Human Rights it was possible to witness strengthening of civil and political rights in many countries, whereas the same observation could not be drawn with regards to economic and social rights. He explained that this inaction was due to a lack, in the Declaration, of an urgent call to regard freedom from hunger as a fundamental right. He concluded that the already included right to food seemed not to be sufficient as it lacked the enumeration of measures that ensure the enjoyment of the right.[13] The following discussion saw differing opinions by those who agreed that adding and specifying the right to freedom from hunger was necessary because lack of adequate nutrition precluded the enjoyment of any human rights, and because it would be important for governments to remember the human right aspect of pertinent actions; and by those who preferred the already simple and clear reference to food. In addition, some states stressed the need to add implementing measures, whereas others preferred to leave only the statement of principles. In parallel, there was widespread agreement on the refusal of paternalism, and on that people should be given 'not only enough to eat but also, and above all, the possibility to provide for their needs through their own efforts'.[14]

As it is known, the final outcome of the works was the adoption of two separate Covenants. The right to food and the right to health figured respectively in Articles 11

13. This intervention was the first engagement of FAO in the preparatory works of the Covenant and was thankful to the new Director General of FAO, which endeavoured to reverse the situation as since then FAO did not engage with the negotiation progress. *See* Julianne C. Traylor, *FAO and the Right to Food*, in *Food as a Human Right* 187, 190-192 (Asbjørn Eide et al., eds, 1984); Asbjørn Eide, Arne Oshaug & Wenche Barth Eide, *The Food Security and the Right to Food in International Law and Development*, in *Transnational Law & Contemporary Problems* 1 (1991): 415.

14. As a reaction, two proposals were presented to follow up the issue. It was proposed by Saudi Arabia (A/C.3/L.1172) to add an article composed by two commas. The first comma would recognize the right to be free from hunger and the urge to undertake programmes, individually and through international cooperation, aimed at achieving the realization of the right 'in the shortest possible time'. The second comma lists a number of actions that states should pay particular attention to:

    (a) policies to ensure that world food supplies are shared on a rational and equitable basis;
    (b) economic, technical and other measures to increase the production of food;
    (c) the adaptation of existing institutions, including systems of land tenure and land use, to the requirements of economic and social progress; and
    (d) the promotion and full utilisation of scientific and technical knowledge and a massive education of the population in order to improve methods of production, conservation and distribution of food.

    A second proposal was presented by Chile, Colombia, Equador, Guatemala and Uganda to add a second comma to the combined Articles 11 (on the right to food, clothes and housing and article) and 12 (on the right to adequate standards of living) a paragraph:

and 12 of the ICESCR, and whereas the right to food is collocated together with the right of adequate standard of living, the additional recognition of the right to be free from hunger accompanies the first paragraph with a statement of principle together with a list of required action for states to fulfil the content of the right. However, in the final draft of the right to health, the reference to nutrition disappears. To sum up, while in the Universal Declaration on Human Rights food and health had an explicit connection, in the ICESCR the right to adequate standard of living and the right to health are defined as two distinct rights. The bridge between the two rights, nutrition, remains only in Article 11: 'Disseminating knowledge of the principles of nutrition' is in fact one of the means through which states are due to improve the methods of production, conservation and distribution of food:

> Article 11
> 1. The States Parties to the present Covenant recognize the right of everyone to an adequate standard of living for himself and his family, including adequate food, clothing and housing, and to the continuous improvement of living conditions. The States Parties will take appropriate steps to ensure the realization of this right, recognizing to this effect the essential importance of international co-operation based on free consent.
> 2. The States Parties to the present Covenant, recognizing the fundamental right of everyone to be free from hunger, shall take, individually and through international co-operation, the measures, including specific programmes, which are needed:
>   (a) To improve methods of production, conservation and distribution of food by making full use of technical and scientific knowledge, by disseminating knowledge of the principles of nutrition and by developing or reforming agrarian systems in such a way as to achieve the most efficient development and utilization of natural resources;
>   (b) Taking into account the problems of both food-importing and food-exporting countries, to ensure an equitable distribution of world food supplies in relation to need.

§2.03 THE SUCCESSIVE INTERPRETATION OF THE RIGHT TO FOOD

Once adopted, the right to food was then to be conceptually and legally interpreted. After its signature, the ICESCR had to wait ten years before its entry into force, and in the meantime the ongoing cold war and economic crisis shifted the international

---

2. The steps to be taken by the States Parties, individually and through international co-operation, to draw up and execute programmes aimed at achieving freedom from hunger shall include those needed:
   (a) to improve methods of production, conservation and distribution of food by making full use of technical and scientific knowledge, disseminating guiding principles of nutrition, and adapting or reforming existing systems of land tenure and land use and systems for the exploitation of natural resources; and
   (b) to help ensure that the worlds food supplies are shared on a rational and equitable basis.

Draft International Covenant on Human Rights, Report of the Third Committee, A/5655, 10 December 1963.

attention on the need to reshape the world economic system.[15] In this scenario, food was portrayed as a component of the New International Economic Order,[16] and articulated in a world food security system 'which would ensure adequate availability of, and reasonable prices for, food at all times, irrespective of periodic fluctuations and vagaries of weather and free of political and economic pressures, and should thus facilitate, amongst other things, the development process of developing countries'.[17] The Declaration on the Eradication of Hunger and Malnutrition, adopted in the same year of the Declaration for the New International Economic Order, 1974, recognizes that '[e]very man, woman and child has the inalienable right to be free from hunger and malnutrition in order to develop fully and maintain their physical and mental faculties'.[18] From the solemn affirmation of the right, the Declaration does not derive entitlements on the individual, but rather a major focus on equity and solidarity between countries on increased food production and more stable international trade of food products. Indeed, the food security-related action is, in this period, focused on the national or international dimension of food security and does not cast much consideration on how to empower the right-holders.[19] In order to follow up the commitments of the Declaration, the World Food Council was established, as a high-level political body aimed at coordinating global actions for world food security.[20]

A few years after, in 1979, closing the agrarian reform era and trying to prosecute the path of the New International Economic Order, the World Conference on Agrarian Reform and Rural Development was held, and at its closing, the Peasants' Charter was adopted. The Charter does not mention the right to food and the right to be free from hunger; however, it can be appreciated for engaging with an in-depth description of states and international agencies required action towards food security and rural development: it covers development, equitable access to natural resources and inputs for food and agriculture, active participation, information and organization of rural population and workers, women's empowerment, environmental protection, fair international food trade, and even the conduct of transnational corporation in the food

15. Nils Gilman, *The New International Economic Order: A Reintroduction*, in *Humanity: An International Journal of Human Rights, Humanitarianism, and Development* 6.1 (2015): 1-16; V. McFarland, *The New International Economic Order, Interdependence, and Globalization*, in *Humanity: An International Journal of Human Rights, Humanitarianism, and Development* 6.1 (2015): 217-233.
16. UN General Assembly Resolution, Declaration on the Establishment of a New International Economic Order, A/RES/3201(S-VI) Adopted at the 2229th plenary meeting, 1 May 1974.
17. Universal Declaration on the Eradication of Hunger and Malnutrition, adopted by the World Food Conference, Rome, U.N. Doc. E/CONF. 65/20, at 1 (1974).
18. *Ibid.*
19. Asbjørn Eide, Arne Oshaug & Wenche Barth Eide, *The Food Security and the Right to Food in International Law and Development*, in *Transnational Law & Contemporary Problems* 1 (1991): 415.
20. The Council was quite successful in developing food aid mechanisms, but did not manage to curb the paradox of high food production, stock and low prices and continuing high rates of world hunger and malnutrition. John D. Shaw, *The World Food Council: The Rise and Fall of a United Nations Body*, in *Canadian Journal of Development Studies/Revue canadienne d'études du développement* 30 (2010): 663.

system.[21] In other words, the Peasants' Charter puts forward the specific needs of rural population for the social, economic, technical and cultural means for effectively achieving rural development, food security and curb rural poverty. It also tailors the needed measures on the material situations of specific social categories such as landless farmers, women, smallholders, local communities. The story tells how the global economic recession of the 1980s changed the agenda and pushed for structural adjustment programmes and a technological turn (the 'green revolution') in agriculture, and the debate for agrarian reforms and rural development faded.[22] During this time, the right to food was included in the Convention on the Elimination of All Forms of Discrimination Against Women of 1979,[23] and more explicitly in the Convention on the Rights of the Child in 1989.[24]

Reflecting on the trends described above, Robert Bald writes in 1985 that whereas '[p]olitical and civil rights concern the kinds of restraints on government that are commonplace in any society recognizing individual rights[, t]he right to food belongs to a second category of international obligations – obligations that consist of pledges to take actions to more equitably share the world's resources' and he concludes that 'the right to food is addressed to areas of governmental conduct that do not lend themselves to control by legal rules'.[25] Of another viewpoint, in the same year, Katarina Tomasevki unveils another perspective of the right and affirms that the right to food acquires significance if looked at in connection with civil and political rights. According to Tomasevski, realizing the right to food necessitates access to resources and land rights, the right to work, the right to freedom of movement and the freedom of association and, finally, participation in decision making.[26]

§2.04 LINKS BETWEEN FOOD AND HEALTH IN INTERNATIONAL LAW

As we saw, the draft Covenant featured the improvement of nutrition among the actions that states had to undergo in order to implement the right to health, but this reference was removed in the final text, and nutrition was rather mentioned in the implementation of the right to food not as a direct objective for states but rather as the object of the state informative endeavour of '[...] disseminating knowledge of the

21. Declaration of principles and programme of action of the world conference on agrarian reform and rural development, World Conference on Agrarian Reform and Rural Development (Rome, 12-20 July 1979); Sudhir Sen, *Agrarian Reform and Rural Development*, in *Worldview* 22.6 (1979): 13-19.
22. D.J. Shaw, *World Food Security: A History Since 1945* (Palgrave 2007).
23. Convention on the Elimination of All Forms of Discrimination against Women New York, 18 December 1979.
24. Convention on the Rights of the Child, Adopted by General Assembly Resolution 44/25 of 20 November 1989, Article 24.
25. Robert L. Bard, *The Right to Food*, in *Iowa Law Review* 70 (1985): 1279, 1289.
26. Katarina Tomasevski, *Human Rights: The Right to Food*, in *Iowa Law Review* 70 (1985). *See also* K. Tomaševski, ed., *The Right to Food: Guide Through Applicable International Law* (Martinus Nijhoff Publishers 1987); Pierre Spitz, *The Right to Food in Historical Perspective*, in *Food Policy* 10.4 (1985): 306-316.

principles of nutrition [...]'.[27] Nutrition is the connecting element between food and health, as it refers to the instrumental role of food which is necessary for the body to performs its functions. Nutrition attains a biological dimension, on how the food is effectively instrumental to fulfil the body functions that biologically enable a person to perform physical and intellectual activities that allow personal human development. Conversely, the food perspective is centred on the conditions that allow the entitlements of an individual with regard to food and involves the economic, social and cultural dimension that surrounds it.

At the beginning of the 1990s, the elaboration of the notion of human development opens a new avenue for the appreciation of food in close relation to health. The first Human Development Report adopted by UN Development Programme in 1990 states that human development is 'about enlarging people's choices', and that '[t]he most critical of these wide-ranging choices are to live a long and healthy life, be educated and to have access to resources needed for a decent standard of living'.[28] In parallel to this new approach, attention on nutrition begins to surface,[29] in consideration of a more refined understanding of the fact that beyond secure access to adequate and sufficient food, the enjoyment of a healthy and dignified life also depends, on the one hand, on a person's nutritional history, that presupposes an adequate nutrition of women during pregnancy and nutrition of children in early age,[30] and on the other hand, on a safe food, unpolluted water and a safe consumption environment.[31] The revived attention to food and nutrition led to substantial development and clarification of the content of both the right to food and the right to health.[32]

The development of the content of the right to food in legal terms owes a lot to the seminal contribution of two authors. Amartya Sen's contribution on the clarification of food entitlements, which describes the relationship of a person with food,[33] and the seminal input to the understanding of the content of the progressive realization of

27. ICESCR Article 11.2.a.
28. HDR 1990, p. 1. *See also* Elizabeth Stanton, *The Human Development Index: A History*, PERI Working Papers (2007) 85.
29. World Summit for Children in 1990, the International Conference for Nutrition in 1992, and World Food Summit in 1996.
30. In the Convention against every form of discrimination against women (1979), Article 12, and in Article 25 of the UN Convention of the Rights of the Child (1989) reference to food is made in this perspective.
31. Besides the persisting number of people that lack their basic dietary needs (780 million), there is a greater number (2 billion) that have vitamin and mineral deficiencies that hamper their normal development and lead to diseases and premature death, whereas hundreds of millions suffer from diseases caused by unbalanced diets. In addition, the consumption of unsafe food and polluted water causes disease and death. World Declaration and Plan of action on nutrition, 1992, para. 1 (plan of action).
32. In 1996 the World Food Conference took place, which gave a new definition of food security including nutrition and safety. World Food Summit in 1996: 'Food security, at the individual, household, national, regional and global levels is achieved when all people, at all times, have physical and economic access to sufficient, safe and nutritious food to meet their dietary needs and food preferences for an active and healthy life.'
33. A. Sen, *Poverty and Famines* (1981), in Eide, *supra*. Sen capability approach also clarified how development is ultimately dependent on a person' individual freedom and choice, and therefore how individual conditions and capacity to act effectively for achieving personal goals and fulfil basic needs are inherently connected to development.

economic, social and cultural rights by Asbjørn Eide. Eide detailed the content of the obligations of those rights in three state duties: obligation to respect, obligation to protect, and obligation to fulfil, which can take the form of facilitating and providing.[34] This contribution became part of the authentic interpretation of the content of the right to food, contained in the General Comment n. 12 adopted by the Committee on the economic, social and cultural rights in 1999. The General Comment n. 12 recognizes that the right to food's core obligations imply 'The availability of food in a quantity and quality sufficient to satisfy the dietary needs of individuals, free from adverse substances, and acceptable within a given culture; The accessibility of such food in ways that are sustainable and that do not interfere with the enjoyment of other human rights.'[35] The CESCR General Comment n. 14, adopted the following year, explicits the connection between food and health, by including food among the 'underlying determinants of health'. The duty to 'ensure equal access for all to the underlying determinants of health, such as nutritiously safe food and potable drinking water [...]' therefore enters into the core states' obligation to facilitate the right to health.[36]

§2.05 EXPANSION OF THE RIGHT TO FOOD

After the release of the General Comment, the progressive realization of the right obtained increased attention, as since 2001, the UN General Assembly adopts a resolution dedicated to the right to food, and the Special rapporteur on the right to food was appointed by the UN Commission on Human Rights (substituted in 2006 by the Human rights Council). The knowledge gap-filling role of the work led by the Special Rapporteurs on the determinants of the right to food, as well as the political attention to the topic, brought to the adoption of other instruments which spell out the content of the right to food and the required actions of states in that regard.[37] The first document is the Voluntary Guidelines on the right to food adopted by the FAO Council in 2004, which represents the first governmentally agreed guide to the implementation of the right to food. The second is the recent UN General Assembly Declaration on the

34. Asbjørn Eide, Arne Oshaug & Wenche Barth Eide, *Food Security and the Right to Food in International Law and Development*, in *Transnational Law and Contemporary Problems University of Iowa* 1:2 (1991): 415-467.
35. CESCR General Comment n. 12 (1999) para. 9. The document then clarifies that '9. Dietary needs imply that the diet as a whole contains a mix of nutrients for physical and mental growth, development and maintenance, and physical activity that are in compliance with human physiological needs at all stages throughout the life cycle and according to gender and occupation. Measures may therefore need to be taken to maintain, adapt or strengthen dietary diversity and appropriate consumption and feeding patterns, including breast-feeding, while ensuring that changes in availability and access to food supply as a minimum do not negatively affect dietary composition and intake.' 'Free from adverse substances' sets requirements for food safety and for a range of protective measures by both public and private means to prevent contamination of foodstuffs through adulteration and/or through bad.
36. CESCR General Comment n. 14 (2000) para. 36.
37. *See* Christophe Golay, Claire Mahon & Ioana Cismas, *The Impact of the UN Special Procedures on the Development and Implementation of Economic, Social and Cultural Rights*, in *International Journal of Human Rights* 15.2 (2011): 299-318.

rights of peasants and other people working in rural areas.[38] This document brings, besides a consolidation of existing and emerging principles of international law, a new description of the content of the right to food as it adapts to the needs of rural population.[39]

Article 15 of the Declaration states that:

> 1. Peasants and other people working in rural areas have the right to adequate food and the fundamental right to be free from hunger. This includes the right to produce food and the right to adequate nutrition, which guarantee the possibility of enjoying the highest degree of physical, emotional and intellectual development. [...]
> 4. Peasants and other people working in rural areas have the right to determine their own food and agriculture systems, recognized by many States and regions as the right to food sovereignty. This includes the right to participate in decision-making processes on food and agriculture policy and the right to healthy and adequate food produced through ecologically sound and sustainable methods that respect their cultures.

This expanded definition of the right to food explicates its components: first, the right to adequate nutrition which, as it was explained, goes beyond the dimension of hunger to encompass a wide range of situations that hamper the right to health due to inadequate food consumption.[40] Second, the right to produce food and the right to food sovereignty, i.e., the right of peasants (and citizens) to determine their food systems and to participate in decision-making processes.[41] This second dimension is particularly significant. Food sovereignty represents the symbol of grassroots struggles against an economic system that tends to exploit resources and excludes the small and subsistence farmers from their land. However, it also brings together instances of

38. A/RES/73/165 – UN Declaration on the rights of peasants and other people working in rural areas.
39. Christoph Golay et al., *The Rights of Peasants, CETIM, Critical Report* 5 (2009).
40. Jessica Fanzo et al., *Tying the Knot: An Interdisciplinary Approach to Understanding the Human Right to Adequate Nutrition*, in *Columbia Journal of Transnational Law* 57 (2018): 62; Jesse B. Bump, *Undernutrition, Obesity and Governance: A Unified Framework for Upholding the Right to Food*, in *BMJ Global Health* 3 (2018).
41. Angelo Rinella & Helen Okoronko, *Sovranità alimentare e diritto al cibo*, in *Diritto pubblico comparato ed europeo* 17.1 (2015): 89-130; Lorenza Paoloni, *I nuovi percorsi della food security: dal 'diritto al cibo adeguato' alla 'sovranità alimentare*, in *Diritto e giurisprudenza agraria, alimentare e dell'ambiente'* 3.1 (2011): 159-165; Chiara Certomà, *Diritto al cibo, sicurezza alimentare, sovranità alimentare*, in *Rivista di Diritto Alimentare* 2 (2010); Raj Patel, *Food Sovereignty*, in *The Journal of Peasant Studies* 36.3 (2009): 663-706. Louis Thiemann & Antonio Roman-Alcalá, *Fast Food Sovereignty: Contradiction in Terms or Logical Next Step?*, in *Journal of Agricultural and Environmental Ethics* 32.5-6 (2019): 813-834; Bina Agarwal, *Food Sovereignty, Food Security and Democratic Choice: Critical Contradictions, Difficult Conciliations*, in *The Journal of Peasant Studies* (2014); Josh Brem-Wilson, *Towards Food Sovereignty: Interrogating Peasant Voice in the United Nations Committee on World Food Security*, in *The Journal of Peasant Studies* 42.1 (2015): 73-95; Priscilla Claeys, *The Creation of New Rights by the Food Sovereignty Movement: The Challenge of Institutionalizing Subversion*, in *Sociology* 46 (2012): 844; Marc Edelman et al., *Introduction: Critical Perspectives on Food Sovereignty*, in *The Journal of Peasant Studies* 41.6 (2014): 911-931; Sofía Monsalve Suárez, *Human Rights and the Food Sovereignty Movement: Reclaiming Control*, in *The Journal of Peasant Studies* 45.1 (2018). Hans Morten Haugen, *Food Sovereignty: An Appropriate Approach to Ensure the Right to Food?*, in *Nordic Journal of International Law* 78.3 (2009): 263-292.

meaningful participation in decision-making of the most vulnerable stakeholders into the agri-food sector, in a similar pattern to what has already been recognized by international law to other categories of people whose lives depend on access to natural resources, such as indigenous peoples and traditional communities.[42] If, on the one hand, the UN Declaration on the Rights of Peasants consolidates a body of emerging standards on rural population in a human rights perspective, and therefore clarifies the content of the right to food in rural areas, the protection of the right to food in urban areas, on the other, is becoming to surface as a new policy issue, and awareness on the importance of food systems and food environments for nutrition is raising, as demonstrated by the adoption of the UN Committee on Food Security Voluntary Guidelines on Food Systems and Nutrition in February 2021.[43]

§2.06 PRESENT AND FUTURE CHALLENGES FOR THE RIGHT TO FOOD: THE COVID-19 PANDEMIC

From 1948 Universal Declaration on Human Rights to the 2018 Declaration on Peasants Rights, we have here described the evolution of the right to food. The status of the right to food in international law is nowadays not contested, and its implementation and justiciability have been widely studied.[44] The content of the right and its understanding vis-à-vis individual and collective entitlements, as well as public policies and standards for private actors, has dramatically evolved and will continue to do so to answer the upcoming challenges.

The COVID-19 pandemic has shown the profound implications that a sudden crisis can have on food systems and food security. One of the main risks that the COVID-19 pandemic has raised is that the health crisis is able to become a food crisis,

42. Elisa Morgera, *Under the Radar: The Role of Fair and Equitable Benefit-Sharing in Protecting and Realising Human Rights Connected to Natural Resources*, in *The International Journal of Human Rights* 23.7 (2019): 1098-1139.
43. Committee on World Food Security, Forty-seventh Session, 'Making a Difference in Food Security and Nutrition', 8-11 February 2021, The CFS Voluntary Guidelines on Food Systems and Nutrition (VGFSyN), CFS 2021/47/7; *see also* HLPE, Nutrition and food systems. A report by the High Level Panel of Experts on Food Security and Nutrition of the Committee on World Food Security, 2017, Rome.
44. Uwe Kracht & Muzammel Huq, *Realizing the Right to Food and Nutrition Through Public and Private Action: Two Commentaries on Drèze's/Sen's Book Hunger and Public Action in the Context of Food and Nutrition Rights*, in *Food Policy* 21.1 (1996): 73-82; G. Kent, *Freedom from Want: The Human Right to Adequate Food* (Georgetown University Press 2005); J. Ziegler et al., *The Fight for the Right to Food: Lessons Learned* (Springer 2011); Naomi Hossain & Dolf te Lintelo, *A Common Sense Approach to the Right to Food*, in *Journal of Human Rights Practice* 10 (2018): 367; C. Courtis, *The Right to Food as a Justiciable Right: Challenges and Strategies*, in *Max Planck Yearbook of United Nations Law Online* 11 (2007): 317; Marc J. Cohen & Mary Ashby Brown, *Access to Justice and the Right to Adequate Food: Implementing Millennium Development Goal One*, in *Sustainable Development Law & Policy* 6 (2005): 54; Ioana Cismas, *The Right to Food Beyond De-mythification: Time to Shed the Inferiority Complex of Socio-Economic Rights*, in *Global Policy* (2014); Francesco Alicino, *Il Diritto al Cibo. Definizione Normativa e Giustiziabilità*, in Rivista AIC N 3.2016 (2016); Antonello Ciervo, *Il diritto al cibo. Presupposti normativi e precedenti costituzionali di un nuovo diritto fondamentale*, in *Parolechiave* 25.2 (2017): 53-68.

and consequently have an impact on the enjoyment of right to food.[45] This final paragraph is dedicated to better understand the consequences of the emergency measures taken during the coronavirus pandemic on the right to food, focusing on the effects in terms of interference with and reconciliation between other fundamental rights, namely the right to health.

The short-term effect of COVID-19 emergency, already witnessed, is a series of negative repercussions on regular access to food. At a domestic level, movement restrictions and lockdowns prevented the usual access to food supply places. Containment measures and bans on gatherings forbid or restricted the opening of local markets, restaurants and canteens, thus hindering or changing the supply abruptly to consumers and the consumption of food. In some cases, this led to an excess production and consequent waste; producers and growers – due to the forced closure of natural buyers – face the risks of non-sale: food loss and waste, reduction in income and consequent exclusion from the market. This effect is further aggravated by what happens internationally, where similar lockdown measures and export restrictions on food and border closures disrupted the global food supply chain.[46] In particular, labour shortages, logistics interruptions and limited access to markets complicate shipping logistics and slow commodity exports around the world. The occurrence of these factors on a global level impedes access to and implies a contraction of international markets.

Limited access to food, due to the effects of the emergency legislation to contain COVID-19, significantly affects the most vulnerable subjects. Among other effects, emergency measures entail that farmers and small producers (especially women) are discouraged from production and harvesting; not so much for fear of contagion, but for the absence of natural commercial outlets (as a rule, local markets), reduction in manpower and/or transport difficulties.[47] This decreased production also has an effect

45. Statement to the Extraordinary Meeting of G20 Agriculture Ministers, 21 April 2020 http://www.g20.utoronto.ca/2020/2020-g20-agriculture-0421.html; 'Mitigating impacts of Covid-19 on food trade and markets', Joint Statement by QU Dongyu, Tedros Adhanom Ghebreyesus and Roberto Azevedo, Directors General of FAO, WHO and WTO http://www.fao.org/news/story/en/item/1268719/icode/; Interim Issues Paper on the Impact of COVID-19 on Food Security and Nutrition (FSN) by the High-Level Panel of Experts on Food Security and nutrition (HLPE) 24 March 2020 http://www.fao.org/fileadmin/templates/cfs/Docs1920/HLPE_2020/New_HLPE_paper_COVID_EN.pdf; COVID-19 and the crisis in food systems: Symptoms, causes, and potential solutions, Communiqué by IPES-Food, April 2020 http://www.ipes-food.org/_img/upload/files/Covid-19_CommuniqueEN.pdf; As evidenced by the 2020 Global Food Crises Report, the year 2019 witnessed the highest level of acute food insecurity and malnutrition at crisis levels compared to the four previous years, and there is the risk that the pandemic will worsen these situations, Food Security Information Network (FSIN), 2020 Global Food Crises Report; City Region Food Systems to cope with COVID-19 and other pandemic emergencies Alison Blay-Palmer, Guido Santini, Jess Halliday, René van Veenhuizen and Makiko Taguchi fao.org/uploads/pics/City_Region_Food_Systems_to_cope_with_Covid-19_and_other_pandemic_emergencies___12.05.2020.pdf.
46. Timothy Sulser & Shahnila Dunston, *Covid-19-Related Trade Restrictions on Rice and Wheat Could Drive up Prices and Increase Hunger*, in *International Food Policy and Research Institute* 15 (2020).
47. FAO, *Covid-19 and Smallholder Producers' Access to Markets* (FAO 2020); FAO, *Gendered Impacts of Covid-19 and Equitable Policy Responses in Agriculture, Food Security and Nutrition* (FAO 2020).

on regular access to food: it contributes to the increase in prices and, given the impossibility of marketing the produce, it entails a contraction of income for these small-scale producers and, consequently, limits their possibility to adequately access food.

Similarly, as a consequence of the lockdown, workers, especially the most defenceless (such as migrants, informal and seasonal workers), suffer a radical contraction in their ability to access food. In fact, following the suspension (or often even the loss) of work and income, food becomes less accessible to this category of buyers due to their reduced purchasing power.[48] Whereas the CESCR in its comment to Article 11 of the Covenant affirms that 'the core content of the right to adequate food implies: [...] The accessibility of such food in ways that are sustainable and that do not interfere with the enjoyment of other human rights', the contrary is also true: it is inacceptable to interfere with the enjoyment of right to food while enacting public health policies. Given the negative effects on food security of lockdown measures, this pandemic represents an emblematic case where a right-based approach has to be adopted if two equally important objectives have to be simultaneously pursued.[49]

An aspect which is illustrative of this risk is the situation of workers of essential sectors, for instance, in the agri-food chain. These workers, if on the one hand do not bear the effect of income loss which affects those occupied in other sectors, on the other hand, they find themselves highly exposed to risk of contagion,[50] which often adds to the often pre-existing exploitative working conditions.[51] At its extreme, the movement restriction measures unveiled how the agricultural sector depends on, and exploits, illegal migration.[52] To sum up, the COVID-19 pandemic has shown how and in what ways, without a careful coordinated intervention, the pursue of a public interest objective can hamper other fundamental rights, such as the right to food, and it also showed how some particularly vulnerable social categories bear the effects of this unduly tension.

The last aspect of the impact of the COVID-19 pandemic on the right to food concerns its socio-cultural dimension as well as sustainability of food systems. Although an incontrovertible conclusion has not yet been reached, scientists seem to

48. FAO, *Impact of Covid-19 on Informal Workers* (FAO 2020).
49. This is particularly true with regard to vulnerable subjects, such as informal workers, migrants, peasants and small producers (especially women). In fact, for such categories, the legislation enacted to guarantee public health (i.e., limitation of movements, lockdowns and export restrictions) could have exponential effects leading even to literally exclude the possibility of access to food. In other words, emergency legislation, abstractly aimed at protecting people's health, impacts in reality so heavily on the possibility for vulnerable subjects to access basic nutritional elements that in the end they impact precisely on the fundamental right which they are intent on protecting.
50. One emblematic case is that of the Slaughterhouse in Germany, where more than 1,500 employees were tested positive https://www.business-humanrights.org/en/germany-1500-workers-test-positive-for-Covid-19-at-meat-processing-plant-company-criticised-for-failure-to-protect-workers.
51. Mark Stabile, Bénédicte Apouey & Isabelle Sola, *Covid-19, Inequality and Gig Economy Workers*, in *VoxEU*. org 01/04, 2020. IPES-Food, *Unravelling the Food–Health Nexus: Addressing Practices, Political Economy, and Power Relations to Build Healthier Food Systems* (The Global Alliance for the Future of Food and IPES-Food 2017).
52. https://blogs.eui.eu/migrationpolicycentre/politics-regularisation-migrant-labour-italy/.

agree that COVID-19 is probably a zoonosis, a human disease of animal origin. It seems that the zoonotic spillover, i.e., the transmission of infection from animal to human, finds opportunities in close contact between wildlife and humans. One such opportunity is the live wildlife trade for human consumption, due to the fact that many different species of wild animals are brought together in the so-called wet markets. Zoonosis is not only connected to wild animal consumption but also to the restless encroachment of natural environment and the loss of continuous ecosystems driven, among others, by intensive agriculture and animal breeding.[53] The pandemic shows in this sense the paradoxes of unsustainable food systems. This occurrence raises questions on how traditional food supply and consumption patterns are to be balanced with other global goals, such as health and environmental protection.[54] Only a right-based approach to public policies can ensure that the contrasting needs are equally and fairly balanced.

§2.07 CONCLUSIONS

Having explained the conundrums unveiled by the coronavirus pandemic, the chapter concludes by illustrating how the content of the right to food speaks to, and should drive the exit strategies from the current crisis. Following the reconstruction of the obligations stemming from the right to food, it derives that states have the obligation to respect the ability of people to produce food for themselves and the ability of people to have economic access to food; they have to respect the cultural dimension of food as well as safeguard and promote sustainable diets and food systems. States have to protect the right to food, hence the duty to refrain privates to cause food prices speculation, or enact unfair practices. Finally, they have the duty to fulfil that entails the obligation to provide food to those who need it. But they also have the duty to facilitate, and this is to be pursued through broader measures such as to protect rural and food chain workers' rights, and design or improve sustainable resilient food policies. A derivate of the principle of non-discrimination is the extraterritoriality of states' obligations for the respect of human rights.[55] The right to food contains an explicit recall to international cooperation. As a consequence, a state has the duty to refrain from imposing unilateral economic sanctions to states (respect), refrain privates to cause food prices speculation or enact unfair practices in their operations abroad (protect), and the duty to cooperate in international forums and with international agencies for safeguarding the right to food.

53. Ewen Callaway, Heidi Ledford & Smriti Mallapaty, *Six Months of Coronavirus: The Mysteries Scientists Are Still Racing to Solve*, *Nature*, 3 July https://www.nature.com/articles/d41586-020-01989-z; Ruth Richardson, *Bending the Arc of Covid-19 Through a Principled Food Systems Approach*, in *Agriculture and Human Values* (2020): 1-2.
54. This topical issue will also be discussed in the Chapter of Ilja Richard Pavone.
55. Skogly Sigrun, *Right to Food: National Implementation and Extraterritorial Obligations*, in *Max Planck Yearbook of United Nations Law* 11 (2007): 339-358.

Measures to fulfil the right to food require comprehensive and coordinated actions and therefore are designed for the middle-long term rather than for the short, but their presence is even more needed in times of crises because they improve the resiliency and equity of a system.

CHAPTER 3

The UN Decade of Action on Nutrition: Opportunities and Challenges in a Time of a Pandemic

Khaled Eltaweel[*]

The last five years witnessed an unprecedented international momentum focusing on mobilizing national and international efforts to eradicate all forms of malnutrition. This contributed to a growing awareness of the interconnectivity between nutrition and other policies such as the economic, social and health ones. It also shed more light on the impacts of conflicts and climate change on hunger and malnutrition. Nevertheless, the world is not on track to achieve this objective. Many of the political commitments were not implemented and the structural challenges of conflicts, climate change, unsupportive economic policies and COVID-19 caused an increase in hunger and malnutrition figures in almost all the regions of the world. Despite its devastating impacts, including those on food security and nutrition, COVID-19 can be used as an opportunity to build better our health, food and economic systems making them more resilient and allowing them to withhold any future pandemic. This can also support the global efforts to achieve Sustainable Development Goal2 and implement the Decade of Action on Nutrition.

§3.01 INTRODUCTION

The last five years witnessed a paradigm shift in the global attention towards the multiple challenges of malnutrition. After the end of the timeframe allocated to the implementation of the Millennium Development Goals (MDGs) in 2000, the global attention moved from the predominant focus on hunger to a broader and more

* All views expressed in this chapter do not necessarily represent the views of any organization.

comprehensive focus on nutrition: targeting all forms of malnutrition (Target 2.2 of the Sustainable Development Goals (SDGs)) and reducing the Non-communicable Diseases (NCDs) (Target 3.4). This represents an important and positive policy development.

Despite the international momentum, political commitment, which is key for a successful outcome of the United Nations (UN) Decade of Action on Nutrition (hereinafter 'the Decade') at the national level, remains below expectations. The global efforts to eradicate malnutrition must be supported by a proactive engagement from all the stakeholders at national, regional and global levels and need to address the political and structural challenges that go beyond the narrow interpretation of nutrition.

In the midst of the implementation of the Decade, the world efforts were interrupted by an unexpected and serious threat that strikes the fundamentals of nutrition: health, food security and economic access. At the end of 2019, the emergence of the new COVID 19 virus affected the global attention on the Decade by risking to move away from building the right atmosphere for better nutrition outcomes to dealing with the threatening and immediate effects of the pandemic.

This chapter discusses the implications of COVID-19 on the global efforts to improve nutrition worldwide. The chapter advocates that while the world continues to confront the health and economic impacts of the pandemic, the world should not lose the momentum to build a world free from all forms of malnutrition building on the clear work programme of the Decade. In other words, COVID-19 could be an opportunity to rethink and rebuild our systems without losing sight of the ultimate objective, that is, a world free from all forms of malnutrition.

§3.02 NUTRITION: A GLOBAL PRIORITY

For many years, nutrition featured among the national and international developmental objectives. Food and Agriculture Organization (FAO) developed the first global indicator on nutrition in 1974 in order to monitor the World Food Summit's (WFS) goal of eradicating hunger in all countries with the target of reducing by half the number of undernourished people by no later than 2015.[1]

Although the indicator focused on measuring hunger reduction progress, the indicator was used to measure undernourishment, which was defined as 'the condition of an individual by which habitual food consumption levels do not provide sufficient dietary energy to cover normal requirements for an active and healthy life'.[2]

The first objective of the MDGs called for eradicating extreme poverty and hunger by 2015. In fact, it enforced the link between the two sub-objectives by implying that there is a strong correlation between poverty and hunger.

The Agenda 2030 for Sustainable Development, which was endorsed in 2015, consolidated the world attention on all forms of malnutrition. Among its seventeen objectives, it included a stand-alone SDG to 'end hunger, achieve food security and

1. The Rome Declaration on World Food Security (1974).
2. The Prevalence of Undernourishment indicator produced by FAO since 1974 and used to monitor the World Food Security Summit (WFS) goal.

improved nutrition, and promote sustainable agriculture' (SDG2). The explicit reference to nutrition in SDG2 is a recognition of its importance in driving socio-economic development and its distinction from food security.

The Decade of Action on Nutrition, adopted by the United Nations General Assembly (UNGA) on 1 April 2016, is considered by many as a breakthrough in the fight against hunger and malnutrition. The UN most universal body's decision came at the peak of an international momentum that, for the first time, put nutrition as a high political priority for the work of the UN and its Member States.

The proclamation of the Decade is also a manifestation of national ownership. It came as a response to the demand of the Member States, that convened at the Second International Conference on Nutrition (ICN2) in November 2014 in Rome with the aim to address the challenges of all forms of malnutrition and its economic, health, social and political implications. This denotes an increasing awareness of the multifaceted nature and complexity of nutrition as well as of its political and economic implications.

The Decade is an unprecedented opportunity for mobilizing and focusing global efforts on the eradication of all forms of malnutrition. For the first time, Member States decided to dedicate a ten-year timeframe to enhanced and focused attention at the national, regional and global levels to realize the objectives of the ICN2, including achieving the global targets on nutrition by 2025 as agreed by the World Health Assembly (WHA) in 2012.[3]

Commitments based on a definite timeframe and evaluating progress based on quantitative indicators could make a significant difference in terms of guiding – and evaluating – national and international efforts towards a world free from all forms of malnutrition, which both governments and UN bodies alike become accountable for.

In response to the Decade, many developed and developing countries adopted national nutrition policies. In some countries, designated Ministries or national bodies were created to be responsible for nutrition and food security policymaking.[4]

§3.03 NUTRITION: THE KEY PLAYERS

The Decade recognizes that the challenges of malnutrition are complex and multidimensional. Those challenges require coordinated work between all relevant stakeholders at the national and international levels.

The primary reasonability of nutrition falls with national governments. Governments have a large policy operating space to impact the final nutrition outcomes. Political commitment is key to bring together all relevant ministries and coordinate the different economic, health and agriculture policies. Governments take the lead to ensure national ownership and bring the private sector and civil society to support their efforts.

Nevertheless, national efforts need to be supported by global coordinated policies and, in many cases, financial resources and best practices.

3. *Global Nutrition Targets* https://www.who.int/nutrition/global-target-2025/en/.
4. Check the WHO Global Database on National Nutrition Policies and Programmes, available at https://www.who.int/nutrition/databases/policies/en/.

At the global level, when dealing with malnutrition, the General Assembly Resolution prioritizes the agriculture and health sectors without undermining the roles of other sectors. Consequently, it identifies the FAO of the UN and the World Health Organization (WHO) as the two leading organizations in the implementation of the Decade.[5]

Additionally, the Resolution recognizes the important role the World Food Program (WFP), the International Fund for Agricultural Development (IFAD) and the United Nations International Children's Emergency Fund (UNICEF) play in the realization of the objectives of ICN2. This is in light of the important roles of these organization in dealing with food crises and malnutrition (WFP); in supporting rural development (IFAD); and in promoting the health and food security of children (UNICEF). [6] The roles of the five mentioned organizations can produce synergies that affect directly and indirectly both nutrition and health outcomes at the national level.

The Resolution also refers to coordination mechanisms, such as the United Nations System Standing Committee on Nutrition (UNSCN) and multi-stakeholder platforms, such as the UN Committee on World Food Security (CFS). This acknowledges the importance of multi-stakeholder agreements involving key players such as the private sector and the civil society.

Working through partnerships is key for the eradication of all forms of malnutrition. Official development assistance plays a key role in addressing the challenges of malnutrition, especially in countries which lack the resources to do so.

§3.04 DIFFERENT FORMS OF MALNUTRITION

While hunger is a form of malnutrition, not all cases of malnutrition are hunger. The WHO and the Global Nutrition Report identify three main forms of malnutrition: undernutrition, overweight and micronutrient deficiency.[7]

[A] Undernutrition

Undernutrition is a physical condition characterized by a nutritional disorder resulting from insufficient food intake (undernourishment) and/or poor absorption and/or poor biological use of nutrients consumed as a result of repeated infectious disease or the lack of proper nutrition, caused by not having enough calories containing substances necessary for growth and health.[8] Undernutrition could be manifested as stunting and wasting in children. Stunting and wasting are forms of growth failure, which develop over a long period of time in children under 5 years of age when growing with limited

5. UNGA Resolution 70/259, para. 3.
6. *Ibid.*
7. WHO classification of Malnutrition https://www.who.int/news-room/fact-sheets/detail/malnutrition.
8. Check UNICEF definition at https://www.unicef.org/progressforchildren/2006n4/undernutritiondefinition.html; Joy Ngo & Lluis Serra-Majem, *Encyclopedia of Food Security and Sustainability* (2019) https://www.sciencedirect.com/topics/food-science/undernutrition.

access and utilization of food.[9] Stunting is measured using the height-for-age nutritional index while wasting takes place when children are thin for their height. Both stunting and wasting can have negative impacts on the child's growth.

[B] Overweight

Overweight is the existence of abnormal or excessive fat accumulation that may impair health. The Body Mass Index (BMI) is used to determine the existence of overweight and obesity in adults. In adults, overweight is defined as a BMI of 25 or more, whereas obesity is a BMI of 30 or more.[10] Overweight and obesity are major causes of many NCDs, including non-insulin-dependent diabetes mellitus, coronary heart disease and stroke. Overweight was identified as one of the risk factors in the infection of COVID-19. People with obesity who contracted SARS-CoV-2 were 113% more likely than people of healthy weight to land in the hospital, 74% more likely to be admitted to an ICU, and 48% more likely to die.[11]

[C] Micronutrient Deficiencies

Micronutrient deficiency is caused by a lack of intake, absorption or use of one or more vitamins or minerals such as zinc, vitamin A, folate, vitamin B12 and iodine.[12] A global indicator of micronutrient deficiency is anaemia reflecting the lack of sufficient iron in the bloodstream.

The SDG2 calls for eliminating all forms of malnutrition in every country. Nevertheless, the world is not on track to achieve this goal. Even before the outbreak of COVID-19, the numbers were alarming. The nutritional status was considered an important determinant in the impact of COVID-19 on the person's health.[13] Better nutritional status could mean better immunity and resistance to COVID-19.

§3.05 A RECENT DETERIORATION OF THE WORLD NUTRITION STATUS

Statistics show that one-third of the countries (48 out of 126) suffer from the coexistence of at least one form of malnutrition.[14] There are common and shared

9. Check WHO Key Facts for malnutrition at https://www.who.int/news-room/fact-sheets/detail/malnutrition#: ~ :text = There%20are%204%20broad%20sub,height%20is%20known%20as%20wasting.
10. Check Obesity at https://www.who.int/health-topics/obesity#tab = tab_1.
11. Obesity Reviews 26 August 2020 https://onlinelibrary.wiley.com/doi/full/10.1111/obr.13128.
12. *See supra* note 10.
13. Faseeha Aman & Sadia Masood, *How Nutrition Can Help to Fight Against Covid-19 Pandemic* (2020) https://www.ncbi.nlm.nih.gov/pmc/articles/PMC7306972/.
14. Barry M Popkin, Camila Corvalan & Laurence M Grummer-Strawn, *Dynamics of the Double Burden of Malnutrition and the Changing Nutrition Reality* (2019) https://pubmed.ncbi.nlm.nih.gov/31852602/.

biological, environmental and socio-economic factors that contribute to the risk or prevalence of all forms of malnutrition.[15]

According to the Global Nutrition Report 2020, a high portion of the world population suffers from at least one form of malnutrition. Analysing the details, more than 821 million people suffer from undernutrition; around 2 billion adults are overweight or obese; and almost other 2 billion people deal with at least one form of micronutrient deficiency.[16] Almost 155 million children are stunted; 52 million children are wasted; 41 million children are overweight.[17]

A country suffers from the double burden of malnutrition when it has the coexistence of undernutrition along with overweight and obesity or with nutrition-related NCDs.[18] The triple burden of malnutrition takes place when undernutrition, overweight and obesity, and micronutrient deficiencies exist at the country level. The fact that the three forms of malnutrition co-exist in many countries is a manifestation of failure of public policies and food systems.

The double and triple burden of malnutrition can happen at the level of single individual, for example, when a person develops obesity with anaemia. When the double burden of malnutrition takes place at the country level, this could put pressures on the national policies with significant economic and health consequences. Certain vulnerable groups can be subject to more negative consequences of the existence of the double burden of malnutrition.[19]

The numbers show that after almost a decade of steady decline in the number of food-insecure people, the numbers of malnutrition started to steadily go up starting in 2017. The deterioration in food security and nutrition status could be attributed to three main reasons: conflicts, climate shocks and unsupportive policies.[20]

Conflicts destroy food systems and enforce famers to migrate. They are driven by internal and international political tensions, competition on scarce natural resources and more recently by the dire impacts of climate change effects on food systems.

The four components of food security (availability, access, utilization and stability) are affected by climate change.[21] Four out of the eight key risks identified by the Intergovernmental Panel on Climate Change (IPCC) have close relations with or direct consequences on food security and nutrition. These are: loss of rural livelihoods and income; loss of marine and coastal ecosystems and livelihoods; loss of terrestrial and inland water ecosystems and livelihoods; food insecurity and breakdown of food

15. *See*: *More than One in Three Low- and Middle-Income Countries Face Both Extremes of Malnutrition* (2019) https://www.who.int/news/item/16-12-2019-more-than-one-in-three-low--and-middle-income-countries-face-both-extremes-of-malnutrition. *Ibid.*
16. *See* the *Global Nutrition Report 2020* at https://globalnutritionreport.org/reports/2020-global-nutrition-report/introduction-towards-global-nutrition-equity/.
17. *Ibid.*
18. World Health Organization, *The Double Burden of Malnutrition* in *Policy Brief* (World Health Organization 2017).
19. FAO, *The Double Burden of Malnutrition: Case Studies from Six Developing Countries* (FAO Food and Nutrition 2006) 84 http://www.fao.org/3/a0442e/a0442e00.pdf.
20. Food Security Information Network, *Global Report on Food Crisis* (2019) https://reliefweb.int/report/world/global-report-food-crises-2019.
21. FAO, *The Future of Food and Agriculture: Alternative Pathways to 2050. Food and Agriculture Organization of the United Nations* (Rome, Italy 2018a) 228 pp.

systems.[22] Those changes also lead to the migration of agriculture workers that risks to undermine the food systems.

Unsupportive public policies could impact food environments and distort food demand and supply. The lack of adequate safety nets undermines access to food and push people into malnutrition.

No country is immune to malnutrition despite the striking difference between regions, since developing and least developed countries (LDCs) suffer from a higher rate of malnutrition. In many cases, hunger and malnutrition could be a result of a low level of income and constrained consumer choices. Obesity could also be a consequence of poverty because consumers tend to eat fatty and low-value products instead of pricy high-nutrient products.

Relative food prices vary systematically across countries and partially explain international differences in the prevalence of undernutrition and overweight adults.[23] Most products are relatively cheap in high-income countries, including sugar- and fat-rich foods. In lower-income countries, healthy foods are generally expensive, especially most animal-sourced foods and fortified infant cereals.

The increasing numbers of all forms of malnutrition are alarming and indicate that if the current trends continue, the world is – and will continue to be – off track to achieve its established targets, including Target 2.2 'ending all forms of malnutrition, and achieving, by 2025, the internationally agreed targets on stunting and wasting in children under 5 years of age'. This will be definitely a lost opportunity.

§3.06 COVID-19 AND NUTRITION

COVID-19 has struck the world in the middle of the Decade of Action established timeframe. This brought additional challenge to the national efforts that were already suffering from the combined impacts of conflicts and climate change on nutrition and food systems.

Unhealthy diets are contributing to pre-existing conditions that put people at more risk from the pandemic. People's nutrition status is one of the major determinants of how they react to the virus. Heart diseases, diabetics and some kinds of cancer can be attributed to metabolic risks, which in turn weaken the immune system and can lead to a high probability of mortality.[24]

While the exact implications of COVID-19 are yet to be seen, the economic implications of the pandemic are affecting both the supply and demand sides of the food systems. The pandemic has constrained the purchasing power of individuals and enforced them to make bad nutritional decisions.

22. IPCC, *Fifth Assessment Report* (2014) https://www.ipcc.ch/report/ar5/syr/.
23. Derek D Headey & Harold H Alderman, *The Relative Caloric Prices of Healthy and Unhealthy Foods Differ Systematically across Income Levels and Continents,* The Journal of Nutrition, Volume 149, Issue 11 (2019) 2020-2033 https://doi.org/10.1093/jn/nxz158.
24. *See* The Global Burden of Disease Report (2019) at https://www.thelancet.com/action/showPdf?pii=S0140-6736%2820%2930752-2.

Many UN organizations, including the FAO and the WFP, have warned against the severe impacts of the pandemic on food security and nutrition. Recent Integrated Food Security Phase Classification analyses point to a worrying deterioration of acute food insecurity in countries already suffering from other crises including conflicts and climate change.[25]

The FAO stressed that COVID-19 has struck at a time when hunger or undernourishment keep rising. An additional 83 million people, and possibly as many as 130 million additional people may go hungry in as a result of the economic recession triggered by the pandemic.[26]

The WFP called for increasing funding to mitigate the possible impact on the most vulnerable warning that the number of acute food insecurity in low- and middle-income countries could double by the end of 2020. That is an increase from 135 million in 2019 to 265 million in 2020.[27]

[A] The Supply-Side Impacts

COVID-19 impacted the supply side of food systems especially in the first few months. While the world adjusted and the impacts are now relatively limited, the long-term effects resulting from the fear of contamination and restrictions on access definitely affected the food systems, food supply chains and production worldwide.

Food supply chains, which include all steps from production to consumption of food, were largely disrupted as a result of COVID-19. The disruption took many forms: restriction on movement of food and factors of production, export restrictions, closure of market, food safety concerns and short-term food price hikes. The stable production of food limited the impacts on food security, but this cannot be taken as a source of confidence especially in the Net Food-Importing Countries and especially if the pandemic continues to exist in the coming years.

The FAO's global survey on COVID-19 demonstrated that the restrictions in the use of public transport (66% of respondents overall) and on the selling of food in public spaces such as parks, squares and streets (68.3% of respondents overall) have highly impacted local food accessibility.[28]

Small-scale producers are facing mounting challenges accessing inputs (seeds and fertilizers) because of the rising prices of these inputs, the severely reduced household incomes, and/or the lack of availability of these inputs in markets.[29]

Reduced food production may have serious implications for food availability as well as nutrition. If planting is reduced, so too are harvests, which means farming

25. *See* FAO, *Novel Coronavirus (Covid-19)* at http://www.fao.org/2019-ncov/en/ and WFP, *Covid-19 Pandemic* at https://www.wfp.org/emergencies/Covid-19-pandemic.
26. *Ibid.*
27. COVID-19 will double number of people facing food crises unless swift action is taken https://www.wfp.org/news/Covid-19-will-double-number-people-facing-food-crises-unless-swift-action-taken.
28. FAO, *Covid-19 and the Role of Local Food Production in Building More Resilient Local Food Systems* (2020).
29. *Ibid.*

families themselves, often among the most acutely food insecure, as well as their communities, will not be able to access sufficient nutritious food down the line. Currently the threat of famine is looming in thirty hunger hotspots including Yemen, South Sudan and Northern Nigeria,[30] which could add to the pressures on the world efforts to achieve SDG2.

The World Trade Organization (WTO) indicated that the world trade is expected to fall between 13% and 32% in 2020 as the COVID-19 pandemic disrupts normal economic activity and life around the world.[31] The trade impact on nutrition could be mixed depending on the context but in these cases, reduced availability combined with reduced access could impact nutrition outcomes negatively.

[B] The Demand-Side Impacts

Consumers' panic led to excessive precautionary demand at the beginning of the crisis, which induced some fears especially in importing countries. The FAO Food Price Index averaged 100.9 points in October 2020, up 3.0 points (3.1%) from September and 5.7 points (6.0%) higher than its value a year ago. The October value, the highest since January 2020, represented the fifth consecutive monthly increase.[32] The short-term increase could be attributed to the overall certainty as a result of COVID-19 and may have a visible effect on consumer nutritional choices.

A recent joint report from the Organisation of Economic Cooperation and Development (OECD) and the FAO found that during the decade 2020-2029 supply growth is going to outpace demand growth, causing real prices of most commodities to remain at or below their current levels.[33]

Access to food is constrained by household income. COVID-19 resulted in job losses and increased unemployment in many countries. There is a positive relationship between income and food demand. The decrease in disposable incomes in low-income countries caused by COVID-19 could decrease demand in the coming years and could further undermine food security.[34] In the long term the pandemic may decrease demand in the next few years, which could have mixed impacts on food security and nutrition.[35]

In many developing countries and LDCs remittances play a key role in supporting livelihood. Decreasing remittances because of job loss impacts food security and nutrition through limitation on access to nutritious food.

30. FAO, WFP, *Hunger Hot Spots Report, March to July 2021 Outlook* (2021).
31. https://www.wto.org/english/news_e/pres20_e/pr855_e.htm.
32. *FAO Food Price Index* http://www.fao.org/worldfoodsituation/foodpricesindex/en/.
33. OECD-FAO, *Agricultural Outlook 2020-2029* (2020) http://www.fao.org/publications/oecd-fao-agricultural-outlook/2020-2029/en/.
34. *Ibid.*
35. http://www.fao.org/news/story/en/item/1298333/icode/.

§3.07 THE MULTI-SECTORIAL NATURE OF NUTRITION

COVID-19 is a serious health threat. Yet, it is also a reminder that our food systems and our economic policies, as they stand now, are not supportive of better nutritional outcomes. The UN Decade of Action on Nutrition emphasizes that tackling malnutrition in all its forms is not a domain of one sector.

The traditional view that considered malnutrition a health challenge is not valid anymore. In addition to health policy, agriculture, social protection, planning, economic and education policies all have a key role to support better nutrition outcomes. Better nutrition can only be achieved through a multifaceted approach that works on those different interconnected policy issues.

The Decade recognizes this cross-sectorial nature. Being the global framework aimed at coordinating national and international actions to eradicate all forms of malnutrition, it structures its work based on six areas of work: (1) sustainable, resilient food systems for healthy diets; (2) aligned health systems providing universal coverage of essential nutrition actions; (3) social protection and nutrition education; (4) trade and investment for improved nutrition; (5) safe and supportive environments for nutrition at all ages; (6) strengthened governance and accountability for nutrition.[36]

These six cross-cutting and interconnected action areas were originally identified under the ICN2 Framework for Action and are key to support better nutrition. In the meantime, the recent experience of the COVID-19 pandemic shows that those six are affected by the pandemic. They are also reflected in many SDGs.

[A] Nutrition and Food Systems

Food systems 'gather all the elements (environment, people, inputs, processes, infrastructures, institutions, etc.) and activities that relate to the production, processing, distribution, preparation and consumption of food, and the output of these activities, including socio-economic and environmental outcomes'.[37] SDG2 refers to promoting sustainable agriculture, which is one of the components of food systems.

One-third of the food produced is lost or wasted across the food supply chain. This affects the availability of food and its nutritional value with implication reflected on the consumer prices. In addition, it represents a major loss of resources, including energy, labour, land and capital used in producing food.

Reducing food losses would contribute greatly to increasing the supply of available food in developing countries, thereby contributing to improving food security and nutrition. Food systems are one of the most visible and direct drivers of nutrition. Working on increasing harmony between food systems and good nutrition outcomes is not an easy objective and requires decisions on different levels of the food supply chain.

36. *See* the Work Programme of the UN Decade of Action on Nutrition https://www.unscn.org/en/topics/un-decade-of-action-on-nutrition?idnews=1791.
37. High Level Panel of Experts, *Food Losses and Waste in the Context of Sustainable Food Systems* (2014).

The ICN2 confirmed what we already know: food systems are distorted. They are not providing adequate, safe, diversified and nutrient-rich food that can lead to healthy diets. The main reasons cited by ICN2 are constraints such as resource scarcity and environmental degradation, as well as unsustainable production and consumption patterns, food losses and waste, and unbalanced distribution.

As a result of the increasing awareness of the importance of food systems, the UN is organizing a food systems summit in September 2021. The event will be held at the UN Headquarters in New York, in conjunction with the UN General Assembly.[38]

The overarching goal of the summit is to help stakeholders better understand and manage the complex choices that affect the future of food systems and to accelerate progress towards the SDGs. Structured around engagement at the national, regional and global levels, the preparatory process towards the summit will enable stakeholders to develop, test and adopt frameworks and decision-making tools and provide platforms for the innovative partnerships and initiatives needed to catalyse significant commitments for action and investment towards more sustainable food systems. The decision of the summit precedes the outbreak of COVID-19. Policymakers will have to consider the impact of this major change on food systems and how to prevent the next pandemic from destroying our food systems.

In the same directions, governments, representatives of the private sector and the civil society organizations have adopted in February 2021, the Voluntary Guidelines on Food Systems and Nutrition. Those guidelines are intended to contribute to reshaping or promoting food systems to ensure that the food that contributes to sustainable and healthy diets is available, affordable, acceptable, safe, and of adequate quantity and quality.

Reforming the food and agriculture systems to make them more nutrition-sensitive features on top of the six areas as key to producing enough nutritious food to overcome the challenges of malnutrition. Currently, there is a weak link between food systems and better nutrition objectives.

The objective of those guidelines is to contribute to the process towards achieving sustainable food systems and improved nutrition, recalling that transformation of food systems should be encouraged in a coherent manner, as appropriate and in accordance with and dependent on national contexts and capacities, in accordance with the three dimensions of sustainable development.[39]

Pandemics such as COVID-19 and the strategies adopted to reduce their transmission may worsen global food insecurity and malnutrition even in the absence of evidence of the transmission via food or food packaging.

FAO and the CFS have requested governments to keep trade corridors open to ensure the continuous functioning of critical aspects of food systems in all countries.[40]

38. The 2021 Food Systems Summit https://www.un.org/en/food-systems-summit.
39. Paragraph 31 of the CFS Voluntary Guidelines and Nutrition and Food Systems http://www.fao.org/fileadmin/templates/cfs/Docs2021/Documents/CFS_VGs_Food_Systems_and_Nutrition_Strategy_EN.pdf.
40. United Nations, *Policy Brief: The Impact of Covid-19 on Food Security and Nutrition* (June 2020).

The FAO is co-leading the implementation of the Decade. In the meantime, the FAO is also supporting the organization of the Food Systems Summit in 2021, which is a recognition of the importance of reforming food systems to support better food security and nutrition outcomes.

[B] Nutrition and Health Systems

Nutrition, food safety and health (SDG3) are interconnected. As a matter of fact, malnourished mothers are more likely to have low-birth-weight babies with higher risk of becoming malnourished children and adults. The effects of malnutrition could lead to an increased vulnerability to NCDs and other chronic diseases. These diseases lead to higher spending on health care, putting significant burdens on national health care systems and economies.

Building modern and efficient health systems leads to better nutrition outcomes. Improved health levels are linked to better food utilization and consequently better nutrition. Some of the causes of malnutrition are rooted in chronic and contagious diseases. Improving health systems can also prevent and treat diseases, which can aggravate undernutrition. According to WHO estimates, each year unsafe food causes 600 million cases of foodborne diseases worldwide and 420,000 deaths.[41] Poor diets are among the top risk factors contributing to the global burden of disease and death today; unhealthy eating habits are linked with one-fifth of deaths worldwide.[42]

The three forms of malnutrition contributing to many diet-related chronic diseases, such as type two diabetes, cancer and cardiovascular diseases, contribute to early deaths.[43] Some estimates calculate that the costs associated with obesity are calculated at approximately USD 2 trillion per year.[44]

In many countries, including some developed countries, health systems failed to deal with high surge of cases because of COVID-19.

The virus depleted human energy and caused organ failures in some cases. In certain cases, nutrition looks like a non-priority compared with the immediate severe health impact of the pandemic. The WHO is co-leading with FAO, the programme of action of the Decade and also the health response to the COVID-19 pandemic. The fight against COVID-19 should not lose sight of the inter-linkages between improving nutrition and dealing with health threats.

41. The Lancet, *The Lancet Study* (2019) https://www.thelancet.com/action/showPdf?pii=S0140-6736%2819%2930041-8.
42. *Ibid.*
43. The Lancet, *Global, Regional, and National Comparative Risk Assessment of 84 Behavioural, Environmental and Occupational, and Metabolic Risks or Clusters of Risks (2017)* https://www.thelancet.com/action/showPdf?pii=S0140-6736%2818%2932225-6.
44. McKinsey Global Institute, *Overcoming Obesity: An Initial Economic Analysis. Discussion Paper* (2014).

[C] Nutrition and Social Protection

Social protection is one of the important drivers of the SDGs. The poverty eradication goal includes an indicator that measures the implementation of nationally appropriate social protection systems and by 2030 achieve substantial coverage of the poor and the vulnerable.[45] The SDG4 on health provides for another indicator that measures efforts towards universal health coverage and achieves access to essential health services and access to affordable medicines and vaccines for all.[46]

Social protection is crucial in ensuring that poor segments of the population are not left behind. It can help target disadvantageous populations and improve their economic access to food.

The International Labor Organization (ILO) concluded that dropping global gross domestic production (GDP) growth by 2%-8%, which is very likely in the short term, would lead to the loss of 5.3-24.7 million jobs.[47] This, in turn, implies large income losses for workers, estimated at USD 860 million to USD 3.44 billion. The situation has recently deteriorated, as there was a 14% drop in global working hours during the second quarter of 2020, equivalent to the loss of 400 million full-time jobs.[48] When the job loss or employment disruption happens in the agriculture sector, it can produce double negative impacts on nutrition in the form of loss of access and lower supply of food.

Cash transfers and other social protection tools were used during the COVID-19 crisis to mitigate the economic and health impacts. Using data and smart approaches to target the neediest is key in determining the success of social protection systems for safeguarding nutrition. Preparing for the next pandemic, governments need to develop advanced social protection and data systems to be able to have an impact on the ground and avoid turning a health crisis into a nutrition one.

[D] Nutrition and International Trade

The ICN2 called on governments, UN agencies, programmes and funds, the WTO and other international organizations to identify opportunities to achieve global food and nutrition targets, through trade and investment policies.[49] It also calls on improving the availability and access of the food supply through appropriate trade agreements and policies and to endeavour to ensure that such agreements and policies have no negative impact on the right to adequate food in other countries.[50] The Agenda 2030 refers to trade as one of the areas that can impact the goals related to food security and nutrition.

45. Indicator 1.3 of SDG1 of Agenda 2030 of the UN (2015).
46. Indicator 3.8 of SDG3 of Agenda 2030 of the UN (2015).
47. ILO, *Covid-19 and the World of Work: Impact and Policy Responses* (1st ed., ILO Monitor 2020) https://www.ilo.org/wcmsp5/groups/public/---dgreports/---dcomm/documents/briefingnote/wcms_738753.pdf.
48. ILO, *Covid-19 and the World of Work: Impact and Policy Responses* (5th ed., ILO Monitor 2020) ilo.org/wcmsp5/groups/public/@dgreports/@dcomm/documents/briefingnote/wcms_749399.pdf.
49. Recommendation 17 of ICN2 (2014).
50. *Ibid.*, Recommendation 19.

Although the empirical evidence on how trade has changed the patterns of consumption is still rather limited, global trade and investment policies are means for improving access and availability of food.

The mixed impacts of trade on nutrition can contribute to increasing food supply, food access, and it can also lead to a situation of more availability of less healthy foods, including ultra-processed foods, which can negatively impact nutrition.

The relationship between trade and nutrition is complex and requires an in-depth understanding of food systems and their evolution. International and regional trade measures should be carefully evaluated to assess their impact on long-term nutritional outcomes.

The forum for negotiating world trade rules, which is the WTO, is not among the organizations mentioned by the UNGA resolution. This is an important challenge as rules-based international trade has a role in supporting better nutrition through the application of transparent and effective food safety measures[51] and rule-based multilateral trade rules, which can help improve access for countries with low agriculture productivity and high food demand.

COVID-19 has significantly disrupted global trade for different reasons, including but not limited to fear of contamination. Many countries have initially imposed trade restricting measures, which limited food consumption to the importers with impacts on food security and nutrition. Countries have applied new sanitary and phytosanitary standards (SPS) measures, tariff reductions, as well as export restrictions.[52]

None of the initial measures was expected to impact negatively on the agricultural sector, which has in fact shown resilience, with a trade performance that has fared better than other sectors as shown by the FAO price index. This is mainly thanks to a coordinated policy response which sought to mend broken supply chains and to help agricultural producers to cope with the 'new normal' situation.[53]

This also reflects the essential nature of food and the resulting relative income inelasticity of demand for it, as well as the fact that most agricultural trade (notably cereals and oilseeds) takes place in bulk marine shipments that have not been subject to major disruptions.[54] While overall merchandise trade fell sharply in the first half of 2020, agricultural and food exports increased by 2.5% during the first quarter of the year compared to the same period in 2019, with an increase of 3.3% in March.[55]

Despite this positive direction, there is a need to be cautious on the future impacts of pandemics on food security and nutrition.

In the meantime, trade policies can be designed in a way that supports better nutrition outcomes. This includes import tariffs, export taxes or subsidies, quantitative restrictions on imports or exports, licensing or customs procedures, domestic support, public stockholding and local procurement, regulation of marketing activities, public research and development in agriculture.

---

51. *See* the WTO Agreement on the Application of Sanitary and Phytosanitary Measures.
52. *See* WTO, *Covid-19 and Agriculture: A Story of Resilience* (2020) https://www.wto.org/english/tratop_e/Covid-19_e/agric_report_e.pdf.
53. *Ibid.*
54. *Ibid.*
55. *Ibid.*

These measures can be important tools for addressing nutrition concerns. The WTO rules, including the Agreements on SPS and Technical Barriers to Trade (TBT), regulate the use of such measures. The SPS and TBT Agreements balance WTO members' rights to regulate for legitimate objectives, such as food safety and consumer protection, and ensure that these regulations do not become discriminatory barriers to trade.

In recent years, many countries implemented nutrition labelling regulations, triggering discussions on these measures in the WTO TBT Committee. These discussions underline the importance of food safety and further work on a commonly agreed international set of standards and guidelines for labelling applicable to all foods.[56]

[E] Nutrition and Supportive Environment

Supportive environment is the fifth action area of the Decade Nutrition policies and outcomes are affected by the surrounding environment. This includes the physical environment such as the school, home, hospital and work environments, food production and urban environments as well as the regulatory and fiscal policies such as labelling and taxation.

Access to safe drinking water and adequate sanitation are essential for the health and prevention of diarrhoeal disease, therefore improving nutrition status. Nutrition actions need to be supported by safe and supportive environments. Conducive legislation and economic policies that put the needs of the population as priority lead to better access to nutritious food and higher level of nutrition. This also requires raising awareness of the role of nutrition and driving socio-economic development.

[F] Nutrition and Governance

Strong governance and accountability systems ensure that nutrition decisions will be implemented and will be accountable for all stakeholders involved. This is fundamental in turning political commitments such as those in ICN2, the CFS Voluntary guidelines on nutrition and Food systems and Agenda 2030 into actions on the ground. It is also key when Governments have to deal with situations of conflict of interests and pressures from different groups and stakeholders.

The programme of work of the Decade provides a clearly defined, time-bound cohesive framework for actions. The Decade confirms the need for coordinated efforts from all stakeholders and was formulated in an inclusive way that was not limited to Member States but included inputs from both the Civil Society Mechanism and the Private Sector Mechanism.

56. FAO & WTO, *Trade and Food Standards* (2017) 72, www.fao.org/3/a-i7407e.pdf.

§3.08 NUTRITION ACROSS AGENDA 2030

In addition to the above-mentioned six areas, nutrition can be traced through many additional SDGs. Across the seventeen SDGs of the Agenda 2030, nutrition features as a catalyst and result of the implementation/lack of implementation of twelve of the SDGs.

According to the analysis of the global nutrition report, five core areas run through the SDGs that nutrition can contribute to, and in turn, benefit from.[57] These areas are explained below.

[A] Nutrition and Infrastructure

A Quality Infrastructure is a system contributing to governmental policy objectives in areas including industrial development, trade competitiveness in global markets, efficient use of natural and human resources, food safety, health, the environment and climate change.[58]

Infrastructure is a key driver of nutrition. Good infrastructure is vital not only when it comes to food access but also utilization and stability through international and local trade.

Health infrastructure such as hospitals and supportive infrastructure that ensures access to safe waters and sanitation are prerequisites for better nutrition. The lack of the latter can increase the risk of infectious diseases such as diarrhoea and cholera.[59]

Establishing functioning school-feeding programmes can provide adequate nutrition, particularly in developing countries. Nevertheless, this requires significant investment in building schools that are equipped with kitchens and – possible – school gardens. The same health and supportive systems play a key role in dealing with the implications of pandemics.

[B] Nutrition, Equity, Gender Equality and Inclusion

The Agenda 2030 calls for reducing inequalities between and within countries. Food insecurity is one of the manifestations of inequality.[60] COVID-19 has deepened existing inequalities, hitting the poorest and most vulnerable communities the hardest, which extends to food security. Social, political and economic inequalities have amplified the impacts of the pandemic. COVID-19 has increased unemployment and decreased the disposable income for food consumption.

57. *Global Nutrition Report* (2017) https://globalnutritionreport.org/reports/2017-global-nutrition-report/.
58. UNIDO, *Report on Quality Infrastructure: Building Trust for Trade* (2016) https://www.unido.org/sites/default/files/2016-05/UNIDO_Quality_system_0.pdf.
59. UNICEF & WHO, *Drinking Water, Sanitation and Hygiene in Schools: Global Baseline Report 2018* (UNICEF & WHO 2018).
60. SDG10 of Agenda 2030.

In every country in the world, there are striking inequalities according to location, age, sex, education and wealth – while conflict and other forms of fragility compound the problem.[61]

The Agenda 2030 and human rights law recognize that gender equality is not only a fundamental human right but a necessary foundation for a peaceful, prosperous and sustainable world. This includes better food security and nutrition outcomes.

There has been progress over the past decades: More girls are going to school, fewer girls are forced into early marriage, more women are serving in parliament and positions of leadership, and laws are being reformed to advance gender equality.[62]

Studies have shown that there is a strong relationship between gender-based discrimination and the different channels through which households and individuals access food – through own-production, access to waged employment, or social protection.[63]

Data also show a relationship between gender inequalities and food insecurity, to the detriment of women, where women are more likely than men to experience food insecurity.[64]

Hunger cannot be reduced or eliminated solely through the provision of adequate food but through systematic interventions that address economic inequality as well as discrimination against women.

Likewise, the food security impacts of COVID-19 are exacerbated for women and girls and people in vulnerable situations such as refugees and Internally Displaced Persons. The pandemic and measures to prevent its spread are driving a disproportionate increase in women's unemployment (as compared to men) and it is also decreasing their overall working time.[65]

This calls for targeted interventions that do not focus only on the provision of food but on addressing the foundation of inequality. Women can be a catalyst for change. Supporting women can lead to better agriculture productivity and better nutrition choices.

---

61. *Global Nutrition Report* (2020) https://globalnutritionreport.org/reports/2020-global-nutrition-report/executive-summary/.
62. Goal 5 of Agenda 2030: Achieve gender equality and empower all women and girls.
63. https://www.adb.org/publications/gender-equality-and-food-security-womens-empowerment-tool-against-hunger.
64. https://docs.wfp.org/api/documents/WFP-0000112500/download/?_ga=2.187656232.1248893545.1599406214-474274742.1596548220.
65. UN WOMEN, Covid-19 and its economic toll on women: The story behind the numbers (2020) https://www.unwomen.org/en/news/stories/2020/9/feature-Covid-19-economic-impacts-on-women.

[C] Nutrition, Peace and Stability

SDG16 calls for creating peace, justice and strong institutions. The increase in hunger in the last three years is mainly because of the combined effects of conflicts and climate change.[66]

Conflicts disturb food systems and force farmers to move away from agriculture. The disturbance of the food systems can undermine their ability to deliver sustainable and healthy diets.

This leads to major adverse effects on the nutritional status of impacted populations and in particular on the most vulnerable ones. In 2017, the crises in South Sudan, Yemen, Somalia and North Nigeria were declared famine.[67]

The combined effects of conflicts and pandemics could be devastating especially when national institutions are not functioning, and international organizations are in a situation where they fail to cope with multiple simultaneous crises.

More recently, the WFP warned that the global hunger crisis caused by conflicts compound with COVID-19 could lead to a wave of famine overwhelming nations already weakened by years of instability.[68]

[D] Nutrition, Poverty and the Economy

Malnutrition, poverty and economic growth are interconnected. Poverty leads to both malnutrition and obesity. Evidence suggests a strong correlation between food insecurity, inequality, poverty and cardiovascular diseases,[69] with a socio-economic gradient of overweight and obesity in many middle- and high- income countries.

Poverty (SDG1) leads to malnutrition, and malnutrition can result in decreased education years and consequently lower levels of income creating a vicious cycle. Higher income could mean more nutrition choices, which results in better access to food and nutrition levels.

The estimated impact on the global economy could be as high as USD 3.5 trillion per year.[70] These enormous costs result from economic growth foregone and lost investments in human capital associated with preventable child deaths, as well as premature adult mortality linked to diet-related NCDs.[71]

---

66. The State of World Food Security and Nutrition in the World (2017) https://docs.wfp.org/api/documents/WFP-0000022419/download/?_ga=2.267071374.1207680118.1605377335-1493320523.1604942628.
67. A famine is declared when at least 20% of households in a given group face extreme food deficits; at least 30% of children in a given group are acutely malnourished; and mortality rates exceed two people per 10,000 population per day.
68. New Wave of Famine could sweep the globe https://news.un.org/en/story/2020/09/1072712.
69. Hester H Vorster & Annamarie Kruger, *Poverty, Malnutrition, Underdevelopment and Cardiovascular Disease: A South African Perspective,* Cardiovascular Journal of Africa Volume 18, Issue 5, 321-324 https://www.ncbi.nlm.nih.gov/pmc/articles/PMC3975540/pdf/cvja-18-321.pdf.
70. The Cost of malnutrition: why policy Action is urgent https://www.glopan.org/cost-of-malnutrition/.
71. *Ibid.*

Stable national institutions may lead to better economic decisions, which result in sustainable agriculture, more food supply and better access to nutritious foods. According to some estimates, the economic consequences of malnutrition represent losses of 11% of GDP.[72]

At the micro-level, poverty limits access to food. It can lead to consuming less food (hunger) or consuming less nutritious food (malnutrition). At the macro-level, recession and economic crises can decrease employment rates, which lead to less disposable incomes and consequently less purchasing power that also contributes to hunger and malnutrition.

The COVID-19 pandemic is estimated to push an additional 88 million to 115 million people into extreme poverty this year, with the total rising to as many as 150 million by 2021, depending on the severity of the economic contraction.[73] This will definitely impact the global efforts to bring the numbers of malnutrition down.

[E] Nutrition and Climate Change

SDG13 calls for taking urgent actions to combat the effects of climate change. Climate change and its negative effects can decrease agriculture yields. Increased carbon dioxide will result in decreased protein, iron, zinc and other micronutrients in major crops consumed by much of the world.[74]

Countries facing both the adverse effects of climate change and conflicts have high levels of malnutrition.[75] Most recently, this is combined with the impacts of COVID-19.

In Sub-Saharan Africa, droughts led to mass exodus and waves of migration to Europe. In other regions, the frequency and severity of extreme weather events decrease crop yields and livestock productivity, as well as result in declines in fisheries and agroforestry in areas already vulnerable to food insecurity.

Irresponsible consumption is threatening world resources and its sustainability. Unsustainable fishing (SDG12) threatens 17% of the world's protein, which is a source of essential micronutrients.

Sustainable and responsible agriculture investment can increase agricultural productivity and the nutritional value. Investment in food system, digitalization and technology transfer can decrease food loss and waste currently estimated at one-third of food produced.

72. *See* The Global Nutrition Report (2017).
73. Data from the World Bank at https://www.worldbank.org/en/news/press-release/2020/10/07/Covid-19-to-add-as-many-as-150-million-extreme-poor-by-2021.
74. IFPRI, *Effects of Rising CO2 on Protein, Iron, and Zinc Availability in Global Diets* (2019) https://www.ifpri.org/blog/effects-rising-co2-protein-iron-and-zinc-availability-global-diets.
75. *Supra* note 72.

[F] Nutrition and Education

SDG4 aims at 'ensuring inclusive and equitable quality education and promote lifelong learning opportunities for all'.

Education is also linked to better nutrition status as people can make better choices when selecting what to eat and how to resist the impacts of mass media when promoting lesser health choices.

The disease affects education throughout childhood; and improving children's health and nutrition brings substantial benefits for education. In the meantime, improving health and nutrition brings benefits to the poor and most vulnerable as health and education reinforce one another.[76]

Malnutrition in children results in reduced stature, poor school performance, reduced economic productivity and opportunities.

School feeding and school meals programmes are designed to support a healthy food environment, help schoolchildren, adolescents and their communities to improve their diets and food choices. With many children staying at home because of COVID-19, the most vulnerable children are hardly hit by the negative impacts.

§3.09 STOCKTAKING OF THE IMPLEMENTATION OF THE DECADE OF ACTION ON NUTRITION

Five years after the world committed to end hunger, food insecurity and all forms of malnutrition, the world is off-track to achieve SDG2 and the planned outcomes of the Decade. Data from the 2020 State of Food Security and Nutrition Report confirms that the world is progressing neither towards SDG Target 2.1, of ensuring access to safe, nutritious and sufficient food for all people all year round nor towards Target 2.2 of eradicating all forms of malnutrition.[77]

The Decade was promulgated as an opportunity for coordinated national and international actions to support the realization of SDG2. Nevertheless, many challenges are arising.

The increasing numbers of hunger and malnutrition were exacerbated further by the COVID-19 pandemic.

The most recent estimate for 2019 shows that prior to the COVID-19 pandemic, almost 690 million people, or 8.9% of the global population, were undernourished. The new estimate for it shows that an additional 60 million people have become affected by hunger since 2014. If this trend continues, the number of undernourished people will exceed 840 million by 2030.[78] COVID-19 pandemic may add an additional 83-132 million people to the ranks of the undernourished in 2020.[79]

---

76. Mattew CH Jukes, Lesley J Drake & Donald AP Bundy, *School Health, Nutrition and Education for All: Levelling the Playing Field* (Wallingford 2007).
77. WFP, *The State of Food Nutrition in the World* (2020) https://docs.wfp.org/api/documents/WFP-0000117811/download/.
78. *Ibid.*
79. *Ibid.*

The impact is not limited to hunger but extends to the different forms of malnutrition. Not one country is on course to meet all ten of the 2025 global nutrition targets and just 8 of 194 countries are on track to meet four targets. Almost a quarter of all children under 5 years of age are stunted. At the same time, overweight and obesity are increasing rapidly in nearly every country in the world, with no signs of slowing.[80]

In 2019, 21.3% (144.0 million) of children under 5 years of age were estimated to be stunted, 6.9% (47.0 million) wasted and 5.6% (38.3 million) overweight, while at least 340 million children suffered from micronutrient deficiencies. Adult obesity is on the rise in all regions for 2030, even without considering a potential global recession.[81]

The Secretary General Report on the Implementation of the UN Decade of Action on Nutrition (2016-2025) acknowledges the important challenges facing the realization of the global nutrition objectives.

Despite some progress in several countries, including the adoption of national policies on nutrition by most of the countries, nutrition is not always a stated objective in national sectoral policies or development plans.[82]

Some regions have achieved notable progress in the achievement of the universal nutrition targets. Nevertheless, there is still a long road ahead to achieve the 2025 and 2030 targets for stunting, wasting, overweight, exclusive breastfeeding, anaemia in women and adult obesity.

In many countries, the business of nutrition is the responsibility of no one. In others, the mandate is divided between different ministries such as agriculture, health and social solidarity with no effective coordination between them.

The Report identifies many recommendations to accelerate progress on all fronts. One key conclusion is that open and inclusive dialogues between all the stakeholders should be arranged at mid-term and, at the end of the Decade, in consultation with Member States.

The Second Global Nutrition policy review, which was conducted by WHO in 2016-2017, indicates that 183 countries have national policies that include nutrition goals and actions, of which 168 countries have specific plans on nutrition, 105 countries have health sector plans with nutrition components, and 48 countries have integrated nutrition objectives in their national development plans.[83]

This number should be taken cautiously, since the existence of a nutrition plan does not necessarily indicate that a country is on track to achieve the nutrition objectives. The non-implementation could result from the lack of funding, the limited coordination between different stakeholders, or the lack of awareness of the importance of nutrition within the national policy framework.

One of the major challenges for a successful outcome of the Decade is that it is necessary to know which foods contribute to health and well-being and which are

80. The Global Nutrition Report (2020) https://globalnutritionreport.org/reports/2020-global-nutrition-report/executive-summary/.
81. *Supra* note 78.
82. Implementation of the UN Decade of Action on Nutrition, Report by the Secretary-General (2018) https://digitallibrary.un.org/record/1486196?ln=en.
83. WTO, *Global Nutrition Policy Review* (2016) http://www.who.int/nutrition/topics/global-nutrition-policy-review-2016.pdf.

unhealthy.[84] This is an area where there is no definite consensus and this is aggravated by over polarization and conflicting interests between countries and different stakeholders, including the private sector and the civil society.

Despite this gloomy picture, there are reasons for optimism. One critical improvement is the increased awareness of the importance of nutrition and its multifaceted nature. Examples of this are shown by the work of nutrition-dedicated bodies such as the UNSCN and CFS as well as the decision to hold a food systems summit in 2021.

Another factor is that the world has gradually accumulated better knowledge and science on what are the causes of malnutrition and what kind of policies can deal with them. This includes, for example, the policies on health diet and national guidelines, the 1,000 days window, fortification of food, breastfeeding and nutrition education and the recently adopted guidelines on nutrition and food systems.

Policymakers are in a better position now in understanding the impacts of their socio-economic policies on nutrition. Why certain segments of the population are suffering from one type of malnutrition and the role of stakeholders and UN agencies in supporting national efforts in achieving better nutrition.

Innovations, digital and new technologies are key drivers of innovation for food systems, which can improve food security and nutrition outcomes especially in developing countries where the productivity is low.

Additionally, the world has access to better data. Data is crucial not only in understanding what kind of policies work but also in measuring progress and making decision-makers accountable for their decisions. Data also can measure and evaluate the effects of different economic, trade and social policies on nutrition. The nutrition-related targets and indicators of SDG2 are quantitative and need to be measured. Data can serve dual objectives as they can also help target the most needy who suffer from the impacts of COVID-19.

§3.10 DEALING WITH THE DUAL CHALLENGE OF MALNUTRITION AND COVID-19

The cross-sectorial nature of nutrition is evident across many of the seventeen SDGs of the Agenda 2030 and consequently requires actions that do not focus only on nutrition and food security but rather on their drivers through what is referred to as double and triple duty actions. The impact of COVID-19 principally on the health and nutrition aspects emphasizes more the need for a holistic approach that seeks to use smart policy interventions to increase the return on investment.

For instance, the socio-economic causes of undernutrition and over nutrition may overlap and hence require coordinated policies and actions to deal with their deep causes in a way that simultaneously address more than one dimension of malnutrition.

Double-duty actions are a smart way of addressing all forms of malnutrition. While double-duty actions are effective, their application varies from one country to

84. Carlos Augusto Monteiro et al., *The UN Decade of Nutrition, the NOVA Food Classification and the Trouble with Ultra-Processing*, Public Health Nutrition, Volume 21, Issue 1, 5-17, doi:10.1017/S1368980017000234.

another and depend on the commitment of the governments and stakeholders and the available human and financial resources dedicated to dealing with malnutrition.

COVID-19 requires a paradigm shift and overhaul of government policies. Government can make use of the lessons learnt from the pandemic to design its health systems and socio-economic policies to prevent the development of malnutrition.

There is no exhaustive list of double-duty actions and new measures depend on the creativity of policymakers. Examples of double-duty actions could include the following ones.

The 1,000 days window, which is an example of double-duty actions that capitalize on biological factors and which are promoted by UN organizations such as UNICEF and WFP. Focused maternal health and the nutrition intakes in the first 1,000 days of life can contribute to the nutrition status of a child during his/her adult life.[85] This is evident in cases of mother's anaemia and/or overweight where this affects the child in terms of nutritional indicators including immune functions, cognitive development and the regulation of energy storage and expenditure.[86] Nutrition interventions during this window of opportunity can have a positive multiplier effect on a person's development and decrease in health care needs and costs during the life cycle.

Investing in water and sanitation infrastructure can improve a person's access and utilization of food. Achieving equitable access to clean water is emphasized under Goal 6 of the SDGs. Without access to safe drinking water, proper sanitation, food is easily contaminated through exposure to unsafe drinking water and pathogens on hands, flies, and unclean surfaces. Handwashing with soap, a basic hygiene practice, can reduce the risk of diarrhoeal disease by approximately 45%,[87] something we appreciate more after COVID-19.

Exclusive breastfeeding to at least 50% by 2025 is one of the targets of the WHA. There is a growing evidence that exclusive breastfeeding in the first six months of life can reduce both the risks of overweight and obesity in adults and protect against stunting and wasting in childhood.[88] On the other hand, it can protect the mother against obesity and some NCDs later in life.[89]

85. WHO, *Double-Duty Actions for Nutrition*; WHO Policy Brief https://www.who.int/publications/i/item/WHO-NMH-NHD-17.2.
86. Kimberley D Bruce & Mark A Hanson, *The Developmental Origins, Mechanisms, and Implications of Metabolic Syndrome,* The Journal of Nutrition, Volume 140, Issue 3 (2010) 648-652, doi:10.3945/jn.109.111179.
87. Val Curtis & Sandy Cairncross, *Effect of Washing Hands with Soap on Diarrhoea Risk in the Community: A Systematic Review,* Lancet Infectious Diseases, Volume 3, Issue 5 (2003) 275-281.
88. WHO, *Exclusive Breastfeeding* http://www.who.int/elena/titles/exclusive_breastfeeding/en/, accessed 2 February 2017.
89. *Exclusive Breastfeeding to Reduce the Risk of Childhood Overweight and Obesity. Biological, Behavioural and Contextual Rationale* (World Health Organization 2014) http://www.who.int/elena/titles/bbc/breastfeeding_childhood_obesity/en/, accessed 2 February 2017.

§3.11 CONCLUSIONS

Eradicating all forms of malnutrition by 2030 is a noble and pragmatic objective. Nutrition is one of the most important investment areas for decision-makers. Nevertheless, this is also a very challenging objective that is being affected by structural challenges as well as the spreading new COVID-19 pandemic.

A comprehensive approach is needed to deal with the causes of malnutrition. Food-based approaches should be complemented with technological approaches, educational inputs and the promotion of the awareness of nutrition-related health problems.

Political commitment is key, yet not enough or not supported by policies, science and resources. National ownership of nutrition policies is the single most important factor that will affect the outcomes of the Decade and the progress it will achieve in eradicating all forms of malnutrition by 2030.

Financing nutrition and the international community's support to developing countries and LDCs is crucial in this process.

The COVID-19 pandemic may have shifted the world efforts away from malnutrition. Nevertheless, this could be an important opportunity for recovery and building back better in a way that will make our food, health and social systems more resilient and more supportive to a world free from all forms of malnutrition where no one is left behind as called by the Agenda 2030 and the UN Decade of Action on Nutrition.

CHAPTER 4

The International Treaty on Plant Genetic Resources for Food and Agriculture and the 2050 Food Challenge

Domenico Pignone

The 2008 spike in food price shed light on possible scenarios of 2050 food security. The world human population is projected to 9.7 billion people by then. Men will have to face a changing climate, the effects of which might be even more devastating than the population increase. Besides temperature increase, climate scenarios imply threats like changes in position and distribution of arable lands, agricultural water availability, spreading of new pests and diseases, death of pollinators, etc.

Many actions are needed to cope with these scenarios, one being breeding new crops producing twice as much food as today and capable of facing new biotic and abiotic stresses. A possible paradigm to address this need is to make use of the vast reservoir of traits present in the world collections of crops' genetic diversity.

Starting with the pioneering works of Nazareno Strampelli in Italy and of Nicolai Vavilov in the former USSR, almost one century ago, and impelled by the quick transformations of agricultural systems following Norman Borlaug's green revolution, after World War II, many countries implemented conservation programmes aimed at safeguarding traditional crop varieties in order to maintain their genetic traits. This vast wealth of genetic resources, estimated in some 7.4 million different crop genotypes, is present in 1,750 different genebanks.

In order to regulate how this wealth of gene could be exploited and how to reward the nations that had conserved them through the efforts of farmers and the poorest, the Food and Agricultural Organization stated negotiations aimed at agreeing to a common framework of actions. The International Treaty on Plant Genetic Resources for Food and Agriculture entered into force on 29 June 2004. The treaty has now been subscribed by 195 parties, including the European Union.

§4.01 INTRODUCTION

By 2050, the food production system worldwide will face the challenge of feeding nine billion people with a quality nourishment produced in a sustainable way, and at the same time reducing soil consumption and shifting water use from agriculture to human needs. The challenge is made even harder in a context of changing climatic conditions, reduction of fossil energy and chemical sources, massive human migrations due to both environmental and political pushes,[1] and to increasing livelihood level of vaster amounts of population in countries with advanced economic level.

To answer these challenges, we need to consider a deep restructuration of our food system, independently of the kind of diet or food style we follow. In the future many different food styles will coexist to allow each one to follow his social, cultural, ethnic, religious, or own sentiment. Independent of lifestyle, one must consider that the very base of any food production is agriculture, which produces both food and feed in addition to raw materials and commodities for non-food applications.[2]

It is then evident that designing our future means designing agricultural plants that need less energy, less water and chemical inputs, less land and less labour to achieve the same production, or, better, to double it.

§4.02 HOW DID WE GET TO THIS POINT

At the end of the last glacial period, some 12,000 YBP, somewhere in the Middle East, men started agriculture by seeding seeds of the plant species they collected from the wild. This apparently simple act is at the basis of human population expansion. It triggered a rapid and profound change in the geology and ecosystem of our planet to the point that this geological epoch is known as the Anthropocene.[3]

The food secured by agriculture allowed rapid growth of the population practising it and allowed people to specialize in specific activities: this is the seed of social organization and the birth of the first states. Men interacted with the genetics of plants providing a selection force driven by human needs and beliefs, thus generating a parallel evolution leading to what we know as crops. Men attained this result by favouring some useful plant characters and getting rid of the unfavourable ones. This process is known as 'domestication', and this led in a few hundred years to an enormous diversification of the plants that men cultivated.[4]

Farmers for centuries have produced their own seeds and forced plants to adapt to environments even very different from the ones where those plants had naturally evolved. This process of empiric breeding has led to a huge wealth of plant diversity, whose peak was achieved around the early nineteenth century, when the growing

1. Tim Searchinger et al., *Creating a Sustainable Food Future: A Menu of Solutions to Feed Nearly 10 Billion People by 2050* (Final Report 2019).
2. Valeria De Laurentiis, Dexter V.L. Hunt & Christopher D.F. Rogers, *Overcoming Food Security Challenges Within an Energy/Water/Food Nexus (EWFN) Approach*, Sustainability 8 (2016) 95.
3. William F. Laurance, *The Anthropocene*, Current Biology 29 (2019) R953-R954.
4. Michael B. Kantar et al., *The Genetics and Genomics of Plant Domestication*, BioScience 67 (2017) 971-982.

industrialization and improvements in agricultural techniques, such as the introduction of guano based fertilization, set up the basis of intensive agriculture.

The twentieth century witnessed a real revolution in agriculture. The rediscovery of Mendel's Laws, the pioneering work of the disowned Italian scientist Nazareno Strampelli on the key role of hybridization in plant breeding,[5] the huge work of Nikolai Vavilov across the newly arose USSR and beyond, leading to the conceptualization of crop diversity and evolution,[6] the open availability of chemical fertilizers[7] were the grounds on which Norman Borlaug, Nobel Laureate for Peace, drew the paradigm of the 'Green Revolution' for agriculture.[8] By applying Borlaug's model, agricultural production made a huge leap forward, especially in developing countries. As an example, cereal production in the East increased over three times in the period 1960-2000. All over the world, agriculture changed into an increasingly intensive activity, largely dependent on external inputs and based on a relatively reduced number of plant varieties.

§4.03 THE 'GENETIC RESOURCES MOVEMENT'

If the green revolution on one side was providing better access to food for many, on the other side, small-scale cultivation scale was disappearing and many local landraces with it. A landrace is a crop variety resulting from empirical selection by the farmers and from adaptation to a specific environment. Until the green revolution, agriculture was mostly based on landraces. Due to their selection/adaptation process, landraces were the repository of the crop's genetic diversity. The rapid substitution of landraces with modern advanced cultivars in compliance with the green revolution paradigm was rapidly bringing the loss of huge amounts of genetic diversity.

The Food and Agricultural Organization's (FAO) Technical Meeting of 1961, taking into account the worries that several scientists were reporting on the loss of genetic diversity, recommended the establishment of exploration centres to be set up in the areas with larger genetic diversity in order to secure it.[9] Nevertheless the case of the Izmir Exploration Center, aimed at preserving the genetic diversity of Middle Eastern crops, proved that the idea was not a practical one.

The theme however returned in evidence with the 1967 FAO/IBP (International Biological Program) technical conference on Exploration, Utilization and Conservation of Plant Genetic Resources, held in Rome, where for the first time panel of experts convened to define a global strategy for conserving genetic resources before they went

5. Sergio Salvi, Oriana Porfiri & Salvatore Ceccarelli, *Nazareno Strampelli, the 'Prophet' of the Green Revolution*, The Journal of Agricultural Science 151 (2013) 1-5.
6. D.R. Harris, *Vavilov's Concept of Centres of Origin of Cultivated Plants: Its Genesis and Its Influence on the Study of Agricultural Origins*, Biological Journal of the Linnean Society 39 (1990) 7-16.
7. Darrell A. Russel & Gerald G. Williams, *History of Chemical Fertilizer Development 1*, Soil Science Society of America Journal 41 (1977) 260-265.
8. Robert E. Evenson & Douglas Gollin, *Assessing the Impact of the Green Revolution, 1960 to 2000*, Science 300 (2003) 758-762.
9. Gian Tommaso Scarascia Mugnozza & Pietro Perrino, *The History of Ex Situ Conservation and Use of Plant Genetic Resources*, Managing Plant Genetic Diversity (2002) 1-22.

completely lost.[10] As a result of that meeting, many conservation institutions were set up, *inter alia*, the Consultative Group for International Agricultural Research network, the Nordic Genebank, and the Italian Laboratorio del Germoplasma, established by Italian National Research Council following suggestions of Prof. Gian Tommaso Scarascia Mugnozza,[11] one of the scientists who represented Italy at the 1967 FAO/IBP Technical Conference and one worldwide leading scientists in wheat breeding.

One of the important outcomes of the FAO/IBP Technical Conference was the strong recommendation to promote germplasm collection and exchange in order to foster the efforts of creating new, more productive varieties. Nevertheless, the Technical Conference concentrated on the scientific aspects regarding the collection, conservation, exchange and utilization of plant genetic resources, without producing any legal framework for the utilization of this wealth of genes or any proposal for the international implications of germplasm exchange.

§4.04 TOWARDS A NEW CONSCIOUSNESS

Immediately after the FAO/IBP Technical Conference, some concerns emerged among the scientific community. Some centres were very efficient in collecting plant genetic resources but less efficient in classifying and exchanging. As a consequence, some scientists felt the collection centres as obstacles to the free availability of genetic material for their experiment; other scientists pointed out the sanitary risks of an unregulated exchange system; some governments, especially in less rich countries, had little or no control on the genetic resources collected and exchanged in their territory, etc. The need for a regulatory framework soon emerged.

During the United Nations (UN) Conference on the Human Environment, held in Stockholm in 1972, some basic principles were set up. Among them, the principle of safeguarding natural resources 'for the benefit of present and future generations through careful planning or management' was asserted.[12] Although strongly environment-oriented, the conference pointed out the need for common position and principles for protecting the environment, especially for those issues being of transnational interest. Some institutions, such as the International Board for Plant Genetic Resources (IBPGR), starting the early 1970s, produced guidelines for a sound collection conservation and exchange of plant genetic resources. Nevertheless these guidelines had no political implications since IBPGR was a technical organ. The FAO had a Commission on Plant Genetic Resources, which could start the political process towards a commonly agreed legal framework, but many different reasons, including budgetary ones, delayed its action.[13] During the 20th Session of the FAO Conference in 1979, several developing countries started setting the issues of the ownership of plant

10. UN General Assembly, United Nations Conference on the Human Environment, 15 December 1972, A/RES/2994.
11. *See supra* note 9.
12. *See supra* note 10.
13. Robin Pistorius, *Scientists, Plants and Politics: A History of the Plant Genetic Resources Movement* (Bioversity International 1997).

genetic resources, on the guarantees of their free exchange, and on the benefits for the countries where the genetic resources had been produced and conserved by farmers.[14]

A first positive step towards a legal frame for the exploitation of plant genetic resources was the voluntary agreement of the International Undertaking on Plant Genetic Resources adopted at FAO in 1983.[15] The undertaking recognizes that 'plant genetic resources are a heritage of mankind to be preserved, and to be freely available for use', and that 'plant genetic resources are indispensable for the genetic improvement of cultivated plants'. Article 5 of this undertaking states 'It will be the policy of adhering Governments and institutions having plant genetic resources under their control to allow access to samples of such resources, and to permit their export, where the resources have been requested for the purposes of scientific research, plant breeding or genetic resource conservation.'

§4.05 THE CONVENTION OF BIOLOGICAL DIVERSITY

During the 1980s the seed of the 1972 UN Stockholm Conference grew in the consciousness of common citizens, due to the evident effects of pollution on the environment. At the same time, the arguments of environmental movements started grounding in the civil conscience. A particular push towards the dramatic effects of human activities on biodiversity was given by some specific campaigns aimed at saving some specific animal under particular threat of disappearance. Eventually, the alarm that the scientific community had raised on the loss of biodiversity became of public domain. Such words like 'biodiversity' became very frequent in the media, but still the real meaning of biodiversity was misunderstood. Even in the scientific community, the term 'biodiversity' was given slightly different meanings according to the discipline of reference.

In 1992, also favoured by the end of the 'cold war', the UN Conference on Environment and Development was organized in Rio de Janeiro. The aim of the conference, also known as the Rio Conference, was to shed common cooperative grounds to afford the environmental challenge of a sustainable development, a too demanding task for single states. Although the arguments discussed within the conference were so different and wide, ranging from socio-economics, to energy and water demand, to environmental protection, the Rio Conference produced key practical results.

One of these results was the Convention on Biological Diversity (CBD). The convention was intended to sustain the conservation and sustainable use of biological diversity and an equitable sharing of benefits deriving from its use. The CBD, signed by 193 countries in 1992 and enacted in 1993, was the first international treaty with legal status to define the biological diversity and regulate its exploitation. The CBD defined the biological diversity as 'the variability among living organisms from all sources, including, "inter alia", terrestrial, marine and other aquatic ecosystems and the

14. José T. Esquinas-Alcázar, *The Role of National, Regional and International Institutions in Germplasm Conservation* (FAO, Unpublished 1989).
15. F.A.O Resolution 8/83. Undertaking on Plant Genetic Resources (Adopted 23 November 1983).

ecological complexes of which they are part: this includes diversity within species, between species and of ecosystems'.[16] Moreover, the CBD recognized that plant genetic resources of agricultural interest, although part of the world's biodiversity, had a special nature.[17]

Nevertheless, the problem of a correct framing of agricultural biodiversity is still an open question. In fact, the CBD does not enlist any plant species. An example is the question of wild crop relatives, that is wild species genetically related to the cultivated ones, and their possible role as gene donors for crop improvement.[18,19] The techniques of plant improvement available at that time did not provide sufficient grounds to allow the reach of a statement on this issue. Most of the crop's genetic improvement was based on the availability of genetic traits of interest in the crop's germplasm or in closely related species from which the genes of interest could be transferred.[20,21] For this reason a regulatory framework for the exploitation of this vast wealth of genes was urgent, to avoid conflicts among countries and to avoid new forms of misdeed towards the less-developed countries or those areas with a lower level of scientific capacity.

§4.06 THE INTERNATIONAL TREATY ON PLANT GENETIC RESOURCES FOR FOOD AND AGRICULTURE

In order to overcome the limitations to the use of crop genetic resources present in the CBD, a long-lasting negotiation process regarding technical, financial, political, institutional and economic issues was started by the FAO Secretariat of the Commission on Genetic Resources, thanks to the tireless efforts of its Secretary Prof. José (Pepe) Esquinas-Alcázar. This long negotiation aimed at producing a comprehensive international agreement, in consonance with the CBD, consenting to guarantee the conservation, exchange and sustainable use of the plant genetic resources for food and agriculture (PGR-FA). In fact, the Secretariat was actually acting as an intergovernmental forum for debating the unresolved issues of the International Undertaking on Plant Genetic Resources and of the CBD regarding crops and the distinctive cropping systems present in different countries.

During the negotiations some concepts were developed and fixed. One very important principle of national sovereignty over local plant genetic resources was established. That is, each and every nation is responsible for safeguarding the crops' genetic resources that are cultivated in its territory, with a special attention to

16. Secretariat, CBD, *Convention on biological diversity*. In Convention on biological diversity. (November 1992) https://www.cbd.int/convention/text/.
17. Ranee K. Panjabi, *The Earth Summit at Rio: Politics, Economics and the Environment* (Northeastern 1997).
18. William B. Lacy, *The Global Plant Genetic Resources System: A Competition-Cooperation Paradox*, Crop Science 35 (1995) 335-345.
19. Nigel Maxted et al., *Towards the Selection of Taxa for Plant Genetic Conservation*, Genetic Resources and Crop Evolution 44 (1997) 337-348.
20. Anthony H.D. Brown et al. (eds), *The Use of Plant Genetic Resources* (Cambridge University Press 1989).
21. David Hoisington et al., *Plant Genetic Resources: What Can They Contribute Toward Increased Crop Productivity?*, Proceedings of the National Academy of Sciences 96 (1999) 5937-5943.

autochthonous genetic resources, e.g., those resulting from the interaction of human culture and preferences and adaptation to specific agro-environments. This is a very important concept, since it establishes that autochthonous crop varieties enclose not only genes but also a mixture of aesthetic preferences, empirical knowledge, cultural heredity, religious convictions, etc. This train of thought allowed the recognition that autochthonous crops' genetic resources have an intangible value that goes aside the economic value of the genetic traits they contain.

A logical consequence of this appreciation is that the communities that have developed, selected, and maintained the autochthonous crop varieties should benefit, somehow, from their exploitation. The concept of farmers' rights, then, emerged side by side with that of breeders' rights. An agreement should therefore contain the guarantee of free access to other countries' genetic resources but should repay the country if a profit would arise from the use of those resources, even though there was no unanimous opinion on the forms of this compensation.

Besides these advancements, still many points were far from an agreement, such as (a) an exact definition of PGR-FA, (b) the application of intellectual property rights to the genetic resources, (c) an exact definition of genetic material, and (d) a list of species to be included in the agreement.

By the end of 2001, an agreement was reached and the International Treaty on Plant Genetic Resources for Food and Agriculture (IT-PGRFA) was adopted on 3 November 2001, during the 31st Session of the FAO Conference held in Rome.[22,23] The Treaty went into effect on 29 June 2004, after being ratified by forty member countries.

The Treaty IT-PGRFA recognizes the universal importance of plant genetic resources for the benefit of humankind and for its food security. It sets rules for the proficient and sustainable preservation and management of countries' genetic resources and for their beneficial exchange. It recognizes farmers' rights and leaves to the countries the regulation regarding specific aspects, such as the protection of traditional knowledge relevant to the PGR-FA, the way of sharing the benefit arising from the utilization of the PGR-FA, the right of citizens to participate in the decision process regarding conservation and sustainable use of PGR-FA. This latter indication actually opened the doors to the formal participation of farmers' organizations and non-governmental organizations (NGOs) into the decisional process regarding the PGR-FA. In some countries, such as Italy or France, this participation is very active and even reflects in the European Union decision-making organs.

The treaty also establishes the Multilateral System of Access and Benefit-Sharing to trace germplasm exchange and fixes the grounds of benefit sharing. The instruments of the Multilateral System are a shared database of the national genetic resources available for exchange and the Standard Material Transfer Agreement (SMTA). This latter is a true contract between the provider of the PGR-FA and the receiver, that is, the entity requesting the resource. The SMTA is, as the name indicates, a standard

22. F.A.O. Resolution 3/2001. Adoption of the International Treaty on Plant Genetic Resources for Food and Agriculture and Interim Arrangements for Its Implementation (2001).
23. F.A.O. International Treaty on Plant Genetic Resources for Food and Agriculture (2009). Official English text available at http://www.fao.org/3/a-i0510e.pdf.

mandatory model that has to be signed by the parties before any exchange could ever take place. The exchange may regard material for research purposes or even for the development of economic activities. In this latter case, the Secretariat of the Treaty can provide a tool for the payment of the rights arising from the benefit-sharing principle and based on the effective economic value of the derived good.[24] Finally the Treaty establishes a list of food crops and forages that was assembled on the basis of food security and country interdependence criteria. These species are enlisted in Annex 1 to the Treaty.

The IT-PGRFA is a good compromise point between different demands arising from the scientific, political, societal and economic sectors. Nevertheless it has to be considered a starting point rather than an endpoint. Changing socio-economic and political positions or new achievements in science are the forces that operate in the sense of revising the treaty. Particularly active is still the debate among scientists.[25,26] Also farmers' organizations and NGOs debate some aspects of the treaty, such as the free exchange and use of autochthones seeds among farmers and communities. Also the list of species in Annex 1 is strongly criticized.

A further source of potential conflict may arise from the adoption of the Nagoya Protocol. The Nagoya Protocol on Access to Genetic Resources and the Fair and Equitable Sharing of Benefits Arising from Their Utilization to the Convention on Biological Diversity, known as the Nagoya Protocol on Access and Benefit Sharing, is a supplementary agreement to the CBD. It was adopted on 29 October 2010 in Nagoya, Japan, and entered into force in October 2014.[27,28] Although subscribed by many countries, this protocol may unfold its effects only after an effective implementation at the domestic level. For this reason the Nagoya Protocol is not yet fully active.

Although the IT-PGRFA is specifically recognized by Article 4 of the Nagoya Protocol, and notwithstanding both agreements regarding the conservation and sustainable use of PGRs and sharing of benefit arising from their use, some differences are evident. The Treaty IT-PGRFA refers to a specific list of species considered of particular importance for food security, Nagoya regards any biological resource. The free utilization of many useful plants might contrast with Nagoya's requirements: cultivated plants not considered in the IT-PGRFA list, plants used as food or condiment and collected from the wild, wild species related to crops (the so-called crop wild relatives). Moreover, even though both consider a system of benefit sharing, its implementation

24. Michael Halewood, Isabel López Noriega & Selim Louafi (eds), *Crop Genetic Resources as a Global Commons: Challenges in International Law and Governance* (Routledge 2012).
25. Michael Halewood, *What Kind of Goods Are Plant Genetic Resources for Food and Agriculture? Towards the Identification and Development of a New Global Commons*, International Journal of the Commons 7 (2013) 278-312.
26. Carolina Roa Rodriguez & Thom Van Dooren, *Shifting Common Spaces of Plant Genetic Resources in the International Regulation of Property*, The Journal of World Intellectual Property 11 (2008) 176-202.
27. CBD International, *About the Nagoya Protocol* (2005) (online) available at http://www.cbd.int/abs/about/.
28. Matthias Buck & Clare Hamilton, *The Nagoya Protocol on Access to Genetic Resources and the Fair and Equitable Sharing of Benefits Arising from Their Utilization to the Convention on Biological Diversity*, Review of European Community & International Environmental Law 20 (2011) 47-61.

is quite different: Nagoya acts directly to the providers, while IT-PGRFA does it through a specific fund.

§4.07 A SIGHT TO THE FUTURE

In the future, the international treaties on the protection, use, and exchange will continue their evolution. New citizens' sensibility, modifications of the socio-economic conditions, political changes, economic interest, NGOs activism, etc., will continue putting pressure on the arguments, as already outlined, and will produce changes in the present agreements or the subscription of new ones. In any case, international agreements such as the IT-PGRFA or Nagoya refer to what already exists in nature. They, in fact, deal with plants possessing genes of interest, and the exploitation of those genes for producing new varieties is thought to happen through traditional breeding techniques. Still there are some grey areas where these protocols have a limited potential of action. One example is the artificial mutagenesis obtained through chemical or physical agents. The Joint FAO/International Atomic Energy Agency mutant variety database enlists some 750 plant varieties obtained by mutation techniques, but independent evaluations estimate that more than 2,200 varieties have been obtained by this process.

Another example of the grey zone are the genetically modified organisms (GMOs). Even though they are not officially considered in the earlier protocols (the specific Cartagena Protocol only deals with their international exchange) GMOs are the evidence that genes from one species may be introduced and function in another species yielding specific characters of agronomic interest. Also, in this case, international regulations, different from country to country, control their use and the sole Cartagena Protocol is aimed at monitoring their international trade.

Recent advances in biotechnology have demonstrated that it is possible to modify in a direct way specific genes in order to make them code for a specific desired trait without modifying the entire genome and often leaving no trace of this genetic surgery. These techniques, known as 'genome editing' techniques, are still at an initial stage of development and their position among the GMOs is plentily debated for ethical and policy implications.[29,30,31]

Nevertheless, these techniques open an interesting potential space of action for plant genetic resources. In fact, most plants genera, even distant ones, share a large number of genes very similar from one species to the other. The small differences present in each species determine the different mode of action of each gene. Nowadays the ease of access to high throughput sequencing facilities is producing a description of

29. Richard Heliwell, Sarah Hartley & Wayne Pearce, *NGO Perspectives on the Social and Ethical Dimensions of Plant Genome-Editing* (Agriculture and Human Values 2019) 1-13.
30. Silvia Friedrichs et al., *Policy Considerations Regarding Genome Editing*, Trends in Biotechnology 37(10) (2019) 1029-1032.
31. Stephan Schleissing, Sebastian Pfeilmeier & Christian Dürnberger (eds), *Genome Editing in Agriculture: Between Precaution and Responsibility – An Introduction*. In *Genome Editing in Agriculture: Between Precaution and Responsibility* (Nomos Nomos Verlagsgesellschaft mbH & Co. KG – Waldseestrasse 3-5 Baden-Baden – Deutschland 2019) 7, 9.

the genetic resources at the whole genome level. It is, at least theoretically, possible to modify a specific gene in one species so that it acts the same way as in another species. This can be done without physical gene transfer between different species. Such a procedure might overcome the precautions imposed on the GMOs and give a new definition and significance to plant genetic resources.[32,33] We should start considering a debate on the need to shift from the paradigm of preserving varieties or landraces to preserving the individual genes they contain.

In a scenario in which the genome editing techniques become mature for a large number of species, and the international regulations will consider edited organisms not as GMOs but as the result of novel breeding techniques, plant genetic resources still maintain a central role and new protocols need to be agreed if the equitable sharing of benefits between receivers and donors remains a priority. This issue is particularly important in as much the major crops, mostly cultivated in the economically advanced countries, have been largely characterized with genomic tools, while the minor and neglected crops still present in the underdeveloped countries are still largely unknown and might reveal to possess genes useful not only for food security but also for the so-called green chemistry, that is, for slowly replacing fossil sources with newly engineered renewable ones. We must look ahead or we will be unprepared leaving grounds for bio-piracy and exploitation of the less well-off.

32. Teodoro Cardi, *Cisgenesis and Genome Editing: Combining Concepts and Efforts for a Smarter Use of Genetic Resources in Crop Breeding*, Plant Breeding 135 (2016) 139-147.
33. Carolina Roa, Ruaraidh Sackville Hamilton, Peter Wenzl & Wayne Powell, *Plant Genetic Resources: Needs, Rights, and Opportunities*, Trends in Plant Science 21 (2016) 633-636.

CHAPTER 5

Codex Alimentarius: Safe, Good Food for Everyone

Tom Heilandt[*]

The Codex Alimentarius Commission, founded jointly by the Food and Agricultural Organization of the United Nations (FAO) and the World Health Organization (WHO) in 1963, is the United Nations body setting international food standards. With 188 Member States and one member organization (European Union), it covers most of the planet and is also open to participation of over 230 observers from all walks of life. Becoming a reference in the World Trade Organization's Agreement on Sanitary and Phytosanitary Measures (WTO-SPS) in 1995 was an important event leading it to systematically integrate science as the basis for all its food safety standards. The Commissions' focus and needs are evolving, as is the environment in which it operates. Population growth and climate change are important issues that have a direct effect on our food supply and vice versa – how we grow, process and consume our food has implications on the environment. Animal and plant health plays an essential role in human health captured in the concept of 'one health'. Codex will need to be proactive and flexible and to respond in a timely manner to the opportunities and challenges that result (contribution to Sustainable Development Goals, new food production and sales methods, new diseases etc.) in accomplishing its mission of protecting consumer health and facilitating fair practice in the food trade.

* I would like to thank my colleague Giuseppe di Chiera for his assistance in the preparation of the chapter

§5.01 FOOD IS A COMMODITY LIKE NO OTHER

[A] We All Need Food

We need food that is safe, sufficient and nutritious – to live full and healthy lives. Beyond keeping us alive, food is an important element of our culture and society. In our increasingly urbanized and globalized world, ever fewer of us produce or even prepare our own food. The food on our plate may have arrived from the other side of the world. Over the last century, the amount of food traded internationally has grown exponentially, and a larger quantity and variety of food than ever before travels the globe today. This has contributed to overall food security but is also not without issues.

In order to feed a growing population, set to reach 9.6 billion by 2050, countries will have to learn to grow what the population needs in a sustainable way and prevent that. Hunger and poverty lead to overexploitation of the fragile resources on which livelihoods depend.

The natural resources base and ecosystems must be managed sustainably to meet people's food requirements and other environmental, social and economic needs. Increased water scarcity and conflicts over access to resources all pose challenges to environmental sustainability and food security. Climate change affecting our planet can make it harder to grow food in some areas and cause safety concerns in others.

[B] Food Is Fragile

Food is a fragile commodity: it can be affected by contamination of microbes, heavy metals or toxins through production methods, soils or poor hygiene.

Though food safety and quality have significantly improved in many parts of the world, the global burden of food-borne diseases remains unacceptably high and more work needs to be done. The World Health Organization (WHO) estimates that yearly 600 million people fall ill because of contaminated food and 420,000 die and 30% of these are children under 5 years of age.[1]

Food can be tampered intentionally via food fraud – either for economic reasons or with the intention to cause harm. Nothing can destabilize a society more than insecurity about food, its safety and availability, and consumers have never been as concerned about food-related risks as today.

Too much food can be as dangerous as not having enough, and a badly composed diet lacking vitamins and minerals can cause health problems. Information on which nutrients are good for us and which are not is at times conflicting, and it changes over time. We need to know what is in a food to compose a healthy diet, but we also need to be aware of what that meant and that a healthy diet is the basis for our health and well-being.

Only the close cooperation of all actors in the food supply chain whether public, private and consumer will achieve our common goal of safe, good food in every home.

1. WHO, *WHO estimates of the global burden of foodborne diseases*, 2015.

§5.02 HISTORY OF STANDARDS AND CODES[2]

[A] From Prehistory to the Greek

Ensuring that food is safe to eat and that consumers are not deceived by dishonest practices have been among the important tasks entrusted to governments since antiquity.

Evidence from the earliest historical writings indicates that governing authorities have always been concerned with codifying rules to protect consumers from dishonest practices in the sale of food. Assyrian tablets described how to determine the correct weights and measures for food grains. Ancient Egyptian scrolls prescribed the labelling to be applied to certain foods. In ancient Athens, beer and wines were inspected for purity and soundness. The Romans had a well-organized state food control system to protect consumers against fraud and bad produce. Food additives - substances that are added to food to maintain or improve the safety, freshness, taste, texture, or appearance of food - have been in use for centuries for preservation, such as salt in dried fish or sugar in marmalade. Similarly, the resins added to Greek wine acted as mild preservatives, and in classical times, the pitch linings of amphorae contributed substances that helped to preserve the wine carried in them.

[B] Codex Austriacus

In Europe during the Middle Ages, individual countries passed laws concerning the quality and safety of eggs, sausages, cheese, beer, wine and bread - and some of these ancient statutes still exist today. In the Austro-Hungarian Empire between 1897 and 1911, a collection of standards and product descriptions for a wide variety of foods was developed as the Codex Alimentarius Austriacus. Although lacking legal force, it was used as a reference by the courts to determine standards of identity for specific foods.

Towards the beginning of the last century, food safety was still at the beginning. In those days the use of unsafe food additives - especially preservatives - was a common practice in many parts of the world. Cold chains were by far not as developed as today and many homes did not have a refrigerator. The sciences such as chemistry began to offer new possibilities to be applied to food especially to keep it from spoiling. Industry quickly embraced such possibilities but as the concept of risk analysis had not yet been developed dealing with one problem (e.g., spoilage) quickly led to other problems (e.g. chemical contamination and food fraud).

[C] Joint Expert Committee on Contaminants and Food Additives

As it became apparent that the chemicals used did not only have beneficial effects, it also became clear that research and regulation were needed.

2. FAO/WHO, *Understanding Codex*, 2018.

Many countries independently developed food laws and regulations, and often found different solutions to ensure that food was safe, up to the quality expected, and that consumers received sufficient and accurate information about the products they were purchasing. However, the differences between national requirements and specifications often made it difficult to trade food across borders.

In 1956 the two major United Nations organizations, Food and Agricultural Organization (FAO) and WHO, created the Joint Expert Committee on Contaminants and Food Additives (JECFA) to scientifically examine the safety of food additives and the impact of contaminants in food.

[D] The Codex Alimentarius Commission

[1] The Mandate

Between 1961 and 1963, FAO and WHO, continuing on the understanding that food safety and quality were a joint concern, created the Codex Alimentarius Commission as part of the Joint FAO/WHO Food Standards Programme to:

(a) protect the health of the consumers and ensuring fair practices in the food trade;
(b) promote coordination of all food standards work undertaken by international governmental and non-governmental organizations;
(c) determine priorities and initiate and guide the preparation of draft standards through and with the aid of appropriate organizations;
(d) finalize standards elaborated under (c) above and publish them in a Codex Alimentarius either as regional or worldwide standards, together with international standards already finalized by other bodies under (b) above, wherever this is practicable;
(e) amend published standards, as appropriate, in the light of developments.

Since its foundation, the Codex system has evolved in an open, transparent and inclusive way to meet emerging challenges.

[2] The Status of Codex Standards

The Codex Alimentarius international food standards, guidelines and codes of practice (in the following short Codex standards) contribute to the safety, quality and fairness of this international food trade. Consumers can trust the safety and quality of the food products they buy, and importers can trust that the food they ordered will be in accordance with their specifications.

Codex standards are recommended to governments and trade for application. They are not a substitute for or alternative to national legislation. Every country's laws and administrative procedures contain provisions with which it is essential to comply.

The reference made to science-based Codex food safety standards in the World Trade Organization's Agreement on Sanitary and Phytosanitary measures (SPS Agreement, 1995) means that Codex has far-reaching implications for resolving trade disputes. World Trade Organization (WTO) members that wish to apply stricter food safety measures than those set by Codex may be required to justify these measures scientifically.

At the heart of the Codex mandate are the core values of collaboration, inclusiveness, consensus building and transparency. Governmental and non-governmental, public and private organizations alike play a vital role in ensuring that Codex texts are of the highest quality and based on sound science. Codex today has 188 member countries and one member organization and over 230 observers.

§5.03 STRUCTURE AND WORK METHODS

[A] An Open Forum: Achievement Through Cooperation

Codex develops standards in a cooperative way. This has made it the forum where the governments of the world meet together with other stakeholders to resolve food safety and quality issues consensually. The Codex agenda is completely driven by its members while the Commission takes into account, where appropriate, the relevant policies, strategies and guidelines of FAO and WHO and cooperates in line with its mandate with other intergovernmental organizations.

With increased globalization and increases in the volume of food traded internationally, the Commission must be capable of responding in a timely manner to the impacts of emerging trends and challenges on consumer health protection or fair practices in food trade, and to the extent that steps to address those impacts are amenable to standardization.

[B] Committee Structure

Codex prides itself to be open, transparent and inclusive. All information about Codex work is publicly available for free on the Codex website, and the work is member driven and strives even in the most difficult cases to take decisions by consensus.

The Commission itself is the ultimate decision body meeting annually in Rome or Geneva and usually attended by more than six-hundred delegates from over one-hundred countries. It is supported by an executive committee consisting of elected members and regional coordinators and by an international secretariat. The technical work is done in horizontal and vertical committees or task forces, each of which is hosted and chaired by a member country that is also responsible for the costs of interpretation and translation. In addition, the FAO/WHO coordinating committees for each of the six Codex regions make sure that specific regional aspects are addressed by Codex. In some cases, these committees develop standards for regional products.

The Commission adopts its food safety standards using the principles of risk analysis and bases its work on the scientific advice provided by the joint FAO/WHO expert bodies and consultations. Codex standards may also address issues related to food quality and labelling.

The structure differentiates between horizontal committees (dealing with all foods) and vertical committees (dealing with a specific food group). Task forces are formed to deal with specific problems and are dissolved once they have achieved their work. Presently one task force is active dealing with the challenges of food-borne antimicrobial resistance.

[C] Work Process and Scientific Basis

The Codex standard-setting process also called 'step-procedure' has eight steps consisting of:

- An initial reflection on which new work is needed (discussion paper).
- Agreement of new work (Step 1).
- Drafting (Step 2).
- Circulation of the draft for comments to all members and observers (Step 3).
- Discussion in the technical committee or task force (Step 4).
- Circulation for comments in view of adoption at step 5 (Step 4).
- Intermediary adoption by the Commission (Step 5).
- Circulation for comments to all members and observers (Step 6).
- Discussion in the technical committee or task force (Step 7).
- Circulation for comments in view of adoption at step 8 (Step 7).
- Adoption as a Codex standard (Step 8).

The Commission reviews a project document presented by a member and decides whether the standard should be developed as proposed. If new work is approved, the Codex Secretariat arranges for the preparation of a proposed draft standard and circulates it to member governments and observer organizations for two rounds of comments. The text also goes to Codex Committees dealing with issues such as labelling, hygiene, additives, contaminants or methods of analysis for endorsement of any special advice in these areas. Once adopted by the Commission, a Codex standard becomes a part of the Codex Alimentarius and published on the website.

The process is also designed to allow sufficient input from all stakeholders to achieve a consensus. It is overall a succession of commenting and discussion steps with ongoing drafting and re-drafting normally in electronic working groups. Projects can be downgraded again from higher steps to lower steps and steps 6 and 7 may be omitted in case of a stable consensus. The overall process can be finished within one year or take longer depending on the complexity of the issue. The process also allows for input received from the FAO/WHO scientific advice provided by standing committees (JECFA – food additives, contaminants and veterinary drugs; JMPR – pesticides; JEMRA – microbiological risks and JEMNU – nutrition).

The FAO and WHO expert bodies for risk assessment establish the scientific basis for Codex standards. These expert bodies are independent of the Commission and its subsidiary bodies, such that their work contributes significantly to the scientific credibility of the Commission's own work. Codex strictly adheres to its established principles of risk analysis that ensures the functional separation/independence of science-based risk assessment from the practical (and political) realities of risk management.

[D] Based on Science: Adopted by Consensus[3]

The debate regarding working by consensus within Codex has a long history but intensified in the late 1990s following a number of decisions taken by vote in the Commission that passed by only a narrow majority – most notably the 1995 and 1997 decisions to adjourn debate on Maximum Residue Limits for bovine somatotropins, and the 1997 decision to adopt the revision of the Codex Standard for Natural Mineral Waters (CXS 108-1981). At that time, the Guidelines for Codex Committees, in the Procedural Manual, already stated that 'the chairperson should always try to arrive at a consensus and should not ask the Committee to proceed to voting if agreement on the Committee's decision can be secured by consensus'.

However, the Commission deemed it necessary to strengthen the importance of consensus further and amended the Rules of Procedure (Rule XII Elaboration and Adoption of Standards) to stress that voting should take place only after all efforts to reach the agreement by consensus on the adoption or amendment of standards have been exhausted.

In 2000, the Commission adopted, in addition, the Guidelines to Chairpersons of Codex Committees and ad hoc Intergovernmental Task Forces and Measures to facilitate consensus (contained in the Procedural Manual), which highlight the need to ensure that Codex texts are scientifically sound, have been thoroughly discussed by the committees and are not forwarded to the Commission for adoption until consensus has been achieved at the technical level. These texts also provide for: the organization of informal meetings of concerned parties; the redefinition of the scope of the texts under consideration to resolve issues on which consensus cannot be reached; the formulation of compromises with a view to advancing texts in the Step-procedure (*see* above); and the involvement and participation of developing countries.

The concept of consensus was also considered by the 2002 Evaluation of Codex.[4] Its findings stressed that active consensus building was vital to the legitimacy of Codex and recommended that Codex develops guidelines for committees on the meaning of consensus and on decision-making in the absence of consensus. The evaluation also highlighted the advantages of consensus building and of intersessional facilitation to take into account the reduced capacity of delegates to consult with their governments during committee sessions.

---

3. D.L. Arietta & L. Wallace, *Consensus building fieldbook.* Minneapolis: University of Minnesota Extension and Hubert H. Humphrey Institute of Public Affair, 2000; L. Dressler, *Consensus through conversation.* San Francisco, CA: Berrett-Koehler Publishers, Inc, 2006.
4. FAO/WHO, *Report of the evaluation of the Codex Alimentarius and other FAO and WHO food standards work*, 2002.

Further discussions on consensus were held in 2009 in the Committee on General Principles following proposals to create a Codex definition of consensus. At the time, it was decided that a definition might be restricting the freedom of Chairpersons to manage the debate and that it was more important to work with Codex Chairpersons to give them the tools to actively contribute to consensus building. The possibility to use facilitators was also introduced to assist Chairpersons in their work.

[E] Achievements: A World Full of Standards

Besides serving as the most important forum for food safety and quality worldwide and creating invaluable links between different food safety authorities by working together, the most important product of the Codex Alimentarius Commission is the Codex standards.

In the 1960s, Codex took the approach of setting many standards for individual foods. This turned out to be impractical, both for keeping standards up-to-date and for their implementation, and gave way to the practice of creating group standards – for example, one general standard for fruit juices and nectars has now replaced the many previous standards for individual fruit juices. This has also been done for other commodities and is being applied when creating new standards such as for spices. The benefits of this approach include the broader coverage it attains and that it allows for innovation in the development of new food products.

[1] An Impressive Score Card

Since 1963 Codex has set hundreds of commodity standards for all major food commodities as well as dozens of guidelines dealing with general issues such as food import and export inspection and certification systems and labelling and Codes of Practice dealing, for example, with guidance on preventing contamination (chemical, physical or microbiological) of food products. In addition, the Commission has created a comprehensive system of thousands of maximum limits for food additives, pesticide and veterinary drug residue limits and maximum limits for a number of important contaminants.

[2] Expectations Require Continued Work

Consumers expect that their government takes legislative and regulatory action to ensure that only safe food of acceptable quality is sold and that the risk of food-borne health hazards is minimized.

The Codex Alimentarius Commission has contributed significantly to securing the place of food on political agendas worldwide. Indeed, governments and food business operators are highly conscious of the political consequences in store should they fail to heed consumers' concerns when it comes to the food they eat.

The right to food for everyone is universally accepted, but it is very important that people have the right to expect their food to be safe, of good quality and suitable for consumption. This makes continued Codex work a necessity. Food-borne illnesses are at best unpleasant; at worst, they can be fatal. Outbreaks of food-borne illness can damage trade and tourism and can lead to loss of earnings, unemployment and litigation. Poor-quality food can destroy the commercial credibility of suppliers, both nationally and internationally. Food spoilage is wasteful and costly and can adversely affect trade and consumer confidence. Food rejections in trade lead to further food waste, which is difficult to tolerate in a world where many still suffer from hunger. This is not a small problem: overall one-third of all food produced for humans is lost or wasted per year having an amount: food lost and wasted could feed the hungry of the world four times over and has an environmental impact which would put it on place three of CO_2 emissions if it was a country.

[3] From Farm to Fork: HACCP – A Codex Signature Achievement[5]

Food production and trade is a complex, growing business. Food business operators have an interest in ensuring that food products are safe, from farm to fork.

One important tool helping them is the Hazard Analysis and Critical Control Point (HACCP) system which identifies specific hazards and measures for their control to ensure the safety of food. HACCP is a tool developed by Codex in 1969 to assess hazards and establish control systems that focus on prevention rather than relying mainly on end-product testing. Any HACCP system is capable of accommodating change, such as advances in equipment design, processing procedures or technological developments.

HACCP can be applied throughout the food chain from primary production to final consumption and its implementation should be guided by scientific evidence of risks to human health. Enhancing food safety and implementation of HACCP can also provide other significant benefits. In addition, the application of HACCP systems can aid inspection by regulatory authorities and promote international trade by increasing confidence in food safety.

The successful application of HACCP requires the full commitment and involvement of management and the workforce. It also requires a multidisciplinary approach; this multidisciplinary approach should include, when appropriate, expertise in agronomy, veterinary health, production, microbiology, medicine, public health, food technology, environmental health, chemistry and engineering, according to the particular study.

HACCP is probably the single tool in food safety that has saved more lives through prevention than any other. It is THE safety belt for food and the Codex Alimentarius Commission is currently finalizing an important revision of its signature tool through the Committee on Food Hygiene.

5. Codex Alimentarius, *Food Hygiene at 50*, 2019.

§5.04 SDGs AND CODEX STRATEGIC PLAN 2020-2025[6]

[A] Codex and SDCs

The Codex Alimentarius Commission was created with the objective of developing and publishing food standards in a 'food code' that would protect public health and ensure fair practices in the food trade. As the United Nations charts the course towards the 'world we want' through the 2030 Agenda for Sustainable Development and its seventeen Sustainable Development Goals (SDGs), food safety and quality, a level playing field for trade, healthy and nutritious diets and consumer information all have significant potential to improve the world we live in.

Codex work has a clear connection to the six following goals for safer, better food for everyone, everywhere.

SDG1: 'No Poverty'

If a country adopts global food safety standards such as Codex standards into national legislation, then local traders can access new markets and increase their trade. They do business and create employment. Reaching this goal would mean an end to poverty in the agriculture sector.

SDG2: 'Zero Hunger'

The first target of this goal is (by 2030) to 'end hunger and ensure access by all people, in particular the poor and people in vulnerable situations, including infants, to safe, nutritious and sufficient food all year round'. There is a strong link between Codex work on food safety and the positive outcome of food security as there can be no food security without food safety. Unsafe food cannot be considered food and is especially dangerous to those already weakened by malnutrition. Codex strives to ensure food safety, thus contributing to food security.

This goal also states the need to 'correct and prevent trade restrictions', which aligns with Codex standards whose function is to harmonize international rules so that food can cross borders safely and without unfair restrictions. This goal also deals with trade and states the need to correct and prevent trade restrictions – another central aspect of the Codex mandate.

Codex is advocating this goal in a positive way by contributing to making it possible to bring safe and nutritious food to every home.

6. Codex Alimentarius, Codex Strategic Plan 2020 – 2025, 2019; FAO, *Statistical Capacity Assessment for the FAO-relevant SDG Indicators 2018/19*, 2019; FAO, *Measuring the SDGs – Improving country data for monitoring SDG achievements and informing policy decisions*, 2019; WHO, *Progress towards the SDGs: A selection of data from World Health Statistics 2018*, 2018; UN, *Transforming our world: the 2030 Agenda for Sustainable Development*, 2015.

SDG3: 'Good Health and Well-Being'

When developing and transition economies engage in the development of Codex standards and then use those standards as the basis for national standards, they are protecting consumer health both within and outside their national borders. Strengthening food safety systems will enable countries to take measures to reduce the burden of food-borne disease.

SDG8: 'Decent Work and Economic Growth'

The targets of this goal are linked primarily to growth, productivity and employment. Engaging in Codex, rather as for Goal 1, will help countries work towards achieving 'full and productive employment and decent work for all'.

Trade is a vital opportunity for growth in this area, and the Codex standards promote fair practices in food trade by eliminating trade restrictions and barriers to trade.

SDG12: 'Food Waste and Management of Chemicals'

One of the targets of Goal 12 is 'halving per capita global food waste at the retail and consumer levels and reduce food losses along production and supply chains'. Codex work on accurate and reliable food labelling links directly to this goal. The goal also calls for sound management of chemicals. Chemicals in food are a worldwide health concern and are a leading cause of trade obstacles. The expert advice provided to Codex by FAO and WHO ensures that correct exposure levels are set in Codex standards to protect consumer health.

SDG17: 'Partnerships for the SDGs'

Partnerships: working together will ensure that no one is left behind in the drive to reach the 2030 SDGs. Codex itself is one of the finest and longest-standing examples of partnership within the United Nations systems FAO and WHO. Codex, together with the World Organization for Animal Health and the International Plant Protection Convention, is also part of another strong partnership when working on global issues having a 'one health' aspect such as antimicrobial resistance or when called upon as the benchmark for standards in WTO trade disputes.

Codex believes in the value of partnerships with all its stakeholders, both members and observers, industry and consumers. In the longstanding partnership with the International Dairy Federation, Codex created standards, guidelines and Codes of Practice for milk and milk products. Codex also closely cooperates with ISO on methods of analysis and sampling and other topics. Codex sees the advent of private standards as an opportunity and cooperates closely with organizations formed by the private sector creating systems that facilitate the application of Codex standards such as the Global Food Safety Initiative.

When Goal 17 describes a 'universal, rules-based, open, non-discriminatory and equitable multilateral trading system', it is pointing directly at the mandate, goals and daily work of the Codex Alimentarius.

[B] Codex Strategic Plan 2020-2025[7]

The plan sets out five strategic goals for the next six years and defines the vision and mission of the Commission.

Codex Vision: 'Where the world comes together to create food safety and quality standards to protect everyone everywhere.'

Codex Mission: 'Protect consumer health and promote fair practices in the food trade by setting international, science-based food safety and quality standards.'

The plan recognizes the important contributions of Codex to achieving the SDGs and using the core values of inclusiveness, collaboration, consensus building and transparency sets out five strategic goals:

- Address current, emerging and critical issues in a timely manner.
- Develop standards based on science and Codex risk-analysis principles.
- Increase impact through the recognition and use of Codex standards.
- Facilitate the participation of all Codex Members throughout the standard-setting process.
- Enhance work management systems and practices that support the efficient and effective achievement of all strategic plan goals.

While Goals 1, 2, 4 and 5 will be working towards the traditional goals of Codex in setting standards, Goal 3 is the task to look further into what happens with the standards once adopted by the Commission and what is their value as international common good.

§5.05 FOOD AND TRADE[8]

[A] Vision of Harmonization and Challenges to Implementation

Peace and prosperity depend on the availability of food. Today, among the principal concerns of national governments the world over is the need to ensure that food imported from other countries is safe and poses no threat to the health of consumers or the health and safety of their animal and plant populations. Consequently, importing countries have introduced laws and regulations to eliminate or minimize such threats. In the area of food, animal and plant control, there is a risk that such measures could lead to barriers to trade in food between countries. In order to trade internationally and have access to markets for high-value products, producers must be able to meet national food regulations. Complying with these requirements in export markets can be

7. Codex Alimentarius, *Codex Strategic Plan 2020–2025*, 2019.
8. FAO/WTO, *Trade and food standards*, 2017.

challenging, especially for smaller producers in developing and emerging economies. The use of international food standards worldwide not only contributes to public health but also helps to reduce trade costs by making trade more transparent and efficient, allowing food to move more smoothly between markets.

Harmonization with a view to promoting free trade was among the concerns underpinning the evolution of Codex – the view that, if every country harmonized towards a single set of international food standards, all countries would encounter fewer barriers to trade, allowing food products to move more freely among countries. This benefits farmers and their households and contributes to reducing hunger and poverty. This concept is recognized in the General Principles of the Codex Alimentarius.

While many countries align with Codex, for others, it can be difficult to integrate Codex standards fully into their national legislation. Varying legal procedures, administrative mechanisms and political systems, and, at times, the influence of national attitudes and concepts of sovereign rights can impede the progress of harmonization and the use of Codex standards. The increasing level of participation by countries in the work of Codex shows that, despite these difficulties, countries value open technical discussion and agree that they are useful to find an international consensus towards which rules and regulations can evolve.

[B] Codex Standards Facilitating Trade

While many trade agreements have implications for food, two WTO agreements are of particular interest with respect to the work of the Codex Alimentarius Commission – the Agreement on the Application of Sanitary and Phytosanitary Measures (SPS) and the Agreement on Technical Barriers to Trade (TBT).

The SPS Agreement contains provisions with respect to measures that may be taken to protect animal, plant and human health. With regard to human health, it acknowledges that governments have the right to take sanitary and phytosanitary measures necessary for the protection of the health of their citizens. However, the agreement requires them to apply those measures only to the extent required to protect human health. It does not permit member governments to discriminate by applying different requirements to different countries where the same or similar conditions prevail, unless there is sufficient scientific justification for doing so. The SPS Agreement specifically identifies the standards, guidelines and recommendations established by the Codex Alimentarius Commission for food additives, veterinary drug and pesticide residues, contaminants, methods of analysis and sampling, and codes and guidelines of hygienic practice. This means that Codex standards are considered scientifically justified and are accepted as the benchmarks against which national measures and regulations are evaluated.

WTO members wishing to set stricter food safety standards than Codex standards may be required to provide evidence as to the scientific and non-discriminatory nature of their measures, should a trade dispute arise. If there is a dispute between two members, WTO will encourage them to resolve the matter amicably; only in rare cases are official dispute settlement procedures initiated at the request of members. The WTO TBT Agreement seeks to ensure that technical regulations and standards, including packaging, marking and labelling requirements, and analytical procedures for assessing conformity with technical regulations and standards, do not create unnecessary obstacles to trade. The TBT Agreement applies to all regulations and standards and is not specific to food.

[C] Not Only for Food Safety: What Is a Sardine?

On 26 September 2002, in one of its first rulings on the TBT Agreement, the Appellate Body of the WTO upheld a panel finding in favour of Peru that sardines caught in the Eastern Pacific (from the Sardinops sagax species) could be marketed and labelled as canned sardines in the European Union (EU). The dispute arose when an EC Council Regulation stated that only sardines from the species Sardinia pilchardus Walbaum (mainly found around the Eastern North Atlantic Coast) could be marketed as preserved sardines, thereby excluding Peruvian sardines. The WTO ruling found that the EC Regulation was inconsistent with the TBT Agreement because it was not based on the relevant international standard established by Codex (CXS 94-1981) for preserved sardines and sardine-type products. That Codex Standard sets out what can be written on a food label and characteristics of twenty-one species from which canned sardine or sardine-type products can be prepared, including both Sardinops sagax and Sardina pilchardus Walbaum. As a result of this dispute, a mutually agreed solution was reached whereby the EC Regulation was amended to address Peru's concerns and allow trade to continue.

§5.06 THE FUTURE

[A] A Lot Has Been Done

For more than five decades, Codex texts have contributed to the safety and quality of the food we eat. The Codex Alimentarius forms a global rule book that everyone in the food chain can follow. At the same time, the Codex Alimentarius Commission's open and participatory standard-setting procedure – gathering together nations to deliberate science-based evidence side by side – also serves as a lifeline to build the capacity of countries working to strengthen their own national food safety control systems. Codex has set the standards for all major issues in food trade and most national legislations are based on what Codex proposes.

Major food safety texts are the general principles of food hygiene (including the essential HACCP system), the general standard for food additives and for contaminants as well as related codes to reduce contamination. The Codex Food labelling system offers all relevant guidance to countries to ensure that consumers receive all relevant information about products and are not misled.

The Codex risk-analysis system, both for application in Codex and direct application by government, offers a comprehensive way for members to protect their population based on sound science. Major breakthrough texts are the risk-analysis guidelines for foods produced using modern biotechnology and AMR. With regards to foods for special dietary purposes, Codex has contributed to improve the situation for people intolerant to gluten as well as giving advice on infant and baby foods and on food supplementation.

Codex nutrition and labelling standards especially on nutrition labelling have contributed to the implementation of the WHO Global Strategy on Diet, Physical Activity and Health.

Food safety is an important topic that many only think about when they encounter a problem. To change this and keep food safety on the agenda constantly, Codex, FAO and WHO together with their members have successfully advocated for creating a World Food Safety Day (7 June every year). This is a constant reminder in the calendar that food safety is everyone's business (and there cannot be food business without safety).

Codex has been creating networks since it was started in 1963, and its goal with the World Food Safety Day is to make food safety a topic that is overall better known.

[B] Overcoming Issues

The new Codex strategic plan will guide Codex work from 2020 to 2025. This will be important to ensure that Codex is setting the right standards in the right way and make sure that the standards serve their purpose and are used by members.

Speed of standard setting and efficient and effective participation of all members are still challenges as is the financing of the scientific advice underlying Codex.

[C] Past and Present Challenges

Codex has faced many challenges to standardization in the past: some of them were solved; others are still waiting for a solution in areas where consensus is difficult to achieve among members. Some examples are:

- Green oranges (solved by changing ripeness criteria from 'orange' to sugar and juice content).
- Labelling of GM food (solved by concentrating on generic guidance and avoiding being overly prescriptive).
- Use of the term 'natural' in labelling (no consensus - work discontinued).
- Follow-up formula (difficult discussions on avoiding misleading consumers on nature and need for this product - ongoing).
- Processed cheese (discontinued because the product is too diverse all over the world).
- Should Codex set standards for alcoholic beverages?
- Use of growth-promoting substances in animal food production (discussions ongoing on some substances, some solved by vote and others by consensus) (*see* section §5.03[D]).

With constant innovations in science and technology, it is now possible to detect minute quantities of radiation from Chernobyl in blueberries exported from Eastern Europe, and ever-smaller residues of pesticides in fruits and vegetables. Uncertainty remains on where the future challenges are likely to arise for national food safety systems and where governments will need to invest to be prepared. Countries will need to be proactive and remain ever watchful, regularly update capacities and stay informed to identify the new challenges.

[D] Kava: An Important Food for Small Islands

Integrating small island developing states in the work of Codex is important. These remote places suffer from specific problems often related to the fact that most of what they eat needs to be imported. But they may also have products which could find their way to international markets if there were international standards that can assure their quality and safety.

Kava (*Piper methysticum*), for example, is an important agricultural commodity for Pacific Island Countries, forming an integral part of cultural, economic and social life. It has been domesticated for around three-thousand years and is being traded within and increasingly outside of the region in important quantities and value. The kava drink, has been consumed in Pacific Island Countries for centuries without any reported ill-effects on the liver, is made from a water extract of the root and/or rhizome of Piper methysticum.

A WHO risk assessment (2007)[9] concluded that 'clinical trials of kava have not revealed hepatoxicity as a problem' suggesting that 'water extracts are devoid of toxic effects' and recommending that 'products should be developed from water-based suspensions of kava'.

After going through the Codex Step-Procedure, the Codex standard for kava products, a work led by Papua New Guinea was adopted by the 43rd Session of the Codex Alimentarius Commission meeting virtually for the first time in its history. A success for Codex and for small island states.

[E] Makgeolli and the Challenge of Dealing with Alcoholic Beverages

Makgeolli is a fermented beverage that contains a small amount of alcohol (3%-8%). It is made from rice, which is mixed with fermentation starter culture. After adding potable water, the mixture is fermented for a certain amount of time at an optimal temperature through a simultaneous two-step fermentation process. Makgeolli has a characteristic cloudy form resulting from the solid matters which come from the main ingredients.

9. WHO, *Assessment of the Risk of Hepatotoxicity with Kava Products*, 2007.

A first discussion paper on a standard for Makgeolli was presented in 2016[10] and triggered questions on the value for Codex to develop regional or international standards for alcoholic beverages. Would a Codex standard for this product promote the use of this alcoholic beverage something which is considered detrimental to health by WHO,[11] one of Codex's parent organizations?

Without prejudice to developing a standard for any particular alcoholic beverage, a more global and comprehensive approach could be pursued by Codex in fulfilment of its objectives to protect consumer health including through provision of information to consumers. In this regard, the base work already exists in the form of the Codex General Standard for the Labelling of Prepackaged Foods and related texts on labelling and claims.

Labelling of alcoholic beverages could inform consumers about the different ingredients in a beverage, its alcohol content and energy value, and also inform consumers about the health risks associated with the products they are considering to consume.

While the Codex labelling standard already provides all the indications for members to implement nutrition labelling for alcoholic beverages (nutrition labelling being mandatory and alcoholic beverages not being excluded), only very few member countries have implemented this approach.

Globally harmonized warning labels for alcoholic beverages on the other hand do not exist presently and could be developed if countries agree. Discussions on this question continue.

[F] Challenges to Consensus

Over the last two years concerns were expressed by a number of Codex Members on the use of the Fourth Paragraph of the Statements of Principle Concerning the Role of Science in the Codex Decision-Making Process and the Extent to Which Other Factors Are Taken into Account (SOP), which provides member countries with the possibility to 'abstain from acceptance of the relevant standard without necessarily preventing the decision by Codex', when Members 'agree on the necessary level of protection of public health but hold differing views about other considerations'.

The subsequent discussions are highlighting the central role of the Chairpersons of Codex Committees and ultimately of the Codex Alimentarius Commission and how they should be advised to ensure adherence to the SOP to advise members not in agreement to clearly indicate their non-acceptance and then a conclusion recorded with the relevant reservations.

While there are still no clear directions provided as to whether achieving consensus should be linked to the SOP, the importance of efforts being made throughout the standard-setting process to achieve consensus remains one of the key

10. Codex Alimentarius, *Report of the Twentieth Session of the FAO/WHO Coordinating Committee for Asia*, 2016.
11. WHO, *Global strategy to reduce the harmful use of alcohol*, 2010; WHO, *Resource tool on alcohol taxation and pricing policies*, 2017.

issues. Providing more guidance on consensus building, not just in relation to the application of the SOP,[12] but to the progression of standards in general, would also be beneficial.

As mentioned before, consensus per se is not defined in Codex, but it is declared by the Chairpersons of Codex Committees and by the procedures of the Commission which makes 'every effort to reach agreement on the adoption of standards by consensus'. However as the Commission itself is composed of human beings, consensus cannot be always reached and voting occurs.

As defined by Arietta and Wallace (2000)[13] 'consensus is a journey and a destination' and as in every journey a number of obstacles can be found on the road before reaching the destination. Voting is just a way to overcome these obstacles although it is not the preferred way.

[G] Change Is a Thing We Can Count On

The future will bring most certainly: more people, climate change, more countries trading, new products and production methods, sustainability, ethics, changed consumer awareness/demands, new sales channels – e-platforms, new diseases, antimicrobial resistance and other unexpected challenges.

More than ever we need to work closely together and innovate together. We need to continue being science and evidence based. We need to properly 'sell' the evidence. We need to be true to our commitment to science and the wish to improve peoples' lives.

[1] From Farm to Fork: Opportunities for Fraud

Recent food scandals make it imperative to investigate solutions to this problem. While a number of initiatives exist to tackle food fraud, which has mainly an economic component but can also pose health risks, Codex is well placed to coordinate efforts towards defining and harmonizing standards related to these issues.

Undertaking a vulnerability assessment, developing an understanding of where the weakest link lies and addressing these aspects as part of a food safety management systems was considered a feasible starting point. Other advancements have been made in terms of traceability systems, electronic documentation, and innovative technology to make labelling more resistant to fraud, and these can all contribute to addressing the problem.

Once definitions have been agreed, a productive approach could be prioritizing certain issues instead of trying to tackle all aspects of food fraud simultaneously.

---

12. *See supra* note 10.
13. D.L. Arietta and L. Wallace, *Consensus Building Fieldbook*. Minneapolis: University of Minnesota Extension and Hubert H. Humphrey Institute of Public Affair, 2000.

[2] A Never-Ending Task

The role of the Codex Alimentarius Commission is constantly evolving taking into account these emerging challenges and the challenges in food production and trade. As science advances, new products and production methods arrive, and the world itself and its climate is changing, creating a food code and keeping it up-to-date is a virtually endless task. The food we buy sits atop the tip of an iceberg of expertise and skills of everyone working in the food chain. Creating standards that protect consumers, ensure fair practices in the sale of food and facilitate trade, is a process that involves specialists in numerous food-related scientific disciplines, together with consumers' organizations, production and processing industries, food control administrators and traders.

More than standards the Codex Alimentarius is not the only result of the work of the Commission, although it is the most important. By providing an international focal point and forum for informed dialogue on issues relevant to food, the Codex Alimentarius Commission builds networks of experts working on all relevant topics along the food chain. Within countries, participation in Codex has led to the introduction of food legislation and Codex-based standards, and the establishment or strengthening of food control agencies to monitor compliance with such regulations. The six regional FAO/WHO Coordinating Committees also provide vital geographical coverage to identify the challenges and needs particular to each region in the area of food standards and food control. These Committees have recently embarked on a process of revitalization aimed at boosting their role as the preeminent *fora* for the discussion of food safety and quality issues at the regional level.

§5.07 CONCLUSIONS

There is a lot to do to achieve safe, tasty, nutritious food in every home all the time. Codex is an excellent international standard-setting tool and the ideal forum to discuss food safety and food trade priorities and issues, but it can only be as good as the members make use of it and how good they are at finding consensus on critical issues and apply the standards in practice.

A longer-term strategic outlook on the future of food and food standards, which possibly includes the goals of the SDGs, will be needed in addition to the medium term in order for Codex to remain relevant and central in an evolving world. Partnerships with other organizations need to be strengthened as food safety and quality are a shared responsibility of all actors in the international supply chains.

The SPS and TBT Agreements both acknowledge the importance of harmonizing standards internationally to minimize or eliminate the risk of sanitary, phytosanitary and other technical standards becoming barriers to trade and encourage members, within the limits of their resources, 'to play a full part' in the work of international standards organizations and their subsidiaries. This has boosted countries' participation in Codex.

The next goal of the Commission should be to discuss how Codex can contribute more to making the world a better place and how to avoid that international standards might be used to do the opposite.

The discussion on the SDGs provides an opportunity for changing a common approach fulfilling at the same time the mission of the Codex Alimentarius: protect consumer health and promote fair practices in the food trade by setting international, science-based food safety and quality standards.

§5.08 AFTERWORD

The year 2020 was supposed to be another busy Codex year. One of the main features of Codex has been since its inception to hold technical meetings in host countries (*see also* section §5.03[B]). This fosters a community of food safety and quality experts that at the same time as going to Codex meetings have the opportunity to study different production and food control systems and learn from each other. Networking is an important part of Codex meetings and people who have worked together in Codex also find it easier to cooperate when other related issues arise. In 2018-2019 Codex held physical meetings on 148 days in 20 countries.

The year 2020 did not turn out the way anyone expected, and Codex held only five days of physical meetings. It was a year of learning, adapting and inventing. While many meetings were cancelled, work did not stop. Codex is a member-driven programme and members were keen to continue the work on international food standards: COVID-19 is not a food-borne disease but hygiene and especially food hygiene is more important than ever. Codex is a pioneer in setting global food hygiene standards. COVID-19 has impacted food trade and inspections, and harmonized rules and standards are important for trade to function safely.

Markets have been named as the culprits for facilitating viruses to jump species. Markets are on the other hand the places where billions of people get their food. Markets need hygiene and reduction of complexity. We need to collaborate to develop the science that allows us to set safe standards for them. There is too much we do not know yet. Best practices need to be defined based on science. The Codex team worked together with FAO and WHO experts on interim guidance for different audiences (available at www.codexalimentarius.org).

The appearance of any new threat to humanity is fertile ground for conspiracy theories which are usually constructed in similar ways.

I drink too much wine (1) thus it is quite probable that I will drop my glass (2). However, if I drop my glass (2) being drunk (1) is only one possibility out of many.

Similar for pandemics: If an evil force releases a virus (1) it is quite probable that this will start a pandemic (2). However, if a pandemic starts (2) an evil force releasing a virus is only one possibility out of many.

In both cases (1) is quite sufficient to imply (2) but (2) is not at all sufficient to imply (1). The skilled conspiracy theorist will make one believe that both are the same to confuse people to receive traction and usually funds.

The need for science-based Codex standards is thus greater than ever before and after an initial learning and adaptation period, the Codex membership decided to go virtual: in just over fourteen days, 147 Codex Members endorsed holding a virtual commission which took place successfully between September and November 2020 adopting important Codex standards. Among those standards was the long-awaited upgrade to the Codex General Principles of Food Hygiene and the HACCP system. Over 133 member countries, 1 member organization (EU) and 54 observer organizations participated with a total of 905 registered participants.

The year 2021 will bring more innovation and for the first time a fully virtual Codex meeting programme. We are working closely with members and observers to innovate together, we continue to be science and evidence based and true to the commitment to improve people's lives when setting international standards. Whether the meetings will be physical, virtual or hybrid in the future, Codex will maintain its values of transparency, inclusiveness, cooperation and consensus building.

CHAPTER 6

Food Safety under WTO Law

Daria Boklan

Food safety is subject to World Trade Organization (WTO) sanitary and phytosanitary (SPS) disciplines. Establishing discrimination under WTO food safety provisions requires comparison not between the products at issue but between the risks at issue. Therefore food-borne risk is a central element of the food safety regime under the WTO law. To protect human, animal or plant life or health from such risk, WTO members have the right to apply SPS measures with certain discretion. This discretion could be inferred, first, from the fact that food-borne risks may include both territorial conditions relevant to the risks (environmental or geographical, for instance) and at the same time, risks found in products. Moreover the analysis may not be limited exclusively to the present risk; the potential risk should be taken into account as well. Second, the discretion to apply food safety SPS measures could be inferred from broad interpretation of the notion of 'directly related to food safety', not limited by an exhaustive list of possible food-borne risks.
Third, WTO members have the right to rely on the precautionary principle as a basis for application of SPS food safety measures and finally they may set their appropriate level of protection basing on both quantitative and qualitative aspects.

§6.01 INTRODUCTION

International food trade has existed for thousands of years, but until not too long ago food was mainly produced, sold and consumed locally. Over the last century, the amount of food traded internationally has grown exponentially, and a quantity and variety of food never before possible travels the globe today.[1]

Food safety is the absence, or safe, acceptable levels, of hazards in food that may harm the health of consumers. Food-borne hazards can be microbiological, chemical or

1. http://www.fao.org/fao-who-codexalimentarius/about-codex/jp/.

physical in nature and are often invisible to the plain eye: bacteria, viruses or pesticide residues are some examples.[2] On the one hand, food safety, nutrition and food security are closely linked;[3] on the other hand they are subject to different World Trade Organization (WTO) agreements. For instance, nutrition labelling and other good-quality measures are within the scope of the Technical Barriers to Trade Agreement (TBT Agreement) and food security issues may fall under the General Agreement on Tariffs and Trade (GATT). According to Article 1.5 of the TBT Agreement, its provisions 'do not apply to sanitary and phytosanitary measures as defined in Annex A of the Agreement on Sanitary and Phytosanitary Measures' (SPS Agreement).

Therefore both SPS and TBT Agreements strike a balance between, on the one hand, members' rights to regulate for legitimate objectives, such as food safety or consumer protection, and on the other hand, ensuring that such regulations do not become unnecessary or discriminatory barriers to trade.[4]

When a measure is an 'SPS measure', as defined in Annex A(1) of the SPS Agreement, the SPS Agreement applies to the exclusion of the TBT Agreement, even if the measure would otherwise be considered a 'technical regulation or standard ... for purposes of the TBT Agreement'. The relationship between the SPS Agreement and TBT Agreement can thus be described as one of the mutual exclusivity.[5]

However we should take into account the position of the panel in *EC – Approval and Marketing of Biotech Products*, according to which 'the requirement at issue, and which would have an autonomous *raison d'etre*, i.e., a different purpose which would provide an independent basis for imposing the requirement'.[6] Therefore one and the same measure could be simultaneously covered by both SPS and TBT Agreements. If the requirement falls within the definition of a 'technical regulation' as defined in Annex 1.1 of the TBT Agreement, it is to be assessed under the TBT Agreement 'to the extent it embodies a non-SPS measure'.[7]

As for the compatibility between SPS Agreement and Article XX(b) GATT,[8] it is worth noting that according to Article 2.4 of the SPS Agreement, SPS measures 'which confirm to the relevant provisions of this Agreement shall be presumed to be in accordance with the obligations of the Members under the provision of GATT 1996 which relate to use of SPS measures, in particular the provisions of Article XX (b)'.

2. http://www.fao.org/food-safety/en/.
3. https://www.who.int/health-topics/food-safety/.
4. Trade and Food Standards, published by the FAO and WTO, 2017, p. 13.
5. Peter Van den Bossche and Werner Zdouc, *The Law and Policy of the World Trade Organization* (Cambridge University Press, 2017), 1077, at 943.
6. Panel Report, *EC – Approval and Marketing of Biotech Products*, WT/DS293/R, 29 September 2006, para. 7.165.
7. *Ibid.*, para. 7.167.
8. According to Article XX (b) of the GATT: 'Subject to the requirement that such measures are not applied in a manner which would constitute a means of arbitrary or unjustifiable discrimination between countries where the same conditions prevail, or a disguised restriction on international trade, nothing in this Agreement shall be construed to prevent the adoption or enforcement by any contracting party of measures (b) necessary to protect human, animal or plant life or health.'

However the opposite is not the case. Measures that are in conformity with the GATT 1994 cannot be presumed to be consistent with the SPS Agreement, as the latter agreement also provides for obligations that clearly do not exist under the GATT 1994.[9]

As far as requirements directly related to food safety are concerned, they are covered by the SPS Agreement.[10]

At Berlin Agriculture Ministers' Conference on the occasion of the Global Forum for Food and Agriculture, held on 18 January 2020, the Communiqué tilted 'Food for All! Trade for Secure, Diverse and Sustainable Nutrition' was issued, where ministers representing seventy-one nations acknowledged that international food safety standards, based on the SPS Agreement, are essential for reaping the benefits of agricultural trade and for avoiding potential risks to human, animal and plant health. They agreed to facilitate trade in agriculture and in safe and nutritious food products by taking appropriate measures in accordance with the WTO Agreement on the Application of Sanitary and Phytosanitary Measures.[11]

Over ten-thousand food safety, plant and animal health requirements have been notified to the WTO, and a growing number of countries are actively providing the information.[12]

Forty-five per cent of all SPS trade concerns are food safety concerns. This shows on the one hand the necessity of food safety regulations under the WTO, but on the other hand difficulty to reach an agreement on such regulations among WTO members.

For instance, Brazil raised concerns about the European Union's (EU's) restrictions on poultry meat and poultry meat preparations. The restrictions affect exporters of meat of domestic ungulates (hooved animals), meat from poultry and rabbits, as well as minced meat, meat preparations and mechanically separated meat, who have been under judicial investigation on alleged charges of non-compliance with food safety standards. Brazil asked the EU to withdraw these measures on the grounds that they are not science-based and responded to the EU's perception that certain export companies cannot be trusted to comply with sanitary requisites for the presence of pathogens.

Brazil also raised concerns regarding the Russian Federation's restrictions on beef and swine meat. According to Russia, this measure was introduced due to numerous detections of the veterinary drug ractopamine in meat products imported from Brazil. As a result, Brazilian exports from sixty establishments were suspended in December 2017. Brazil said it has opened an investigative process in order to assess possible irregularities and stated its commitment to establishing control systems and processes that guarantee compliance with, and fulfilment of, the sanitary requirements of Brazilian meat products exported to the Russian market.[13]

This problem was reflected in the last Review of the Operation and Implementation of the SPS Agreement of 2014. The adoption of this document has taken over three

9. Peter Van den Bossche and Werner Zdouc, *The Law and Policy of the World Trade Organization* (Cambridge University Press, 2013), 1045, at 903.
10. https://www.wto.org/english/tratop_e/sps_e/sps_issues_e.htm#definitions.
11. https://www.gffa-berlin.de/wp-content/uploads/2020/01/2020-GFFA-Communique.pdf.
12. https://www.wto.org/english/tratop_e/sps_e/sps_issues_e.htm#definitions.
13. https://www.wto.org/english/news_e/news18_e/sps_12jul18_e.htm.

years due to members' disagreement over standards on food safety. Members finally reached a compromise by introducing wording suggesting that members are unable to agree on that recommendation.[14]

Nevertheless the SPS Agreement covers all types of measures aimed at the protection of human or animal life or health from food-borne risks. Such measures may concern requirements for final products, process and production, inspection and certification, packaging and labelling.

§6.02 SCOPE OF THE AGREEMENT ON SANITARY AND PHYTOSANITARY MEASURES

The Preamble of the SPS Agreement enshrines that no member should be prevented from adopting or enforcing measures necessary to protect human, animal or plant life or health and at the same time SPS measures are not to be applied in a manner that constitutes: a means of arbitrary or unjustifiable discrimination between members or a disguised restriction on international trade. Further, the right to apply SPS measures is enshrined in Article 2.1 of the SPS Agreement, according to which 'members have the right to take sanitary and phytosanitary measures necessary for protection of human, animal or plant life or health [...]'. However, the rights to apply SPS measures are limited by obligation of not to arbitrarily or unjustifiably discriminate between WTO Members, enshrined in Article 2.3 of the SPS Agreement.

The panel elaborated three cumulative elements which are required for a violation of Article 2.3 of the SPS Agreement: (1) the measure should discriminate between the territories of members other than the member imposing the measure, or between the territory of the member imposing the measure and that of another member; (2) the discrimination should be arbitrary or unjustifiable; and (3) identical or similar conditions prevail in the territory of the members compared.[15]

According to the Appellate Body, these conditions should 'relate to the particular objective pursued and risks addressed by the SPS measure in question'.[16] They may include both territorial conditions, like ecological or environmental relevant to the risks addressed by an SPS measure and at the same time, 'those found in products and not just the territory of an exporting or importing Member'.[17] Moreover, the analysis under Article 2.3 entails consideration of all relevant conditions that may not yet have manifested in products but are relevant in light of the regulatory objective and specific SPS risks at issue.[18] The analysis may not be limited exclusively to the risk present on the products.[19] The potential risk should be taken into account as well.

14. https://www.wto.org/english/news_e/news18_e/sps_06mar18_e.htm.
15. Panel Report, *Australia – Measures Affecting Importation of Salmon – Recourse to Article 21.5 by Canada*, WT/DS18/RW, 18 February 2000, para. 7.111.
16. Appellate Body Report, *Korea – Import Bans, and Testing and Certification Requirements for Radionuclides*, WT/DS495/AB/R, 11 April 2019, para. 5.59.
17. *Ibid.*, 5.63.
18. *Ibid.*, para. 5.64.
19. *Ibid.*, para. 5.65.

Therefore discrimination under Article 2.3 requires a comparison not between products at issue like under the GATT or TBT Agreement but between risks at issue. The panel in *Australia – Measures Affecting Importation of Salmon – Recourse to Article 21.5 by Canada* underlined that 'discrimination in the sense of Article 2.3, may also include discrimination between *different* products, e.g. not only discrimination between Canadian salmon and New Zealand salmon, or Canadian salmon and Australian salmon; but also discrimination between Canadian salmon and Australian fish including non-salmonids, as referred to by Canada in this case'.[20] When dissimilar products pose the same or similar health risks, they should be treated in the same way.[21] This approach to discriminatory treatment is connected with the specific nature of the SPS measures and food safety.

SPS measures include those which have the purpose of protecting human, animal or plant life or health from particular risks. Namely risks arising from the entry, establishment or spread of pests, diseases, disease-carrying or disease-causing organisms; additives, contaminants, toxins or disease-causing organisms in food, beverages or feedstuffs; diseases carried by animals, plants or products thereof.

The SPS measures include all relevant laws, decrees, regulations, requirements and procedures including, *inter alia*, labelling requirements directly related to food safety.

Interpretation of 'directly related to food safety' was made in *EC – Approval and Marketing of Biotech Products*, where the Panel noted that '[t]he term "food safety" as it is used in the Agreement encompasses the safety of such substances as food additives, contaminants (including pesticide residues), etc.' and ruled that GMO can be covered by the SPS Agreement.[22]

Further this approach was developed in a recent case *Korea – Import Bans, and Testing and Certification Requirements for Radionuclides* where the panel did not disagree with position of Korea, where it described the measures at issue as covered by the SPS Agreement and referred to 'two incidents in May 2016 in Tochigi where a food stand had accepted mislabelled wild edible plants that had actually been sourced from a restricted area that exceeded the reference level (100 Bq/kg) by up to 2,100 Bq and bamboo shoots served for lunch at a local elementary school were found to contain 234 Bq/kg of caesium. The mislabelling was discovered through a purchase survey by MHLW.'[23]

Therefore the panel interpreted 'directly related to food safety' broadly, not only relying on wording of Article 1 of Annex A of the SPS which contains pests, diseases, disease-carrying organisms, additives, contaminants, toxins or disease-causing organisms in food. This means that Article 1 of Annex A of the SPS agreement does not

20. Panel Report, *Australia – Measures Affecting Importation of Salmon – Recourse to Article 21.5 by Canada*, WT/DS18/RW, 18 February 2000, para. 7.112.
21. Peter Van den Bossche and Werner Zdouc, *The Law and Policy of the World Trade Organization* (Cambridge University Press, 2017), 1077, at 951.
22. Panel Report, *EC – Approval and Marketing of Biotech Products*, WT/DS293/R, 29 September 2006, paras 7.410, 7.387-7.388.
23. Panel Report, *Korea – Import Bans, and Testing and Certification Requirements for Radionuclides*, WT/DS495/R, 22 February 2018, para. 7.286.

contain an exhaustive list of potential food-borne risks and panels may enlarge it on a case-by-case basis.

§6.03 SCIENTIFIC BASIS

Scientific certainty and confidence in scientific evidence relate to the principle of prevention and not to precaution. Preventive measures are well recognized in WTO law and can be invoked by party to justify an import ban on products whose hazardous or dangerous nature is established.[24]

Article 2.2 of the SPS Agreement enshrines that SPS measures should be 'based on scientific principles and is not maintained without sufficient scientific evidence [...]'. The Appellate Body ruled in this respect that 'the obligation in Article 2.2 that an SPS measure not be maintained without sufficient scientific evidence requires that there be a rational or objective relationship between the SPS measure and the scientific evidence. Whether there is a rational relationship between an SPS measure and the scientific evidence is to be determined on a case-by-case basis and will depend upon the particular circumstances of the case, including the characteristics of the measure at issue and the quality and quantity of the scientific evidence'.[25] Further this approach was developed by the panel in *US – Certain Measures Affecting Imports of Poultry from China*, where it was stated that 'the scientific evidence must bear a rational relationship to the measure, be sufficient to demonstrate the existence of the risk which the measure is supposed to address, and be of the kind necessary for a risk assessment'.[26] At the same time, Article 2.2 of the SPS Agreement stipulates an exception from this scientific-based rule. This exception is foreseen by Article 5.7 of the SPS Agreement, which according to the Appellate Body 'operates as a qualified exemption from the obligation under Article 2.2 not to maintain SPS measures without sufficient scientific evidence'.[27]

The Appellate Body held that Article 5.7 of the SPS Agreement must be interpreted keeping in mind that the precautionary principle finds reflection in this provision.[28] That is the case when precautionary principle of international environmental law enshrined in a treaty on international trade.

The obligation to act consistently with the precautionary principle is crystallizing as a rule of customary international law.

---

24. Makane Moise Mbengue and Urs P. Thomas. 'The Precautionary Principle: Torn Between Biodiversity, Environment-Related Food Safety and the WTO' (2005) 5(5) *Global Environmental Issues* 41.
25. Appellate Body Report, *Japan – Measures Affecting Agricultural Products*, WT/DS76/AB/R, adopted 22 February 1999, para. 84.
26. Panel Report, *US – Certain Measures Affecting Imports of Poultry from China*, WT/DS392/R, adopted 29 September 2010, para. 7.200.
27. Appellate Body Report, *Japan – Measures Affecting Agricultural Products*, WT/DS76/AB/R, adopted 22 February 1999, para. 80.
28. Appellate Body Reports, *Canada – Continued Suspension of Obligations in the EC – Hormones Dispute*, WT/DS321/AB/R, adopted 16 October 2008, para. 680.

There is certainly sufficient evidence of state practice to support the conclusion that this principle has now received sufficiently broad support to allow a strong argument to be made that it reflects a principle of customary law.[29]

The concrete substance of precautionary principle is still disputable; however, it is clear that it includes obligation to prevent SPS risks when there is lack of full scientific certainty.

Precaution contributes to the interpretation of international instruments in a manner that will enhance the protection of the environment in cases of scientific uncertainty as to the impact of a particular activity.[30]

The Appellate Body noted that it is 'perfectly legitimate for a Member to seek to halt the spread of a highly risky product while allowing the use of a less risky product in its place'.[31] Such interpretation could be regarded as interpretation in light of the precautionary principle.

The Appellate Body recognized that members had the right to establish their own level of sanitary protection, which may be higher than implied in existing international standards, guidelines and recommendations.[32]

According to Article 5.7 of the SPS Agreement, 'in cases where relevant scientific evidence is insufficient, a Member may provisionally adopt sanitary or phytosanitary measures on the basis of available pertinent information [...]'.

The Appellate Body elaborated a special test to interpret and apply Article 5.7 of the SPS, according to which the measure to fall under the mentioned article should satisfy four cumulative criteria, namely the measure must (1) be imposed in respect of a situation where relevant scientific evidence is insufficient, (2) be adopted on the basis of available pertinent information, (3) not be maintained unless the member seeks to obtain the additional information necessary for a more objective assessment of risk and (4) be reviewed accordingly within a reasonable period of time. The latter two requirements highlight the provisional nature of measures adopted pursuant to Article 5.7.[33] As for the first criterion, the panel underlined that Article 5.7 refers to 'relevant scientific evidence' which implies that the body of material that might be considered includes not only evidence supporting Japan's position but also evidence supporting other views.[34] Article 5.7 was obviously designed to be invoked in situations where little, or no, reliable evidence was available on the subject matter at issue.[35] It is triggered not by the existence of scientific uncertainty but rather by the insufficiency of

29. Philippe Sands and Jacqueline Peel, *Principles of International Environmental Law* (Cambridge, 2018), 239.
30. *Ibid.*, 240.
31. Appellate Body Report, *European Communities – Measures Affecting Asbestos and Asbestos-Containing Products*, WT/DS135/AB/R, adopted 12 March 2001, para. 168.
32. Abdul Hasseb Ansari and Sri Wartini, 'Application of Precautionary Principle in International Trade Law and International Environmental Law: A Comparative Assessment' 2014 13(1) *Journal of International Trade Law and Policy* 22.
33. Appellate Body Reports, *Canada – Continued Suspension of Obligations in the EC – Hormones Dispute*, WT/DS321/AB/R, adopted 16 October 2008, para. 676.
34. Appellate Body Report, *Korea – Import Bans, and Testing and Certification Requirements for Radionuclides*, WT/DS495/AB/R, adopted 11 April 2019, para. 5.107.
35. *Ibid.*, para. 8.219.

scientific evidence.[36] That means the concept of insufficiency of scientific evidence and the concept of scientific uncertainty are not interchangeable[37] and the panel and the Appellate Body used narrow interpretation of Article 5.7 of the SPS Agreement. In addition the Appellate Body underlined that 'insufficient' within the meaning of Article 5.7 does not allow, in qualitative or quantitative terms, the performance of an adequate assessment of risks as required under Article 5.1 (of the SPS Agreement).[38] Thus the trigger for applicability of Article 5.7 is the insufficiency of the scientific evidence, not the provisional nature of the measure at issue.[39] Alongside that the Appellate Body ruled that WTO Members should be permitted to take a provisional measure where new evidence from a qualified and respected source puts into question the relationship between the pre-existing body of scientific evidence and the conclusions regarding the risks.[40]

As for the second criterion, it works when there is some evidentiary basis indicating the possible existence of a risk, but not enough to permit the performance of a risk assessment. Rational and objective relationship between the information concerning a risk and the provisional SPS measure is required.[41]

The third criterion contains three requirements: the WTO member must make best efforts to remedy the insufficiency, seek to obtain additional information and such information should be appropriate to conduct a risk assessment within the meaning of Article 5.1 of the SPS Agreement.[42]

And finally with respect to the last criterion the Appellate Body stated that 'reasonable period of time' depends on the specific circumstances of each case, including the difficulty of obtaining the additional information necessary for the review and the characteristics of the provisional SPS measure.[43]

§6.04 INTERNATIONAL STANDARDS

International food standards contribute to public health and make trade more transparent. However, at the same time, food safety requirements may constitute barriers to international trade for protectionist purposes.

Article 3 of the SPS Agreement reflecting objective of the Preamble enshrines three alternative obligations regarding international standards. First option is to base

36. Appellate Body Report, *Japan – Measures Affecting the Importation of Apples*, WT/DS245/AB/R, adopted 26 November 2003, para. 184.
37. Peter Van den Bossche and Werner Zdouc, *The Law and Policy of the World Trade Organization* (Cambridge, 2017), 969.
38. Appellate Body Report, *Korea – Import Bans, and Testing and Certification Requirements for Radionuclides*, WT/DS495/AB/R, adopted 11 April 2019, para. 5.106.
39. Peter Van den Bossche and Werner Zdouc, *The Law and Policy of the World Trade Organization* (Cambridge, 2017), 970.
40. Appellate Body Reports, *Canada – Continued Suspension of Obligations in the EC – Hormones Dispute*, WT/DS321/AB/R, adopted 16 October 2008, para. 703.
41. *Ibid.*, para. 678.
42. *Ibid.*, para. 679.
43. Appellate Body Report, *Japan – Measures Affecting Agricultural Products*, WT/DS76/AB/R, adopted 22 February 1999, para. 93.

SPS measures on international standards (Article 3.1), second option is to conform to international standards (Article 3.2) and third option is to introduce higher level of SPS protection. Article 3.4 directly refers to Codex Alimentarius Commission as one of the relevant international standards, which is the main international food safety standard.

Codex is an intergovernmental body created in 1963 by the Food and Agricultural Organization (FAO) and the World Health Organization (WHO) under the Joint FAO/WHO Food Standards Programme to develop food standards, guidelines and recommendations. Codex is recognized in Annex A(3) of the SPS Agreement as the source for international standards, guidelines and recommendations for food safety in respect of contaminants.[44] Codex standards contain requirements for food aimed at ensuring for the consumer a safe, wholesome food product free from adulteration, correctly labelled and presented.[45] However, the non-binding standards set by international standard-setting organizations do not become binding by virtue of the SPS Agreement. It suffices that some of the elements of the standard are adopted and that the measure does not contradict the standard.[46]

§6.05 RISK ASSESSMENT AND APPROPRIATE LEVEL OF SANITARY AND PHYTOSANITARY PROTECTION

The term 'risk assessment' refers to the scientific process of identifying the existence of a risk and establishment the likelihood that the risk may actually materialize according to the measures that could be applied to address the risk.[47] Risk assessment is one of the key issues in proving food safety. Article 5 of the SPS Agreement contains provisions on the risk assessment and enshrines obligation to ensure that SPS measures are based on an assessment, as appropriate to the circumstances, of the risks to human, animal or plant life or health, taking into account risk assessment techniques developed by the relevant international organizations (Article 5.1). With respect to food safety, according to paragraph 4 of Annex A to the SPS Agreement, the 'risk assessment' includes the evaluation of the potential for adverse effects on human or animal health arising from the presence of additives, contaminants, toxins or disease-causing organisms in food, beverages or feedstuffs.

The right to apply SPS measures, including food safety measures, is limited by obligation provided in Article 5.6 of the SPS Agreement not to apply more trade-restrictive measures than required to achieve their appropriate level of sanitary or phytosanitary protection. According to this article a measure is not more trade

44. Specifically, Annex A(3)(a) states 'for food safety, the standards, guidelines and recommendations established by the Codex Alimentarius Commission relating to food additives, veterinary drug and pesticide residues, contaminants, methods of analysis and sampling, and codes and guidelines of hygienic practice' are considered 'international standards, guidelines and recommendations'. Panel Report, *Korea – Import Bans, and Testing and Certification Requirements for Radionuclides*, WT/DS495/R, 22 February 2018, para. 2.22.
45. http://www.fao.org/fao-who-codexalimentarius/about-codex/jp/.
46. Peter Van den Bossche and Werner Zdouc, *The Law and Policy of the World Trade Organization* (Cambridge, 2017), 953.
47. *Ibid.*, 955.

restrictive than required unless there is another measure, reasonably available taking into account technical and economic feasibility, that achieves the appropriate level of sanitary or phytosanitary protection (ALOP)[48] and significantly less trade restrictive.

A complainant must establish that an alternative measure: (i) is reasonably available taking into account technical and economic feasibility; (ii) achieves the member's ALOP; and (iii) is significantly less restrictive to trade than the contested SPS measure. These cumulative elements entail an assessment of a proposed alternative measure that serves as a conceptual tool to be used for the analysis under Article 5.6.[49] The Appellate Body has said that a member's ALOP is an 'objective' and that an SPS measure is the instrument chosen to attain or implement that objective. It is the 'prerogative' of a member to set the level of protection that it deems appropriate. At the same time, members adopting SPS measures must determine their ALOP with sufficient precision to enable the application of the relevant provisions of the SPS Agreement. While a member is not required to set the ALOP in quantitative terms, a member may not establish its level of protection with such vagueness or equivocation as to render impossible the application of the relevant disciplines of the SPS Agreement, including the obligation set out in Article 5.6.[50] A panel must ascertain the respondent's ALOP on the basis of the totality of the arguments and evidence on the record, which may include the level of protection reflected in the SPS measure actually applied.[51] A panel examining a claim under Article 5.6 of the SPS Agreement is charged with, *inter alia*, ascertaining the respondent's ALOP on the basis of the totality of the arguments and evidence on the panel record. A panel is also required to identify the level of protection that would be achieved by the alternative measure proposed by the complainant.[52]

§6.06 CONCLUSIONS

Discrimination under WTO food safety provisions requires a comparison not between products at issue but rather between risks at issue. Therefore food-borne risk is a central element of the food safety regime under the WTO law. To protect human, animal or plant life or health from such risk WTO members have the right to apply SPS measures with certain discretion. This discretion could be inferred, first, from the fact that food-borne risks may include both territorial conditions, like ecological or environmental relevant to the risks and at the same time, risks found in products. Moreover such food-borne risks may not yet have been manifested in products but are relevant in light of the regulatory objective of the SPS measure. In addition the analysis may not

48. Appropriate level of sanitary and phytosanitary protection – The level of protection deemed appropriate by the member establishing a sanitary or phytosanitary measure to protect human, animal or plant life or health within its territory (SPS Agreement, Annex A, paragraph 5).
49. Appellate Body Report, *Korea – Import Bans, and Testing and Certification Requirements for Radionuclides*, WT/DS495/AB/R, adopted 11 April 2019, para. 5.21.
50. *Ibid.*, para. 5.23.
51. *Ibid.*, para. 5.24.
52. *Ibid.*, para. 5.38.

be limited exclusively to the risk present on the products; the potential risk should be taken into account as well.

Second, the discretion to apply food safety SPS measures could be inferred from broad interpretation of the notion of 'directly related to food safety', not limited by an exhaustive list of possible food-borne risks.

Third confirmation of the discretion is right to rely on precautionary principle as a basis for application of SPS food safety measures. And finally the right of WTO members to set their ALOP is taken into consideration not only in quantitative terms but also in qualitative aspects.

CHAPTER 7

Checking Compliance with Food Law: Control, Inspection and Approval Procedures under the WTO SPS Agreement*

Denise Prévost

The Sanitary and Phytosanitary (SPS) Agreement has been the subject of much academic scrutiny and public attention, as it mediates a difficult tension between the liberalization of agri-food trade and the protection of health. However, this attention has focused on the disciplines that this agreement imposes on World Trade Organization (WTO) Members' regulatory measures in the area of health protection. This chapter argues that, although less prominent, of no less importance are the rules in the SPS Agreement dealing with procedures applied by Members to ensure compliance with their SPS requirements. These procedures are gaining importance due to the difficulties inherent in ensuring compliance with food regulations in the context of fragmented food production in global value chains (GVCs), on the one hand, and the recognized importance of allowing producers in developing countries to participate in GVCs, on the other. The trade/health balance aimed at by the SPS Agreement can be undermined if compliance procedures are not appropriately disciplined. A too stringent interpretation of the disciplines of these procedures may unacceptably weaken the ability of WTO Members to ensure that their SPS requirements are complied with, thereby endangering health, while a too lax interpretation allows broad scope for protectionism. This chapter closely examines the rules on control, inspection and

* This contribution partly draws upon the following publications by the same author, *Balancing Trade and Health in the SPS Agreement: The Development Dimension.* Wolf Legal Publishers, Nijmegen (2009) and Prévost, D., 'National Treatment in the SPS Agreement: A Sui Generis Obligation' in A. Kamperman Sanders (ed.), *The Principle of National Treatment in International Economic Law: Trade, Investment and Intellectual Property,* Edward Elgar, Cheltenham (2014).

approval procedures in the SPS Agreement to assess whether, in the context of food production in GVCs, they contribute to, rather than undermine, the careful balance between trade and health objectives sought by the SPS Agreement.

'In God we trust; everything else we measure'[1]

§7.01 INTRODUCTION

Control, inspection and approval procedures, also known as conformity assessment procedures, are rapidly gaining importance in food regulatory systems, due to the increasingly fragmented nature of the food production chain.[2] These procedures are essential to ensure that all steps in the supply chains for food production comply with the applicable food-safety requirements in importing countries. They respond to consumer demands for reliable verification that food-safety standards are met, in the wake of several food-safety scares, such as that regarding melamine in baby milk formula and animal feed.[3] However, the complex, costly and burdensome nature of these conformity assessment procedures has increased greatly, reflecting the difficulty of controlling dispersed food production chains, particularly in the processed food sector.[4] Regulating the safety of food throughout the production chain, 'from farm to fork', entails traceability, compliance assessment and certification at several critical points involving different actors and is prone to overlaps, duplication of efforts, delays and inefficiencies. In addition, improved analytic and testing capacity and proliferating

1. Slogan attributed to the Total Quality Management (TQM) movement, based on the ideas of William Edwards Demming (1900-1993) who advocated a systems-wide approach to improving manufacturing processes and measuring quality. *See* Martínez-Lorente, A., Dewhurst, F. and Dale, B. (1998) 'Total Quality Management: Origins and Evolution of the Term' 10(5) *The TQM Magazine* 378-386. The TQM is seen as the forerunner of the International Organization for Standardization's ISO 9000 series of standards for assessing the adequacy of the quality control systems in production processes.
2. As noted in the vision paper of the Dutch Presidency of the EU in 2015 entitled *The EU and Global Value Chains: Implementing sustainable business through EU aid and trade policies*, 'Global value chains – where the different stages of the production process are located across different countries – have come to be a dominant feature of world trade. More than 70% of world trade consists of intermediate goods, services and capital.' *See* https://www.euandgvc.nl/documents/leaflet/2015/09/10/2-pager (accessed 29 October 2019). The increased role of global value chains in the agri-food industry is detailed in the ITC, OECD, UNCTAD, World Bank Group and WTO *Background Note for the G20 Argentina Presidency 2018 Agriculture and Food Global Value Chains* (2018).
3. Melamine is an industrial chemical, which Chinese producers had used to falsely inflate the apparent protein content of watered-down milk products to meet the levels required by regulation. Melamine-contaminated products spread rapidly and were soon found in forty-six other countries. In 2009, the ingestion of this chemical by infants in milk formula led to kidney damage, with 6 deaths and approximately 294,000 cases of illness, of which 51,900 required hospitalization. *See* Keck, F. (2009) 'The Contaminated Milk Affair' 1 *China Perspectives* 88.
4. As noted by Marks, food supply chains are becoming more complex, and food risks are not only connected to growers but also increasingly to food processors or handlers. Failure to properly remove contaminants in a single production step can result in contaminated food reaching millions of consumers, given the current system of centralized production and transatlantic shipment. Marks, A.B. (2015) 'The Risks We Are Willing to Eat: Food Imports and Safety' 52(1) *Harvard Journal on Legislation* 125-172.

certification systems in importing countries necessitate quality control systems that are far from universal in exporting countries.[5]

As such, conformity assessment procedures can operate as a de facto barrier to entry to food supply chains. This is particularly so for those suppliers that lack the financial resources and technical capacity to *demonstrate compliance* with food-safety requirements of importing countries in accordance with the applicable compliance procedures, even if their products in fact meet these substantive requirements. It has been noted that the costs of obtaining the necessary compliance certification may exclude disadvantaged groups, including 'small producers, small farms, women and older producers'.[6] Shepherd argues that that global value chains (GVCs) 'rely on the ability to move goods quickly, cost effectively, and reliably across borders' and that this 'business model simply cannot work in the presence of long border delays, or other supply chain disruptions'.[7] It is therefore important to ensure that agri-food suppliers of developing countries can reap the benefits of participation in GVCs by addressing delays, complexities and costs in conformity assessment procedures that may operate to exclude them.[8]

Many of the substantive obligations in the World Trade Organization (WTO) Agreement on Sanitary and Phytosanitary Measures (SPS Agreement) function as a filter to separate measures legitimately designed to protect health from risks in agri-food products from measures that are a disguised form of protectionism. In this way, the SPS Agreement tries to balance the often-competing goals of trade liberalization and health protection.[9] However, this delicate balance can be undermined if WTO Members are free to use procedural requirements to make it difficult for agri-food exporters to access their markets, for example, by imposing discriminatory, costly, burdensome or lengthy procedures to test for conformity with their sanitary and phytosanitary (SPS) requirements; to approve additives; or to set tolerances for contaminants, thereby greatly limiting the potential for suppliers, particularly those in developing countries, to participate in GVCs for food production. However, the sensitive trade/health balance aimed at by the SPS Agreement also could be disturbed if WTO Members are prevented from reliably checking the conformity of imported

5. Tran, N., Wilson N.L.W. and Anders S. (2012) 'Standard Harmonization as Chasing Zero (Tolerance Limits): The Impact of Veterinary Drug Residue Standards on Crustacean Imports in the EU, Japan, and North America' 94(2) *American Journal of Agricultural Economics* 496-502.
6. Kaplinsky, R. and Morris, M., *How Regulation and Standards Can Support Social and Environmental Dynamics in Global Value Chains*. Geneva: International Centre for Trade and Sustainable Development (2017) 12.
7. Shepherd, B., *Trade Facilitation and Global Value Chains: Opportunities for Sustainable Development*. Geneva: International Centre for Trade and Sustainable Development (2016) 1.
8. An example of the trade impact of the difficulty in demonstrating compliance with food-safety requirements in the context of complex supply chains is provided in a study of the shrimp industry of Bangladesh, *see* Redden, J., *The Role of Aid for Trade in Building the Capacity of Developing Country Firms to Meet Sustainability Standards*. Geneva: International Centre for Trade and Sustainable Development (2017) 30. Similar difficulties were identified in a study of the shrimp supply chain in Vietnam, *see* Tran, N. et al. (2013) 'Governance of Global Value Chains in Response to Food Safety and Certification Standards: The Case of Shrimp from Vietnam' 45 *World Development* 324-336.
9. For a discussion of the rules of the SPS Agreement on substantive SPS measures, *see* Chapter 6 of this book.

agri-food products with their SPS requirements. In view of the vast differences in regulatory infrastructure and enforcement capacity among the 164 WTO Members and of the dispersed nature of the food production chain, it is reasonable to expect that an importing Member would need to have procedures in place to ensure that the products it imports, and the inputs and services used in their production chains, meet its regulatory requirements to address food-safety risks or risks from pests or diseases of plants and animals. As recently noted more generally, conformity assessment procedures are 'essentially about establishing trust in trading relationships' in that they enable importing Members 'to have confidence that products are safe and of good quality'.[10]

In order to prevent the misuse of compliance procedures to restrict market access and prevent participation in food supply chains, but still respect the policy room left to Members to protect health in their territories by the relevant substantive rules of the SPS Agreement, this agreement includes rules on control, inspection and approval procedures. These rules, contained in Article 8 and Annex C of the SPS Agreement, aim to limit the delays, costs and administrative burden of compliance procedures and to prevent their discriminatory application.

§7.02 LEGAL FRAMEWORK FOR CONTROL, INSPECTION AND APPROVAL PROCEDURES

To address the trade-restrictive effects of control, inspection and approval procedures, Article 8 of the SPS Agreement provides:

> Members shall observe the provisions of Annex C in the operation of control, inspection and approval procedures, including national systems for approving the use of additives or for establishing tolerances for contaminants in foods, beverages or feedstuffs, and otherwise ensure that their procedures are not inconsistent with the provisions of this Agreement.

Annex C contains detailed rules on control inspection and approval procedures, which broadly aim to ensure that procedures are not lengthier and more burdensome than is reasonable and necessary and that they do not discriminate against imports. This annex is an integral part of the SPS Agreement[11] and is expressly referred to in Article 8. It is therefore essential to read Article 8 together with Annex C, as a violation of the rules in Annex C would automatically result in a violation of Article 8 of the SPS Agreement.[12] It is thus useful to examine Annex C in detail to assess how it mediates the tension between trade liberalization and health protection.

Annex C contains three paragraphs. In particular, Annex C.1 contains a list of nine requirements in subparagraphs (a) to (i) applicable to procedures to check and ensure the fulfilment of SPS measures (commonly known as conformity assessment

10. Statement made by the WTO Secretariat at the Committee on Technical Barriers to Trade, *Thematic Session on Conformity assessment procedures: National quality infrastructure*, G/TBT/GEN/275, 11-12 November 2019.
11. Article 1.3 of the SPS Agreement.
12. Panel Report, *EC – Approval and Marketing of Biotech Products*, para. 7.1569.

procedures). Further, Annex C.1 contains an additional unnumbered subparagraph, which addresses the thorny issue of prior approval systems and tolerance determinations. The remaining two paragraphs of Annex C are rather limited in scope, dealing with two specific situations in a facultative way, imposing no obligations on importing Members. More specifically, Annex C.2 addresses the situation where SPS measures specify control at the level of production and requires Members in whose territory the production takes place (i.e., the exporting Member) to facilitate such control as well as the work of the controlling authorities. Annex C.3 provides that nothing in the SPS Agreement shall prevent Members from carrying out reasonable inspection in their own territories.

As the most relevant disciplines on control, inspection and approval procedures are to be found in Annex C.1, this provision and its scope of application merit detailed attention.

§7.03 SCOPE OF APPLICATION

The first issue to be examined is the precise coverage of the disciplines of Annex C.1, as set out in its introductory sentence and footnote 7 to this annex.

The broad scope of application of Annex C.1 was emphasized in several WTO dispute settlement rulings. The panel in *US – Poultry* found that it covers 'any procedure' as long as it is aimed at 'checking and ensuring the fulfilment of sanitary or phytosanitary measures', and is undertaken in the context of 'control, inspection, or approval'.[13] In this regard, a Member's characterization of its measure is not decisive.[14] The panels in *US – Poultry, US – Animals* and *Russia – Pigs (EU)* found that Annex C.1 covers not only procedures that address products but also procedures that deal with the consideration or determination of equivalence and of the disease status of a particular geographic region.[15] Further, not only the control, inspection and approval procedures themselves but also measures that affect their operation,[16] or amount to their application,[17] have been held to fall within the scope of application of Annex C.1. However, to fall under Annex C.1, a link is required between the relevant procedure and an SPS measure that the Member seeks to check and ensure the fulfilment of.[18]

13. Panel Report, *US – Poultry (China)*, para. 7.363.
14. *Ibid.*, para. 7.372.
15. Panel Report, *US – Animals*, para. 7.69 and Panel Report, *Russia – Pigs (EU)*, para. 7.515.
16. *See* Appellate Body Report, *Australia – Apples*, para. 438, where the Appellate Body held that actions that prohibit, prevent or impede undertaking and completing control, inspection and approval procedures in accordance with the obligations in Annex C.1 can be challenged under its provisions.
17. Panel Report, *EC – Approval and Marketing of Biotech Products*, paras 7.1492 and 7.1785. In this case the complainants did not challenge the European Community's prior approval system for biotech products itself, but instead the manner in which it was applied, which was characterized by a blocking of the approval process by certain EC Member States. As Annex C.1 disciplines approval procedures and their application, the panel found that the EC was obliged to comply with its provisions.
18. Panel Report, *Korea – Radionuclides*, para. 7.378. Similarly *see* Panel Report, *US – Animals*, para. 7.73.

It is useful to note that the procedures covered by Annex C are themselves SPS measures in their own right, as evinced by the fact that among the illustrative list of 'SPS measures' in Annex A.1 are 'testing, inspection, certification and approval procedures'. As a result, such procedures are subject *not only* to Article 8 and Annex C but also to all the other relevant rules of the SPS Agreement. This is expressly stated in Article 8, as cited above.[19] The disciplines in Annex C thus apply *in addition to* (not instead of) the remaining obligations in the SPS Agreement.

Other SPS measures laying down substantive requirements for agri-food products are not subject to Article 8 and Annex C.[20] It follows that substantive SPS measures must be distinguished from procedural SPS measures for purposes of determining the applicability of Annex C.1.[21] However, the fact that a substantive SPS requirement and the procedure to assess conformity with it are combined in a single measure does not form an obstacle to the applicability of Annex C.1.[22]

The broad applicability of the rules in Annex C means that these rules have significant implications for the governance of GVCs in food production as many commonly used procedural requirements fall within their scope.

§7.04 RULES ON CONTROL, INSPECTION AND APPROVAL PROCEDURES

It is now necessary to examine the disciplines which Annex C.1 sets out for control, inspection and approval procedures to assess whether they achieve a trade/health balance that is appropriate to the reality of the food production supply chain. This chapter focuses on the obligations of greatest relevance for food GVCs. It first examines the prohibitions on undue delay and discrimination in the operation of conformity assessment procedures, and the requirement of equitable fees. It then turns to the controversial disciplines on prior approval and tolerance determination systems. The obligations of Annex C.1 are assessed in light of their contribution to the dual objective of facilitating participation in food GVCs and not undermining Members' ability to achieve their chosen food-safety levels through governance of the food supply chain.

19. It is interesting to note that the US in *Japan – Apples* did not challenge Japan's inspection and control requirements for apples under the disciplines of Annex C.1, but rather their scientific basis under Articles 2.2 and 5.1 of the SPS Agreement. This did not present any problems since control and inspection procedures are, as just explained, themselves SPS measures and subject to all the relevant disciplines of the SPS Agreement.
20. Panel Report, *Australia – Salmon (Article 21.5 – Canada)*, paras 7.154-7.157, where information requirements imposed by Australia on imported Canadian fish were found to be substantive SPS measures and thus outside the scope of Annex C.1.
21. Scott criticizes this distinction as unnecessary on the basis that whether the SPS measures are substantive or procedural, they still have to meet the science-based requirements of the SPS Agreement. If they fail to do so, judicial economy could be used so as not to turn to Annex C. Scott, J., *The WTO Agreement on Sanitary and Phytosanitary Measures: A Commentary*. Oxford: Oxford Commentaries on the GATT/WTO Agreements, Oxford University Press (2007) 220.
22. Panel Report, *Korea – Radionuclides*, para. 7.378.

[A] Undue Delay

Lengthy control, inspection and approval procedures can have an important trade-restrictive effect, especially in the case of perishable food products.[23] The efficient operation of food GVCs depends on the timely, reliable supply of input products. Delays in approval procedures can therefore operate to exclude the affected suppliers from GVC participation in the food sector. Nevertheless, reliable verification of compliance with SPS requirements in the context of dispersed value chains may take time.

The first obligation imposed by Annex C.1, contained in the first clause of paragraph (a), prohibits 'undue delays' in undertaking or completing control, inspection and approval procedures. The words 'undertaken and completed' indicates that the prohibition on undue delays applies at all stages of these procedures, from commencement to conclusion.[24] Consequently, even if only the final step of a procedure is delayed (i.e., the final decision on approval or rejection), this delay would be caught by Annex C.1(a).[25]

The case law clearly distinguishes the obligation to initiate, conduct and conclude a conformity assessment procedure without undue delay (envisaged by Article C.1(a)) from any requirement to come to a particular outcome (*not* envisaged by this provision). In other words, the requirement embodied in Annex C.1(a) 'is simply to issue a final determination regardless of whether it be positive or negative'.[26] This interpretation reflects an awareness of the need to balance two objectives: that of preventing conformity assessment procedures being dragged out to evade the obligations on substantive SPS requirements; and that of allowing importing Members sufficient time to reliably assess compliance with their SPS requirements.

As held by the Appellate Body in *Australia – Apples*, Annex C.1(a) prohibits 'unwarranted, or otherwise excessive, disproportionate or unjustifiable' delays.[27] It is thus not the *length* of the delay in itself but rather whether there is a legitimate reason or *justification* for it, which is relevant for this assessment,[28] determined on a

23. For example, in 2018, the European Commission reported undue delays in the approval of its exports of apples and pears to the US, pending since 2008. This issue was repeatedly raised and discussed in the WTO SPS Committee, which provides a forum for WTO Members to discuss 'specific trade concerns' (STCs) with regard to each other's SPS measures. *See* WTO SPS Information Management System, STC nr. 439, *US import restrictions on apples and pears*, available at http://spsims.wto.org/en/SpecificTradeConcerns/View/439 (accessed 31 October 2019).
24. Panel Report, *EC – Approval and Marketing of Biotech Products*, para. 7.1494; Panel Report, *US – Poultry (China)*, para. 7.353; and Panel Report, *US – Animals*, para. 7.112.
25. This situation is illustrated by STC 439 (*supra* note 23) where the EU raised a concern of 'undue delay' under Annex C.1(a) because the last administrative step (publication of approval for apple and pear imports) had been put on hold by the US.
26. Panel Report, *Russia – Pigs*, para. 7.527, with reference to Panel Report, *US – Animals*, para. 7.112.
27. Appellate Body Report, *Australia – Apples*, para. 437.
28. Panel Report, *EC – Approval and Marketing of Biotech Products*, para. 7.1496, where it was held the mere fact that a particular delay is short would not preclude a panel from finding that it is 'undue'. Similarly, a lengthy delay is not sufficient to establish that the delay is 'undue' (unless no adequate explanation is provided).

case-by-case basis.[29] It has been emphasized that Members must be allowed to take the time reasonably needed to determine with adequate confidence that their SPS requirements are met.[30] The nature and complexity of the conformity assessment procedure is a relevant consideration,[31] which creates the necessary flexibility for verification of compliance in multifaceted supply chain production systems. The exigencies of trade therefore do not trump Members' right to protect health in their territories by reliably determining compliance with their SPS requirements.

Logically, a Member is only responsible for delays that are attributable to it, thus not for delays caused by the applicant, for example, by refusing to allow access for inspection or by tardy provision of SPS-related information. However, if an importing Member makes unnecessary requests for information,[32] that goes far beyond what is needed for the relevant assessment of SPS compliance, or if it delays the completion of the approval procedure because of outstanding non-SPS-related information, this would entail a violation of Annex C.1(a).[33]

In view of the reality of changing sanitary status and evolving scientific data, when new or additional information becomes available, the need to assess this information may justify a delay.[34] However, where a Member delays a procedure by requesting reconfirmation or updating of existing information, this is not seen as justifying a delay in the completion of the procedure.[35] To find otherwise would create a 'dangerous loophole' in the disciplines of Annex C.1(a) by allowing a Member to 'indefinitely postpone the completion of a procedure by invoking the need to reconfirm information that had become outdated by virtue of its own inaction'.[36]

However, care must be taken that this does not preclude a precautionary or prudent approach in identifying, assessing and managing a risk. A precautionary approach may necessitate requests for additional information before a decision can be taken, thus extending the timeframe for the procedure. The rules on SPS measures in the SPS Agreement allow room for precaution in Article 5.7 but subject this policy space to disciplines to prevent its abuse.[37] Similarly, in the context of the prohibition on 'undue delay', in Annex C.1(a), the panel in *EC – Approval and Marketing of Biotech Products* noted the need to determine whether a particular request for additional information 'is a reflection of genuine caution and prudence or whether it is a pretext

29. Appellate Body Report, *Australia – Apples*, para. 437. *See also* Panel Report, *EC – Approval and Marketing of Biotech Products*, paras 7.1496-7.1498.
30. Panel Report, *EC – Approval and Marketing of Biotech Products*, para. 7.1498.
31. Panel Report, *US – Animals*, para. 7.114.
32. Panel Report, *Russia – Pigs (EU)*, para. 7.583, where Russia's information requests regarding surveillance and control measures in EU Member States not affected by African Swine Fever were held to be excessive and unjustified, and thus causing 'undue delay'.
33. Panel Report, *Indonesia – Chicken*, paras 7.528-7.534, where Indonesia's delay in approving a veterinary health certificate for a Brazilian chicken-exporting enterprise, which had already submitted the required information on its food-safety system, pending the submission of information regarding its halal assurance system was seen as unjustified for purposes of Annex C.1(a) as it was not needed to ensure compliance with Indonesia's SPS requirements.
34. Panel Report, *EC – Approval and Marketing of Biotech Products*, para. 7.1498.
35. Panel Report, *US – Animals*, para. 7.143.
36. *Ibid.*, para. 7.143.
37. For a discussion on Article 5.7 of the SPS Agreement, *see* Chapter 6 of this book.

to delay the completion of an approval procedure',[38] finding that there is 'no inherent tension' between a prudent or precautionary approach and the obligation to complete approval procedures without undue delay. However, this flexibility is 'subject to reasonable limits, lest the precautionary approach swallow the discipline imposed by Annex C(1)(a), first clause',[39] by allowing a Member to endlessly defer substantive decisions due to its choice of a precautionary approach.

Consequently, the panel did not regard a precautionary approach in a situation where science is complex, uncertain or evolving, such as in the case of biotech products, as justifying a *deferral* of a substantive SPS decision.[40] Instead, the panel noted that substantive decisions need not 'give a straight yes or no answer' to applicants but may include time-limited or conditional approvals, or rejections subject to the possibility of a review when the state of scientific knowledge changes.[41] Thus Members retain the ability to take 'differentiated, proportionate action' to protect health from potential but uncertain risks,[42] also in their conformity assessment procedures. To allow procedural delays to *replace* substantive decisions in cases of uncertainty (i.e., to be misused as a tool for risk management) would make it possible for Members to 'evade the obligations to be observed in respect of substantive SPS measures, such as Article 5.1, which requires that SPS measures be based on a risk assessment'[43] thus undermining the effectiveness of the other provisions of the SPS Agreement. The panel's nuanced approach ensures that the trade/health balance of the SPS Agreement is not skewed in cases where Members choose a precautionary approach.

[B] Non-discrimination

Discriminatory application of control, inspection and approval procedures is a cause for concern, as this could be used to favour domestic producers in order to protect them from import competition. In the context of food production chains, this could lead to greater sourcing of input products from domestic than from foreign producers, restricting the possibilities for the latter to participate in food GVCs. However, there may be legitimate reasons to treat foreign agri-food products differently from those sourced from domestic producers, including the difficulty in ensuring traceability in fragmented supply chains, concerns regarding the reliability of foreign inspection, testing and certification systems, and food-safety incidents relating to imported products. It is therefore important that the obligation of non-discrimination takes this reality into account.

38. Panel Report, *EC – Approval and Marketing of Biotech Products*, para. 7.1522.
39. *Ibid.*, para. 7.1523.
40. *Ibid.*, para. 7.1526.
41. *Ibid.*, para. 7.1527.
42. *Ibid.*
43. *Ibid.*, para. 7.1517.

The core non-discrimination obligation is contained in the second clause of Annex C.1(a),[44] requiring that Members ensure that procedures to check and ensure the fulfilment of SPS measures are:

> undertaken and completed ... in a no less favourable manner for imported products than for like domestic products.

In order to establish a violation of this provision, a two-step analysis is necessary, namely: (i) whether domestic and imported products are 'like'; and (ii) whether the latter are treated in a less favourable manner than the former in the undertaking and completion of the challenged procedures.[45]

As this provision clearly lays down a national treatment obligation, interpretative guidance has been sought in the jurisprudence on the national treatment obligation in Article III:4 of the General Agreement on Tariffs and Trade (GATT) 1994.[46] Under GATT case law on national treatment, the likeness of domestic and imported products depends on the nature and extent of the competitive relationship between them, and 'less favourable treatment' exists if there is a detrimental impact on the conditions of competition of imported products.[47] The national treatment obligation is thus in essence a prohibition on internal measures that protect domestic producers from import competition.

The first step of the analysis, and the trigger for the application of the non-discrimination obligation in Annex C.1(a), is that the products compared be 'like'.[48] It is only with regard to 'like' products that the obligation to conduct conformity assessment procedures in a 'no less favourable manner' applies. Extensive GATT case law regarding 'likeness' in the national treatment obligation provides interpretative

---

44. Non-discrimination obligations applicable to conformity assessment procedures, are also reflected in Annex C.1(d) and (g) dealing with the confidentiality of information about imported products provided in the context of control, inspection and approval procedures; and the criteria used in the siting of facilities used in the procedures and in the selection of samples, respectively. Panel Report, *Korea – Radionuclides*, para. 7.391. The panel also referred to Annex C.1(f), but as this provision requires 'equitable' rather than 'no less favourable' treatment of imports, it is discussed separately in section §7.04[C] below.
45. Panel Report, *Russia – Pigs*, para. 7.539, followed in *Korea – Radionuclides*, para. 7.385. *See also* Panel Report, *EC – Approval and Marketing of Biotech Products*, para. 7.2400.
46. Panel Report, *EC – Approval and Marketing of Biotech Products*, para. 7.2401, referring to case law on the GATT national treatment obligation in Appellate Body Report, *EC – Asbestos*, para. 100 and Appellate Body Report, *Dominican Republic – Import and Sale of Cigarettes*, para. 96.
47. *See* for example, Appellate Body Report, *Korea – Various Measures on Beef* (2001), para. 137.
48. It is interesting to note that, as discussed in Chapter 6 of this book, the scope of the non-discrimination obligations applicable to substantive SPS measures, contained in Articles 2.3 and 5.5 of the SPS Agreement, is not delimited by a requirement of 'like' products. Instead they apply even if the affected products are not like (i.e., not in a competitive relationship), as long as the SPS risk posed by the compared products is similar (i.e., 'similar conditions' prevail). *See* further on this point, Prévost, D., 'National Treatment in the SPS Agreement: A Sui Generis Obligation' in A. Kamperman Sanders (ed.), *The Principle of National Treatment in International Economic Law*. Edward Elgar Press, Cheltenham (2014) 125-160. In *Korea – Radionuclides*, the panel distinguished the concept of 'similar conditions' in Article 2.3 of the SPS Agreement from that of 'like products' in Annex C.1(a), noting that the former is broad and can encompass specific products, specific risks, or specific territorial differences (such as the presence of a pest or disease). Panel Report, *Korea – Radionuclides*, para. 7.392.

guidance,[49] requiring a determination of the nature and extent of the competitive relationship between the products compared using four traditional indicators.[50]

However, under GATT case law, if a distinction is made between products purely on the basis of their origin, it can be presumed that the products are 'like',[51] thus an analysis of the nature and extent of their competitive relationship on the basis of the traditional likeness test is not necessary. In *Korea – Radionuclides,* Japan relied on this case law to argue that products from Japan were to be presumed 'like' Korean domestic products, as Korea's measures (additional testing requirements for radionuclides following the nuclear accident at Fukushima) targeted only Japan and were therefore origin based. The panel, and on appeal the Appellate Body, disagreed with this argument, noting that the additional testing requirements did not distinguish between Japanese and Korean products based *solely* on origin. In fact, the Appellate Body doubted whether such a presumption of likeness is possible under the SPS Agreement due to the fact that SPS measures, by definition,[52] are measures applied to protect human, animal, or plant life or health from risks in food or feed, or from pests or diseases, or to prevent or limit certain damage from pests. This definition of an SPS measure raises the question of 'whether a procedure to check and ensure the fulfilment of SPS measures is at all capable of making a distinction between products based exclusively on their origin and thus whether likeness may be presumed in the context of Annex C(1)(a)', according to the Appellate Body.[53] In the case at hand it was unnecessary to decide this question as it was clear that origin was not the sole basis of the additional testing requirements imposed by Korea.[54] Instead, the Appellate Body recognized that Korea's measures could not be separated from the public health concerns underlying them, following the Fukushima nuclear accident,[55] and thus no presumption of likeness could be made. This important ruling shows regard for the health-related regulatory objectives inherent in distinctions in conformity assessment procedures, even when they target specific countries, making a presumption of 'likeness' unsuitable.

Where likeness cannot be presumed, it is necessary to establish the nature and extent of the competitive relationship between the products compared to determine whether they are 'like'.[56] For this purpose, case law traditionally relies on an open list of factors, including the physical characteristics of the products, their end use,

49. Panel Report, *Korea – Radionuclides*, para. 7.393. Here the panel concluded that 'the same likeness criteria under Article III:4 of the GATT 1994 are appropriate for an analysis under Annex C(1)(a).'
50. Appellate Body Report, *EC – Asbestos*, para. 99. *See also* Panel Report, *Korea – Radionuclides*, para. 7.391.
51. *See* Panel Reports, *Canada – Autos*, para. 10.74; *India – Autos*, paras 7.174-7.176; *China – Publications and Audiovisual Products*, paras 7.1496-7.1498.
52. The definition of an SPS measure is found in Annex A.1 of the SPS Agreement.
53. Appellate Body Report, *Korea – Radionuclides*, para. 5.233.
54. *Ibid.*, para. 5.234.
55. *Ibid.*, paras 5.220-5.241.
56. Appellate Body Report, *EC – Asbestos*, para. 99. This competition-oriented perspective was reiterated in Panel Report, *Korea – Radionuclides*, para. 7.393.

consumer tastes and habits and the tariff regimes of other Members.[57] The regulatory objective underlying the different treatment is, in principle, irrelevant to the 'likeness' analysis.[58] As a result, the fact that the discriminatory treatment inherent in a particular conformity assessment measure was intended to address a health risk rather than to protect the domestic industry would be irrelevant to the determination of whether the products at issue are 'like'.

However, this is not to say that the health risks inherent in a product can never be of relevance to the 'like product' analysis, and thus to the question of whether the regulatory measure at issue falls within the scope of the national treatment obligation. In *EC – Asbestos*, in examining the national treatment obligation in Article III:4 of the GATT 1994, the Appellate Body considered the health risks associated with chrysotile asbestos fibres, which are carcinogenic, as pertinent in the examination of likeness between these products and cement-based products containing polyvinyl-alcohol, cellulose and glass fibres, under the likeness criteria of physical properties and consumer tastes and habits.[59] It is clear, therefore, that the SPS risk inherent in a particular product would be a relevant consideration to be taken into account by a panel or the Appellate Body when determining the likeness of the products involved, if it affects the nature and extent of the competitive relationship between the products compared, for instance, if it is reflected in the product characteristics (e.g., an increased level of toxins) or affects consumer preferences in a manner that sufficiently weakens the competitive relationship between the products involved to render them not 'like'. Where the difference in SPS risk does not undermine the competitive relationship between the products, however, the products are 'like' and the obligation to treat the imported product in a no less favourable manner applies. This highlights the economic or 'competition-oriented perspective' to the interpretation of the national treatment obligation,[60] which leaves no room for consideration of regulatory objectives in themselves.[61] This may raise concerns, as legitimate health policy reasons may

57. Panel Reports, *US – Poultry (China)*, para. 7.425 and *Korea – Radionuclides*, para. 7.393; following the GATT jurisprudence on 'like products' in the GATT Working Party Report on *Border Tax Adjustments*, para. 18 and further developed in Appellate Body Reports, *Japan – Alcoholic Beverages II*, p. 20 and *EC – Asbestos*, para. 101. These criteria have been developed in the case law to 'assist in the task of sorting and examining the relevant evidence' regarding the 'likeness' analysis but are, as emphasized by the Appellate Body, 'neither a treaty-mandated nor a closed list of criteria that will determine the legal characterisation of products.' *See* Appellate Body Report, EC – Asbestos, para. 102.
58. *See* Panel Report, *Japan – Alcoholic Beverages II*, paras 6.16-6.17, implicitly affirmed in Appellate Body Report, *Japan – Alcoholic Beverages II*, 115.
59. Appellate Body Report, *EC – Asbestos*, para. 113.
60. Panel Report, *Korea – Radionuclides*, para. 7.393.
61. Note, however, that one Appellate Body member wrote a separate concurring opinion in *EC – Asbestos*, arguing that the extent of the scientific evidence showing that chrysotile asbestos fibres are carcinogenic means that even in the absence of evidence regarding differences in physical characteristics and consumer tastes and habits, cement-based products containing chrysotile asbestos fibres are not 'like' cement-based products containing PCG fibres. This Appellate Body Member rejected the decisive nature of the test of the competitive relationship of the products on the market, stating: 'the necessity or appropriateness of adopting a "fundamentally" economic interpretation of the "likeness" of products under Article III:4 of the GATT 1994 does not appear to me to be free from substantial doubts.' Appellate Body Report, *EC – Asbestos*, para. 154.

underlie distinctions in conformity assessment procedures with respect to competing products.

Interestingly, unlike the GATT 1994, the SPS Agreement does not contain an exceptions provision justifying less favourable treatment of like imported products when that is necessary to protect health.[62] In the non-discrimination obligation applicable to substantive SPS measures, in Article 2.3 of the SPS Agreement, this does not present problems, as its prohibition extends only to 'arbitrary' or 'unjustifiable' discrimination between countries where 'identical or similar conditions prevail'. Thus, where a health justification for discriminatory treatment exists or there are differences in the SPS situations in the relevant countries, no violation of Article 2.3 can be found since the prevailing SPS-conditions are not 'similar' or the different treatment is not 'arbitrary or unjustifiable'. However, the non-discrimination obligation applicable to conformity assessment procedures in Annex C.1(a) is not similarly restricted but instead prohibits *all* 'less favourable' treatment of 'like' products in control, inspection or approval procedures. This seems to call for more flexibility in the interpretation of the national treatment obligation in Annex C.1(a) of the SPS Agreement, in order to achieve the trade/health balance aimed at by the agreement.[63]

In light of this problem, panel in *EC – Approval and Marketing of Biotech Products* considered that 'less favourable manner', in the second step of the national treatment analysis of Annex C.1(a), entails more than just differentiation between products that have been found to be 'like'.[64] It viewed as insufficient the mere proof that the approval procedure was conducted in a manner unfavourable for a particular imported product, 'if the relevant Member's conduct is explained by factors or circumstances unrelated to the foreign origin of the product'.[65] In that case, the panel was of the view that it had not been established that the alleged less favourable manner of processing applications for imported biotech products was explained by the *foreign origin* of these products rather than, for instance, by a 'perceived difference between biotech products and novel non-biotech products in terms of the required care in their safety assessment, risk for the consumer, etc.'.[66] It thus found no violation of the second clause of Annex C.1(a). As there was no appeal in this case, the Appellate Body has not had the opportunity to review this ruling.

62. Article XX of the GATT contains the general exceptions that justify a violation of any GATT obligation, thus including the non-discrimination obligations, provided that the conditions set out in the relevant exception are met, and the measure is not applied in a manner constituting arbitrary or unjustifiable discrimination or a disguised restriction on trade. The relevant exception for measures necessary to protect the life or health of humans, animals of plants is contained in para. (a) of Article XX.
63. This balance is reflected in the Preamble to the SPS Agreement which emphasizes the objective to strike a balance between Members' rights to adopt or enforce measures necessary to protect human, animal or plant life or health with the requirement that the measures not be applied in a manner which would constitute a means of arbitrary or unjustifiable discrimination or a disguised restriction on international trade. As noted by the panel in *Korea – Radionuclides*, '[t]his balance is similar to that expressed by the national treatment rule in Article III:4 as qualified by the exceptions in Article XX of the GATT 1994.' (para. 7.391).
64. Panel Report, *EC – Approval and Marketing of Biotech Products*, para. 7.2408.
65. *Ibid.*, para. 7.2408.
66. *Ibid.*, para. 7.2411.

This understanding of 'less favourable'[67] treatment departs from established case law on the GATT national treatment obligation, in that it allows 'less favourable' treatment of like imported products in conformity assessment procedures if this is explained by something other than their foreign origin, for example by the regulatory objective underlying the different treatment.[68] It requires the complainant to show not only that the procedure modifies the conditions of competition to the detriment of the imported product but also that such detrimental impact is due to the foreign origin of the product, rather than due to other factors. An examination of the rationale or regulatory objective of a measure allows for justification of the measure as part of the initial test of 'less favourable' treatment, contrary to the traditional national treatment analysis.

This less intrusive interpretation of the prohibition on 'less favourable' treatment of imports in conformity assessment procedures is arguably necessitated by the balancing objective of the SPS Agreement. In view of the fact that, unlike the GATT 1994, there is no general exceptions provision in the SPS Agreement that could justify discriminatory treatment due to its regulatory objective, and that, unlike the non-discrimination obligations in Articles 2.3 and 5.5 of the SPS Agreement that apply to substantive SPS measures, the prohibition on less favourable treatment in Annex C.1(a) is not limited to arbitrary or unjustifiable distinctions, the panel's examination of the possible justification for the different treatment in its examination of the 'no less favourable' treatment criterion is understandable.[69]

A similar approach has been taken in the line of case law on the national treatment obligation in Article 2.1 of the WTO Agreement on Technical Barriers to Trade (TBT Agreement), where regulatory purpose has been considered in the 'less favourable treatment' analysis, in the absence of an exception provision allowing justification of discriminatory treatment.[70] A line of reasoning analogous to that

67. This ruling seems based on a misunderstanding of the finding of the Appellate Body in *Dominican Republic – Cigarettes*, where the Appellate Body held that there is no 'less favourable treatment' under Article III:4 of the GATT if the detrimental effect of the measure on imports can be explained by factors unrelated to the foreign origin of the product. *See* Appellate Body Report, *Dominican Republic – Import and Sale of Cigarettes*, para. 96. Note that subsequently the Appellate Body clarified this ruling, explaining that it did not mean to imply that regulatory justifications are relevant to the 'less favourable treatment' analysis in Article III:4 of the GATT, but only that a 'genuine link' is needed between the challenged measure and the detrimental impact on imports. *See* Appellate Body Report, *US – Clove Cigarettes (2012)*, fn. 372 to para. 179 and Appellate Body Reports, *US – COOL (Article 21.5) (2015)*, para. 5.358.
68. This approach has been consistently rejected in GATT jurisprudence. *See* for example, Panel Reports, *Canada – Wheat Exports and Grain Imports* (2004), para. 6.214.
69. Scott, *supra* note 21, 230 sees this finding as coming close to endorsing a 'quasi-exception within the [national treatment] rule itself' similar to the 'mandatory requirements' doctrine in the EC. She notes that this exception is broader than that in Article XX of the GATT, as it makes room for new and diverse concerns. However, she regards the allocation of the burden of proof on the complainant to demonstrate that the differential treatment is explained by factors other than the foreign origin of the products as 'less than appropriate'.
70. Appellate Body Report, *US – Clove Cigarettes*, WT/DS406/AB/R, para. 174. Here the Appellate Body referred to the sixth recital of the Preamble of the TBT Agreement and stated that 'the object and purpose of the TBT Agreement is to strike a balance between, on the one hand, the objective of trade liberalization and, on the other hand, Members' right to regulate'. On this basis, and taking into account that the context for interpretation of the national treatment

followed in the case law on the TBT Agreement would seem to form a more appropriate basis for finding that the national treatment obligation to undertake conformity assessment procedures in a 'no less favourable' manner in Annex C.1(a) of the SPS Agreement only prohibits distinctions that do not stem exclusively from legitimate regulatory distinctions. Support for such an interpretation could best be sought in the object and purpose of the SPS Agreement, namely to balance trade liberalization with the legitimate right of Members to regulate to protect health in their territories, as reflected in its preamble;[71] and in the context for Annex C.1(a) which includes the absence of an exceptions provision to allow justification of legitimate regulatory distinctions.

As developed in the TBT case law, this assessment should be based on an objective examination of the design, structure, operation, and application of the measure at issue and not on mere 'perceived differences' in risk, as allowed by the panel in *EC – Approval and Marketing of Biotech Products*. The latter seems to go too far, allowing less favourable treatment that does not respond to actual differences in SPS risk. It is to be hoped that, if faced with this issue in a future dispute, the Appellate Body will clarify the reasoning behind the more limited interpretation of the 'no less favourable' manner requirement along the lines of the TBT case law.

Nevertheless, it is clear that an interpretation of the prohibition on a 'less favourable' manner of conducting conformity assessment procedures as including an enquiry into the legitimate regulatory purpose of the different treatment is correct. It would be unsustainable, in light of the balancing objective of the SPS Agreement, to impose an absolute prohibition on differences in the manner in which control, inspection and approval procedures are carried out if they modify the conditions of competition to the detriment of imported products. This would leave no scope for justified distinctions in procedures that are founded on legitimate regulatory concerns, such as the poor credibility of the certification system of the exporting country, the weakness of its laboratory testing facilities or inspection capacity or the pervasiveness of zoonosis in the exporting region. Such an approach would risk undermining WTO Members' ability to ensure compliance with their SPS regulations effectively and to protect against SPS risks, contrary to the stated objective of the SPS Agreement.

[C] Equitable Fees

Not only lengthy and discriminatory procedures but also high costs for conformity assessment procedures and certifications can prevent producers of agri-food products, particularly small producers in developing countries, from demonstrating compliance with substantive SPS measures, and thus exclude them from participation in food

obligation in the TBT Agreement includes the lack of an exceptions provision, the Appellate Body found that this obligation 'should not be interpreted as prohibiting any detrimental impact on competitive opportunities for imports in cases where such detrimental impact on imports stems exclusively from legitimate regulatory distinctions.'

71. This objective is reflected in the first recital of the Preamble of the SPS Agreement.

supply chains.[72] Fees for these procedures and certifications may be misused to protect domestic producers from competition.

To address this problem, Annex C.1(f) contains the requirement of equitable application of fees imposed for the procedures at issue. While what is 'equitable' is defined in relation to the fees charged to domestic producers and other Members, this is not a non-discrimination provision in the strict sense. The criterion of equity rather than no less favourable treatment in respect of fees seems to be intended to reflect the fact that actual costs of procedures may justifiably differ depending on the origin of the products (e.g., if inspectors have to travel further to inspect a production site in a particular Member, or if the SPS status of a Member necessitates more frequent or complex controls and testing than that of another).

Aside from the above-mentioned relational standard, subparagraph (f) also contains an objective standard, namely that the relevant fees 'should' be no higher than the actual cost of the service. This seems to be a hortatory element in the provision and would arguably allow higher fees when considerations of equity would not prevent this. Read in light of Article 10.1 of the SPS Agreement that obliges Members to take account of developing country Members' needs in applying their SPS measures, equity could be seen to allow Members to apply differential fees for Members at different levels of development,[73] thereby facilitating developing country producers' participation in GVCs.

[D] Systems of Prior Approval and Tolerance Determination for Food or Feed

The most controversial aspect of the rules in the SPS Agreement on control, inspection and approval systems, as already apparent in the negotiations towards this agreement,[74] relates to the disciplines to be applied to prior approval systems (also called pre-marketing approval). The final outcome of the negotiations on this issue is the brief unnumbered provision found at the very end of Annex C.1 dealing with systems for prior approval and the establishment of tolerance levels for contaminants. This paragraph states:

> Where an importing Member operates a system for the approval of the use of food additives or for the establishment of tolerances for contaminants in food, beverages or feedstuffs which prohibits or restricts access to its domestic markets for products based on the absence of an approval, the importing Member shall

72. *See for example* Redden, J., *The Role of Aid for Trade in Building the Capacity of Developing Country Firms to Meet Sustainability Standards.* Geneva: International Centre for Trade and Sustainable Development (2017) 28-29 reporting that a mango producer in Burkina Faso struggled to obtain the required Hazard Analysis and Critical Control Points certification due to the very high costs of the certification process and foreign consultant's fees.
73. Scott, *supra* note 21, 221-222.
74. Breen, J.M., 'Agriculture' in Terence P. Stewart (ed.), *The GATT Uruguay Round: A Negotiating History (1986–1992), Vol. IV: The End Game.* Kluwer, The Hague/London/Boston (1999) 41-45, 233-234.

consider the use of a relevant international standard as the basis for access until a final determination is made.

While the rest of Annex C.1 deals in general with conformity assessment procedures in relation to substantive SPS measures, this subparagraph addresses a more specific situation. This is the situation where the procedures in place condition market access for food or feed[75] on prior approval of the relevant additives by the importing Member or restrict access pending the determination of a tolerance level for the relevant contaminants. Such procedures amount to provisional import bans or import restrictions, pending the decision on approval or tolerance level.[76] They are not based on an assessment of risk but are rather in the nature of precautionary measures in place until a final decision is taken on approval or tolerance determination.

In practice, two situations can be distinguished in this regard. The first is where the regulating Member maintains the import ban or restriction temporarily, while an assessment is made of whether the food additive is safe and should be approved, or of what level of contaminants in food are safe and should be tolerated. Examples of this situation abound in the area of food-safety.[77] One illustration is the application by Australia and New Zealand of a 'limit of determination' level for residues of agricultural or veterinary chemicals in food, pending the conduct of a risk assessment to determine the safe residue level.[78] Another example is the prior approval system in place in the European Union (EU) for genetically modified foods.[79] In principle, the importing Member will proceed to obtain the necessary evidence to carry out a risk assessment on which to base its final determination. While this situation may lead to (sometimes lengthy) delays in gaining market access, the onus is on the importing Member to demonstrate the safety risk or lift the restriction on market access. Unjustifiable delays in the operation of prior approval systems would be caught by the discipline of Annex C.1(a), as discussed above.[80]

However, a second type of situation arises where an importing Member does not have a strong interest in the product involved, for example, with respect to exotic fruits which are imported in small quantities, or in the harmful substance at issue, for example, outdated pesticides, and is therefore unwilling to commit the necessary resources to conduct a risk assessment on the basis of which to decide on approval or

75. It is interesting to note that this obligation is limited to food or feed and does not apply to risks from pests or diseases that are not food-related.
76. *See* Panel Report, *EC – Approval and Marketing of Biotech Products*, para. 7.1359. While the EU's prior approval system for the marketing of biotech products was not challenged in that case, the complainants preferring to focus on the delays in the *application* of this prior approval system, the panel did note that the prior approval system itself amounted to a provisional marketing ban.
77. As noted by Foster, most developed countries have prior approval systems in place. Foster, C. (2008) 'Prior Approval Systems and the Substance: Procedure Dichotomy under the WTO SPS Agreement' 42 *Journal of World Trade* 1203-1217, 1207.
78. Food Standards Australia New Zealand, *Australia New Zealand Food Standards Code* - Standard 1.4.2 http://www.foodstandards.gov.au/code/Pages/default.aspx (accessed 31 October 2019).
79. Regulation (EC) No. 1829/2003 of the European Parliament and of the Council of 22 September 2003 on genetically modified food and feed, OJ L 268, 18/10/2003 p. 0001–0023.
80. *See* Panel Report, *EC – Approval and Marketing of Biotech Products*, para. 8.6, where delays in the application of the EU's prior approval system for marketing of biotech products were found to be unjustified and in violation of Annex C.1(a).

tolerance levels. In such prior approval systems, the market access restriction remains in place indefinitely, or until the *exporting* Member can bring sufficiently convincing scientific evidence assessing the risk and establishing its safety to the satisfaction of the importing Member. An example is the EU Novel Foods Regulation,[81] which imposes a prior approval requirement for foods that are considered 'novel', namely those derived from new technological processes and those that have no significant history of consumption in Europe before 1997. It thus catches traditional products of biodiversity from several developing countries that have been safely consumed in those countries for centuries and are important sources of export revenue. Approval of these novel foods requires the exporter to present scientific evidence demonstrating the safe consumption of the novel food in question for at least twenty-five years. The high costs and duration of the application procedure deter exporters from applying for such approval.[82] Another example is the 2005 EU regulation on pesticide residue levels, which sets a maximum residue level (MRL) of 0.01 mg/kg (i.e., the limit of determination) for those pesticides that had not been authorized on a particular product or for which no data was available to prove their safety.[83] Reassessment of MRLs is based on scientific information provided by the pesticide industry, and as this industry has no interest in funding research on older pesticides, it no longer markets, no data is available and the default strict MRL remains applicable. Such prior approval or tolerance determination systems can lead to serious market access barriers.

It is therefore important to ensure that prior approval and tolerance determination systems are disciplined to address their significant trade-restrictive effects beyond those caused by undue delays, discrimination or procedural irregularities. However, the last subparagraph of Annex C.1 applies only a very weak discipline to such systems, requiring Members to 'consider' conditioning market access in such cases on the relevant international standard, until a final determination is made. If prior approval and tolerance determination systems were seen as covered only by this soft discipline, there is a risk that a broad loophole could be created in the rules of the SPS Agreement. This is because the obligation in the last subparagraph of Annex C.1 is a far cry from the disciplines in the rest of the SPS Agreement, which require that an SPS measure *must* be based either on an international standard or on a risk assessment meeting the requirements in the relevant provisions of the agreement.[84] Precautionary measures are only allowed where scientific evidence is insufficient to permit a risk assessment to

81. Regulation (EU) 2015/2283 of the European Parliament and of the Council of 25 November 2015 on novel foods, amending Regulation (EU) No. 1169/2011 of the European Parliament and of the Council and repealing Regulation (EC) No. 258/97 of the European Parliament and of the Council and Commission Regulation (EC) No. 1852/2001 OJ L 327, 11.12.2015, pp. 1-22.
82. The EU Novel Foods Regulation has been the subject of extensive discussions in the SPS Committee, which provides a forum for WTO Members to discuss STCs with regard to each other's SPS measures. *See* WTO SPS Information Management System, STC nr. 238, *Application and modification of the EU Regulation on Novel Foods* http://spsims.wto.org/en/SpecificTradeConcerns/View/11 (accessed 31 October 2019).
83. Regulation (EC) No. 396/2005 of the European Parliament and of the Council of 23 February 2005 on maximum residue levels of pesticides in or on food and feed of plant and animal origin and amending Council Directive 91/414/EEC, OJ L 70, 16.3.2005, pp. 1-16.
84. These disciplines are discussed in Chapter 6 of this book.

be conducted, and where the imposing Member has complied with the remaining requirements of Article 5.7, including the obligation to seek to obtain the necessary information for a proper risk assessment and to review the measures within a reasonable period.[85]

Systems of prior approval and tolerance determination sit uncomfortably with these substantive disciplines.[86] This is because they are premised on the idea that the need for precaution is exceptional, arising only in situations of insufficient scientific evidence, i.e., where a risk assessment is impossible. In other cases, measures must be firmly based on science, embodied in either an international standard or a risk assessment. However, in the second situation mentioned above, systems of prior approval and tolerance determination adopt a precautionary approach *not* due to the impossibility of conducting a risk assessment, but due to the choice of a Member not to allocate resources to assessing risks in areas that are not a priority for that Member. To protect health in the absence of a risk assessment to determine the safety of the product or substance at issue, Members prohibit such products or adopt very restrictive measures, such as 'limit of determination' residue levels.

The question of the relationship between the last subparagraph of Annex C.1 and the rest of the SPS Agreement is problematic. As stated above,[87] Annex C is an integral part of the SPS Agreement and must be read together with it. SPS measures that fall within its scope of application, also those covered by the last subparagraph of Annex C.1, are also subject to all the relevant disciplines of the SPS Agreement, as clearly stated in Article 8. However, the application of all the remaining rules of the SPS Agreement to systems for prior approval and tolerance determination would seem to make redundant the Annex C.1 provision dealing *specifically* with these systems. The flexibility allowed by its weak discipline would effectively be eliminated entirely by the application of the normal SPS disciplines on harmonization and risk assessment. Such a result would be contrary to the principle of effective treaty interpretation. Further concerns have arisen that this would mean that most prior approval systems are inconsistent with the SPS Agreement, a 'far-reaching and untenable' consequence,[88] which could 'potentially expose the SPS Agreement and the WTO itself to ridicule'.[89] An appropriate interpretation of Annex C.1 is thus needed that gives meaning to its terms while not undermining the trade/health balance of the SPS Agreement.

As mentioned above, the disciplines to be applied to prior approval systems were a contentious aspect of the negotiations towards the SPS Agreement, and agreement was reached to include only the very watered-down discipline we currently find in the last subparagraph of Annex C.1. Nevertheless, no explicit carve-out was provided for

85. On the requirements under Article 5.7 of the SPS Agreement, *see* Chapter 6 of this book.
86. This tension between pre-marketing approval systems and the rules of Articles 2.2 and 5.1 is noted in Downes, C., *The Impact of WTO SPS Law on EU Food Regulations*. Springer, Cham (2014) 137 and Foster, *supra* note 77, at 1213.
87. *See supra* section §1.03.
88. Downes, *supra* note 86, at 137.
89. Foster, *supra* note 77, at 1213.

prior approval systems. This seems to indicate an instance of 'constructive ambiguity'[90] resulting from a compromise reached in the negotiations on this contentious issue. A treaty interpreter, faced with a future challenge to a system of prior approval or tolerance determination under the last subparagraph of Annex C.1, would be obliged to give some meaning to this provision, in light of the principle of effective treaty interpretation.

The object and purpose of Annex C.1, as seen from its remaining provisions, appears to be to apply additional disciplines to control, inspection and approval procedures to prevent them undermining the trade liberalization gains from the remaining disciplines of the SPS Agreement. This is in keeping with the overall objective of the SPS Agreement, which aims to reduce the trade-restrictive effects of legitimate SPS measures by disciplining those aspects that can unnecessarily increase their negative impact on trade. Consequently, reading the last subparagraph of Annex C.1 in the context of Article 8, and in light of the object and purpose of Annex C.1 and of the SPS Agreement as a whole, this subparagraph can be seen as establishing an additional discipline on the types of systems covered by it, rather than creating a wide loophole for such systems to escape the remaining rules of the SPS Agreement. In this light, the last subparagraph of Annex C.1 can be regarded as aiming to reduce the great trade-restrictive effect of the use of systems of prior approval and tolerance determination by encouraging reference to international standards to fill the gap *pending the final decision* on approval or tolerance determination on the basis of scientific risk assessment.

More specifically, during the reasonable period of time allowed by Article 5.7 for seeking additional information to conduct a risk assessment and review a provisional measure, which in the case of prior approval systems can be rather lengthy, Annex C.1 would oblige Members to consider allowing market access for products conforming to relevant international standards. The normal requirements of Article 5.7 would continue to apply as well, and the Member would have to seek to obtain the additional information necessary to conduct a risk assessment and review its measure in a reasonable period of time. These disciplines would serve to mitigate the problems experienced by exporting Members caused by *justifiable* delays in prior approval and tolerance determination procedures while risks are assessed, while still allowing an importing Member sufficient space to assure itself of the safety of the products at issue before allowing importation. However, when prior approval systems are in place with no efforts from the importing Member to seek additional information to conduct a risk assessment, or to review the measure in a reasonable period of time, the last subparagraph of Annex C.1 would not 'save' such systems from the substantive obligations of the SPS Agreement. Instead, such systems would fall foul of the obligation of a scientific basis in Articles 2.2 and 5.1 of the SPS Agreement and not meet

90. As noted by former WTO Director-General Mike Moore, WTO negotiators resorted to what has been called 'constructive ambiguity' in framing treaty provisions on controversial issues vaguely, as a diplomatic means of enabling consensus to be reached. Moore, M., *A World Without Walls: Freedom, Development, Free Trade and Global Governance*. Cambridge: Cambridge University Press (2003) 111.

the requirements of Article 5.7 for exemption from these disciplines, leaving no room for the application of the last paragraph of Annex C.1.

This reading of the relationship between Annex C.1 and the rest of the SPS Agreement would ensure that Members do not use prior approval and tolerance determination systems in a manner that undermines the sensitive trade/health balance sought by the SPS Agreement by avoiding the need to have (or seek) a scientific basis for trade-restrictive SPS measures. Yet it respects the right of Members to use prior approval systems as a tool to keep out potentially risk food products pending a determination of their safety.

§7.05 CONCLUSIONS

The balance struck in the substantive rules of the SPS Agreement in order to distinguish legitimate health protection from disguised protectionism can be undermined if the procedures used to determine compliance with SPS requirements are undisciplined. These procedures may be abused to throw down practical barriers that restrict the possibilities for suppliers to access the markets of their trading partners and to benefit from participation in GVCs for food production. These problems may be especially acute for suppliers in less-developed WTO Members and particularly for small- and medium-sized enterprises, due to their lack of resources to devote to complex and costly procedural requirements to demonstrate compliance with SPS measures. This would diminish the possibilities for these Members and their producers to share in the gains of trade.

Article 8 and Annex C of the SPS Agreement bring some discipline to conformity assessment procedures and prior approval systems used by Members. Their provisions broadly speaking aim to ensure that such procedures are not lengthier, costlier or more burdensome than is reasonable and necessary, and that they do not discriminate against imports. By doing so they address some of the most important procedural constraints to GVC participation in the food sector, and thereby prevent the misuse of control, inspection and approval procedures for protectionist purposes.

However, it is important that this liberalizing effect does not come at the cost of effective conformity assessment procedures. The increasing fragmentation of the supply chain for food production makes it difficult for Members to regulate the various stages of, and inputs in, food production. Consequently, conformity assessment procedures gain importance to ensure the safety of traded agri-food products. Unreasonable limits on control, inspection and approval systems would undermine the confidence of importers in the safety of foreign agri-food products and thus be counterproductive. Reliable conformity assessment systems operate to generate the necessary trust for trade in the sensitive area of food by protecting the integrity of food regulatory systems.

The resulting need for a careful balance between trade and health objectives in the interpretation and application of Annex C rules has been repeatedly recognized in the jurisprudence. Working with sometimes vague or ambiguous provisions and in the context of factually complex cases, WTO panels have shouldered their responsibility to protect this balance within the limits imposed by the negotiated rules. It is to be hoped that the WTO dispute settlement system will survive the current institutional crisis it faces and continue to serve the Members in this way,[91] also with regard to the future interpretation of the rules on prior approval systems and their controversial relationship with the rest of the SPS Agreement. While direct challenges to the latter systems have yet to materialize, this contribution proposes an interpretation of the relevant rules that could serve to secure the trade/health balance that is at the core of the SPS Agreement.

91. At the time of writing, the WTO dispute settlement system faces an imminent threat of collapse, as the United States' continued blocking of the process for appointment of new Appellate Body members has made it impossible for appeals to be heard, and therefore also for appealed panel reports to be adopted and become binding. While a discussion of this crisis is outside the scope of this contribution, it forms the context for this discussion as, without a functioning dispute settlement system, the possibility for rules-based resolution of trade disputes through reasoned interpretation and application of negotiated rules, as reflected in the case law discussed in this chapter, will be a thing of the past.

CHAPTER 8

Food Production and Animal Welfare: An International Law Perspective

Ilja Richard Pavone

Despite growing societal concerns for animals, incremental legal reforms, and new advances in moral and political philosophy, our relationship with animals remain inherently hostile by far. Be it Concentrated Animal Feeding Operations (CAFOs), live animal markets, encroachment of wildlife habitats, we keep animals in conditions of systemic and ongoing exploitation. In countries around the world, the demand for animal meat rises as the world population increases. Animal welfare concerns are also gaining more attention as consumers perceive the links between animal health, animal welfare, and human well-being. The challenge is how to combine the unavoidable increase in food animal production while simultaneously ensuring high animal welfare standards and protecting food security.

As witnessed by the COVID-19 pandemic, which probably originated in a wet market in Wuhan, where minimum health and welfare standards are simply inexistent, animal welfare is a matter that has a direct impact on the health of the human being.

This chapter surveys the state of the art of animal law in the field of meat production, focusing on existing standards set up by the Office International des Epizooties (OIE). Against this background, the failures and weaknesses of international law in addressing the animal issues - that have a transnational dimension - will be highlighted.

§8.01 INTRODUCTION

Since the end of World War II, there has been a progressive shift towards more intensive systems of meat production, especially in the more densely populated areas of Northern Europe, South East Asia and North America.

Statistical data show an inexorable and substantial increase in the use of animals both in agriculture and in science. In particular, the global demand for meat is rising in light of population growth (steady increase in beef and poultry's demand).[1]

Global meat output in 2018 was estimated at 336,4 million tonnes (up 1.2% from 2017): the principal meat producers are the United States (US), the European Union (EU), and emerging economies such as Brazil, China and Russian Federation.[2]

By 2050, the Food and Agricultural Organization (FAO) appraises that meat production and meat consumption will double, in particular in developing countries.[3] China, in particular, if it were to continue at the same rate of growth in meat production and import (it is the world's largest meat importer), is expected to become the first country in the world for meat consumption.[4]

The rise in meat demand has gone along with a significant transformation of the livestock sector of the agriculture industry in the past few decades, shifting from traditional family farm to large farms (Concentrated Animal Feeding Operations (CAFOs)).[5]

Modern farms are much more efficient than traditional farms, since they allow to produce cheaper and faster meat and poultry, and meat- and poultry-related products (milk and eggs).

Industrial livestock production raises, however, environmental (land degradation, impact on global warming, resource consumption), health (food insecurity, transmission of zoonotic diseases, antimicrobial resistance),[6] as well as animal welfare (conditions of slaughtering and of transportation) issues.

---

1. According to FAO statistical data, in 2014 meat consumption especially in developing countries has been growing at 56%, http://www.fao.org/faostat/en/#data/QL.
2. World poultry meat output increased by 1.3% in 2018 to 123.9 million tonnes, as productions expanded in the United States of America, the European Union, India and China, among others. Meat Market Review March 2019, Overview of global meat market developments in 2018, http://www.fao.org/3/ca3880en/ca3880en.pdf.
3. World Agriculture Towards 2030/2050, ESA Working Paper No. 12-03, http://www.fao.org/3/a-ap106e.pdf.
4. https://www.euromeatnews.com/Article-China-to-remain-the-worlds-main-consumer-of-beef/3780. The COVID-19 pandemic – according to FAO – has had a limited impact on livestock production, mainly related to the increased difficulty in transporting live animals and animal products like milk, meat and eggs to markets given that the system has showed a great resilience. *See* 'FAO Guidelines to mitigate the impact of the Covid-19 pandemic on livestock production and animal health', Rome, 2020, http://www.fao.org/3/ca9177en/CA9177EN.pdf.
5. Nowadays, most of meat is produced in CAFOs, which are high-density facilities that house hundreds or thousands of animals in confinement, where feed is brought to the animals (as opposed to livestock on grazing lands). The main attributes of CAFOs highlighted by the literature are: 'confinement feeding, separation of feed and livestock production, specialization, large size, and close vertical linkages with buyers'; J. Mac Donald, *CAFOs: Farm Animals and Industrialized Livestock Production* (Oxford Research Encyclopedias, Environmental Science, 2018), https://oxfordre.com/environmentalscience/view/10.1093/acrefore/9780199389414.001.0001/acrefore-9780199389414-e-240.
6. As stated by EFSA in its Special Report No. 31/2018 (Animal Welfare in the EU): 'The safety of the food chain is indirectly affected by the welfare of animals, particularly those farmed for food production, due to the close links between animal welfare, animal health and food-borne diseases', https://www.efsa.europa.eu/en/topics/topic/animal-welfare.

Several food-borne outbreaks have been caused by the livestock sector,[7] often aggravated by the lack of compliance with animal welfare standards;[8] indeed, it is commonly accepted that the welfare of farmed animals is strictly related to the safety of the food chain.[9]

To date, both international and domestic law have failed to address these interrelated issues. A global regulation of meat production would be instead necessary given its transboundary dimension (meat as well as living animals are imported and exported worldwide), in order to avoid a jeopardized protection. A global regulation of livestock production would be in line with the Manhattan Principles, *One World, One Health* (2008) that recognize the essential link between human, domestic animal and wildlife health.[10]

The COVID-19 pandemic has taught us that we must transform the global food system production into a mechanism that should be first based on respect of animal welfare as a pre-condition for protecting human health and the environment. Indeed, the main driver of zoonotic diseases is related to the asymmetric relationship between the human being and animals.[11] Consumption of meat from both farmed and wild animals is, indeed, a source of comorbidities.[12]

7. World Health Organization, *Food Safety Fact Sheet,* (4 June 2019), https://www.who.int/en/news-room/fact-sheets/detail/food-safety.
8. A. Brunet Marks, *A New Governance Recipe for Food Safety Regulation,* 47 Loyola University Law Journal 3, 907-968 (2016).
9. http://www.efsa.europa.eu/en/topics/topic/animal-welfare.
10. Contributing to One World, One Health: A strategic Framework for Reducing Risks of Infectious Diseases at the Animal–Human–Ecosystems Interface, FAO, OIE, UNICEF, World Bank, UNSIC (United Nations System Influenza Coordinator), https://oneworldonehealth.wcs.org/About-Us/Mission/The-Manhattan-Principles.aspx. With specific reference to zoonotic diseases – originated either from farmed or wild animals – the One Health approach, that links human health, animal health, environmental health, should deserve particular attention. For details, *see* UNEP Report, 'Preventing the Next Pandemic. Zoonotic diseases and how to break the chain of transmission', UNEP's Frontiers Report Series, 2020, section IV, pp. 39-44, Preventing the next pandemic – Zoonotic diseases and how to break the chain of transmission | UNEP – UN Environment Programme. On its application to the livestock sector, A. Peters, *Covid-19 as a Catalyst for the (Re-) Constitutionalisation of International Law: One Health – One Welfare,* ESIL Research Paper Series No. 2020-44, 1-10, at 7 (2020).
11. The risks of disease spillover from wild animals have been widely documented, as witnessed by the cases of SARS, the H5N1 bird flu virus R.G. Webster, *Wet Markets: A Continuing Source of Severe Acute Respiratory Syndrome and Influenza?,* The Lancet 363, 541-562 (2015).
12. There are several examples of infectious diseases in humans that originated in animals. For instance, HIV/AIDS was transmitted to man from a chimpanzee, probably due to the practice of bush meat trade; SARS-CoV-2 (the virus that causes COVID-19) probably spread the wet market of Wuhan through the illegal selling of the Chinese Pangolin. In 2016 this mammal was, *inter alia,* transferred from Appendix II to Appendix I of CITES. Amendment to Appendices I and II of the Convention adopted by the Conference of the Parties at its 17th meeting, Johannesburg (South Africa), 24 September-4 October 2016, https://cites.org/sites/default/files/notif/E-Notif-2016-063.pdf.

    K.G. Andersen et al., *The Proximal Origin of SARS-CoV-2,* Nature 26, 450-452 (2020); *see also* R. Espinosa, D. Tago & N. Treich, *Infectious Diseases and Meat Production,* 76 Environmental and Resource Economics 1019-1044 (2020).

For instance, the emergence of avian influenza viruses has been clearly linked to intensified poultry production systems.[13]

The issue of wet markets and zoonosis is just part of the wider problem of zoonotic disease outbreaks related to the global meat industry. Indeed, any mechanism that involves an extremely high density of animals that come into contact with human will lead to an increased risk of disease transmission.

Paradoxically intensive animal farming - under the profile of food safety - is preferable to live animal market, where animals are directly slaughtered on site with an increased risk of zoonosis.[14]

Besides health matters, the spread of CAFOs worldwide represents a damaging and ultimately unsustainable form of agriculture. The vast majority of farmed animals are raised in indoor confinement systems, where they have no sunshine, clean air, enough space. A significant implication of the shift towards factory farms has been the movement of large numbers of animals from pastures and open-air lots into confined spaces with no grass or vegetation for grazing. Factory farms have particularly severe implications for beef cattle welfare, including the intensive confinement of farmed animals in enclosures that prevent them from moving comfortably or expressing the most basic natural behaviours.

Since the side effects of meat production on the environment and human health are transnational, in this chapter I will argue that a global and harmonized regulation is necessary. Normative gaps, such as the lack of a reflection on animal welfare in environmental law and the legal weakness of animal welfare standards issued by the Office International des Epizooties (OIE), will be discussed.

§8.02 ANIMAL PROTECTION AND THE LEGAL GAP

Concern about the living conditions of farmed animals is not a novel issue. In 1964, Ruth Harrison published her well-known bestseller *Animal Machine* where she revealed the cruel realities of the factory farming in the United Kingdom (UK) and inspired the first farm animal welfare legislation.[15] In response to the huge impact of her book on the public opinion, the British authorities appointed a committee to investigate the welfare of farmed animals. The resulting account - known as The Brambell Report[16] - is the first official document addressing the problem of animal welfare. The report listed five freedoms that should be guaranteed to farmed animals, namely freedom from hunger and thirst by ready access to fresh water and a diet to

13. M.S. Dhingra, *Geographical and Historical Patterns in the Emergences of Novel Highly Pathogenic Avian Influenza (HPAI) H5 and H7 Viruses in Poultry* (Frontiers in Veterinary Sciences, 5 June 2018).
14. X. Zhang, Y. Zhao & G. Mu, *Economic Factors Contributing to the Outbreaks of Indigenous Major Infectious Diseases from Domestic Animals in China Between 2000 and 2016: A Multicountry Study*, The Lancet 390:S48 (2017).
15. R. Harrison, *Animal Machines: The New Factory Farming Industry* (Ballantine Books, 1966); C.J.C. Phillips, *The Animal Trade: Evolution, Ethics and Implications* (CABI, 2015) 55.
16. Report of the Technical Committee to Inquire into the Welfare of Animals Kept under Intensive Livestock Husbandry Systems. *See* M. Eilsher, *The Five Freedoms: A History Lesson in Animal Care and Welfare, MSU Extension 4-H Animal Science* (Michigan State University, 2019).

maintain full health and vigour; freedom from discomfort by providing an appropriate environment including shelter and comfortable resting area; freedom from pain, injury or disease by prevention or rapid diagnosis and treatment; freedom to express normal behaviour by providing sufficient space, proper facilities and company of the animal's own kind; freedom from fear and distress by ensuring conditions and treatment which avoid mental suffering.

The five freedoms offered a scientific and philosophical background in order to protect animals under human custody from unnecessary forms of cruelty.

The development of animal welfare science has proved that not only terrestrial animals but also fish experience pain and suffering, overwhelming the previous mechanistic view of animals.[17]

The ethical debate which arose in the 1980s on the concepts of animal rights and animal welfare prompted several countries such as Australia,[18] Canada,[19] New Zealand,[20] and the United States[21] to enact welfare legislation. The minimum of modern animal welfare legislation is represented by the recognition of animal sentience,[22] which means accepting animals are capable of experiencing positive and negative feelings and prohibiting unnecessary cruelty.

---

17. Sentience is the ability to perceive or feel things and is commonly accepted as a distinctive characteristic of terrestrial and marine mammals and of invertebrates, such as cephalopods. Sentience in fish, insects, and crustaceans is, instead, still questioned. S. Proctor et al., *Searching for Animal Sentience: A Systematic Review of the Scientific Literature*, Animals 3,882-906 (2013). Directive 2010/63/EU clearly states that 'New scientific knowledge is available in respect of factors influencing animal welfare as well as the capacity of animals to sense and express pain, suffering, distress and lasting harm' (6th paragraph, preamble), and that, 'In addition to vertebrate animals including cyclostomes, cephalopods should also be included in the scope of this Directive, as there is scientific evidence of their ability to experience pain, suffering, distress and lasting harm' (8th paragraph preamble).
18. *See*, Australian Animal Welfare Standards and Guidelines, Australian Government Department of Agriculture, Water and the Environment, http://www.agriculture.gov.au/animal/welfare/standards-guidelines. Australia has developed national standards and guidelines addressing the welfare of farmed animals (sheep, cattle, poultry, exhibited animals, livestock at saleyards and depots are at various stages of development).
19. D. Fraser et al., *Toward a Harmonized Approach to Animal Welfare Law in Canada*, 59 The Canadian Veterinary Journal 293-302 (2018). In Canada, all provinces and territories have laws addressing animal welfare. The Criminal Code of Canada prohibits anyone from wilfully causing animals to suffer from neglect, pain or injury (section 446). There are, however, exceptions for 'generally accepted practices' and, furthermore, the anti-cruelty regulation only applies to 'unnecessary' cruelty.
20. *See*, Animal Welfare Matters New Zealand Animal Welfare Strategy, Ministry for Primary Industries (2013). Section 4 of the Animal Welfare Act includes under the Definition of physical, health, and behavioural needs: (a) proper and sufficient food, (ab) proper and sufficient water, (b) adequate shelter, (c) opportunity to display normal patterns of behaviour, (d) physical handling in a manner which minimizes the likelihood of unreasonable or unnecessary pain or distress, (e) protection from, and rapid diagnosis of, any significant injury or disease. The needs are however targeted according to 'the species, environment, and circumstances of the animal.'
21. *See*, Animal Welfare Act, National Agricultural Library U.S. Department of Agriculture (last visited 3 May 2020), https://www.nal.usda.gov/awic/animal-welfare-act. In the United States, the Animal Welfare Act of 1966 is a federal law that covers the welfare of animals in research, exhibition, and transport.
22. I. Roberston, *To Feel or Not to Feel; That Is the Legal Question*, The New Zealand Law Journal 10 et seq. (2017). In New Zealand, for instance, animals have been recognized as sentient through an amendment to the Animal Welfare Act ('Animal Welfare Amendment Act') adopted on 5 May

Animal welfare is a key element in agricultural and development policies, as well as one of the key components of the safety and the quality of agro-food products.[23] The EU recognized in Article 13 of the Treaty of Lisbon (Treaty on the Functioning of the European Union (TFEU)) that animals are 'sentient beings',[24] spawning secondary legislation (directives and regulations) envisaging minimum welfare standards on rearing, slaughter and transport of farm animals and specific requirements for certain species (pigs, calves, laying hens, broilers).[25]

Despite these developments, animals are worse off today than they were in the past. How could it happen? One of the reasons is that, to date, international law has failed to address the globalized factory farming. The lack of harmonized rules raises the issues of double standards and outsourcing: the higher levels of protection of animal welfare envisaged, for instance, at domestic or regional level (EU), do not apply abroad. In fact, industries in the meat sector override stricter domestic regulations by simply relocating their business. A concrete case is represented by the practice of transferring horses for slaughter from the southern borders of the United States to Mexico, where lower animal welfare standards are met.[26] This trend is on the rise due to the policy of multinational firms to produce meat directly in developing countries ('outsourcing'),[27] where less legal constraints and lower costs are met. For instance, the rise of factory farming in China has been reported in several studies.[28]

Then, as highlighted by the Animal Protection Index, there is a lack of animal welfare legislation, that are still missing in most developing countries.[29] This is highly problematic, because the main producers of meat and poultry are developing countries (Columbia, Indonesia, Iran, Mexico) or emerging economies (BRICS - Brazil, Russia, India, China, South Africa) (with the only exception of US).[30]

2015. The amended Animal Welfare Act now states 'An Act to reform the law relating to the welfare of animals and the prevention of their ill-treatment; and in particular (i) to recognize that animals are sentient.'.

23. L.J. Lara & M.H. Rostagno, *Animal Welfare and Food Safety in Modern Animal Production, Food Science, Technology and Nutrition* (Woodhead Publishing, 2018) 91 et seq.
24. Consolidated Version of the Treaty on the Functioning of the European Union, 9 May 2008, 2008, O.J. (C115) 47 (hereinafter 'TFEU'). Article 13 – which draws on the Protocol on the protection and welfare of animals, and broadens its scope – states that 'In formulating and implementing the Union's agriculture, fisheries, transport, internal market, research and technological development and space policies, the Union and the Member States shall, since animals are sentient beings, pay full regard to the welfare requirements of animals, while respecting the legislative or administrative provisions and customs of the Member States relating in particular to religious rites, cultural traditions and regional heritage.' On the value of Title II of the Lisbon Treaty, *see* P. Craig, *The Treaty of Lisbon: Process, Architecture and Substance*, 33 European Law Review 137-166 (2008).
25. For an overview on EU secondary legislation on farmed animals, I.R. Pavone, *Animal Welfare and Protection of Farm Animals in the European Union*, 45 L'Observateur des Nations Unies 7-30 (2018).
26. https://www.ams.usda.gov/mnreports/al_ls635.txt.
27. T. Kelch, *Globalization and Animal Law: Comparative Law, International Law and International Trade* (Wolters Kluwer, 2017).
28. C.J.C. Phillips, *The Animal Trade: Evolution, Ethics and Implications* (CABI, 2015) 55.
29. https://api.worldanimalprotection.org/.
30. OECD/FAO Agricultural Outlook 2018-2027, http://www.agri-outlook.org/commodities/Agricultural-Outlook-2018-Meat.pdf.

§8.03 THE CURRENT LEGAL FRAMEWORK

Despite the problem related to the lack of harmonized rules regulating transnational animal law, several states have adopted anti-cruelty laws in the last decade in line with the 'explosive rise of animal law'.[31] While animal welfare is increasingly protected in domestic jurisdictions, animal rights are still hardly recognized.[32] In fact, domestic laws on animal protection present a common structure ('anti-cruelty laws') since they – although prohibit unnecessary forms of cruelty on animals – admit violence and exploitation on animals when it is deemed as 'necessary', such as in the case of meat production, hunting, fishing, experiments.

For instance, the UK's Animal Welfare Act (AWA) 2006 prohibits 'unnecessary suffering' of animals under human control. In Italy the act against cruelty to animals, clandestine fighting and unauthorized competitions that amended the Penal Code ('Title IX-Bis, Crimes against Sentiments for Animals') envisages, in particular, the crimes of 'animal killing' (Article 544 *bis*) and 'animal abuse' (Article 544 *ter*).[33]

The ethical framework of anti-cruelty laws is based on so-called welfarism in contrast to the animal rights or abolitionist position.[34] This current of thought admits animal exploitation, but at the same time affirms that a minimum standard of welfare must be guaranteed to non-human animals and animal utilization must be strictly regulated.[35]

Against this background, a growing number of states have not only enacted anti-cruelty laws but has adopted specific policies that promote human treatment of animals and their welfare.[36]

However, animal law is jeopardized throughout the world since the same key concept of 'unnecessary suffering' is dependent upon several factors, such as advancement of science, changes in public attitudes, cultural habits, religious belief.

31. R.L. Kupp Jr, *Bioethics and the Explosive Rise of Animal Law*, 9 American Journal of Bioethics 1-2 (2009).
32. A. Peters, Toward International Animal Rights, In Studies in Global Animal Law Chapter X: 109-120 (A. Peters ed., Springer, 2020).
33. Legge 20 luglio 2004, n.189, 'Disposizioni concernenti il divieto di maltrattamento degli animali, nonché di impiego degli stessi in combattimenti clandestini o competizioni non autorizzate', in *Gazzetta Ufficiale* n. 178 del 31 luglio 2004.
34. On the difference between the animal welfare and the animal rights position, *see* G. Francione, R. Garner, *The Animal Rights Debate: Abolition or Regulation?* (Columbia University Press, 2010).
35. J. Rossi & S. Garner, Animal Welfare: A Critical Examination of the Concept, in *Encyclopedia of Food and Agricultural Ethics* (P.B. Thompson & D.M. Kaplan eds, 2014).
36. Some developing countries do have legal provisions on the protection of animals. In Northern Africa, Egypt's 2014 Constitution established under Article 45 the duty to perform 'kind treatment of animals' (alrifq bilhayawan). In India, due to the influence of the Hindu religion, which banishes the killing of cows as sacred animals as well as the consumption of beef products, animals enjoy a higher standard of protection compared to neighbouring countries. Article 5(G) of the Indian Constitutions states that 'It shall be the duty of every citizen of India to protect and improve the natural environment including forests, lakes, rivers and wildlife, and to have compassion for living creatures' and a Prevention of Cruelty to Animals Act was enacted in 1960. *See* J. Eisen, *Animals in the Constitutional State*, 15 International Journal of Constitutional Law 909-954 (2017).

In this framework, the most relevant changes have been registered in the EU, where a cruel practice such as leg-hold trap has been prohibited.[37] Furthermore, the EU has placed a ban on the import and commercialization of seals and seal products.[38] These shifts in the legislation followed a strong input by the European public opinion that requested to prohibit some of the most controversial practices on animals.

The EU has set a high level of protection for farmed animals, probably the highest in the world, spawning secondary legislation (directives and regulations) envisaging minimum welfare standards on rearing, slaughter and transport of farm animals and specific requirements for certain species (pigs, calves, laying hens, broilers). The resulting 'EU animal welfare law', which stems from the recognition of animal sentience in Article 13 TFEU (Lisbon version), protects not only farmed animals but all animals kept in captivity (laboratory animals, pets and animals in zoos).

The various categories of animals protected by EU animal welfare law can be summarized as: farmed animals, wildlife animals,[39] experimental animals, zoo animals,[40] and companion animals.[41] In the first category, farmed animals, one can highlight three different sets of rules: (1) directives and regulations which lay down minimum standards concerning the welfare of specific kinds of animals, such as laying hens,[42] calves,[43] pigs,[44] and chickens reared for meat;[45] (2) directives and regulations which contain provisions that affect all animals, including fish, bred or kept for the production of food, wool, skin or fur, or for other farming purposes (the most important act is commonly referred to as the General Farm Animals Directive,[46] followed by the

37. Council Regulation (EEC) No. 3254/91. of 4 November 1991 prohibiting the use of leghold traps in the Community and the introduction into the Community of pelts and manufactured goods of certain wild animal species originating in countries which catch them by means of leghold traps or trapping methods which do not meet international humane trapping standards.
38. Regulation (EC) No. 1007/2009 of the European Parliament and of the Council on trade in seal products.
39. With reference to wild animals and the protection of biodiversity, in 2010, the EU adopted an ambitious biodiversity strategy (2011-2020) based on six targets (protect species and habitats; maintain and restore ecosystems; achieve more sustainable agriculture and forestry; make fishing more sustainable and seas healthier; combat invasive alien species; help stop the loss of global biodiversity) and horizontal measures for its implementation (financing, partnership, knowledge base). The relevant legislation is provided by the Birds Directive and by the Habitat Directive which set up the Natura 2000 ecological network, whose legal foundation is provided by Article 192 TFEU ('Environment').
40. Council Directive 1999/22 of 29 March 1999 relating to the keeping of wild animals in zoos, 1999 O.J. (L 94) 24.
41. *See* P.D. Villa, *The EU Explores Options to Define a Policy Framework on Dog and Cat Welfare*, Welfare of companion animals in Eur.: views and perspectives (European Commission), July 2013.
42. Council Directive 1999/74, of 19 July 1999 laying down minimum standards for the protection of laying hens, 999 O.J. (L203) 53. O.J. (L 203) 53 (EC) (although there are still shortcomings, i.e., millions of male chicks are slaughtered immediately after hatching).
43. Council Directive 2008/119, of 18 December 2008 laying down minimum standards for the protection of calves, 2008 O.J. (L 10) 7 (EC).
44. Council Directive 2008/120, of 18 December 2008 laying down minimum standards for the protection of pigs, 2008 O.J. (L 47) 5 (EC).
45. Council Directive 2007/43, of 28 June 2007 laying down minimum rules for the protection of chickens kept for meat production, 2007 O.J. (L 182) 19 (EC).
46. Council Directive 1998/58, of 20 July 1998 concerning the protection of animals kept for farming purposes, 1998 O.J. (L 221) 23 (EC). One fundamental provision in the 1998 Directive is Article

EU Regulation on the protection of animals at the time of killing);[47] (3) regulations concerning food safety and animal health ('Hygiene Package').[48]

In contrast with the European area, US, one of the main producer, importers and exporters of meat and meat-related products, does not have a legislation at the federal level which comprehensively protects farmed animals. Indeed, broad strokes can be identified in the US legislation on farmed animals. The federal AWA, as a limited scope, since it only applies to '*live dogs, cats, monkeys (nonhuman primate mammals), guinea pigs, hamsters, and rabbits*'. In fact, paragraph g. of AWA is clear in this point: 'excluded from the field of application of this law are (1) birds, rats of the genus Rattus, and mice of the genus Mus, bred for use in research, (2) horses not used for research purposes, and (3) other farm animals, such as, but not limited to livestock or poultry, used or intended for use as food or fiber, or livestock or poultry used or intended for use for improving animal nutrition, breeding, management, or production efficiency, or for improving the quality of food or fiber'.

Therefore, farmed animals used in the production of food and fibre, such as horses, chicken, rabbits raised for food, veal, cattle, are not protected by this federal act. It follows that care of farmed animal welfare relies almost exclusively on science-based animal care guidelines and legislations of single states.

For example, the Humane Methods of Livestock Slaughter Act requires that livestock is rendered unconscious before slaughter.[49] The other species, such as poultry, can therefore be slaughtered without previous stunning.

3, which requires EU Member States to 'make provisions to ensure that the owners or keepers take all reasonable steps to ensure the welfare of animals under their care and to ensure that those animals are not caused any unnecessary pain, suffering or injury'.

47. Council Regulation (EC) No. 1099/2009 of 24 September 2009 on the protection of animas at the time of killing, 2009 O.J. (L 303) 1.
48. Council Regulation (EC) No. 429/2016 on the European Parliament and of the Council of 9 March 2016 on transmissible animal diseases and amending and repealing certain acts in the area of animal health ('Animal Health Law'), 2016 O.J. (L 84) 1 (explaining EU legislation on the prevention of the transmission of animal diseases to human beings, focusing on the scope and content of the recent Regulation on transmissible animal diseases); Council Regulation (EC) No. 882/2004 on the European Parliament and of the Council of 29 April 2004 on official controls performed to ensure the verification of compliance with feed and food law, animal health and animal welfare rules, 2004 O.J. (L 165) 1 (explaining that in fact, the EU recognizes that animal health and animal welfare are strictly interconnected with and contribute to food safety and the EU adopted one of the highest standards of protection of human health in this field).
49. The law was enacted on 27 August 1958 and was amended in 1978. § 1902. Human methods of slaughtering: 'In the case of cattle, calves, horses, mules, sheep, swine, and other livestock – all animals must are rendered insensible to pain by a single blow or gunshot or an electrical, chemical or other means that is rapid and effective, before being shackled, hoisted, thrown, cast, or cut.' The law also regulates the transport of equines for slaughter and regulates the handling of 'downed' animals. Downed animals are those that are too weak, sick or injured to stand. The act also did not cover downed veal calves. However, the USDA's Food Safety and Inspection Service announced in 2016 that facilities must provide humane euthanasia for veal calves who are sick, disabled or dying. Heretofore, the common practice was to toss the calves aside and hope they recover enough to walk to the abattoir on their own. This meant that suffering calves would languish for hours before being put out of their misery. With this new regulation, these calves must be humanely euthanized immediately and held back from production of food for humans.

In fact, the conventional US poultry slaughter method is represented by electric immobilization followed by throat slitting, which results in extreme suffering for birds. Controlled atmosphere killing (CAK) is a better way to kill birds and, in addition to being a cleaner and more efficient system, it eliminates many of the animal welfare problems.[50]

People for the Ethical Treatment of Animals and the Humane Society of the US support CAK as a more humane method of slaughter because the birds are unconscious before they are hung upside down and slaughtered. CAK can undoubtedly increase the efficiency of the poultry process system.[51]

There is also a federal law that covers the transport and slaughter of animals kept for food production.[52] Unfortunately, this law also does not apply to birds (chicken and turkeys) as well as aquatic species.

This limited legal framework is evidence of the power of the corporations that are involved in the meat industry. The lack of a comprehensive federal law that protects the welfare of all species of animals while they are in the CAFO or otherwise being raised for food is a serious legal gap that undermines the process towards the improvement of living conditions of livestock and animals in captivity.

§8.04 LOOKING FOR INTERNATIONAL STANDARDS

To date, reference to the welfare of animals in international law is scarce. The only treaties specifically dealing with animal welfare have been adopted at regional level by the Council of Europe (CoE). The CoE enacted in 1976 the European Convention for the Protection of Animals Kept for Farming Purposes which is a framework convention introducing principles for the housing and management of farmed animals, in particular for animals in intensive farming systems.[53] It is complemented by twelve recommendations for specific species (including goats, sheep, pigs, cattle, turkey and other domestic fowl) set up by the Standing Committee of the Convention.[54] Then, in 1979, it also approved the European Convention for the protection of animals for slaughter that covers the treatment of animals in slaughterhouses and slaughter operations. In particular, Article 12 of the Convention envisages the prerequisite of 'prior stunning' before slaughter ('animals shall be stunned by an appropriate method').[55]

International environmental law, on its own, does not deal at all with the several issues raised by livestock production (animal welfare, food safety, environmental degradation).

50. https://www.peta.org/features/case-controlled-atmosphere-killing/.
51. G.L. Francione & R. Garner, *The Animal Rights Debate: Abolition or Regulation?* (Columbia University Press, 2010) 32.
52. The so-called 'Twenty-Eight Hours Law' was adopted on 3 March 1873.
53. The Convention was followed by a 'Protocol of Amendment to the European Convention for the Protection of Animals kept for Farming Purposes' (ETS No. 145), opened for signature on 06/02/1992, not yet into force.
54. https://www.coe.int/t/e/legal_affairs/legal_cooperation/biological_safety_and_use_of_animals/farming/A_texts_documents.asp.
55. Article 17.

More in general, however, environmental law does not address the welfare of animals under human control, but, rather, it is mainly devoted to wild animals.[56] Indeed, they are mainly protected by wildlife law (Convention on International Trade in Endangered Species of Wild Fauna and Flora - CITES, International Convention for the Regulation of Whaling - ICRW) as a species under threat of extinction, but a reflection on the welfare of the single animal is, however, absent in environmental law.[57]

Since meat production has a deep impact in terms of global warming, the lack of any reference to this problem in the Paris Agreement is surprising.[58]

Intensive farming - as highlighted in detail in Chapter 12 of Justo Corti Varela - has high carbon costs: according to FAO statistics, 14.5% of all anthropogenic greenhouse gas (GhG) emissions originate from the livestock supply chain. Cattle are the main source of GhG emission contributing to 65% of the livestock sector's emissions (2,495 and 2,128 million tonnes CO_2-eq).[59]

Livestock production has a negative impact in terms of environmental degradation in two ways. First, it has a direct repercussion related to the entire industrial food and farming cycle, including inputs, equipment, production, processing, distribution, heating, cooling and waste. Then, it also has an indirect effect associated with land degradation and deforestation: in fact, natural ecosystems are mainly devoted to crop production for feeding livestock that implies lost opportunities for storing carbon that the land would offer were it not being farmed.

The International Panel on Climate Change (IPCC) Report on Climate Change and Land (2019)[60] has recognized the negative impact of beef cattle production on the environment and included a policy recommendation to reduce meat consumption, since the carbon costs of farming are very high and cutting carbon from energy and transport 'is not enough'.[61] According to the IPCC, about 23% of anthropogenic GhGs stems from agriculture and land use; therefore, the whole process related to meat production (that involves raising livestock, exploiting land, using fertilizer) is a key driver of global warming.

In fact, radical changes in the agriculture sector, achieving emissions reductions requires basic reversals in the agriculture sector, particularly in animal farming. Given

56. S.R. Harrop, *The Dynamics of Wild Animal Welfare Law*, 9 Journal of Environmental Law 287-296 (1997).
57. D. Cao & S. White (eds), *Animal Law and Welfare: International Perspectives* (Springer, 2016).
58. H. Harwatt et al., *Scientists Call for Renewed Paris Pledges to Transform Agriculture*, The Lancet (11 December 2019), https://www.thelancet.com/action/showPdf?pii=S2542-5196%2819%2930245-1.
59. http://www.fao.org/news/story/it/item/197623/icode/. *See also* the report by Greenpeace 'Farming for Failure. How European Animal Farming Fuels the Climate Emergency', September 2020, https://storage.googleapis.com/planet4-eu-unit-stateless/2020/09/20200922-Greenpeace-report-Farming-for-Failure.pdf.
60. IPCC Special Report on climate change, desertification, land degradation, sustainable land management, food security, and greenhouse gas fluxes in terrestrial ecosystems, https://www.ipcc.ch/srccl/.
61. Q. Schiermeier, *Eat Less Meat: UN Climate-Change Report Calls for Change to Human Diet*, News in Focus, Nature, 291-292 (2019).

that environmental law does not deal at all with these problems, an answer should be provided by animal law strengthening current standards.

§8.05 IN SEARCH OF INTERNATIONAL STANDARDS

To date, international animal law does not properly address animal welfare issues; indeed, there are scarce rules addressing domesticated animals.[62] In particular, welfare problems of farmed animals have been only recently and cautiously dealt with by intergovernmental organizations (IGOs). The only binding treaty on the matter is represented by a regional agreement, the already mentioned European Convention for the Protection of Animals for Slaughter.

At United Nations (UN) level, despite the absence of specific reference to the topic of animal welfare, the FAO Committee on World Food Security endorsed the recommendations contained in the report by the High Level Panel of Experts on Food Security and Nutrition on 'Sustainable Agricultural Development for Food Security and Nutrition: What Roles for Livestock?' (2016).[63] The novelty is that a part of the document is expressly devoted to animal welfare[64] and the incorporation of this paragraph in a UN official document is quite relevant:[65] In essence, the issue of animal welfare is now included within the classic domain of 'sustainability' ('society', 'economics', and 'environment'), and might become one of the key elements of sustainable agricultural policy.[66] Although animal welfare is not explicitly mentioned in the Sustainable Development Goals (SDGs),[67] the improvement of animal welfare can be considered as one of the main tools to achieve Goal 12 'Sustainable Consumption and Production'.[68]

To date, the only existing global standards on animal welfare were set up by the OIE, the most specialized IGO in the field of animal issues. The OIE was set up in 1924 in response to the threats posed to agricultural production by the spread of animal diseases.[69] Indeed, OIE focused originally on animal disease prevention and did not deal with animal welfare issues, since it aimed at protecting human economic activities that could be seriously undermined by food-borne outbreaks.[70] Rather, the OIE's

62. A. Peters, *Studies in Global Animal Law* (Springer, 2020).
63. http://www.fao.org/3/a-i5795e.pdf.
64. Paragraph VIII, 'Animal health and welfare'.
65. H. Buller, H. Blokhuis, P. Jensen & L. Keeling, *Towards Farm Animal Welfare and Sustainability*, Animals (Basel), 8(6) 1-13 (2018).
66. UNEP, Perspective Series Issue No. 34: Why is Animal Welfare Important for Sustainable Consumption and Production?, https://www.unenvironment.org/resources/perspective-series/issue-no-34-why-animal-welfare-important-sustainable-consumption-and.
67. https://sdgs.un.org/goals.
68. L. Keeling et al., *Animal Welfare and the United Nations Sustainable Development Goals*, 6 Frontiers in Veterinary Science 1-12 (2019). The SDGs and their impact on food and nutrition have been deeply analysed in the previous chapters of this book (*see* the contributions of Uche Ewelukwa Ofodile and Khaled Eltaawel).
69. https://www.oie.int/en/about-us/our-members/member-countries/. OIE is not a UN Specialized Agency. Presently OIE counts 182 Member States.
70. Appendix to the International Agreement Organic Statutes to the Office International des Epizooties; Article 4 of the Organic Statutes states as follows: 'The main objects of the Office are:

attention on animal disease prevention stemmed from a desire to safeguard human economic activity, not to protect animals against harm for the animals' own sake.[71]

OIE is a technical organization that issues general standards, guidelines and manuals on scientific issues surrounding animals, such as prevention of epizootic diseases, antimicrobial resistance, animal diseases diagnosis, promotion of animal welfare.[72] Similar to the World Health Organization (WHO) or the World Meteorological Organization, OIE acquires its legitimacy before its Member States in light of its independence from the decision-making process of politics and its scientific expertise. OIE has progressively widened its original scope now also including animal welfare.[73]

Indeed, it was not until the OIE's Strategic Plan for 2001-2005 that animal welfare was recognized as a priority (OIE, 2011f), almost eighty years after the OIE's establishment.[74] However, at the OIE General Session (1993), the OIE International Committee had already recognized the strict connection between animal welfare and animal health. Animal welfare is also one of the three pillars of the 'One Health' concept which was introduced in early 2000, affirming that human and animal health (which is strictly associated to animal welfare) are strictly interdependent and related to the health of the ecosystems.[75]

In this framework, OIE has developed a solid cooperation with FAO and WHO through a specific programme (*The Tripartite's Commitment*), with the goal of addressing risks at the human-animal-ecosystems interface.[76] Since then, the cooperation between the three Organizations has resulted in the development of the Global Action Plan on Antimicrobial Resistance.[77]

The Strategic Plan was then followed by the OIE Global Animal Welfare Strategy (2017) ('A world where the welfare of animals is respected, promoted and advanced,

---

a. To promote and co-ordinate all experimental and other research work concerning the pathology or prophylaxis of contagious diseases of livestock for which international collaboration is deemed desirable. b. To collect and bring to the attention of the Governments or their sanitary services, all facts and documents of general interest concerning the spread of epizootic diseases and the means used to control them. c. To examine international draft agreements regarding an animal sanitary measures and to provide signatory Governments with the means of supervising their enforcement.'

71. International Agreement for the Creation of an Office International des Epizooties in Paris with Appendix: the Organic Statutes of the Office International des Epizooties of 25 January 1924 (57 LTNS 135).
72. Examples of the technical role of OIE are provided by The Manual of Diagnostic Tests and Vaccines for Terrestrial Animals and the Manual of Diagnostic Tests for Aquatic Animals.
73. International Committee of the OIE, 'Animal Welfare Mandate of the OIE', Resolution No. XIV of May 2012, para. 11 (The OIE incorporate animal welfare considerations within its major functions and assume the following specific roles and functions: development of standards and guidelines leading to good animal welfare practice), available at, https://www.oie.int/about-us/key-texts/basic-texts/new-mandates/.
74. A. Petrini & D. Wilson, *Philosophy, Policy and Procedures of the World Organisation for Animal Health for the Development of Standards in Animal Welfare*, 24 Revue Scientifique et Technique 665-771 (2005).
75. https://www.oie.int/en/for-the-media/onehealth/. V.S. Slorach, *Coordination des politiques de surveillance de la santé animale et de la sécurité sanitaire des aliments 'de l'étable à la table'*, Revue scientifique et technique (OIE editeur, 2013).
76. www.oie.int/fileadmin/home/eng/Media_Center/docs/pdf/onehealthportal/Tripartite_2017.pdf.
77. https://www.who.int/antimicrobial-resistance/global-action-plan/en/.

in ways that complement the pursuit of animal health, human well-being, socio-economic development and environmental sustainability.'). The four pillars of the Global Strategy are (i) development of animal welfare standards; (ii) capacity building and education; (iii) communication with governments, organizations and the public; (iv) implementation of animal welfare standards and policies.

The OIE has devised international standards on animal welfare addressed to terrestrial animals (Terrestrial Animal Health Code) and farmed fish (Aquatic Code). Current standards on terrestrial animals include guidelines related to the transport (by sea, by land, by air), the use of animals in research and education, production systems (beef cattle, broiler chickens, dairy cattle, pigs).

The OIE's Terrestrial Animal Health Code has been described as '[t]he one intergovernmental animal regulatory instrument that encompasses a wide variety of animals, and not just endangered animals'.[78]

OIE standards are formally recognized by the World Trade Organization Agreement on the Application of Sanitary and Phytosanitary Measures as the international reference for animal health.[79]

Animal welfare - which is a key element in the Code - is defined: 'how an animal is coping with the conditions in which it lives. An animal is in a good state of welfare if (as indicated by scientific evidence) it is healthy, comfortable, well nourished, safe, able to express innate behaviour, and if it is not suffering from unpleasant states such as pain, fear, and distress. Good animal welfare requires disease prevention and appropriate veterinary treatment, shelter, management and nutrition, humane handling and humane slaughter or killing. Animal welfare refers to the state of the animal; the treatment that an animal receives is covered by other terms such as animal care, animal husbandry, and humane treatment'.[80]

Since the adoption of an amendment in 2005, the code also addresses the most pressing welfare issues regarding farmed animals, particularly (1) those arising during the transport of animals by land, sea or air; (2) the slaughter of animals for human consumption; and (3) the killing of animals for purposes of disease control (section A).[81]

However, a careful analysis of OIE standards on farmed animals discloses their significant limits. The standards - that are not binding upon Member States - do not envisage any specific prohibition of most cruel practices, nor *in situ* inspection. For instance, there is no mention of ritual slaughtering, an ancient practice that does not

78. C. Otter, S. O'Sullivan & S. Ross, Laying the Foundations for an International Animal Protection Regime, 2 *Journal of Animal Ethics* 1, 53-72 at 53 (2012); *see also* A.B. Thiermann, *International Standards: The World Organization for Animal Health Terrestrial Animal Health Code*, 34 Revue Scientifique et Technique 1, 277-281 (2015).
79. Article 3, and Annex A, para. 3(b), WTO, Agreement on the Application of Sanitary and Phytosanitary Measures, http://www.wto.org/english/docs_e/legal_e/15sps_02_e.htm. It specifically recognized the 'animal health and zoonoses, the standards, guidelines and recommendations developed under the auspice of the International Office of Epizootics'.
80. Article 7.1.1, of the Terrestrial Animal Health Code.
81. https://www.oie.int/standard-setting/terrestrial-code/.

foresee prior stunning.[82] It is, however, admitted on the basis of the freedom of religious belief both by the CoE's Convention for the Protection of Animals for Slaughter and EU Regulation 1099/2009 (Article 4, paragraph 4), which provide that Member States may allow derogations from the stunning requirement to allow for ritual slaughter (it is however banned in some European countries).[83] Other areas of concern regard, in particular, pig tail docking, extreme confinement of some farm animals for their entire lives, long-distance transport and slaughterhouse stunning.

The fact that the worst practices of industrial agriculture have not yet been eradicated raises the issue of incomplete implementation of current standards, whose poor record is a significant shortcoming in animal welfare law. The OIE standards (animal code and terrestrial code) entail detailed principles that are addressed to the whole process of meat production, but, to date, 'evidence on the actual uptake of OIE standards in domestic legislation remains scarce'.[84]

The implementation gap, as distinct from the enforcement of animal law, depends upon a range of factors. These include not only the lack of binding force of OIE's standards but their legal nature. First, these standards are the mere list of technical recommendations that are drafted by independent experts and not by politicians, while the welfare of farmed animals is a political issue; therefore, they could be considered by states as a specific tool when they adopt specific domestic legislations on farmed animals only if there is a domestic policy in this direction. While this list can be helpful to craft national laws, it does not represent an actual standard that limits or prohibits specific practices that are harmful to animal welfare, nor can it be expected to do so as OIE is not charged with such an important responsibility. Unlike other IGOs like WHO, for instance, that has the power to adopt binding regulations,[85] the OIE Constitution does not foresee this function.[86] Its power mainly relies on its 'technical nature', since its recommendations should be exclusively driven by scientific considerations.

However, the existence of this organization does not diminish the need for an international animal welfare treaty that directly seeks to deal with issues of public policy.

82. C.M. Zoethout, *Ritual Slaughter and the Freedom of Religion: Some Reflections on a Stunning Matter*, 35 Human Rights Quarterly 3, 651-672 (2013).

83. *See* Report Legal Restrictions on Religious Slaughter in Europe, March 2018, https://www.loc.gov/law/help/religious-slaughter/religious-slaughter-europe.pdf. In the Advisory Opinion of Advocate General Hogan, ICJ, 10 September 2020, Case C-336/19, it was clearly stated that 'that the practice of ritual slaughter of animals without prior stunning will result, in certain circumstances, in the products derived from that ritual being treated differently than products that have been derived from slaughter carried out in a manner which observes higher standards in the area of animal welfare' (para. 60). Therefore, consumers must be aware through a specific logo if the meat consumed, deriving from ritual slaughtering does not fully respect animal welfare standards.

84. OECD Study on the World Organization for Animal Health (OIE) Observatory: Strengthening the Implementation of International Standards, https://www.oecd-ilibrary.org/sites/c88edwww.googbcd-en/index.html?itemId=/content/publication/c88edbcd-en.

85. WHO Constitution, Arts 21-22.

86. International Agreement for The Creation of an Office International des Epizooties in Paris, 25 January 1924.

§8.06 THE TERRESTRIAL CODE AND THE WELFARE OF FARMED ANIMALS

Section 7 of the Terrestrial Code, introduced in 2005, is especially devoted to the welfare of farmed animals with reference to transport, slaughter and production systems.

Against this background, Chapter 7.5.1 of the Terrestrial Code is addressed to the 'Slaughter of Animals'. The goal of the recommendations contained in this chapter is to 'address the need to ensure the welfare of food animals during pre-slaughter and slaughter processes, until they are dead'.[87] They apply to slaughter carried out in slaughterhouse and abattoirs of domestic animals such as cattle, buffalo, bison, sheep, goats, camelids, deer, horses, pigs, ratites, rabbits and poultry.

As to the stunning methods, the guiding principles are related to the appropriate training and competence of the operators. The guidelines underline the fundamental role of the personnel engaged in all the procedures that lead to the killing of the animal; in fact, they must have a specific certificate released from a competent authority. Then, they affirm that the animals should be adequately restrained,[88] stunned[89] and slaughtered[90] 'as soon as possible'. The 'golden rule' is, therefore, that animals in restraint must be stunned, and once stunned they must be promptly bled out. The necessity of previous stunning is to date widely recognized at European level. The EU regulation on the Protection of Animals at the Time of Killing (Council Regulation (EC) No. 1099/2009) states that 'any particular, any avoidable pain, distress, or suffering during their killing shall be avoided' (Article 3). As a general requirement, stunning is compulsory before slaughtering to ensure that each animal loses consciousness and reaches a state of apathy, which must be held up until the moment of death (Article 4, paragraph 1).[91] Also the CoE's Convention for the Protection of Animals for Slaughter asserts that 'animals shall be stunned by an appropriate method' (Article 12). Technical recommendations are then made with reference to mechanical stunning ('a mechanical device should be applied usually to the front of the head and perpendicular to the bone surface')[92] and electrical stunning.[93]

Chapter 7.9 of the Terrestrial Code (Animal Welfare and Beef Cattle Production Systems) states that each slaughterhouse/abattoir should have a dedicated plan for animal welfare.

Animals should be transported to slaughter in a way that minimizes adverse animal health and welfare outcomes, and the transport should be conducted in

87. Chapter 7.5.1, para. 1.
88. Article 7.5.7, para. 1, *a*.
89. Article 7.5.7, para. 1, *b*.
90. Article 7.5.7, Para. 1, *d*.
91. Article 4, para. 1 of the Regulation states 'Animals shall only be killed after stunning in accordance with the methods and specific requirements related to the application of those methods set out in Annex I.' According to Article 2 lect. (f) of Regulation 1099/2009, stunning means 'any intentionally induced process which causes loss of consciousness and sensibility without pain, including any process resulting in instantaneous death'.
92. Article 7.5.7, para. 2.
93. Article 7.5.7, para. 2.

accordance with the OIE recommendations for the transportation of animals (Chapters 7.2. and 7.3.). In particular, animals should be handled in such a way as to avoid harm, distress or injury. Violent acts to move animals, such as crushing or breaking tails of animals, grasping their eyes or pulling them by the ears should not be allowed under any circumstances. Animal handlers should never apply an injurious object or irritant substance to animals and especially not on sensitive areas such as eyes, mouth, ears. The throwing or dropping of animals, or their lifting or dragging by body parts such as their tail, head, horns, ears, limbs, wool, hair or feathers, should not be permitted.

Measurable criteria for the welfare of beef cattle have been introduced in the Terrestrial Code. Outcome-based measurables, specifically animal-based measurables, can be useful indicators of animal welfare.[94] These are: behaviour, morbidity rates, mortality rates, changes in weight and body condition, reproductive efficiency. Reproductive efficiency can be an indicator of animal health and animal welfare status. Poor reproductive performance can indicate animal welfare problems. Examples may include: anoestrus or extended post-partum interval, low conception rates, high abortion rates, high rates of dystocia. Other criteria listed are physical appearance,[95] handling responses (improper handling can result in fear and distress in cattle),[96] complications due to routine procedure management.[97]

As to the welfare at slaughter of birds, specific considerations on the electrical stunning of birds using a waterbath are then provided; indeed, the duration between hanging on shackles and stunning should be kept to the minimum and *should not exceed one minute*.[98]

Specific standards are then established with regard to animal welfare and broiler chicken production systems. General conditions regard thermal conditions and the environment,[99] lighting,[100] air quality (with a threshold of ammonia concentration

94. Article 7, para. 9.
95. Article 7.9.4, para. 6 affirms 'Physical appearance may be an indicator of animal health and animal welfare, as well as the conditions of management. Attributes of physical appearance that may indicate compromised welfare include: presence of ectoparasites, abnormal coat colour or texture or excessive soiling with faeces, mud or dirt, dehydration, emaciation.'
96. Article 7.9.4, para. 7 states 'Indicators could include: chute or race exit speed, chute or race behaviour score, percentage of animals slipping or falling, percentage of animals moved with an electric goad, percentage of animals striking fences or gates, percentage of animals injured during handling, such as broken horns, broken legs, and lacerations, percentage of animals vocalizing during restraint.
97. Article 7.9.4, para. 8 highlights that 'Surgical and non-surgical procedures are commonly performed in beef cattle for improving animal performance, facilitating management, and improving human safety and animal welfare. However, if these procedures are not performed properly, animal welfare can be compromised. Indicators of such problems could include: post procedure infection and swelling, myiasis, mortality.'
98. Article 7.5.7, para. 3, *b*.
99. Article 7.10.4, para. 2, Lect. *a* ('thermal conditions of broilers should be appropriate for their stage of development, and extremes of heat, humidity and cold should be avoided').
100. Article 7.10.4, para. 2, Lect. *b* ('there should be an adequate period of continuous light … . there should also be an adequate period of continuous darkness').

which should not exceed 25 ppm at broiler level),[101] noise,[102] nutrition,[103] flooring, bedding, resting surfaces and litter quality (with particular welfare requirements for day-old birds, that 'should be placed on an appropriate type of flooring suitable for their size', Lect. *f*).[104]

With reference to the problem of overcrowding, which affects the free movement of broiler chicken, the Code envisages vague standards regarding stock density rather than a specific space requirement. Indeed, the Code foresees that broilers should be housed at a stock density that allows them to access feed and water and *to move and adjust their posture normally*.[105]

As to the poultry slaughter standards, one of the most cruel practices, such as 'poultry scalding', where live birds are immersed in a scalding tank, is not explicitly prohibited by the Terrestrial Code, as well as intense confinement of pigs and broiler chickens. However, the practical effectiveness of OIE standards should not be exaggerated; as Favre observes about the OIE's standards on live animal transportation, for example, they 'read like a checklist of issues that should be considered if you are going to engage in live animal transport' rather than 'an actual standard that limits or prohibits practices that are harmful to animal welfare'.[106]

In brief, the limits of OIE standards are due to two factors: the first is obvious and is related to the nature of soft law instruments that are themselves characterized by a lack of binding force.[107] The second issue is related to the fact that OIE standards are adopted by consensus ('OIE's consensus-based approach'), and it requests the absence of objectors among states; it is therefore obvious that the agreement is usually found at the lower level and the most controversial issues are not dealt.

§8.07 CONCLUSIONS

It is now commonly accepted that animal welfare, environment protection and human health are interrelated phenomena. A high standard of animal welfare means less probability of transmission of pathogens into human populations from other species.

101. Article 7.10.4, para. 2, Lect. *c* ('Adequate ventilation is required at all times to provide fresh air, to remove waste gases such as carbon dioxide and ammonia, dust and excess moisture content from the environment. Ammonia concentration should not routinely exceed 25 ppm at broiler level').
102. Article 7.10.4, para. 2, Lect. *d* ('[...] exposure of broilers to sudden or loud noises should be minimised where possible to prevent stress and fear reaction, such as piling').
103. Article 7.10.4, para. 2, Lect. *e* ('Broilers should always be fed a diet appropriate to their age and genetics, which contains adequate nutrient to meet their requirements for good health and welfare').
104. Article 7.10.4, para. 2, Lect. *f* ('The floor of poultry house should be preferably be easy to clean and disinfect').
105. Lect. h of Article 7.10.4, para. 2.
106. D. Favre, *An International Treaty for Animal Welfare*, Animal Law, 18, 237-280, at 252 (2012).
107. J. Friedrich, *Codes of Conduct*, Vol. II (The Max Planck Encyclopedia of Public International Law, 2012) 264-275.

This relation is clearly recognized in the Guiding Principles on Animal Welfare of the Terrestrial Code.[108]

The recent 'One Welfare' concept emphasizes the link between animal welfare, human well-being, biodiversity and the environment.[109] It builds upon and complements the development of the 'One World, One Health' scheme to achieve fully comprehensive approaches in support of global sustainable development. Indeed, the UN 2030 Agenda proposes a development model 'in which humanity lives in harmony with nature and other living species are protected', although animal welfare is not yet included among the SDGs, and in particular SDG 12.

A new shift in global animal law is, however, necessary. The fact that the worst practices of industrial agriculture have not yet been eradicated raises the issue of incomplete enforcement ('implementation gap'), whose poor record is a significant shortcoming in EU animal welfare law. The starting point must be a correct implementation of OIE standards that, despite their limits, are comprehensive and – with particular reference to farmed animals – cover all the phases of farming, from transport by sea, air, land, to slaughtering, expressly requesting prior stunning.

The most pressing issue is how to reinforce the legal value of OIE's codes and to guarantee a wide implementation, diminishing the existing gap between ambition and action on the ground. While the decision to respect animal welfare standards relies upon single governments, it is still open to the question of how the international system can assist countries to address the animal welfare gap. At the same time, law reforms must begin from a change in habits in our societies.

As outlined by the IPCC, there is an urgent need for dietary change, particularly in high-income societies in order to reduce meat and dairy demand and free up pressure on land. Low-meat diet may have additional benefits beyond its large mitigation of greenhouse gas emission, particularly in avoiding or reversing land degradation and in food security.

In the long term, a more comprehensive and sophisticated regulatory mechanism devoted to meat production establishing specific animal welfare standards should be established. It should address through a holistic approach both industrialized and wildlife production systems and their potentials for food security.

108. Article 7.1.2, para. 1, affirms that 'That there is a critical relationship between animal health and animal welfare.'
109. https://www.onewelfareworld.org/about.html.

PART II Selected Cases and Legislations and European Food Law

CHAPTER 9

Right to Food and Food Security: A Comparative Perspective

Francesco Alicino

In the past three decades, the right to food has evolved, multiplied and diversified in such a way that it has led to an innovative definition of food security, also in the light of global health emergencies. This has also revealed the multisectorial and multidimensional aspects of the rights related to food, whose implementation requires the appropriate use of new technologies and scientific innovations and the benefits of which should be available for the whole society, including future generations. In this chapter, the author focuses on the attention of the essential features of the international human right to food, its evolution and its impact on regional and national legal systems. This enhances the role of the framework laws regulating the monitoring and evaluation mechanisms of the right to food and food security which, on the other hand, explains the function of the judiciary and the justiciability of economic, social and cultural rights. That implies the right to equal access to adequate food and the right to live in an inclusive, safe, non-polluted environment.

§9.01 INTRODUCTION

In the rich part of the world people no longer eat food. They do consume it. In this context, normally individuals do so in such a way that, alongside the energy needed to drive cars and heat houses, food has a significant impact on the environment through pollution, depletion of phosphorus, chemical products and the over-exploitation of land and water resources.[1] At the same time, different regions of the planet are still

1. Hanna Ritchie & Max Roser, *Environmental Impacts of Food Production* (2020), published online at OurWorldInData.org. Retrieved from https://ourworldindata.org/environmental-impacts-of-food (last accessed 4 February 2020). For a specific example of that *see also* Jenifer Huang McBeath & Jerry McBeath, *Environmental Change and Food Security in China* (Springer 2010).

experiencing famine situations.[2] Many of them are conflict-driven and starvation of civilians is often used as a method of warfare or for exacerbating cleavages based on social, political, religious and even ethnic identity.[3]

For these reasons, the food (production, transportation, distribution, marketing) system cannot be seen as a consequence of isolated and innocent acts.[4] On the contrary, this system reflects a dynamic chain of causes and effects, the consequences of which are now so damaging that many support radical transformations in the relations among people, politics and food, in order to make it more economically, socially and ecologically acceptable. In other terms, the world vitally needs a sustainable food system, which entails better farming methods, healthy eating behaviours and democratic countries valuing food that is not only profitable for industries, political lobbies and the large landowners it relies on but also safe, nutritious, inclusive and environmentally friendly. The search for these changes has thus stimulated interdisciplinary debates, including those related to the right to food and the relative legal commitments.[5] Their implementation does indeed encompass multiple actions, such as fostering governance of land tenure and natural resources, strengthening nutrition-sensitive social protection mechanisms, addressing inequalities and violent conflicts, reducing consumption of meat and other animal-derived foods, improving responsible investments in agriculture and in rural areas as well as in health, education and democratic policy-making.

As a result, in the past three decades, the right to food has evolved, multiplied and diversified in such a way that it has led to an innovative definition of food security: a definition that stresses the guarantee of human dignity and democracy, making both public authority and every single individual agency of positive evolutions. This also reveals the multisectorial and multidimensional aspects of the rights related to food, whose implementation also demands the appropriate use of new technologies and scientific innovations,[6] the benefits of which are due to be available for the whole society, including future generations.[7] That is even more significant when focusing the

2. World Health Organization (WHO), *World Hunger Is Still Not Going Down after Three Years and Obesity Is Still Growing* (15 July 2019).
3. The number of chronically hungry people worldwide hit 821 million in 2018, up from 777 million just three years before. Ten out of the thirteen largest hunger crises in the world are conflict-driven, and 60% of the people who are food insecure live in conflict zones. *See* World Food Programme, *Fact Sheet Hunger & Conflict* (January 2019), available at https://docs.wfp.org/api/documents/WFP 0000105972/download/?_ga= 2.128824716.1450031486.1569440059-184252046.1569440059 (last accessed 7 February 2020).
4. On the definition of the notion of 'food System' *see* European Commission, *Executive Summary. Recipe for Change: An Agenda for a Climate-Smart and Sustainable Food System for a Healthy Europe. Report of the EC FOOD 2030 Independent Expert Group* (2018).
5. IAP, *Opportunities for Future Research and Innovation on Food and nutrition Security and Agriculture: The InterAcademy Partnership's Global Perspective* (InterAcademy Partnership 2018).
6. Paola De Bernardi & Danny Azucar, *Innovation in Food Ecosystems: Entrepreneurship for a Sustainable Future* (Springer Nature 2019).
7. This is clearly affirmed in Article 27(1) of the Universal Declaration of Human Rights ('[e]veryone has the right freely to participate in the cultural life of the community, to enjoy the arts and to share in scientific advancement and its benefits') and Article 15 of the International Covenant on Economic, Social and Cultural Rights ('[t]he States Parties to the present Covenant recognize the right of everyone: (a) to take part in cultural life; (b) to enjoy the benefits of scientific progress and

attention on the connection among the notions of 'adequate food', 'free from hunger', and 'human rights law', as developed at the international, regional and national levels.

Nevertheless, it is precisely this connection that has also revealed how the human rights-based approach to food system still remains trapped in theoretical and practical difficulties, which are not easily solved via traditional legal instruments. The right to be free from hunger, for example, derives from the assertion that the society, starting but not ending with the State, has enough resources, both economic and institutional, to ensure that everyone is adequately nourished. Difficulties, however, arise when trying to flesh out this right and translate it into specific prerogatives and responsibilities. These same difficulties, after all, also explain the efforts of many national and supranational actors in identifying ways of making the rights to food and food security more concrete and efficient. This is even more necessary in regional contexts facing nutrition crises, further aggravated by the current environmental problems, such as the process of land degradation and desertification.

In the first part of this chapter, I will focus the attention on the essential features of the international human right to food, its evolution over the past decades and its impact on the regional and national legal systems. This will allow me to underscore the multidimensional and multisectorial aspects of the right to food, which are more evident in the light of the notions and the questions related to sustainability. From here stems the role of the framework laws regulating the monitoring and evaluation mechanisms, which normally oblige the competent authority to submit periodic reports and determine a procedure for possible cases of infringement of the right to food and food security. It, on the other hand, explains the function of the judiciary, which will lead to the broader issues concerning the justiciability of economic, social and cultural rights, including the right to equal access to adequate food and the right to live in an inclusive, safe, non-polluted environment.

§9.02 THE INTERNATIONAL HUMAN RIGHTS TO FOOD

Article 1 of the 1948 Universal Declaration of Human Rights (UDHR) stipulates that 'all people are born free and equal in dignity and rights'. This reveals the basic idea of the inviolable rights of the person, both as an individual and in the social groups where human personality is expressed. One of these rights refers to a suitable standard of living, which includes adequate food, a major premise for a free and dignified life.[8]

This relationship is also confirmed in the Covenant containing economic, social and cultural rights (ICESCR)[9] that, adopted by the United Nations (UN) General Assembly on 16 December 1966, came into force on 3 January 1976. It should be noted that two years before the Universal Declaration on the Eradication of Hunger and

its applications'). In this sense see also: Article XIII of the American Declaration of the Rights and Duties of Man; Article 14.1(c) of the Additional Protocol to the American Convention on Human Rights in the Area of Economic, Social and Cultural Rights (also known as the Protocol of San Salvador); Article 42 of the Arab Charter on Human Rights; Article 32 of the ASEAN Human Rights Declaration.

8. Article 25 UDHR.
9. Article 11.

Malnutrition had been approved at the World Food Conference: it stated that increasing food production and sharing resources more adequately are key elements in order to combat hunger and malnutrition, a common responsibility to the international community. Two decades later, however, the Food and Agricultural Organization (FAO) realized that these goals were going to fail anyway. It therefore organized the 1996 World Food Summit bringing together representatives from 185 States, who clarified the content of the right to adequate food: this implies the fundamental right of everyone to be free from hunger, whose implementation and progressive realization must be seen as a means of achieving food security for all. In response, in 1999, the Twentieth Session of the Committee on Economic, Social and Cultural Rights adopted the General Comment 12 on Article 11 ICESCR, thus defining the right to adequate food more precisely: the right to life is strictly associated with the notion of adequate food which, however, suggests a broader concept as it entails the need to establish the economic, political and social conditions necessary to enable people to achieve food security on their own.[10] In doing so, the Committee pointed out the States' obligations to *respect*, *protect* and *fulfil* the right to adequate food.

On the one hand, the Member States must refrain from adopting measures that could prevent, restrict or deprive people of the ability to feed themselves (*duty to respect*). On the other, the States must adopt specific actions, either legislative or of a different sort, to regulate both public and private activities in order to ensure that they do not interfere with the exercise of the right to food of any sector of the population (*duty to protect*). To stimulate more positive activities, the Members States should also elaborate policies and programmes that provide food directly to individuals or groups who, for reasons beyond their control, cannot nourish themselves (*duty to fulfil*). All of this aims at guaranteeing freedom from hunger within a State and promoting knowledge of the human right to food among individual, social groups and authorities.

It must nonetheless be underlined that these obligations infer cooperation and assistance, which prevent a Member State from imposing measures that could interfere with the ability of another country to enable its inhabitants to exercise their right to adequate food. It means that under no circumstance shall food system be used to exercise political pressure or, worse, as a method of warfare, nor shall food aid be contingent upon socio-economic crises or natural calamities. Instead, Countries with extremely limited resources must seek international assistance when necessary to prevent situations of famine and malnutrition.

Thus, in the early 2000s, section 10 of the World Food Summit mandated the FAO to establish an international working group (IWG) to draw a set of voluntary guidelines in order to support the Member States' efforts to achieve the progressive realization of

10. *See* para. 6 of the CESCR General Comment No. 12: The Right to Adequate Food (Document E/C.12/1999/5): '[t]he right to adequate food is realized when every man, woman and child, alone or in community with others, have physical and economic access at all times to adequate food or means for its procurement. The right to adequate food shall therefore not be interpreted in a narrow or restrictive sense which equates it with a minimum package of calories, proteins and other specific nutrients. The right to adequate food will have to be realized progressively. However, States have a core obligation to take the necessary action to mitigate and alleviate hunger'.

the right to adequate food in the context of national food security. During its 123rd session (28 October-2 November 2002), the FAO Council installed this IWG which, few years later, adopted the final version of the guidelines. The document does not infer legally binding rules. It, however, provides guidance on strengthening legal and accountability frameworks, founding them on three fundamental concepts: *adequacy*, *availability* and *accessibility*.

In other words, food should not only be available in sufficient quantity to satisfy the dietary needs of people. It should also be sustainable, which implies a long-term availability of the right to adequate food, the realization of which is conceived in a way that does not inhibit the enjoyment of other rights. For these reasons, food system should aim at improving the management of natural resources, scientific developments, and human rights. This system, then, should be conceived in ways that may help to produce food that is not only sufficient for the whole population but also healthful to eat, free from adverse substances, economically stable and acceptable within both the household's livelihood and a given socio-cultural context. International cooperation in augmenting the availability and accessibility of adequate food is also relevant, especially in the light of the increasing speed of scientific and technological findings in some crucial sectors – the example is given by the molecular genetics of pathogenicity, which has been being studied for the past three decades in order to find alternative agricultural approaches that may reduce the use of agrochemicals.[11]

Despite their strictly interrelation, there are some differences among these concepts to such an extent that accessibility suggests more physical and economic attributes whereas adequacy has quantitative and qualitative attributes. At the same time, availability relates not only to the amount of food but also refers to a combination of local food production, commercial food imports and exports, food aid, and domestic food stocks. In this sense, availability requires organizing the food system in a way that is adequate to a given geopolitical and socio-economic context as well as accessible to all individuals, starting from the poorest and most disadvantaged.

From these points of view, the UN 2030 Agenda[12] constitutes a further effort towards an effective implementation of food security, in a sustainable sense of the term. It underscores the fact that in the past five decades, resource-intensive farming has contributed to deforestation, water scarcity, soil depletion and high levels of greenhouse gas emissions. As a consequence, on the planet, there are now more people to feed with less water and productive lands to rely on. The 2030 Agenda solemnizes the need to conserve natural resources and biodiversity. This suggests that agriculture and food systems must be transformed away from wasteful and exploitative approaches, while ensuring higher governance standards and more inclusive decision-making. In this manner, the 2030 Agenda highlights the importance of interrelation

11. *See ex plurimis* Guus Bakkeren & Les J. Szabo, *Progress on Molecular Genetics and Manipulation of Rust Fungi* (Phytopathology 2019) available at https://apsjournals.apsnet.org/doi/pdf/10.1094/PHYTO-07-19-0228-IA (last accessed 9 February 2020); Roberto Sierra et al., *Discovery of Phytophthora Infestans Genes Expressed in Planta Through Mining of cDNA Libraries*, 3 PLoS One, 5 (2010).
12. I am referring to the Resolution adopted by the General Assembly on 25 September 2015, *Transforming our world: the 2030 Agenda for Sustainable Development*, 70/1.

among people, worldwide economy, sustainable environment, international cooperation and food. The agenda is therefore able to recognize that food systems should be better balanced in order to make it more equitable, less inefficient and an ally of the ecological concerns. To reach this goal there is an urgent need to increase investment, including through a more developed international cooperation, in rural infrastructure, agricultural research, technology development, and livestock gene banks. This can help to enhance agricultural productive capacity in poor countries, while preventing trade distortions in food markets and limiting the volatility of the asset prices.[13]

§9.03 THE SECTORIAL, REGIONAL AND CONSTITUTIONAL RIGHTS TO FOOD

The evolution of the UN strategy on the implementation of the rights related to food and food security is reflected in specific international legal documents. Many of them aim at protecting a particular group of individuals[14] while others are related to regional contexts[15] that, sometimes, are in a better position to evaluate the multidimensional

13. *See ex plurimis*, FAO, *Food and Agriculture in the 2030 Agenda* (2016).
14. In this sense reference can be made to: Article 27 of the International Covenant for the Rights of the Child; Article 28 of the Convention on Persons with Disabilities, and in the context of healthcare and pregnancy; Article 12(2) of the Convention on the Elimination of All Forms of Discrimination against Women in the context of healthcare and pregnancy; Article 24 (1)(b) of the Convention relating to the Status of Refugees; Article 27 of the International Convention on the Protection of the Rights of All Migrant Workers and Members of Their Families, Articles 24-26 of the Convention on the Rights of the Child. These documents show that, although all individuals have equal human rights, the human right to food often devotes peculiar attention to those who belong to vulnerable groups. This is evident in the light of Article 24 of the Convention on the Rights of the Child which, related to the right to health, calls for appropriate measures to combat disease and malnutrition, including through the provision of nutritious food and safe drinking water. At the same time, Article 28 of the Convention on the Rights of Persons with Disabilities recognizes the right of persons with disabilities to a suitable standard of living, which implies adequate food. At the regional level, Article 14 of the African Charter on the Rights and Welfare of the Child affirms that every child shall has the right to enjoy the best attainable state of physical, mental and spiritual health, which includes the provision of nutritious food. The right to adequate nutrition of children is also enshrined in Article 15 (para. 3) of the Protocol of San Salvador.
15. The examples are given by: Article 12 of the Additional Protocol to the American Convention on Human Rights in the Area of Economic, Social and Cultural Rights, the 1988 so-called Protocol of San Salvador; Article 17 of the 1990 Cairo Declaration on Human Rights in Islam; Article 34 of the 2000 Charter of Fundamental Rights of the European Union; Article 15 of the Additional Protocol to the 2000 African Charter on Human and Peoples' Rights on the Rights of Women in Africa of 2000. *See also* the African Charter on Human and Peoples' Rights, which adopted on the initiative of the Organisation of African Unity (OAU) – since 26 May 2001 the African Union (AU) – in 1981 and entered into force in 1986: the right to adequate food is not specifically recognized in the Charter, although Article 21 stipulates that 'all peoples shall freely dispose of their wealth and natural resources'. In addition, Article 15 of the Additional Protocol to the African Charter on Human and Peoples' Rights and the Rights of Women in Africa explicitly recognize the right to food security for women. Moreover, in 1990 the OAU adopted the African Charter on the Rights and Welfare of the Child that stipulates the right to adequate food in Articles 14 and 20. The 1988 San Salvador Additional Protocol to the American Convention on Human Rights recognizes the right to adequate food in Article 12. In 2009 the AU also adopted the African Union Convention for the Protection and Assistance of Internally Displaced Persons in Africa (Kampala Convention), under which the States Parties pledge themselves to provide internally

nature of the right to food and its close link with other human rights. This is the case of the right to water, necessary to produce and cook food. The same can be said about the right to property, which implies the access to land and other productive resources needed to produce food. And, from a legal point of view, we must take into account the right to health, under which proper biological use of food can be contingent on the person's state of wellbeing and his/her possibility of access to basic health care.[16] It also implies the right to work and the right to just and favourable remuneration, such as to ensure workers and their families an existence worthy of human dignity, which includes adequate food. All individuals have equal dignity and are equally free before the right to food, without unreasonable discriminations based on sex, religion, political opinions as well as on personal and social conditions.[17]

Authorities must guarantee that measures affecting the livelihood and the ability to exercise the right to food are adopted in a manner that respects the absolute value of persons, based on the simple fact that they are human beings, irrespective of their status. It, on the other hand, entails treating certain categories of people differently from the rest, which may sometimes be necessary in order to remove economic and social obstacles: problems and difficulties that constrain freedom and equality of some vulnerable individuals, thereby impeding the development of their personality and their effective participation in the country's life. This is even more important in relation to the governments' decisions that affect the ability of people to feed themselves; which implies the governments' obligations to ensure that information regarding laws, budgets and actions elaborated within the framework of the rights to food and food security is transparent, published in a language accessible to ordinary people and disseminated through appropriate media.

It is evident that many spheres of the State activity involve the rights relating to food, whose primary references may be affirmed in the constitutional provisions. This

---

displaced persons with adequate humanitarian assistance, including food and water. It should be noted that this Convention states that members of armed groups 'shall be prohibited from denying internally displaced persons the right to live in satisfactory conditions of dignity, security, sanitation, food, water, health and shelter'. To this respect it is important to remember that the Colombian Constitutional Court has developed a strong jurisprudence in the field of internal displacements of poor rural population due to armed conflicts. *See* the following decisions: T-227/1997, SU-1150/2000, T-1635/2000, T-327/2001, T-1346/2001, T-098/2002, T-215/2002, T-268/2003, T-419/2003, T-602/2003, T-721/2003, T-025/2004, T-078/2004, T-097/2005, T-312/2005, T-563/2005, T-882/2005, T-1076/2005, T-086/2006, T-138/2006 and T-585/2006. In these cases, the Colombian Constitutional Court has considered that food security is one of the rights threatened by forced displacements. On the basis of these premises, the court has included food relief as a component of the 'right to a vital minimum', thus ordering political authorities to adopt positive measures to fulfil this right. The court has also urged public authorities to develop and implement programmes to achieve the reestablishment of the displaced population, including adequate nutrition, access to work and, when possible, return to their homes and places of origin.

16. Take, for example, Article 17 the Protocol of San Salvador, where it is stated that '[e]veryone has the right to special protection in old age', which requires the Member States 'to take progressively the necessary steps to make this right a reality and, particularly, to provide suitable facilities, as well as food and specialized medical care, for elder individuals who lack them and are unable to provide them for themselves'.
17. Dubravka Bojic Bultrini et al., *The Right to Food Within the International Framework of Human Rights and Country Constitutions* (FAO 2014).

can be done in different ways: explicit and direct recognition of the right to food for all individuals or for certain groups, such as children or indigenous peoples;[18] implicit recognition in broader human rights;[19] explicit recognition as a goal, or as a directive principle of State policy.[20]

Incorporating the rights relating to food in Constitutions represents a strong statement that a State wishes to progress towards their realization for all individuals. The fact is that constitutional provisions alone cannot ensure combined actions necessary to achieve this end. Framework laws regulating effective programmes and monitoring processes should assist those provisions as well. This is also because, since the rights to food and food security are multidimensional and cross-sectorial in nature, a framework law is essential to assign responsibility to public and private actors while ensuring coordination and direction for programmes and monitoring processes. This kind of law should provide the scope and content of the right to adequate food in more details, setting out the obligations of authorities and stakeholders. In other words, an effective framework law should also establish institutional mechanisms and the normative content of the right to food and food security, providing legal instruments for its enforcement at the administrative, judicial and quasi-judicial levels.

§9.04 FRAMEWORK LAWS AND MONITORING MECHANISMS

Given the multifaceted nature of the right to food, the framework law should designate the competent public authority and establish its legal responsibility. This could be done taking into serious account the territorial structure of a State, its different levels of democratic participation (provincial, cantonal, regional and other sub-unit territorial governments). The framework law, however, does not have to provide full details,

18. The examples of Constitutions that explicitly recognize the right to food for all, or for certain groups such as the minors of age and of the elderly and/or indigenous peoples, are given by the Constitutions of Belarus (Article 21), Bolivia (Article 16), Brazil (Title 2, Chapter 2 Article 6), Colombia (Articles 44, 46, and 65), Costa Rica (Article 82), Congo (Article 47), the Dominican Republic (Article 57), Ecuador (Articles 13, 32, 45, and 66), Egypt (Article 79), Fiji (Chapter 2, section 36; Chapter 2, section 41), Guatemala (Article 51), the Republic of Guyana (Article 40), Haiti (Article 22), Honduras (Article 123), Kenya (Article 43), Malawi (Articles 30.2 and 42), Maldives (Article 23), Mexico (Article 4), Moldova (Article 47(1)), Nepal (Article 18(3)), Nicaragua (Article 63), Niger (Article 12), Panama (Article 56; Article 110; Article 118), Paraguay (Article 54), Philippines (Article 15), South Africa (Article 27, 28, and 35), Suriname (Article 24), Ukraine (Article 48), Zimbabwe (Articles 77, 19-2, 81-1, and 50-5).
19. The examples are given by the Constitutions of Argentina (section 75.22), Belgium (Article 23), Bosnia & Herzegovina (Article 2), Armenia (Article 34), Cuba (Article 9.a), Cyprus (Article 9), Egypt (Article 38), Ethiopia (Article 43), Indonesia (Article 28c and 28h), Japan (Article 25), Nicaragua (Article 4; Article 98), the Republic of Peru (Article 2), and many others.
20. One of the most famous example refers to the Constitution of India (Article 47). But that also is the case of the Constitutions of Armenia (Article 48), Austria (Article 5), Bangladesh (Articles 15 and 18), Brazil (Articles 208, 227), Burundi (Article 17), Cuba (Article 9.b), the Democratic People's Republic of Korea (Article 25), Ecuador (Article 3), Ethiopia (Article 90), Gambia (Article 216(4)), Guatemala (Article 99), Honduras (Article 347), Iran (Articles 3(12) and 43), Ireland (Article 45), Malawi (Article 13), Myanmar (Part 2 (26/b)), Namibia (Article 95), Nigeria (Articles 16.2 and 17.3), Pakistan (Article 38), Papua New Guinea (Article 1.4), South Sudan (Article 35(2)), Sri Lanka (Article 27), Swiss (Article 104), Uganda (XIV), Venezuela (Article 305), Zimbabwe (Article 289).

which should be left to lower-level provisions. More importantly, the framework law should establish transparent, fair and non-discriminatory eligibility criteria to identify minimum amount of adequate food that allows individuals not only to be free from hunger but also to have a free and dignified life. Food requirements are what a person needs to maintain normal organic and cognitive functions and be able to develop properly his/her human existence throughout childhood.[21]

The framework law must also affirm appropriate monitoring and evaluation mechanisms, which oblige the competent authority to submit periodic reports and determine a procedure for possible cases of infringement. These mechanisms must be simple, easily accessible and free of charge. They must include the regular analysis, interpretation and dissemination of relevant information in order to evaluate the progress of the realization of the rights to adequate food and food security among all members of society. It means making sure that the State's law is provided in accordance with relevant human rights principles. But this also infers that national authorities, including judiciary, should deal with violations of the right to adequate food making reference to the provisions established at regional and international levels, or even to case laws decided in other legal contexts. That is more evident where the so-called multilevel constitutionalism is already operational, which means where the State law and supranational institutions are seen as interdependent components of a legal system governed by constitutional pluralism instead of sovereign and rigid hierarchies.[22]

That is the case of the European Union's (EU)'s legal system where, however, there is neither express notion of the right to food nor the reference to the right to adequate food. Nevertheless, some provisions of the EU Charter of Fundamental Rights may indirectly provide effective recognition of these rights.[23] In addition, after the

21. So, on the basis of these premises, in 1995 the Swiss Federal Court (*Tribunal fédéral suisse, V. v. Einwohnergemeinde X und Regierungsrat des Kanton Bern*, BGE/ATF 121 I 367, 371, 373 V. JT 1996, 27 October 1995) provided example of the minimum content strategy, ruling that in the Swiss Constitution there is an implicit right to a minimum level of subsistence (*conditions minimales d'existence*): as such, this right needed to be enforced by the judiciary. In this case, the plaintiffs were three stateless persons, who found themselves in Switzerland with no money. As they had no papers, they could neither work nor leave the country. For the same reason, they were not eligible for social assistance. The Swiss Court considered that they had a right to basic minimum conditions, including food: this is necessary in order to prevent a situation where people 'are reduced to beggars, a condition unworthy of being called human'. Therefore, the court ordered political authorities to grant the plaintiffs relief. To this respect *see also* the German Federal Constitutional Court and Federal Administrative Court (*BVerfGE 1, 97, 104* et seq.; *BVerwGE 1, 159, 161*; *BVerwGE 25, 23, 27*; *BVerfGE 40, 121, 134*; *BVerfGE 45, 187, 229*) which derives from the constitutional principles positive State obligations to provide an 'existential minimum' or 'vital minimum', comprising access to food, housing and social assistance to persons in need. *See also BVerfGE 82, 60 (85), BVerfGE 87, 153 (169)*, with the German Federal Constitutional Court provides an interesting example: it has held in several cases that the state tax power cannot extend to the material means necessary to cover the 'existential minimum' which includes food needs. Thus, the legislature has a duty to respect the means for basic livelihood and cannot impose taxes beyond these limits.
22. Ingolf Pernice, *Multilevel Constitutionalism and the Crisis of Democracy in Europe*, 11 European Constitutional Law Review, 3, 541-562 (2015).
23. *See*, for example, Articles 1 (human dignity), 2 (right to life) 3 (right to the integrity of the Person), 21 (non-discrimination), and 22 (cultural, religious and linguistic diversity).

publication of the 1997 Green Paper on the general principles of food law[24] and the 2000 White Paper on food safety,[25] in January 2002, the European Commission presented a general food law regulation defining the procedure of food safety.[26] This regulation affirms that, in this field, the legislation of each Member State shall pursue a high level of protection of life and human health, as well as protection of consumers' interests, including fair practices in food market.[27] Particular attention should also be paid to the protection of animal health and welfare, plant health and the environment, as regards food additives, food enzymes and food flavourings.[28] The EU legal framework on food also implies the *Codex Alimentarius*, which provides international food standards as well as some advisory provisions called code of practice, which mainly address food business and contribute to the safety, quality and fairness of the worldwide food market.[29] It is clear that the main aim of the EU framework law is not to guarantee access to adequate food for all individuals, but to ensure that food is safe for human beings, for the consumers' best interest, and for the effective functioning of the European Single Market.[30]

Similarly, in the context of the Council of Europe the European Convention of Human Rights (ECHR) does not contain an express notion of the rights to food and food security. Also in this case, these rights can be regarded as being legally linked to other rights and principles, like those related to the right to life,[31] the prohibition on inhuman and degrading treatment,[32] the right to private, home and family life,[33] the right to non-discrimination,[34] and the protection of property.[35]

---

24. Brussels, 30 April 1997 COM(97) 176 final.
25. Brussels, 12 January 2000 COM(1999) 719 final.
26. Regulation (EC) No. 178/2002 of the European Parliament and of the Council laying down the general principles and requirements of food law, establishing the European Food Safety Authority and laying down procedures in matters of food safety, 28 January 2002 (OJ L 31, 1.2.2002, 1).
27. Ines Härtel & Dapeng Ren, *Agri-Food Law: Term, Development, Structures, System and Framework, in Handbook of Agri-Food Law in China, Germany, European Union* 10-55 (Ines Härtel ed., Springer 2018).
28. The Regulation established the European Authority on food security. The European food legislation shall be supplemented by the so-called food hygiene package (Regulation EC 852/2004; 853/2004; 854/2004) and by the Food Improvement Agents package, which would lead to the definition of a Common Authorisation Procedure for food additives, food enzymes and food flavourings.
29. *See* B. van der Meulen, *The Codex Alimentarius, in Roadmap to EU Food Law* 31-41 (Irene Scholten-Verheijen et al. eds, Den Haag 2011).
30. B.M.J. van der Meulen, *The Structure of European Food Law,* 2 Laws, 69-98 (2013).
31. Article 2 ECHR.
32. Article 3 ECHR.
33. Article 8 ECHR.
34. Article 14 ECHR.
35. Article 1 of the 1952 Protocol to ECHR. That is clearly affirmed by the jurisprudence of the European Court of Human Rights (EctHR) which, for example, has held that forced evictions, forced displacements and destruction of homes and property may amount to a violation of the right to privacy, family life and home, to a violation of the right to property, and even to inhuman and degrading treatment. *See ex plurimis* ECtHR: *Moldovan and others (2) v. Romania*, 12 July 2005, paras 105, 108-110; *Cyprus v. Turkey*, of 10 May 2001, paras 187-189; *Selçuk and Asker v. Turkey*, of 24 April 1998, paras 77-80; *Aakdivar and others v. Turkey*, of 16 September 1996, para. 88; *Cyprus v. Turkey*, 10 May 2001, paras 174-175; *Yöyler v. Turkey*, of 10 May 2001, paras

The fact is that in most of these legal scenarios, including the European one, there are difficulties in the identification of a firm legal basis to bring a case to the court regarding the right to adequate food. This is even more evident where there is no express constitutional basis for this right, and there is no clear statutory basis either. In these situations, directly arguing a case on the source of the supranational law and on the soft law documents[36] can be a highly uncertain bet. And if this difficulty is present in the monistic legal systems, where international law is directly part of domestic law and can be directly invoked before judicial courts, it increases in dualistic systems, where supranational law is not automatically incorporated into domestic law.

Incorporation, however, can certainly contribute to the realization of the right to adequate food and food security at the national level.[37] In these legal systems holders of those rights are more able to turn to courts if they feel the rights related to food have been violated. Moreover, in their judgments, the ordinary courts may include the redress deemed appropriate (not only an end to the infringement but also a guarantee of non-repetition, for example) and may also order temporary protective measures until a final decision is delivered.

§9.05 THE JUDICIARY

Some case laws illustrate that indirect recognition of the right to adequate food through interpretation of other human rights is also possible. Moreover, many times the courts have interpreted the scope and normative content of the right to food and food security in a way that involves a range of issues, such as those concerning the protection of categories of people from extreme poverty and severe malnutrition. Other cases are linked to access to food by individuals that are discriminated on grounds of their

79-80; *Demades v. Turkey*, 31 October 2003, paras 31-37; *Selçuk and Asker v. Turkey*, 24 April 1998, paras 86-87; *Bilgin v. Turkey*, 16 November 2000, paras 108-109; *Ayder v. Turkey*, of 8 January 2004, paras 119-121.

36. That the case of the General Comment No. 12 and the FAO Voluntary Guidelines. *See supra*.
37. *See ex plurimis* the Constitutions of Albania (Article 5), Andorra (Article 3), Angola (Articles 12 and 13), Armenia (Article 6), Azerbaijan (Articles 148 (II), 151 and 12), Benin (Article 146), Bhutan (Articles 145, 146, 147 and 40), Bolivia (Articles 410 and 13), Bulgaria (Article 5), Burkina Faso (Article 151), Burundi (Chapter XIII), Cabo Verde (Article 11(4)), Cameroon (Article 45), the Central African Republic (Article 72), Chad (Article 221), Chile (Article 5.2), Comoros (Article 10), Costa Rica (Article 7), Côte d'Ivoire (Article 87), Croatia (Article 140), the Czech Republic (Article 49), Djibouti (Article 70), El Salvador (Article 44), Estonia (para. 123), France (Article 55), Georgia (Article 6), Germany (Article 25), Greece (Article 28), Guatemala (Article 46), Guinea (Article 151), Honduras (Articles 16-18), Hungary (Foundation/article Q/3), Italy (Article 10), Kazakhstan (Article 4), Lithuania (Article 138), Madagascar (Article 137), Montenegro (Article 9), Morocco (Preamble), Netherlands (Articles 91-94), Paraguay (Article 137), Poland (Articles 87, 89 and 91), Portugal (Article 8), Moldova (Article 4(2)), Romania (Articles 11 and 20), Russia (Article 15(4)), Rwanda (Article 190), San Marino (Article 1(4)), Senegal (Article 98), Seychelles (Article 48), Slovenia (Article 8 and 153), South Africa (Article 231), South Sudan (Article 243), Spain (section 95), Tajikistan (Article 10), Macedonia (Article 8), Timor Leste (section 9), Tunisia (Article 20), Turkey (Article 90), Turkmenistan (Article 6).

religious, political and ethnic affiliation[38] or because they are being held under restrictive conditions, like police custody and detention.[39]

In Guatemala, for example, in May 2013, the Child and Adolescent Court of the Zacapa Department held that the State had failed to take decisive actions in combating child malnutrition in the Camotán municipality. For these reasons, Guatemala violated the right to food, the right to life, the right to housing and the right to an adequate standard of living. In its decision, the court expressly mentioned not only Article 51 of the Constitution, which protects the right to food for children, but also Article 11 ICESCR and Article 25 UDHR. The court also made reference to General Comment 12.[40]

An analogous case was decided by the Supreme Court of Canada, which in 1996 partly struck down a criminal prosecution directed against a member of an indigenous community who had been charged for fishing without a requisite license in a natural reserve. The Supreme Court held that the requirement of a license infringed the existing (aboriginal) right to fish for food.[41] As opposed to the right to fish commercially, the right to fish for food is a right that should be given first priority that, however, does not necessarily undermine the importance of the preservation of natural resources.[42]

In this sense, the case of South Africa seems to be highly significant. Here the Constitution states that everyone has the fundamental right to have access to basic needs, including 'sufficient food and water'. The Constitution also establishes that 'the State must take reasonable legislative and other measures, within its available resources, to achieve the progressive realisation of each of these rights';[43] which is even more urgent to address when 'basic nutrition, shelter, basic health care services and social services' of children are taken into consideration.[44] However, given that there is no common definition of reasonableness, the Constitutional Court of South Africa (CCSA) has corroborated it with other three detailed obligations. In particular, the

38. *See* Inter-American Commission of Human Rights, *Maya Indigenous Community of the Toledo District v. Belize* address, 12 October 2004, Case 12.053, where it is stated that the use of natural resources on indigenous lands by certain private third parties undermines the indigenous population's right to food. *See also* African Commission on Human & Peoples' Rights, *Social and Economic Rights Action Center & the Center for Economic and Social Rights v. Nigeria* (27 May 2002, 155/96) in which the African Commission held that Nigeria had violated the right of the indigenous Ogoni people by not involving them in the decision-making process that affected the development of their community's lands and livelihood. *See also* Human Rights Committee, *Womah Mukong v. Cameroon,* Communication No. 458/1991, U.N. Doc. CCPR/C/51/D/458/1991 (1994), where it is stated that the deprivation of food during detention constitutes a form of cruel, inhuman and degrading treatment.
39. For example, on 12 May 2000, the High Court of Fiji (*Tito Rarasea v. State*) struck down a punishment imposed by the prison authorities to an inmate, consisting in reducing his food rations by half. The High Court considered that the reduction of food rations and the use of food as a means of control was not consistent with Article 11(1) of the ICESCR.
40. *Juzgado de la niñez y la adolescencia e de Adolescentes en Conflicto con la Ley Penal del Departamento de Zacapa* (Carpeta judicial No. 19003-2011-0064I-of.1°), 31 May 2013.
41. *R v. Cote* (1996) 138 DLR (4th) 385, of 3 October 1996.
42. *Ibid.*, para. 62. To this respect *see also* Inter-American Court of Human Rights: *Yakye Axa Indigenous Community v. Paraguay*, of 17 June 2005; *Sawhoyamaxa Indigenous Community v. Paraguay*, 29 March 2006, *Mayagna (Sumo) Awas Tingni Community v. Nicaragua*, 31 August 2001.
43. Section 27 Constitution of the Republic of South Africa (CSA).
44. Section 28(c).

court has affirmed that, in order to meet the reasonable test, in this area, a State policy should: not exclude a disproportionate percentage of the population; consider the situation of vulnerable social groups; address the needs of individual in increasingly desperate conditions.[45] This, on the other hand, has emphasized the fact that many times courts need to interpret other constitutional rights and freedoms (such as equality[46] dignity,[47] life[48] health care,[49] education)[50] in ways that have positive impacts on the right to food and food security.[51]

While the human rights crisis at hand cannot wait for the slow wheels of justice to find solutions for all, a judicial decision can at least set precedents and provide opportunities for future development of access to adequate food and the relative entitlements afforded by supranational laws, Constitutions and legal frameworks.

Thus, in 2001, the Supreme Court of India issued several interim orders requiring the government to effectively implement various measures under the right to food, which ensures the fundamental right to life with human dignity. As part of the constitutional rights, right to food imposes on the governments, both federal and local, the duty to apply it in the most effective way possible. To achieve this end a special Commission was set up to collect and analyse data regarding the obligations of the State and federal governments.[52] Hence, since 2001, the Supreme Court's interim orders have served to define with increasing detail the right to food in at least three ways: by recognizing the right to food as a fundamental right within the meaning of the rights to life and human dignity; by spelling out in detail the entitlements that make up the right food and making it more enforceable; and by creating a mechanism for the continuous monitoring and reporting of the implementation of the court's decisions.[53]

The same observations were made on the other hemisphere of the world where, in 2007, the *defensor del pueblo de la nación*, a national ombudsman, requested the Supreme Court of Argentina to order the federal government and the government of the Chaco Province to adopt urgent measures in favour of the Toba indigenous communities. The complaint was founded on domestic legislation as well as on regional and international human rights laws, such as those referring to the American Convention, the American Declaration, UDHR, ICESCR, and CEDAW. More specifically, members of the Toba community were living in extreme poverty and hunger. The Supreme Court

45. CCSA, *Government of the Republic of South Africa & Others v. Grootboom & Others*, 2000 (11) BCLR 1169, paras 43, 44 and 64.
46. Section 9 CSA.
47. Section 10 CSA.
48. Section 11 CSA.
49. Section 27(1)(a) CSA.
50. Section 29 SCA.
51. CCSA, *Minister of Health and Others v. Treatment Action Campaign and Others* (2002) AHRLR 189; *Khosa & Others v. Minister of Social Development & Others*, 2004(6) BCLR 569 (CC). *See also* Yared Teka Tsegay et al., *Hidden Hunger in South Africa: The Faces of Hunger and Malnutrition in a Food-Secure Nation* (Oxfam 2014).
52. *See* the Supreme Court's Interim Order of 2 May 2003, *People's Union for Civil Liberties v. Union of India & Ors,* Writ Petition No. 196 of 2001.
53. Poorvi Chitalkar & Varun Gauri, *India: Compliance with Orders on the Right to Food, in Social Rights Judgments and the Politics of Compliance: Making It Stick* 288-314 (M. Langford, C. Rodríguez-Garavito & J. Rossi eds, Cambridge University Press 2017).

attributed this situation to the government's inaction and failure to discharge its obligations under national and supranational law. On this basis, the court ordered that the indigenous communities' right to food had to be secured. Moreover, the Argentinian judges charged the national government and the government of Chaco Province to adopt a series of detailed and emergency measures for immediate distribution of food and safe drinking water to those communities. In the judgment, the Supreme Court also addressed the proper role of the judiciary in tackling such issues and issuing specific remedial actions: courts are guardians of constitutional dispositions, which entail ensuring the effectiveness of relative rights and avoiding their violation. Here are the reasons why the courts' intervention could not be seen as an improper interference on the part of the judiciary vis-à-vis other branches of the State, including the legislative power.[54]

Four years later, the Supreme Court of Nepal published a key decision regarding a similar situation. Aside from the availability of food, the Nepalese Court put emphasis on the respect, protection and fulfilment of the right to food. Thus, the attention was focused on the links between the right to food and other human rights, such as the right to employment and social security. In doing so the Supreme Court cited and analysed all relevant documents of the international law – including ICESCR, UDHR, CEDAW – to which Nepal is a State party. In this manner the Nepalese judges reinforced the responsibility and duty of the local government to fully ensure the achievement of the right to food for every individual. As the case was filed to redress food supply in food-insecure districts, the Supreme Court also issued specific directives that clearly recall the above-mentioned Right to Food Guidelines. As a result, the decision encouraged the government of Nepal to comply with the constitutional obligation to supply food in a timely manner by any means of transportation and save people from hunger and malnutrition, including those who are in state of detention.[55] The basic international and constitutional human rights impose the States an unequivocal obligation to ensure that the right to adequate food of detainees is fulfilled, especially when related to particularly vulnerable people (very young children, the elderly, pregnant women and those with a chronic medical condition). The 2019 decision of the 9th U.S. Circuit Court serves as an important example of that.

The case had its origin in 2017, when Donald Trump's Executive Order on immigration was subject to review by the US District Judge Dolly M. Gee. The Judge found that children in U.S. Customs and Border Protection custody did not have adequate food, clean water or basic hygiene items and were held in conditions that deprived them of sleep. The Trump administration appealed arguing that authorities were not required to provide specific accommodations under the settlement's requirement that facilities be safe and sanitary and asked the Circuit Court to weigh in. A three-judge panel of the 9th U.S. Circuit Court disagreed. On 15 August 2019 the court

54. *Defensor del Pueblo de la Nación c/ Estado Nacional y otra (Provincia del Chaco) s/ proceso de conocimiento*, (2007) D. 587. XLIII. In this sense *see also* Buenos Aires Administrative Trial Court, *C.M.D. y otros c. GCBA s/amparo*, No. 3, 11 March 2003; Administrative Court, *González Rayco, Artidoro c. GCBA s/amparo*, No. 4, 19 May 2005.

55. *See* FAO, *Monitoring Framework for Implementation of Human Right to Adequate Food in Nepal* (2017).

rejected the appeal on the basis that children were not kept in safe and sanitary conditions: 'assuring that children eat enough edible food, drink clean water, are housed in hygienic facilities with sanitary bathrooms, have soap and toothpaste, and are not sleep-deprived are without doubt essential to the children's safety', wrote Judge Marsha S. Berzon. Moreover, together with William A. Fletcher and A. Wallace Tashima, Judge Berzon upheld a requirement that government officials work to release detained children from custody as soon as possible because of the detrimental impact that detention can have on their mental and physical health.[56]

In this sense, it should also be noted that the US Courts, while not referring to a human or constitutional right to food, have frequently dealt with statutory food stamp programmes. In 1973, for instance, the US Supreme Court held that a statutory restriction in the eligibility conditions for a food stamp programme was unconstitutional, thus confirming a lower court's decision to include plaintiffs in the programme.[57]

Programmes like this, however, also remind us that rights concerning food and food security can imply negative protection against inadequate food products, which can be considered as potential threats to human beings. Quite illustrative in this respect is the 1996 decision issued by the Supreme Court of Bangladesh, which interpreted the constitutional dispositions enshrining the right to life in a way that the government had to remove threats posed by a consignment of powdered milk with levels of radiation above the acceptable limits. The Supreme Court stated that the right to life includes the protection of health and normal longevity of an ordinary human being.[58]

It is also important to remember that the rights related to food and food security might be protected by means of quasi-judicial appeals, which in some legal systems are dealt with by human rights bodies. Normally, in these cases, the procedures are simpler and less expensive than other types of legal actions, which make them more accessible to the poorest and disadvantaged. But this should not detract from the fact that the quasi-judicial institutions are used to address deeper and structural causes and consequences of the violations of the rights related to food and food security.[59] Indeed,

56. United States Court of Appeals for the Ninth Circuit, No. 17-56297 D.C. No. 2:85-cv-04544-DMG-AGR, 15 August 2019.

57. *U.S. Department of Agriculture v. Moreno*, 413 U.S. 528, 25 June 1973. *See also* the 1996 judgment issued by the a U.S. Federal District Court (*U.S. District Court, 2nd district, Robidoux v. Kitchel, 876 F. Supp. 575, D. Vt. 1995*), which held that eligibility decisions concerning food stamp programmes by administrative authorities should be delivered promptly, within statutory guidelines.

58. Supreme Court of Bangladesh (High Court Division), *Dr. Mohiuddin Farooque v. Bangladesh and Others (no. 1)*, 1 July 1996.

59. Over the past two decades a number of States have adopted adequate food framework laws, establishing institutional guidance for the governance of their food security systems and also recognize the right to food and/or take a human rights-based approach. That is the case of Argentina (2003), Brazil (2010), Ecuador (2009-2010), Guatemala (2005), Honduras (2011), Indonesia (2012), Mexico (2004, 2013), Nicaragua (2009), Turkmenistan (2000), Venezuela (2008 (one law amended 2009), Tanzania (2011), Zanzibar (2011). These States score a full point under the FAO monitoring methodology, as does Armenia (2002) that has a food security legislation addressing a number of aspects of food security and recognizing the right to food, but does not establish an institutional framework. Many of these laws explicitly address nutrition as well as food security, as demonstrated by the case of Azerbaijan (1999/2011), Colombia (2009),

litigation-based legal strategies are only one means to ensure that States comply with their obligations in connection with those rights. Furthermore, it should be stressed that, when determining the best approach for advancing the right to food, the use of legal litigation should be carefully balanced against the advantages and disadvantages of other remedies, such as social mobilization, political negotiation, and civil society participation.

And yet, while the judiciary should not be seen as the only means for the realization of the right to adequate food and food security, the complete absence of any resource to courts of law in this matter clearly downgrades the span of mechanisms available for victims, which also makes State accountability weaker and fosters impunity.[60] After all, it is found that a clear and sufficient legal framework at domestic level, widening of standing rules, active participation of civil society, non-governmental organizations in the protection and promotion of human rights in a domestic legal system enhance the justiciability of the right to food, and, for this way, improve its implementation.[61]

§9.06 CONCLUSIONS

Food plays a vital role in many aspects of human existence, including death. This is evident in the light of starvation[62] and diet-related diseases[63] that kill millions of people around the world each year. Food, however, does not only bring about biological

---

Djibouti (2009, 2010), France (2009, 2010), Japan (2005), the Kyrgyz Republic (2008), and Tajikistan (2010). There are also States that have adopted governmental or ministerial decrees establishing a coordination framework for food security, which contain human rights-based provisions on the right to food: these include the Angola (2008), Cabo Verde (2013), El Salvador (2009), Mozambique (2010-2013), Peru (2013) and Venezuela (2014). Also at regional level there have been recent efforts in this sense. That is the case of the Latin American Parliament that, in November 2012, adopted a Regional Framework Law on the Right to Food, Food Security and Food Sovereignty: on the basis of this law Latin American States agree to establish at the national level human rights-based legislations on adequate food, food security and food sovereignty. On this question *see* Margret Vidar, Yoon Jee Kim & Luisa Cruz, *Legal Developments in the Progressive Realization of the Right to Adequate Food*, FAO Legal Office (2014), available at http://www.fao.org/right-to-food/resources/resources-detail/en/c/271813/ (last accessed 4 February 2020), where the authors affirms that it would be very helpful if the framework law stipulates that the national human rights institutions are responsible for legal assistance and investigation of cases of violation of the right to adequate food.

60. Christian Courtis, *The Right to Food as a Justiciable Right: Challenges and Strategie, in Max Planck Yearbook of United Nations Law* 317-337 (A. von Bogdandy & R. Wolfrum eds, Koninklijke Brill N.V. 2007).
61. International Development Law Organization (IDLO) & Irish Aid, *Realizing the Right to Food. Legal Strategies and Approaches* (2029).
62. FAO, *2019 Food Security and Nutrition in the World: Safeguarding Against Economy Slowdowns and Downturns*, FAO (2019), where it is stated that more than 820 million people worldwide are still going hungry.
63. Ashkan Afshin et al., *Low Intake of Healthy Foods and High Intake of Unhealthy Foods Is the Leading Cause of Mortality, Globally and in Many Countries*, 393 The Lancet 10184, 1958-1972 (2019): '[g]lobally, in 2017, dietary risks were responsible for deaths of all deaths among adults. Cardiovascular disease was the leading cause of diet-related deaths, followed by cancers deaths and 20 million and type 2diabetes. More than 5 million diet-related deaths occurred among adults aged younger than 70 years'.

effects, beneficial or dangerous as they may be. It also implies political and socio-economic concerns that form important parts of today's global society which, among other things, is now facing three major challenges: to produce enough safe food to feed a growing world population; to make more efficient and prudent use of environmental assets; and to combat famine in countries caught in local conflicts, economic difficulties and natural disasters.[64]

In this perspective, the human rights-based approach aims at affirming the rights related to adequate food and food security as constant values beyond the volatility of the economy and the instability of politics, both national and international. Recognizing and protecting human rights remains a basic challenge for today's global society, even though the universal-invariable conception of these rights is constantly confronted with various task and problems. Indeed, getting all public and private stockholders to translate the right to food into justiciable legal commitments as well as into operational strategies and actions still presents formidable task and interlocking democratic concerns, the relative importance of which varies from location to location.

This is also due to the fact that in the past decades, different actors, such as food retailers, have become more prominent in the global food chain, while the increased population, urbanization, and economic interdependence have reduced barriers to the flow of food products. As a result, the food system has become more intensive and complex, accentuating existing challenges (not only the eradicating of hunger and malnutrition but also food health and food security), the solutions of which will depend on effective governance systems.

However, it should be clear that strict interdependencies exist between right to food and many other parts of a broad sustainable development agenda, like those referring to inclusive economic growth, decent employment and remuneration, social protection as well as access to clean water, energy, health, sanitation, and natural resource management. But, for the same reasons, difficulties related to today's food system may offer a valuable space for learning to eliminate, or at least reduce, the unreasonable discriminations and unsustainable social injustice.

Such an inclusive attitude, however, cannot arise from simply affirming food security and the human right to food. On the contrary, these concepts deserve to be taken seriously, which means to meet their corresponding commitments and implement them in a worthwhile system capacity and recovery performance.

64. *See*, for example, TEEB, *TEEB for Agriculture & Food Scientific and Economic Foundations Report*, UN Environment (2018).

CHAPTER 10

Regulating Health Claims: An International Comparison

Jill E. Hobbs, Stavroula Malla & May T. Yeung

The chapter examines the regulatory environment for the use of health claims on food products and (dietary) supplements across various countries. The challenge in establishing a balanced approach to the regulation of health claims on food products and supplements is viewed through the twin lenses of market failure (information asymmetry, negative externalities) and non-market (government or regulatory) failure. An international comparison of the approach to regulating the use of health claims on food products and supplements is provided, including a discussion of the health claims regulatory environment in the United States, Canada, the European Union, Japan, Australia and New Zealand. Recent changes to the regulatory environments within these countries are noted. Differences in the definition of the health food sector, functional foods, and supplements are explored, along with the implications of allowing product-specific versus generic health claims. The scope of permitted health claims varies internationally, including the types of disease risk reduction claims permitted, the use of structure/function claims, and the process for verifying and validating scientific evidence supporting new health claims.

§10.01 INTRODUCTION

A growing awareness of the link between diet and health, coupled with ageing and affluent populations, has led to an increased demand for food products that deliver health benefits beyond basic nutrition. Functional foods and dietary or food supplements (also known as nutraceuticals, natural health products (NHPs), and complementary medicines) have emerged as a new category of products promising health benefits to consumers. Examples of functional foods include foods with enhanced levels of omega-3 fatty acids for heart health, foods enhanced with probiotics for digestive health, or calcium for bone health. Supplements are typically isolated or purified from food (plant, animal, microorganism or marine based) and may include ingredients such as amino acids or vitamins. Firms market supplements in a dosage form such as pills, capsules, powders, or liquids.

The emergence of new health claims, sometimes encompassing new or novel food products, has required adaptations in the regulatory environment for food and supplements. Regulation needs to balance the imperative of protecting consumers from false and misleading health claims while encouraging research and development into products offering socially beneficial health outcomes.

The health foods sector is diverse and can be difficult to define. Health foods are defined differently, regulated differently, and encompass different types of products in different countries. The terms functional foods, nutraceuticals, supplements, natural health products, complementary medicines are variously used in different jurisdictions to refer to products with health-enhancing attributes. Differences in definitions matter - governing how these products are regulated and positioned in the market, determining what types of health claims are allowed, and creating complexities for firms seeking to navigate access to export markets. This chapter examines the overarching regulatory objectives with respect to health foods and provides an international comparison of the approach to regulating health claims in the United States (US), Canada, the European Union (EU), Japan, and Australia.

Health claims can be classified with respect to the scope of the claim (generic or product-specific), as well as the nature of the claim (disease risk reduction or structure/function claim). Generic health claims specifying relationships between a food component and a health benefit are available for use on any food product that meets the requirements for the use of the claim; for example, the relationship between a food component and lower cholesterol levels, a risk factor in coronary heart disease. In contrast, product-specific health claims are tied to a specific product that has undergone a registration process for the use of the claim and may not be permitted for use on other products.[1,2] The use of generic health claims is more common than a product-specific approach.

The nature of the health claim, whether disease risk reduction or structure/function, and the approach to regulating these types of claims is the source of more significant regulatory divergence across different jurisdictions. A disease risk reduction claim indicates a relationship between the consumption of a nutrient and the reduced risk of a health condition. For example, several countries (US, Japan, Canada, Australia) permit health claims linking the presence of calcium and/or vitamin D and the reduced risk of osteoporosis. Structure/function claims suggest a link between the presence of a specific nutrient and the normal growth, development or functioning of the human body. An example is the presence of calcium and/or vitamin D and proper

1. Jill E. Hobbs, Stavroula Malla, Eric K. Sogah & May T. Yeung, *Regulating Health Foods: Policy Challenges and Consumer Conundrums* (Edward Elgar Publishing Ltd. 2014), 266pp.
2. Muriel Subirade, *Report on Functional Foods* (Food and Agriculture Organization of the United Nations 2007).

bone structure, a structure/function claim permitted in several countries, including the EU, US, and Canada.

The chapter is organized as follows: section §10.02 explores the overarching regulatory issues with respect to why governments regulate the use of health claims, together with common challenges in devising a regulatory strategy. Section §10.03 summarizes the health claims regulatory environment in the US, Canada, the EU, Japan, and Australia. Section §10.04 concludes with an assessment of the similarities and differences in regulatory approaches.

§10.02 REGULATORY OBJECTIVES AND PITFALLS

The use of health claims on food products is subject to regulatory oversight in most countries. Health claims regulation balances several objectives, including encouraging healthier diets, protecting consumers from false or misleading health claims, and establishing a clear and transparent set of rules for firms operating in this space. The process for assessing the scientific evidence in support of a health claim, together with the types of health claims permitted, influences the incentives for innovation and product development in the health foods sector. Consumer confidence in the regulatory oversight of health claims shapes their trust in health claims. A lax regulatory environment, or one which permits a confusing array of conflicting health claims, weakens consumer confidence and trust, while an overly restrictive regulatory approach stifles incentives to invest in the sector. A regulatory balancing act is required, taking into consideration the potential for both market and non-market failures.

The concept of market failure recognizes that, left to their own devices, markets sometimes fail to produce a socially optimal allocation of resources. Four sources of market failure exist: public goods and externalities, imperfect information (including information asymmetry), monopoly rents, and distributional equity.[3] Economists have long recognized that government intervention to correct a market failure is justified if the intervention yields a Pareto improvement[4] and if the benefits of the intervention outweigh the costs. While the notion of market failure is well established in the economics literature, Coase[5] observed that the potential for government or regulatory failure also exists, with the theory of non-market failures subsequently gaining traction[6,7]. Non-market (regulatory) failure occurs when a policy intervention creates additional inefficiencies.

Wolf[8] posits four sources of non-market (government or regulatory) failures: (i) the tendency to use more resources than is necessary given the disconnection between

3. Charles Wolf, *Market and Non-market Failures: Comparison and Assessment*, Journal of Public Policy, 7(1) 43-70 (1987).
4. A Pareto improvement makes at least one individual better off without making another individual worse off.
5. Ronald Coase, *Discussion*, American Economic Review, 54(3) 194-197 (1964).
6. Charles Wolf, *A Theory of Non-market Failure: Framework for Implementation Analysis*, Journal of Law and Economics, 21(1) 107-139 (1979).
7. Wolf, *supra* note 3.
8. *Ibid.*

revenues (e.g., tax revenue) and costs; (ii) internalities or self-interested behaviour – where private or organizational goals are oriented towards agency performance rather than the achievement of socially optimal market outcomes; (iii) derived externalities – unintended consequences of public policy that are not considered by public agencies; and (iv) distributional inequities caused by power and privilege emerging as drivers of decisions, rather than the income and wealth incentives that characterize markets. A balanced approach to regulation therefore requires consideration of the extent to which the intervention addresses a market failure (leading to a Pareto improvement) while avoiding the pitfalls of regulatory (non-market) failure.

Two consumption-related market failures arise in the context of health foods: information asymmetry and negative externalities.[9,10] The health-enhancing properties of functional food (or supplements) are credence attributes: consumers cannot evaluate the presence (or quality) of a credence attribute even after use,[11,12] thus creating information asymmetry. In the absence of credible labelling, consumers are unaware of (or do not trust) potential health benefits arising from the consumption of functional foods or supplements, resulting in underconsumption of these products from a social welfare perspective. Establishing a regulatory environment that facilitates credible health claims allows consumers to identify foods with specific health benefits, thereby addressing the market failure due to information asymmetry. Establishing a clear, transparent and enforceable regulatory environment for health claims also reduces uncertainty for firms investing in this sector, as well as reducing the potential for damage to the collective reputation of the industry from spurious health claims promulgated by unscrupulous firms.

Addressing the market failure due to information asymmetry and the need to protect consumers from false and misleading health claims is the most powerful motivator behind health claims regulation. Providing useful, credible information to consumers requires an appropriate regulatory balance. An overly restrictive labelling environment complicates rather than facilitating the consumer decision-making process, particularly if consumers must navigate a series of small-print riders and qualifying statements to evaluate a health claim. A relatively lax regulatory system allowing the use of contradictory or obtuse language, or permitting health claims for which little scientific evidence exists, however, creates doubt as to the veracity of health claims.

A second motivation for regulation arises due to negative (consumption) externalities. Even in the presence of credible labelling, consumers may under-consume healthier foods if the costs of ill health are not borne entirely by the individual. Publicly funded health care systems (or even private health care insurance markets) mean that

9. Hobbs et al., *supra* note 1.
10. Jill E. Hobbs, Stavroula Malla & Eric K. Sogah, *Regulatory Frameworks for Functional Food and Supplements*, Canadian Journal of Agricultural Economics, 62(4) 569-594 (2014).
11. Michael Darby & Edi Karni, *Free Competition and the Optimal Amount of Fraud*, Journal of Law and Economics, 6, 67-88 (1973).
12. Jill E. Hobbs, *Heterogeneous Consumers and Differentiated Food Markets: Implications for Quality Signaling in Food Supply Chains*, Canadian Journal of Agricultural Economics, 67(3) 237-249 (2019). DOI: 10.1111/cjag.12202.

an insured individual does not bear the full costs of poor health, resulting in the consumption of foods with health benefits at a level below the social optimum. While there may be little that labelling can do to alleviate this aspect of market failure, strategies to encourage healthier diets (including facilitating appropriate health claims on food products) are an important aspect of general public policy.[13]

Positive spillover effects (externalities) may be present in the approval process for new health claims. Obtaining approval for a new health claim typically involves lengthy and complex procedures for assessing the scientific evidence to support the claim, with the costs of obtaining approval incurred by the firm or organization applying for the health claim. When health claims are generic, these are sunk costs to the individual innovating firm (or organization) applying for the health claim that reduce entry costs for subsequent firms entering the market. New entrants can free-ride on the efforts of the innovating firm. Since the benefits of pursuing a new health claim accrue to others in addition to the innovating firm, suboptimal levels of resources will be allocated to new product development and new health claims approval. This is another form of market failure.[14]

Policymakers face a delicate balancing act: an overly complex or onerous regulatory process for the approval of new health claims (or the registration of new products) risks introducing elements of non-market (regulatory) failure. Firms operating in the sector face higher costs that deter investment if the regulatory process for the approval of a new health claim is slow, demanding and expensive, or lacks transparency. Regulatory inefficiencies reduce the incentive to invest in the health foods sector, resulting in fewer of these foods being available to consumers. Yet regulation of health claims is necessary to protect consumers from false or misleading information, to encourage consumption of healthier food products, and to create a level playing field and transparency for firms investing in the sector. As the discussion in the next section indicates, similarities, as well as some striking differences, exist in how countries have approached this regulatory balancing act.

§10.03 REGULATION OF HEALTH CLAIMS IN SELECTED COUNTRIES

[A] United States

The Food and Drug Administration (FDA) has regulatory responsibility over the US food sector, primarily under the Fair Packaging and Labeling Act, Federal Food, Drug and Cosmetic Act and the Nutrition Labeling Education Act. The majority of prepackaged foods must display nutrition labelling, while food labels with nutrient content claims and/or health claims must meet specific requirements. Applicable regulations and their requirements change frequently. The FDA does not pre-approve individual labels for food products.

13. Hobbs et al., *supra* note 1 and *supra* note 10.
14. Hobbs et al., *supra* note 1.

Conventional foods include most prepared foods and raw produce. The terms functional foods and nutraceuticals are not formally defined by the FDA but are in common use in the industry. Dietary supplements are a special category of products under the general umbrella of foods with a unique labelling regime.[15] A food product is regulated according to its intended use, its labelling and accompanying information, which includes nutrition information, nutrient content claims and health claims. The FDA classifies a product as either a food or a drug depending on the intended use. Manufacturers and producers of food products must therefore definitively choose whether to market their product as a food or as a drug and, in doing so, de facto select their regulatory category and its specific requirements. If a manufacturer chooses to market its product as a functional food, the product can be regulated as a conventional food or a dietary supplement.[16] The FDA allows three types of claims on food and dietary supplement labels – health claims (risk reduction), structure/function claims, and nutrient content claims.

Risk reduction health claims indicate a relationship between a food, a component of food or a dietary ingredient, and a reduction in disease risk or change in health condition and are subject to a pre-market review and authorization process by the FDA. The FDA permits authorized health claims only after an evidence-based review process, where the food/disease connection has met the significant scientific agreement (SSA) standard. As of January 2018, the FDA had approved twelve SSA-based Health Claims.[17] Examples include calcium, vitamin D and osteoporosis; dietary saturated fat and cholesterol and risk of coronary heart disease; plant sterol/stanol esters and risk of CHD. In addition, Authoritative Statement Health Claims are approved for conventional food products only, based upon an authoritative statement from specific US scientific bodies.[18] Examples include potassium and risk of high blood pressure and strokes; wholegrain foods and risk of heart disease and certain cancers; and saturated fat, cholesterol and trans fat and reduced risk of heart disease.

Qualified health claims are authorized after the same evaluation procedure and are supported by credible but inconclusive evidence; thus, qualified health claims are not held to the same level of qualified expert consensus.[19] A qualification or small-print rider must be included with the health claim. More than thirty qualified health claims are currently approved in the US. Examples include green tea and cancer; omega-3 fatty acids and coronary heart disease (CHD); tomatoes and/or tomato sauce and prostate cancer. All authorized health claims (including qualified claims) are generic in that,

15. Food and Drug Administration, *Food Labeling and Nutrition* https://www.fda.gov/food/food-labeling-nutrition, accessed 25 October 2019.
16. Hobbs et al., *supra* note 1.
17. Food and Drug Administration, *Authorized Health Claims that Meet the Significant Scientific Agreement Standard* (12 January 2018) https://www.fda.gov/food/food-labeling-nutrition/authorized-health-claims-meet-significant-scientific-agreement-ssa-standard#approved.
18. Food and Drug Administration, *Label Claims for Conventional Foods and Dietary Supplements* (19 June 2018) https://www.fda.gov/food/food-labeling-nutrition/label-claims-conventional-foods-and-dietary-supplements.
19. Food and Drug Administration, *Qualified Health Claims* (14 June 2019) https://www.fda.gov/food/food-labeling-nutrition/qualified-health-claims.

once authorized, any food product may use the claim so long as it meets the claim's criteria of use.

Structure/function claims are permitted by the FDA without a pre-market review and do not require approval before marketing. They describe the role of an ingredient or nutrient in affecting the normal structure or function of the body, or the means by which it does so. The claim must not be misleading, and while the manufacturer must be able to substantiate its claim, the substantiation is not presented to the FDA. There is no need for conventional food manufacturers to notify the FDA of structure/function claims and a disclaimer is not required on the labels.[20] Consequently, the FDA does not approve or maintain a register of structure/function claims.

Nutrient content claims describe the level of a nutrient in the product. They must be approved by the FDA, only use the language specified by the FDA and be accompanied by additional information, usually the presence of nutrition labelling. The regulation ensures that descriptive terms such as free, low, high, more, reduced, lite common in nutrient content claims are used consistently and have meaning for consumers.[21]

Dietary supplements are regulated by the 1994 Dietary Supplements Health Education Act (DSHEA). The same generic authorized and qualified health claims can be made for dietary supplements as conventional foods since the FDA applies the same standards in assessing health claims for both conventional foods and dietary supplements.[22,23] Dietary supplements can also use structure/function claims by notifying the FDA within thirty days of being marketed with the claim. A dietary supplement making a structure/function claim must be labelled with the disclaimer that the FDA has not evaluated the claim and the supplement is 'not intended to diagnose, treat cure or prevent any disease'.[24] In addition to the nutrient content claims available to conventional foods, dietary supplements are permitted the use of percentage claims which describe the percentage level of an ingredient that may not have a recommended daily intake in the supplement.[25] Dietary supplements are not subject to pre-market approval or registration prior to marketing and sale, even when using novel ingredients or those for which the scientific evidence is lacking or showing potential harm.[26,27] Product offerings, as well as sales, in the dietary supplement category have experienced exponential growth, attributable not only to strong consumer demand but also to the ease of market entry. Given that new products are not tested by the FDA for safety, purity or quality, nor is substantiation required when making structure/function

20. Food and Drug Administration, *Structure/Function Claims* (14 December 2017) https://www.fda.gov/food/food-labeling-nutrition/structurefunction-claims#conventional.
21. Food and Drug Administration, *supra* note 18.
22. Hobbs et al., *supra* note 1.
23. Taylor C. Wallace, *Twenty Years of the Dietary Supplement Health and Education Act: How Should Dietary Supplements Be Regulated?*, Journal of Nutrition, 145, 1683, 1686 (2015).
24. Food and Drug Administration, *supra* note 20.
25. Food and Drug Administration, *supra* note 18.
26. Wallace, *supra* note 23.
27. Hobbs et al., *supra* note 1.

claims, the cost of market entry is significantly reduced.[28] Firms can implement highly flexible marketing strategies based on permissive structure/function claims as well as the availability of a large selection of generic authorized claims. The relatively relaxed regulatory structure encourages firms to undertake research and development. While this creates an environment conducive to innovation and growth in the dietary supplement industry, it does so at the expense of greater consumer protection.[29]

The US has been undertaking a process of review and reform of the dietary supplements regulatory environment. In September 2017, the FDA announced a public meeting seeking comment on the development of a pre-DSHEA list of dietary ingredients.[30] The status of this list is still under development at time of writing.[31] In February 2019, FDA announced plans to revise the new dietary ingredients notification process, undertake greater enforcement actions against adulterated or unlawful products or misleading labelling and claims and create a rapid communications strategy to alert consumers about unlawful marketing of dietary supplements.[32] In April 2019, the FDA announced the Dietary Supplement Ingredient Advisory List, which is a means to rapidly alert the public when ingredients in dietary supplements are unlawfully marketed.[33] Concurrently, the FDA announced a public meeting seeking comments from interested parties to help facilitate 'responsible innovation in the dietary supplement industry while preserving the FDA's ability to protect the public from unsafe, misbranded, or otherwise unlawful dietary supplements'.[34] A range of topics is under review, including the scope of substances that are considered dietary ingredients, ways to incentivize responsible innovation, strategies to encourage compliance with and

28. James Hamblin, *Why Vitamins and Other Dietary Supplements Can Contain Anything*, The Atlantic (26 June 2016) https://www.theatlantic.com/health/archive/2016/06/supplements-make-tobacco-look-easy/488798/ accessed 24 February 2020.
29. Hobbs et al., *supra* note 1.
30. Federal Register, *Development of a List of Pre-dietary Supplement Health and Education Act Dietary Ingredients; Public Meeting; Request for Comments*, Federal Register Notice (6 September 2017) https://www.federalregister.gov/documents/2017/09/06/2017-18812/development-of-a-list-of-pre-dietary-supplement-health-and-education-act-dietary-ingredients-public.
31. Daniel Fabricant, *Responsible Innovation in Dietary Supplements: Promoting Overall Compliance with the Premarket Notification Requirement Through Enforcement*, presentation made at FDA Public Meeting (16 May 2019) https://www.fda.gov/media/126623/download (accessed 24 February 2020).
32. Food and Drug Administration, *Statement from FDA Commissioner Scott Gottlieb, M.D., on the Agency's New Efforts to Strengthen Regulation of Dietary Supplements by Modernizing and Reforming FDA's Oversight*, Food and Drug Administration Statement (11 February 2019) https://www.fda.gov/news-events/press-announcements/statement-fda-commissioner-scott-gottlieb-md-agencys-new-efforts-strengthen-regulation-dietary.
33. Food and Drug Administration, *FDA Statement from Deputy Commissioner for Food Policy and Response Frank Yiannas on New Steps to Protect Consumers from Unlawful Ingredients in Dietary Supplements* (16 April 2019) https://www.fda.gov/news-events/press-announcements/fda-statement-deputy-commissioner-food-policy-and-response-frank-yiannas-new-steps-protect-consumers.
34. *Ibid.*

implement meaningful enforcement of regulations, and a potential mandatory pre-market product registry.[35,36] The industry has emphasized the need to balance effective regulation of supplements without stifling commercial incentives in the sector.[37]

The US regulatory environment for dietary supplements is evolving, with the FDA undertaking several significant initiatives intended to modernize and reform its oversight. Such efforts will be complicated, requiring consultation, collaboration and engagement of industry stakeholders; the process will be lengthy and broad in scope. The regulatory environment for health foods and dietary supplements in the US will therefore be in a gradual state of change for the foreseeable future.

[B] Canada

The Canadian regulatory approach to health foods or functional food products has been evolving. Canada makes a clear regulatory distinction between supplements (known as NHPs) and food. Health Canada is responsible for regulating health claims on food under the Food and Drug Regulations (FDR), while the Canadian Food Inspection Agency (CFIA) is responsible for enforcing food labelling regulations. Regulatory responsibility for NHPs lies with the Natural and Non-prescription Health Products Directorate (NNHPD) within Health Canada and is governed by the Natural Health Products Regulations (NHPR) which came into force in 2004.

Functional food is defined by Health Canada[38] 'as similar in appearance to, or may be, a conventional food, is consumed as part of a usual diet and is demonstrated to have physiological benefits and/or reduce the risk of chronic disease beyond basic nutritional functions' (p. 3). A health claim relates to the consumption of a food product or food ingredient and health. The assessment of new food-health claims is based on three main criteria: causality, generalization, and quality assurance. A comprehensive list of studies that involve original research in humans on the food-health relationship is also required to establish a causal link between a food and healthiness.[39] Permitted generic health claims on food products in Canada include disease risk reduction claims, therapeutic claims, function claims (including nutrient

35. Megan Olsen & Andrew Shao, *New Dietary Ingredients (NDI) and Innovation in Dietary Supplements: A Call for New Compliance and Enforcement Strategies*, Food and Drug Law Institute (April/May 2019) https://www.fdli.org/2019/07/new-dietary-ingredients-ndi-and-innovation-in-dietary-supplements/.
36. Sebastian Krawiec, *NDI Problems Take Center Stage at FDA Public Meeting with Industry*, Nutritional Outlook (20 May 2019) http://www.nutritionaloutlook.com/regulatory/ndi-problems-take-center-stage-fda-public-meeting-industry.
37. *Ibid.*
38. Health Canada, *Nutraceuticals/functional Foods and Health Claims on Foods*, Health Canada, (1998) http://www.hc-sc.gc.ca/fn-an/label-etiquet/claims-reclam/nutra-funct_foods-nutra-fonct_aliment-eng.php, accessed 20 June 2014.
39. Health Canada, *Guidance Document for Preparing a Submission for Food Health Claims*, Health Canada (2009) http://www.hc-sc.gc.ca/fn-an/alt_formats/hpfb-dgpsa/pdf/legislation/health-claims_guidance-orientation_allegations-sante-eng.pdf, accessed 15 April 2010.

function claims, probiotic claims), general health claims, and implied health claims.[40,41,42]

Disease risk reduction claims correlate the consumption of food or a food ingredient and the risk of developing a diet-related disease.[43] Therapeutic claims refer to the relationship between the consumption of a certain nutrient or food and the treatment or mitigation of a disease or condition, or restoring or otherwise modifying an existing function. Function claims denote the effects of a food or food component on the normal functions of the human body.

Further, general health claims are broad claims that promote health through healthy eating or that provide dietary guidance, without referring to a specific or general health effect, health condition or disease (e.g., 'part of a healthy diet'). These claims are permitted on foods that meet the recommendations of Canada's Food Guide, a nutrition guide produced by Health Canada. Implied health claims can consist of logos, symbols or words that contribute to an overall impression about a food product and are evaluated on a case-by-case basis (e.g., probiotic, antioxidant).

Sixteen disease risk reduction or therapeutic claims are currently permitted in Canada. Examples include: sodium and hypertension; calcium and osteoporosis; psyllium products, barley products, ground whole flaxseed and lower blood cholesterol; vegetables and fruit and heart disease.[44] *See* §10.05, Appendix for a full list.[45] Canada also allows structure/function claims (known as function claims), which describe the beneficial effects that the consumption of a food or food constituent has on the normal functions of the body. Three have been approved: coarse wheat bran and regularity; green tea and antioxidant effect on blood; and psyllium and regularity.[46]

Nutrient function claims (formerly known as biological role claims) and probiotic claims are subcategories of function claims.[47] Nutrient function claims describe the well-established roles of energy or nutrients essential for the maintenance of good health or normal growth and development.[48] There are twenty-eight acceptable nutrient function claims,[49] including, for example, 'calcium aids in the formation and

40. Canadian Food Inspection Agency and Health Canada, *Guide to Food Labeling and Advertising* (2009) http://www.inspection.gc.ca/english/fssa/labeti/guide/toce.shtml, accessed 8 March 2010.
41. Canadian Food Inspection Agency, *Health Claims on Food Labels*, 2019 http://www.inspection.gc.ca/food/requirements-and-guidance/labelling/industry/health-claims/eng/1392834838383/1392834887794?chap=0.
42. Canadian Health Food Association, *Resources Advertising and Labelling* (2019) https://chfa.ca/en/Regulatory/Food-Regulations/Resources, accessed 11 October 2019.
43. Canadian Food Inspection Agency and Health Canada, *supra* note 40.
44. Health Canada, *Health Claim Assessments*, Health Canada, (2017) https://www.canada.ca/en/health-canada/services/food-nutrition/food-labelling/health-claims/assessments.html, accessed 11 October 2019.
45. A number of health claims have been reviewed by Health Canada but not accepted including: Dietary Fibre, Grain Products and Cancer (2001); Dietary Fat and Cancer (2005); Whole Grains and Coronary Heart Disease (2012). Health Canada ruled that the balance of scientific evidence did not support these health claims, however, they have been approved in the US.
46. Canadian Food Inspection Agency, *supra* note 41.
47. *Ibid.*
48. Canadian Food Inspection Agency, *supra* note 40.
49. Canadian Food Inspection Agency, *supra* note 41.

maintenance of bones and teeth', 'iron factor in red blood cell formation, or helps build red blood cells'. The second subcategory of function claims, probiotic claims, refer to microorganisms in food that are beneficial to human health.[50,51] Probiotic claims can also take the form of therapeutic or disease risk reduction claims but typically tend to be function claims and may be either strain-specific or non-strain specific. Strain-specific probiotic claims refer to the health benefits or effects of specific strains of probiotics, while non-strain-specific probiotic claims indicate the general effects of probiotics on body function. Sixteen acceptable non-strain specific claims for probiotics are currently approved,[52] including for example: 'Bifidobacterium adolescentis probiotic that naturally forms part of the gut flora', 'Lactobacillus salivarius provides live microorganisms that contribute to healthy gut flora'. Health Canada has not yet accepted any strain-specific claims. Health Canada defines NHPs as 'naturally occurring substances that are used to restore or maintain good health' and may derive from plants, animals, microorganisms and marine sources.[53] According to the NHPR, NHPs include vitamins and minerals, herbal remedies, homoeopathic medicines, traditional medicines (such as Chinese medicines), probiotics, and other products, such as amino acids and essential fatty acids.[54] Labelling requirements under the NHPR include product name, quantity, ingredient listing and recommended conditions of use. The latter includes purpose, dosage, route of administration and any cautionary statements. Health claims on NHPs are product specific, requiring manufacturers to prove ingredient content in order to obtain mandatory pre-market approval.[55] Health Canada is currently updating its approach to regulating labelling and health claims on NHPs. Proposed changes include the use of a standardized format for the presentation of essential risk information, along with the use of plain language to ensure that information on labels can easily be understood.[56] In summary, Canada has a smaller list of approved disease risk reduction claims for food products and a stronger requirement for the use of structure/function claims compared to that of the US. In general, Canada has a fairly stringent regulatory procedure, and updates to the labelling requirements for NHPs aim to add a further layer of consumer protection. Canada is also unique in that it allows therapeutic claims on food. As with other jurisdictions, the use of generic health claims for functional food may create free-rider

50. *Ibid.*
51. Canadian Food Inspection Agency, *supra* note 42.
52. Canadian Food Inspection Agency, *supra* note 41.
53. Health Canada, *Natural and Non-prescription Health Products Directorate*, Government of Canada (2019) https://www.canada.ca/en/health-canada/corporate/about-health-canada/branches-agencies/health-products-food-branch/natural-non-prescription-health-products-directorate.html, accessed 13 November 2019.
54. *Ibid.*
55. A detailed review of Canada's NHP Regulations lies beyond the scope of this chapter. Interested readers are referred to Hobbs et al., *supra* note 1 and C. Tamayo & F.A. Hoffman, *Canada's Natural Health Products: A Regulatory Overview*, Pharmaceutical Regulatory Affairs, 5, 174 (2016) doi: 10.4172/2167-7689.1000174.
56. Health Canada, Forward Regulatory Plan 2019-2021: Self-Care Framework, Health Canada, Government of Canada, 2019 https://www.canada.ca/en/health-canada/corporate/about-health-canada/legislation-guidelines/acts-regulations/forward-regulatory-plan/plan/self-care-framework.html, accessed 13 November 2019.

problems, reducing incentives for firms to invest the resources necessary to establish a new health claim, but creates opportunities for positive spillover effects once a health claim is established.

[C] The European Union

Prior to 2006, the EU did not have a harmonized health claims system, and different approaches were in use across the Member States. Following regulatory harmonization in 2006, the European Food Safety Authority (EFSA) assumed regulatory responsibility for evaluating the scientific evidence supporting health claims. The approval process for a new health claim consists of a series of steps. First, the applicant provides information to a national authority in a Member State, after which an opinion is issued by EFSA with respect to whether the health claim is substantiated by scientific evidence and is in compliance with European Health Claims Regulation (EU 1924/2006). The EFSA-approved health claims are then forwarded to the European Commission (EC) which decides whether or not to permit the health claim and maintains the EU Register of Nutrition and Health Claims Made on Foods.[57]

A number of criteria exist for making new health claims and nutrient content claims in accordance with EC 1924/2006. The claim must have some established positive nutritional or physiological effect; nutrients in the food must be either high or low enough to achieve the desired effect; and the consumer needs to only consume a reasonable amount of the product to achieve the desired nutritive or physiological effect.[58]

A food is defined as a functional food by the European Commission Concerted Action on Functional Food Science in Europe if: 'it is satisfactorily demonstrated to affect beneficially one or more target functions in the body, beyond adequate nutritional effects, in a way that is relevant to either an improved state of health and well-being and/or reduction of risk of disease. Functional foods must be in the form of conventional foods and they must demonstrate their effects in amounts that can normally be expected to be consumed in the diet: they are not pills or capsules, but part of a normal food pattern'[59] (p. 1).

The EU defines supplements as concentrated sources of nutrients (i.e., minerals and vitamins) with nutritional or physiological effects that are marketed in dose form (e.g., pills, capsules, or liquids). The EU regulates supplements as foods; thus, health and nutrition claims for foodstuffs may also apply to food supplements. However, the list of nutrients eligible for food supplement status is fairly restrictive. If a substance intended for use in a food supplement does not have a history of safe use in the EU prior

57. https://ec.europa.eu/food/safety/labelling_nutrition/claims/health_claims_en.
58. European Commission, EC Regulation No. 1924/2006 of the Parliament and of the Council of 20 December 2006 on nutrition and health claims made on foods (2006) https://eur-lex.europa.eu/LexUriServ/LexUriServ.do?uri=OJ:L:2006:404:0009:0025:EN:PDF, accessed 24 February 2020.
59. Alexander J. Stein & Emilio Rodríguez-Cerezo, *Functional Food in the European Union* (Institute for Prospective Technological Studies, Technical Report Series EUR 23380 EN–2008 2008).

to 1997, EFSA must provide a scientific opinion on its safety under the auspices of the EU novel foods regulations.[60,61]

Three broad types of health claims are permitted in the EU: function health claims (Article 13 claims); risk reduction claims (Article 14(1)(a) claims); and claims referring to children's development (Article 14(1)(b) claims).[62] Function health (Article 13) claims are 'relating to the growth, development and functions of the body, or referring to psychological and behavioural functions, or on slimming or weight-control'.[63] Two subcategories of Article 13 claims exist: Article 13(1) health claims (generic structure/function) and Article 13(5) health claims (product specific, new or proprietary). For example, 'calcium is needed for the maintenance of normal bones' and 'calcium is needed for the maintenance of normal teeth' are Article 13(1) (function) claims. Examples of Article 13(5) (product-specific, new or proprietary) claims include: 'Carbohydrates contribute to the recovery of normal muscle function (contraction) after highly intensive and/or long-lasting physical exercise leading to muscle fatigue and the depletion of glycogen stores in skeletal muscle' and 'Lactitol contributes to normal bowel function by increasing stool frequency.' Currently, the EU has approved 241 function health claims, including 229 Article 13(1) claims and 12 Article 13(5) claims.

Risk reduction (Article 14(1)(a)) claims refer to the reduction of a risk factor in the development of a disease. Examples include 'calcium and vitamin D help to reduce the loss of bone mineral in postmenopausal women. Low bone mineral density is a risk factor for osteoporotic bone fractures' and 'Sugar-free chewing gum helps reduce tooth demineralisation. Tooth demineralisation is a risk factor in the development of dental caries.' Currently, there are fourteen authorized risk reduction claims in the EU[64] (*see* §10.05 Appendix to this chapter).

The final category of health claims are health claims pertaining to children (Article 14(1)(b)). In contrast to other countries such as Canada which prohibit the use of health claims on products intended for children under the age of 2, the EU has approved twelve health claims pertaining to the normal health and development of children under Article 14(1)(b).[65] Examples include 'calcium and vitamin D are needed for normal growth and development of bone in children'; 'Iron contributes to normal cognitive development of children.'[66]

60. European Food Safety Authority, *Food Supplements* (2019) https://www.efsa.europa.eu/en/topics/topic/food-supplements, accessed 13 November 2019.
61. A detailed discussion of food supplements in the EU lies beyond the scope of this chapter. We refer interested readers to Hobbs et al., *supra* note 1 and European Food Safety Authority, *supra* note 60.
62. European Commission, *EU Register of nutrition and health claims* (2019) https://ec.europa.eu/food/safety/labelling_nutrition/claims/register/public/?event=search, accessed 19 November 2019.
63. *Ibid.*
64. *Ibid.*
65. For the complete dataset of nutrition and health claims *see* European Commission, *supra* note 62.
66. European Commission, *supra* note 62.

In general, the regulatory stringency of the EU system appears to be high as indicated by the relatively short list of approved disease risk reduction claims and an extensive list of health claims (2,076 by November 2019) that remain unauthorized due to the failure to meet standards of scientific evidence.[67]

[D] Japan

Responsibility for regulating the health foods sector in Japan lies with the Ministry of Health, Labour and Welfare (MHLW). Japan was one of the first countries to regulate functional foods, recognizing that food products could positively affect the physiological system of the human body.[68] Japan does not make a regulatory distinction between dietary supplements and functional food, using the same approach to health claims regardless of whether the product is marketed as a food or a dietary supplement. In contrast to the approach in other countries such as the US, the EU, and Canada, health claims in Japan are product specific. Claims must be approved prior to use.

A set of approved health claims was established for foods (and dietary supplements) under the classification Food for Specified Health Uses (FOSHU). FOSHU encompasses food that 'is intended to be consumed for the maintenance/promotion of health or for special health uses by people who wish to control health conditions, including blood pressure or blood cholesterol'.[69] Health claims in this category are generally known as Regular FOSHU.

Additional categories of health claims include Qualified FOSHU, Standardized FOSHU and Reduction of disease risk FOSHU (sometimes called Specific FOSHU) based on different strengths of assurance with respect to the health benefit. Qualified FOSHU includes foods for which the evidence supporting a health function is weaker and does not meet the level of regular FOSHU. Standardized FOSHU is for food processing ingredients that are well established in FOSHU claims.[70] Reduction of Disease Risk FOSHU are products allowed to carry a reduction of disease risk claim 'when reduction of disease risk is clinically and nutritionally established in an ingredient'.[71] Examples of FOSHU approved products include foods with gastrointestinal benefits, foods related to blood cholesterol levels, blood sugar levels, and blood pressure (*see* §10.05 Appendix to this chapter).

Two approved disease risk reduction claims exist. The first refers to a link between calcium and osteoporosis ('Intake of proper amount of calcium contained in healthy meals with appropriate exercise may support healthy bones of young women and reduce the risk of osteoporosis when aged'). The second claim relates to folic acid and neural tube defect ('Intake of proper amount of folic acid contained in healthy

67. *Ibid.*
68. Ministry of Health, Labour and Welfare, *Food for Specified Health Uses (FOSHU)*, Government of Japan http://www.mhlw.go.jp/english/topics/foodsafety/fhc/02.html, accessed 24 February 2020.
69. *Ibid.*
70. Hobbs et al., *supra* note 1.
71. Ministry of Health, Labour and Welfare, *supra* note 68.

meals may support women to bear healthy babies by reducing the risk of neural tube defect, such as spondyloschisis, during fetal development').[72]

For FOSHU approval, the MHLW requires that the effectiveness of the food on the human body be clearly proven. The absence of any safety issues must also be shown (e.g., through animal toxicity tests, confirmation of the effects of excess intake). The use of nutritionally approved ingredients is required; for example, no excessive use of sodium. The use of established quality control methods, including clear specification of all products and ingredients, processes and methods of analysis, is also necessary.[73] Additionally, a safety assessment is mandated and the efficacy of functional attributes must be established in order for a food to be approved as FOSHU.

Japan also introduced the category of Food with Nutrient Function Claims (FNFC), which present evidence of a relationship between a vitamin or mineral and a health function or structure. Currently, twelve vitamins and five minerals have met the necessary evidence standards for inclusion as FNFC. These include: 'Niacin helps to maintain healthy skin and mucosa.' 'Magnesium is necessary in the development of bone and teeth, maintains proper blood circulation, and helps the proper function of many body enzymes and energy generation.'[74] An FNFC is comparable to a product with a generic structure/function claim in the US, EU or Australia. These generic FNFC claims can be made on food without prior approval for that specific product as long as the product meets the requisite standards and specifications.

A new regulatory classification, Foods with Function Claims (FFC), was established in 2015 based on the Dietary Supplement Health and Education Act (DSHEA) system in use in the US. The FFC rules exist as an additional regulation alongside the FOSHU system. The new FFC regulatory system is more flexible than the FOSHU system in terms of health claims, the protocol for clinical studies, the required results, the acceptance of scientific reviews instead of clinical studies, and the lack of a requirement for governmental approval. The FFC regulation covers all FOSHU health claims, as well as health claims relating to skin, eyes, mental stress, joints, memory, sleep, bones, fatigue, circulation, body temperature, muscles, liver, walking, backache, and other functions. It also covers structure/function health claims that are not approved in the FOSHU system. The FOSHU system restricts health claims to fatty acids, triglyceride, blood pressure, blood sugar, cholesterol GI tract, teeth care, calcium/mineral uptake. FFC health claims are product specific. According to the Consumer Affairs Agency:[75] 'Information on the evidence supporting the safety and effectiveness of the product are submitted to the Secretary-General of the Consumer Affairs Agency before the product is marketed. However, unlike FOSHU, the product is not individually pre-approved by the Secretary General of the Consumer Affairs Agency

72. *Ibid.*
73. *Ibid.*
74. Ministry of Health, Labour and Welfare, *Food with Nutrient Function Claims (FNFC)*, Ministry of Health, Labour and Welfare, Government of Japan (n.d.) http://www.mhlw.go.jp/english/topics/foodsafety/fhc/01.html, accessed 17 October 2019.
75. Food Labeling Division, Consumer Affairs Agency, Government of Japan (translation) (2015) What are 'Foods with Functions Claims' https://www.caa.go.jp/policies/policy/food_labeling/information/pamphlets/pdf/151224_1.pdf (accessed 24 February 2020).

... The submitted information is disclosed on the website of the Consumer Affairs Agency.' (pp. 2, 3). In 2019, the number of FFC products was 1,753, while the number of approved FOSHU products was 1,063.[76]

According to Iwatani and Yamamoto (p. 100)[77] after the introduction of the FOSHU system in 1991, the market for FOSHU products increased, peaking in 2007 and then declining. A number of reasons are suggested for this downward trend in FOSHU, including difficulty detecting a significant effect in healthy volunteers in clinical studies; regulatory inertia in the form of the long period from approval to registration and slow responses to additional requests; and low return on research and development expenditures. As a consequence, firms are hesitant to apply for FOSHU approval and instead have refocused their efforts towards the new FFC category of functional products. The introduction of the new FFC regulatory system appears to have revitalized the sector, with the total market reported to be worth USD 8 billion by 2018.[78] The new regulatory system has addressed some of the non-market (regulatory) failures apparent in the FOSHU system, with a more flexible approach to health claims and categories and a more relaxed approach to scientific evidence that allows the use of scientific reviews as evidence rather than purely clinical studies,[79] similar to Australia's new Assessed Listed designation. This appears to have ameliorated some of the uncertainty faced by firms investing in this sector.

Japan's regulatory system provides a mix between a purely generic system and a purely product-specific one, although the system is decidedly more product specific. The system has undergone significant changes in recent years to address some of the non-market failures caused by regulatory inertia. Nevertheless, the large number of product-specific health claims and the weaker standards for scientific evidence may threaten consumer confidence in the credibility of health claims.

[E] Australia (and New Zealand)

Australia and New Zealand coordinate their regulatory efforts in food safety (and many other food-related matters) via the Food Standards Australia New Zealand Agency (FSANZ). The Food Standards Code 1.2.7 governs nutrition, health and related claims on most food labels while Food Standards Code 1.2.8 regulates nutrition labelling.

Food manufacturers are permitted the voluntary use of nutrition (nutrient) content claims and health claims for food. Nutrition content claims focus on a substance or nutrient contained in a food while health claims focus on the relationship between a food product and health. There are two categories of health claims allowed by FSANZ: general level health claims and high level claims.

General level health claims under FSANZ are similar to the US category of structure/function claims for conventional foods in that they describe a relationship

76. Shun Iwatani & Naoyuki Yamamoto, *Functional Food Products in Japan: A Review*, Food Science and Human Wellness, 8(2) 96-101 (2019).
77. *Ibid.*
78. *Ibid.*
79. *Ibid.*

between the nutrient and a health function.[80] There is a list of 200+ pre-approved general level food-health relationship claims available to a manufacturer for use. Pre-approved general claims are generic in that any manufacturer can use the claim so long as their product meets the criteria established for the claim. General health claims cannot refer to serious disease or biomarkers of serious disease. Examples of pre-approved general level health claims include: 'calcium is necessary for normal teeth and bone structure' or 'chromium contributes to normal macronutrient metabolism'.[81]

Manufacturers can also use a general level health claim not from the pre-approved list by self-substantiating a nutrient-health relationship. This process includes certifying that the desired food-health relationship claim has been established according to the requirements dictated by Standard 1.2.7 and notifying FSANZ, which maintains a list of notified food-health relationships.

Examples of self-substantiated general level claims are provided in Table 10.1.

Table 10.1 Examples of Self-Substantiated General Level Claims (Australia)[82]

Owner	*Claim*
Lion Dairy and Drinks, Australia	Prebiotics increase beneficial bifidobacterium to support digestive health
Nature's Sunshine Products Australia Pty	Bovine hydrolysed collagen supports bones and joints Bovine hydrolysed collagen promotes youthful/healthy hair Bovine hydrolysed collagen promotes youthful/strong nails
Kellogg (Aust) Pty Ltd	Increasing grain fibre intake increases feelings of fullness
Webster Limited/Walnuts Australia	Walnuts contribute to heart health without causing weight gain Walnuts contribute to heart health

Unlike a structure/function claim in the US, or an FSANZ pre-approved general health claim, a self-substantiated general level food-health relationship claim is partially specific to the manufacturer(s) making the claim. Should another manufacturer wish to use a self-substantiated food-health relationship that is already listed, they must undertake their own review and notification process to FSANZ.[83] Therefore, the use of the specific self-substantiated claim is limited to manufacturers who undergo the review and notification process. For example, both Lion Dairy and Drinks and Vitasoy Australia Products Pty have separately notified the claim that 'Prebiotics

80. Hobbs et al., *supra* note 1.
81. Food Standards Australia New Zealand, *Schedule 4: Nutrition, Health and Related Claims* http://www.foodstandards.gov.au/code/Documents/Sched%204%20Nutrition%20and%20health%20claims%20v159.pdf, accessed 24 February 2020.
82. Food Standards Australia New Zealand, *Notified Food-Health Relationships to Make a Health Claim* http://www.foodstandards.gov.au/industry/labelling/fhr/Pages/default.aspx, accessed 24 February 2020.
83. Food Standards Australia New Zealand, *Nutrition Content Claims and Health Claims* (April 2016) http://www.foodstandards.gov.au/consumer/labelling/nutrition/Pages/default.aspx, accessed 24 February 2020.

increase beneficial bifidobacterium to support digestive health.'[84] Similar to the US FDA's stance on structure/function claims, FSANZ maintains a disclaimer pertaining to the list of notified self-substantiated claims. The agency does not 'guarantee and assumes no legal liability or responsibility for the accuracy, currency, completeness or interpretation of any information contained in the list of notified food-health relationships. FSANZ is not responsible for the enforcement of Standard 1.2.7 and does not assess compliance of the notified food-health relationships. (Their) role is only to administer the notification process. Publication by FSANZ does not indicate acceptance, approval or validation of the notified food-health relationship'.[85] High level health claims refer to a nutrient and a serious disease or biomarkers thereof – they are the equivalent of disease risk reduction claims. FSANZ has pre-approved thirteen high-level claims based upon a food-health relationship. High-level health claims are generic, hence any manufacturer can use them on their product so long as the conditions of use for the claim are met. Examples of approved high-level claims include fruits and vegetables and coronary heart disease; calcium (with or without Vitamin D) and osteoporosis; saturated fatty acids reduce cholesterol.[86] All high-level health claims must be substantiated with scientific evidence to a specified certainty and can only be used on foods that meet FSANZ nutrient profiling scoring criterion.[87] If a manufacturer wishes to use a high-level health claim beyond the approved list of thirteen, it must obtain pre-market approval from FSANZ, based on an assessment of whether there is convincing scientific evidence supporting the food-health relationship basis of the claim. Claims with insufficient or probable supporting evidence will not be approved. FSANZ does not undertake enforcement of any food safety and labelling standards. FSANZ and Food Standards 1.2.7 and 1.2.8 only regulate foods. Dietary supplements, nutraceuticals and complementary medicines are regulated separately by each country: Australia under the Therapeutic Goods Administration (TGA) and New Zealand under the New Zealand Medicines and Medical Devices Safety Authority (Medsafe). Efforts to form a joint regulatory authority to oversee both countries' medical devices and therapeutic goods markets were halted in November 2014.[88] The remaining discussion focuses on Australia, which has been undertaking significant revisions to the regulatory environment for therapeutic goods.

The TGA oversees the registration and sale of complementary medicines (CM). CM are therapeutic goods that contain one or more active ingredients including but not limited to amino acids, plant or herbal materials, lipids, minerals and vitamins. All medicines, including CM, are regulated with a risk-based approach. Depending upon their ingredients and the indications (claims) made for the product, lower risk

84. Food Standards Australia New Zealand, *supra* note 82.
85. *Ibid.*
86. Food Standards Australia New Zealand, *Reviews of Food Health Relationships for High Level Health Claims* http://www.foodstandards.gov.au/consumer/labelling/nutrition/Pages/reviewsforhighlevelc3090.aspx, accessed 24 February 2020.
87. Food Standards Australia New Zealand, *supra* note 83.
88. Stewart Eisenhart, *Australia and New Zealand Abandon Plan for Single Medical Regulatory Agency*, Emergo (20 November 2014) https://www.emergobyul.com/blog/2014/11/australia-and-new-zealand-abandon-plan-single-medical-regulatory-agency, accessed 24 February 2020.

medicines *can* be *listed* (becoming a listed CM) on the Australian Register of Therapeutic Goods (ARTG) while higher risk medicines *must* be *registered* (becoming a registered CM). Most CM are listed.[89]

A listed CM on the ARTG can only contain pre-approved low-risk ingredients, must be manufactured using GMP and as of 2018, can only use pre-approved structure/function indications for therapeutic benefits. Successful listing results in a unique AUST L registration number which must be displayed on the product label. Listed CM are treated similarly to dietary supplements in the US, as the TGA does not evaluate the product for safety, quality or efficacy prior to listing to enable rapid market access.[90] Prior to 2018, a sponsor (usually the manufacturer) of a listed CM could cite their own indication(s) (similar to a claim on a US dietary supplement) and/or choose indications from the TGA's pre-approved list. This resulted in listed CM with multiple indications, many questionable. As of 2018, indications must only be from the TGA-approved permitted indications list.[91] These indications are generic in that any listed CM product that meets the specifications of the claim can use it.[92] This is similar to the regulations under FSANZ applied to structure/function claims in conventional food.

A registered CM is considered of higher risk than a listed medicine due to their ingredients or the indications made. A product must be registered if it uses indications that are not on the permissible list or if it is not solely comprised of approved ingredients.. A registered CM will undergo full critical assessment by the TGA for quality, safety and efficacy resulting in an assigned unique AUST R number which must be displayed on its label[93] and is subject to more stringent post-marketing surveillance.[94] As of September 2018, forty-six registered CM have been evaluated by TGA for safety, efficacy and quality. Many of these have been submitted by large pharmaceutical companies,[95] indicating that the level of scrutiny for a registered medicine is high. Large companies will have the technical expertise and resources necessary to sponsor a successful CM registration.

A TGA 2016 review of CM showed increasing compliance breaches in the areas of labelling, advertising and evidence. Similar to the US market for dietary supplements, Australia's CM industry was riddled with products of doubtful efficacy, exaggerated or

89. Therapeutic Goods Administration, *An Overview of the Regulation of Complementary Medicines in Australia* (25 March 2013) https://www.tga.gov.au/overview-regulation-complementary-medicines-australia, accessed 24 February 2020.
90. Therapeutic Goods Administration, *Overview of Listed Complementary Medicines: ARGCM Part B: Listed Complementary Medicines* (29 October 2017) https://www.tga.gov.au/overview-listed-complementary-medicines#indications, accessed 24 February 2020.
91. *Ibid.*
92. Therapeutic Goods Administration, *Permitted Indications for Listed Medicines* (12 June 2019) https://www.tga.gov.au/permitted-indications-listed-medicines, accessed 24 February 2020.
93. Therapeutic Goods Administration, *Registered Complementary Medicines* (25 March 2013) https://www.tga.gov.au/registered-complementary-medicines, accessed 24 February 2020.
94. Ken Harvey, *Regulation of Complementary Medicines*, Internal Medicine Journal, 47, 983,985 (2017) https://onlinelibrary.wiley.com/doi/epdf/10.1111/imj.13548.
95. Therapeutic Goods Administration, *List of Evaluated Registered Complementary Medicines* (11 September 2018) https://www.tga.gov.au/list-evaluated-registered-complementary-medicines, accessed 24 February 2020.

unsubstantiated claims, lack of supporting evidence and little research[96] where ease of market access likely came at the expense of consumer protection. TGA subsequently began regulatory reforms for CM,[97] with the goals of minimizing the regulatory and administrative burden for businesses, while ensuring timely access to high-quality CM for consumers.[98]

As of 2018, AUST L products can only use pre-approved ingredients and indications; both lists are currently undergoing evaluation; thus existing labels and products will need to comply with forthcoming new regulations.[99] A significant regulatory change is the addition of the assessed listed (AUST AL) designation which is a new, third, intermediate level of risk and health claims tier. AUST AL products undergo a pre-market assessment of the efficacy *evidence* supporting their unique indication assessed by TGA and are labelled as such, i.e., the use of a claimer.[100,101] An AUST AL product may use intermediate indications, which can be a disease risk reduction claim or refer to a non-serious form of disease, ailment, defect or injury; they must have at least one intermediate risk indication and may also present lower risk indications but evidence for all levels of indications will be subject to pre-market assessment.[102]

Another noteworthy reform is the granting of exclusivity for the development of a new ingredient and its accompanying indication. The existing registration system for both the permissible ingredients and approved indications allowed for use by CM are generic; 'once an ingredient is included in the Permissible Ingredients Determination, it may be used in any listed CM, provided any requirements for use are complied with'.[103] Similarly, once an indication is approved and listed, it is available for use by any product that meets the requirements of the indication.

This lack of exclusivity causes a form of market failure as the generic nature of both permissible indications and ingredients lists allows free-riders to benefit from the innovation and resources of one firm. If one manufacturer undertakes the effort to seek regulatory approval of a new CM ingredient or change in use of an existing one, once the approval is achieved, many firms then can use that approved ingredient without having to incur the expense of innovating its research and development. The situation

96. Harvey, *supra* note 94.
97. Therapeutic Goods Administration, *Complementary Medicines Reforms* https://www.tga.gov.au/complementary-medicines-reforms, accessed 29 October 2019.
98. Complementary Medicines Australia, *Australia's Complementary Medicines: Industry Snapshot 2018* (2018) http://www.cmaustralia.org.au/resources/Documents/Australian%20Complementary%20Medicines%20Industry%20snapshot%202018_English.pdf, accessed 29 October 2019.
99. Therapeutic Goods Administration, *Upcoming Changes to the Permissible Indications Determination* (14 August 2019) https://www.tga.gov.au/upcoming-changes-permissible-indications-determination (accessed 29 October 2019).
100. Harvey, *supra* note 94.
101. Therapeutic Goods Administration, *supra* note 92.
102. *Ibid.*
103. Therapeutic Goods Administration, *Overview of Evaluation of a Substance for Use in Listed Complementary Medicines: ARGCM Part C: New Complementary Medicine Substance Evaluation*, (9 September 2019) https://www.tga.gov.au/overview-evaluation-substance-use-listed-complementary-medicines, accessed 29 October 2019.

is exacerbated should the approval/registration process be slow, strenuous, rigorous and/or expensive.

Although less costly in terms of time and expense, the same is true for new CM indications. A single firm will commit time and resources to undertake the application and approval of a new indication for use in the permissible indications determination. Once approved, the indication is not exclusive to that firm. Others may use that indication so long as they meet regulatory requirements in doing so. As a result, there has been little incentive for manufacturers to invest in R&D towards new ingredients for CM. In an effort to correct the free-rider problem in CM and provide incentives for innovation, regulatory reforms have now included a two year period of exclusivity for firms that undertake research and development for new ingredients.[104]

Australia continues the process of implementing regulatory reforms for complementary medicines; thus the regulatory environment will continue to evolve. These regulatory reforms are intended to find balance between consumer protection, regulatory effort and risk while also providing the industry with incentives to conduct R&D and improve the efficacy of and the evidence supporting their products.[105] Consumers are provided with improved transparency and better information from which to make informed decisions regarding their health-related purchases. The regulatory approach therefore attempts to address the potential for both market and non-market failures. Monitoring the progress and success of these regulatory reforms is worthwhile for other countries facing similar situations.

§10.04 CONCLUSIONS

The regulation of health claims on food and related products is complex and continues to evolve. As the examples discussed in this chapter illustrate, despite broad similarities in regulatory objectives, the approach to regulating health claims differs internationally. In some countries (e.g., the US, Canada, and Australia), a separate regulatory structure exists for health claims on foods (often referred to as functional foods) versus supplements (NHPs, complementary medicines). Other countries (e.g., Japan) do not make a regulatory distinction between health claims on food versus non-food supplements, with the same health claims available across both types of products. The international regulation of health claims of non-food products based on animal, plant, marine materials or microorganisms is further complicated by the mismatch in categorization of these products across countries, from dietary supplements to food supplements, to NHPs, and complementary medicines. The differences extend beyond mere terminology: what is considered an NHP in Canada may encompass a dietary supplement in the US or a complementary medicine in Australia, or a food supplement in the EU, but the categories do not map precisely, and the definitions differ. Firms exporting these products must navigate a complex and often conflicting array of definitions and regulatory approaches in different markets.

---

104. *Ibid.*
105. *Ibid.*

Beyond differences in definition and product categorization, the types of health claims that are permitted in different countries, the degree of scientific evidence required for verification of a claim, the process of regulatory approval for new claims, and the extent to which health claims are monitored and health claims regulations enforced, also differs internationally. Thus, (structure) function claims that have been pre-approved by the relevant regulatory authority are permitted for use in some countries (e.g., Canada, Australia, the EU), while the US takes a much looser approach to regulating this type of health claim. Disease risk reduction claims are subject to stronger regulatory oversight in the US (as in other countries); however, the use of qualified claims (subject to less conclusive scientific evidence) is permitted in the US and Japan, but not in Canada, the EU, Australia or New Zealand.

A further regulatory distinction arises in the use of generic versus product-specific health claims. Generic health claims - which are available for use on any product meeting the necessary conditions - are used on food products in the US, Canada, the EU, and Australia, while the Japanese regulatory structure is largely embedded in a product-specific approach. Both product-specific and generic systems are in evidence in the international regulation of dietary supplements/natural health products/complementary medicines. From a regulatory perspective, generic health claims have the advantage of allowing a wider range of products to use a health claim, encouraging competition, and avoiding a profusion of similar-sounding health claims. The disadvantage of a generic system is the potential for free-rider problems to deter private sector investment in the R&D necessary to substantiate a new health claim, as well as pursue approval of a new health claim, often a lengthy process.

The regulatory environment for health claims internationally continues to evolve, with notable changes underway recently, particularly with respect to the use of health claims on dietary supplements (US), NHPs (Canada), and complementary medicines (Australia). Concerns over misleading or exaggerated claims or the profusion of confusing and conflicting claims in use in the sector have spurred these changes. Evidentiary standards, types of health claim, language in use on labels and in advertising are all under review to differing degrees across these countries.

The regulation of health claims on foods and related products entails a delicate balancing act. At its heart is the need to protect consumers from false, fraudulent or misleading claims. A lax regulatory environment weakens consumer confidence and exposes firms marketing genuine health food products to competition from less scrupulous firms. Yet, an overly complex regulatory environment, with slow and uncertain approval processes for new health claims, deters investment in the sector, resulting in reduced consumer access to health-enhancing products. A balanced and transparent approach to the regulation of health claims creates a more stable commercial environment for firms in the health foods sector, while bolstering consumer trust.

Science does not standstill. Scientific discoveries will continue to offer foods with enhanced health properties and new ways to deliver improvements in nutrition and health. Ongoing changes to the regulatory environment will continue to be necessary, as will efforts to ensure that the divergence in international regulatory approaches does not continue to widen.

§10.05 APPENDIX

CANADA

Approved disease risk reduction or therapeutic health claims, along with the date of approval:

- Sodium and Hypertension (2000).
- Dietary Fat, Saturated Fat, Cholesterol, Trans Fatty Acids and Coronary Heart Disease (2000).
- Fruits, Vegetables and Cancer (2000).
- Calcium and Osteoporosis (2000).
- Plant Sterols (Phytosterols) (2010).
- Oat Products and Blood Cholesterol Lowering (2010).
- Psyllium Products and Blood Cholesterol Lowering (2011).
- Unsaturated Fat and Blood Cholesterol Lowering (2012).
- Barley Products and Blood Cholesterol Lowering (2012).
- Sugar-Free Chewing Gum and Dental Caries Risk Reduction (2014).
- Ground Whole Flaxseed and Blood Cholesterol Lowering (2014).
- Soy Protein and Cholesterol Lowering (2015).
- Vegetables and Fruit and Heart Disease (2016).
- Polysaccharide Complex (Glucomannan, Xanthan Gum, Sodium Alginate) and Cholesterol Lowering (2016).
- Eicosapentaenoic Acid, Docosahexaenoic Acid and Triglyceride Lowering (2016).
- Polysaccharide Complex (Glucomannan, Xanthan Gum, Sodium Alginate) and a Reduction of the Post-Prandial Blood Glucose Response (2016).

Source: Health Canada.[106]

THE EUROPEAN UNION

Approved Risk Reduction (Article 14(1)(a)) Claims

- Calcium and vitamin D help to reduce the loss of bone mineral in post-menopausal women. Low bone mineral density is a risk factor for osteoporotic bone fractures.
- Calcium helps to reduce the loss of bone mineral in post-menopausal women. Low bone mineral density is a risk factor for osteoporotic bone fractures.
- Vitamin D helps to reduce the risk of falling associated with postural instability and muscle weakness. Falling is a risk factor for bone fractures among men and women 60 years of age and older.

106. Health Canada, *supra* note 44.

- Replacing saturated fats with unsaturated fats in the diet has been shown to lower/reduce blood cholesterol. High cholesterol is a risk factor in the development of coronary heart disease.
- Supplemental folic acid intake increases maternal folate status. Low maternal folate status is a risk factor in the development of neural tube defects in the developing foetus.
- Barley beta-glucans has been shown to lower/reduce blood cholesterol. High cholesterol is a risk factor in the development of coronary heart disease.
- Barley beta-glucans has been shown to lower/reduce blood cholesterol. High cholesterol is a risk factor in the development of coronary heart disease.
- Chewing gum sweetened with 100% xylitol has been shown to reduce dental plaque. High content/level of dental plaque is a risk factor in the development of caries in children.
- Oat beta-glucan has been shown to lower/reduce blood cholesterol. High cholesterol is a risk factor in the development of coronary heart disease.
- Plant stanol esters have been shown to lower/reduce blood cholesterol. High cholesterol is a risk factor in the development of coronary heart disease.
- Plant sterols and plant stanol esters have been shown to lower/reduce blood cholesterol. High cholesterol is a risk factor in the development of coronary heart disease.
- Plant sterols have been shown to lower/reduce blood cholesterol. High cholesterol is a risk factor in the development of coronary heart disease.
- Sugar-free chewing gum helps neutralise plaque acids. Plaque acids are a risk factor in the development of dental caries.
- Sugar-free chewing gum helps reduce tooth demineralisation. Tooth demineralisation is a risk factor in the development of dental caries.

Source: European Commission (2019). EU Register on nutrition and health claims, European Commission, https://ec.europa.eu/food/safety/labelling_nutrition/claims/register/public/?event=search.[107]

JAPAN

Table A1 Approved FOSHU Products

Specified Health Uses	Principal Ingredients (ingredients exhibiting health functions)
Foods to modify gastrointestinal conditions	Oligosaccharides, lactose, bifidobacteria, lactic acid bacteria, dietary fiber 8 ingestible dextrin, polydextrol, guar gum, psyllium seed coat, etc.

107. European Commission, *supra* note 62.

Specified Health Uses	Principal Ingredients (ingredients exhibiting health functions)
Foods related to blood cholesterol level	Chitosan, soybean protein, degraded sodium alginate
Foods related to blood sugar levels	Indigestible dextrin, wheat albumin, guava tea polyphenol, L-arabiose, etc.
Foods related to blood pressure	Lactotripeptide, casein dodecaneptide, tochu leaf glycoside (geniposidic acid), sardine peptide, etc.
Foods related to dental hygiene	Paratinose, maltotriose, erythritol, etc.
Cholesterol plus gastrointestinal conditions, triacylglycerol plus cholesterol	Degraded sodium alginate, dietary fiber from psyllium seed husk, etc.
Foods related to mineral absorption	Calcium citrated malate, casein phosphopeptide, heme iron, fructo-oligosaccharide, etc.
Foods related to osteogenesis	Soybean isoflavone, MBP (Milk basic protein), etc.
Foods related to triacylglycerol	Middle chain fatty acid, etc.

Source: Ministry of Health, Labour and Welfare[108]

108. Ministry of Health, Labour and Welfare, *supra* note 68.

CHAPTER 11

Food Safety in the United States

Alexia Brunet Marks

Consumers see the world as a giant grocery store. Over the past decade, the volume of food imports in the United States (US) has doubled and the import share of overall consumption has steadily risen. The increase in food trade has, ultimately, expanded the menu of food safety risks to now include risks related to lengthy supply chains as well as differing food safety standards and varying hygienic practices. Ensuring the safety of the increasing volume and diversity of food has become an enormous challenge. This chapter highlights two unique features of the US food safety system. First, food safety regulation in the US is not focused on direct regulation but rather on cooperative engagement. Regulation involves the interplay between direct regulation (rulemaking, monitoring, and enforcement), indirect regulation (legal liability), and private regulation (farmers, private auditing and certification organizations, retailers and industry groups). Second, while the goal is to strike a delicate balance of regulatory techniques (from public to private and from low-interventionist to highly prescriptive obligations) to foster a culture of food safety, the chapter shows that this balance is difficult (if not impossible) to achieve.

§11.01 INTRODUCTION[1]

Food safety is a hotly debated issue. While food nourishes, sustains, and enriches our lives, it can also kill us. Without proper incentives to encourage food safety, microbial pathogens can and do enter the food source, so much so that according to the United States (US) Centers for Disease Control (CDC), the federal agency that tracks food-borne illnesses and collaborates with state and local health departments and other

1. Alexia Brunet Marks, A New Governance Recipe for Food Safety Regulation, 47 Loy. Univ. L.J. 3 (2016); Alexia Brunet Marks, The Risks We Are Willing to Eat: Food Imports and Safety, 52 Harv. J. on Legis. 125 (2015).

federal agencies to investigate food-borne outbreaks, each year roughly 1 in 6 Americans (or 48 million people) gets sick, 128,000 are hospitalized, and 3,000 die of food-borne diseases.[2] The cost of food-borne illness, meanwhile, is estimated at USD 15.6 billion per year.[3] Guaranteeing food safety is hard, if not impossible. Over fifty years ago, most farmers in the US were small and sold goods locally but today, at any given meal, our menu comes from a dozen different sources. As author John Fagan writes, back then, '[w]hen Grandmother went shopping, she would look the farmer or butcher in the eye and ask, "Is this fresh and flavorful?" ... In that day, there was a personal basis upon which trust was developed between buyer and seller',[4] and the supplier knew that if he or she did not answer accurately, Grandmother would go to a different vendor next week. This kind of trust no longer exists in the food industry. Serious food-borne outbreaks have occurred on every continent in the past decade,[5] often exacerbated by increasing food supply chains, globalized trade, and distribution networks.[6]

§11.02 A COOPERATIVE NEW GOVERNANCE APPROACH TO REGULATING FOOD SAFETY

In the US, food safety regulations exist at the federal, state and local levels. At each level, health and safety regulators are faced with the problem of making decisions involving large scientific uncertaintics, public perceptions at odds with professional perceptions, uncertain and conflicting public values expressed through the political process, and difficult judgments of equity when risk and benefit are borne by different groups.[7]

Great debate surrounds the optimal level of regulation and legal scholars differ on whether regulations are necessary and if so, what amount of regulation is sufficient regulation.[8] Legal scholars Cass Sunstein,[9] John Braithewaite,[10] Stephen Shavell and

2. U.S. Centers for Disease Control, https://www.cdc.gov/foodsafety/cdc-and-food-safety.html.
3. *Ibid.*
4. John Fagan, *Cert ID: A Successful Example of an Independent, Third-Party, Private Certification System 1* (28 January 2003), http://www.farmfoundation.org/ projects/documents/fagan.pdf.
5. *Food Safety Fact Sheet,* World Health Org. (4 June 2019), https://www.who.int/en/news-room/fact-sheets/detail/food-safety.
6. Alexia Brunet Marks, A New Governance Recipe for Food Safety Regulation, 47 Loy. Univ. L.J. 3 (2016); Alexia Brunet Marks, The Risks We Are Willing to Eat: Food Imports and Safety, 52 Harv. J. on Legis. 125 (2015).
7. Chauncey Starr & Chris Whipple, A Perspective on Health and Safety Risk Analysis, 30 Mgmt. Sci. 1, 1 (1984).
8. Stephen Breyer, *Regulation and Its Reform,* 15-34 (1982).
9. Cass Sunstein, *Risk and Reason: Safety, Law and the Environment* 28-52 (2002) (noting the need for regulation to achieve safety through a 'cost-benefit' state that compensates for the faulty risk perception of an irrational public).
10. John Braithwaite, *Restorative Justice & Responsive Regulation* 54-70 (2002) (noting that 'responsive regulation' should follow a pyramid approach. Restorative justice is suitable for a virtuous actor, deterrence for a rational actor, and incapacitation for an incompetent or irrational actor. The regulator escalates the pyramid when cooperative or rational approaches fail. Similarly, adequate enforcement of compliance with private regulation will depend on the attitude of regulated firms.).

Mitchell Polinsky[11] would all argue that regulations are a necessary deterrent for negative behaviour. Shavell and Polinsky believe that regulation is better than legal liability from a deterrence perspective. They state that in the case of product liability lawsuits involving domestically manufactured food products, legal liability is unlikely to serve as a deterrent due to the high transaction and information costs that deter plaintiffs from bringing cases forward; moreover, deterrence is possible due simply to market forces (loss of sales) and regulation.[12] In contrast, legal scholar Kip Viscusi would argue that much regulation is an overreaction to relatively low probability risks that cannot be justified by a strict cost-benefit analysis.[13]

For argument sake, assume that regulations contain a deterrent value. Is food safety regulation any different than regulation in general? When it comes to food safety, should we favour strong federal, state regulation of business or deregulation? In reality regulation occurs in many settings[14] and consists of rulemaking (standard setting), monitoring compliance, and enforcement that involves legislature, agencies and the court system.[15] Today, traditional command-and-control regulation by the state is increasingly being replaced in political theory as well as in practice by alternative, flexible, less state-centred forms of regulation, such as self-regulation, co-regulation, management-based regulation, private systems of governance, and empirically informed regulation.[16] This transition challenges existing conceptualizations of regulation in that traditional top-down regulatory theory, based on a state-centred conception of regulation and premised on improving compliance and regulatory techniques, is inadequate to deal with these new arrangements.[17] Pragmatically, this new type of regulation includes not only state institutions but also second- and third-party actors,

11. A. Mitchell Polinsky & Steven Shavell, The Uneasy Case for Product Liability, 123 Harv. L. Rev. 1437, 1443-1458 (2010) (noting that market forces and regulation are sufficient to form deterrence in product liability cases. However, since they do not reference food-borne illness cases as a separate category from product liability cases, we cannot presume that their results hold with respect to food-borne illness cases.).
12. *Ibid.*
13. Kip Viscusi, *Fatal Tradeoffs: Public and Private Responsibilities for Risk,* 149-160 (1995).
14. Ian Ayres & John Braithwaite, *Responsive Regulation: Transcending the Deregulation Debate,* 84-99 (1992).
15. Sol Picciotto, Reconceptualizing Regulation in the Era of Globalization, 29 J.L. Soc'y 1, 1-11 (2002); Colin Scott, Private Regulation of the Public Sector: A Neglected Facet of Contemporary Governance, 29 J.L. Soc'y 56, 56-76 (2002).
16. Marius Aalders & Ton Wilthagen, Moving Beyond Command-and-Control: Reflexivity in the Regulations of Occupational Safety and Health and the Environment, 19 Law & Pol'y. 415, 415-444 (1997); John Braithwaite, Enforced Self-Regulation: A New Strategy for Corporate Crime Control, 80 Mich. L. Rev. 1466, 1466-1507 (1982); John Braithwaite, The New Regulatory State and the Transformation of Criminology, 40 Brit. J. Criminology 222, 222-238 (2000); Cary Coglianese & David Lazer, Management-Based Regulation: Prescribing Private Management to Achieve Public Goals, 37 Law & Soc'y Rev. 691, 691-730 (2003); Franco Furger, Accountability and Systems of Self-Governance: The Case of the Maritime Industry, 19 Law & Pol'y 445, 445-476 (1997); Neil Gunningham & Darren Sinclair, Regulatory Pluralism: Designing Policy Mixes for Environmental Protection, 21 Law & Pol'y 49, 49-76 (1999); Cass R. Sunstein, Empirically Informed Regulation, 78 Chicago L. Rev. 4, 1 (2011).
17. Darren Sinclair, Self-Regulation Versus Command and Control? Beyond False Dichotomies, 19 Law & Pol'y 529, 529-559 (1997).

such as firms, associations, and non-governmental organizations, acting as rule makers as well as monitoring or enforcement agencies.

As the following paragraphs will show, food safety regulation in the US is a cooperative enterprise and one which entails the interplay between three key forces: direct regulation, indirect regulation (legal liability) and private regulation. Direct regulation involves federal and state government agencies engaged in command-and-control regulation: rulemaking, monitoring, and enforcement. Indirect regulation refers to legal liability. Private regulation involves the food industry and third parties (farmers, private auditing and certification organizations, retailers and industry groups). The following sections describe this delicate balance and describe the broad range of regulatory techniques (from public to private and from low-interventionist to highly prescriptive obligations) that the actors in each of these groups cover.

§11.03 DIRECT REGULATION

Regulating the safety of the US food supply is as complex as the sourcing and delivery of food itself. Food safety regulations are made by several entities. Food safety regulations may be declared by legislative bodies, such as US Congress, while state and local regulatory agencies handle the retail food segment and other food safety issues through state legislative bodies or local town ordinances and bylaws. State and local regulatory agencies may adopt or modify the federal standards. If they adopt the minimum federal standards with changes, however, these changes must be more stringent than the federal minimum standards.

[A] Federal Regulation: Agencies and Legislation

After a product enters the stream of commerce, it is not a simple task to map which agency oversees its transhipment. While there are twelve federal agencies tasked with some form of food regulation, these three federal agencies play key roles to ensure food safety in the US: the Food Safety and Inspection Service (FSIS) of the US Department of Agriculture (USDA), the US Food and Drug Administration (FDA), and the CDC). The USDA and FDA, as mandated by Acts of Congress, regulate food safety interstate under their respective statutory authorities, codified in the US Code of Federal Regulations. Both the FDA and USDA have provisions written into the acts that regulate their segment of the food supply individually, yet they also have cooperative inspection programmes that work together. Each of these agencies will be discussed in turn as they have oversight over certain food groups. First, the FSIS, an agency under the USDA, founded in 1862 and one of the oldest agencies in existence, is responsible for developing and executing federal laws related to farming, forestry, rural economic development, and food. The FSIS is responsible for ensuring that the nation's commercial supply of meat, poultry, and processed egg products is safe, wholesome, and correctly labelled and packaged.[18] Next, the FDA was founded in 1930 and is charged

18. US Food Safety Inspection Service, https://www.fsis.usda.gov/wps/portal/fsis/home.

with protecting the public health by assuring that foods (except for meat from livestock, poultry and some egg products which are regulated by FSIS) are safe, wholesome, sanitary and properly labelled; that cosmetics and dietary supplements are safe and properly labelled; that human and veterinary drugs, and vaccines and other biological products and medical devices intended for human use are safe and effective; regulating tobacco products; and protecting the public from electronic radiation.[19] One cannot overlook the vast scope of FDA regulatory authority and the phenomenal number of products that the FDA regulates. For example, the FDA comprises seven product-oriented centres and offices and is responsible for the safety of the nation's domestically produced and imported foods, cosmetics, drugs, biologics, medical devices, and radiological products. According to agency estimates, consumers spend 25 cents of every consumer dollar on food, dietary supplements and cosmetics regulated by the FDA, through its most active centre – the Center for Food Safety and Applied Nutrition (CFSAN).[20] Of the 25 cents, approximately 75% is spent on foods.[21] CFSAN regulates USD 417 billion worth of domestic food, USD 49 billion worth of imported foods, and over USD 60 billion worth of cosmetics sold in interstate commerce.[22] The FD&C Act regulation takes place from the point of import entry or domestic processing to the point of retail sale. There are over 377,000 registered food facilities (including approximately 154,000 domestic facilities and 223,000 foreign facilities) that manufacture, process, pack, or hold food consumed by humans or animals in the US and several thousand cosmetic firms. These figures do not include restaurants, institutional food service establishments, or supermarkets, grocery stores, and other food outlets regulated by state, local, and tribal authorities that receive guidance, model codes, and other technical assistance from CFSAN to promote uniform coverage of food establishments and retailers. Finally, the FSIS and FDA work closely with the CDC, which, founded in 1946, leads federal efforts to gather data on food-borne illnesses, investigate food-borne illnesses and outbreaks,[23] and monitors the effectiveness of prevention and control efforts in reducing food-borne illnesses. The CDC also plays a key role in building state and local health department epidemiology, laboratory, and environmental health capacity to support food-borne disease surveillance and outbreak response.[24]

19. US Food and Drug Administration, https://www.fsis.usda.gov/wps/portal/fsis/home.
20. *Ibid.*, 7 (noting that CFSAN, in conjunction with the nationwide field force of the US Office of Regulatory Affairs, is responsible for the safety, nutrition and proper labelling of foods and cosmetics).
21. *Ibid.*, at 8.
22. *Ibid.*
23. A food-borne outbreak occurs when two or more people get the same illness from the same contaminated food or drink. When an outbreak is detected, public health and regulatory officials work quickly to collect as much information as possible to find out what is causing it so that they can prevent more illnesses. This action includes warning the public when there is clear and convincing information linking illness to a contaminated food. Federal, state and local officials may investigate an outbreak, depending on how widespread it is.
24. US Centers for Disease Control, https://www.cdc.gov/.

[1] *Challenges with Food-Borne Illness*

The FDA and USDA enforce key pieces of food safety legislation, each regulation introduced at a critical point in the history of food safety in the US. At the turn of the twentieth century, food safety was best depicted by author Upton Sinclair's 1906 fictitious novel, *The Jungle*, which described the horrific conditions and practices of the meatpacking industry.[25] While it was published as fiction, US President Theodore Roosevelt's investigative team reported back to the president that the conditions noted in the book were accurate. That same year, US President Roosevelt passed the Pure Food and Drug Act and the Meat Inspection Act, both in 1906. The Pure Food and Drug Act prohibited interstate commerce in adulterated and misbranded food and drugs.[26] Although it was not known by its present name until 1930, FDA's modern regulatory functions began with the passage of the Pure Food and Drugs Act. Meanwhile, the Meat Inspection Act, enforced by the USDA, makes it a crime to adulterate or misbrand meat and meat products being sold as food and ensures that meat and meat products are slaughtered and processed under strictly regulated sanitary conditions.

In 1938, after a legally marketed toxic elixir killed 107 people, including many children, US Congress moved to replace the Pure Food and Drug Act with the Federal Food, Drug, and Cosmetic Act (FD&C Act).[27] The FD&C Act completely overhauled the public health system by authorizing the FDA to demand evidence of safety for new drugs, issue standards for food, and conduct factory inspections. The next overhaul to the food safety regulatory system would not come for another seventy years, after several high-profile food-borne illness outbreaks and a notable rise in global trade in food.

From 1938 to 2012, a number of high-profile food-borne illness cases tested the USDA and FDA's ability to handle (and to coordinate with the US Department of Justice) large-scale outbreaks. While there are too many to discuss in this short chapter, a few are worth mentioning. Many outbreaks involved the fast-food industry. The first fast-food restaurant in the US was White Castle™ in 1921, selling inexpensive hamburgers, and today, American-founded fast-food chains such as McDonalds™ (established in 1940) and Kentucky Fried Chicken™ (established in 1952) are multinational corporations with outlets across the globe. The 1970s was called the 'decade of the fast-food business' as fast-food businesses appeared and became common fare. But the rise in demand for fast-food and the location of franchises across the country was not without a cost. The most significant fast-food outbreak, the 1993 Jack in the Box™ *E.coli* outbreak, led to significant policy and inspection changes with the US agency that regulates meat and poultry, the USDA. Referred to as 'the most infamous food

25. Upton Sinclair, The Jungle (1905).
26. FDA History, https://www.fda.gov/about-fda/history-fdas-fight-consumer-protection-and-public-health.
27. The Federal Food, Drug, and Cosmetics Act, 21 U.S.C. §§321 et seq., https://www.fda.gov/regulatory-information/laws-enforced-fda.

poison outbreak in contemporary history', and the '9/11 of the industry',[28] this outbreak involved seventy-three fast-food restaurants in California, Idaho, Washington, and Nevada and resulted in nearly 750 reported cases of food-borne pathogen from contaminated beef patties. The outbreak killed 4 children and permanently injured 178 young victims with kidney and brain damage.[29] Within a year, the USDA initiated research into new inspection policies and proposed establishing a Pathogen Reduction Program[30] in federally inspected meat-processing facilities, which included food-safe handling labels on all packages of raw meat and poultry.[31] These specific policy changes would require a radical change in how the USDA viewed pathogens. The FDA, meanwhile, was tasked with responding to other outbreaks which implicated leafy green vegetables, cantaloupes, and peanuts. In 2006, the California vegetable industry experienced a multistate food poisoning incident, which resulted in 205 illnesses and 3 deaths from bagged spinach tainted with *E.coli*.[32] Altogether, the past decade saw 19 *E. coli* outbreaks associated with contaminated lettuce and other leafy greens.[33] Another outbreak involved a 2011 Listeria outbreak implicating Jensen Farms™ involving cantaloupe, which resulted in 150 infected persons from twenty-eight states and at least 33 deaths.[34] In their subsequent federal trial, the owners received USD 3 million in fines and five years of probation. Other notable outbreaks included the Peanut Corporation of America™ *Salmonella* outbreak of 2008-2009 which led to more than 700 infected persons from forty-six states and 9 deaths.[35] This incident involved a massive recall of more than 3,900 different types of products from 350 companies.[36] Notably, the court found Peanut Corporation of America's owner and his brother guilty on a combined ninety-seven federal criminal charges sentencing the chief executive officer to twenty-eight years in federal prison, his brother to twenty years in federal prison, and three other quality assurance and plant managers from three to six years in federal

28. Darin Detwiler, Questioning Effectiveness of Meat and Poultry Handling Labels, Food Quality and Safety (31 March 2014), https://www.foodqualityandsafety.com/article/do-meat-and-poultry-handling-labels-really-convey-safety/.
29. US Centers for Disease Control, *Emerging Infectious Diseases,* 21:8 (1 August 2015), https://wwwnc.cdc.gov/eid/pdfs/vol21no8_pdf-version.pdf.
30. Economic Research Service, U.S. Department of Agriculture, *Part II. Empirical Investigation: A Closer Look at Food Safety Drivers in the Meat Industry* (15 April 2004), https://www.ers.usda.gov/publications/pub-details/?pubid=41636.
31. US Department of Agriculture Safe Handling Label, https://www.fsis.usda.gov/wps/wcm/connect/fa5e85b6-1f58-4af8-ab5e-3fef6c468eab/safe_handling_label_hi.jpg?MOD=AJPERES.
32. Bill Marler, *How Is This Acceptable: At Least 583 Sickened with E.Coli Linked to Leafy Greens in the U.S. and Canada Since 2017,* Marler Blog (20 December 2019), https://www.marlerblog.com/legal-cases/how-is-this-acceptable-at-least-583-sickened-with-e-coli-linked-to-leafy-greens-in-the-us-and-canada-since-2017/.
33. *Ibid.*
34. US Centers for Disease Control, *Multistate Outbreak of Listeriosis Linked to Whole Cantaloupes from Jensen Farms, Colorado (Final Update)* (27 August 2012), https://www.cdc.gov/listeria/outbreaks/cantaloupes-jensen-farms/index.html.
35. US Centers for Disease Control, *Multistate Outbreak of Salmonella Typhimurium Infections Linked to Peanut Butter, 2008-2009 (Final Update) Listeriosis* (11 May 2009), https://www.cdc.gov/salmonella/2009/peanut-butter-2008-2009.html.
36. US Centers for Disease Control, *Multistate Outbreak of Salmonella Typhimurium Infections Linked to Peanut Butter, 2008-2009 (Final Update) Listeriosis* (11 May 2009), https://www.cdc.gov/salmonella/2009/peanut-butter-2008-2009.html.

prison.[37] Finally, the 2012 DeCoster™ Egg *Salmonella* outbreak resulted in nearly 2,000 infected persons reported to the CDC, although the CDC estimates that up to 56,000 people may have been affected. In the subsequent federal trial, the owners were sentenced to three months in prison.[38] The outbreaks signalled gaps in FDA's regulatory power and specifically that the FDA needed more power to recall foods (a power which the USDA already had) and to ensure the produce was safe. These outbreaks provided an impetus for an overhaul of the 1938 FD&C Act.

[2] Challenges with International Trade

Consumers see the world as a giant supermarket. Over the past decade, the volume of food imports in the US has doubled and the import share of overall consumption has steadily risen.[39] Today, over 15% of our food supply comes from imports and this percentage is even larger percentage for specific products. Nearly 20% of fresh vegetables we eat, 50% of the fresh fruits we eat, and 80% of the fish we eat come from imports.[40] Every year, consumers in the US purchase USD 2 trillion worth of imported products from 825,000 importers through more than 300 ports of entry, and these numbers are rising. As food travels from local farms to processors to importers and distributors, and so on, the opportunities for contamination increase with every step in the system. Imported food can be risky[41] which makes ensuring the safety of the increasing volume and diversity of food an enormous challenge.

Rising global trade, with numerous sectors and global production chains generating trillions in annual revenues, serves as a constant reminder that our food system is vulnerable to threats from beyond US borders.[42] CDC experts reviewed outbreaks reported to their outbreak surveillance system from 2005 to 2010 for implicated foods that were imported to the US and found that during those years, 39 outbreaks and 2,348 illnesses were linked to imported food from fifteen countries.[43] Nearly half (17 outbreaks) occurred in 2009 and 2010, with 45% of the imported foods causing the

37. Dan Flynn, *5 of Stewart Parnell's 28-Year Prison Sentence May Not Stand*, Food Safety News (2 May 2017), https://www.foodsafetynews.com/2017/05/25-of-stewart-parnells-28-year-prison-sentence-may-not-stand/#.WoMnsROPIch.
38. US Centers for Disease Control, *Multistate Outbreak of Human Salmonella Enteritidis Infections Associated With Shell Eggs (Final Update)* (2 December 2010), https://www.cdc.gov/salmonella/2010/shell-eggs-12-2-10.html.
39. Andy Jerardo, What Share of U.S. Consumed Food Is Imported?, 6 Amber Waves 1, 36-37, (February 2008).
40. FDA, *Proposed Rules to Ensure the Safety of Imported Food*, http://www.fda.gov/Food/GuidanceRegulation/FSMA/ucm359450.htm.
41. US Centers for Disease Control, *CDC Research Shows Outbreaks Linked to Imported Foods Increasing* (14 March 2012), http://www.cdc.gov/media/releases/2012/p0314_foodborne.html (Also noting that CDC figures underestimate the true number of outbreaks due to imported foods as the origin of many foods causing outbreaks is either not known or not reported).
42. IMAP, Food & Beverage Industry Global Report-2010 (2010), http://www.imap .com/imap/media/resources/IMAP_Food__Beverage_Report_WEB_AD6498A02CAF4.pdf.
43. Alexia Brunet Marks, The Risks We Are Willing to Eat: Food Imports and Safety, 52 Harv. J. on Legis. 125 (2015).

outbreaks came from Asia.[44] Fish (17 outbreaks) were the most common source of implicated imported food-borne disease, followed by spices (6 outbreaks).[45]

If the 2008 Chinese infant formula scandal[46] taught regulators anything, it is that a food scandal can have global implications. In 2008, Chinese food manufacturers intentionally adulterated milk with melamine, a high nitrogen compound which appears to have been added to diluted milk to give the appearance of normal protein levels, and which later was discovered in baby formula and animal feed.[47] As officials assured the American public that no Chinese manufacturers of infant formula were registered to sell infant formula in the US[48] the scandal was wreaking havoc on many economies - affecting global contracts, instilling an irreversible loss of confidence for Chinese food, and perpetuating a general scepticism for food trade. Even still, global agricultural trade has been rising by 3.6% per year for the last two decades, facilitated by technological change, productivity gains, and trade liberalization.[49] With the growth of supply chains, and often in new geographical areas, it can be particularly difficult to verify that new supply chain partners can provide the requisite regulatory framework and sufficiently robust public health measures for ensuring the safety of the foods and foodstuffs offered for international trade.[50] As trade and supply chains continue to expand, concern over food safety will only intensify.

The rise in global trade, with a growing number of outbreaks implicating imported foods, again signalled gaps in FDA's regulatory power. Given the globalization of the world's food supply, regulators became acutely aware that coordination of efforts internationally is vital to ensuring food safety.[51] Cooperation is required in the rapid detection of incidents, identification of causative agents and foods, and the prompt and effective response to contain and mitigate any adverse health and economic effects. This includes maintaining sensitive and rapid alert systems, detailed and well-tested preparedness plans and rapid and effective emergency response systems with links to relevant international networks.[52] An overhaul of the 1938 FD&C Act was needed to accomplish these goals.

44. *Ibid.*
45. *Ibid.*
46. Mark McDonald, From Milk to Peas, a Chinese Food-Safety Mess, N.Y. Times (21 June 2012 12:02 PM EDT), http://rendezvous.blogs.nytimes.com/2012/06/21/from-milk-to-peas-a-chinese-food-safety -mess/?ref = topics&_r = 0 (explaining that in 2008, 6 children died and some 300,000 fell sick from melamine, an industrial chemical used to make fertilizer and plastic pipe, found in Chinese- manufactured infant formula).
47. United Nations Food and Agriculture Organization, *Melamine Contamination of Dairy Products in China* (2008), http://www.fao.org/food/food-safety-quality/a-z-index/melamine/en/.
48. US Food and Drug Administration, *Melamine Contamination in China* (5 January 2009), http://www.fda.gov/NewsEvents/PublicHealthFocus/ucm179005.htm (noting USD 7 trillion in annual revenue).
49. Jayson Beckman et al., *U.S. Department of Agriculture, Economic Research Service, The Global Landscape of Agricultural Trade, 1995-2014* (2017), https://www.ers.usda.gov/publications/pub-details/?pubid = 85625.
50. *See supra* note 6, at 1947.
51. Alexia Brunet Marks, The Risks We Are Willing to Eat: Food Imports and Safety, 52 Harv. J. on Legis. 125 (2015).
52. Food & Agriculture Organization, *International Cooperation on Food Contamination and Food-borne Disease Surveillance*, http://www.fao.org/docrep/meeting/008/y5871e/y5871e0n.htm.

[3] New Legislation to Address These Challenges

The Food Safety Modernization Act (FSMA) was passed in 2011[53] signalling a shift in the FDA's focus on food safety regulation from reactive to proactive with the agency mandating a series of risk-based preventive controls.[54] As of January 2020, the FDA has finalized eight major rules to implement FSMA, recognizing that ensuring the safety of the food supply is a shared responsibility among many different points in the global supply chain for both human and animal food. The FSMA rules, described at length on the FDA website,[55] are designed to make clear specific actions that must be taken at each of the below points to prevent contamination.[56]

Four rules look expressly at import safety. First, *Accredited Third-Party Certification*, establishes the framework, procedures and requirements for accreditation bodies seeking recognition by the FDA, as well as requirements for third-party certification bodies seeking accreditation. Second, the *Foreign Supplier Verification Programs*, requires that importers perform certain risk-based activities to verify that food imported into the US has been produced in a manner that meets applicable US safety standards. Third, *Mitigation Strategies to Protect Food Against Intentional Adulteration* is aimed at preventing intentional adulteration from acts intended to cause wide-scale harm to public health, including acts of terrorism targeting the food supply. Rather than targeting specific foods or hazards, this rule requires mitigation (risk-reducing) strategies for processes in certain registered food facilities. Fourth, the *Voluntary Qualified Importer Program* is a voluntary fee-based programme that provides expedited review and import entry of human and animal foods into the US for participating importers. Both consumers and importers will benefit from this programme.

Four rules focus on domestic food safety concerns. The *Sanitary Transportation of Human and Animal Food* advancing FDA's efforts to protect foods from farm to table by keeping them safe from contamination during transportation. The goal of this rule is to prevent practices during transportation that create food safety risks, such as failure to properly refrigerate food, inadequate cleaning of vehicles between loads, and failure to properly protect food. And the *Standards for the Growing, Harvesting, Packing, and Holding of Produce for Human Consumption* (known as the produce safety rule) establishes, for the first time, science-based minimum standards for the safe growing, harvesting, packing, and holding of fruits and vegetables grown for human consumption. Two rules deal expressly with good manufacturing practices. *Current Good Manufacturing Practice and Hazard Analysis and Risk-Based Preventative Controls for Human Foods*, requires food facilities to have a food safety plan in place that includes an analysis of hazards and risk-based preventive controls to minimize or prevent the identified hazards. And *Current Good Manufacturing Practice and Hazard Analysis and*

53. FDA Food Safety Modernization Act, Pub. L. No. 111-353, 124 Stat. 3885 (2011) (codified as amended in scattered sections of 21 U.S.C.) (amending the Federal Food, Drug, and Cosmetic Act (codified as amended at 21 U.S.C. § 301-399f)), https://www.fda.gov/food/guidance-regulation-food-and-dietary-supplements/food-safety-modernization-act-fsma.
54. *Ibid.*
55. *Ibid.*
56. *Ibid.*

Risk-Based Preventive Controls for Food for Animals requires animal food facilities to have a food safety plan in place that includes an analysis of hazards to determine which ones need control and risk-based preventive controls to minimize or prevent those hazards.

[B] State and Local Agencies

Food safety regulations in the US are made at several levels. Food safety regulations may be declared by legislative bodies while state and local regulatory agencies handle the retail food segment and other food safety issues through state legislative bodies or local town ordinances and bylaws. For example, as noted earlier, the FDA CFSAN provides technical assistance, model codes, and other guidance to local food establishments and retailers such as restaurants, institutional food service establishments, or supermarkets, grocery stores, and other food outlets regulated by state, local, and tribal authorities. State and local regulatory agencies may adopt or modify the federal standards. If they adopt the minimum federal standards with changes, however, these changes must be more stringent than the federal minimum standards.

Most states have a Health and Safety Act which can apply criminal, regulatory and administrative sanctions on manufacturers that sell adulterated or contaminated food. State Food Protection Programs, such as a state's department of agriculture or public health, are responsible for the enforcement of regulations adopted by state legislation. During an investigation of food-borne illness or a recall, federal government agencies may work with state agencies such as the state department of public health[57] or the state department of agriculture.[58]

§11.04 INDIRECT REGULATION: LEGAL LIABILITY

The US relies on legal liability to influence legislation and to motivate the food industry to increase food safety.[59] In a perfectly competitive market, firms receive negative signals about their errors and the market corrects itself. In the context of food safety, for firms to alter corporate behaviour to invest in food safety, manufacturers must face costs when they violate rules. What are some of the negative signals (costs) that firms receive in order to modify their food safety practices? The costs are regulatory, market-oriented, and legal in nature. Can the legal system serve as a deterrence mechanism to raise food safety levels; in other words, can food-borne illness lawsuits impact firm behaviour in a socially desirable way by providing correct signals and adequate incentives to avoid harmful conduct?

57. Healthfinder.gov, https://healthfinder.gov/FindServices/SearchContext.aspx?show=1&topic=820.
58. State Departments of Agriculture, https://www.nasda.org/states/state-directory.
59. Jean Buzby & Peter Frenzen, Food Safety and Product Liability, 24 Food Pol'y 637, 637-651 (1999); Spencer Henson & Julie Caswell, Food Safety Regulation: An Overview of Contemporary Issues, 24 Food Pol'y 589, 589-603 (1999); and Kip Viscusi, Toward a Diminished Role for Tort Liability: Social Insurance, Government Regulation, and Contemporary Risks to Health and Society, 6 Yale J. on Regul. 65, 65-107 (1989).

Take for example the deterrence effects associated with tort law or the law of personal injury. In the US, tort liability is meant to shift the costs from the victims to the offenders and signal the potential wrongdoers to implement precautionary measures. The central concern of the economic theory of liability is how to induce an injurer to take the socially appropriate level of care – the level that minimized the sum of the cost of taking care and the losses to victims.[60] The tort system can work as a deterrent if benefits from taking the socially appropriate level of care and making investments to reduce risk and external costs from harmful activities are internalized.[61]

While several examples of food-borne illness lawsuits have been noted above, another example is the famous *E.Coli* food-borne illness outbreak implicating Odwalla™ unpasteurized apple juice in 1996.[62] The outbreak resulted in the death of one child and seventy injuries and ultimately led Odwalla™, the producer, to discontinue the sale of unpasteurized juice.[63] It also resulted in substantial monetary loss for Odwalla™: a voluntary product recall (valued at USD 12.5 million), a 17% drop in revenue during the first six months after the outbreak, and a record of USD 1.5 federal fine for interstate shipment of an adulterated food product (the largest fine ever assessed in a food case by the FDA), and twenty-one personal injury lawsuits.[64]

This example shows how direct regulation (by the FDA) combines with legal liability and market mechanisms to curtail firms from placing unsafe food in the marketplace. And yet, as CDC estimates reveal, food-borne illness outbreaks continue to occur, and gaps in food safety persist. What lessons can regulators learn from the Odwalla™ incident and others, to fine-tune the balance of deterrence mechanisms that are at play? In the end, Odwalla™ received several different signals (regulatory, legal and market) and the firm implemented positive food safety changes. In many cases, however, firms do not receive adequate signals, either because market failures are present or for other reasons. Regulators can learn from instances when different signals (regulatory, legal and market) succeed and fail.

For instance, while one may hear that an outbreak of food-borne illness was followed by a record-breaking verdict for the plaintiff, this is not the norm. Not every plaintiff makes it to trial. Market failures exist in that not all victims sue (lawsuits are long, expensive and transaction costs are prohibitive), information (on traceability) is limited, and plaintiffs have to overcome causation. Of note, in a study of food-borne

60. A. Mitchell Polinsky & Daniel L. Rubinfeld, The Welfare Implications of Costly Litigation for the Level of Liability, 27 J. Legal Stud., 151 (1988).
61. Susan Rose-Ackerman, *Product Safety Legislation and the Law of Torts*, in *Product Liability and Innovation: Managing Risk in an Uncertain Environment* 151 (Janet R. Hunziker & Trevor O. Jones eds, 1994), http://www.nap.edu/openbook/0309051304/html/151.html; Guiseppe Dari -Mattiacci & Francesco Parisi, *The Economics of Tort Law: A Precis*, in *The Elgar Companion to Law & Economics* (Edward Elgar Publishing, 2d ed. 2006), http://papers.ssrn.com/sol3/papers .cfm?abstract_id=458701.
62. Pam Belluck, Juice Maker Pleads Guilty and Pays $1.5 million in Fatal Poising Case, N.Y. Times (24 July 1998 12:02 PM EDT); *See also*, Editorial, Rotten Fruit, Black Crud and the End of Odwalla, Seattle Times (16 January 1998 12:02 PM EDT), http://community.seattletimes. nwsource.com/archive/?date=19980116&slug=2728990.
63. Pam Belluck, Juice Maker Pleads Guilty and Pays $1.5 million in Fatal Poising Case, N.Y. Times (24 July 1998 12:02 PM EDT).
64. *Ibid.*

illness lawsuits, the results suggest that food-borne illness litigation sends a moderate signal to firms to increase food safety practices, but mostly through settlements.[65] Some plaintiffs have cases resolved in confidential proceedings prior to filing; some have cases resolved through arbitration prior to trial and after filing.[66] In this way, high transaction costs and information costs may lead to less than desirable levels of food safety. Only when firms expect to bear the costs of injuries will they invest more resources in reducing contamination. If firms are made to incur costs, they will increase the precautions they take.[67]

§11.05 PRIVATE REGULATION

Over the last ten years, discussion has intensified over the private sector role in regulating food safety. As countries feel pressure to raise food safety standards they are realizing that the same formal rules and practices that promise greater trade may, in fact, be limiting their regulatory options.[68] Frequent budget shortfalls reduce the capacity to perform periodic inspections to assess compliance[69] and formal international commitments (treaties) keep countries from setting higher-than-the-default food safety standards that could be perceived as protectionist.[70] These comments suggest that governments lack nimbleness and flexibility to easily adopt higher food safety standards. In contrast, private companies have shown their agility to adopt higher standards to meet their supply chain needs by adopting third-party certification, public-private partnerships, and voluntary standards. The evolving structure of global food production with multinational enterprises, supply chains,[71] and different available standards necessitates an evolution from traditional regulation to something else.[72] In the last ten years, private food safety codes and supply chain contracts crossing international boundaries have proliferated, setting the stage for a transition in how food safety is regulated on a global scale. This transition from overseeing all food

65. Alexia Brunet Marks, Check Please: Using Legal Liability to Inform Food Safety Regulation, 50 Hous. L. Rev. 3, 723-785 (2013).
66. In most cases, these settlements may be lower than their initial demands. Settlements do not affect a firm's bottom line because there is no market mechanism in the report of a jury verdict.
67. Denis W. Stearns, On (Cr)edibility: Why Food in the United States May Never Be Safe, 21 Stan. L. & Pol'y Rev. 245, 252 (2010).
68. Kenneth W. Abbott & Duncan Snidal, Strengthening International Regulation Through Transnational New Governance: Overcoming the Orchestration Deficit, 42 Vand. J. Transnat'l L. 501 (2009); Ching-Fu Lin, Comment, SPS-Plus and Bilateral Treaty Network: A 'Global' Solution to the Global Food-Safety Problem?, 29 Wis. Int'l L.J. 694 (2012).
69. Paul Verbruggen & Tetty Havinga, *Food Safety Meta-Controls in the Netherlands* 6 (Nijmegen Sociology of Law Working Paper Series, No. 2014/07, (July 2014)), http://www.researchgate.net/publication/270585728_Food_Safety_Meta-Controls_in_the_Netherlands.
70. Simon Lester, *Talk of a 'Right to Regulate' is Hurting the Trade Debate*, Huffington Post Blog (21 July 2015), http://www.huffingtonpost.com/simon-lester/talk-of-a-right-to-regula_b_7839680.html.
71. John Gerard Ruggie, Business and Human Rights: The Evolving International Agenda, 101 Am. J. Int'l L. 819, 823 (2007) ('[S]eventy-seven thousand transnational firms span the global economy today, with some 770,000 subsidiaries and millions of suppliers – Wal-Mart alone is reported to have more than sixty thousand suppliers.').
72. *See supra* note 67, at 505.

safety functions to 'co-regulating' might be labelled, at least by some, as a form of New Governance.

Generally perceived as opposite to 'command and control' regulation, New Governance is marked by increased collaboration of stakeholders and non-state actors, decentralization and devolution, flexibility and context specificity, and adaptability and dynamic learning.[73] The phenomenon of New Governance refers to a regulatory paradigm defined by privatization, decentralization, public participation, horizontal coordination, experimentation, and a solution-oriented focus.[74]

The private sector regulates food safety in ways that consumers may not always be aware of. The following are a few examples of how private regulation is able to set higher standards by adopting third-party certification to complying with food safety standards that exceed public FDA or USDA standards. For an early example of private-retailer-imposed certification: in 1999, Safeway™ supermarket, then the third-largest food retailer, required all of their suppliers of certain commodities to verify, through third-party certification, that they follow USDA Good Agricultural Practices for production and Good Manufacturing Practices for packinghouses for domestic and imported produce[75] which, at that time, exceeded federal regulations. For another example, in 2008, Wal-Mart™ required retailers to provide real-time details on where suppliers fall short in food safety on a plant-by-plant basis,[76] a process standard that exceeds US food safety requirements.[77] Finally, Whole Foods Market™ and Wal-Mart™ provide two additional examples of private retail standards. All suppliers to the Whole Foods Market™ chain must meet detailed standards that include: acceptable and unacceptable ingredients, storage and handling of products, and welfare standards for livestock which provide meat, poultry, eggs, and dairy products.[78] Another example is Wal-Mart's™ announcement of corporate-wide efforts to have fresh produce suppliers follow the Produce Traceability Initiative Protocol and institute a '100% money back' guarantee on freshness by 2014, with no mention of exemptions or exclusions for small

---

73. Orly Lobel, The Renew Deal: The Fall of Regulation and the Rise of Governance in Contemporary Legal Thought, 89 Minn. L. Rev. 342 (2004).
74. Amy J. Cohen, *Negotiation,* Meet New Governance: Interests, Skills, and Selves, 33 Law & Soc. Inquiry 503 (2008).
75. Linda Calvin, *Produce, Food Safety, and International Trade: Response to U.S. Foodborne Illness Outbreaks Associated with Imported Produce,* Int'l Trade & Food Safety 90 (2004), http://www .ers.usda .gov/media/321547/aer828g_1_.pdf.
76. *Wal-Mart, Wal-Mart Becomes First Nationwide U.S. Grocer to Adopt Global Food Safety Initiative Standards* (4 February 2008), http://news.walmart .com/news-archive/2008/02/04/wal-mart-becomes-first-nationwide-us-grocer-to-adopt-global-food-safety-initiative-standards (noting that in 2008, Walmart became the first US grocery chain requiring their factories to be certified against one of the internationally recognized Global Food Safety Initiative (GFSI) standards under which producers of Walmart and Sam's Club private label and other foods sold in the US must be audited by independently trained, approved, and licensed auditors who are experts in their industry).
77. *Ibid.* (noting that GSFI schemes are not only consistent with but sometimes exceed the FSMA rules).
78. Whole Foods Market, Whole Body Supplier Guidelines, Version 2 (2013), http://www. wholefoodsmarket.com/sites/default/files/media/Global/Company%20Info/PDFs/Whole_Body_Supplier_Guidelines.pdf.

farms or local produce.[79] Unlike governments, firms do not have to be fair or inclusive; for instance, standard vendor agreements that supermarkets use essentially serve as supplier contracts and often include provisions that supersede the small business exemptions proposed for the FSMA.[80] In other words, the contracts apply to all suppliers regardless of their size.

Supply chains may have their own standards in place, in the case of a supplier-buyer relationship like Wal-Mart™, and this standard may or may not be benchmarked against a private global food safety scheme. Generally private 'schemes,' which include a set of standards plus a governance structure for certification and enforcement with these features (accreditation, certification, standard setting, adoption, implementation, conformity assessment, and enforcement)[81] emerged due to: (1) a shift in regulatory responsibility for food safety and quality to industry, (2) the increased international sourcing of products, (3) heightened consumer concerns over food safety resulting from food-borne illness outbreaks, and (4) changing consumer attitudes in relation to their interest in product features beyond food safety.

Schemes are not as visible in the US as they are in Europe, where over 85% of all Western European retailers require GlobalGAP certification.[82] Yet, scheme certification is a growing trend in the US as more and more consumers are shopping in retail stores and expressing demand for certain product attributes. In the US, consumers spend 64% of their food dollars on supermarket purchases, compared to 16.3% at warehouse clubs and supercentres, 5.9% directly at farms, processors, or wholesalers, 2.9% home delivered or mail order, 2.7% at convenience stores, 2.3% at speciality food stores and the remainder in other venues.[83] When consumers demand specific quality attributes such as organic, free range, cage free, hormone free, grown without pesticides, or express concerns over fair trade, child labour, and overexploiting natural resources, retailers respond by regulating their transnational suppliers,[84] often requiring that their suppliers comply with a universally accepted auditing scheme.[85] The auditing scheme

79. Rodney B. Holcomb et al., Food Safety Policies and Implications for Local Food Systems, 28 Choices 4, 1-2 (2013), http://www.choicesmagazine.org/choices-magazine/theme-articles/developing-local-food-systems-in-the-south/food-safety-policies-and-implications-for-local-food-systems.
80. Even with small business exemptions from the FSMA, local producers are generally encouraged to follow Good Agricultural Practices and Good Handling Practices protocols.
81. Spencer Henson & John Humphrey, *The Impacts of Private Food Safety Standards on the Food Chain and on Public Standard-Setting Processes*, FAO (2009), http://www.fao.org/3/a-i1132e.pdf.
82. Grace Chia-Hui Lee, *Private Food Standards and Their Impacts on Developing Countries*, Eur. Comm'n 27 (2006), http://trade.ec.europa.eu/doclib/docs/2006/november/ tradoc_127969.pdf.
83. US Dep't of Agric. Food Expenditures: *Table 14: Sales of Food at Home by Type of Outlet (Including Sales Tax)* (2016), http://www.ers.usda.gov/data-products/food-expenditures.aspx.
84. Tetty Havinga, Private Regulation of Food Safety by Supermarkets, 28 Law & Pol'y 515, 518 (2006) at 521 (noting that grocery retailers respond to consumer preferences for food safety and quality and may set more stringent standards than public regulators).
85. Global Food Safety Initiative, *Enhancing Food Safety Through Third Party Certification* (2011), http://www.mygfsi.com/gfsifiles/GFSI_White_Paper_-_Enhan cing_Food_Safety_Through_Third_Party_Certification.pdf.

could include, for example, firm-specific guidelines on suppliers' abilities to perform a product recall or maximum pesticide residue limits that exceed national standards by 25%-80%.[86]

That scheme could exceed national food safety standards. Of course, retailers may also require supplier compliance with a scheme for various other reasons: to increase coordination among food safety management activities all along the food chain, to strengthen the legal responsibility of food chain operators for the safety of food that they produce, to improve transparency and accountability for public food safety decision making,[87] or to market their products by offering conformity with global standards and in a way, to engage in non-price competition.[88]

These examples are representative of the increasing phenomenon in the US, EU, and elsewhere, that each retailer has its own marketing channel with its own set of vendor agreements, compliance regulations, and costs. This is unique in two respects. First, unlike national governments, which are tied to World Trade Organization (WTO) regulations and rules, retailers are free to draft buyer-driven requirements that can exceed national standards.[89] As legal scholars Louise and David Trubek explain, having the standard regulatory framework in place motivates these entities to self-regulate, while the opportunity to opt out allows them to create innovative approaches to ultimately enhance regulatory efficacy.[90] In this way, food retailers are uniquely positioned to take advantage of higher food safety standards - which include stricter numerical and process standards, as well as product specifications, product analysis, purchasing procedures, internal audit, and full product or ingredient traceability - because the private sector is out of reach of WTO and other economic law constraints. Second, from a sociological perspective, the growing influence of the private sector in food safety means that the focus on the state for providing food safety is no longer adequate.[91]

While there are numerous costs and benefits to using New Governance - particularly third-party certification features - anecdotal evidence indicates that the use of third-party certification leads to greater food safety transparency, cooperation and fewer food safety recalls.[92] While these are benefits, one of the most challenging

86. *Ibid.*, at 2.
87. Jennifer Brown, *Walmart Settles with Cantaloupe Victims from Colorado Outbreak*, DENV. POST (13 May 2014 2:34 PM EDT), http://www.denverpost.com/news/ ci_25755216/walmart-settles-cantaloupe-victims-from-colorado-outbreak (noting that previously retailers could escape liability through contracting; in recent years this has changed).
88. Maki Hatanaka & Lawrence Busch, Third-Party Certification in the Global Agrifood System: An Objective or Socially Mediated Governance Mechanism?, 48 Sociologia Ruralis 73 (2008), http://onlinelibrary.wiley.com/doi/10.1111/j.1467-9523.2008.00453.x/full.
89. Alexia Brunet Marks, A New Governance Recipe for Food Safety Regulation, 47 Loy. U. Chi. L.J. 3 (2016).
90. David M. Trubeck & Louise G. Trubek, New Governance & Legal Regulation: Complementarity, Rivalry, and Transformation, 13 Colum. J. Eur. L. 1, 20 (2006).
91. Lawrence Busch & Jim Bingen, *Introduction: A New World of Standards*, in *Agricultural Standards: The Shape of the Global Food and Fiber System* (Jim Bingen & Lawrence Busch eds, 2006).
92. Timothy D. Lytton & Lesley K. McAllister, Oversight in Private Food Safety Auditing: Addressing Auditor Conflict of Interest, 2 Wis. L. Rev. 289, 289-294 (2014) (noting the role of private actors in food safety governance).

issues highlighted by the 2011 Colorado *Listeria* outbreak is the credibility of food safety audits and third-party certifications.[93] In the Colorado *Listeria* outbreak, the auditors had given the farm nearly perfect food safety ratings. Food safety scholars Timothy Lytton and Lesley McAllister note the structural conflict of interest that exists when private auditors are paid for by the auditees - a conflict between the financial interest of the auditor and protecting the public from food safety risks.[94] The 2011 Colorado *Listeria* outbreak underscores the potential weakness of the New Governance framework and serves as a food safety challenge.

[A] Examples of a Modern, Co-regulation, New Governance Approach

Despite its shortcomings, New Governance - described as an increased collaboration of stakeholders and non-state actors, decentralization and devolution, flexibility and context specificity, and adaptability and dynamic learning - is being used in legislation today. Recent US food safety legislation, the FSMA of 2011,[95] passed in response to growing levels of imports, diminishing resources to inspect, and heightened food safety risks,[96] adopts key New Governance features: third-party certification[97] voluntary standards[98] and public-private partnerships.[99] The new rules illustrate a role model for emerging food safety practice, though not one without challenges. In some cases, more legislative authority or guidance is necessary: for example, with respect to conflicts of interest, third-party auditors are not prevented from working in-house for their clients, and auditors are not prevented from performing other services for their auditees; the

93. Tom Karst, *Wal-Mart Files Suit in Jensen Cantaloupe Case*, Produce Retailer (14 February 2014 5:10 PM EDT), http://www.produceretailer.com/produce-retailer-news/Wal-Mart-files-suit-in-Jensen-canta loupe-case-245591681.html. (noting that in the Listeria outbreak, a wrongful death claim was brought against the retailer, Walmart who in turn, filed a complaint in 2014 in a Wyoming court asserting third-party claims against the grower (Jensen Farms), the distributor (Frontera Produce Ltd.) and the third-party auditors (Primus Group Inc. and Bio Food Safety Inc.). Primus subcontracted Bio Food Safety to undertake the on-site audit of the cantaloupe farm, which resulted in a nearly perfect rating. While this case involved an unsuccessful audit to a domestic producer, it revealed possible 'blind spots' in the privatization of third-party certification).
94. *See supra* note 91, at 290.
95. *See* FDA Food Safety Modernization Act, Pub. L. No. 111-353, 124 Stat. 3885 (2011) (codified as amended in scattered sections of 21 U.S.C.) (amending the Federal Food, Drug, and Cosmetic Act (codified as amended at 21 U.S.C. § 301-399f)).
96. Alexia Brunet Marks, The Risks We Are Willing to Eat: Food Imports and Safety, 52 Harv. J. on Legis. 125 (2015).
97. Third-party certification means that an independent organization has reviewed the manufacturing process of a product and has independently determined that the final product complies with specific standards for safety, quality, or performance. Certified products bear the certifier's mark on their package.
98. 21 U.S.C. § 384b (2012) (explaining that for importers who want to voluntarily participate in the programme, the Voluntary Qualified Importer Program provides for the expedited review and importation of food offered for importation).
99. *Ibid.*, at § 381. For a description of several voluntary system recognition agreements, *see FDA Recognizes New Zealand as Having a Comparable Food Safety System*, FDA (13 December 2012), http://www.fda.gov/food/newsevents/constituentupdates/ucm331276.htm.

'checklist mentality' should be addressed by requiring a certain number of unannounced visits, as is being considered by the Global Food Safety Initiative. To be sure, the food safety challenges mentioned in the chapter will test the new FSMA rules.

FDA regulators were unaware that considering third-party certification and moving away from traditional regulation was a step towards embracing New Governance. But there are examples that the FSMA responds to New Governance thinking. Under FSMA, the state continues to play a significant role in orchestrating the alignment of public-private contacts. For instance, under FSMA, private actors (exporters) are encouraged to seek certification for their exported products by incentives such as the VQIP - which provides expedited entry for certified foods for approved exporters.[100] To summarize, although the FSMA rules contain elements of Transnational New Governance, the rules most closely resemble an attempt to incorporate New Governance features into a traditionally command-and-control governance framework.

There is evidence, however, that they were aware that considering third-party certification and moving away from traditional regulation was a step towards enhanced food safety. In 2004, based on a conclusion that seafood imports were unsafe to eat, the General Accounting Office issued a seafood safety report recommending that the FDA explores the possibility of certifying third parties to conduct inspections of foreign seafood processors and domestic importers, similar to the FDA's third-party inspection programme for medical devices.[101] Then, in 2008, a programme referred to as the Shrimp Pilot was launched to examine the potential FDA use of third-party certification.[102] The Shrimp Pilot succeeded in teaching the FDA that third-party certification could lead to gains in screening imports and that direct accreditation, in which the FDA accredits and provides direct oversight to third-party certification bodies, would be 'costly and administratively burdensome'.[103] Ultimately, the FDA decided to include the use of third-party audits as a part of import controls in FSMA.[104]

Evidence shows that third-party certification can reduce an industry's regulatory burden. In 2006, the FDA and Health Canada initiated the pilot, Multipurpose Audit Program.[105] The pilot explored the potential benefits to medical device manufacturers and agencies of using a single third party to conduct both FDA and Health Canada inspections and audits at the same time in one joint audit-inspection. The hope was

100. FSMA, Pub. L. No. 111-353, 124 Stat. 3885 (2011) (codified as amended in scattered sections of 21 U.S.C).
101. US Gov't Accountability Office, GAO-04-246, *Food Safety: FDA's Imported Seafood Safety Program Shows Some Progress, but Further Improvements Are Needed* (2004).
102. US Food & Drug Admin., *Assessment of the Third-Party Certification Pilot for Aquacultured Shrimp*, 73 Fed. Reg. 39705 (10 July 2008), http://www.fda.gov/food/guidanceregulation/guidancedocumentsregulatoryinformation/seafood/ucm265934.htm.
103. Accreditation of Third-Party Auditors/Certification Bodies to Conduct Food Safety Audits and to Issue Certifications, 78 Fed. Reg. 45,782, 45,786 (proposed 29 July 2013) (to be codified at 21 C.F.R. pts. 1, 16).
104. David Acheson, *Third-Party Audits: Their Crucial Role in Moving Forward with FSMA and Food Safety*, Food Safety News (27 November 2012), http://www.foodsafetynews.com/2012/ 11/third-party-audits-their-crucial-role-in-moving-forward-with-fsma-and-food-safety/.
105. US Food & Drug Admin., *Global Engagement* 1-4 (2012), http://www.fda.gov/downloads/aboutfda/reportsmanualsforms/reports/ucm298578.pdf.

that using one third-party to simultaneously meet FDA and Health Canada regulatory requirements for systems quality could potentially reduce the industry's regulatory burden.[106] The results from the ten joint audit-inspections under the pilot showed that the joint approach reduced the time spent in manufacturing facilities by about one-third, on average, compared to the estimated time required for separate FDA and Health Canada audits and inspections, thereby reducing the regulatory burden for the industry.[107] In addition, the FDA and Health Canada gained a better understanding of their respective audit and inspection approaches, providing a foundation for leveraging inspection resources in the future.[108]

§11.06 EXAMINING FUTURE CHALLENGES AND CONCLUSIONS

We are living in a new regulatory reality, driven by changes in consumer demand and the production and supply of food. Consumer preferences and food production and supply are changing due to changes in the variability of our climate and changing to include more central processing and widespread distribution. Consumers, meanwhile, are demanding more transparency in their food system, particularly as it relates to animal welfare and climate change, and are pushing for more nutritional information to make more informed decisions regarding their diets. These changes are driving advances in food science and in food production leading to new food innovations (like cellular meat and alternative proteins) and a future of individually based diets.

Rising global trade and innovation in food technology will continue to threaten food safety in unpredictable ways, challenging regulators, litigators, and private industry to develop new rules. While regulators continue to solve recurring food safety problems (particularly with respect to *E.coli* and romaine lettuce, and with respect to *Hepatitis-A* in the restaurant food sector), new and emerging bacteria, toxins, and antibiotic resistance and unexpected sources of food-borne illness (such as flour and meal replacement shake mixes)[109] will be met with better detection of multistate outbreaks and advances in testing to diagnose food-borne illness.

Regulation needs to continue to evolve, as it has in the past twenty years, into a co-regulatory framework embracing the elements of New Governance. Finding a careful balance between the three elements of the food regulatory system, namely federal and state regulators, consumer litigation, and private industry, is essential. At the same time the food agencies need to continue to work together. The FDA and the USDA have worked closely over the years to oversee the nation's food supply and will continue to collaborate. One example of this is in the area of cellular meat: here, the USDA and FDA jointly decided to take active steps to jointly regulate the development of this new food. These agencies are partnering in many key areas, including the implementation of produce safety measures and biotechnology efforts.

106. *Ibid.*
107. *Ibid.*
108. *Ibid.*
109. Centers for Disease Control, https://www.cdc.gov/foodsafety/challenges/index.html.

As history shows, the emergence of new antibiotic-resistant pathogens[110] and new food-borne illness risks will continue to put pressure on all national regulatory systems. Even with the new innovative rules under FSMA, the success of this new legislation will be tested by the growing complexity of modern food supply chains and by pressure exerted by international trade obligations to harmonize national regulatory standards in a downward manner.

110. Examples of antibiotic-resistant pathogens are *E.coli 0157:H7* and different strains of *Salmonella – Salmonella Typhimurium* and *Salmonella Newport*.

CHAPTER 12

CAFOs: Climate Change, Livestock Production and the Law

Justo Corti Varela[*]

Climate change policy is currently focused on the decarbonization of the economy. Although in the Paris Agreements there are some references to non-energy related policies, national plans centre their measures on either green energy production or energy efficiency. Little is said about the impact of agriculture on climate change beyond CO_2 emissions (deforestation, desertification), and how our model of food consumption, too focused as it is on livestock products, also has other negative impacts on the environment and human health.

Intensive livestock production and feedstuffs-related trade have multiple implications for climate change (direct emissions, indirect emissions and reduction of carbon absorption capacity) as well as health implications – for consumers and rural population – in different countries. Consequently, an integrated (climate change/health) international law approach is necessary. This contribution will analyse the different strategies employed on how to include water consumption and land use in international climate change agreements, as well as how to quantify and redistribute environmental and health costs, particularly regarding livestock production and the feedstuffs trade.

* I would like to thank Prof. Stéphanie Dagron for her comments during the workshop on *Health and the Environment in International Law: Actors, Norms and Responsibilities* in the Max Planck Institute for Comparative Public Law and International Law (Heidelberg, 17-18 October 2018). I also thank Dr Pedro Villarreal and Dr Allan Francis Tatham for their invaluable comments and deep reading of former versions of the paper. As usual, any remaining error and omission remains with the author.

§12.01 INTRODUCTION

Climate change policy is currently focused on the decarbonization of the economy, mainly on the creation of a global carbon market.[1] Although in the Paris Agreements there are some references to non-energy related policies,[2] the tendency of national plans establishing Nationally Determined Contributions (NDC) centre on measures of either green energy production or energy efficiency.[3] Despite the fact that the main source of CO_2 emissions is related to burning of fossil fuels for producing energy, non-direct energy emissions (particularly agriculture-related and land-use changes) have an impact of one-third of the total emissions worldwide.[4] Moreover, in climate change reports little is being said about the impact of agriculture on climate change beyond emissions, and how our model of food consumption – to focused as it is on livestock products – also has other negative impacts on the environment and human health.

Food is, at the end of the day, an energy source and this problem concerns the difficult equilibrium between two sensible systems: the environment and health. As has happened with the economy, human beings have always tried to increase their sources of energy in order to grow. While the middle class emerge in the old 'Global South',[5] animal-sourced foods expand globally. Annual meat production is projected to increase from 218 million t in 1997-1999 to 376 million t by 2030.[6] Recent studies predict a global rise in demand for animal food products of up to 70% by 2050, driven

1. This issue was at the core of COP25 Summit (Chile-Spain 2019) but, unfortunately, there was not agreement and finally the issue was postponed to COP26. Euronews, *Watch again: COP25 talks end with no deal on carbon markets* (16 December 2019), https://www.euronews.com/2019/12/14/cop25-climate-conference-extended-after-failure-to-reach-agreement.
2. For example, Article 5 encourages parties to develop 'policy approaches and positive incentives for activities relating to reducing emissions from deforestation and forest degradation'; or Article 7, which fosters a 'global goal on adaptation of enhancing adaptive capacity, strengthening resilience and reducing vulnerability to climate change'. UNFCCC, *Paris Agreement* (2015), https://unfccc.int/sites/default/files/english_paris_agreement.pdf.
3. For example, the NDC of the EU is focused on energy (Fuel Combustion, Fugitive emissions from fuels and CO2 transport and storage) and industrial processes and product use. Agriculture, waste and land use, in this order, are situated at the end of the plan. *See* EU, *Intended Nationally Determined Contribution of the EU and its Member States* (2015), https://www4.unfccc.int/sites/ndcstaging/PublishedDocuments/European%20Union%20First/LV-03-06-EU%20INDC.pdf.
   Similarly, in the Chinese proposal, the NDC is centred on 'Building Low-Carbon Energy System', 'Building Energy Efficient and Low-Carbon Industrial System', 'Controlling Emissions from Building and Transportation Sectors', and 'Promoting the Low-Carbon Way of Life'; all of them being energy-related policies. 'Increasing Carbon Sinks' (basically afforestation) and 'Enhancing Overall Climate Resilience' are left in second place. *See* China, *Enhanced actions on climate change: China's intended nationally determined contributions* (2015), https://www4.unfccc.int/sites/ndcstaging/PublishedDocuments/China%20First/China%27s%20First%20NDC%20Submission.pdf.
4. T. Stocker et al. eds, *Climate Change 2013: The Physical Science Basis* (Intergovernmental Panel on Climate Change & Cambridge University Press, 2014).
5. Diane E. Davis, The Sociospatial Reconfiguration of Middle Classes and Their Impact on Politics and Development in the Global South: Preliminary Ideas for Future Research 241-267 (Julian Go ed., Political Power and Social Theory, Emerald, 2010).
6. WHO *Availability and changes in consumption of animal products* (World Health Organization, 2018), http://www.who.int/nutrition/topics/3_foodconsumption/en/index4.html.

by urban consumers in emerging economies.[7] Livestock currently uses almost a third of the world's entire land surface, mostly permanent pasture, but also one-third of the world's arable land for providing livestock feed. Livestock production is not only very intensive in its use of natural resources, putting at risk the equilibrium between climate and environmental systems, but the concentration of energy that animal products provide, at least at the levels that they are consumed in high-income countries, could alter our health systems, increasing the risks of cancer and cardiovascular problems.[8] The paradox is that while globalization expands, Western food habits into middle-income countries, low-income ones have augmented their food dependency due to the assignment of arable land to the lucrative production of feed-related crops for export.[9] Using the case of livestock products, this chapter links the environmental and health challenges to international law. Submission to international law is justified for three reasons. First, because livestock production is a major source of greenhouse gas (GHG) emissions and hence it fits in the global climate change strategy. Second, because livestock production, with a much internationalized market of feeding, is global and cannot be regulated on a national basis. Finally, because there are clear interconnections between the pressure that livestock production exerts on the environment and the rise of new global health challenges, as pandemics. The structure of the chapter is divided into two parts. In the first step it focuses on environmental and health problems directly related to an animal protein diet. Second, it pays attention to those problems that are a consequence of the internationalization of feed markets. Finally, the chapter makes some proposals on how to integrate health and environmental approaches under the umbrella of the climate change framework.

§12.02 DIRECT IMPACTS OF AN ANIMAL PROTEIN DIET

Livestock production is responsible for 14.5% of carbon emissions,[10] but, at the same time, it makes exceptional demands on scarce resources like water and land, either directly for keeping the animals alive or indirectly for producing their feed. Moreover,

7. PierreJ. Gerber et al., *Tackling Climate Change Through Livestock: A Global Assessment of Emissions and Mitigation Opportunities* (Food and Agriculture Organization, 2013), http://www.fao.org/3/a-i3437e.pdf.
8. Many studies link high consumption of meat and cancer and cardiovascular problems. For a good review of the literature *see* Alison J. McAfee, et al. *Red Meat Consumption: An Overview of the Risks and Benefits*, 84 *Meat Science* 1, 1-13 (2010). Specifically, on cancer risks, *see* Giuseppe Lippi, Camilla Mattiuzzi & Gianfranco Cervellin *Meat Consumption and Cancer Risk: A Critical Review of Published Meta-Analyses*, 97 *Critical Reviews in Oncology/Hematology* 1-14 (2016).
9. There are no global studies on this matter. However, looking at the evolution of exports of typical animal feed crops, like maize or soybeans, the assumption can be confirmed. For example, Mozambique exported 0 tons of maize from 1974 to 2001. It started exportations in 2002 with a peak of 103,000 tons in 2006. Similarly, Ethiopia started maize exportations in 1998, with a peak of 60,000 tons in 2011; and soybean exportations in 2001, with a peak of 42,000 tons in 2013. Of course, these figures are far away from those of big middle-income exporters like Brazil (around 20 million tons of maize and 50 million tons of soybean) or Argentina (around 20 million tons of maize and 10 million tons of soybean), but they show a trend. *See*, http://www.fao.org/faostat/en/#data/TP.
10. *Ibid.*

red meat consumption – the most environmentally costly food produced from livestock – increases the risk of dying prematurely by 13%[11] and, in 2015, the World Health Organization (WHO) certified it as probably carcinogenic to humans:[12] diets clearly link environmental and human health.[13]

[A] On the Environment

Traditionally, livestock was a way to *recycle* low-quality vegetable protein or even agricultural waste into high-quality animal nutrients. However, as the ratio of land to population decreases, farmers are induced to adopt technologies that raise returns on land at the expense of a higher input of labour, like breeding. As Boserup explained already in 1965,[14] in modern agriculture, there are close crop-livestock interactions and any growth in demand for animal products have a multiplier effect on the agricultural demand on natural resources.[15] Of course, in a second agricultural revolution[16] context, this means an increase in GHG emissions related to energy inputs. It is worth recalling that fossil fuels are used not only for direct agricultural activities like mobility, heating or processing but also to produce nitrogenous fertilizers that are energy-intensive. But other inputs, like arable land, fresh water and waste disposal capacity, are near to their limits.[17] The rise of consumer expectations on animal protein has these other environmental impacts that, indirectly, reduce the capacity to dispose of important natural resources, thereby reversing climate change policies.

11. An Pan, et al. *Red Meat Consumption and Mortality: Results from 2 Prospective Cohort Studies*, 172 Archives of Internal Medicine 7, 555-563 (2012).
12. IARC Red Meat and Processed Meat IARC Monographs on the Evaluation of Carcinogenic Risks to Humans, 114 International Agency for Research on Cancer (World Health Organization 2015), http://publications.iarc.fr/Book-And-Report-Series/Iarc-Monographs-On-The-Evaluation-Of-Carcinogenic-Risks-To-Humans/Red-Meat-And-Processed-Meat-2018. Véronique Bouvard, et al. *Carcinogenicity of Consumption of Red and Processed Meat*, 16 *The Lancet Oncology* 16, 1599-1600 (2015).
13. David Tilman & Michael Clark *Global Diets Link Environmental Sustainability and Human Health*, 515 *Nature* 7528, 518 (2014).
14. E, Boserup, *The Condition of Agricultural Growth: The Economics of Agrarian Change under Population Pressure* (Aldine Publishing Company, 1965), https://www.biw.kuleuven.be/aee/clo/idessa _files/boserup1965.pdf. For a recent development of this theory *see* J. Bruinsma, *World Agriculture: Towards 2015/2030 – An FAO Study* (FAO/Earthscan/Routledge, 2017).
15. H. Steinfeld, *Livestock's Long Shadow: Environmental Issues and Options* (Food and Agriculture Organization, 2006), http://www.fao.org/docrep/010/a0701e/a0701e00.HTM.
16. The First Agriculture Revolution was, basically, the domestication of plants (10,000 BC). The Second Agriculture Revolution meant the introduction of mechanization and fertilizers (XIX century). The Third Agriculture Revolution (or green revolution) implied the generalization of these changes, including technological improvements such as cheap agrochemicals and high-yielding varieties, in developing countries. Although results were more evident during the green revolution, the basis of nowadays agriculture (mechanization and agrochemicals) started with second agriculture revolution. For more details about the different agriculture revolutions *see* M. Mazoyer & L. Roudart, *A History of World Agriculture: From the Neolithic Age to the Current crisis* (NYU Press, 2006).
17. Jelle Bruinsma, The Resources Outlook: By How Much Do Land, Water and Crop Yields Need to Increase by 2050? 233-278 (P. Confort, ed., Agricultural Development Economics Division Economic and Social Development Department, FAO, 2011).

[1] GHG Emissions

GHG emissions of the agriculture sector represent 22% of total global emissions, quite similar to those of industry and slightly more than what transport produces. Although official reports estimate that livestock production is responsible for 35% of agricultural GHG emissions[18] when agriculture and related transport emissions are combined, the impact of animal products rises up to 80% of the combined sector's emissions.[19] In this sense, the livestock sector alone would produce 7.1 gt CO_2-eq per annum, that is 14.5% of human-induced GHG emissions.[20]

However, inside the livestock sector, there are strong differences among species. While beef (41%) and cattle milk (20%) are the major polluters, pig meat (9%) and eggs (8%) have a much less important impact.[21] Emission intensity regarding per protein basis also shows that beef is the most polluting, with an average of over 300 kg CO_2-eq per kg of protein.[22] Small ruminants emit half of that amount (between 165 and 112 kg CO_2-eq per kg of protein), while pork and chicken are below 100 kg CO_2-eq per kg of edible protein.[23] That means, from a protein source perspective, beef is three times more negative for climate change than pork, chicken and eggs.

When direct breeding activities are distinguished from other related emissions, like feed production and post-farm transport and processing, it is noticeable that almost half of emissions are not related to animal digestive gas emissions. Feed production, with 45% of the total, is the key element, with 3.3 gt of emissions. It does not include transport when crops are imported from foreign countries, as it will be explained in section §12.03[A]. below. Finally, regarding the type of gas emitted, 44% is methane (CH_4), 29% nitrous oxide (N_2O) and only 27% CO_2. It is worth recalling that methane is thirty-four times stronger than CO_2 if its effects on climate change in the long term are compared. It has been responsible for 60% of the equivalent radioactive force caused by CO_2 emissions since the onset of the Industrial Revolution.[24]

18. N. Stern, *The Economics of Climate Change: The Stern Review* (Cambridge University Press, 2006).
19. Anthony J. McMichael, et al. *Food, Livestock Production, Energy, Climate Change, and Health*, 370 *The Lancet* 9594, 1253-1263 (2007).
20. Gerber, *supra* note 7.
21. *Ibid*. These are global figures but there could be important differences depending on the type of production, the weather and geographic characteristics or the methodology used. For an example of these differences *see* A. Leip et al., *Evaluation of the Livestock Sector's Contribution to the EU Greenhouse Gas Emissions* (Joint Research Centre, European Commission, Institute for Environment and Sustainability, Climate Change, 2010), http://agritrop.cirad.fr/558780/1/document_558780.pdf.
22. C. Opio et al., *Greenhouse Gas Emissions from Ruminant Supply Chains: A Global Life Cycle Assessment* (FAO, 2013), http://www.fao.org/docrep/018/i3461e/i3461e.pdf.
23. M. MacLeod et al., *Greenhouse Gas Emissions from Pig and Chicken Supply Chains: A Global Life Cycle Assessment* (FAO, 2013), http://www.fao.org/docrep/018/i3460e/i3460e.pdf.
24. Philippe Ciais, et al. Chapter 6: Carbon and Other Biogeochemical Cycles, 465-570 (T.F. Stocker et al. ed., Climate Change 2013: The Physical Science Basis. Contribution of Working Group I to the Fifth Assessment Report of the Intergovernmental Panel on Climate Change, Cambridge University Press, 2013), https://www.ipcc.ch/report/ar5/wg1/.

[2] *Intensity in the Use of Land and Water*

The use of land and water in livestock production depends on the kind of system used. Extensive grazing systems demand large quantities of land, with serious risks of deforestation and land degradation, and relatively small amounts of water.

Regarding land, the Food and Agricultural Organization (FAO) estimates that livestock uses 70% of all agricultural land, which is 30% of the total land surface of the Earth. Extensive systems produce nearly 9% of total meat, mixed 46% and the landless system 45%. These last two also require land for feed-cultivation that represents 33% of all arable land used. In total, livestock consumes more than 80% of all agricultural land but, taking into account outputs, extensive systems are much more land demanding since they are responsible for around two and a half times more land-use change than intensive systems.[25]

Although the big picture seems to say that extensive livestock is the most negative for climate change, when the attention is focused on the evolution of the production systems in practice, there is a clear connection between the expansion of feed crops (mainly soybean) and the decrease in forest area in Latin America, particularly in Brazil, Argentina and Paraguay.[26] From a climate change point of view, deforestation is the land-use change process generating most GHG emissions.[27]

Concerning water, agricultural production consumes 70% of freshwater used. While each human being consumes 30 litres-300 litres of water per day for domestic purposes, it is necessary to use more than 3,000 litres per day to grow their food.[28] There is no agreement, however, on the total water used in the livestock sector and figures change considerably depending on the system (from 0 litres per day in extensive grazing to 125 litres per animal, per day in industrial landless pig production).[29] The greatest controversies refer to grain-fed beef where variations could be from 15,000 litres per kg to 100,000 litres per kg.[30]

[3] *Waste and Biodiversity Loss*

Livestock production has important impacts on land and water pollution. The FAO has underlined the relation between livestock waste and how nutrients, heavy metals and

25. Figures compiled from several FAO documents by T. Garnett, *Intensive Versus Extensive Livestock Systems and Greenhouse Gas Emissions* (Food Climate Research Network briefing paper, 2010), https://fcrn.org.uk/sites/default/files/FCRN_int_vs_ext_livestock.pdf.
26. Gerber, *supra* note 7.
27. Climate Change 2007: Mitigation (Bert Metz et al. eds, Contribution of Working Group III to the Fourth Assessment Report of the Intergovernmental Panel on Climate Change, Cambridge University Press, 2007).
28. K. Turner et al., *Economic Valuation of Water Resources in Agriculture: From the Sectoral to a Functional Perspective of Natural Resource Management* (FAO Paper Reports No. 27, 2004), http://www.fao.org/docrep/007/y5582e/y5582e00.htm.
29. P.K. Thornton & M. Herrero, *The Inter-Linkages Between Rapid Growth in Livestock Production, Climate Change, and the Impacts on Water Resources, Land Use, and Deforestation* (The World Bank, 2010), https://elibrary.worldbank.org/doi/abs/10.1596/1813-9450-5178.
30. Donald Peden, et al., Water and Livestock for Human Development 485-514 (David Molden ed., Comprehensive Assessment of Water Management in Agriculture, Earthscan/IWMI, 2007).

pathogens in livestock go into the water and accumulate in the soil.[31] In intensive livestock systems, there is also pollution from feed and fodder production in the form of nutrient loadings and pesticides.[32]

A recent study in the European Union (EU) concluded that livestock contributes to 78% for terrestrial biodiversity loss, 80% for soil acidification and air pollution (ammonia and nitrogen oxide emissions) and 73% for water pollution. According to the same article, livestock is one of the major contributors to these environmental impacts, ranging between 12% for global warming and 59% for water quality impact.[33]

[B] On Health

Animal proteins are a very effective source of nutrients. Fogel[34] attributes the remarkable gains in life expectancy in modern Western populations to their expanding food supplies, particularly with an animal origin. In the same vein, animal diets have also transformed childhood growth and size attained in adulthood, reducing infections, particularly at the beginning and end of our lives. However, in the second half of the twentieth century, the combination of a sedentary life and workstyle and a continuous growth in protein and calories have started to neutralize these health benefits producing other effects, mainly related to cardiovascular diseases and cancer. Moreover, health gains from abundance in food have not been generalized, and still 815 million people remain energy undernourished.[35]

The ideal scenario – as was already highlighted in Chapter 8 written by Ilja Richard Pavone – would be to reduce consumption of animal products in high-income countries and thus lower the ceiling of the consumption level to which low-income and middle-income countries would then converge.[36] In developing countries, adequate policies should be taken since multiple forms of malnutrition (undernutrition and obesity) coexist.[37]

[1] Carcinogenic Impact

When in 2015 the International Agency for Research on Cancer (IARC (WHO)) linked dietary patterns or metabolism and cancer and declared that the high consumption of

31. Steinfeld, *supra* note 15.
32. Thornton & Herrero, *supra* note 29.
33. Adrian Leip, et al. *Impacts of European Livestock Production: Nitrogen, Sulphur, Phosphorus and Greenhouse Gas Emissions, Land-Use, Water Eutrophication and Biodiversity*, 10 *Environmental Research Letters* 11, 115004 (2015).
34. R.W. Fogel, *The Escape from Hunger and Premature Death, 1700–2100: Europe, American and the Third World* (Cambridge University Press, 2004).
35. FAO, *The State of Food Insecurity and Nutrition in the World 2017* (FAO, 2018), http://www.fao.org/3/a-I7695e.pdf.
36. *See supra* note 19.
37. Benjamin Caballero, *A Nutrition Paradox: Underweight and Obesity in Developing Countries*, 352 *New England Journal of Medicine* 15, 1514-1516 (2005).

red meat (group A2) and processed meat (group 1)[38] was associated with an increased risk of colorectal cancer, there was an interesting debate in the media. However, the issue was not new, as indicated in earlier medical literature.[39]

The IARC stated that red meat, taking into account limited evidence from epidemiological studies, could be associated with the development of colorectal cancer. Red meat would be included in group A2 (probable carcinogens) like glyphosate or androgenic (anabolic) steroids. Processed meat, however, was classified as group 1 (carcinogenic to humans) since there was sufficient evidence of carcinogenicity in humans. Other products in this category are asbestos, aflatoxins, plutonium, arsenic, radon, tobacco smoking or ultraviolet radiation.[40] Meat eating was associated mainly with colorectal cancer, and it also found evidence of links with pancreatic cancer and prostate cancer.

According to the WHO Global Burden of Disease Project,[41] meat could be responsible for 50,000 cancer deaths per year worldwide, which is much less than the 1 million cancer deaths per year globally due to tobacco smoking, 600,000 per year due to alcohol consumption, and 200,000 per year due to air pollution.

Risks of meat consumption increase with the amount consumed. For every 50 g portion of processed meat and 100 g portion of red meat eaten daily, the risk of colorectal cancer increases by about 18% and 17%, respectively.[42]

[2] Chemicals in Meat Production

The use of nitrites (to cure meat and give them a healthy colour) and veterinary drugs are, in the EU, the main concern related to chemicals in the meat industry. Not authorized in the EU but in the United States (US),[43] the use of hormones as growth promoters in cattle and sheep is also an important source of alarm in other regions. According to scientists, all these chemicals - administered under supervision and under the security thresholds - should not represent a risk to human health.[44]

38. IARC, *Red Meat and Processed Meat*, 14 IARC Monographs on the Evaluation of Carcinogenic Risks to Humans (2018), https://monographs.iarc.fr/wp-content/uploads/2018/06/mono114.pdf.
39. Manjinder S. Sandhu, Ian R. White & Klim McPherson, *Systematic Review of the Prospective Cohort Studies on Meat Consumption and Colorectal Cancer Risk: A Meta-Analytical Approach*, 10 *Cancer Epidemiology and Prevention Biomarkers* 5, 439-446 (2001).
40. A full list of products at, https://monographs.iarc.fr/list-of-classifications-volumes/.
41. WHO, *Disease burden and mortality estimates* (Institute for Health Metrics and Evaluation, 2016), http://www.who.int/healthinfo/global_burden_disease/estimates/en/index1.html.
42. IARC, *supra* note 38.
43. For an interesting debate about the safety of these drugs in meat production *see* the Panel and Appellate Body decision of the WTO EC-Hormones.
44. The debate, related to the risk to human health of the administration of hormones to cows when used in accordance with good animal husbandry practice, was developed in the *EC-Hormones* case within the WTO's Dispute Settlement Body. As it was appointed by the EC, sometimes it is not easy to clarify what constitutes good animal husbandry practice. *See WTO – EC-Hormones*, Panel Report, paras 4.180 ss.

The main concerns relate to the use and abuse of antibiotics, particularly in intensive systems where the risk of infections is very high and its massive administration is a routine practice. Recent studies have linked the generalized use of antibiotics in intensive livestock and resistances that appeared in humans, and the failure of surveillance programmes currently in force.[45]

[3] Fat and Obesity

Livestock products are rich in fats and calories. The consumption of foods high in fats and sugars and reduction in physical activity are, according to official studies, the main reasons for the increase in obesity and related diseases.[46] These include metabolic and cardiovascular diseases, in particular, type 2 diabetes and ischemic heart disease and, less certainly, some cancers. Developing countries, where there are large differences in income within a single society, face the double burden[47] of undernutrition due to nutritional deficits in parts of their populations and an increase in obesity-related chronic diseases due to increased availability of foods of an animal origin.[48]

[4] Zoonotic Infections

The rapid change from extensive livestock production to an intensive one, particularly in developing countries where isolation and best techniques are not always available, is reducing human contact with new infectious agents. There is scientific evidence to show the effect of agricultural intensification and environmental changes on the risk of zoonoses for which there are epidemiological interactions between wildlife and livestock. Such environmental incursions and commercial practices have facilitated the emergence of zoonotic infections, including various viral haemorrhagic fevers, bird flu, Nipah virus from pig farming, and, probably, BSE in cows and its human variant.[49] Both N1H5 influenza (avian) and N1H1 influenza (pigs) (as well as the COVID-19 pandemic) produced international health crises. The first one was probably the first global zoonotic crisis with an impact on international health law[50] and the second one, declared a *pandemic* by the WHO in 2009, produced changes in protocols and the way

45. Remco Schrijver et al., *A Review of Antimicrobial Resistance Surveillance Programmes in Livestock and Meat Thereof in Europe with a Focus on Antimicrobial Resistance Patterns in Humans*, 24 *Clinical Microbiology and Infection* 6 (2017), doi: 10.1016/j.cmi.2017.09.013.
46. Joint WHO/FAO Expert Consultation, *Diet, Nutrition and the Prevention of Chronic Diseases*, 916 World Health Organization Technical Report Services (2003).
47. Ricardo. Uauy & Noel W. Solomons, *The Role of the International Community: Forging a Common Agenda in Tackling the Double Burden of Malnutrition*, 32 *UN Standing Committee on Nutrition* (2006) 24-37.
48. Gerard Anderson & Edward Chu, *Expanding Priorities: Confronting Chronic Disease in Countries with Low Income*, 356 *New England Journal of Medicine* 3, 209-211 (2007).
49. Bryony Anne Jones, et al. *Zoonosis Emergence Linked to Agricultural Intensification and Environmental Change*, 110 *Proceedings of the National Academy of Sciences* 21, 8399-8404 (2013).
50. D.P. Fidler, *Global Outbreak of Avian Influenza A (H5N1) and International Law*, ASIL Insights (The American Society of International Law, 2004).

that international health institutions interact with national authorities and media in an interconnected world.[51]

§12.03 THE HIDDEN SIDE: FEEDSTUFFS TRADE

[A] Protein Deficit

The EU population consumes around 100 g of protein per capita per day, 59% from livestock. Livestock products are officially almost all produced in the EU;[52] however, when the attention is focused on the origin of that protein (which is the EU balance sheet for protein-rich feed materials), 69% is imported[53] basically from South America (Brazil and Argentina). The EU only produces 3% of its needs in soybean meal, the main raw material of feeds. Soybean meal represents 64% of the protein-rich feed materials and is the major source of essential amino acid lysine for monogastric livestock (pigs and poultry) which are the lesser polluters regarding GHG emissions.[54] In fact, there is a close correlation between the increases in monogastric livestock, for environmental and GHG emission reasons and the importation of soybean meal as a recent study of the European Parliament has underlined.[55] Although the protein deficit is not new (it started in the 1960s with the EEC-US agreements for the acceptance of the EU Common Agricultural Policy (CAP) in the General Agreement on Tariff and Trade (GATT) and the reduction of European maize tariffs as a compensation),[56] it has become particularly important since the prohibition of animal protein in feeds because of the BSE crisis. It creates distortions in both EU environmental and health (food safety) policies and casts doubt on one of the key elements of the CAP, viz., as the guarantee of supply of food through a policy that would permit the EU to be

51. Bradly J. Condon & Tapen Sinha, *The Effectiveness of Pandemic Preparations: Legal Lessons from the 2009 Influenza Epidemic*, 22 *Florida Journal of International Law* 1, 1-30, 2010. L.O. Gostin, *Influenza A (H1N1) and Pandemic Preparedness under the Rule of International Law*, 301 *Journal of the American Medical Association* 22, 2376-2378 (2009).
52. 96% for meat and 99% for diary. European Commission, *Short Term outlook for arable crops, meat and dairy markets*, Short Term Outlook 5 (DG for Agriculture and Rural Development, Winter 2013), https://ec.europa.eu/agriculture/sites/agriculture/files/markets-and-prices/short-term-outlook/pdf/2013-03_en.pdf.
53. A. Bouxin, *Feed & Food Statistical Yearbook 2012* (European Feed Manufacturers' Federation, 2013), www.fefac.eu.
54. G.D. Cromwell, *Soybean Meal an exceptional Protein Source*, https://en.engormix.com/feed-machinery/articles/soybean-meal-exceptional-protein-t40451.htm.
55. Andrea Bues et al., *The Environmental Role of Protein Crops in the New Common Agricultural Policy*, Ref. 2012-067 (DG for Internal Policies -Agriculture and Rural Development- of the European Parliament, 2013), http://www.europarl.europa.eu/RegData/etudes/etudes/join/2013/495856/IPOL-AGRI_ET(2013)495856_EN.pdf.
56. For an explanation of the historical reasons of the protein deficit *see* M. Häusling, *The EU Protein Deficit: What Solution for a Long-Standing Problem?*, Ref. 2010/2111(INI) (Committee on Agriculture and Rural Development of the European Parliament, 2011), http://www.europarl.europa.eu/sides/getDoc.do?type=REPORT&reference=A7-2011-0026& language=EN.

self-sufficient in agricultural products. Unfortunately, the tendency has been that it will be even worse in subsequent years.[57]

[B] On the Environment

[1] Delocalization of Environmental Costs

The EU imports annually 28 million t of soybeans. It represents 14% of the global soya harvest and about 15 million hectares of arable land, mostly in South America. Putting the figures into context, that represents almost all the arable land of France (18 million hectares). China is three times more dependent on soybean imports, with 95 million t of imported soybean (90% of the total consumption), mainly from South America and the US.

Since soybean is largely traded internationally, emissions in Latin America are actually attributed to production units around the world. However, other environmental costs such as water or land-use change are not taken into account in these calculations. The increasing demand for meat in developing economies is forcibly extending intensive agriculture into the tropical rainforests of South America, especially Brazil, Bolivia, and Paraguay.[58] Soybean production is the subject of much-learned discussion on deforestation and environmental impacts.[59]

[2] International Transport Costs

International transport environmental costs are not taken into account in the assignment of emission units in the protein trade. Looking at UK Department for Environment, Food & Rural Affairs figures, international shipping produces 10 CO_2 gr t/km. That is 28 million t of soybean imported from America to the EU could represent around 2.8 million t of supplementary emissions.

57. Cornelis Leonardus Maria de Visser, et al. *The EU's Dependency on Soya Bean Import for the Animal Feed Industry and Potential for EU Produced Alternatives*, 21 OCL-Oleagineux Corps Gras Lipides 4 (2014), doi https://doi.org/10.1051/ocl/2014021.
58. Rosamond Naylor, et.al. *Agriculture. Losing the Links Between Livestock and Land*, 310 Science 5754, 1621-1622 (2005).
59. Laureen Elgert, *Shifting the Debate about 'Responsible Soy' Production in Paraguay: A Critical Analysis of Five Claims about Environmental, Economic, and Social Sustainability*, Working Paper No. 23 (Land Deal Politics Initiative and the Institute for Development Studies of the University of Sussex, 2012), https://assets.publishing.service.gov.uk/media/57a08a1de5274a27b2000425/LDPI_WP_23.pdf. K. Minderhoud, *Round Table for Responsible Soy Association: Breaking Ground for Responsible Soy – An Institutional Response to Agricultural Expansion and Intensification in Argentina*, (International Development Studies of the University of Utrecht, 2010), https://dspace.library.uu.nl/handle/1874/44520.

[C] On Health

[1] Lack of Controls on Herbicides and Pesticides: Impact on Consumers and Foreign Farmers

Countries that export feedstuffs to the EU are genetically modified (GM) crop producers. Almost 95% of the soybean cultivated in Brazil, US and Argentina has been GM to be herbicide resistant that allows the use and abuse of glyphosate during its cultivation. In practice, farmers use more pesticides when they sow GM seeds than with traditional crops, and the keeping of good practices is difficult to control.[60] Pesticide resistance in weeds grows each year[61] and this, in turn, forces farmers to use even higher doses. For that reason chemical companies are starting to commercialize new crops engineered to tolerate 2,4-D and dicamba, older herbicides that are considered more toxic to human health and the environment than glyphosate.[62]

In 2015, the IARC classified glyphosate as a 'probable carcinogen' but the European Food Safety Authority (EFSA) insisted on the safety of the product.[63] Denmark prohibited it in 2003 and the Netherlands (2014) and France (2015 for gardening and since 2021 for any use, unless there is no credible alternative)[64] have followed suit. The EP is currently debating the renewal of the relevant authorization, always for local use, never for the importation of agricultural products cultivated using glyphosate. A draft EP report of September 2018[65] cast doubt on the transparency of EFSA assessments, driven basically by Germany (through the *Bundesinstitut für Risikobewertung*) acting as the rapporteur EU Member State, particularly because the close connections of some members with the German chemical industry,[66] a sensitive issue now that Bayer has taken over Monsanto.[67]

---

60. L.K. Finnegan, *Glyphosate: The Fragile Power Behind Argentina's Soy Complex* (Norwegian University of Life Sciences, 2017), https://brage.bibsys.no/xmlui/handle/11250/2465280.
61. Jerry M. Green & Michael D.K. Owen, *Herbicide-Resistant Crops: Utilities and Limitations for Herbicide-Resistant Weed Management*, 59 *Journal of Agricultural Food Chemistry* 11, 5819-5829 (2011).
62. Carmen Bain, et al. *'Superweeds' or 'Survivors'? Framing the Problem of Glyphosate Resistant Weeds and Genetically Engineered Crops*, 51 *Journal of Rural Studies* 211-221 (2017).
63. For a discussion on that *see* Justo Corti Varela, Butterfly Effect of International Scientific Organizations' Reports: The Unexpected Consequences of the IARC Decision on Glyphosate, 170-187 (Maria Isabel Torres Cazorla & José Manuel Sánchez Patrón eds, International Biolaw: human rights, public health and environment, Tirant lo Blanch, 2018).
64. S. Elzas, *Macron Backs Down on Pledge to Ban Glyphosate in France* (Radio France International, 25 January 2019), http://en.rfi.fr/environment/20190125-macron-backs-down-pledge-ban-glyphosate-france.
65. European Parliament, *Draft Report on the Union's authorisation procedure for pesticides*, Ref. 2018/2153(INI) (Special Committee on the Union's authorisation procedure for pesticides, 2018), http://www.europarl.europa.eu/sides/getDoc.do?pubRef=-%2f%2fEP%2f%2fNONSGML%2bCOMPARL%2bPE-627.625%2b01%2bDOC%2bPDF%2bV0%2f%2fEN.
66. The report was criticized because it did not reveal its authorship (mean while some members of its Committee for Pesticides and Their Residues were under suspicions of having links with the industry); and because the review of some of the published toxicology studies was conducted by

Without entering into the debate either about the health safety of GM crops or about glyphosate carcinogens, the point is that it does not matter whether or not its use is permitted in the EU because: first, the EU depends on GM feed protein for animal production;[68] second, EU consumers are not informed about that because EU label regulation excludes animal products from livestock fed with Genetically Modified Organisms (GMO);[69] and, finally, GM soybean encourages the abuse in use of herbicides by farmers in exporting countries and thereby allows for its introduction into the European food chain.[70]

[2] *No Traceability of Imported Foodstuffs*

There is no traceability of foodstuffs imported into the EU supply chain. One of the conclusions of the CoExtra project,[71] a mega research initiative promoted by the European Commission in order to find solutions to the proposed *coexistence* of three chains (GM, traditional and organic), was that it was not possible or too costly to impose full traceability on EU suppliers of feedstuffs. Six years later, the technology to do so is now available and apparently affordable.[72]

Traceability could introduce benefits both for the environment and human health as the EFSA underlines.[73] It would permit tracing back to the origin of the protein that people are consuming, not only the country of birth, of fattening or of slaughter as it is

Glyphosate Task Force, a consortium of chemical companies that lobbies in favour of glyphosate. The Guardian, *EU scientists in row over safety of Glyphosate weedkiller* (13 January 2015), https://www.theguardian.com/environment/2016/jan/13/eu-scientists-in-row-over-safety-of-glyphosate-weedkiller.

67. *See*, for example, Financial Times, *Monsanto Risk Takes root with Bayer Investors. Worries Over Cost of Glyphosate Cancer Link Wipe €25bn from Market Value* (20 March 2019), https://www.ft.com/content/ba67adba-4b26-11e9-bbc9-6917dce3dc62.
68. The EU dependency on imports of protein-rich feedstuffs, for which there are no substitutes in the short term, is calculated in the 65% of EU needs. *See* József Popp, et al. *Economic Impact of GM Hysteria on EU Feed Market*, 4 *American Journal of Plant Sciences* 8, 1547-1553 (2013).
69. For economic reasons, they are out of the strict labelling policy on EU food. *See* statement 16 of Regulation EC 1830/2003 of the European Parliament and of the Council of 22 September 2003 concerning the traceability and labelling of genetically modified organisms and the traceability of food and feed products produced from genetically modified organisms and amending Directive 2001/18/EC. OJ L 268, 18.10.2003, pp. 24-28. For a comment, *see* J. Corti Varela *Organismos genéticamente modificados y riesgos sanitarios y medioambientales: Derecho de la Unión Europea y de la Organización Mundial del Comercio*, 267 (Reus, 2010).
70. For a good overview of recent studies *see* Marek Cuhra, *Review of GMO Safety Assessment Studies: Glyphosate Residues in Roundup Ready Crops Is an Ignored Issue*, 27 *Environmental Sciences Europe* 1, 20 (2015).
71. Yves Bertheau, *Genetically Modified and Non-genetically Modified Food Supply Chains: Co-existence and Traceability* (John Wiley & Sons, 2012).
72. Joelma Leão-Buchir, et al. *Real-Time PCR for Traceability and Quantification of Genetically Modified Seeds in Lots of Non-transgenic Soybean*, 34 *Bioscience Journal* 1, 34-41 (2018).
73. It is, in fact, a central element of the EU food safety policy. *See* Regulation (EC) No. 178/2002 of the European Parliament and of the Council of 28 January 2002 laying down the general principles and requirements of food law, establishing the European Food Safety Authority and laying down procedures in matters of food safety. OJ L 31, 1.2.2002, pp. 1-24.

compulsory in EU legislation as a result of the BSE crisis,[74] but also the origin and composition of the feed that the livestock was eating and the feeding system used.

§12.04 CLIMATE CHANGE AND INTERNATIONAL TRADE LAW: LIMITATIONS AND OBSTACLES

Environmental regulation is normally based on a life-cycle analysis, which takes into consideration the production, consumption and end-of-life phases of a product. States establish product standards or recycling methods that reduce environmental harm but also regulate the way that products are sold in their market, including those coming from third countries. There is, however, a problem of jurisdiction when the production is done beyond its borders, which may raise an issue of extraterritoriality. Moreover, if the measure chosen is a trade restriction, there could be a conflict with international trade rules.

[A] Process and Production Methods and Likeness under GATT/WTO Law

Since the beginning of the 1990s, GATT/WTO (World Trade Organization) case law was dealing with the possibility of imposing trade exceptions based on Process and Production Methods (PPMs), first in a negative manner with the *US-Tuna* reports, and afterwards opening such possibility with *US-Shrimp*. A key element of PPMs is the concept of like product. As it was said in *Japan – Alcohol II*,[75] it evokes the image of an *accordion*. The scope of *like products* may be different in each particular provision referring to it.[76] Traditionally, GATT and WTO have examined likeness according to the 1970 Report of the Working Party on Border Tax Adjustments, which refers to their physical characteristics, the end uses, consumers' tastes and habits and the tariff classification.[77] In the *US-Tuna* cases, nevertheless, only the first criterion was used, which led to the product-process distinction. Two physically identical or similar products could not be treated differently because of their production processes. The Panel in *US-Tuna I* stated that, since regulations governing the by-catch of dolphins during tuna fishing 'could not possibly affect tuna as a product', the US could not grant a less favourable treatment to Mexican tuna compared to US tuna based on differences in production methods (paragraph 5.15). The idea was reproduced in *US-Tuna II* (paragraph 5.9). However, both reports have never been adopted by parties, and the

74. Beef Labelling Regulation (EC) No. 1760/2000 of the European Parliament and of the Council of 17 July 2000 establishing a system for the identification and registration of bovine animals and regarding the labelling of beef and beef products and repealing Council Regulation (EC) No. 820/97. OJ L 204, 11.8.2000, pp. 1-10.
75. Appellate Body Report, p. 21.
76. Mainly Article III, but also Articles II.2, VI.1, IX.1, XI.2.c, XIII.1, XVI.4 and XIX; as well as specific provisions of the TBT and SPS Agreements.
77. For a connection between this report and the GATT/WTO case law *see* EC-Asbestos, Appellate Body Report, para. 113.

Appellate Body never confirmed this product-process doctrine, so it should not be understood as a settled case-law.[78]

The change came with *US-Shrimp* which was, from a factual point of view, comparable to *US-Tuna*. The Panel followed a similar reasoning as that of *US-Tuna*, but the Appellate Body reversed it. The change was, basically, that the Appellate Body did not follow the first criterion of likeness of the Working Party but the second one, that is, consumers' tastes. Two products with identical physical characteristics but different PPMs could be considered unlike if consumers treat them differently. This vision is widely shared by the literature,[79] and it was confirmed by the Panel and the Appellate Body in *US-Tuna II* (Mexico).[80]

[B] Labelling and Other Consumer Information Measures

Once, under certain conditions, two products could be considered different because consumers perceived them as distinguishable due to their way of production (e.g., environmentally friendly or not), the next question is which measure could be imposed to respond to this differentiation. The necessity test of Article XX GATT, as well as similar wording in Sanitary and Phytosanitary (SPS) and Technical Barriers to Trade (TBT) agreements, is, probably, the key element for this question. Case law demands no alternative measure reasonably available to achieve the level of protection chosen.[81] The selection of the level of protection is essential. It should not be so high, particularly in comparison with other products in competition, that the number of measures available is so reduced that only trade ban could be available.[82] The experience (GMOs, fishing, hormones, etc.) shows that bans that are *necessary* to protect public interests,

78. David Sifonios, *Environmental Process and Production Methods (PPMs) in WTO Law*, 103 (Springer, 2018). This author criticizes the literature that considered this approached as a consolidated jurisprudence. *See* particularly *infra* note 91.

79. Gabrielle Marceau & Joel P. Trachtman, *A Map of the World Trade Organization Law of Domestic Regulation of Goods: The Technical Barriers to Trade Agreement, the Sanitary and Phytosanitary Measures Agreement, and the General Agreement on Tariffs and Trade*, 48 *Journal of World Trade* 2, 351-432, 412 (2014); Joost Pauwelyn, *Recent Books on Trade and Environment: GATT Phantoms Still Haunt the WTO*, 15 *European Journal of International Law* 3, 575-592, 586 (2004), Christiane R. Conrad, *Processes and Production Methods (PPMs) in WTO Law: Interfacing Trade and Social Goals*, 227 (Cambridge University Press, 2011). Sifonios, *supra* note 78, 115.

80. *See* Panel Report, para. 7.249: 'The information presented to the Panel does suggest that US consumers have certain preferences with respect to tuna products, based on their dolphin-safe status, and we do not exclude that such preferences may be relevant to an assessment of likeness. To the extent that consumer preferences, including preferences relating to the manner in which the product has been obtained, may have an impact on the competitive relationship between these products, we consider it a priori relevant to take them into consideration in an assessment of the likeness.' The likeness was not under discussion in the Appellate Body Report, *see* para. 230.

81. *See*, for example, US-Section 337, Panel Report, para. 5.26; Thailand-Cigarettes, Panel Report, para. 75; US-Gasoline, Panel Report, para. 6.25.

82. *See*, for example, EC-Hormones, para. 194.

such as human health or the environment, are much more difficult to demonstrate than other measures founded on consumer information, like labelling.[83]

However, the 2012 report of the Appellate Body in the *US-Tuna II* (Mexico) case proves that even labelling could be illegal under GATT/WTO law. The US labelling 'dolphin-safe' (a clear environmentally based PPM) was analysed through the TBT Agreement, including the no less favourable treatment to like products (Article 2.1) and the necessity of the measure (Article 2.2). The Appellate Body found that the way in which the US' refusal to grant the label to tuna products caught by chasing and encircling dolphins with a purse seine net in order to catch the tuna swimming beneath them, as Mexico did, was not compatible with WTO law since there was no scientific evidence that *setting on* dolphins with a purse seine net was likely to kill or injure them.[84] Consequently, even labelling should be based on a clear, sound-science basis and not just on assumptions.

To sum up, climate change labelling is normally founded on PPM distinctions. Nowadays, WTO case law permits such differentiation when consumers make distinctions. Even though labelling is normally considered the less restrictive measure to tackle public interests (like human health or the environment), or in other words, the least difficult means to prove that the measure is necessary; labelling could not be based on assumptions but on sound science evidence.

§12.05 TOWARDS AN INTEGRATION OF ENVIRONMENTAL AND HEALTH TARGETS IN A COMMON CLIMATE CHANGE STRATEGY?

As part of the discussion, this chapter develops some proposals on how to integrate environmental and health targets in a common climate change strategy.

The Paris Agreements have left the onus on each country to put together their own *national* climate action plans (Intended Nationally Determined Contributions)) and the selection of the necessary targets and strategies to achieve the proposed reduction aims.[85] Regarding livestock, as in other sectors, the main strategies proposed by both FAO[86] and the Intergovernmental Panel on Climate Change[87] are centred on adaptation and mitigation, basically accelerating the change from extensive to intensive production systems (and from ruminants to monogastric meat production) as well

83. For a good overview of the GATT/WTO law on the issue *see* Erich Vranes, Climate Labelling and the WTO: The 2010 EU Ecolabelling Programme as a Test Case under WTO Law (Christoph Herrmann & Jörg Philipp Terhechte eds, European Yearbook of International Economic Law, Springer, 2011).
84. US-Tuna II, Appellate Body Report, para. 297.
85. *See* Articles 3 and 4 of Paris Agreements.
86. Gerber, *supra* note 7.
87. IPPC, *Climate Change 2014. Mitigation of Climate Change* (Working Group III Contribution to the Fifth Assessment Report of the Intergovernmental Panel on Climate Change, 2015), http://www.ipcc.ch/pdf/assessment-report/ar5/wg3/ipcc_wg3_ar5_full.pdf.

as improving feed additives to reduce some animal emissions (particularly of NH_3). The EU has, basically, followed the same strategy of adaptation.[88]

There is no comprehensive strategy that could cover both health and environmental problems related to livestock production, that is, the unbalanced overconsumption of animal protein; and the lack of clear information about the origin, impact and functioning of the international protein trade system.

[A] Equalize Animal Protein Consumption Through Feed Carbon-Pricing

According to recent studies, meat consumption of around 90 g/day would be the better balance between health benefits and risks related to this animal protein.[89] That would mean reducing by half the consumption in high-income countries and doubling in lower- income ones. Information measures, as will be discussed in the next point, and pricing measures are necessary in order to modulate the demand for animal protein. In the short term, removing state subsidies for animal feed could, via increases in retail prices, help to reduce meat consumption and redirect grain harvests to local low-income country diets. In the medium term, carbon-pricing of greenhouse-gas proxies, such as livestock feeds, would be a way to tackle different environmental and health problems that intensive feeding systems in high-income countries encompass.[90] However, this initiative clashes with the problem of lack of data. It would be necessary to develop a comprehensive study in order to fully calculate the GHG emission footprint of imported feed. Pricing feed-related carbon emissions is essential, including international transport, water use, and deforestation pressure. For doing that, probably, it is necessary to implement detailed traceability systems - extending current label information included in feeding - in order to identify, specifically, the field where feed crops have been sowed. New technology such as the QR code and big data could help. This information would also be very interesting for the future accountability of non-climate-change issues such as the accomplishment of best agricultural practices (including pesticides use), respect for biodiversity or recognition of workers' minimum rights.

Table 12.1 Meat Consumption

	Daily Meat Consumption Per Person (g)
Africa	31
East and South Asia	112
West Asia (incl. Middle East)	54

88. European Commission, *EU agriculture and climate change* (Factsheet 2015), https://ec.europa.eu/agriculture/sites/agriculture/files/climate-change/factsheet_en.pdf.
89. Teresa Norat, et al. *Meat, Fish, and Colorectal Cancer Risk: The European Prospective Investigation into Cancer and Nutrition*, 97 *Journal of the National Cancer Institute* 12, 906-916 (2005). Teresa Norat, et al. *Meat Consumption and Colorectal Cancer Risk: Dose-Response Meta-Analysis of Epidemiological Studies*, 98 *International Journal of Cancer* 2, 241-256 (2002).
90. Nicholas Stern, *The Economics of Climate Change: The Stern Review* (Cambridge University Press, 2006).

	Daily Meat Consumption Per Person (g)
Latin America	147
Developing countries	47
Developed countries	224
Average	101

Source of Data: FAOSTAT. Available at http://faostat3.fao.org/.

[B] Empowering Consumers on Health and Environmental Costs of Animal Protein

As Akerlof explained in his famous article on the market for *lemons*,[91] information asymmetry between buyers and sellers could lead to market dysfunction. It is necessary to transmit, in a simple way, environmental and health costs and advantages on different kinds of animal proteins.

By inserting a QR code in the label of a product and a free app plus a big database that encapsulates the extensive traceability system of the feed-food chain (including FAO/WHO recommendations for each one), all the information necessary to make choices about what they want to eat could be easily transmitted to consumers. Concerns about both products and processes affect consumers in making their choices. Making this information available to them is, probably, the least trade-restrictive measure that can be taken.

§12.06 CONCLUSIONS

This chapter has tried to demonstrate the underlying mutual interrelations between health and environmental issues arising from livestock food and how climate change policy could be attuned to tackle both of them. The problems clearly flow beyond national borders and have an international dimension: not only because they are related to possible similar health problems in different countries, or even in the origin of global pandemics (as it happened with the H1N1 virus - swine flu - or could happen, in the near future, with the H5N1 virus -avian flu),[92] but also mainly because the feed-livestock trade and the environmental impact (mainly on climate change) of animal agriculture are global. This research has discovered that there is no comprehensive information about the environmental impact of the feed trade, and when some information is available (like GM grain feeding), it is not put at the consumers' disposal. Agriculture and particularly breeding are seen as local activities when, in fact,

91. George A. Akerlof, *The Market for 'Lemons': Quality Uncertainty and the Market Mechanism*, 84 *Quarterly Journal of Economics* 3, 488-500 (1970).
92. The first was declared as a pandemic by the WHO in June 2009. *See* Justo Corti Varela, *Quelles responsabilités pour les décisions des organisations scientifiques internationales? Le cas de la grippe porcine (A-H1N1) et l'OMS*, 33-50 (Etienne Vergès dir., Droit, sciences et techniques: quelles responsabilités?, LexisNexis 2011). The second one has created trade conflicts, for example, *see* the WTO Panel and Appellate Body Report in *India – Agricultural Products*.

they are highly internationalized. Equalization and stabilization of animal protein consumption is a common measure for health and environmental/climate change policy. The two measures that this chapter proposes - carbon pricing of imported protein and informing consumers about the origin and proceedings of animal products along the entire food chain - require a comprehensive and international feed-food traceability system. The combination of an extensive database and new technologies for making this information available to consumers in an understandable manner is probably the main challenge. This tool could have benefits beyond health/climate change policies, permitting consumers to make better choices regarding animal welfare and human rights protection in places of production overseas, at the same time that WTO requirements are fulfilled.

CHAPTER 13

An Overview of EU Food Law

Luchino Ferraris[*]

This chapter aims at introducing the origin, the structure and the nature of European Union (EU) food law. After having briefly recalled the historical developments that led to the creation (or the radical restructuring) of European food law, the inherent interdisciplinarity of the subject and its numerous legal sources will be identified and discussed. In fact, European legal sources are largely influenced by arrangements taken in the international arena and are somehow limited by the powers of Member States to implement and complement this policy. It will be shown how, besides the 'framework' of the General Food Law (GFL) Regulation, many other pieces of legislation have been adopted on a number of interrelated and often cross-cutting issues. This patchwork of sources gives rise to a heterogeneous body of legislation, although some common principles and trends are still identifiable. Lastly, a special focus will be placed on ongoing policy initiatives and on the matter of whether the current pandemic crisis determined by the spread of the COVID-19 virus may have any impact on the future of (EU) food law.

§13.01 EU FOOD LAW: ORIGIN AND DEFINITION OF A POLICY DOMAIN

If food law can be very simply defined as the entirety of laws and policies regulating the food sector, European Union (EU) food law is nothing but the circumscription of this regulatory activity within the EU territory.

While this seems straightforward in theory, EU food law is a highly problematic sector of law. This is true mainly for three broad reasons, namely due to its historical

* This contribution represents solely the views of its author and cannot in any circumstances be regarded as the official position of the European Commission.

development, the jumble of its sources and its inherent interdisciplinarity. It is worth spending a few words on each of these aspects.[1]

From a historical perspective, it is important to seize that food law at the European level was born almost involuntarily as a corollary of the setting up of the internal market. The first big turning point is therefore the *Cassis de Dijon* case,[2] which paved the way to mutual recognition as overarching principle for the free movement of goods in the EU.[3] Mutual recognition, however, though accompanied by a number of remarkable exceptions in EU law, has the drawback of leading to a harmonization through the lowest common denominator, as 'manufacturers established in Member States with the most lenient safety or technical requirements or legal procedures do gain a competitive advantage'.[4] A further step was thus needed. The impetus was given by the well-known Bovine Spongiform Encephalopathy (BSE) crisis, burst in Britain between the late 1980s and across the 1990s. This triggered increasing concerns for European consumers that could very simply not be addressed on the basis of the legal framework then in place. From that moment onwards, numerous policy discussions led to the publication of the White Paper on Food Safety,[5] which constituted the policy foundation for the second big turning point in the history of food law, namely the adoption of the 'General Food Law' (GFL) Regulation.[6] This piece of legislation can be deemed to be the 'father' of EU food law, in the sense that it lays down the benchmarks of the subject, the main principles and rules, as well as the architecture of the institutional framework with the establishment of the European Food Safety Authority (EFSA). As a result, the skeleton of EU food law nowadays revolves around the two key notions of 'food security', namely the security to have sufficient food supplies, and 'food safety', namely the hygienic, sanitary and nutritional security of food (on this notion and on the detailed content of the GFL, *see infra*, Chapter 14).

Second, food law in Europe is the result of a jumble of sources that gives rise to an extremely complex multilevel governance of the food sector in Europe. As will be seen *infra*, in the next paragraph of this chapter, the EU regulatory capacity in laying

---

1. For a more extensive consideration of the EU food legal framework, which would not be suitable to the introductory overview of this chapter, *see* F. Albisinni, *Strumentario di diritto alimentare europeo* (2nd edn, UTET 2015); L. Costato & F. Albisinni, *European and Global Food Law* (2nd edn, Wolters Kluwer 2016).
2. Case 120/78 *Rewe v. Bundesmonopolverwaltung für Branntwein* [1979] ECR 1979-00649.
3. Literature on the *Cassis de Dijon* case is of course boundless. In the context of food/agricultural sector, *see* A. Germanò, *Manuale di diritto agrario* (8th edn, Giappichelli 2016); L. Costato, *Sull'interpretazione dell'art. 30 del Trattato CEE*, 2 Rivista di diritto agrario 26 (1981); L. Costato, *Troppo (o troppo poco) Cassis de Dijon*, 2 Rivista di diritto agrario 3 (1998); L. Russo & L. Costato, *Corso di diritto agrario italiano e dell'Unione Europea* (4th edn, Giuffrè 2015). On the more general repercussion of the decisions on EU law, *see* A. Mattera, *L'arrêt 'Cassis de Dijon': une nouvelle approche pour la réalisation et le bon fonctionnement du marché intérieur*, 23 Revue du Marché Commun 505 (1980).
4. B.M.J. van der Meulen, *The Structure of European Food Law*, 2 Laws 69, 75 (2013).
5. White paper on food safety of 12 January 2000, COM/99/0719 final.
6. Regulation (EC) No. 178/2002 of the European Parliament and of the Council of 28 January 2002 laying down the general principles and requirements of food law, establishing the European Food Safety Authority and laying down procedures in matters of food safety. For the details of policy developments that led to this turning point, *see* B. van der Meulen (ed.), *EU Food Law Handbook* (Wageningen Academic Publishers 2014).

down the food legal system is eroded both from the top - due to the numerous international legal sources that have to be complied with - and from the bottom - due to the competences that need to be shared with Member States (and/or their regions) in the implementation and enforcement of the policy.

Lastly, and partly linked to the latter point, EU food law is an incredibly cross-cutting sector. This is true first of all from an intra-legal perspective, as it gives rise to rights/duties of civil law and administrative law and contributes to defining rights/duties that have a relevance in criminal law; and it is also true from the point of view of many other non-legal subjects involved, such as agriculture, consumer and environmental protection, as well as intellectual property rights. Moreover, it is virtually impossible to have an understanding of the subject without diving into hard sciences, such as toxicology, epidemiology and so forth.

As a result, given this complex and scattered patchwork, it is of fundamental importance to retrace first and foremost the legal sources of EU food law.

§13.02 THE SOURCES AND COVERAGE OF EU FOOD LAW

As mentioned above, it is quite challenging to detect the sources of EU food law, due to the interdisciplinarity of the topic.

First and foremost, there are international legal sources. Part I of this book dwells in great detail on the international legal sources of EU food law: it is therefore more appropriate to refer to those contributions. Among all these international sources, however, at least from a certain point of view the World Trade Organization (WTO) Agreement on Sanitary and Phytosanitary (SPS) Measures can be singled out for having played an essential role in shaping the architecture of EU food law.[7] As will be seen in the next paragraph, the whole functioning of the EU food system should be based on risk analysis, which is something that Article 6 of the GFL takes directly from Article 5 of the SPS Agreement. For situations of scientific uncertainty, namely when risk assessment is inconclusive but gives scientific reasons to suspect a food safety risk, public authorities are legitimized to take action. This substantiates the precautionary principle, which - albeit being more thorough in the version of Article 7 GFL - ensues directly from Article 5(7) of the SPS Agreement.[8] Likewise, where international standards exist or their completion is imminent, they shall be taken into consideration

7. Agreement on the Application of Sanitary and Phytosanitary Measures (Marrakesh, Morocco, 15 April 1994), Marrakesh Agreement Establishing the World Trade Organization, Annex 1A, The Legal Texts: the Results of the Uruguay Round of Multilateral Trade Negotiations 59 (1999), 1867 U.N.T.S. 493.
8. Indeed, the WTO case law has shown progressive openness vis-à-vis the cases in which resort to the principle may be allowed. WTO Appellate Body Report, European Communities - Measures Concerning Meat and Meat Products (*Beef Hormones*) DS26/AB/R [1998], adopted 13 February 1998, para. 120; WTO Appellate Body Report, Japan - Measures Affecting the Importation of Apples (*Japan Apples*) DS245/AB/R [2003], adopted 10 December 2003, paras 179-185; WTO Panel Report, European Communities - Measures Affecting the Approval and Marketing of Biotech Products (*EC-Biotech*), DS291/R [2006], adopted 21 November 2006, para. 7.1522. One author concluded from this overall case law that '[t]he precautionary principle does not provide a separate basis for the adoption of SPS measures where the underlying science is uncertain,

in the development or adaptation of food law, except where such standards or relevant parts thereof would be an ineffective or inappropriate means (Article 5(3) GFL, largely replicating Article 3 of the SPS Agreement). These are just a couple of (relevant) examples to show how some essential parts of EU food law are internationally driven.[9]

As far as European sources of food law are concerned, it is important to clarify that the EU treaties do not explicitly provide for any legal basis for food law. Therefore, the Treaty provisions used in the past were either those linked to the free movement of goods (Articles 28-37 TFEU) or to other EU competences that, although conceived for other sectors, were more or less directly or indirectly related to food production, transformation and distribution (rules on approximation of laws: Articles 114-118 TFEU; public health: Article 168 TFEU; consumer protection: Article 169 TFEU; common commercial policy: Article 207 TFEU; and common agricultural policy: Article 43 TFEU).

Against this background, a great deal of legislation was adopted, starting in particular with the GFL, as mentioned above. In essence, the latter lays down rules on food products to secure a high level of protection of public health and consumers, particularly through the establishment of the overarching principles of the system and of the EFSA. Largely on the basis of this benchmark, numerous pieces of legislation were subsequently adopted and in particular, just to give some of the most prominent examples: the Genetically Modified Organisms (GMOs) package;[10] food labelling;[11] health claims;[12] novel foods;[13] Food Improvement Agents Package for additives, flavourings and enzymes;[14] pesticides;[15] geographical indications;[16] and official controls.[17] As a result, it can be said that overall EU food law aims at combining the

---

though a precautionary approach to risk assessment may be warranted in such circumstances'. *See* P. Sands & J. Peel, *Principles of International Environmental Law*, 847 (3rd edn, Cambridge University Press 2012).

9. C. Downes, *The Impact of WTO SPS Law on EU Food Regulations* (Springer 2014); M. Bronckers & R. Soopramanien, *The Impact of WTO Law on European Food Regulation*, 3 Eur. Food & Feed L. Rev. 361 (2008).
10. Directive No. 2001/18/EC on the deliberate release of GMOs into the environment; Regulation (EC) No. 1829/2003 on genetically modified food and feed; Directive (EU) No. 2015/412 amending Directive 2001/18/EC as regards the possibility for the Member States to restrict or prohibit the cultivation of GMOs in their territory; Regulation (EC) No. 1830/2003 concerning the traceability and labelling of genetically modified organisms and the traceability of food and feed products produced from genetically modified organisms; Directive No. 2009/41/EC on contained use of genetically modified micro-organisms; Regulation (EC) No. 1946/2003 on transboundary movements of GMOs.
11. Regulation (EU) No. 1169/2011 of the European Parliament and of the Council on the provision of food information to consumers.
12. Regulation (EC) No. 1924/2006 of the European Parliament and of the Council on nutrition and health claims made on foods.
13. Regulation (EU) 2015/2283 of the European Parliament and of the Council on novel foods.
14. Regulation (EC) No. 1331/2008 of the European Parliament and of the Council establishing a common authorization procedure for food additives, food enzymes and food flavourings; Regulation (EC) No. 1332/2008 of the European Parliament and of the Council on food enzymes; Regulation (EC) No. 1333/2008 of the European Parliament and of the Council on food additives; and Regulation (EC) No. 1334/2008 of the European Parliament and of the Council on flavourings and certain food ingredients with flavouring properties for use in and on foods.
15. Directive No. 2009/128/EC of the European Parliament and of the Council of 21 October 2009 establishing a framework for Community action to achieve the sustainable use of pesticides.

producer's perspective with a solid grounding of consumer's protection, the balance being struck in a different way in each specific case.

It follows from the above that the competence of Member States to regulate food law is apparently much more limited than some decades ago; equally, if European integration continues at its normal pace, it will be increasingly more so in the future. However, their role nowadays is still predominant for the adoption of technical regulations and implementation of the EU food policy; moreover, the regulation of liability and consumer's rights fall outside the scope of EU regulation; likewise, the EU does not have a competence in criminal law proceedings relating to food crime. More generally, it should be borne in mind that because the EU mostly relies on Member States' administration, the latter becomes decisive for the overall functioning of the system. In light of the above, Member States' role in defining and enforcing EU food law keeps on being remarkable.[18]

§13.03 THE SEARCH FOR AN ESSENCE OF EU FOOD LAW

As for any subject, it is uneasy – and also to an extent arbitrary – to pin down the 'essence' or the 'soul' of EU food law. However, the fact remains that there are some benchmarks in the system that connote this field of study by comparison with any other.

It is the author's opinion that this essence is to be found in, or hammered out from, the general principles and structure of the GFL. In fact, in the absence of an 'EU food law constitution' in the EU Treaties, the GFL has extensively carried out this task of cornerstone, although at the level of secondary sources. Article 5 GFL mentions five key principles that shape inevitably the architecture of the whole system. Apart from the reference to the free movement of goods, the second regards the pursuit of the highest levels of human life and health, which includes the fact of giving priority to safety rather than trade. The third and fourth principles are consumers' protection and information to consumers against fraudulent and deceptive practices, adulteration of food and any other misleading action. The fifth and sixth principles are precautionary principle and transparency principle, that are general principles of Union law well-known even outside the food sector.[19] These principles embed and pull together the architecture of a system made up of public powers, incident management and rules on products, processes and presentation of the products for food business operators.[20]

In this connection, an author argued that there is one actual provision of the GFL that in a way summarizes the spirit of any other EU food legal provision, namely the

16. Regulation (EU) No. 1151/2012 of the European Parliament and of the Council on quality schemes for agricultural products and foodstuffs.
17. Regulation (EU) No. 2017/625 of the European Parliament and of the Council of 15 March 2017 on official controls and other official activities performed to ensure the application of food and feed law, rules on animal health and welfare, plant health and plant protection products.
18. On these aspects, including an insight of the Italian constitutional framework for food law, *see* L. Costato et al., *Compendio di diritto alimentare* (7th edn, Wolters Kluwer 2015).
19. J. Tulumovic, *Food Law of European Union*, 18 Rev. Eur. L. 83, 86 (2016).
20. van der Meulen, *supra* note 4, 71.

ban to place unsafe food on the market established by Article 14 GFL.[21] According to this author, the negative formulation of Article 14 GFL, which clarifies when a product is unsafe and not when it is safe, does not cover the 'grey area' of the border-line cases when a food is halfway between the one and the other; Article 14(2) GFL only clarifies that a food is unsafe when it is injurious to health and/or unfit to human consumption; all 'grey' cases are left to the much 'more specific provisions that ban foods that while possessing a certain defect cannot be said to fulfil the requirements of Article 14 GFL'.[22] In sum, in this system, compliance to safety leads to a 'refutable presumption of safety'.[23] However insightful this construction is, it is also very important to remind that food law, from a broader perspective, can be phrased as the struggle to find a balance between the enhancement of free movement of goods, on the one hand, and the pursuit of important societal values, such as consumer protection, the preservation of the natural environment, food security, the right to food and local development, on the other. EU food law brings this struggle at the EU level and therefore requires to consider it on the basis of the specific EU rules.

From this brief reasoning, it could be concluded that the real 'core' of EU food law can indeed be seen in the struggle to find a balance in law between producers' prerogatives, consumers' rights and public interest on the basis of the existing reliable science. This balance is struck in the so-called 'risk analysis', made up of a risk assessment, a risk management and a risk communication, as laid down in Article 6 GFL. In particular, the risk assessment is to be conducted by EFSA and the other two steps by the Commission. However, as perceptively observed,[24] EFSA does not produce binding scientific decisions, but only scientific advice that flows into an overall decision, which is formally issued by the Commission.[25] EFSA's rules were deeply revised in 2019 on the occasion of the reform of the GFL,[26] but the revision mostly had to do with transparency within EFSA and its structure, while its fundamental role of risk assessor remained unchanged. Therefore, EFSA issues case-specific decisions and not general norms on the scientific positions to be taken by the EU. It is fundamental that the role of science in food law is understood keeping this connection in mind. The contentious issue concerning the role of science in food law also shapes another key principle of the system, namely the precautionary principle. While – as seen above – the principle is applied in the EU more restrictively than it is, for instance, in the WTO system, from an analysis of the case law it would still appear that this principle works

21. B.M.J. van der Meulen, *The Core of Food Law: A Critical Reflection on the Single Most Important Provision in All of EU Food Law*, 7 Eur. Food & Feed L. Rev. 117 (2012).
22. *Ibid.*, 118-119.
23. *Ibid.*, 125.
24. van der Meulen, *supra* note 4, 89.
25. This is also why it is not easy to challenge judicially EFSA's opinion. On this topic, *see* M. Cocconi, *Le garanzie del cittadino rispetto ai giudizi scientifici contenuti nei pareri dell'Autorità europea per la sicurezza alimentare*, 3 Rivista di diritto alimentare 4.
26. Regulation (EU) No. 2019/1381 of the European Parliament and of the Council on the transparency and sustainability of the EU risk assessment in the food chain.

more as a flexible political tool than a clearly defined intellectual concept.[27] In any case, it is another perfect example showing how the existence of relevant, sufficient and reliable science is supposed to play a crucial role in the production of the norms and their content.

§13.04 LOOKING BACKWARDS AND FORWARDS: COVID-19 PANDEMIC CRISIS AS AN EARTHQUAKE FOR EU FOOD LAW?

In this introductory contribution on EU food law, the origin, the scope and the nature of this sector of law were explored. It is now time to contextualize our findings in the broader picture of the current period, in order to try to depict an evolutionary trend and to figure out how this field could change in the future. To do so, it is necessary to briefly outline the recent developments and future challenges.

Concerning recent developments, three important acts have been lately adopted by the EU that are likely to play an important role in the EU regulatory framework for food. First of all, in 2019, an extremely important reform of the GFL was concluded, as a result of a fitness check launched in 2014, but also as a follow-up on a citizen's initiative to ban glyphosates.[28] The result was Regulation (EU) No. 2019/1381 of the European Parliament and of the Council of 20 June 2019 on the transparency and sustainability of the EU risk assessment in the food chain. The main objectives were to improve transparency, to strengthen cooperation, to attract excellent scientists and to improve the communication strategy with all parties involved. The most innovative part of this regulation clearly has to do with the restructuring of EFSA. This authority has in the past often been blamed for not being able to ensure adequate transparency, reliability and independence in the risk assessment procedure. In this connection, one of the most contentious issues was the need to ensure that the risk assessment is based only on published studies that are commissioned by competent public authorities and not by the industry. In fact, this widespread disappointment against the industries' practice – on the one hand – to submit only studies that revealed positive outcomes for them, while carefully hiding the disclosure of the others; and – on the other hand – to impede the publication of these studies entrenching behind confidentiality reasons. A compromise was found in the new Article 39 of the GFL, where it will be for EFSA to strike a balance between societal interests that would require divulging relevant data

27. L. Bergkamp & J.C. Hanekamp, *European Food Law and the Precautionary Principle: Paradoxical Effects of the EU's Precautionary Food Policies*, in H. Bremmers & K. Purnhagen (eds), *Regulating and Managing Food Safety in the EU* (Springer 2018).
28. In January 2017, a citizen's initiative led by Pesticide Action Network aimed at stopping glyphosates in the EU, but also at reforming the pesticide approval procedure and set EU-wide targets for pesticide use. The Commission in the Communication on the European Citizens' Initiative 'Ban glyphosate and protect people and the environment from toxic pesticides', C(2017)8414 final, replied on the one hand that there was no sufficient scientific or legal ground to stop glyphosates; on the other, it made clear that it would accept to focus on the better implementation of the directive on Sustainable Use of Pesticides. The 2019 Regulation was one of the responses the EU provided to that initiative. The citizens' initiative in question and the Commission's replies are available at https://europa.eu/citizens-initiative/initiatives/details/2017/000002_en (accessed 6 April 2020).

and the industries' interest to avoid this disclosure; at the same time, only exceptionally will the Commission be able to ask EFSA to directly commission additional studies (new Article 32d). Besides the reform of the GFL, other important recent developments that need to be flagged are the publication of a new regulation on organic farming,[29] as well as the new regulation on official controls.[30]

Concerning the future challenges, indeed, these seem at present more numerous than ever. First of all, in December 2019, the European Green Deal was published by the Commission.[31] The Green Deal is supposed to be the flagship of the newly established von der Leyen Commission and to drive a transition towards a society 'where economic growth is decoupled from resource use'[32] and which will become carbon neutral by 2050. This will require a holistic approach consisting of the restructuring of the whole economy, including food production and consumption. The Communication also anticipates the Farm to Fork strategy, then published in full in spring 2020.[33] The Communication makes already clear that the Farm to Fork strategy will 'launch a broad stakeholder debate covering all the stages of the food chain, and paving the way to formulating a more sustainable food policy'; it will contribute to circular economy and 'reduce the environmental impact of the food processing and retail sectors by taking action on transport, storage, packaging and food waste', while stimulating more sustainable food production and consumption.[34]

Unfortunately, this process – which as can be seen would constitute an extremely ambitious effort to largely reconceive the food sector – is likely to be (at least) postponed due to the outbreak of the COVID-19 crisis. This of course concerns not only Europe, but also the whole planet and will require to dedicate to it every available resource on the matter with immediate effect. The question should then be raised of whether and how this pandemic will affect and shape the European food sector in the near future. Though scientific uncertainty and the state of emergency, at the time of writing, do not enable one to make reliable predictions, some possible consequences may at least be sketched.

The first, and quite obvious, is that – as mentioned above – every other reform will be stuck for an indefinite period. This does not only concern the Farm to Fork

29. Regulation (EU) 2018/848 of the European Parliament and of the Council on organic production and labelling of organic products. *See* a commentary by H. Schmidt, *Regulation (EU) 2018/848: The New EU Organic Food Law*, 14 Eur. Food & Feed L. Rev. 15 (2019).
30. Regulation (EU) 2017/625 of the European Parliament and of the Council of 15 March 2017 on official controls and other official activities performed to ensure the application of food and feed law, rules on animal health and welfare, plant health and plant protection products. *See* a commentary by F. Albisinni, *Regulation (EU) 2017/625: Official Controls, Life, Responsibilities, and Globalization*, 14 Eur. Food & Feed L. Rev. 118 (2019).
31. Communication from the Commission to the European Parliament, the European Council, the Council, the European Economic and Social Committee and the Committee of the Regions: the European Green Deal, C(2019)640 final.
32. *Ibid.*, 2.
33. Communication from the Commission to the European Parliament, the Council, the European Economic and Social Committee and the Committee of the Regions – A Farm to Fork Strategy for a Fair, Healthy and Environmentally-Friendly Food System, COM(2020)381 final.
34. *Ibid.*, 12. On the Green Deal and the Farm to Form strategy, cf. L. Ferraris, Green Deal *e agricoltura, la vera sfida è a livello globale*, 1 Il diritto dell'agricoltura 21 (2020).

strategy but also an increasingly necessary update of the directive on Sustainable Use of Pesticides, the ongoing reform of the Common Agriculture Policy 2021-2027 and a number of other policy initiatives on which DG SANTE was currently working. In other words, this unattended shock will imply a complete overhaul of the agenda.

A second possible consequence could be the revival of food security. The latter concept is rooted in EU food and – even more – agricultural policy since time immemorial, but given the recent times of prosperity in Europe, at least concerning the availability of supplies, the trend seemed to be that of trying to go behind this concept to strengthen food safety and other environmental matters. Now, more than ever in recent history, the stability of food supplies has rapidly become seen once again as essential and the halt to (intra-EU and worldwide) cross-border movements may have an impact on the circulation of foods. As far as the current scientific uncertainty can enable us to draw conclusions, it seems quite clear that COVID-19 is very different from the BSE crisis. While the latter triggered a common mistrust vis-à-vis a certain food, the former is likely to trigger on the contrary people's craving for food. The consequence is that while BSE-like phenomena may lead to the temptation to use safeguard measures for reasons of public health, therefore hampering free movement of goods, COVID-19 pandemic may rather foster increased production and circulation of food products. This is demonstrated by the efforts already undertaken by the Commission to create cross-border 'green lanes' in order to facilitate circulation of essential goods like food, which also includes easing food safety checks.[35] This picture may be altered in case of failure of some states to assure the availability of supplies in the country via domestic production; this may in turn prod it to stop the export. This scenario may become likely if and when agri-food companies are no longer in the conditions to produce and/or – even worse – they go bankrupt. This may result in a domino effect in the whole chain of the world economy, which all of a sudden seems in some respects less globalized than it has ever been in the last century.

35. Cf. https://ec.europa.eu/commission/presscorner/detail/en/ip_20_510, accessed 6 April 2020.

CHAPTER 14

EU Agricultural Law and the Common Agricultural Policy

Alberto Germanò & Eva Rook Basile

This chapter 14 of the book *International Food Law* has the aim to make known the content and trends of the complex system of European agricultural law, built on incentive law and regulatory law. This work takes long account of European Union agricultural law until December 2017 and briefly considers the following legal measures, as well as the consequences of Brexit on the European food law, the European Commission proposals to reform the Common Agricultural Policy (CAP), and the European Commission Communication 'farm to fork strategy' relating to a strategy aimed at ensuring food security in the present time of COVID-19 pandemic.

§14.01 EUROPEAN AGRICULTURE IN THE CAP AND NON-EXCLUSIVE AREAS OF UNION COMPETENCE

While it is the task of the European Union (EU) to define and implement a 'common agricultural policy' (CAP),[1] agriculture is a shared competence and not an area of exclusive competence of the Union.[2]

The attribution to the Union of the definition and implementation of a common policy concerning agriculture means that there is no simple regulation of agricultural products in European Community law,[3] but rather that there is a common policy for the

1. The incipit of Article 38 of the Treaty on the Functioning of the European Union (TFEU).
2. Article 4.2, letter d) TFEU which refers to agriculture and fisheries. Note, however, with regard to fishing that 'the conservation of the marine biological resources' is exclusive to the Union.
3. Here some words are useful, words to be reported immediately at the beginning of this chapter on the European law of agriculture. Article 38 of the TFEU is worded as follows: '1. The Union shall define and implement a common agriculture and fisheries policy. // The internal market shall extend to agriculture, fisheries and trade in agricultural products. "Agricultural products" means the products of the soil, of stock farming and of fisheries, and products of first-stage processing

entire agricultural sector. This means that the Union has the power to carry out programmatic and regulatory interventions on both the production and market of agricultural products. The need therefore arises to clarify what the interference is between the 'CAP', whose implementation lies with the Union, and the 'shared competence' in the event of a disciplinary action in agriculture.

Although the regulation of the internal market of production and trade of agricultural (and fish) products is, therefore, and by express provision in regulation, not exclusively attributed to the EU, Union action encounters a series of objectives which condition it and legitimize its normative dispositions.

In other words, any intervention that the Union takes in agriculture finds precise boundaries in the purposes that define the CAP and which determine a sort of limit beyond which intervention would become abusive.

While the analysis of these goals will be taken up later, here it is necessary to refer to the other aspect of the problem, namely that of the shared competence of agriculture in the legal system of the Union. It should be noted, therefore, that in this system, the principle of subsidiarity applies according to which the Union intervenes in areas that are not within its exclusive competence, 'only' if and in so far as the objectives of the proposed action cannot be sufficiently achieved by the Member States but rather, by reason of the scale or effects of the proposed action, be better achieved at Union level.[4] Therefore, even in non-exclusive but shared competences, such as agriculture, the Union is not without legislative powers.

So the fact cannot be ignored that to constitute an agricultural market defined as 'internal' and therefore single, there is a need for it to be subject to the same single legislation. So we are forced to conclude that the establishment and functioning of a single market of agricultural products to be preferred over non-EU countries' products and with cost sharing among the Member States can only be governed and managed directly by the EU.[5] As, moreover, seems to be confirmed by paragraph 4 of Article 38 which states that 'the operation and development of the internal market for agricultural products must be accompanied by the establishment of a common agricultural policy'. Therefore, the explicit definition of agriculture as a shared competence needs further clarification as soon as it is specifically linked to the definition and implementation of the CAP.

directly related to these products. References to the common agricultural policy or to agriculture, and the use of the term "agricultural", shall be understood as referring to fisheries, having regard to the specific characteristics of this sector.- 2. Save as otherwise provided in Articles 39 to 44, the rules laid down for the establishment and functioning of the internal market shall apply to agricultural products.- 3. The products subject to the provisions of Articles 39 to 44 are listed in Annex I.- 4. The operation and development of the internal market for agricultural products must be accompanied by the establishment of a common agricultural policy.' This formulation should be kept in mind throughout this study.

4. Article 5 of the Treaty on European Union.
5. Court of Justice of 29 November 1978, Case 83/78, *Pigs Marketing Board*.

§14.02 OBJECTIVES OF THE CAP

Paragraph 1 of Article 39 of the TFEU (Treaty on the Functioning of the European Union) identifies the objectives of the CAP, which are to increase productivity by promoting technical progress and ensuring better use of production factors; to ensure a fair standard of living for the agricultural community, particularly by increasing individual earnings of persons engaged in agriculture; to stabilize agricultural markets; and to assure both availability of supplies and reasonable prices for consumers.

An analysis of the aforementioned purposes immediately evidences both their amplitude and the difficulty in complying with all of them concurrently. It is enough to consider the difficulty of combining farmers' interests in a fair standard of living with consumers' interests in receiving agricultural products at reasonable prices, or the difficulty in simultaneously achieving increased productivity in agriculture and stabilizing the agricultural market. Thus, the Court of Justice has had to clarify that these objectives may not be pursued in the same way all simultaneously. What is required is that Community institutions be concerned with ensuring the contemporary pursuance of objectives even if, in any specific legislation, temporary precedence is given to one or another in relation to the particular circumstances in which community institutions' wide powers of discretion are employed.

This coveted co-pursuance, however, appears ever more difficult considering the evolution of the CAP in the 2003 and 2009 reforms and the regulations in force in 2013-2020. The requirement to decouple premiums/production (i.e., decoupling) seems neither to satisfy the aim of production increases nor those of guaranteeing self-supplying, farmers' incomes and reasonable consumer prices. The most appropriate interpretation of the laws on CAP objectives seems to be that they are concerned with guaranteeing the social and territorial cohesion that is alluded to in the first letter of paragraph 2 of the same Article 39 of the TFEU.

One of the objectives of the Union's agricultural policy is that of supply security. In the immediacy of the entry into force of the Treaty of Rome, this goal responded to a primary need for the reconstruction of Europe following the disasters of the Second World War. Today this aim might have taken on the Union's commitment to carry out a joint action to make the protection of human rights in general effective, among which there is the right to freedom from hunger. In actual fact, the adoption of 'decoupling' and the strict environmental requirements introduced by the CAP has actually caused the disappearance of that food superabundance which in the 1980s and 1990s had allowed the European Community, once a group of states with insufficient food availability, to become a real-world food power, a great exporter of natural or transformed agricultural products. Now, in the new century, the disappearance of Community surpluses is causing supply problems in the EU itself in various agricultural years for this or that product and, in any case, strong price fluctuations.[6] We are starting to fear food insecurity for European citizens accompanied by food price

6. With the medium-term reform of the CAP, the granting of aid to farmers became commensurate with the eligible hectares they hold even if they do not cultivate them which has constituted a strong disincentive to cultivate areas less fertile or at greater meteorological risk so land

increases, which patently infringes the other stated purposes of Article 39 of the TFEU, i.e., of ensuring market stability, reasonable consumer prices and a fair standard of living for farmers.

It is in this perspective, then, that the EU's current renewed attention to agricultural production must be considered.[7] The previous period was characterized by market interventions related to the free circulation of goods, consumer protection and agricultural product safety; today, we are witnessing an accentuation of the 'food security' goal. The food production objective, in fact, has come back into the regulations in the modified 2013 CAP. Food safety was once an essential prerequisite of the European food market; today it does not seem to have the same visibility. Nowadays, 'food security', in the sense of guaranteeing food sufficiency, is gaining importance. So perhaps the conclusion can be drawn that the EU is evolving into a system that goes beyond market boundaries to affect more intimate and fundamental aspects of civil society. The current shared economic objectives are being replaced by the development of absolute values, such as ensuring that the world is free from hunger. This, not new but rather newly interpreted, objective in Article 39 TFEU needs to be kept in mind every time the Union legislates in the field of agriculture in order to implement the CAP.

§14.03 ON 'SHARED COMPETENCE' REGARDING AGRICULTURE AND NUTRITION

The question of the nature of Union competence in the field of agriculture first of all requires mention of the principle of subsidiarity, according to which the Union intervenes in matters which are not within its exclusive competence, 'only if and in so far as the objectives of the proposed action cannot be sufficiently achieved by the Member States but rather, by reason of the scale or effects of the proposed action, be better achieved at Union level'.

As will be explained later, the CAP was split and is still split into two interdependent sectors: price policy and structural policy, with the creation of Common Market Organizations (CMOs) for a large number of agricultural products.

The competence of the Union in the agricultural field, therefore, can have a different effect on national rights depending on whether it is a matter of regulating the market (prices) or structures (the subjects). Indeed, the need for a European market governed by single prices should be immediately apparent; on the other hand, unified legislation to govern European agricultural structures might be less necessary, even though the effect on the single agricultural market of the impact of the various domestic regulating of agricultural enterprises must be kept in mind.

The need for a 'single' regulatory framework in terms of prices, levies and aid is evident in Article 43 of the TFEU: paragraph 2 establishes the co-decisional procedure of Parliament and Council as the ordinary procedure for 'the common organization of the agricultural markets and [for] the other provisions necessary for the pursuit of the

(including fertile land) has been used for other activities such as the production of energy, also because it has become cheaper to turn to the world market for the purchase of food.

7. 'A strong agriculture is vital for the EU food industry and *global food security*'.

objectives of the common agricultural policy and the common fisheries policy'; but paragraph 3 states that it is the sole responsibility of the Council, on a proposal from the Commission, (to) adopt measures on fixing prices, levies, aid, and quantitative limitations and on the fixing and allocation of fishing opportunities.[8]

However, even in the field of common market structures and organizations, there is an increasingly frequent use of Union regulations which impose a single legislative framework on aspects related to the agricultural structures of all the Member States. In other words, the ever more frequent use of regulations rather than directives in legislating on agricultural matters has given rise to laws common to the whole of the Union, not only with regard to prices but also with regard to the said structures. Therefore, also in virtue of the primacy of EU law, the regulating of agriculture, as a whole, would seem to lie with the normative provisions of the Union.

These considerations, which might have been legitimate before the Treaty of Lisbon, no longer sound correct after its entry into force. Indeed, the Lisbon Treaty in Article 4 of the TFEU expressly inserts agriculture into the list of shared competences.

However, Article 2 of the TFEU explains the meaning of the term 'shared competence'. The law clarifies that shared competence does not mean that the 'main' institution is responsible for the determination of principles and the other institutions are responsible for regulation of the details, with the coexistence of two levels of government having equal possibility to intervene in regulating the subject. European law expressly states that 'when the Treaties confer on the Union a competence shared with the Member States in specific areas [including agriculture], the Union and the Member States may legislate and adopt legally binding acts in that area'; with the clarification that 'the Member States shall exercise their competence to the extent that the Union has not exercised its competence'[9] and shall again exercise it 'to the extent that the Union has decided to cease exercising its competence'.

In the matter of agriculture, the distinction between limits deriving from the exclusive competence of the Union and limits linked to the contents of legislation on sharing is very slight. Already the content of the Union legislation can substantially preclude the legislative activity of the Member States such as the case of Union provisions on the harmonizing of domestic laws. This situation occurs when the Union lays down rules regarding CMOs, which, in order to be 'common', can only be the same for all European agricultural operators, so there are necessarily the same rules here.

And confirmation can be drawn from the fact that in the matter of the CAP, the Union uses the instrument of regulation and not directives.

8. In the orbit of subsidiarity, a 'legislative' sui generis procedure is envisaged, for which (only) the Council provides on a proposal from the Commission. The purpose of this exception to the ordinary legislative procedure (Council and Parliament in co-decision on a proposal from the Commission) is to allow the Council to legislate without the intervention of the Parliament in cases where some promptness is needed. The fact is that, due to the close relationship between basic agricultural policy and price fixing, withdrawals, aid and quantitative limitations, the procedure will, in practice, be extremely complicated.
9. Previously, among the measures aimed at strengthening Community competences, the Court of Justice had supported the so-called pre-emption mechanism, in addition to the theory of so-called implicit powers, under which state action was precluded when the Community exercised its activities in a specific field of competence of the Member States 'by occupying the field *at first*'.

Moreover, the formula of the Lisbon Treaty is in the sense of the inclusion of agriculture among shared competences. With it, the EU wanted to give strength to the principle of subsidiarity, redesigning the spaces of legislative sovereignty of the Member States. Thus, in the current policy of 2013 agricultural structures, states are increasingly assigned tasks, especially in terms of promotional initiatives. As a consequence, Union institutions have lost their centrality in identifying individual choices for economic intervention typical of traditional incentivizing Union law, but this loss is offset by the growing weight of regulatory Union law by virtue of the adoption of very incisive definitions requiring Member States to act within a unitary regulatory framework. While domestic political motivations regarding the environment and territory can take on importance, the rules, even those of expenditure, market and competition, remain centralized in actual unified texts of unitary regulation.

The matter of nutrition is not mentioned in the Treaty, but it ends up being a subject of shared competence by virtue of the close relationship between food and public health and consumer protection, both of which are mentioned in Article 4 of the TFEU among the areas of shared competence.[10] However, it must be immediately said that the same 'invasion' that the EU has made into the matter of agriculture is repeated in that of food security, through the construction of extensive legal regulation of the food system.[11]

To speak of food law is, in fact, to talk about the legal regulation of agricultural production and the marketing of healthy and safe agricultural products, because all foods are of agricultural origin. The introduction of the marketing aspect of agricultural products into the study of food law makes food take on the quality of 'goods' in a market that is expanding. The food market is no longer a local market where the parties to the exchange contract know each other and interact with each other; it is a national market, and then European, and thereafter worldwide, which requires new and different ways of relating producers to consumers. After all, modern industrial techniques for the conservation and processing of food products, the development of a transport network and the diffusion of commercial distribution systems determine the progressive removal of food from its place of production and make it necessary for the consumer to be informed of the type, quality and origin of the product, that is, of its peculiarity as a marketable good and also of its cultural identity, broadly speaking. Thus, the information mode acquires fundamental importance in the market of

10. On the other hand, Articles 168 and 169 of the TFEU respectively state that Union action complements domestic health policies and helps to protect health through a policy of support of the measures carried out by States.
11. The subject of food, in terms of its safety and healthiness, was taken up by the Union when, on 28 January 2002, it issued Reg. No. 178/2002 on food security. This regulation has as its legal basis Articles 37 (now 43) on agriculture, 152 (now 168) on health, 133 (now 207) on the common commercial policy and 95 (now 114) on the approximation of legislation. However, the reference to the legal basis 'agriculture' makes it possible to consider that the provisions on food and feed, on ingredients and food additives, on solvents, preservatives and sweeteners, on allergenic substances, on genetically modified organisms contained in food and on food hygiene – in essence, all aspects of food law – 'are' within the competence of the EU which, pursuant to Article 38 TFEU, has jurisdiction over agriculture, fisheries and trade in agricultural products.

agricultural product as food, since it allows both the producer and the consumer to communicate and understand what the specific food offered on the market is. To the producer, the removal of anonymity provides a competitive advantage while the removal of product homogeneity favours the consumer in his freedom of choice; improved communication tools reduce the information asymmetries linked to going beyond the territorial boundaries of old-fashioned local markets.

§14.04 THE DEFINITION OF AGRICULTURE IN EU LAW

For Article 38 of the TFEU, 'the internal market shall extend to agriculture, fisheries and trade in agricultural products'. But paragraph 1 goes on to state that 'agricultural products means the products of the soil, of stock farming and of fisheries, and products of first-stage processing directly related to these products'.

The formula embraces both the methods of obtaining agricultural products and their trade, and the standard focuses on the ontological distinction between agricultural and industrial products, with the consequence of differentiating the related markets. An agricultural product is then further defined by the same Article 38, which states that 'agricultural products' are only those listed in Annex I in section §14.05.

The affirmation of the principle that the products of agriculture (and of fisheries) are different from the products of industry and services is the whole basis of this part of the Treaty dedicated to the regulation of the agricultural market, characterized not only by its own rules due to special exemptions to basic EU antitrust rules but also by a set of rules in the CAP that clearly take into consideration the special status of this productive sector.

The 'agrarian' derogation from the basic rules on competition will be discussed later. Here it is necessary to clarify the meaning of the Union's definition of agriculture. And there are two observations to be made. The first concerns the systematic importance of the notion of agricultural product; the second concerns the content of Annex I, that is, the list of products to which the exception to the fundamental anticompetitive rules applies.

Article 38 specifies that the internal market includes agriculture and trade in *agricultural products*; that *agricultural products* are those in Annex I; that EU agricultural law is characterized by exemption from the anticompetitive rules of agreements and from public aid systems when they concern the agricultural products listed in the annex. This provision evidences the fact that the specifically different agricultural legislation of the Union revolves around the 'product' – the 'good' – and not the activity, that is the 'business'. A confirmation of this can be found, for example, in the ruling that banned an agreement between Danish breeders of fur animals aimed at requiring members to sell only through the cooperative formed by themselves. Thus former Article 36 (now Article 42) which allows greater flexibility in competition restriction in the agricultural sector,[12] which as we have said will be discussed later,

12. This refers to the judgment of the Court of First Instance of 2 July 1992, T-61/89, Dansk Pelsdyravlerforening.

was not applied. In other words, the Court of First Instance stated that fur, not being included in Annex I, is not an agricultural product, even if, on the contrary, fur animals are agricultural products and their breeding is agriculture, as they, under the item 'live animals', are included in the annex.[13]

Today, however, it should be understood that the EU law's definition of agriculture comprises a reference to activity. Indeed, it is not possible to ignore that for the Union law in force[14] 'agricultural activity' is the 'production, rearing or growing of agricultural products, including harvesting, milking, breeding animals and keeping animals for farming purposes', as well as 'maintaining the land in good agricultural and environmental conditions'[15] and maintaining it 'suitable for grazing or cultivation'.[16] It is true that the agricultural 'product' is still the element which constitutes the reference point for TFEU rules relating to agriculture,[17] but it is equally certain that the above provisions have introduced notions related to the activity into the Union system of agricultural legislation, whose importance contributes to the qualification of agriculture from an ontological point of view without mortifying the determination of the sector by the product.

However, whatever the possible conclusion on the meaning of agriculture according to EU law, the annex with its list of agricultural products continues to be of fundamental importance as it is on this basis that exemptions from the ban on restrictive agreements and state aid, which represent the specific nature of EU agricultural legislation, are made.

§14.05 ANNEX I OF THE TREATY

Annex I of the TFEU contains not only plant and animal products but also fish, crustaceans and molluscs. It also contains products obtained from industrial processing such as bran, gluten, inulin, sugar, molasses and margarine. It also lists live plants and cork, but not wood; it includes flax, but not cotton, or silk, or wool. It does not distinguish between animals for meat, or work, sports and leisure.

13. Confirmation of the importance of the product in the EU agricultural system can also be found in the Court of Justice judgment of 25 February 1999, C-164 and 165/97, *Parliament v. Council*, which declared forestry regulations nn. 307 and 308/1997 illegitimate for violation of the prerogatives of the pertinent European Parliament in environmental matters, because trees and wood are not included in the annex and, therefore, do not pertain to agriculture whose 'legal basis' is the current Article 43 of the TFEU. Consequently, under EU law, wood production – that is forestry – is not agriculture.
14. Starting with directive 72/159 of 17 April 1972 on the role of primarily agricultural entrepreneur characterized by the prevalence of work time dedicated to agricultural activity (today, the role of primarily agricultural entrepreneur no longer exists), continuing with Reg. 1782/2003 of 29 September 2003 in the medium-term reform of the CAP, ending with Reg. 73/2009 of 19 January 2009.
15. *See* Article 2 of Reg. 73/2009.
16. So now Reg. 1307/2013.
17. But in its possible aspect of 'maintaining the land in good agronomic and environmental conditions', agricultural activity could also give rise to no product other than a generic or general environment.

Attempting to identify the authorizing criterion for the list of the annex is a formidable task. The exclusion, on the one hand, of wood, silk and cotton could prima facie suggest that the list revolves around the idea of agriculture destined for food. But immediately one realizes that this is not so since linen, hemp, flowers and tobacco are included. Perhaps another sort of criterion could be used; that is, we should not forget that in as much as they are food, the markets of both agro-industrial products and fish from the sea are subject to the same economic laws of King and Engel that govern the market of agro-food products.[18] But we cannot fail to recognize that this does not apply to all the products listed in the annex, that is to say those - and there are many - that are not foodstuffs. One could therefore think of the criterion of the biological cycle, but it does not apply to all the 'products' listed in the annex, even if there is no doubt that it occurs in the basic products from which listed products such as sugar, margarine or animal and vegetable fats are industrially produced.

Much more simply, it can be said that what the 'constituent fathers' had in mind were the traditional cultures spread throughout the six original countries of the Community, as demonstrated by the fact that at the time of the Treaty and Annex compilation, the Member States were invited to integrate the list using the activities found in their respective geographic areas.[19] So the absence of some products in the annex rather than being the result of precise systematic logic seems to be the result of the activity or inactivity of the founding states in completing the list. So, we must understand the empirical criterion guiding the six states that, in 1958, gave rise to the European Economic Community (EEC).

A word should be said regarding the meaning of the formula 'raw material processing' used in Article 38 of the TFEU. As a general rule, this expression means basic processed products; however, Annex I also includes products that strictly speaking cannot be defined as 'first-stage processing'. So what should be considered is the rationale for inclusion in the list. A need was felt to ensure homogeneous treatment of agricultural products whether they were marketed in their natural state or after even second-stage processing.[20] This protection of products of agricultural origin made it necessary to not only include substitutes for (true) agricultural products in the list,[21] but also extend the system to second-stage products[22] and to include products indistinguishable from (true) agricultural products.[23] The various cases all have a

18. King's (economic) law holds that the demand for agro-food products is not elastic with respect to their price; Engel's (economic) law says that the demand for agro-food products is not elastic with respect to consumer income.
19. The annex could be amended up to two years after the entry into force of the Treaty, so that, correctly, after the amendments in Regulation Nos 7-bis/59 of 18 December 1959 no further additions were made. However, on the occasion of the acts of accession, first of Greece and then of Spain and Portugal, an 'almost-agricultural' regulation was drawn up for cotton and silk, that are excluded from the annex.
20. This is the case, for example, of syrups, gluten, inulin and ground products.
21. This is the case for honey and vinegar substitutes, or lard imitations.
22. This is the case for bread, pasta, biscuits and chocolate.
23. This the case for pure glucose and lactose which, even if excluded from the annex, would not have been distinguishable from agricultural glucose and lactose.

common justification. The intention was always to protect the trade of basic agricultural products. In other words, the inclusion in the same law of agricultural products and food products derived from them allowed for the protection of the activities constituting the first link in the food chain. In essence, in concrete terms, the interpreter is not required to go in search of the meaning of the term 'first-stage processing' because what holds true is the rule of inclusion/exclusion in Annex I list of the subject under consideration.

The conclusion is that the annex constitutes a 'narrow' but exhaustive list of products to which Union legislation on agriculture applies; that such products are 'goods' resulting (as a rule) from the cultivation of the soil and breeding of animals; that such 'goods' are perceived here (and above all) as objects of exchange or 'merchandise'; that agricultural products as 'goods' are essentially governed by the legislation of the agricultural sector broadly speaking, that is, as the regulation of 'subjects' producing certain specific goods.

§14.06 THE SPECIAL FEATURES OF EU AGRICULTURAL LAW

The special features of European agricultural matters once included the particular rules of the Union law forming process.[24] Today the particularity of EU agricultural law is due to the 'derogations' to the provisions prohibiting restrictive agreements between undertakings and state aid. But it should be added that the matter of European agriculture is 'special' by virtue of the freedom in judgment enjoyed by the EU institutions here. In the production of law, they can apply to a lesser extent or even cease to apply the competition rules. The vagueness and intrinsically contradictory nature of the purposes referred to in the aforementioned Article 39 of the TFEU allow the pursuance of any one of them without all or any other of them necessarily being present at the same time; but above all, these objectives prevail over the fundamental principles of the common market itself. The Court of Justice itself evidenced this when it judged the advantages granted to some producers and traders of bananas to be legitimate as being consistent with the objectives that the Treaty has assigned to agriculture.[25]

In order to understand agricultural 'derogations', it is necessary to look at the 'rules' revolving around the principle of protection of the freedom of competition which is the cornerstone of EU law.

24. Indeed, it should be recalled that before the Treaty of Lisbon, the adoption of 'agricultural' acts had a specific procedure. By virtue of Article 37 of the Treaty of Rome, the Community legislation on agriculture was approved, by a qualified majority, by the Council on a proposal from the Commission and on the (non-binding) opinion of the European Parliament. This specific *modus procedendi* was characterized by the fact that it required neither the unanimity of the Council nor the co-decision of the Parliament, with the consequence of allowing greater flexibility in the adoption of 'agricultural' measures. The Lisbon Treaty has confirmed the rule that agricultural acts are adopted on a proposal from the Commission, but has overturned the system, because it requires the participation of both Parliament and Council, after consulting the Economic and Social Committee.
25. Judgment of 5 October 1994, C-280/93, *Commission v. Germany*.

The objective of the Treaty of Rome was to create a market (at first, common, and now internal) within which the effective circulation of people, goods, services and capital must be assured. Then a regime need to be created to ensure that competition is not distorted in the market and this is why in Article 3 of the Treaty of Lisbon the EU is attributed exclusive power over the establishment 'of the competition rules necessary for the functioning of the internal market'.[26]

Traditionally, the purpose of competition is identified firstly as that of ensuring the triumph of the most worthy entrepreneur economically; that is, competition is seen first and foremost as competition between entrepreneurs. But traditionally there is another purpose that is taken into consideration: the safeguarding of consumer interests.

This has always implied that decisions on supply and demand must be *freely* adopted by producers and consumers: the former seeking to optimally use their respective production capacities to improve products and reduce their prices in order to acquire customers, the latter aspiring to enjoy a wide selection of similar products differing in quality and price. In order to achieve such objectives, preference needs to be given to the market economy, that is, to precisely that economic system whose freedom of competition corresponds to the community's founding and, therefore, 'constitutional' principle.

The realization of a market economy requires rules preventing undertakings from behaviours incompatible with a fair, effective and undistorted tender system. Furthermore, there is a need for other rules aimed at making measures proposed by Member States for their markets or national undertakings compatible with competition principles. Under this dual profile are, respectively, the rules prohibiting restrictive agreements between undertakings and the abuse of dominant positions on the one hand, and the rules on state aid on the other.

[A] Competition Law: General Rules

The competition rules applicable to undertakings are contained in Articles 101 and 102 of the TFEU and consist of the prohibition of 'all agreements between undertakings, decisions by associations of undertakings and concerted practices which may affect trade between Member States and which have as their object or effect the prevention, restriction or distortion of competition within the internal market' (Article 101), and the prohibition of 'any abuse by one or more undertakings of a dominant position within the internal market or in a substantial part of it' (Article 102).

Prejudicial to the brief analysis of the aforesaid norms is an understanding of the meaning of the term 'undertaking' used by community antitrust law. In EU law it is any 'economic unit':[27] more precisely, it is any entity that regularly and continuously

26. Freedom of competition is included in the Protocol on the Internal Market and on Competition, annexed to the Lisbon Treaty which, as stated in Article 51 of the TEU, has the same legal significance as the Treaty.
27. Court of Justice 31 October 1974, C-15/74, Sterling.

carries out economic activities on the market, regardless of its legal status, the way it works, its organizational or business elements, and even its profits.[28]

If freedom of competition carries the unavoidable assumption that *each* undertaking establishes its own commercial strategy independently, it is easy to foresee that the coordination of the conduct of *several* undertakings on the market is capable of altering competition. However, not only agreements, concerted practices, decisions taken together but also contracts imposed by one party to another and even the exchange of information as expression of a common will to maintain certain behaviour are prohibited by Article 101 of the TFEU. They are declared null when their object or in any case their effect is that of distorting or restricting competition.[29] However, there is also a need to consider the 'extent' of the effects of such agreements on the market. In the assessment of the impact that the agreements are purported to have on the market, the concept of 'relevant market' acquires importance. It is to be understood as 'the set of products that according to their characteristics are particularly suited to satisfy constant needs and are not very interchangeable with other products',[30] and this in order to be able to assess in concrete whether the victim of the alleged abusive behaviour can avoid it by turning to suppliers of equivalent goods or services. Consequently, this threshold of 'sensitivity' is not reached by '*de minimis*' agreements – those between undertakings holding a modest share of the market – due to their inappreciable effects on competition.[31]

With regard to this aspect, it should be added that the Court of Justice case law has also elucidated the principle of reasonableness or rule of reason. By virtue of this principle and a comparative analysis of the elements of the various agreements, restrictions on the freedom of action of undertakings are 'saved' when they are concretely offset or overcome by other competition incentives.[32] Therefore, to ascertain whether a situation renders an agreement lawful, an actual financial analysis of the

28. Court of Justice 22 January 2002, C-218/00, Soc. Cisal; Court of First Instance 4 March 2003, T-319/99, Federación Nacional de Empresas. Confirmation in the agricultural sector, already given by Article 1.4 of Reg. 3508/92 of 27 November 1992, now results from the Article 4 of the Reg. 1307/2013 which again defines the farmer as 'a natural or legal person or a group of natural or legal persons, regardless of the legal status granted to such group and its members by national law, whose holding is situated within the territorial scope of Treaties (...) and who exercises an agricultural activity'. *See also* the judgments of the Court of Justice of 23 April 1991, C-41/90, Höfner; 17 February 1993, C-159 and 160/91, Poucet and Pistre; 19 January 1994, C-364/92, Sat Fluggesellschaft Mbh; 16 November 1995, C-244/94, *Féderation française des sociétés d'assurance*.
29. For examples of restrictive agreements on competition, *see* Court of Justice 1 February 1977, C-47/76, *De Norre*.
30. Commission decision of 7 March 2003, *Michelin*.
31. *See* Court of Justice of 9 July 1969, C-5/69, *Völk*.
32. With regard to the understanding of the term 'reasonableness', it is useful to note that the third paragraph of Article 101 of the TFEU excludes from the prohibition agreements which 'contribute to improving the production or distribution of goods or to promoting technical or economic progress, while allowing consumers a fair share of the resulting benefit' and which 'impose on the undertakings concerned restrictions which are not indispensable to the attainment of these objectives and afford such undertakings the possibility of eliminating competition in respect of a substantial part of the products in question'. To this end, cf. the judgments of the Court of Justice 11 July 1985, C-42/84, Remia Bv; 8 June 1982, C-258/78, Nungesser; 28 January 1985, C-161/84, Pronuptia; 28 February 1991, C-234/89, Delimitis.

performance of the agreements in the juridical context in which they occur must be carried out.[33]

Article 102 TFEU prohibits the abuse of a dominant position. It is forbidden, that is, to exploit the economic power possessed by one or several undertakings which enables them to hinder potential competitors' access to the market.[34] In other words, Article 102 of the TFEU governs the distortive use of the dominance of one or a few undertakings able to neutralize any type of potential competition.[35]

So that Article 102 of the TFEU can be operative; however, the dominance of the undertaking needs to take place over a large part of the product market. Here it should be recalled what has already been said in this regard: that the market we are speaking of is not only a geographical market, but that of a product, which is identifiable by bearing in mind the actual competition between similar products participating in the competition, which are presumed to be interchangeable according to their use and so overlap those offered by the undertaking in question.

[B] Competition Law: The Agricultural Derogation

Therefore, the fundamental principle of EU law is that of the freedom of competition, which is considered to be an instrument of economic progress, a source of collective prosperity, a cause of advantages for consumers. However, in such a context and as a different rule, Article 42 of the TFEU states that the rules on competition apply to production of and trade in agricultural products only to the extent determined by the European Parliament and the Council.

With Regulation 26/62 of 4 April 1962, the Council declared the applicability of the anticompetitive provisions (at that time contained in Articles 81 and 82) to the matter of agriculture but provided for the possibility of agreements between agricultural producers for the concentration of their supply and for the issuing of common production rules.[36]

33. Thus, agreements justified by environmental protection requirements (1983 Commission decision in Carbon Gas Technologie), by social policy on selective distribution systems (Court of Justice 25 October 1977, C-26/76, Metro I, 22 October 1986, C-75/84, Metro II) and by energy policy (Commission decision of 1991 in Scottish Nuclear) have been declared admissible.
34. Court of Justice 14 February 1978, C-27/76, United Brands-Chiquita.
35. Therefore the application of unfair commercial conditions, discriminatory practices, restrictions on the production or distribution of goods or services, or all forms of exploitation of suppliers and customers are prohibited, to which, due to the reduction or absence of competition, undertakings that already hold significant market power could be induced.
36. Article 3 of Reg. 26/62, dictated the exceptions to the rule of the previous Article 2, distinguishing three different situations: first of all, the rule on prohibition of agreements does not apply to agreements 'as form an integral part of a national market organization'; second, the rule does not apply to agreements 'that are necessary for attainment of the objectives set out in the then current Article 33 (now 39)'; third, the rule does not apply 'to agreements, decisions and practices of farmers, farmers' associations or associations of such associations belonging to a single Member State, which concern the production or sale of agricultural products or the use of joint facilities for the storage, handling or processing of agricultural products, and under these no obligation to charge a identical price, unless the Commission finds that competition is thereby excluded or that the objectives of the Article 33 of the Treaty (now, Article. 39 of the TFEU) are jeopardised'.

Regulation 26/62 was repealed by Regulation 1184/2006, but Article 176 of the subsequent Regulation 1184/2006 and then Article 209 of the current Regulation 1308/2013 of 17 December 2013 on the single CMO substantially repeat the provision of Article 3 of the old Regulation 26/62. Therefore, Article 206 of Regulation 1308/2013 includes agreements between agro-food industrial enterprises and agro-food traders under the general discipline of Articles 101 and 102 of the TFEU, but the subsequent Article 209 excludes agreements between 'exploitants agricoles';[37] more precisely, the provision 'saves' agreements between farmers belonging to a single Member State on condition that they do not impose a specific sale price, do not totally exclude competition and are not in conflict with the purposes of Article 39 of the TFEU.[38]

It is worth highlighting that, in the provisions of Articles 101 and 102 of the TFEU, transactions and behaviours implemented by undertakings in violation of competition rules are automatically null; instead, merely by virtue of the 'exception' established by Article 209 of Regulation 1308/2013, in the case of agreements between farmers a sort of 'presumption' of lawfulness and coherence with Article 39 of the TFEU occurs. In fact, for agreements between farmers, the Commission has the power to ascertain the negative impact on the purposes of Article 39 of the TFEU of said agreements but only afterwards, i.e., *ex post*, can it contest them, with the further and most important consequence that the verification of a 'defect' in agricultural agreements does not have retroactive effect.[39]

Therefore, it can also be concluded that with Regulation 1308/2013, a clear distinction between agricultural 'producers' on the one hand and all those who work in the agricultural sector on the other has been reiterated. While the latter – agro-food

---

37. Article 209 of Reg. 1308/2013 on the single CMO substantially preserves the provisions of Article 176 of Reg. 1234/2007 but in a different formulation for which Articles 101 and 102 of the TFEU apply to the agricultural sector 'only to the extent determined in Articles 207 to 210 of this Regulation'. Note also that in Articles 207 and 208 are given the definitions of 'relevant market' and 'dominant position' as already understood by the Court of Justice in the judgment of 13 February 1979, Hoffmann-La Roche.
38. More precisely, Article 209 states in para. 1.1 that Article 101 of the TFEU does not apply to the agreements, decisions and practices necessary for the attainment of the objectives set out in Article 39 of the Treaty; in para. 1.2 that Article 101 of the Treaty does not apply to agreements, decisions and concerted practices of farmers, farmers' associations, associations of such associations, or producer organizations which concern the production or sale of agricultural products or the use of joint facilities for the storage, treatment or processing of agricultural products, unless the objectives of Article 39 of the Treaty are jeopardized; and in para. 1.3 that this paragraph shall not apply to agreements, decisions and concerted practices which entail an obligation to charge an identical prices or by which competition is excluded. Lastly, para. 2 of Article 209 establishes that proof of the violation of Article 101 of the Treaty is the responsibility of those who allege this violation, while proof that the requirements of the exemptions are satisfied is borne by the person who invokes them.
39. It is useful to note that Article 1 of Reg. 1/2003 declares in general that 'agreements, decisions and concerted practices caught by Article 101 of the TFEU shall be prohibited, no prior decision to that effect being required', and that the 'verification' of the non-compliance with the conditions dictated by para. 3 of Article 101 of the TFEU takes place *a posteriori*, following an official finding or complaint, also with regard to agreements other than those between farmers. For the effect there is a substantial equation of the originally different situations; however, it seems to us that the presumption of lawfulness of the agreements between farmers is always valid with the consequent *ex nunc* effectiveness of the eventual ascertainment of the infringement.

industrial enterprises and agro-food merchants – are subject to the strict prohibition of agreements pursuant to Article 101 of the TFEU, the former are exempted by a general provision, which starts with the assumption that their agreements are essentially lawful. In fact, the rationale of the provision rests on the fact that the legal and economic structure of European agriculture consists of a very large number of farmers operating in the market. Given their number, they do not have the possibility of acquiring a dominant position from which to abuse their power, no do they have the strength to reach agreements capable of distorting competition in their sector whose supply is so fragmented as to be a place of competitive excellency.

In this way the Community's freedom of competition principle is presumed in agriculture through the filter of adapting the general rules to the needs of the sector. So a *specific rule* is set for European agriculture: among the tools to be used to achieve the objectives set out in Article 39 of the TFEU, that of guaranteeing the freedom of competition is in a subordinate position.[40] Therefore, it can be concluded that competition is only an instrument for the pursuit of EU agricultural policy, so much so that it can be 'sacrificed' in order to pursue the objectives set forth in Article 39 of the TFEU.

To have confirmation of what has been said so far, it is sufficient to look at the attention the EU dedicates to farmer associations and even interbranch organizations, to whom it also provides with financial support. Here, in fact, there are both agreements between farmers associated with recognized producer organizations, as well as practices agreed upon by interbranch organizations.

[C] The Prohibition of Public Aid: General European Legislation

Prior to the establishment of the European Common Market (1958), Member States used to support national 'industries' with aid, in order to prevent them from succumbing to competition with foreign 'industries'. With the Treaty of Rome the choice of the competitive market model was made, which is incompatible with the adoption of protectionist instruments.

The peremptory nature of the ban on public aid, however, is mitigated when it is felt that, in critical economic sectors, it is necessary or appropriate to grant direct or indirect public aid to related companies. In principle, Article 107 of the TFEU prohibits aid to undertakings to the extent that it may 'affect trade between Member States (...) and distort or threaten to distort competition'. It is a rule meant to guarantee the prohibition of discrimination between citizens and undertakings of the various Member States, as well as the principles of free movement of goods, persons and capital, and the principle of freedom of competition.

But this provision, as are Articles 108-109 of the TFEU, is part of those reflecting the need to reconcile freedom of competition, on the one hand, and with the need, on the other, for public measures essential to achieving objectives worthy of protection.

40. Court of Justice 5 October 1994, C-280/93, *Germany v. Council*, with regard to the banana war to which reference has already been made.

In order for 'aid' to be defined as forbidden, a benefit of a patrimonial nature must be granted with public resources by the state or other subject in favour of some undertakings or production – thus, selectively – so as to alter the conditions of competition within the common market. In other words, aid is banned because public money would confer a position of advantage to some entrepreneurs to the detriment of their direct competitors. Consequently, 'aid' is not only 'positive' services such as financial subsidies but also measures reducing the burden that would normally weigh on the balance sheet of an undertaking.[41]

More specifically, two requirements are essential: that of the public provenance of the aid and that of the actual distortive impact of the aid on trade. The first requirement implies a specific negative judgment on the allocation of aid in the public budget and, therefore, against all taxpayers, when it gives rise to an unjustified flow of resources from the public budget to only some of the competing entrepreneurs in the market.[42] The second requirement expresses the need for the aid to be capable of affecting competition and intra-Community trade. It is for this reason that it has been established that every national aid project must be notified to the Commission in order to examine whether the aid produces potential and not necessarily current injury,[43] and whether the measure of support is compatible with the provisions concerning competition protection. The need to take note of the impact of all aid on competition suggested the introduction of the *de minimis* rule, for which, when it is below a certain threshold, aid is not to be notified and does not fall into the interdiction of Article 107 of the TFEU.[44]

But the ban on public aid to companies is not absolute. That is, aid is possible and the Treaty itself distinguishes between aid permitted by law (social aid granted to final consumers, aid to repair damage caused by natural disasters or other exceptional events), aid cleared by the Commission and aid permissible following the Council's decision. The second category of permissible subsidies includes those which give substance to state aid policies and which the Treaty of Rome and the TFEU allow only if they are aimed at achieving precise and certain objectives: the economic development of backward regions; remedy for a serious disturbance in the economy of a state; the development of certain activities or of certain economic regions (not necessarily in a crisis or underdeveloped); the realization of projects of common European interest.

41. *See* Court of Justice of 15 March 1994, C-387/92, Banco Exterior de España.
42. Interventions which cannot be strictly qualified as subsidies but which in various forms relieve the burdens on the undertaking are also considered aids, so that their assessment must be carried out according to their effects. *On the point v. the judgments of the Court of Justice* 5 October 1999, C-251/97, *France v. Commission*; 14 February 1990, C-301/87, *France v. Commission*.
43. *See* Court of Justice of 10 December 1969, C-6 and 11/69, *Commission v. France*.
44. On 6 March 1996 the Communication on *de minimis* aid was issued in sectors other than agriculture. It was then superseded by Reg. 69/2001 of 12 January 2001 and, thereafter, by Reg. 1535/2007 of 20 December 2007. Regulations 69/2001 and 1535/2007 are no longer in force.

If aid is not lawful, the Member State which granted it must work to recover it. However, restitution is not a sanction. The objective is to restore the situation to what it was prior to payment of aid.[45]

The use of block exemption regulations was also recognized as being appropriate for state aid. With regard to aid in sectors other than agriculture, the Commission has issued Regulation 1407/2013 and Regulation 651/2014 declaring that aid of minor importance, as well as those for small and medium-sized enterprises (SMEs), is compatible with the internal market.

In conclusion, therefore, it is legitimate to state that EU law does not demand the total abolition of financial aid to undertakings but rather wants transparent and temporary aid regimes inserted in a programmatic framework to avoid giving rise to forms of trade war between Member States of the EU. In other words, the prohibition of state aid is neither absolute nor unconditional.[46]

[D] The Prohibition of Public Aid: The Agricultural Derogation

All this, however, is fully valid only for the economic operators of industry. For those of agriculture, instead, Article 42, paragraph 2, of the TFEU allows the Council to authorize the granting of state aid 'for the protection of enterprises handicapped by structural or natural conditions' (letter a), or 'within the framework of economic development programmes' (letter b).

Various regulations on CMOs and now Article 211 of Regulation 1308/2013 on the single CMO declare the provisions of Articles 107-109 of the TFEU applicable, and therefore determine that states may not give their own aid to farmers.[47] However, the Structural Funds establish both fully EU-funded price support measures for certain specific agricultural products and, especially, EU contributions to the financing of public, semi-public or private projects to improve agricultural production, processing and sales. Thus, it can be noted that the structural regulations and, most recently, Regulation 1305/2013 on rural development and Regulation 1308/2013 on the single CMO provide subsidies to farmers and, therefore, pursuant also to paragraph 1 of Article 42 of the TFEU, national structural aid.[48]

45. *See* Court of Justice of 4 April 1995, C-24/95, *Commission v. Italy*. In the topic *see also* the judgments of the Court of Justice 20 September 1990, C-5/89, *Commission v. Germany*; 15 January 1986, C-52/84, Commission v. Belgium; 7 June 1988, C-63/87, *Commission v. Greece*; 27 June 2000, C-404/97, Portugal v. Commission; 3 July 2001, C-378/98, *Commission v. Belgium*; 18 July 2007, C-119/05, *Ministry of Industry v. Lucchini spa*.
46. *See* Court of Justice of 22 March 1977, C-78/76, Steinike and Weinlig.
47. In principle, the provisions of the TFEU on State aid applied to the production and marketing of agricultural products: *see*, Court of Justice of 26 June 1979, C-177/78, *Pigs and Bacon Commission v. Mc Carren and Company Limited*.
48. So the Parliament and the Council together can authorize direct aid: to reduce production costs; to promote diversification and qualitative improvement of production; to protect and improve the conditions of hygiene and animal welfare: to provide support for agricultural activity in areas where it is essential for the reorganization of the territory; to intervene with transitory support for agricultural income; to sensitize farmers to environmental problems; to solicit the establishment of producer groups; to support the marketing sector of agricultural products through these associations, provided that they are not surplus production.

In order to indicate the criteria to be followed in judging the admissibility of national aid in the agricultural sector, in 2000, the Commission issued a Guidance Communication on the Guidelines it would follow to judge this admissibility for both agricultural production and the processing and marketing of its products. The subsequent Regulation 1857/2006 with reference to aid to agricultural SMEs renounced the method of the Communication and made a clear distinction between agriculture and agro-industry, the latter being included in the ordinary regime for industrial products, given that agricultural product processing companies have significant similarities to industrial enterprises in the food processing sector. Now, however, Regulation 702/2014 of 25 June 2014 governs the conditions necessary for all SMEs in the agricultural sector – both those in production (Articles 14-16) and those in the processing and marketing of agricultural products (Article 17) – to obtain state aid.

It can therefore be concluded that in the general context of the prohibition of public subsidies to economic operators, agriculture is the sector which is the beneficiary of extensive derogations in the field of competition due to its structural and economic peculiarities. However, we cannot forget that Article 39 paragraph 2 of the TFEU establishes that the CAP must take into account the special nature of agricultural activity due to the social structure of agriculture and the structural and natural disparities of the different geographical areas, and therefore strive to smooth out differences because 'agriculture is a sector intimately linked to the whole economy'.

§14.07 THE CAP: PREMISE

At the time of the drafting of the Treaty of Rome, the then existing structural differences in agriculture of the six founding countries were the first obstacle to the realization of the common market; therefore, the need was felt to modernize their agricultural structures with the aim of defending both producers and consumers and of guaranteeing supply security. The concrete legal instruments to achieve these Community objectives appeared to be simultaneous: (a) manoeuvres on product prices; (b) actions on productive structures. In fact, it was clear that price support meant guaranteeing an adequate income for economic operators while financial aid to agricultural structures would end up affecting the price of the product they put onto the sales market to the benefit of consumers. And so Community price support and Community support of structures had to be closely correlated.

However, due to the greater ease of managing price interventions, the market for agricultural products began to be affected by European legislation as early as 1962, while the policy of structures was substantially inaugurated with the directives of 1972.

[A] Price Policy

In 1962 the Community began regulating the market of agricultural products by regulating its organization, product by product. The gradual creation of a single organization for each productive sector eliminated the previous national organizations and took away the states' jurisdiction to intervene in granting support to the various productions covered by what were now the CMOs, unless they were specifically authorized.

The main feature of the common agricultural market organizations was the fact that they were focused on price regulation.[49] In fact, having created a CMO for each agronomic sector,[50] each originally had its own specific legislation dictated by a special regulation in which there was greater or lesser recourse to the adoption of the various types of price interventions that had been conceived: guaranteed minimum prices;[51] production aid;[52] few intervention tools.[53]

Thus, each CMO had its own provisions on prices. As regards the internal market, the target price was that which the Community bodies fixed each year as the target price of the market, bearing in mind the most deficient area of the EU. On the basis of this price, the entry price was fixed, that is, the price that guaranteed the protection of the common market from the lowest world market prices through the determination of mobile duties (the so-called import levies) which determined the increase of entry price of non-Community products into the Union area. This prevented the entry of non-Community agricultural products into the European market at a cost lower than that of domestic production, protecting the interests of Community producers. On the basis of the target price, the intervention price was then fixed, that is to say, the price paid by state intervention agencies for products farmers gave them when the market price fell below the intervention price. Subsequently, in order to induce Community producers to place their products on the world market, naturally at world prices which were usually lower than Union production costs, it could grant export refunds calculated on the difference between Community costs and lower world prices.[54]

As a last consideration, it should be noted that the CAP rested mainly and concretely on 'guaranteed' prices and on the related CMOs that focused on production. The consequence of the coupling of financial support and production was the increase in some productions with consequent formation of food surpluses at enormous expense to the Community because of intervention prices. So at the end of the 1980s it was felt that the policy of the CAP had reached a critical point and that it was necessary to change it.

---

49. It is for this reason that the Court of Justice has defined the CMO as 'that set of legal provisions and instruments which the competent bodies use to control and normalize the market [of the product] in question': judgment of 13 November 1964, C-90 and 91/63, *Commission v. Luxembourg*.
50. Since the introduction of the CAP, the Council has set up twenty-one COM for a product or group of products, repeatedly amended and integrated. Now there is only Reg. 1308/2013 on the single CMO.
51. As in the case of cereals, butter, sugar.
52. As in the case of tobacco, oilseeds and protein plants.
53. As in the case of flowers and eggs.
54. In other words, price regulation was based on four main measures, two on the internal market, two on the non-EU market. When prices rose due to the decline in the supply of agricultural products, sale by the national intervention agencies and/or the consent to greater imports guaranteed that the price did not exceed the target price set by the Union, with protection in the interests of consumers. Mirroring this measure, when, on the other hand, the quantity produced caused the price to fall on the free market to the point of not providing producers with a fair income, demand by the national bodies at the intervention price set by the Union guaranteed price support with protection of producers' interests.

Today, of the so-called institutional prices, only the intervention price survives, and only in part. Indeed, since the MacSharry reform and Regulation 3290/94 following the approval of the Marrakesh Treaty establishing the World Trade Organization, the Union has abolished the variable import levies (the so-called threshold price) and limited the granting of export subsidies. Then, with Regulation 1782/2003 on medium-term reform of the CAP, the Union decoupled premiums from production, excepting some products and some Member States.

In 2005 the EU price policy, which had been financed for over forty years by the Guarantee Section of the European Agricultural Guidance and Guarantee Fund (EAGGF), was affected by the reform which divided the original EAGGF into two separate funds, one of which became the European Fund Agricultural Guarantee (EAGF). The reform of the EAGF was followed by a general reform of CMOs under Regulation 1234/2007. This was followed by Regulation 1308/2013, so-called on the single CMO, which unified the previous legislation of the various CMOs, while the contemporary Regulation 1307/2013 regulated a new system of price payments. These last two are in effect for the period 2014-2020.

In order to understand the changes, it should be recalled that at the end of the 1980s, the Union began to think of a system based on the principle of the decoupling of financial support from production but without depriving farmers of an income inducing them to remain on their landed properties to protect the territory and continue producing foodstuffs for the market. This was initially provided by the rule of the single payment scheme (SPS) introduced by Regulation 1782/2003 where a farmer is the recognized receiver of income aid on the basis of the average coupled aid he received in the previous three years 2000-2002, with reference to certain productions.[55] Subsequently, in order to create a system in which 'support' was 'more targeted', Regulation 1307/2013 provided for the 'unpacking' of the SPS into seven different types: basic payments, ecological or greening payments, voluntary redistributive payments, payments for areas subject to natural constraints, payments for young farmers, simplified payments for small farmers and, again, coupled payments for strategic productions. Furthermore, it was established that support is granted only to active farmers.[56]

As for the achievement of the aim of having 'fairer support', the Union has intervened on the methods of distributing direct payments. More precisely, it was decided to establish: progressive penalization of those receiving higher amounts (the capping code); the abandonment of the criterion of the 'historical period' of premiums enjoyed for the calculation of payments; and the extension to all Member States of the 'regionalization' model of decoupling that some states (those that entered the Union

55. The SP) replaces the amount of premiums already provided for by the various CMOs, and a single aid is divided into quotas (the so-called payment entitlements) in relation to the 'eligible hectares' used by the beneficiary. The subdivision into quotas is planned to make it possible to move the premium with or without land, thus giving a single aid the appearance of a 'good' of the holding to the extent that is possible for it to circulate autonomously and, consequently, have its own economic value. Indeed, a single aid can be circulated simultaneously with the transfer of land or independently of it.
56. The purpose of the limitation of the beneficiaries' base (the active farmers) is to avoid having support going to subjects that have little to do with agricultural activity.

after 2000) had already adopted since 2003. This last provision is an attempt by the EU to achieve a process of convergence between Member States and thereby succeed in reducing the existing disparities in the distribution of support.

[B] Structure Policy

The six founding countries of the European Common Market each had a policy in their respective legal systems to protect their agriculture through the use of tools ensuring both adequate income for their own farmers and the coverage of their citizens' food needs. More precisely, *economic reasons* advised increasing exports and reducing imports of agricultural products by acting on levers, tax and customs, respectively; *social reasons* required guaranteeing long-term employment on the land and increasing the level of food consumption; *political reasons* suggested securing local food production to support food needs in the case of detestable, but possible wars. Satisfying these needs was accomplished by different methods. These mainly included: land reforms and land leases; special legislation for credit, subsidies and deferred payments for the mechanization and industrialization of agriculture; reduction of distribution costs for agricultural products in the internal market and in the world market; national market organization in various agricultural sectors; legislation on compulsory stockpiling; raising incoming customs duties; tax reduction in the case of production going abroad. The use of these methods was different from country to country, both in terms of intensity and mechanisms, and this was obviously in relation to the specific structural and environmental situations of the distinct agriculture and respective institutions of the different countries; but all these methods were marked by the common denominator of strong public intervention and economic protectionism in the agricultural sector.

The remarkable differentiation between the six founding countries had at first suggested that agriculture remains outside the European Common Market. In fact, in the course of the negotiations that were to give rise to the EEC, there had been long discussions on the advisability of excluding agricultural products from the common market. The liberal approach of the Treaty, with its consequent guarantee of a regime of free circulation of goods, workers, services and capital, was ill-suited to the agricultural sector where numerous small agricultural enterprises lacked sufficient economic strength to effectively dialogue on equal terms with the agro-food industry and the commercial agricultural product oligopolies. Only in the end did the thesis prevail that agriculture could not be excluded from the general economic system that was being planned and so it came to be part of the Treaty. But then it was necessary to intervene on the structures of the various Member States to make them homogeneous.

In July 1958, a Conference of Member States was convened in Stresa 'to proceed to the comparison of their policies, establishing in particular the balance of their resources and their needs', with the aim of 'tracing the guidelines of a common agricultural policy'. In its conclusions, the Conference pressed for a policy to improve the agricultural structures of the six and proposed replacing national market organizations with CMOs. But when the 1960 and 1968 projects (the so-called Mansholt Plan) containing strong intervention on agricultural structures failed,[57] it was considered easier to immediately provide for the realization of a price policy. In its immediacy, this seemed able to ensure the necessary adaptation time to intervene later on improving structures. In short, while specific intervention on structures was necessary, it was essential on prices. Price intervention soon translated into strong protectionism of the internal agricultural market.

The specific interventions on structures were not resumed until 1972 when Directive 159/1972 was adopted. This elaborated the role of the 'farmer who practices farming as his main occupation' as the sole receiver of EU subsidies. This physical or legal subject was characterized by adequate occupational skill and competence, either through educational qualification or experience of agricultural activity, enabling him to keep accounting books and draw up a business development plan that within a maximum of six years would bring the farm up to a level of earned income comparable to that received for non-agricultural work in the region in question, who was involved in agricultural activity for at least 50% of his working time and who earned at least 50% of his total income from it. The 1972 Community legislator therefore made a clear choice in favour of a *highly productive agriculture* model.

Since then interventions on structures have multiplied with the increasing realization of the perverse effects of a price policy linked to production quantity. The urgent need to confront the risk of surpluses has led, first of all, to a change in the criterion of productive development as quantity. Regulation 797/1985 focused on *improving quality*, subsidizing only productions that could be allocated to the market.[58] However, it was foreseen that while aid needed to be given to producers of agricultural products destined for the market, besides agricultural production, other activities could be carried out which would enhance the identifiable potential of any single farm.[59] It was the beginning of the discourse on 'multifunctional agriculture' and the provision of its financial support.

Performing these other activities, in fact, not only contributed to greater and better exploitation of farm resources but was also able to determine synergies between the production and service management sectors, with the potential for great improvements in the production sector. This gradually undermined the system that up to that moment had been founded on a model of farm efficiency as being only productive of goods, to become the backbone of the CAP in the years following the 1990s and form

57. The '1980 Agricultural Programme' or the 2nd Mansholt Plan of 21 December 1968 on structures provided for the conversion of polyculture farms to monoculture undertakings, the so-called Production Units, or the establishment of larger undertakings through the use of associative or corporate instruments, the so-called modern agricultural enterprises.
58. Regulation 797/85 significantly changes the name of 'business plan' in the 1972 directives into 'improvement plan' and therefore clarifies that investments are made to achieve objectives other than simply increasing production.
59. It is useful to refer in particular to Article 16 of Reg. 797/1985 which allowed farmers who worked in the mountains and in less-favoured areas to receive compensatory compensation for their work in these geographical areas, due to the environmental protection objectives that their work could carry out. Reg. 797/1985 is no longer in force.

the basis of Regulation 2088/1985 on Integrated Mediterranean Programs[60] and Regulation 2052/1988 on the modification of the Structural Funds.[61]

A significant change of course takes place, however, with Regulation 3808/1989 dedicated to the acceleration of agriculture structure adaptation. The peculiarity of the 1989 provision lies not so much in the fact of its opening up the CAP to subjects whose profession was not agriculture,[62] but rather in the fact of providing for the support of 'investments aimed at *diversifying* the sources of income' to all farmers, not just those in less-favoured areas.[63]

The worthiness of European contributions now lies with a model of multifunctional business, in which qualifying a holding as 'agriculture' not only does not prejudice the exercise of extra-agricultural activities, but these activities actually promote the finding of further opportunities for the integration of the undertaking into its rural territory. So the CAP does not intend to address producers only for the quantity or quality of their agricultural products but expands its scope to include those who play a role in preserving rural areas[64] by working and living on the land.

After all, Regulation 1760/1987 and Regulations 1094/1988 and 1097/1988 had already repudiated the principle of maximizing production at all costs, providing for direct aid for land to be set aside land, for converting and 'extensifying' productions, for foresting holdings, for severing income support from production and introducing co-responsibility levies or 'penalties' for overrunning certain production quotas.[65]

60. The Reg. 2008/1985 intended to improve the socio-economic structures of the southern regions of the EU, providing for a unitary and joint action in the sectors of agriculture, fisheries, agro-food industries, energy and craft industry, construction, public works, services and tourism, in a global view. Reg. 2088/1995 is no longer in force.
61. The modification of the Structural Funds makes clear the design of a community policy aimed at resolving the disparities existing between the various regions of Europe, through interventions capable of contributing to the development of the *whole social tissue* of the area and therefore, where territories are predominantly agriculture, of what is now called rural space.
62. Reference to a 'farmer who practices farming as his main occupation' has been abandoned, and therefore it is not necessary to refer to both working time destined to agriculture and income from agriculture.
63. Tourism or craft businesses and the manufacture and sale of products of the enterprise on the farm are mentioned. Aid is now destined to 'farmers who, while they do not practice farming as their main occupation, derive at least 50% of their total income from farming, forestry, tourism or craft activities, or activities for maintaining the countryside which quality for public aid, carried out on the holding, provided that the proportion of income deriving directly from farming on the holding is not less than 25% of the farmer's total income and that off-farm activities do not account for more half the farmer's total working time' (Article 1 of Reg. 3808/1989).
64. So the talk of part-time farmers starts, who are also worthy of aid.
65. With the new regulations, the EU first intervenes in some surplus productions, prohibiting the planting new vineyards and introducing co-responsibility levies designed to contain production. Second, the Union sees environmental policy as an instrument to affect agricultural production, first by including environmental conservation among the new declared purposes of the CAP (Reg. 1760/87) and then highlighting the negative effects on the environment of productions based solely on the economic calculation of the cost/intervention price. Thus the European legislator also grants incentives to those farmers who strive to: reconvert surplus production into other productions that are still insufficient in the European economy; cease using land intensively by adopting or re-adopting extensive cultivation methods; 'freeze' for at least five years the cultivation of a portion of their respective holdings, thus 'putting aside' some lands in

In the 1990s the aforementioned orientation found further reasons for confirmation in the measures that accentuated its direction. In the Uruguay Round, the point of greatest friction had turned out to be the policy of aid to agriculture, so much so that in 1992 the Community had already approved distinct intervention programmes aimed at influencing the productive structure of agricultural enterprises through manoeuvres on prices, incentives and grants. The 1992 reform[66] is representative of a significant change in the CAP, so much so that it can be said that structural policy and market policy converge into one from then on. From this point, the CAP appears to be based on two pillars of equal value (production and rural space) so agriculture loses its monolithic production approach centralized on the CMOs and where structural measures were simply accompaniments to price policy. Regulations 2081/1992 and 2082/1992 on protected designations of origin are also from the 1990s, in which protected geographical indications and traditional specialities are guaranteed in order to give farmers more opportunities to find new spaces on the market for quality agricultural products, while Regulation 1953/1995 (later integrated, for animal production, from Regulation 1804/1999) regulates cultivations not using synthetic chemicals and closely links organic productions to respect for the environment: all measures which, although they concern commercial aspects of European agricultural policy, can also be considered structural measures.

In the last year of the century, structural policy decisively steps towards anti-productive purposes and the encouragement of rural development. In the evolution of the CAP, the May-June 1999 regulations 'on rural development' confirm the reduction of guaranteed minimum prices and the establishment of producer income aid. In particular, Regulation 1257/99 integrates agricultural policy with that of the territory, convinced of the inadequacy of sectorial interventions and the need, on the contrary, for a global approach on a territorial basis. From the integration of Regulation 1257/99 with Regulation 1259/99, the rule is that the provision of aid is in exchange for agro-environmental commitments and that funding is subordinate to compliance with both general and specific environmental requirements (the so-called cross-compliance). In essence, the 1999 CAP reform assigns the farmer the task of highlighting the 'territoriality' of his action. Thus, alongside agriculture characterized by mass production of commodities, the reform first proposes quality agriculture whose characteristics are differentiation and typicality, 'centralized' on the natural and cultural particularities of the territory in which the farmer operates; and, second, agriculture elevated to protective guardian of the countryside and landscape and consumers' food choices.

Actions on the CAP continue. First of all, there is the replacement of Regulation 1257/99 on rural development with Regulation 1782/2003 of the mid-term reform of

---

the global management of their businesses; transform arable land into wooded land, diverting land from the production of cereals to produce timber, still subject to significant imports (Reg. 1094/1988 and Reg. 1096/1988).

66. A set of provisions were adopted (Reg. 1765/92, 1766/92, 2078/92, 2079/92 and 2080/92 of 30 June 1992), which constitute what has been called the 'MacSharry reform' from the name of the Commissioner of agriculture at that time.

the CAP,[67] then with Regulation 1698/2005,[68] then Regulation 73/2009[69] and finally with Regulation 1305/2013 on rural development.

Regulation 1305/2013 of 17 December 2013 – which is effective for the period 2014-2020 – confirms the structure of the already existing rural development policy. In the overall framework of structural policies, the rural development regulation is characterized by entrusting the Member States with the task of finishing strategic choices and managing them in a multilevel system because they are oriented, co-financed and controlled by the Union. In order to achieve agricultural and forestry sector competitiveness, sustainable natural resource management and balanced territorial development of rural areas,[70] six 'priorities' have been identified[71] with the specific provision that each Member State has the right to identify areas of more specific interest in its Rural Development Program and with measures that respond mainly to the needs of small businesses, mountain areas, women in rural areas, climate change mitigation and short agro-food supply chains.[72]

However, what is worth highlighting is that the 2013 regulations maintained the structure of the two-pillar CAP. They impose mandatory annual general application measures for the first pillar, which are complemented by voluntary measures responding to national specificities in the framework of multi-annual programming of the

67. The focal point of the new legislation lay in the belief that public spending on European agriculture must be justified by specific offsets demanded from farmers and that beneficiaries must uphold them. The specific nature of the reform lay in the fact that aid was conditional to the effective achievement of these goals (the so-called cross-compliance or conditionality), with a consequent reduction or revocation of the benefit in the event of non-compliance. Reg. 1782/2003 is no longer in force; it was repealed by Reg. 73/2009, which in turn was repealed by Reg. 1307/2013 on 'direct payments'.
68. Reg. 1698/2005 aimed to affect the second pillar of the common agricultural policy in consideration of the fact that over half of the population of the EU (then 25 Member States) lived (and lives) in rural areas occupying 90% of the territory and that agriculture and forestry were and remain the predominant forms of land use and management of natural resources in rural areas of Europe. The new regulation identified 'three political axes' which concerned: increasing agricultural sector competitiveness by promoting its restructuring; enhancing the environment and rural space through land management support; improving the quality of rural life by diversifying economic activities through measures aimed at the agricultural sector and other components of the rural way of life. Reg. 1698/2005 is no longer in force; it was repealed by the Reg. 1305/2013 on rural development.
69. It is worth noting that Article 28, para. 2 of Reg. 73/2009 established that starting in 2010 Member States could order the not granting of direct payments to a subject 'whose agricultural activities form only an insignificant part of its overall economic activities', or 'whose principal business does not consist of exercising an agricultural activity'. Reg. 73/2009 is no longer in force; it was repealed by Reg. 1307/2013 on 'direct payments'.
70. In this regard, reference is made to mitigating climate change, protecting biodiversity, protecting water and promoting renewable energy.
71. They are: (1) stimulation of knowledge transfer and innovation; (2) strengthening of competitiveness in all types of agriculture and sustainable forest management; (3) promotion of their organization, processing and marketing included, and of the risk management of the food chain; (4) restoration, protection and improvement of ecosystems; (5) promotion of resource efficiency and transition to a low carbon economy; (6) promotion of social inclusion, poverty reduction and economic development in rural areas. Cf. Article 5 of Reg. 1305/2013 on rural development.
72. With an analysis of the situations in terms of strengths and weaknesses and of the opportunities and risks (the so-called swot analysis) of the geographical areas affected by the programs whose definitions are given.

second pillar. In this context then, and with respect to Regulation 1305/2013, it is possible to resume analysis of the contemporary Regulation 1307/2013 on direct payments which influences the 'formation' of farm structures by dictating the provisions on aid to farmers.

If you will recall, Regulation 1307/2013 'unpacked' the system of direct payments, keeping basic decoupled payment mandatory (Articles 21-35) in relation to the number of eligible hectares.[73] Also laid down is compulsory decoupled ecological or greening payment in the amount of 30% of the national ceiling (Articles 43-47).[74] It also introduced a simplified payment scheme for 'small farmers'[75] who are exempt from bureaucratic burdens and environmental obligations related to the ordinary payment

73. Eligible hectares are land held on 15 May 2014. The law also demands that the farmer be an 'active farmer' and that he have presented the sole application in 2011, i.e., that he 'activated' a title in 2011. On the definition of 'active farmer' *see* Article 9 of Reg. 1307/2013, according to which it is one who: (1) in the most recent fiscal year for which evidence is available has obtained, for direct payments, an amount at least 5% of the total receipts that it obtained from non-agricultural activities; (2) whose agricultural activities are not insignificant; (3) whose principal business consist of exercising an agricultural activity. In other words, a subject who, even if he does not derive most of his income from agriculture, nevertheless does not derive an infinitesimal amount from it. In this regard *see* Article 28 of Reg. 73/2009 as above, note 69. Article 3, para. 3, letter d) of the most recent Reg. 2017/2393 of 13 December 2017 establishes that the Member States may decide that only one or two of the three criteria listed in Article 28 may be invoked by interested parties to demonstrate that they are active farmers; while the letter (a) of the same para. 3 of the Article 3 of Reg. 2017/2393 provides that Member States may decide that no direct payments are to be granted to farmers who are not registered, for their agricultural activities, in a national fiscal or social security register.
74. This is support payment for agricultural practices beneficial to the climate and the environment for farmers who receive basic payment and who also provide jointly on their respective eligible hectares the presence of at least two or three different crops on arable land, the maintenance of permanent grasslands and, now, the presence of 7% of areas of ecological interest (Article 46.1, Reg. 1307/2013). On the topic *see also* Reg. 1306/2013 – the so-called horizontal regulation –, which provides for administrative sanctions to those who do not respect the rules of conditionality. On the new definitions of 'meadow' and 'permanent pasture' *see* Article 3, para. 1, of Reg. 2017/2393.
75. Even in the absence of a specific definition, 'small farmers' should be understood as those who carry out 'the minimum activity defined by the Member States' on their agricultural land that is ('maintained in a state suitable for grazing or cultivation without preparatory action going beyond usual agricultural methods and machineries'). Therefore, the 'small farmer' cannot be a mere landowner in rural areas because at the very least he must maintain the surface of his land in good agro-economic and environmental conditions. There is no specific provision to determine 'smallness'. For this purpose, however, it is possible to consider that Article 10, para. 1, letter b) of Reg. 1307/2013 prescribes that Member States shall decide 'not to grant direct payments to farmers where the eligible area of the holding (…) is less than one hectare'; and that Article 63, para. 1, letter b), prescribes that the amount of annual payment to small farmers cannot exceed 'the amount corresponding to the national average payment per hectare, multiplied by a figure corresponding to a number of hectares not exceeding five'. It could be inferred that a farmer is 'small' if he cultivates more than one hectare but no more than five hectares.

regime, i.e., from greening obligations and cross-compliance rules.[76] Finally, it provided payment for disadvantaged areas;[77] payment for young farmers;[78] coupled payment;[79] and a further type of direct aid, i.e., the 'distribution for the first hectares'.[80]

Now, the criteria of 'active farmer', 'young farmer' and 'small farmer', those of the compulsory greening measure and the optional 'coupled' and 'redistributive' measures necessarily influence the form, the consistency, and the competitive capacity of farms. In this way price policy is integrated with that of structures.[81]

The 2013 regulations have undergone meticulous modification in Regulation 2017/2393 of 13 December 2017, which in essence represents a mini-reform of the CAP. Besides those already considered in the previous notes regarding ecological payment rules, the favouring of young farmers and small farmers and the definition of 'active farmer', the changes concern the field of action of producer organizations, the strengthening of agricultural insurance and farmers' income stabilization tools.

As for ideas on what the CAP should be after 2020, the Commission presented a Communication in November 2017 proposing ideas for reforming the EU's agricultural policy, and in June 2018, a Proposal to amend all Regulations of 17 December 2013 for the period 2021-2027. The Commission considers that the maintenance of the two CAP pillars should be confirmed as should the various types of payments, introducing, however, a ceiling for direct payments, a system of decreasing payments for large undertakings and greater use of payment redistributive payment. But above all, the Commission proposes to modify the CAP's implementation model to centralize it on subsidiarity so that states would have a more decisive role in implementing CAP programmes. Thus it would be for the Union to set the basic parameters of objectives, the main types of intervention and the basic requirements, while the Member States would draw up the strategic plans to achieve the specific objectives established by

76. Article 2, para. 6 of Reg. 2017/2393 of 13 December 2017 added an exemption from the obligation to declare also the parcels for which no application for payment is requested.
77. Under the 'direct payments' regulation, Member States may grant payments up to 5% of the annual national ceiling to farmers in areas with specific natural constraints, in order to maintain agricultural activity and the presence of farmers in areas subject to specific natural constraints.
78. According to the Article 50 of Reg. 1307/2013 young farmers were farmers 'aged forty or less than forty years'. The formula has been modified by Article 1 of Reg. 2017/2393 for which a 'young farmer is a person no more than 40 years of age at the moment of submitting the application'.
79. *See* Article 52 and those following of Reg. 1307/2013. Member States may allocate up to 8% of the national ceiling to grant coupled support in sectors or regions where specific types of farming or specific agricultural sectors that are particularly important for economic or social or environmental reasons, undergo certain difficulties, establishing that the coupled support may only be granted to the extent necessary to create an incentive to maintain current levels of production in the sectors or regions concerned. On the new definition of 'coupled support' *see* Article 3, para. 11 of the Reg. 2017/2393.
80. Member States may use a share of their national allocation to provide a payment system for farmers for at most thirty hectares, which would favour a significant redistributive effect among farmers receiving direct aid (Article 41(4), Reg. 1307/2013).
81. At this point it is worth noting that Article 3, para. 5 of Reg. 2017/2393 modifies Article 14 of Reg. 1307/2013 on direct payments with regard to the flexibility between the pillars. Starting from 2019, Member States will be more able to adapt supports to their specific needs as they will be allowed to revise their decisions on the transfer of funds from their direct payment ceiling to their rural development programmes and vice versa.

common agreement. Finally, future CAP regulation should be more coherent with other Union policies, which in the near future will increasingly concern migration, research, the fight against climate change and sustainable development.

§14.08 TRENDS IN AGRICULTURAL LAW IN THE EU IN THE LAST YEARS

In the early years of this new century, certain interventions by the EU appear to have been characterized by a change in the structure of its agricultural law.

The discipline of agriculture in place in the EU seems to be considerably detached from that of the past because underlying the current design of community institutions is basically a different philosophy - so to speak. One has the impression that the normative corpus concerning agriculture - from the CAP to rural development, from the original single market organizations to the single CMO -[82] is changing its skin and going from the right to incentivize to the right to regulate.

At the start date of the CAP in 1962, European agricultural law was mainly characterized by its promotional aspect, as was clearly evident from what was actually contained in the CAP. The most incisive manifestation of this promotional function was the importance of the role of the first pillar of the CAP, that of the regulation of financial interventions on agricultural markets, with its provisions on prices. Nor were things different for the second pillar on rural development, which was intended to encourage the advent and implementation of stronger and more competitive structures in an agricultural economy which, while it never ceased to be a market economy, was distinguished (and is still partly distinguished) by the 'protection' afforded by European and national support and aid. In other words, the system required the presence of a 'regulated' market.

The starting point was (and is) that the structural weaknesses of the agricultural market made (and makes) a minimum of protectionism essential to allow freedom of initiative to be combined with a balanced development of the system, so the concrete governance of the European agricultural economy was (and still is) expressed through the levers of intervention on prices and markets. In this way these interventions have progressively replaced the corresponding legislation of the Member States, which, in fact, emerged in an age of national agricultural protectionism. We can safely say that the institutional unity of Europe was based on its level of economy.

Today, absolute liberalism, a consequence of globalization, is reducing promotional law and economic incentives because they are deemed to distort the free market and free competition at the world level. Thus European institutions are progressively foregoing direct intervention with financial incentives in many sectors of agricultural production, while the space given over to local dimensions of government and national choices has increased, especially due to the importance the second pillar is acquiring. In fact, the second pillar has its basis in the natural and structural differences in

82. And to go beyond the topics of this chapter, from food law to quality packaging or mandatory and voluntary information on food.

agriculture of the different regions of the EU, which thus 'demand' different interventions by the Member States.

However, almost as a counterpart to this 'flight' of European economic interventions from the centre to the periphery, there has been more incisive intervention by the EU on the content of the legal discipline of the various sectors of its competence, in order to continue to guarantee the institutional unity of Europe, but now in terms of law.

Thus, EU law is turning into a law of rules which not only identifies the disciplinary framework within which it is to be implemented each time at a peripheral level but even precisely determines the legislation that we all must obey, dictating definitions and establishing rules of behaviour. So that, it could be said that when the legal component of adopted rules dominates the economic regulation of the sectors considered, the centralized use of regulatory instruments is what enables the institutional unity of Europe to remain firmly established.

This consideration is confirmed by the fact that from the multiplicity of provisions first disseminated in a multitude of normative acts, we have moved to their reorganization and their systematization in a formally single act – a sort of 'code' – which has expansive force because it is capable of attracting to itself norms of sectors not included in the original text and to extend its definitions to other disciplines with which it can coordinate.

So, and in conclusion, it is useful to remember that in the Communication of November 2017, the Commission, wondering about the future of the CAP after 2020, has foreseen that it will be characterized precisely by the tendency to constitute itself as a legislation of rules rather than of incentives. Thus, the future discipline of domestic rights, on which the elaboration of national strategic plans will be based in order to achieve the objectives established jointly by the Union and the Member States, will be pervaded by 'common' rules of law.

On 31 January 2020, the United Kingdom (UK) ceased to be a Member State of the EU. The UK and the EU have signed a 'withdrawal agreement' which provides a legal framework for the process of British exit. The scenarios of the significant economic consequences on the matter of the European agricultural law particularly concern: (i) the reintroduction of a customs border between Northern Ireland (a part of the UK) and the Republic of Ireland (an EU Member State) and the free movement of people and goods across the border; (ii) the UK firms have no need to comply with the next agricultural and food regulations fixed by the EU, particularly on food and feed safety, on the authorization and labelling of genetically modified organisms, on quality schemes for agricultural products with protected designations of origin and protected geographical indications; (iii) UK will not be subjected to the opinions of the European Food Safety Authority which is the EU's risk assessment body providing scientific advice on food to the EU. This has implications for future patterns of trade in agricultural and food products between EU and UK.

The new proposals from the European Commission refresh the CAP providing strengthened support for farmers and rural areas in the years to come. The proposals aim to ensure that the CAP can continue to provide strong support for European farming, enabling prosperous rural area and the production of high-quality food. In other words, the next CAP will make the EU's agricultural policy more responsive to current and future challenges, continuing to support the active needs of European farmers. On 1 June 2018 the European Commission presented a legislative proposal on the CAP, after the above-mentioned Communication 'The Future of Food and Farming' (29 November 2017) presented to the European Parliament, the Council, the European Economic and Social Committee and the Committee of the Regions. The priorities for the new CAP are: food security, fair trade, maintaining farming activity, food quality, preserving biodiversity, environmental protection, fair remuneration for the public goods supplied by farmers, rural development based on the creation of green jobs. On 20 October 2020 the EU Council agreed its negotiating position on the post-2000 CAP reform package. This agreed position puts forward some strong commitments from Member States for higher environmental ambition with instruments like mandatory eco-schemes and enhanced conditionality. The agreement is described, by Julia Klockner, Federal Minister for food and agriculture of Germany, as 'a milestone for Europe's agricultural policy. Members States demonstrated their ambition for higher environmental standards in farming and at the same time supported the needed flexibility in ensuring farmers' competitiveness'. This agreement fulfils the aspiration of greener, fairer and simpler CAP. These documents of the European Commission and Council confirm the continuity of the European policy headed, a long time ago, for the integration of the productive activities with the environmental protection.

On 19 March 2020, the European Commission Communication 'Temporary framework for State aid measures to support the economy in the current Covid-19 outbreak' notes that the COVID-19 outbreak is a severe public health emergency for citizens and societies. Therefore this Communication sets out the possibilities that Member States have under EU rules to ensure liquidity and access to finance for undertakings. Besides this general communication the Commission Implementing Regulation 2020/466 of 30 March 2020 – amended by the Commission Regulation 2020/1667 of 10 November 2020 – decrees temporary measures to contain risks to human, animal and plant health and animal welfare during serious disruptions of Member State's control systems due to coronavirus disease (COVID-19). The Regulation 2017/625 had introduced an official system of controls that provided national authorities with the necessary power to ensure effective enforcement of regulatory requirements and with mechanism that allowed the full cooperation of all parties involved in ensuring the correct application of the law across national borders; now the coronavirus disease requires the introduction of new rules for the circulation of agricultural and food products and new procedures for international controls. And already the European Commission Communication 'Farm to fork strategy. For a fair, healthy and environmentally-friendly food system' 2020 noted: 'food systems cannot be resilient to crises such as the Covid-19 pandemic if they are not sustainable', stating that 'the Covid-19 pandemic has underlined the importance of a robust and resilient food system that functions in all circumstances, and is capable of ensuring access to a sufficient supply of affordable food for citizens'. In other words, Article 39(d) of the Treaty on the Functioning of the EU which ensures the availability of supplies, returns in a prominent place, confirming a policy that has never forgotten, among the EU purposes, the central purpose of *food security* with which the further purpose of *food safety* is complemented: this latter purpose has been and will be the central corollary of the former, but will never be its substitute.

CHAPTER 15

Food Safety System in the EU

Maria Pia Ragionieri

Food safety, in its different meanings of hygienic-sanitary, toxicological and nutritional safety, implies the definition of food as 'any substance that can be ingested', either with reference to food for human consumption or feed for the nutrition of animals (which in turn are destined for human consumption). With reference to these food and feed, the rules dictated by the Community Regulations about food safety regard all the operations, from production-collection to processing and distribution, influencing all the moments and places of the path, for profit or non-profit. In the food market only safe and healthy food should necessarily circulate and therefore 'at risk' foods cannot be placed on the market. It follows that we need to define: what is the risk; who is legitimated to intervene in case of risk; the intervention strategies; who should assess the risk; who should manage and communicate it. The European Union (EU) shall dictate the hygienic-sanitary prescriptions and regulate the responsibility for damages caused by defective food products, where the 'defect' is assessed in relation to the harmless of the thing. The EU shall assume the responsibility for control and prevention interventions by pivoting on the precautionary principle as guideline, by virtue of which scientific uncertainty shall assume the quality of legally relevant fact, suitable to produce the effect of the prohibition or authorization. The last safety issue, certainly not marginal, concern the safety information, the correct and exhaustive communication to the consumer of the food characteristics, patterns and quantities of its consumption. This chapter is dedicated to the rule of the different mentioned aspects and to the critical issues.

The expression 'food safety' is correlated with the expressions food law and food security, in order to define the wide range of rules concerning food products, starting from the agricultural raw material, throughout the agri-food chain.

Food law, a set of public, private and criminal law disciplines, represents a subject characterized in its essence by interdisciplinarity. We must also note that the globalization of the economy and the strategic role that the food import and export processes have taken on in the various countries, to reduce customs barriers, have assigned to food law the role of a technical barrier. This is precisely a consequence of the diversity of contents regulated by the different models of food regulations adopted by several countries worldwide. The path towards the accentuation of contaminations between different models makes it possible the realization of an 'international food law' in parallel with the emergence of a Global Food System.[1]

Food security concerns the security of food availability and supply, the security of having sufficient food; therefore, it is linked to a quantitative criterion.[2]

Food safety concerns, instead, the quality profile of the food, based on the acquired food security.[3]

In the European context, the subject of food law is based on a set of principles and rules whose pillar is represented by Regulation 178/2002 on food safety,[4] a system regulation, which has organically provided, as stated in the same Article 4 of the regulation, a general framework of horizontal legislation to comply within the adoption of sectoral measures.

The specificity of the food rules derives from its subject, the food (or food product or foodstuff), defined by Article 2 of the regulation as 'any substance or product processed, partially processed or unprocessed, intended to be ingested, or which is reasonably expected to be ingested by humans' – food for humans, and feed for animals, animals which in turn are destined to become food for humans.

The rule dictated by the regulation concerns all the operations at the various stages of production, processing, transport, up to the distribution on the market of the products intended for food, in order to guarantee the consumers safety and protection.

The food market must be a market for safe and healthy foods only. The so-called 'unsafe' foods, pursuant to Article 14 of the regulation shall not therefore be put into circulation.

The Regulation 178/2002 marks a significant milestone in food discipline, since it goes beyond the traditional rule of the hygienic and health safety of the product, which is based on prohibitions and sanctions; it suggests a food safety rule based on both prevention and control, mentioning expressly the precautionary principle, and the separation between management and assessment of the risk, as well as the centrality of the traceability processes of the products, and the regulation of the entrepreneurial responsibility of producers and distributors.

If unsafe foods cannot circulate in the food market, defining the concept of risk becomes crucial. Unsafe foods are injurious to human health, and also those that are unfit for human consumption, when the product is contaminated, putrefied or deteriorated or decayed.

1. A. Jannarelli, Il mercato agroalimentare europeo, in Diritto agroalimentare, n. 2, 2020, p. 318.
2. E. Rook Basile, Sicurezza e qualità degli alimenti, in M. Goldoni, E. Sirsi, Per uno studio interdisciplinare su agricoltura e alimentazione, Milano 2011, p. 151.
3. *See* P. Borghi, Sicurezza alimentare e commercio internazionale, in Prodotti agricoli e sicurezza alimentare, Atti del III congresso nazionale UMAU, Pisa-Siena 5-9- novembre 2002.
4. A. Germano, M.P. Ragionieri, E. Rook Basile, Diritto agroalimentare, Le regole del mercato degli alimenti e dell'informazione alimentare, Torino 2019, pp. 41 ss.

Pursuant to Article 14 of the regulation, foods that shall have negative effects on the physical well-being of the consumer are injurious to human health, even if the harmful effect is long-term or occurs to the detriment of the subsequent generations, or if it is produced by accumulation of several distinct food ingested portions.

The risk is determined by the probability of an adverse effect on human and animal health consequential to a hazard.

It is an element of hazard and therefore can constitute a hazard: the biological, chemical or physical agent contained in the food, or the condition in which the food or feed is found, and also the intrinsic composition of the product, with reference to the toxicological safety.[5]

The risk must be analysed along a process that consists of three phases: risk assessment, risk management and risk communication.[6]

The risk must be assessed by an authority having the requisite third-party nature and independence, composed of scientists, namely the European Food Safety Authority (EFSA);[7] managed by the European Commission, which is responsible for the political choices among the various options of intervention, that are based on the results of scientific assessment. The European Commission is also responsible for risk communication, which is the interactive exchange, throughout the process of analysis, information and opinions, between those responsible for the different stages, consumers, businesses, academic community and all stakeholders.

The centrality of the process, achieved with Regulation 178/2002, assigns to the EU the responsibility for prevention and control interventions, based on that principle, which is the precautionary principle, assumed as the guideline of the European action. The application of this principle to food safety is established by Article 7 of the regulation, which raises the scientific uncertainty to a legally relevant fact by providing: 'According to this principle, in specific circumstances where, following an assessment of available information, the possibility of harmful effects on health is identified but scientific uncertainty persists, provisional risk management measures necessary to ensure the high level of health protection chosen in the Community may be adopted, pending further scientific information for a more comprehensive risk

5. L. Costato, Il diritto al cibo nelle fonti internazionali, europee e italiane, in L. Costato, et al., Compendio di diritto alimentare, Milano 2019, p. 2; M. Valletta, Biotecnologia, agricoltura e alimentare: il nuovo regolamento sui cibi geneticamente modificati ed il processo di sistematizzazione del quadro giuridico comunitario, in Riv. Pubbl. Comp. Eur., 2003, p. 1493.
6. *See* the reasons relating to greater transparency and sustainability of the risk analysis that led to the adoption of Regulation 2019/1381 of 30 June 2019 (which amends Regulation 178/202, among other things, regarding the objectives and general principles of risk communication, the General plan of risk communication, the consultation of interested third parties), L. Costantino, La ricerca dell'equilibrio tra scienza e governance della sicurezza alimentare. Riflessioni sulla proposta di Regolamento e l'analisi del rischio, in Costato, Germanò e Rook Basile, Trattato di diritto agrario, vol. 3, Il diritto agroalimentare, Torino 2011, p. 641; *see also* 'Società del rischio', E. Rook Basile, La mano invisibile del rischio, in I diritti della terra e del mercato agroalimentare, Liber amicorum, Alberto Germanò, Tomo II, p. 1075.
7. *See*, F. Viti, l'Autorità europea per la sicurezza alimentare e l'analisi del rischio, in L. Costato, A. Germanò, E. Rook Basile, Trattato di diritto agrario, vol. 3. Il diritto agroalimentare, Torino 2011, p. 641; F. Adornato, The European Food Safety Authority, in L. Costato, F. Albisinni (eds), European and Global Food Law, Milano 2016, p. 203; V. Paganizza, L'Autorità europea per la sicurezza alimentare, in L. Costato, et al., Compendio di diritto alimentare, Milano 2019, p. 86.

assessment.'[8] However, it is worth mentioning that in the provision in question, the 'possibility' and not the compulsory nature of the application of the precautionary principle (instead provided for the risk analysis) shall be attributed to the Commission. It should however be noted that together with the discretion in adopting precautionary measures, it shall be provided that such measures must be provisional, proportionate, necessary and aimed at ensuring a high level of health protection.

Thanks to the valuable contribution provided by EU jurisprudence through the Luxembourg Court, the application of the precautionary principle must be inspired by the teachings of the Court of Justice such as: the need that scientific information shall be weighted without manifest errors of assessment; the adoption of restrictive measures must presuppose a sufficiently documented risk assessment on the basis of available scientific data; the compliance with the principle of proportionality in cases where provisional precautionary measures are adopted.[9]

Food safety, in its interpretation of health and hygiene safety, requires the coordination of the provisions of Regulation 178/2002 with those of the so-called hygiene package consisting in particular of three rules: Regulation 852/2004, of a general nature, on hygiene foodstuffs, which replaced Directive 93/43 on Hazard Analysis Critical Control Points (Haccp); the second, Regulation 853/2004 provides specific hygiene rules for food of animal origin; the third, Regulation 854/2004 regulates the organization of official controls on products of animal origin intended for human consumption. Besides the above-mentioned provisions, Regulation 882/2004 concerning official controls ensures the verification of compliance with food and feed law, animal health and animal welfare rules. Regulations 854 and 882 were then repealed by Regulation 2017/625 of 15 March 2017, which provided a single framework for all official controls. The three regulations (nn 852, 853, and 854) extended the Haccp system (previously addressed only to food industries) to the production and distribution of all food products, therefore also to primary food production. Article 1, paragraph 2 of Regulation 852, states that the regulation is inapplicable to primary production only when it takes place for private domestic use and to the direct supply of small quantities of primary products from the producer to the final consumer or to local retailers who supply the final consumer directly.

Chapter II of the above-mentioned regulation, entitled 'Food Business Operators Obligations', expressly states that for primary production and related operations, in accordance with Annex 1, the general hygiene requirements set out in Part A of Annex 1 apply.

Part ii of Annex 1, letter a), provides for stricter rules on documents and registrations for breeders and those who produce primary products of animal origin.

8. P. Borghi, Il rischio alimentare e il principio di precauzione, in Trattato di Diritto agrario, vol. II, L. Costato, A. Germanò, E. Rook Basile (eds), Torino 2011, pp. 53 ss.; A. Germanò, Corso di diritto agroalimentare, Torino 2007, pp. 49 ss.
9. *See* Court of Justice 5 June 1998, C-180/96 on the well-known issue of Bovine Spongiform Encephalopathy, so-called Mad cow, between the United Kingdom and the European Commission; the ruling of the Court of Justice on genetically modified organisms between Greenpeace France and the French Ministry of Agriculture 21 March 2000, C-6/99.

For the food industry operators, who carry out any phase of production, processing and distribution of animals, following the primary production activity and activities associated with it, the general hygiene requirements set out in Annex II apply.

In addition to the general hygiene requirements addressed, the food industry operators must comply with specific hygiene measures, if necessary, and among these in particular the microbiological criteria for foodstuffs covered by Regulation 2073/2005. The term 'microbiological criterion' means 'the acceptability of a product, a batch of foodstuffs or a process, based on the absence, presence or number of microorganisms, and/or on the quantity of their toxins/metabolites, per unit/s of mass, volume, area or batch'. In order to guarantee this microbiological safety, operators are required to take samples according to the methods indicated in Chapter III of Appendix 1, which establishes the rules for sampling and preparation of samples for analysis. For traditional products, meaning those products that according to Regulation 2074/2005 are historically recognized as traditional products, or manufactured according to registered or codified technical references, or according to traditional methods, or protected as traditional food products by national or EU legislation, Article 13 of Regulation 852/2004 recognizes the Member States the power to adopt national measures to conform to the requirements of the regulation itself. This is in order to allow the continuous use of traditional methods in one of the stages of production or processing of the food. To this last EU regulation is linked the national discipline represented primarily by the Legislative Decree No. 173 of 30 April 1998, which is directed to the enhancement of our gastronomic heritage, promoting typical products historically recognized as traditional products, providing for derogations from the general EU legislation on hygiene. It is also worth recalling Law No. 526 of 21 December 1999, which allows the marketing of typical products even if the methods of the strict provisions on Haccp are not observed and the production premises do not comply with them. For the typical products, indeed, the traditional methods of production are indispensable to guarantee the organoleptic characteristics that distinguish them.[10]

The fundamental need to ensure the health and hygiene safety of food has led the EU legislator to provide for the 'traceability' of food, animal feed for human consumption and any other substance intended incorporated into a food or feed at all stages of food chain, mandatory under Article 18 of Regulation 178 of 2002 from 1 January 2006. This term indicates the possibility to reconstruct backwards and follow the entire path of the food along the supply chain, at all stages of production, processing and distribution, so as to establish the identity, history and origin of the product.[11]

10. A. Germanò, M.P. Ragionieri, E. Rook Basile, Diritto agroalimentare. Le regole del mercato e dell'informazione alimentare, Torino 2019, pp. 62 ss.
11. F. Albisinni, Rintracciabilità di filiera nelle produzioni animali per la sicurezza alimentare, in Quaderni dei Georgofili, Atti della giornata di studio, Firenze, 2 dicembre 2004; P. Borghi, Tracciabilità e precauzione: nuove e vecchie regole per i produttori mediterranei nel mercato globale, in Diritto e giurisprudenza agraria e dell'ambiente, 2004; S. Rizzioli, in L. Costato, et al., Compendio di diritto alimentare, Milano 2019, p. 111; S. Masini, Corso di Diritto alimentare, Milano 2018, p. 160; L. Calcagni, Rintracciabilità delle carni bovine: garanzia per il benessere dei consumatori, in Diritto e giurisprudenza agraria e dell'ambiente, 2000, pp. 236-249,); *see also* J.R. Pavone, *Animal Welfare and Protection of Farm Animals in the European Union*, in

The food operator must be equipped with tools aimed at providing all the information required for the various stages of the food chain (name and address of the supplier, quantity, date of supply, batch number, if any) so as to be able to proceed with any withdrawal of products, targeted and accurate, and at the same time to provide information to consumers and officials responsible for controls.[12]

Traceability also responds to another need, which is the identification of subjects involved in the production process, differentiating the individual operators for the purposes of responsibility,[13] bringing the final product back to the different sources of production.

With regard to liability for food product defects, the EU legislator with Directive 99/44 has extended the factual responsibility of the producer, already provided for the producer of processed products by Directive 85/374, also to producers of agricultural commodities.

The defectiveness of the food product is linked to the concept of safety. Article 6 of the directive states that a product is defective when it does not offer the safety that can legitimately be expected.

And this in relation to the manner and timing in which it was introduced on the market and the intended use of the product. A safety obligation arises on the producer's part, inherent to the harmlessness of the product, different from the faulty concept which considers only defects that diminish the value of the use of the good, that is its exchange value.[14]

In order to assess the safety of the food product, all the instructions and warnings for the consumer contained in the main information tool, the label, must also be considered.

The further declination of food safety is, therefore, highlighted, as information security, which means suitable and exhaustive communication to the consumer of food both of the characteristics and of the modalities and quantity of food consumption.[15] As

L'Observateur des Nations Unies, vol. 45, pp. 7-30; M.P. Ragionieri C. Losavio, Traceability and the Hygiene Package, in L. Costato, F. Albisinni (eds), European Food Law, 2012; G. Maccioni, La sicurezza alimentare nel sistema di tutela multilivello, Pisa 2010, p. 166.

12. On official controls, V. Paganizza, Controlli ufficiali e regime sanzionatorio nel settore alimentare, in L. Costato, et al., Compendio di diritto alimentare, Milano pp. 325 ss.; F. Aversano, Sul controllo ufficiale nella filiera agroalimentare: antiche questioni e nuovi modelli, where the author stresses a possible 'coexistence', on the security and environmental side, assigning to the institutions a task of protection no longer limited to food safety, but of wider scope, as evidenced by the Communication from the Commission to the European Parliament, the Council, the Economic and Social Committee and the Regional Committee, A Farm to Fork Strategy for a fair, healthy and environmentally friendly food system of 20 maggio 2020, in Diritto Agroalimentare, n 2, 2020, p. 249.
13. *See* G. Palmieri, La responsabilità dell'impresa alimentare, in L. Paoloni, Alimenti, danno e responsabilità, Milano 2008, p. 93; M. Giuffrida, Responsabilità per danno da prodotto difettoso, in IV Dig /Civ, Agg, Torino 2009, p. 453.
14. A. Germanò, M.P. Ragionieri, E. Rook Basile, Diritto agroalimentare, Le regole del mercato degli alimenti e dell'informazione alimentare, Torino 2019, p. 50.
15. L. Costato, S. Rizzioli, Voce Sicurezza alimentare, in Digesto disc. Priv. Sez. civ., 2010; Costato, in L. Costato, et al., cit., p. 2.

an example, we recall the mandatory indication on the label of the possible presence of allergenic substances in food, such as, among others, eggs, milk, cereals.[16]

The European Union (EU) has paid particular attention in guaranteeing information to the final consumer of food, in order to overcome the 'information asymmetry' of modern contractual relations in which the consumer lacks the cognitive tools to make a conscious choice of the food being purchased.[17]

Only the informative obligation on food producers allows the correction of this information asymmetry, guaranteeing the consumer a preventive protection, no longer based, according to civil law, on the remedy after the damage.[18]

The label becomes the primal means of information on all those elements that attest to the safety of the product, its quality and price. The content of the label acquires the qualification of a 'technical rule', containing the mandatory indications for all foods, with now uniform regulations for all Member States of the EU, dictated by Regulation 1169 of 25 October 2011.[19]

This regulation, of a horizontal nature, is linked to regulatory measures of a particular kind by product, such as the Directive on Mineral Waters (Dir. 2009/54), the regulations on protected designations of origin, geographical indications or traditional specialities guaranteed (DOP, PGI, STG, Regulation 1151/2012), the Directive on Food Supplements (Dir. 2002/46), which integrate the requirements in general provided for by Regulation 1169/2011 for the labelling of all foods.

Voluntary indications may be added to the mandatory indications, both those defined by the aforementioned community regulations regarding PDO, IGP and STG,[20] and those of religious and ethical importance,[21] or those voluntary indications relating to the territory of production, i.e., simple geographical indications, and voluntary indications quality.[22]

16. M.P. Ragionieri, L'informazione sugli allergeni negli alimenti a seguito dell'entrata in vigore del regolamento 1169/2011, in I diritti della terra e del mercato agroalimentare, Liber Amicorum, Alberto Germanò, cit. p. 1539.
17. E. Sirsi, Il diritto all'educazione del consumatore di alimenti, in Riv,dir.agr., 2011, I, p. 508; S. Masini, Diritto all'informazione ed evoluzione in senso 'personalista' del consumatore, in Riv.dir.agr. 2011, I, 576; S. Bolognini, Linee guida della nuova normativa europea relativa alla fornitura di informazioni sugli alimenti ai consumatori, in Nuove leggi civ. comm., 2012, p. 613.
18. In this perspective, the market becomes the place of competition between businessmen, in which the system of information provided allows to pose on an equal level producers and consumers, A. Iannarelli, La disciplina dell'atto e dell'attività: i contratti fra imprese e tra imprese e consumatori, in N. Lipari, Diritto privato europeo, vol. II, Padova 1997, p. 505.
19. All the elements that make up the food must be indicated on the label: ingredients, additives and enzymes, flavours, sweeteners, colourings and preservatives, net quantity, actual alcoholic strength by volume for alcoholic beverages, instructions for use and storage conditions, name of the manufacturer, place of origin or provenance if omission is the possible cause of error, food supplements, GMOs and allergenic substances, nutritional values, expiry date, price.
20. I. Canfora, La valorizzazione dei prodotti agricoli regionali fra politiche territoriali e vincoli europei, in I diritti della terra e del mercato agroalimentare, Liber Amicorum, Alberto Germanò, cit., Tomo II, p. 1357.
21. M. Alabrese, Prodotti di qualità e alimenti halal, in A. Massart e F.M. Orsini, Diritti, culture e migrazioni (problemi di frontiera del settore agroalimentare), Pisa 2011, p. 77.
22. On these indications and the information 'Mountain product' and 'Product of the islands' and 'Product from organic farming', *see* A. Germanò, M.P. Ragionieri, E. Rook Basile, Diritto agroalimentare, cit., pp. 130 ss.; N. Lucifero, Il reg.(UE) 2018/848 sulla produzione biologica.

Consumer and human health protection at a high level emerges from the detailed regulatory framework. The so-called Rapid Alert System for Food and Feed (RASFF) integrated into its discipline and extended to the risks arising from the use of food or feed by Articles 50 and 52 of Regulation 178/2002 and of the implementing provisions referred to in Regulation 16/2011.

Member States, non-EU countries that have decided to join it, the European Free Trade Association, EFSA and the European Commission participate in the rapid alert system. The latter, having verified the correctness of the information received, transmits it to all parties on the network. If the refusal of food goods occurred at the EU border, the third countries concerned are also involved.

Each subject of the RASFF, all members of the network, identifies a contact point that must guarantee constant availability. The information, relating to a serious risk to human health deriving from food or materials in contact with them, for animal health deriving from feed, or for the environment, must contain all the elements to identify the product. Once the formal control of the information has been carried out, it is retransmitted by the Commission to all subjects of the network so that they can take the most appropriate measures to deal with any danger. In turn, these measures are communicated to the Commission, which transmits them to all members of the network. At the same time, citizens are informed about the measures adopted or to be adopted according to the nature, severity and extent of the risk.

If the countries concerned cannot set up adequate measures to deal with serious health risks for human health, animal health and environmental, in emergency situations (due to the extent of the risk or its spread or the characteristics of the hazard), the management of the same is entrusted at centralized level to the Commission alone, on own initiative or on the initiative of a Member State, in accordance with the provisions of Article 53 of Regulation 178/2002 and following the procedure of Article 58 of the regulation itself, which provides for the assistance and opinion of the Standing Committee on the Food Chain and Animal Health.

However, in particular cases of urgency, the Commission may, without the opinion of the Committee, take provisional and proportionate measures.

If the food crisis is such that the serious risk may require the intervention of all institutional subjects and scientists, the Commission establishes a crisis unit in which EFSA participates. The task of the Crisis Unit is to identify the best strategy to prevent, limit or reduce the risk to an 'acceptable level', involving any public or private entity that can help resolve the crisis.[23]

From the set of rules on RASFF, on emergency situations and on food crises, an articulated framework of guarantees emerges to prevent and manage the risks related

Principi e regole del nuovo regime nel sistema del diritto agroalimentare europeo, in Riv. Dir. agr., 2018, I, p. 477; I. Canfora, Organic food, in L. Costato, F. Albisinni, European and global food law, Milano 2016, p. 463.

23. V. Paganizza, Profili e criticità del RASFF, in Studi in onore di Luigi Costato, Napoli 2004, p. 289; Il sistema di allarme rapido per gli alimenti e i mangimi, in L. Costato, et al., Compendio di diritto alimentare, cit., p. 117.

to the food products that place the EU at the top of the protection of human and animal health, ensuring the consumer of food a suitable communication information.[24]

These rules combine to outline a European model of approach to the critical issues that may occur along the food supply chain, rigorous and synergistic, assigning defined roles and functions to the various participants.

The effectiveness of the system outlined is based on the execution of control and analysis of production processes and food, through inspections. The authorities that must carry out the inspections ensure that they are also carried out in exceptional circumstances such as the COVID-19 pandemic.[25]

The European Commission, precisely to ensure that food safety is not compromised by restrictions on circulation, aimed at limiting the spread of COVID-19, has adopted a regulation that allows Member States to carry out controls in ways and forms compatible with the aforementioned restrictions.[26]

24. S. Bolognini, La disciplina della comunicazione business to consumer nel mercato agroalimentare europeo, Torino 2012, pp. 2 ss.
25. We note that at the current state of scientific knowledge it does not appear that food represents a means of possible spread of the pandemic in relation to COVID-19, nor that there is a risk of contracting the infection from contaminated food packaging, even if recent studies report that the biological agent of COVID 19 (SARS-Cov-2) survives twenty-four hours on cardboard, and several days on hard surfaces, such as steel and plastic 'under experimental conditions – such as an environment with controlled relative humidity and temperature'.
26. *See* EU Commission Implementing Regulation 2020/466, of 30 March 2020 'on temporary measures to contain risks to human animal and plant health and animal welfare during certain serious disruptions of Member states control systems due to coronavirus (Covid-19)'.

CHAPTER 16

Food Waste in EU Food Law

David Röttgen & Francesca Allocco[*]

The topic of reducing food waste and, therefore, preventing food wastage has gradually become a priority in the European Union (EU) political agenda.
The authors have adopted a historical approach in order to illustrate the genesis of food waste in EU Food Law. The reduction of food waste is not a merely local/national issue, but a universal topic that involves many issues such as the environment, the economic effects, besides social, health and food safety issues. In the early days of this debate, the EU legislator had not fully understood the complexity and innovative scope of this matter.
At the beginning, a definition directly related to food waste has been missing: EU Institutions focused their activities on the general management of waste while food waste was still only addressed under the concept of 'bio-waste'.
Over the years, many EU Acts, as well as working documents, have been progressively implementing the regulatory basis to create a collective awareness of food waste production also allowing to create new opportunities.

§16.01 GENERAL OVERVIEW

Besides having an economic and environmental impact, food waste also has a social impact. The issue of reducing the production of food waste is one of the contemporary challenges that States and international institutions have to promptly face in relation to the progressive consumption of environmental resources for food production. At the same time, the pressing demand for raw materials, due to the increase of world population, must also be faced. The increase of hardship in some territories, stricken either by war or by poverty, or areas affected by unexpected climatic events, highlights

* We would like to thank E. Fidelbo and D. Morelli for contributing to the preparation of this chapter.

food waste as one of the most obvious paradoxes of contemporary reality. For all these reasons, international, European Union (EU) and national institutions have begun to take action as illustrated further on.

In 2019, Food and Agricultural Organization (FAO) published its annual report 'The state of food and agriculture: Moving forward on food loss and waste reduction':[1] this document reports the outcomes of the survey of food waste trends at the global level and throughout the food supply chain. It is interesting to note that in the more developed countries, food waste is produced more during the final stages of the food supply chain, i.e., sales and consumption, while in the less developed countries, production of food waste is concentrated more in the initial phase, i.e., agricultural production and post-harvesting.

Before any in-depth examination of the status of EU legislation, it is necessary to clarify that the concept of 'food waste' has not immediately acquired a unanimous definition.

Indeed, the EU Institutions have progressively implemented the legislation, which initially was not very exhaustive, with increasingly specific definitions: from the concept of 'biodegradable waste'[2] introduced by the Directive 1999/31/EC of 26 April 1999 on the landfill of waste (Landfill Directive), to the concept of 'bio-waste'[3] introduced by the Directive 2008/98/EC of the European Parliament and of the Council of 19 November 2008 on waste, also known as 'Waste Framework Directive' (WFD), to the targeted concept of 'food waste'[4] introduced only in 2018 thanks to Directive (EU) 2018/851 of the European Parliament and of the Council of 30 May 2018, amending Directive 2008/98/EC on waste (Directive 2018/851).

In any case, the definition most representative of the general meaning of 'food waste' – and which will be adopted in this paper – is that set out by FAO in 2019. In accordance with the implicit provisions of the Sustainable Development Goals of Agenda 2030 (SDGs), in particular 'Target 12.3', which will be treated in §16.05, the terms 'food loss' and 'food waste' have been interpreted as 'the decrease in quantity or quality of food along the food supply chain'.[5]

Food loss represents an event that occurs during the process phases along the food supply chain, from production to harvesting and processing of the food (e.g., slaughtering). Therefore, 'food losses as occurring along the food supply chain from harvest/slaughter/catch up to, but not including, the retail level'.[6] As a result, it is estimated that 'globally, around 14 percent of all food from post-harvest up to, but not excluding, retail is lost'.[7]

1. FAO. *The state of food and agriculture: Moving forward on food loss and waste reduction* (2019).
2. Council Directive 1999/31/EC of 26 April 1999 on the landfill of waste. Article 2(m).
3. Directive 2008/98/EC of the European Parliament and of the Council of 19 November 2008 on waste and repealing certain Directives. Article 3(4).
4. Directive (EU) 2018/851 of the European Parliament and of the Council of 30 May 2018 amending Directive 2008/98/EC on waste. Article 1(3)(c).
5. *See supra* note 1, xii.
6. *Ibid.*, xii.
7. *Ibid.*, 22.

The above-mentioned phases are, indeed, the moment when the real food waste as defined by the FAO occurs, i.e., 'Food waste, which occurs at the retail and consumption level'.[8] This also includes the transport and logistics of food products, the positioning on the shelves and the selection of products by large-scale retailers. Moreover, the administration and consumption of food, leading to the inevitable elimination of those products which, during the journey, have lost the freshness and/or integrity of the packaging, or those foods close to the expiry date which have been discarded by retailers or by consumers themselves. Food waste is also spawned in stocks: there are large quantities of food that remain in warehouses or refrigerators at home for a long time and which, due to being unused, must necessarily be discarded because they are no longer edible. In addition, another factor in the production of food waste is represented by food administration, distribution and consumption activities (i.e., in restaurants, 'fast food' production and sale points and in hospital, school and company canteens).

Pursuant to the provisions included in the SDGs Target 12.3, as described in §16.05 below, recently FAO has removed food used for other economic purposes, such as feed and seed production, from the above definitions. Likewise, non-edible organic parts included in the food itself have been excluded.[9]

Within the first stage of the food supply chain, there are several causes that encourage the growth of food loss. The most representative are: (i) overproduction in the agri-food industry, (ii) defective product composition (unsuitable size or shape), (iii) deterioration of the product and/or its packaging, (iv) marketing strategies in product selection, (v) inadequate management of food stocks.

It should also be added that food waste is often the result of (a) inadequate planning of purchases, (b) compulsive over-purchasing, (c) confusion over labels ('best before' and 'use by'), (d) poor conservation or management of food at home, (e) the preparation of excess food and (f) the failure to reuse leftovers for the preparation of new foods.[10]

§16.02 MONITORING: QUANTITATIVE ESTIMATES

According to an estimate by FAO still in 2011 'Roughly one-third of the edible parts of food produced for human consumption, gets lost or wasted globally, which is about 1.3 billion ton per year.'[11]

'Every year in Europe a growing amount of healthy, edible food – some estimates say up to 50% – is lost along the entire food supply chain, in some cases all the way up to the consumer and becomes waste.'[12] A 'study published by the Commission estimates annual food waste generation in the 27 Member States at approximately 89

8. *Ibid.*, xii.
9. *Ibid.*, xiii.
10. *See supra* note 4, 39.
11. FAO. *Global food losses and food waste: Extent, causes and prevention* (2011), 4.
12. Resolution of European Parliament of 19 January 2012 on how to avoid food wastage: strategies for a more efficient food chain in the EU [2011/2175(INI)], Whereas(A).

million tonnes, or 179 kg per capita'.[13] Furthermore 'post-harvest losses amount to about 14% of total production and another 15% is lost in distribution and in household waste, three-fifths of the total supply increase needed by 2050 could be achieved if we simply stopped wasting food'.[14] All the above figures reveal that Europe's total food waste costs EUR 143 billion a year.[15] Only by optimizing the collection and distribution phases, it would be possible to reduce the amount of food wasted each year by almost a third.[16] According to the forecast made by the European Parliament in 2012, in the absence of resolute action, it was estimated that 'total food waste will have risen to approximately 126 million tonnes (a 40% increase) by 2020 unless additional preventive actions or measures are taken'.[17] In 2021, the European Commission assessed that '88 million tonnes of food waste are generated in the EU each year with associated costs estimated at €143 billion'.[18]

It is also to be noted that despite the lack of a general and widespread application of the common methodology for data collection, recent studies state that there is still a moderately high uncertainty regarding estimates of the amount of food waste generated in Europe: 'the approximate 95% confidence interval is ± 14 million tonnes (or ± 16%). The results for the production and processing sectors in particular are likely to change once more studies become available'.[19]

And further, it should also be mentioned that in 2050 the world's population will reach almost 10 billion.[20] Therefore, the 'global demand for agricultural outputs is forecast to increase by 35-50 percent between 2012 and 2050 as a result of population and income growth'.[21]

However, the growth trend of the population does not imply that there will be an increase in the quality of life and also in the food supply. In fact, in 2018, 815 million people in the world suffered from chronic malnutrition.[22] Within just one year, this estimate increased further to 820 million people.[23] It is clear that an increase of 5 million undernourished people in a single year is a serious wake-up call, especially in

13. *Ibid.*, Whereas(B).
14. *Ibid.*, Whereas(F).
15. FUSIONS, Estimates of European food waste levels https://ec.europa.eu/food/safety/food_waste/stop_en (March 2016); K.L. Thyberg & D.J. Tonjes, *Drivers of food waste and their implications for sustainable policy development*, Resour. Conserv. Recycl., Vol. 106 (January 2016) 110-123.
16. *See supra* note 11.
17. *See supra* note 13.
18. https://ec.europa.eu/food/sites/food/files/safety/docs/fw_lib_reduce-food-waste-eu_faqs.pdf.
19. EU FUSION, *European project FUSIONS releases EU-28 estimates of food waste levels and a Food Waste Quantification Manual*, Newsletter 2 March 2020.
20. T. Searchinger et al., *Creating a sustainable food future: a menu of solutions to feed nearly 10 billion people by 2050*. WRI. Washington DC (2018).
21. *See supra* note 1, 90.
22. UN SDG 2. World Food Day: A #ZeroHunger World by 2030 is possible, available on http://sdg2advocacyhub.org/actions/world-food-day-2018 (October 2018).
23. *See supra* note 1, Foreword.

comparison to its 'nemesis': in 2017 a scientific study was published stating the presence of 600 million people suffering from obesity in 2015.[24]

Looking at Europe, to date '79 million people are still living below the poverty line in the European Union' (...) 'of these, 16 million have received food aid from charitable institutions',[25] while 43 million people cannot afford a quality meal every second day.[26]

In Italy, the economic value of wasted food is about EUR 13 billion per year, with an average of 149 kg of wasted food per person.[27]

Another interesting consideration concerns the effects of food waste on climate change: the large amount of food waste plays a significant role in global warming, leading to the production of carbon dioxide and methane. According to the provisions of the European Parliament Resolution of 19 January 2012, as confirmed five years later by the Resolution of 16 May 2017:

> for every kilogram of food produced, 4,5 kg of CO_2 are released into the atmosphere; whereas in Europe the approximately 89 Mt of food wasted produce 170 Mt CO_2 eq./yr, broken down thus: food industry 59 Mt CO_2 eq./yr, domestic consumption 78 Mt CO_2 eq./yr, other 33 Mt CO_2 eq./yr; whereas the production of the 30% of food which ends up not being consumed accounts for an additional 50% of use of water resources for irrigation, while producing a kilogram of beef requires 5-10 tonnes of water.[28]

As regards greenhouse gas (GHG) emissions associated with food losses, according to the latest estimates of FAO,[29] the largest contribution is attributed to cereal and legume crops, followed by roots, tubers and plant crops. Due to food perishability, careless storage in both warehouses and transports may end up in decreased food integrity or even food waste.

According to the International Panel on Climate Change (IPCC) 'By 2050, agricultural GHG emissions associated with production of food that might be wasted may increase to 1.9-2.5 Gt CO2-eq yr-1.'[30] Therefore, the growth of food waste will inevitably lead to an increase in CO_2 emissions on the planet, thereby directly exacerbating the effects of climate change. A rigorous overall strategy to reduce food waste would be beneficial to the reduction of GHG, indeed acting 'as a climate change mitigation measure that provides synergies with food security and land use'.[31]

24. The New England Journal of Medicine, 'Health Effects of Overweight and Obesity in 195 Countries over 25 years' http://www.nejm.org/doi/full/10.1056/NEJMoa1614362; Global Burden of Disease Study 2015, 'Obesity and Overweight Prevalence 1980-2015' (GBD 2015).
25. *See supra* note 12, Whereas(C).
26. *See supra* note 15.
27. Federalimentare, *Food recovery and waste reduction foodward project*, 2015; ISPRA, *Food waste: a systemic approach for structural prevention and reduction*, Report n. 267/2017.
28. *See supra* note 12, Whereas(L); Resolution of European Parliament of 16 May 2017 on initiative on resource efficiency: reducing food waste, improving food safety (2016/2223(INI)), Whereas(D).
29. *See supra* note 1.
30. IPCC, *Climate Change and Land* (SRCCL) Chapter 5: Food Security, 2019, 81.
31. *Ibid.*, 81.

§16.03 THE FIRST (SOFT) REGULATORY ACTIONS IN EUROPE

The first thoughts of the EU Institutions on food waste may be identified in the Landfill Directive. Indeed, the Council Directive 75/442/EEC of 15 July 1975 and the subsequent amendments introduced by Council Directive 91/156/EEC of 18 March 1991, both relating to waste, do not deal - not even incidentally - with this matter.

Thus, in the Landfill Directive of 1999, although there was no specific definition of food waste, it provided for the reduction of disposal in landfills of the so-called biodegradable waste, i.e., 'any waste that is capable of undergoing anaerobic or aerobic decomposition, such as food and garden waste, and paper and paperboard'.[32] The aim of such provision, however, was to reduce the on-site production of methane gas and, consequently, the increase in global warming.[33] To achieve these goals, Member States had to draw up within two years after the adoption of the Directive a national strategy for the reduction in the amount of biodegradable waste going to landfills. The idea was to provide containing measures by encouraging separate collection, recycling, composting, biogas production and energy recovery, in order to reach within 2016 a progressive reduction of more than 50% of biodegradable municipal waste produced and surveyed in 1995.[34]

Article 5(2) provided for reduction targets but did not impose compliance on Member States. Therefore, the failure to meet the reduction thresholds has not led to any liability on the part of the Member States many of which have continued to landfill biodegradable waste.

Only a few years later, EU Institutions faced the need to develop the regulation of the food sector, through the enactment of Regulation (EC) No. 178/2002 of the European Parliament and of the Council (Food Safety Regulation): Article 2 identifies what was legally meant by 'food' i.e.:

> any substance or product, whether processed, partially processed or unprocessed, intended to be, or reasonably expected to be ingested by humans. 'Food' includes drink, chewing gum and any substance, including water, intentionally incorporated into the food during its manufacture, preparation or treatment. It includes water after the point of compliance as defined in Article 6 of Directive 98/83/EC and without prejudice to the requirements of Directives 80/778/EEC and 98/83/EC.[35]

This definition of food therefore makes it possible to include in its general meaning all food generated along the food supply chain, from production to the last stage of consumption. In the definition of food are also included those non-edible parts which, however, cannot be separated until the moment of consumption. Feeding stuffs are excluded. Similarly, by-products of the food industry, which by their nature fulfil the criteria of Article 5(1) of the WFD, cannot be included in the definition of food.

---

32. *See supra* note 2, Article 2(m).
33. *Ibid.*, Whereas (16,17).
34. *Ibid.*, Article 5(2).
35. Regulation (EC) No. 178/2002 of the European Parliament and of the Council of 28 January 2002 laying down the general principles and requirements of food law, establishing the European Food Safety Authority and laying down procedures in matters of food safety. Article 2.

The Food Safety Regulation has regulated the phases of (a) production, (b) processing and (c) distribution of food, but not the post-consumption/distribution phase, in which food waste is generated. Furthermore, it does not contain any provisions for the transfer of food surpluses. This is because when the Food Safety Regulation was written no common methods that could precisely quantify the scale of the problem had yet been developed. As a consequence, it was impossible to define the real extent of food waste and the projection of food waste reduction targets in terms of tonnes.

Under such perspective, Food Safety Regulation represented the first regulatory act in the field of food products, also adopted for this function by means of an EU Regulation. However, it cannot be considered as a regulatory instrument in the field of food waste, precisely because these are different disciplines, even though they share the same origin of their subject matter, that is to say, food.

§16.04 WFD 2008/98/EC AND 'GREEN PAPER'

Since 2008, EU Institutions have been increasing their efforts in the field of 'bio-waste' and, indirectly, food waste.

Pursuant to the precautionary principle and to the prevention principle in the environmental field, as laid down in Article 174(2) of the Treaty establishing the European Community (TEC), reiterated in Article 191 of the Treaty on the Functioning of the European Union (TFEU), the WFD was adopted by the European Parliament and of the Council on 19 November 2008.[36]

For the first time some elements - as detailed below - have been introduced providing important guidance for food waste.

The WFD, at that time, set as main objectives for the Member States the achievement of a recycling society (nowadays: circular economy), through efficient systems that comply with the priority order of the waste (treatment) hierarchy based on: (a) prevention; (b) preparing for re-use; (c) recycling; (d) other recovery, e.g., energy recovery; (e) disposal.[37]

As to the production of food waste, while it is true that in 2008 the same waste had not been specifically examined by the EU legislator, the WFD demands, in accordance with the waste hierarchy, to support the separate collection and appropriate treatment of organic waste in order to reduce emissions from landfill,[38] as per Article 5 of the Landfill Directive. Thereby, over the years, the WFD has played a fundamental role in resolving environmental problems concerning the production and management of waste. The WFD provides a framework legislation that allows the application of general principles both to legislation differentiated by type of waste (i.e., biodegradable waste, batteries, end-of-life vehicles, packaging, Polychlorinated Biphenyls (PCB), Polyvinyl Chloride (PVC), waste water, ships, Waste Electrical and Electronic Equipment (WEEE), waste mineral oil, tyres, radioactive waste) and to

36. *See supra* note 3.
37. *Ibid.*, Article 4.
38. *Ibid.*, Whereas 35.

specific legislation for various types of treatment (i.e., incineration, landfill, material recycling, other recovery and, last but not least, reuse and prevention, etc.).

In order to ensure the protection of the environment by means of the so-called recycling society, the WFD intends to achieve reduction in waste production. This also included the food sector indirectly through the establishment of prevention plans and programmes, allowing Member States to use different approaches in relation to the collection of household waste,[39] which inevitably includes a part of food waste, only providing for an increase in the quantity destined to reuse and recycle by 2020.[40] Further measures adopted by the WFD were and still are the mechanisms of definition of so-called By-products, referred to in Article 5, and of the status of 'End of Waste' (EoW) referred to in Article 6 below.

These legal provisions may represent one of the most effective ways of managing some of the 'causes' of food waste. In particular, the By-product and EoW definitions can be applied to every type of waste and to every treatment carried out, including food waste.

The concept of By-product is fundamental for achieving waste-prevention, set at top of the waste hierarchy. To qualify as a 'By-product', a substance/object resulting from a production process that is not primarily intended for the production of the same substance/object, must satisfy all the following conditions at the same time:

a) further use of the substance or object is certain;
b) the substance or object can be used directly without any further processing other than normal industrial practice;
c) the substance or object is produced as an integral part of a production process; and
d) further use is lawful, i.e., the substance or object fulfils all relevant product, environmental and health protection requirements for the specific use and will not lead to overall adverse environmental or human health impacts.[41]

The concept of By-product is to be strictly distinguished from the concept of EoW. The acknowledgement of the status of EoW is an indispensable lever to achieve the recycling society. The reasons for the application of EoW and its widespread use can be briefly outlined in the following points: (1) encouraging the production of high-quality goods or materials; (2) improving consumer confidence; (3) avoiding unnecessary trade barriers and promoting the internal market. These aims can be achieved through the fulfilment of the criteria identified in Article 6, which are:

(a) the substance or object is commonly used for specific purposes;
(b) a market or demand exists for such a substance or object;
(c) the substance or object fulfils the technical requirements for the specific purposes and meets the existing legislation and standards applicable to products; and

39. *Ibid.*, Whereas 41.
40. *Ibid.*, Article 11(2)(c).
41. *Ibid.*, Article 5(1) By-products.

(d) the use of the substance or object will not lead to overall adverse environmental or human health impacts.[42]

Moreover, Article 3(4) of WFD introduced for the first time the concept of 'bio-waste' corresponding to:

> biodegradable garden and park waste, food and kitchen waste from households, restaurants, caterers and retail premises and comparable waste from food processing plants.[43]

However, in the WFD form 2008, the concept of food waste had not yet acquired its conceptual autonomy. It still remained absorbed in the overall meaning of 'organic waste'. Consequently, the indication of the objectives set out in Article 22, which encourage the separate collection of bio-waste and provide for treatment in a way that fulfils a high level of environmental protection and the use of environmentally safe materials produced from bio-waste, was not yet relevant to the detailed determination of the production and management of food waste.[44] This is due to the fact that it has not yet been separately identified as different from organic waste. In any case, although in 2008, the WFD had not directly addressed the issue of reducing food waste, it was the main benchmark for the adoption of a proper waste management system. An essential prerequisite to this is the importance of the definitions in the WFD, necessary to enable subsequent research to have a common reference point.

After the definition of 'bio-waste' and the publication of the WFD in 2008, the European Commission published the 'Green Paper on the management of bio-waste in the European' ('Green Paper').[45] This document analysed the numerous data on the 2008 state of the art as to the application of the different methods of management of biodegradable waste in different Member States.

Given that Green Paper adopted the same definition of 'bio-waste' as the WFD,[46] any data related to this research represents the general levels of production and management of the comprehensive kind of 'bio-waste' in Europe. Therefore, it cannot be considered symptomatic of the mere trend of food waste flows.

It was first noticed that the management of 'bio-waste' is not unique and exclusive: several treatment operations (i.e., pre-treatment for landfill, incineration with more or less energy recovery, anaerobic digestion for biogas production, high-quality composting, etc.) can be carried out by each Member State according to its preferences.[47] In other words, economic and territorial factors necessarily force every State to make different choices with regard to different treatment options, both in terms of energy availability and soil conditions, as well as the costs of supply. Nevertheless,

42. *Ibid.*, Article 6(1) End-of-waste status.
43. *Ibid.*, Article 3(4).
44. *Ibid.*, Article 22 Bio-waste.
45. European Commission, *Green Paper on the management of bio-waste in the European Union* [COM(2008) 811 final].
46. *Ibid.*, 14.
47. *Ibid.*, 15.

the best treatment option must take into account an inherent characteristic of bio-waste: it is putrescible and wet. The Green Paper states that 'kitchen waste' specifically - the current wet fraction - contains up to 80% water.[48] This leads to the conclusion that incineration of bio-waste is not advantageous if there is a high percentage of wet waste causing lowcalorific performance capacity.

In 2010, in accordance with the Green Paper, the European Commission developed an impact assessment document on the management of bio-waste which included different treatment options and future recycling targets.[49] Its main purpose was to identify measures appropriate to ensuring better management of bio-waste in Europe for the next ten years, also involving additional aspects of operational management, such as the more political aspects of environmental, economic and social impact. Studies have been carried out on the different treatment systems for each phase in which bio-waste is generated: from prevention in the wider sense, to home composting, to the evaluation of an obligation to separate collection, to the composting strategy in large scale, to the analysis of anaerobic digestion for biogas production. This outstanding assessment has been consolidated later by a European Commission document, which sets out actions the Member States could carry out in order to increase efficiency and reduce the production of bio-waste, notably in the following areas:[50]

- development of waste prevention plans and programmes in accordance with the waste hierarchy;
- promotion of separate collection and biological treatment and composting of bio-waste;
- promotion of minimum quality standards for the use of compost and digestate in agriculture in order to preserve/restore soil conditions;
- stopping landfilling of bio-waste in order to produce high-quality compost for CO_2 reduction purposes;
- production of fuels from the bio-waste treatment process.

Subsequently Regulation 1169/2011 on the provision of food information to consumers was introduced.[51] It provides for the appropriate use of labels indicating a food's 'best before' and 'use by' dates, defining the limits of the two labels: in the case of highly perishable food, the expiry date replaces the date of minimum durability, after which the food is defined as a risk to human health. This contributes to preventing the production of food waste. However, the consumer is not always aware of the difference between these two definitions. Consequently, there are cases where the use of labelling has led to an increase in food waste, with the misconception that health damage could be caused if the minimum shelf life date is passed. This clearly shows that correct and

48. *Ibid.*, 2.
49. European Commission DG Environment, *Assessment of the options to improve the management of bio-waste in the European Union*, Final Report (February 2010), 89-93-120-124.
50. Communication from the Commission of 18 May 2010 on future steps in bio-waste management in the European Union [COM(2010)235 final].
51. Regulation (EU) No. 1169/2011 of the European Parliament and of the Council of 25 October 2011 on the provision of food information to consumers. Article 2, 24; Annex X.

widespread consumer information is an essential instrument for the complete reduction of the food waste generated.

European Parliament Resolution of 19 January 2012 was a first approach in exclusively focusing on food waste.[52] It encouraged public institutions, housing, schools, hospitals and food banks to collect and redistribute unused, but still edible food, to people in need, as an additional and not a substitute measure to current social protection systems. Furthermore, this Resolution emphasizes the need for citizens to be informed not only about the causes and consequences of waste but also on how to reduce it. However, while this Resolution is overall beneficial, it had not yet developed an independent definition of food waste, thus leaving the debate open.

§16.05 'SUSTAINABLE DEVELOPMENT GOALS' AND 'CIRCULAR ECONOMY PACKAGE'

The years which followed the regulation have been characterized by an increasing attention of international and EU literature as to the analysis of the exclusive phenomenon of food waste. Working tables and groups as well as programmes have been set up in order to identify and give priority to actions aimed at the prevention and reduction of the quantities of food loss and food waste produced.[53,54,55]

Therefore, on 25 September 2015, the United Nations (UN) General Assembly adopted the Sustainable Development Goals (SDGs) of Agenda 2030:[56] such sustainability programme, supported and endorsed by 193 UN Member States, consists of seventeen different targets for the initiation of sustainability in a wide range of fields of application. SDGs Target 12 'Ensure sustainable consumption and production patterns' aims to progressively ensure sustainable models of the entire production and consumption cycle, through a systematic approach and the involvement of all stakeholders in the sector, right down to the final consumers. The purpose is to achieve the goal of halving the amount of global food waste per capita in the retail and consumption phase by 2030, as well as reducing the amount of food loss from the food production and supply chain, including the post-harvest phase (SDGs Target 12.3).[57]

As a result, at the EU level the European Commission adopted the Communication 'Closing the loop – An EU action plan for the Circular Economy' (hereinafter

52. *See supra* note 12.
53. UN General Assembly Resolution A/Res/66/288 of 27 July 2012 on the outcome of the Rio + 20 Conference, entitled 'The Future We Want'.
54. EC Health and Consumers Directorate-General, *Member State Working Group on Food Losses and Food Waste Draft Terms of Reference (ToR)*, Ref. Ares (2014)2332096 – 14 July 2014.
55. Decision N. 1386/2013/EU of the European Parliament and of the Council of 20 November 2013 on a General Union Environment Action Programme to 2020 'Living well, within the limits of our planet'.
56. UN, Sustainable Development Goals (SDG) of the 2030 Agenda for Sustainable Development, (2015).
57. *Ibid.*, SDG 12: Responsible Consumption and Production in https://unric.org/it/obiettivo-12-garantire-modelli-sostenibili-di-produzione-e-di-consumo/ (31 October 2019-24 January 2020).

'Action Plan')[58] on 2 December 2015: it summarizes the work that preceded it and indicates the way to future decisions and it contains draft amendments to six relevant directives: the amendment referred to the WFD, the Directive 94/62/EC (packaging and packaging waste), the Landfill Directive and a group of directives consisting of No. 2000/53/EC (end-of-life vehicles), No. 2006/66/EC (batteries and accumulators) and No. 2012/19/EU (WEEE).

Through this Action Plan, the European Commission has drafted a timeframe of actions aimed at defining ad hoc measures to implement sustainability principles in the different areas where the benefits of the circular economy are felt throughout the life cycle of the product (extraction of raw materials, production, consumption). This also included waste management (encouraging the use of EoW) and the examination of the single relevant sectors (plastics, food waste, essential raw materials, construction and demolition waste, biomass and organic products). In particular, with regard to food waste and in order to reach SDGs Target 12.3, the European Commission acknowledged interventions carried out and undertook to set up a platform in order to develop scheduled actions, such as:

- to develop a common methodology to quantify food waste and define its indicators;
- to share best practice in waste prevention and raising awareness on waste prevention;
- to adopt measures to clarify Union legislation on waste, food and feed;
- to facilitate the donation of food and the safe use of food and by-products from the food chain and from the feed production;
- to review the food labelling system in compliance with the provisions of the Food Safety Regulation.

All Member States are represented in the European Platform for Food Loss and Food Waste (FLW Platform),[59] established the following year and active until 2021. It makes it possible to discuss the most appropriate measures on this topic with EU Institutions, industry experts and selected stakeholders in order to achieve objectives defined together. These are divided into several sub-groups for debate, each for a specific theme: (1) food donation; (2) food waste measurement; (3) action and implementation; (4) date marking and food waste prevention.

With the adoption of the Action Plan and in order to support the achievement of the agreed sustainability objectives, the European Commission adopted on 2 December 2015 a second proposal amending Directives 2008/98/EC, so-called Proposal 2015(595).[60] The first one was presented by the European Commission in 2014[61] but in

58. Communication from the Commission to the European Parliament, the Council, the European economic and social Committee and the Committee of the regions, *Closing the loop – An EU action plan for the Circular Economy* [COM(2015) 614 final].
59. EU Platform on Food Losses and Food Waste available on http://ec.europa.eu/food/safety/food_waste/eu_actions/eu-platform_en. and https://ec.europa.eu/food/safety/food_waste/eu_actions/food-donation_en, last visiting on 7 May 2020.
60. Proposal for a directive of the European Parliament and of the Council amending Directive 2008/98/EC on waste [COM (2015)595 final].

December of the same year the European Commission decided to withdraw a pending legislative proposal on waste with a view to proposing a new package covering the entire economic cycle and not just waste reduction targets by the end of 2015. The main reason for this change was that recent trends have made EU institutions even more aware of the need for more careful resource management, from both an environmental and economic point of view.

As regards the reduction of food waste, the Proposal 2015(595) presented measures according to the Action Plan, ensuring the separate collection of bio-waste and recommending Member States to adopt a common methodology for the data acquisition monitoring food waste production. It seems obvious that adopting an EU strategy to reduce food waste without a common monitoring methodology would significantly undermine all the work done: it is first of all necessary to define how to gather data, otherwise it is difficult to understand if and how much progress the measure has achieved. Proposal 2015(595) intended to incorporate the actions set out in the Action Plan and, consequently, the SDGs indicated by the UN. However, as to food waste, once again no autonomous concept of food waste was proposed and, therefore, any action aimed at monitoring and preventing it would have been flawed at the origin and ineffective in achieving the objectives set. In fact, although there was a marginal change in the definition of 'bio-waste' in Proposal 2015(595) as:

> 4. 'bio-waste' means biodegradable garden and park waste, food and kitchen waste from households, restaurants, caterers and retail premises, comparable waste from food processing plants and other waste with similar biodegradability properties that is comparable in nature, composition and quantity;[62]

it was neither persuasive nor so ambitious, as it was still stuck in considering food waste a necessary part of the macro-definition of 'bio-waste'. Therefore, Proposal 2015(595) had not made a significant contribution to the development of the legislation in question about food waste.

For this reason, as will be better explained in §16.07 below, Proposal 2015(595) itself underwent a thorough revision which, in 2018, ended with the adoption of the final text of Directive 2018/851 amending the WFD dating from 2008.

§16.06 LEGALLY DEFINING FOOD WASTE: FIRST ATTEMPTS

The scarce incisiveness of the efforts so far taken at European and international level made EU Institutions aware that the major shortcomings were arising from the enduring absence of an autonomous food waste definition.

When, in 2016, the FLW Platform was being established, the European project FUSIONS 'Food Use for Social Innovation by Optimising Waste Prevention Strategies'

61. Proposal for a Directive of the European Parliament and of the Council amending Directives 2008/98/EC on waste, 94/62/EC on packaging and packaging waste, 1999/31/EC on the landfill of waste, 2000/53/EC on end-of-life vehicles, 2006/66/EC on batteries and accumulators and waste batteries and accumulators, and 2012/19/EU on waste electrical and electronic equipment. [(COM(2014)397); (COM(2014)398)].
62. *Ibid.*, Article 1(2)(c).

(FUSIONS),[63] funded by the European Commission Framework Program No. 7, terminated.

Run from 2012 to 2016, FUSIONS brought together universities, businesses and consumer organizations from thirteen Member States in order to implement a harmonized food waste data monitoring system. This latter would enable policymakers to develop guidelines for a common European policy in order to achieve European Commission's target of a 50% reduction of food waste by 2030, in accordance with SDGs Target 12.3. A first final report, presenting estimates of food waste arising in the EU-28,[64] played a crucial role for the subsequent legislation. As it intended to collect in sixteen categories the European food waste production data, a common definitional framework was needed. The report thus holds the first definition of 'Food Waste':[65]

> Fractions of 'food and inedible parts of food removed from the food supply chain' to be recovered or disposed (including – composted, crops ploughed in/not harvested, anaerobic digestion, bioenergy production, co-generation, incineration, disposal to sewer, landfill or discarded to sea).

As a very last outcome of the FUSIONS project, a further report had been issued addressing recommendations to EU Institutions and Member States.[66] First of all, it recommended a common framework for food waste definition and a standardised methodology for data collection strengthening the FLW Platform. In addition, the report recommended to (1) develop guidelines for policy interventions stimulating social innovation to achieve food waste reduction/prevention, (2) facilitate food donations supporting a favourable EU and national legislative framework, harmonizing value-added tax (VAT) rules for donating food. In conclusion, FUSIONS's fact-based approach has provided copious and punctual information, which enabled decision-making bodies to define policy targets and operational guidelines for subsequent EU regulatory interventions.

Such informational heritage has been the basis for the adoption of the European Parliament Resolution of 16 May 2017 on resource efficiency to reduce food waste (hereinafter 'Resolution').[67] The Resolution takes into account FUSIONS' final report and the outcomes of the Action Plan, pushing to establish a comprehensive action plan on food waste covering the various policy areas and outlining the strategy for the years ahead. The Resolution stated that circular economy tools have to be implemented and adapted to the food supply chain; By-product and EoW, as laid down by the WFD, are crucial to optimize the use of food unavoidably lost or discarded. Following FUSIONS recommendation, the European Parliament has submitted the first Food Waste definition held by EU institution:

---

63. FUSIONS, *Food Use for Social Innovation by Optimising Waste Prevention Strategies*, available on https://www.eu-fusions.org/.
64. FUSIONS, *Estimates of European food waste levels*, March 2016.
65. *Ibid.*, 7.
66. FUSIONS, *D3.5 Recommendations and Guidelines for a European common policy framework on food waste prevention*. 3-8 July 2016.
67. Resolution of the European Parliament of 16 May 2017 on 'Resource efficiency: reducing food waste, improving food safety' [2016/2223(INI)].

> food waste means food intended for human consumption, either in edible or inedible status, removed from the production or supply chain to be discarded, including at primary production, processing, manufacturing, transportation, storage, retail and consumer levels, with the exception of primary production losses.

The Resolution, as a non-binding act of the European Parliament, calls on European Commission, Council and Member States to explore modalities for donating food, in order to remove legal and administrative barriers, both local and supranational, that still prevent from using such an environmental and social sustainability tool.[68]

As a good practice, European Parliament pointed out the Italian Good Samaritan legislation (hereinafter 'Law 155/2003').[69] In particular, according to Law 155/2003, non-profit organizations, where acting as food donors to the needy, were recognized the legal status of end consumer, thus preventing them from criminal or civil liability and ensuring a better conservation, transport, storage and use of food.

Following the European Parliament's Resolution exhortation, on 28 August 2017, European Commission adopted the Decision (EU) 2017/1508 on the reference document on Best Environmental Management Practices for the food and beverage manufacturing sector (BEMPs food and beverage)[70] in order to stimulate the use of by-products and to prevent food waste.[71] Being such BEMPs food and beverage adopted by means of a decision, they are directly applicable and binding on those to whom they are addressed.[72] In this case, BEMPs food and beverage are addressed to Eco-Management and Audit Scheme (EMAS)-registered organizations in the food and beverage manufacturing sector and are intended to tackle the most significant direct and indirect environmental aspects for food supply chain manufacturers and the related main environmental pressures.[73] Thus, even though the reference document in hand is not meant to solely deal with food waste, this latter is necessarily encompassed in the suggested BEMP scope.

BEMPs food and beverage provide for general measures aimed at tackling specific shortcomings, as well as sector-specific benchmarks of excellence (manufacture of bread, biscuits and cakes; cheese-making operation; production of meat and poultry meat products; manufacture of olive oil; manufacture of wine; manufacture of beer; processing of coffee; manufacture of fruit juice).

Food losses reduction strategies primarily focus on the first stage of the food supply chain, i.e., the production phase. BEMPs food and beverage convey best available techniques (BAT) already experienced in the sector and which have now

---

68. *Ibid.*, paras 96-110.
69. Law 25 June 2003 No. 155, *Discipline of the distribution of food products for social solidarity purposes* (G.U. 1 July 2003 No. 150).
70. Decisions (EU) 2017/1508 of 28 August 2017 on the reference document on best environmental management practice, sector environmental performance indicators and benchmarks of excellence for the food and beverage manufacturing sector under Regulation (EC) No. 1221/2009 of the European Parliament and of the Council on the voluntary participation by organizations in a Community EMAS.
71. *Ibid.*, Whereas n. 2.
72. TFEU Article 288 (former TEC Article 249).
73. *See supra* note 70, Chapter 3.1.9. Avoiding food waste in manufacturing operations.

become of general relevance due to said Decision (EU) 2017/1508 on BEMPs food and beverage.

In particular, as regards food waste, BEMPs food and beverage provide benchmarks of excellence for each sector given, for instance:

- fruit residues from manufacture of fruit juice are recovered as valuable products (e.g., pectin, essential oils), or used as animal feed or as co-substrate in an anaerobic digestion plant (BEMP 3.7.1);
- cheese-making operations: the whey is recovered and treated in order to obtain other products intended for human consumption, based on market demand. Excess whey is employed instead for animal feed or for anaerobic digestion. (BEMP 3.8.1);
- bakeries, i.e., manufacture of bread, biscuits and cakes: 100% of the selling-points of produced bread participate in an appropriate take-back scheme for the unsold bread (BEMP 3.9.1).

Once dealt with food loss resulting from the first stage of the supply chain, i.e., the production, on 25 October 2017, a notice relating EU guidelines on food donations (hereinafter 'Notice')[74] has been issued by European Commission. Again, the Notice is the outcome of the previous European Parliament Resolution pressures, as the former complies with the latter's recommendations. The Notice defines 'surplus food' as follows:

> Surplus food, consisting of finished food products (including fresh meat, fruit and vegetables), partly formulated products or food ingredients, may arise at any stage of the food production and distribution chain for a variety of reasons. Foods which do not meet manufacturer and/or customer specifications (e.g. variations in product colour, size, shape, etc.) as well as production and labelling errors can generate surplus in the agricultural and manufacturing sectors for instance.[75]

The document describes the problems that may arise in every production process. Surplus food may be redistributed essentially provided that (a) it is fit for human consumption and (b) it complies with all food safety requirements as specified by EU rules on food safety and food information to consumers as well as relevant national rules. Other key issues, in order to ensure highest rate of participation to the redistribution supply chain, are the conditions of traceability, labelling and food composition. Also, the legal and fiscal barriers which prevent to distribute surplus food have been outlined, including taxation on surplus food distribution. The European VAT Committee agreed on 7 December 2012 on guidelines to ensure the uniform application of the VAT Directive[76] across EU Member States. As to food donations, the Committee has held that:

74. European Commission, Commission notice, EU guidelines on food donation (2017/C 361/01).
75. *Ibid.*, 2(2).
76. Council Directive 2006/112/EC of 28 November 2006 on the common system of value added tax (VAT).

> the donation of foodstuffs to the poor, made by a taxable person free of charge, shall be treated as a supply of goods for consideration, in accordance with the first paragraph of Article 16 of the VAT Directive, unless this donation meets the conditions laid down by the Member State to be considered as a gift of small value within the meaning of the second paragraph of Article 16 of the VAT Directive.[77]

Therefore, in cases where such a donation must be treated as a supply of goods for consideration, the taxable amount shall be the purchase price of the goods donated, adjusted to the state of those goods at the time when the donation takes place, as provided for in Article 74 of the VAT Directive. Nonetheless, this provision has had a different implementation across Member States. In some Member States, little or no VAT is paid when food is donated to food banks as the national authorities consider that the value of the donated food close to its 'best before' or 'use by' date is small or zero. Other Member States consider the price of a product ready to be donated to be determined as if the product were subject to a usual commercial transaction, and therefore subject to VAT, with negative consequences for food donation. The Notice also calls on Member States to provide fiscal incentives, such as tax deductions or tax credits. In particular, corporate tax incentives in place in a few Member States (e.g., France, Spain and Portugal) have proved their effectiveness in encouraging donation of food production surplus. Some Member States have provided corporate tax credits, meaning that food donors are able to deduct a percentage of the value of the donated food from the corporate tax on their revenue. Indeed, tax deductions are more common across Member States: food donations are treated as a deductible tax expense, thus reducing the taxable income. The Notice, therefore, aims at limiting generated food waste at the final stages of the food supply chain, i.e., distribution and consumption, still not encompassed by the scope of the aforementioned BEMPs food and beverages.

Many non-governmental organization (NGO), acting at Member States' level in order to foster food donations, collection and distribution, are represented, at EU level, by the European Food Banks Federation. National and supranational food banks foster social cohesion between all the constituents of societies at local national and European levels as well as solidarity between themselves whatever the countries they are active in.[78]

§16.07 THE 'CIRCULAR ECONOMY PACKAGE'

After a two-year-and-a-half legislative procedure, on 30 May 2018, the 'Circular Economy Package'. Hereby European Parliament and the Council adopted four new directives amending six previous directives: waste, packaging, landfill, electric and electronic equipment waste, end-of-life vehicles and batteries. Member States shall comply with them by 5 July 2020.

Directive 2018/851, amending the WFD dating from 2008, has deepened the waste legislation approach to food waste.[79] In particular, due to the crucial intervention

77. *See supra* note 74, 7 Fiscal rules.
78. Available on https://www.eurofoodbank.org/, visited on 15 May 2020.
79. *See supra* note 4.

of the European Parliament's Environment, Public Health and Food Safety Committee (hereinafter 'Environment Committee'), in 2017 the Proposal 2015(595) has been amended.[80] The revision aimed at a change of pace from the Proposal 2015(595)'s approach: the new directive should not have been a mere WFD update but rather head towards more ambitious targets and purposes.

Over the years, in fact, a general awareness of the pressing need to reduce waste (every kind of waste, including food ones) has been reached, also for the purposes of combating global warming and the increasing loss of natural resources. It drove policymakers to tackle the inefficiencies of the market and of the international manufacturing, which, year after year, has constantly increased waste production.

This led the European Parliament to brush aside the weak Proposal 2015(595), no longer adequate to cope with new challenges. Instead, it was necessary to adopt new definitions and implement mechanisms to create a more modern and competitive, as well as more innovative and sustainable, EU economy. Waste would no longer have been seen as a mere 'burden' to manage, but a real anthropic 'resource' to exploit, in order to decrease the use of natural ones. New legal tools would have to redefine product's standard to meet market demand in tackling waste production. The explanatory statement of the report on the amendments proposed by the Environment Committee (hereinafter 'Report 2017') indicates the following specific objectives:[81] (1) strengthening of waste prevention measures; (2) encouraging the development of an efficient secondary raw materials market.

More ambitious objectives have been laid down in order to extend the life cycle of the products by avoiding losses, using by-products, providing new business models based on extended producer responsibility schemes and targets for reuse and recovery of municipal waste. As to the food waste reduction, the Report 2017 shows that European Parliament has a strong commitment in complying with Agenda 2030 SDGs to reduce waste food by 30% by 2025 and by 50% by 2030.[82]

To this regard, national waste prevention programmes would play a crucial role in food waste reduction and prevention. Prevention and reduction require an adequate measurement of the collected data, which the Parliament supports and boosts by committing Member States to report on an annual basis, rather than biennial as previously provided by the Proposal 2015(595).[83]

80. *See supra* note 60.
81. European Parliament, Report A8-0034/2017 of 9 February 2017 on the proposal for a directive of the European Parliament and of the Council amending Directive 2008/98/EC on waste (COM(2015)0595–C8-0382/2015 – 2015/0275(COD)), 142.
82. *Ibid.*, Amendment (78).
83. *Ibid.*, Amendment (36) on Recital 12: '(12) Member States should take measures to promote prevention *and reduction* of food waste in line with the 2030 Agenda for Sustainable Development, adopted by the United Nations General Assembly on 25 September 2015, and in particular its target *of reducing* food waste *by 50 %* by 2030. These measures should aim to prevent *and reduce the total generation of* food waste *and reduce food losses along the whole supply chain, including primary production, transportation and storage.* Having regard to the environmental, social and economic benefits of preventing food waste, Member States should establish specific food waste prevention measures, *including awareness campaigns to demonstrate how to prevent food waste in their waste prevention programmes. With these measures, Member States should aim to achieve a Union-wide food waste reduction target of 30 % by 2025 and of 50 % by 2030.*

European Parliament intervention is of historical relevance, since WFD Article 3 now encompasses a Food Waste definition which was still lacking in the Proposal 2015(595). The Report 2017 adopted the following definition:[84]

> 20d. 'food waste' means food intended for human consumption, either in edible or inedible status, removed from the production or supply chain to be discarded, including at primary production, processing, manufacturing, transportation, storage, retail and consumer levels, with the exception of primary production losses.

A definition that entails the production as well as the consumption phase. Furthermore, the definition is not strictly separated from the 'bio-waste' definition as the latter is basically considered as the subsequent stage. Report 2017 proposes a bio-waste definition[85] which still encompasses waste from household, restaurant and from processing plants.

The amendments suggested in Report 2017 have been adopted by the European Parliament on 14 March 2017.[86]

As to the fight against food losses, European Parliament approved the amendments on the definition of Food Waste, as quoted above. In particular, a specific food waste hierarchy has been proposed. This special waste hierarchy was intended to prioritize the prevention, even taking financial measures to facilitate donations, and the edible food rescue for human consumption.[87] Nevertheless, this reform has not been accepted in the Directive 2018/851 final version. Furthermore, pursuant to the prevention principle, European Parliament accepted stakeholders' requests of drawing attention to consumer empowerment: the necessity to improve consumer awareness of the precise meaning of 'use by' dates has been thus assessed and declared.

Discussions on WFD amendments have been then carried over to the Council. Eventually, a legislative Resolution of the Parliament has been issued: as an agreement had been reached between Parliament and Council, the Resolution corresponded to the

---

Member States should *also* measure progress *made* in *the reduction of* food waste *and food losses. To measure this progress and to* facilitate exchange of good practice across the EU both between Member States and between food business operators, a common methodology for such measurement should be established. Reporting on food waste levels should take place on *an annual* basis.' (emphasis added).

84. *Ibid.*, Amendment (98), Article 1(1)(2) point (fe) (new).
85. *Ibid.*, Amendment (84): '4. "bio-waste" means biodegradable garden and park waste, food and kitchen waste from households, restaurants, caterers and retail premises, comparable waste from food processing plants and other waste with similar biodegradability and compostability properties'.
86. European Parliament, Amendments adopted by the European Parliament on 14 March 2017 on the proposal for a directive of the European Parliament and of the Council amending Directive 2008/98/EC on waste (COM(2015)0595 - C8-0382/2015 - 2015/0275(COD)) (P8_TA(2017)0070).
87. *Ibid.*, Amendment 107: 'Article 4a. Food waste hierarchy. 1. The following specific food waste hierarchy shall apply in order of priority in food waste prevention and management legislation and policy:(a) source prevention; (b) edible food rescue, prioritising human use over animal feed and the reprocessing into non-food products; (c) organic recycling; (d) energy recovery; (e) disposal. 2. Member States shall provide incentives for the prevention of food waste, such as setting up voluntary agreements, facilitating food donation or, where appropriate, taking financial or fiscal measures.', 56.

final legislative act (i.e., Directive 2018/851 final version).[88] The Food Waste definition adopted, amending the previous one proposed in the Report 2017, although more comprehensive, seems to miss some peculiarities of the sector in hand. Here below, the new Directive 2018/851 definition:

> 'food waste' means all food as defined in Article 2 of Regulation (EC) No 178/2002 of the European Parliament and of the Council that has become waste.

The Institutions did not elaborate an autonomous definition, as proposed by Environment Committee, instead referring to 'food' definition as enshrined in Food Safety Regulation. Some shortcomings have been arising from such drafting techniques, since WFD's objectives and scope do not entirely coincide with Food Safety Regulation's. In particular, the latter deals with food supply chain from production to consumption but does not encompass the subsequent stages.

Moreover, it is noteworthy that European Parliament acknowledged FLW Platform outcomes on a common methodology for a uniform measurement of food losses levels. Actually, in its declaration on the availability of data and reporting obligations issued just prior to the Directive 2018/851 adoption, the European Commission stated that pursuant to prevention principle and thanks to the common understanding reached between the co-legislators, Member States will ensure that the reporting of data will cover 2020.[89]

In conclusion, Directive 2018/851, amending WFD, though not providing an ad hoc food waste hierarchy, is, however, an important change of pace for food waste reduction as:

- thanks to Parliament, waste prevention has been encouraged whose implementation needs data collected by Member States on the basis of a common methodology;[90]
- a new and autonomous definition of Food Waste, pursuant to WFD Article 3(4a), has been adopted;[91]
- the adoption of a common methodology for the measurement of food waste has been recommended and its implementation has been carried on;[92]
- it provides that consumer awareness of the meaning of 'use by' and 'best before' dates should be improved;[93]

88. European Parliament, legislative Resolution of 18 April 2018 on the proposal for a directive of the European Parliament and of the Council amending Directive 2008/98/EC on waste (COM(2015)0595 – C8-0382/2015 – 2015/0275(COD)).
89. Declaration by the Commission on the availability of Data and Reporting Obligations on 17 May 2018 (8502/2018 ADD 1 REV 2).
90. *See supra* note 4, Article 1(10).
91. *Ibid.*, Whereas (9). Article 1(3)(c): 'food waste' means all food as defined in Article 2 of Regulation (EC) No. 178/2002 of the European Parliament and of the Council that has become waste.
92. *Ibid.*, Whereas (31).
93. *Ibid.*, Whereas (32).

- it ensures EU to be on track towards the attainment of Agenda 2030 UN SDGs;[94]
- economic and fiscal measures to foster food donations for food waste prevention purposes have been encouraged;[95]
- 'bio-waste' encompasses waste from restaurants and from food processing plants;[96]
- by 31 December 2023 Member States should have provided that bio-waste is either separated and recycled at source, or is collected separately and is not mixed with other types of waste, encouraging the recycling, including composting and digestion and promoting the use of materials produced from bio-waste;[97]
- Member States should adopt specific food waste prevention programmes.[98]

Last but not least, Annex IVa, titled 'Examples of economic instruments and other measures to provide incentives for the application of the waste hierarchy referred to in Article 4(3)', provides incisive measures to tackle food waste.[99]

§16.08 MEASURES TAKEN AFTER 2018/851 DIRECTIVE

As 'Circular Economy Package' has been enacted and environmental resources scarcity has become clear, EU Institutions pushed towards the implementation of a more synergic approach to face environmental issues within the period 2021-2027.[100] Not just the manufacturing sector needs a change of pace towards prevention and precautionary principle, envisaging new schemes for corporate responsibility, but even public authorities competent for soil or biodiversity protection have to reshape their way to tackle these issues, being provided with instruments of waste prevention.

To this regard, a 'sustainable bioeconomy' should be implemented. It means an overarching shift of the business models which would lead to more efficient measures in order to enable the major economic players to better compete at the global level. It has to be necessarily implemented where dealing with economic activities having direct impacts on soil or biodiversity: thus, new food, biological and agricultural systems are needed to reduce waste production and natural resources consumption.

94. *Ibid.*, Whereas (31).
95. *Ibid.*, Whereas (15).
96. *Ibid.*, Whereas (9); Article 1(3)(b): 'bio-waste' means biodegradable garden and park waste, food and kitchen waste from households, offices, restaurants, wholesale, canteens, caterers and retail premises and comparable waste from food processing plants;'.
97. *Ibid.*, Article 1(19).
98. *Ibid.*, Article 1(22)(c).
99. Directive 2018/851, Annex IV-bis 'Fiscal incentives for donation of products, in particular food', No. 3.
100. Communication from the Commission to the European parliament, the Council, the European economic and social Committee and the Committee of the regions. A sustainable Bioeconomy for Europe: Strengthening the connection between economy, society and the environment COM(2018) 673 final.

To this end, it seems crucial to provide incentives to enable enterprises to develop close supply chains, such as 'zero waste' or circular systems, as well as empowering consumer by laying down labelling schemes, both for product and process certification, in order to promote best practices.

Indeed, strategic fields are those related to bio-waste recovery activities in order to progressively substitute fossil fuels. Biogas and biofuels plants are crucial in order to low or eradicate CO_2 production.[101]

As to the Action Plan's implementation, European Commission gave a high contribution; it has focused on some issues of foremost concern, such as plastics, construction and demolition waste, biomass plants, bio-based products, as well as food waste.[102]

In the waste legislation field, guidelines have been provided to foster separate collection of that waste not reaching optimal recovery rate yet, such as plastics, textiles and bio-waste.

Regarding the food waste, the working paper has drafted how SDGs Target 12.3 has affected Directive 2018/851, as well as FLW Platform impact on the latter, with a particular focus on a harmonized food waste data monitoring system aimed at waste prevention. It has also recommended the implementation of measures to reduce food waste at every stage of the supply chain.

Further, referring to food donations measures as pointed out in §16.06, European Commission calls on for a European food redistribution project. It should explore the policy, regulatory and operational frameworks existing in the Member States and, thus, promote dissemination of the EU food donation guidelines as well as stakeholder engagement in this regard. In fact, facilitating food donation is crucial to fight food poverty and prevent food waste. Lastly, a market study published by the European Commission found that up to 10% of the 88 million tonnes of food waste generated annually in the EU are linked to date marking (i.e., 'use by' and 'best before' dates). In regard to the role of date marking in food waste prevention, it has been held that the differentiation between the concepts of 'use by' and 'best before' will be improved so as to facilitate common understanding and use of date marking. Technical guidance is currently under preparation, with support of the FLW Platform, in order to promote more consistent date marking practices in line with EU date marking rules.

As the first measure is consequently taken, European Commission issued a common methodology and minimum quality requirements for the uniform measurement of levels of food waste. Such Decision (EU) No. 2019/1597 commits Member States to separately measure the amounts of food waste for the following stages of the food supply chain: (a) primary production; (b) processing and manufacturing; (c) retail and other distribution of food; (d) restaurants and food services; (e) households.[103]

101. Directive (EU) 2018/2001 of the European Parliament and of the Council of 11 December 2018 on the promotion of the use of energy from renewable sources; Communication of Commission of 30 January 2019, Reflection Paper Towards a Sustainable Europe by 2030.
102. Commission Staff Working Document of 4 March 2019 [SWD(2019) 90 final].
103. Commission Delegated Decision (EU) 2019/1597 of 3 May 2019 supplementing Directive 2008/98/EC of the European Parliament and of the Council as regards a common methodology and minimum quality requirements for the uniform measurement of levels of food waste.

The measurement covers food waste that is classified under European List of Waste (ELW) codes referred to in Annex II of Decision (EU) No. 2019/1597 'Waste codes included in the European list of waste for types of waste which typically include food waste' for each supply chain stage. Actually, some shortcomings could arise from this provision: ELW codes associated to 'Restaurants and food services' stage (20 01 08; 20 01 25; 20 03 01) coincide with those related to the categories 'Households' and 'Retail and other distribution food', except for the code 20 03 02 (Waste from markets) encompassed just in the latter. This could lead to potential heterogeneity in measurement methodology, unless good practices will emerge across Member States.

Simultaneously, the European Commission has laid down a timetable to take measures aimed at implementing the Environment Action Programme, in particular envisaging a food waste reduction targets revision by 2023.[104]

As to enact measures and strategies laid down in its programmes, European Commission has then issued sector-based provisions, particularly intended to tackle food waste produced in the entire fresh fruits and vegetables food supply chain.

In such context it is, for example, to be referred to Regulation (EU) No. 2019/801 which has authorized the use of mono- and diglycerides of fatty acids (E 471) as food additives. Within the common authorization procedure for food additives, food enzymes and food flavourings' preliminary activity (referred to in Regulation 1331/2008),[105] it has in fact been ascertained that mono- and diglycerides of fatty acids, when used as a glazing agent for a surface treatment of fresh fruits and vegetables, form a thin, inert, physical barrier layer against moisture loss and oxidation capable to protect the nutritional quality and extend the shelf life.

Such pattern is illustrative of the constant interaction between various pieces of legislation involved within the food waste sector: here, the European Commission has basically exercised its food safety authorization powers for the submitted additives, under reserve to apply it on fruits of which the peels are usually not consumed. Once ascertained such additives were of safety concern for human health, the Union list of food additives has been updated thus approving their use for citrus fruit, melons, pineapples, bananas, papayas, mangoes, avocados and pomegranates.[106]

Another number of specific sector-based provisions deal with food storage schemes, particularly referred to transportation and delivery stages.[107] It has in fact been noticed that Ecodesign and Energy Labelling provisions still lack requirements that contribute to circular economy and extended producer responsibility objectives laid down by 2018/851 Directive such as for product reparability and recyclability and,

104. Commission Staff Working Document of 15 May 2019 on Evaluation of the 7th Environment Action Programme to 2020 *'Living well, within the limits of our planet'* [COM(2019) 233 final], 166.
105. Regulation (EC) No. 1331/2008 of the European Parliament and of the Council of 16 December 2008 establishing a common authorization procedure for food additives, food enzymes and food flavourings.
106. Commission Regulation (EU) 2019/801 of 17 May 2019 amending Annex II to Regulation (EC) No. 1333/2008 of the European Parliament and of the Council as regards the use of mono- and diglycerides of fatty acids (E 471) on certain fresh fruits.
107. Commission Staff Working Document Impact Assessment of 1 October 2019 [SWD(2019)341 final].

thus, also for the purpose of food waste prevention. Food storage, both in private households and in food services, plays an important role in food waste reduction and prevention. Studies show that:[108]

> Another element relevant for material efficiency is food waste caused by spoilage and bad planning. Food production 'from farm to fork' constitutes almost 20% by weight of the EU's total Domestic Material Consumption (DMC). End-users, i.e. private households and food services, waste 18% of those resources. Of this end-use waste, 60% is due to food spoilage and bad planning and thus avoidable.

Refrigerating appliances would ensure optimized food preservation thus contributing to prevent food spoilage.

The Commission has then proposed Measure No. 7 aimed at making consumers properly informed about correct food storage specifying each type of perishable food preservation standards (temperatures and compartments).[109] Such information shall be available on appliances instruction manuals for end-users and installers or on free access website.[110] Optimizing these new storage conditions will gain a reduction by almost 60% of the food waste due to 'not-used-in time', estimated at 23 Mt/year in the period 2011-2012. An additional 20% can be saved on food waste from leftovers and too much food prepared or served.[111]

Moreover, in accordance with the extended producer responsibility principle, clear price signals and transparency of the markets would represent important measures to tackle food spoilage.[112]

§16.09 THE EUROPEAN GREEN DEAL

On 11 December 2019, European Commission presented 'The European Green Deal',[113] an action working paper setting out the next strategy aimed at transforming the EU into a fair and prosperous society, with a modern resource-efficient and competitive economy and where economic growth is decoupled from resource use. Such approach is fully consistent with SDGs and part of the priorities announced in new Commission President von der Leyen's political guidelines.

As to the food sector, the strategy pursues an inherent reshaping of the food supply chain towards a 'food value chain'. The Commission states to be fully aware that agricultural and food industry sectors still results in loss of biodiversity and climate change and consumes excessive amounts of natural resources, while an important part of food is wasted. Such phenomena are even exacerbated due to air, water and soil

108. *Ibid.*, 11.
109. *Ibid.*, 26.
110. *Ibid.*, 27.
111. *Ibid.*, 33; Preparatory/Review Study on Commission Regulation (EC) No. 643/2009 and Commission Delegated Regulation (EU) No. 1060/2010, Final report. VHK, March 2016.
112. Commission Staff Working Document of 1 October 2019, *Market transparency in the EU's food supply chain* [COM(2019) 6908 final], 48.
113. Communication From The Commission of 11 December 2019 to the European Parliament, the European Council, the Council, the European economic and social Committee and the Committee of the regions, *The European Green Deal* [COM(2019) 640 final].

pollution, whose negative impact is going to raise proportionately with population size, thus worsening the poverty rate as well as food safety and security.

To implement the strategy, on 20 May 2020, the European Commission published the long-awaited 'From farm to fork' (FFTF) strategy.[114] The FFTF provides a framework for future European objectives concerning the creation of more sustainable food systems. The aim is to value the whole food supply chain, helping to create conditions leading to higher incomes for primary producers thus increasing the competitiveness of the European agri-food sector worldwide.

The FFTF strategy is one of the key elements of the European Green Deal, the major inspiring framework for EU acting.

The primary goal of the FFTF strategy consists of addressing the need to reduce dependence on chemical pesticides and antimicrobials, reduce over-fertilization, enhance organic farming, improve animal welfare and halt biodiversity loss.

These targets can only be achieved through a fair transition from traditional agri-food systems to the most innovative and sustainable ones, set by the European Commission with the following sub-objectives:

(1) to reach the objective of at least 25% of the EU's agricultural land under organic farming by 2030;
(2) to reduce the overall use and risk of chemical pesticides by 50% and the use of more hazardous pesticides13 by 50% by 2030;
(3) to spend EUR 10 billion under the Horizon 2020 and Horizon Europe programme on R&I on food, bioeconomy, natural resources, agriculture, fisheries, aquaculture and the environment as well as the use of digital technologies and nature-based solutions for agri-food;
(4) to integrate objectives of the common agricultural policy in order to give industry more funding tools to achieve sustainable transition;
(5) to enhance the bio-based economy by increasing the number of advanced biorefineries that produce bio-fertilizers, protein feed, bioenergy, and biochemicals, offering opportunities for the transition to a climate-neutral European economy;
(6) to increase the GHG emission reduction target (in particular methane and nitrous oxide generated by livestock farms) by investing in anaerobic digestion systems for the production of biogas from waste, agricultural residues and livestock manure;
(7) to accountably manage excess of nutrients (especially nitrogen and phosphorus) through the decrease of the use of fertilizers by at least 20% by 2030 and the reduction of nutrient losses by at least 50%, while ensuring that there is no deterioration in soil fertility through the adoption of an integrated nutrient

114. Communication from the Commission of 20 May 2020 to the European Parliament, the Council, the European Economic and Social Committee and the Committee of the Regions, *A Farm to Fork Strategy for a fair, healthy and environmentally-friendly food system* [COM(2020) 381 final].

management action plan to address nutrient pollution at source and increase the sustainability of the livestock sector;

(8) to increase efficiency in food processing, commerce up to final distribution, in order to reduce the amount of food waste generated throughout the food production chain, also by completely redesigning the design and performance of food packaging.

In order to reduce food waste, the European Commission has set out to achieve Target 12.3 SDGs, i.e., to halve the amount of food waste per capita by 2030. This should be done through the application of the common methodology and minimum quality requirements for the uniform measurement of levels of food waste, as set out in EU Decision 2019/1597 (*see* §16.08) on the basis of which each Member State will transmit reference data from 2022 onwards. Accordingly, the European Commission will set precise targets for reducing food waste, which for the first time will be legally binding on the Member States.

Moreover, in order to better reduce the amount of food waste produced, the European Commission will proceed to clarify the use of 'use by' and 'best before' food labels, which are still a source of confusion for citizens today and therefore cause additional domestic food waste due to improper food conservation.

The transition to more sustainable food systems also requires, according to the European Commission, a change in the nutritional plans commonly adopted by citizens. In this regard, the European Commission will propose in 2022 the standardization of nutrition information on food packaging through the use of a new labelling system based on the nutri-score model and traffic light labelling. However, this can only contribute to increasing the value of the general food system if the European Commission simultaneously proposes mandatory labelling of the origin and provenance of food products, increasing the mandatory range.

Finally, given that European food quality already represents excellence in terms of food safety, measures aimed at reducing sales of antimicrobials for farm animals in Europe by 50% will be taken. Europe will also continue to raise the standard of controls on food imported from extra-EU countries which must comply with all European food safety regulations and requirements in order to be admitted.

§16.10 FOOD WASTE AND BAT CONCLUSIONS

It is to be noted that food waste is also tackled by more specific sectoral legislation.

From the second half of the 1990s, EU Institutions have set up different plants authorization and control regimes for each industrial sector, aimed at tackling pollution arising from industrial activities. Directive No. 2010/75/EU, known as 'Industrial Emission Directive' (IED), has brought to unity these various regimes.[115] As to the sector in hand, it is worth to focus on the various BAT reference documents, which

115. Directive 2010/75/EU of the European Parliament and of the Council of 24 November 2010 on industrial emissions (integrated pollution prevention and control).

describe each industrial sector applied techniques, present emission and consumption levels and, in particular, BAT and any emerging technique, as well as so called sectoral 'BAT conclusions'. These documents result from the exchange of information between Member States, the industries concerned, NGO promoting environmental protection and the Commission, pursuant to Article 13 of IED Directive.

In the wake of Decision 2018/1508 on BEMPs food and beverage,[116] the Commission has issued sector-based BEMPs for agriculture,[117] whose conversion to sustainability requires reduction of food losses.

For instance, as to the waste management, BEMPs for agricultural sector suggest, wherever possible, anaerobic digestion or composting of organic waste, preferably in-site or, when off-site, as nearly to the farm as possible.

Instead, BATs for waste treatment[118] do not encompass the sector in hand, except for the definition of 'Liquid biodegradable waste' where 'Waste of biological origin with a relatively high water content (e.g. fat separator contents, organic sludge, catering waste)' is included.

Lastly, BATs for food, drink and milk industries, recently issued,[119] establish best practices for water loss reduction in industrial processes. Although the document does not refer to food waste treatment, attention is nonetheless drawn on this latter to the extent the single techniques listed deal with the category 'Residue' which encompasses both waste and by-products and, thus, even substances relevant as food loss or food waste. The document focuses on the food industry production process rather than on the product.

§16.11 MOST SIGNIFICANT LEGAL DEVELOPMENTS IN MEMBER STATES

Before focusing on measures taken at national level, the attention should be drawn on the EU research project REFRESH,[120] funded by the 'Horizon 2020' framework programme and established in 2016 in the wake of the FLW Platform. Experts from twelve European countries and China work towards the project's goal to contribute towards SDGs Target 12.3 to halve per capita food loss at the retail and consumer level by 2030 and reduce food losses along the food production and supply chains. On this basis, strategic partnerships between governments, enterprises and local stakeholders are

116. *See supra* note 70.
117. Commission Decision (EU) 2018/813 of 14 May 2018 on the sectoral reference document on best environmental management practices, sector environmental performance indicators and benchmarks of excellence for the agriculture sector under Regulation (EC) No. 1221/2009 of the European Parliament and of the Council on the voluntary participation by organizations in a Community EMAS.
118. Commission Implementing Decision (EU) 2018/1147 of 10 August 2018 establishing best available techniques (BAT) conclusions for waste treatment, under Directive 2010/75/EU of the European Parliament and of the Council.
119. Commission Implementing Decision (EU) 2019/2031 of 12 November 2019 establishing best available techniques (BAT) conclusions for the food, drink and milk industries, under Directive 2010/75/EU of the European Parliament and of the Council.
120. Refresh, available on https://eu-refresh.org/about-refresh.

encouraged in four leading countries (Spain, Germany, Hungary and Netherlands) in order to elaborate policy recommendations at Union level and to foster new ad hoc technologies.

There are several examples of excellence created by local entrepreneurs from different Member States, financed by the European 'Life' projects or the 'Horizon 2020' programme. The present paragraph outlines some of the various techniques and innovation projects categorized by the different stages of the food supply chain.

First of all, a better and more prudent food waste management would lead to creating new raw materials or food by-products for different uses. From a legal perspective, WFD, as amended by Directive 2018/851, provides the relevant mechanisms, i.e., by-products or EoW.

As to waste from fruit and vegetables production, in Italy, the 'Orange Fiber' project[121] has been established. It produces an organic and natural fabric from citrus juice by-products. In Spain, two kinds of products have been made up from pruning citrus trees: as to the leaves, they are treated to obtain essences, as well as fertilizers and animal feed; the wood has been transformed into pellets for fuel and animal bedding.[122]

A number of projects focus on grapes skins as production residue from wine industry. In Spain, such waste has been qualified as by-products for producing tannin suitable for use by the leather industry.[123] Further, in Italy, the first vegan technical fabric, 'Vegea', has been recently created in Italy, produced from the marc, i.e., the wine production residues. 'Vegea' is a Horizon 2020 funded project and has been awarded by the European Parliament in the context of the 'European TOP 50 competition', 2017 edition, which annually selects the new millennium's fifty best business ideas.[124]

Improper food storage conditions may lead to relevant product losses and deterioration. As to tackle this issue, a company funded under the Horizon 2020 programme developed a wire-less remote monitoring system.[125]

Citrus residues may also be used in organic packaging and cosmetics. The former, in particular, would be a solution of significant relevance in order to avoid plastics.[126]

Lastly, as to post-consumption stage where the most relevant rate of food waste comes from, a twofold approach arises from Member States practices.

As to the former, it has been developed in the United Kingdom (UK), where 40% of food waste was landfilled.[127] In 2013, UK established to get rid of food waste landfill disposal by 2020 and set up the project 'Vision: 2020 UK Roadmap to Zero Food Waste

121. Orange Fiber, available on http://orangefiber.it.
122. Life Ecocitric – Citric Waste Integrated Management LIFE13 ENV/ES/000889.
123. Grape Tannins – Saving of forest exploitation for obtaining of tanning extracts through valorisation of wine waste LIFE04 ENV/ES/000237.
124. Vegea, available on https://www.vegeacompany.com (November 2019).
125. Koolzone, available on https://www.koolzone.com (November 2019).
126. Life Citruspack – Revalorization strategies within the circular economy for the use of citrus waste in green packaging and cosmetics LIFE16 ENV/ES/000171.
127. DEFRA government review 2011 of waste policy in England, available on https://www.vision2020.info/ban-food-waste/.

to Landfill'.[128] It combined measures intended to spread information across the population with more concrete measures aimed at planning and implementation of energy recovery or anaerobic digestion plants.

The latter approach comes from Italy, where a Life project, called 'Life.Food-.Waste.StandUp',[129] was established in 2016. It is an awareness-raising project addressing agri-food, supply chain enterprises and end-consumers to prevent food waste and to manage food surplus. The project brought together no profit organizations (Fondazione Banco Alimentare Onlus), trade associations (Federalimentare) and consumer associations (Unione Nazionale Consumatori), all of them with a twofold aim: reducing the food waste and contributing to provide healthy meals to the needy.

In September 2019, three years after the project's launch, the first outcomes have been disclosed: more than 10,000 agri-food businesses involved, 12,000 sales points trained on the procedures of the management of food surplus, 1,500,000 consumer reached. Such figures have also been achieved thanks to the approval of the Law No. 166/2016 (hereinafter 'Gadda Law'),[130] a new legislation enhancing Law 155/2003 and representing a landmark for other European countries.

As an awareness-raising project, the field chosen was twofold. On the one hand, food supply chain businesses: fighting waste and fostering donations have been pursued relying on management's professional development and employees' engagement. On the other hand, food waste issues were brought to the Italian cities, spreading information across citizens and consumers on how crucial is fighting against food waste and losses.

In this regard, the Gadda Law combined with the 'Food Waste Prevention National Programme'[131] established in 2014, has been aiming at reducing food waste, encouraging food surplus and pharmaceutical recovery and donation for solidarity purposes.

The Gadda Law is addressed to public and private bodies pursuing non-profit civic and solidarity purposes (the 'donees', pursuant to Gadda Law Article 2). Food sector operators may transfer free of charge surplus food (compliant with food safety standards) to donees, which in turn have to donate it as a priority to the needy. Should the foodstuff be no longer fit for human consumption, it may be conferred as animal feed or for self-composting. Transfer may also regard baking and dough of flour products from baking plants which have not been sold or distributed within twenty-four hours after production. Seized food products may further be freely transferred. The Gadda Law has promoted information campaigns aimed at fostering best practices for waste prevention in food services such as customer's take-away of leftover food.

128. Vision 2020: UK Roadmap to Zero Food Waste to Landfill, available on https://www.vision2020.info/.
129. Life Food Waste Stand Up available on http://www.lifefoodwastestandup.eu/it.
130. Law 19 August 2016, No. 166, '*Provisions concerning the donation and distribution of food and pharmaceutical products for the purpose of social solidarity and for the limitation of waste*' (G. U. 30 August 2016 No. 202).
131. Ministerial Decree (Ministry of Environment) 8 July 2014, No. 185, '*Piano Nazionale di Prevenzione degli Sprechi Alimentari*' (PINPAS); Ministerial Decree (Ministry of Environment) 27 June 2017, No. 168, '*Piano Nazionale di Prevenzione degli Sprechi Alimentari*' *(PINPAS)*.

Lastly, in 2018, the Italian Government, Regions, Autonomous Provinces of Trento and Bolzano and other local entities reached an agreement[132] to define Guidelines intended to enable hospital, school and military canteen-managing institutions to prevent or reduce food waste. In fact, according to data gathered by Banco Alimentare and Caritas, such food services, managing 3 million tonnes of food, generates every year around 210,000 tonnes of food surplus in Italy, of which just 12% is recovered (25,000 tonnes of food).

§16.12 THE PANDEMIC'S EFFECTS ON FOOD WASTE PRODUCTION AND MANAGEMENT[133]

COVID-19 has modified the way food access, control and food safety and consequently the amount of food waste produced.

Primarily, it would be useful to state that it is not known, with scientific accuracy, the real extent – in quantitative terms – of the variables relating to food waste when this work, carried out in the first months after the beginning of the pandemic, was drafted. Two are the main reasons. First, each State has acted individually taking different precautions and virus containment measures coherent with the national approach adopted locally. Therefore, in countries such as Italy, France and Spain, access to social and restaurant facilities has been completely precluded, except for delivery services, but clearly with a lower yield. Other countries, mainly northern European ones, have made a different choice: restaurants have been closed shortly or have never closed. Second, due to the short time elapsed from the beginning of the pandemic to the writing of this chapter, no official data on the tonnes of food waste generated at the time of the COVID-19 were provided by the EU Institutions. These reasons do not allow to have a uniform overview of the effects that the COVID-19 has generated on food waste, although this does not prevent to carry out a broad-spectrum analysis. However, it is necessary to bear in mind another consequence of the pandemic, i.e., the general increase in the number of poor people as a result of the economic crisis resulting from the spread of lockdown measures and therefore of import/export blockades in general. As a response, Member States have promoted numerous solidarity initiatives consisting of the distribution of food that would otherwise have been wasted, due to the waste that the pandemic has anyway generated.[134]

132. Unified Conference State Regions of 19 April 2018 *'Guidelines to bodies managing school, company, hospital, social and community canteens, in order to prevent and reduce the waste associated with the administration of food'*.
133. For more details http://www.fao.org/2019-ncov/q-and-a/impact-on-food-and-agriculture/en/; http://www.fao.org/2019-ncov/resources/policy-briefs/en/; https://ec.europa.eu/food/safety_en; https://ec.europa.eu/food/safety/food_waste/library_en; https://ec.europa.eu/food/sites/food/files/safety/docs/fw_lib_gfd_eu-plt-prevent-flw-covid-19.pdf; https://www.ifpri.org/landing/covid-19-blog-landing-page,visited on 7-8 May 2020.
134. https://www.ecowatch.com/stop-food-waste-day-organizations-45871951.html?rebelltitem=1#rebelltitem, visited on 5 May 2020.

In this regard, ReFED[135] has carried out a broad-spectrum study on a sample of food companies and non-profit organizations that distribute food donations on the effects produced by the pandemic at all stages of the food supply chain.

Agro-food production, an essential activity in times of lockdown, has operated relentlessly, but at the same time faced difficulties in finding labour for harvesting activities in the fields. It has also recorded an increase in so-called immediate and short-term waste (i.e., waste produced in the first phase of the food supply chain) due to the large volumes of warehouse stock, to the catering interruption, to cruise line and airline cancellations, as well as the import/export of products, which make up a large part of the market demand.

This is reflected in the few statistics available, i.e., the change in food price indices. In fact, the 'FAO Food Price Index (FFPI)', which measures the most common international food prices, in April 2020 recorded -3.4% from March 2020 (one month) and -10% from January 2020 (three months). This means that in April 2020 world food prices fell for the third consecutive month. Another interesting statistic is the 'FAO Sugar Price Index', which in just one month recorded -14.6%, due to the collapse in international crude oil prices that led sugar factories to switch more sugar cane for sugar production instead of ethanol. This widened the availability of sugar exports, also contracted by reduced demand due to the COVID-19.[136]

The large-scale distribution has increased retail sales, as a result of quarantine or travel restrictions, reducing the amount of unsold food, but at the same time, the amount of packaging waste has increased, which will be added to those resulting from home delivery of food by the few restaurants remaining open.[137]

By contrast, in the beginning, the pandemic hindered much more seriously the distribution, due to the ban on movements. A considerable amount of food waste has thus been generated. The industry is now re-planning its activities, in order to deal with online purchasing.[138]

As to health and food safety, in its document, 'Covid-19 and food safety. Questions and Answers',[139] the European Commission makes it clear that 'there has been no report of transmission of Covid-19 via consumption of food to date'.[140] It is, nonetheless, required the implementation of such food production and distribution safety measures.

135. ReFED is a multi-stakeholder non-profit, powered by an influential network of the nation's leading business, non-profit, foundation, and government leaders committed to reducing U.S. food waste, available on https://www.refed.com/content-hub/refeds-covid-19-u-s-food-system-review/, visited on 5 May 2020.
136. http://www.fao.org/worldfoodsituation/foodpricesindex/en/, visited on 7 May 2020. Further data, released on 7 May 2020, show that 'The FAO Cereal Price Index' averaged nearly 164.0 points in April, down marginally from March but still up almost 4.0 points (2.4%) from April 2019. 'The FAO Dairy Price Index' recorded in April a -3.6% from March 2020 and fell by -8.8% from April 2019. Again, in April 2020, 'The FAO Meat Price Index' fell by -2.7% within a month.
137. *See supra* note 135.
138. *Ibid.*
139. European Commission, Directorate-General for health and food safety, Crisis management in food, animals and plants. Food hygiene, 'Covid-19 and food safety. Questions and Answers', 8 April 2020.
140. *Ibid.*, para. 1.1.

In the beginning of the pandemic, the European Commission has also issued guidelines for a sound waste management in the context of the COVID-19 crisis, aimed at ensuring a high protection of human health and environment.[141] First of all, the document points out that '[a]ccording to the European Centre for Diseases Prevention and Control (ECDC), there is currently no evidence to infer that standard waste management procedures are unsafe or insufficient in terms of the risk for Covid-19 infection or that household waste plays a role in the transmission of SARS-CoV-2 or other respiratory viruses'.[142] Anyway, according to the ECDC, specific measures are required as regards infection prevention and control for suspected or confirmed coronavirus cases self-isolating at home.[143] Guidelines have then recalled that for the 2014-2020 period, Member States have allocated EUR 4.9 billion of cohesion policy funding to waste management, including support to waste prevention and awareness-raising, separate collection systems (incl. equipment and vehicles).[144] By the end of 2019, 31% of this amount has not yet been allocated to specific project: the European Commission thus suggests to use such funds also under other priorities, such as disaster risk management or healthcare.[145] This would also improve waste management system, as long as it is an essential service to the society. In this context, improvements would even regard food waste and packaging waste fractions management.

Official data on food waste produced in Europe by the beginning of the pandemic are not yet available, to date. It is nonetheless clear that food consumption and food losses are going to be subject to major changes, due either to the forecast population growth by 2050, either to the awareness of the agriculture and livestock production impact.[146]

§16.13 CONCLUDING REMARKS

A common and universal 'food waste' definition is still lacking. Such circumstance plunges its roots into the WFD's timeless 'waste' definition shortcomings. While FAO provided a definition for 'food waste' and 'food loss', this does not coincide with the EU 'food waste' definition, which refers to 'food' as enshrined in Food Safety Regulation. In this regard, for instance, it is doubtful whether or not EU 'food waste' is encompassed in FAO 'food loss'. Nonetheless, besides such further improvements and

141. European Commission, Waste management in the context of the coronavirus crisis, 14 April 2020.
142. *Ibid.*, 2.
143. ECDC technical report 'Infection prevention and control in the household management of people with suspected or confirmed coronavirus disease (Covid-19)', 30 March 2020, available on https://www.ecdc.europa.eu/en/publications-data/infection-prevention-control-household-management-covid-19 (visited on 7 May 2020).
144. https://cohesiondata.ec.europa.eu/stories/s/xqec-t5kv (visited on 8 May 2020).
145. *See supra* note 6, 5.
146. Sustainable Development Foundation, 'Pandemia e sfide green del nostro tempo', web conference available on https://www.fondazionesvilupposostenibile.org/presentato-dossier-pandemia-e-sfide-green/, visited on 8 May 2020.

considering production's as well as consumer conducts' unevenness, it is possible that EU Institutions have achieved – at least at a prescriptive level – satisfactory solutions.

Since 2008, WFD has been providing legal tools (i.e., by-products and EoW) to enable businesses to develop innovative industrial practices aimed at preventing and reducing food losses, particularly at food supply chain stages preceding the retail. Nonetheless, as pointed out, by-products and EoW regime has always been underscoring some practical shortcomings, mainly due to Commission and Council's inertia in laying down the relevant statutory instruments (i.e., implementing acts, as defined after Lisbon).

Such normative reticence may also occur on purpose, pursuant to the subsidiarity principle as enshrined in TFEU Article 5(3). It is thus possible that EU Institutions have intervened, according to the subsidiarity as well as the conferral principles, to the extent EU law allows in the matter(s) in hand, i.e., setting general principles and objectives whose implementation mainly weighs on national administrations. Environmental issues are exemplary of such approach: their normative qualification as shared competences, pursuant to TFEU Article 4(2)(e), reflects Europe's geographical and climatic diversity, which in turn entails different cultivations, agricultural techniques, supply chain in each region, requiring different institutional as well as economic answers.

In this regard, stakeholders' participation through European projects developed at national level, but co-funded by the Union, such as 'Life' or 'Horizon', is crucial. Such projects fulfil the duty to convert legal provisions in industrial innovative practices aimed at food losses reduction, fostering technological innovation, energy savings. Although it is clear that food losses and waste would unlikely be totally eliminated, a substantial reduction is nevertheless of remarkable importance for the environment.

CHAPTER 17

The EU Policy to Protect Bees: The Restrictions on the Use of Neonicotinoids and the Emergency Authorizations Granted by MS – In Search of a Long-Term Strategy on Pesticides

Daniela Corona

In order to halt the loss of honeybees, since 2010 the European Commission has adopted increasingly severe restrictions to the use of *neonicotinoids*, the most widely used class of insecticides in the world. Such restrictions, however, have been bypassed by the Member States who have repeatedly adopted emergency authorization in accordance with Article 53 of the Regulation (EC) 1107/2009 on plant protection products. Moreover, they have not yet fully implemented Directive 2009/128/EC that aims to achieve a sustainable use of pesticides in the European Union (EU) by reducing the risks and impacts of pesticide use on human health and the environment and promoting the use of integrated pest management and of alternative approaches or techniques, such as non-chemical alternatives to pesticides. The lack of national compliance with key EU legislative instrument envisaged to protect biodiversity and, in particular, bees poses some doubts as to the likelihood that the EU could attain its ambitious objectives set in the Farm to Fork Strategy adopted in May 2020.

§17.01 INTRODUCTION

The use of pesticides[1] in modern agriculture is commonly considered fundamental in order to guarantee stable food production. Since the 1940s, indeed, with the discovery of the effects of DDT,[2] the sale and the use of pesticides has constantly grown, together with consumers' concerns about the possible toxic effects of such substances. According to the last available data collected by Food and Agricultural Organization (FAO), global pesticides use (in tonnes of active ingredient) increased by 46% during the period 1996-2016.[3] At present, such trend seems unstoppable. In fact, the world population is projected to reach about 9.7 billion by 2050;[4] as a consequence, food production must increase by 70%.[5] How will it be possible to meet such growing demand taking into consideration that there is limited scope for significantly expanding agricultural land? The answer commonly given to this question is that the use of pesticides is the only way to protect agricultural production; its use is immediately effective and simple and can boost agriculture productivity of the developing countries where alternative methods – less environmentally impacting – are too expensive and not readily available.

The European Union (EU) has adopted one of the strictest regulatory frameworks governing the authorizations of active substances and the use of plant protection products in the world. It aims at ensuring a high level of protection of both human and animal health and the environment. Also, it provides for a range of actions to achieve a sustainable use of pesticides. In particular, with the adoption of Regulation (EC) 1107/2009 concerning the placing of plant protection products on the market (PPP Regulation),[6] EU legislators have decided to strengthen the safety standards regarding the approval of active substances and the use of pesticides containing them. By the same vein, Directive 2009/128/EC on the sustainable use of pesticides[7] (Sustainable Use Directive) provides for a range of actions to achieve a more sustainable use of the chemical compounds in the EU by reducing the impact of such substances on human health and on the environment and promoting the use of integrated pest management

1. The term 'pesticide', in the context of this chapter, refers to plant protection products as defined by Article 3(10)(a) of Directive 2009/128/EC.
2. H. Bouwman, R. Bornman, H. van den Berg & H. Kylin, 'DDT: fifty years since silent spring', in *Late lessons from early warnings: science, precaution, innovation*, EEA Report, No. 1/2013, p. 240.
3. Global situation of pesticide management in agriculture and public health, Report of a 2018 WHO-FAO survey, 2019.
4. United Nations, Department of Economics and Social Affairs, *World Population Prospects 2019*, available at: https://population.un.org/wpp/.
5. FAO, How to feed the world in 2050, available at: http://www.fao.org/fileadmin/templates/wsfs/docs/expert_paper/How_to_Feed_the_World_in_2050.pdf.
6. Regulation (EC) No. 1107/2009 of the European Parliament and of the Council of 21 October 2009 concerning the placing of plant protection products on the market and repealing Council Directive 79/117/EEC and 91/414/EC, in OJ L 309 of 24.11.2009, p. 1.
7. Directive 2009/128/EC of the European Parliament and of the Council of 21 October 2009 establishing a framework for Community action to achieve the sustainable use of pesticides, in OJ L 309, 24.11.2009, p. 71.

(IPM)[8] and of alternative approaches or techniques, such as non-chemical alternatives to pesticides.

The strict requirements that an active substance (and the pesticide containing it) must comply with before reaching the market have led to an approximate 50% reduction in the number of approved active substances in the EU.[9] This is the consequence of the constant engagement of the European Commission (EC) in reviewing the authorizations granted; indeed, according to Article 21(1) and (3) of the PPP Regulation, the EC 'may review the approval of an active substance at any time, including where, in the light of new scientific and technical knowledge, there are indications that the substance no longer satisfies the approval criteria laid down in Article 4 of that regulation'.[10]

The 'European Green Deal'[11] presented in December 2019 and the 'Farm to Fork Strategy'[12] of May 2020 stressed even more the urgency to act against the loss of biodiversity. The latter, in particular, provides that the 'EC will take additional action to reduce the overall use and risk of chemical pesticides by 50% (...) by 2030' (... .) and 'it will revise the Sustainable Use of Pesticides Directive, enhance provisions on integrated pest management and promote greater use of alternative ways of protecting harvests from pests and diseases'. Furthermore, the EC sets the objective of at least 25% of the EU's agricultural land under organic farming by 2030.

In this chapter, we will single out the EU action on halting the losses of honeybees, a phenomenon that has been characterizing worldwide agriculture. We will first briefly analyse the EU policy actions adopted over the years to combat the loss of biodiversity and, more in particular, of the bees population. Then, we will focus on a particular aspect, namely, the restrictions on the use of *neonicotinoids*, the class of pesticides the use of which has been found to be particularly dangerous for insects and bees, adopted by the EC. We will also see how Member States (MS), by making use of an emergency tool contained in the PPP Regulation, are allowed to bypass such restrictions. Finally, we will make some remarks on the current gap between the EU long-term strategy on the protection of biodiversity (including the actions to protect

8. For the definition of IPM, *see* Article 3 point 6 of the Directive 2009/128/EC: (...) '"integrated pest management" means careful consideration of all available plant protection methods and subsequent integration of appropriate measures that discourage the development of populations of harmful organisms and keep the use of plant protection products and other forms of intervention to levels that are economically and ecologically justified and reduce or minimise risks to human health and the environment. "Integrated pest management" emphasises the growth of a healthy crop with the least possible disruption to agro-ecosystems and encourages natural pest control mechanisms (...)'.
9. *See* the EU Pesticides Database, available at: https://ec.europa.eu/food/plant/pesticides/eu-pesticides-database/public/?event=homepage&language=EN.
10. Case C-616,17, *Blaise and Others*, judgment of 1 October 2019, EU:C:2019:800, para. 99.
11. Communication from the Commission to the European Parliament, the European Council, the Council, the European Economic and Social Committee and the Committee of the Regions – The European Green Deal, Brussels, 11.12.2019, COM(2019)640 final.
12. Communication from the Commission to the European Parliament, the Council, the European Economic and Social Committee and the Committee of the Regions – A Farm to Fork Strategy for a fair, healthy and environmentally friendly food system, 20.5.2020, COM(2020)381 final.

bees) and the lack of implementation of some key legislative instruments by MS envisaged to attain this objective.

§17.02 THE EU ACTIONS TO COMBAT THE LOSS OF HONEYBEE POPULATIONS

Neonicotinoids are active substances used in plant protection products to control harmful insects. They are systemic pesticides, which means that they are taken up by the plant and transported throughout the plant (leaves, flowers, roots and stems, as well as pollen and nectar); in doing so, they come into contact with insects when the latter feed on the plant. Neonicotinoids have been introduced in the early 1990s and have become the most widely used class of insecticides in the world.[13]

Since 2005 the EC has approved the use of five neonicotinoids in the EU (*see* Table 17.1 below). Between 2008 and 2009, substantial losses of honeybee colonies due to the accidental releases of those active substances were reported by several MS. As a consequence, in 2010, the EC adopted the first restriction to the use of clothianidin, thiamethoxam and imidacloprid, the three active substances that – as we will in the next section – have later been the object of conflict between the EC and some MS as regards the need to enact more severe restrictions.

Indeed, the debate around the so-called bee colony collapse disorder had already started in the mid-1990s in France where beekeepers had reported alarming clinical signs in bees after a pesticide containing imidacloprid was first used in the country.[14] A number of studies analysing the decline of honeybees were subsequently published; according to them, even though the possible causes are diverse (land use practices, climate change, intensive agriculture system etc.), most of them have linked such decline with the use of neonicotinoids.[15] The decline of honeybee population in the world and, more in general, of natural pollinators is a matter of serious concern. According to the EC Communication, 'EU Pollinators Initiative',[16] it is estimated that 5%-8% of current global crop production is directly attributed to animal pollination. In the EU alone, around 84% of crop species and 78% of wildflower species[17] depend, at least in part, on animal pollination. As regards the contribution of insect pollinators to

---

13. L. Maxim & J. van der Sluijs, 'Seed-dressing systemic insecticides and honeybees', in *Late lessons from early warnings: science, precaution, innovation*, *supra*, p. 369.
14. *Ibid.*
15. J.-M. Bonmatin, E.R. Bengsch, R. Charvet & M.-E. Colin, *Effets des produits phytosanitaires sur les abeilles. Analyse d'imidaclopride dans les pollens de maiös. Rapport de résultats n°14*, 2002, CNRS-CBM, INRA, Orléans; J.-M. Bonmatin et al., 'Behaviour of Imidacloprid in Fields: Toxicity for Honey Bees', in: E. Lichtfouse, J. Schwarzbauer, D. Robert (eds), *Environmental Chemistry: Green Chemistry and Pollutants in Ecosystems*, 2005, Springer, pp. 483-494; L. Chensheng, M. Kenneth Warchol, R.A. Callahan, *In Situ* Replication of Honey Bee Colony Collapse Disorder, *Bulletin of Insectology*, June 2012.
16. Communication from the Commission to the European Parliament, the Council, the European Economic and Social Committee and the Committee of the Regions, 'EU Pollinators Initiative', Brussels, 1.6.2018, COM(2018)395 final.
17. *Ibid.*

the EU's annual agricultural output, it is valued at almost EUR 15 billion.[18] A recent research article on insects confirmed that over 40% of insect species are threatened with extinction; one of the most affected species is bees.[19]

With a view to facing the decline in honeybee and its consequences, over the years, the EC has enacted a series of actions directly and indirectly addressing this phenomenon. The Habitats Directive adopted in 1992 aims at protecting a wide range of rare, threatened or endemic animal and plant species including, *inter alia*, fifty-six species of wild insect pollinators.[20] Together with the Birds Directive,[21] the Habitats Directive forms the Natura 2000 Network whose aim is to ensure the long-term survival of Europe's most valuable and threatened species and habitats listed under both directives.[22]

Starting from 2006, the EC has launched several initiatives to halt the loss of biodiversity, with growing attention towards the decline of wild pollinators.[23] With those initiatives the EC has tried to put in place a synergic strategy by including measures affecting pollinators in existing legislative frameworks in the areas of the environment, pesticides, agriculture, cohesion and research and innovation. The PPP Regulation adopted in 2009, for instance, has strengthened the requirements for the approval of active substances in relation to the exposure of honeybees. In particular, point 3.8.3 of Annex II to the PPP Regulation requires that the exposure of honeybees to the active substance in question be only 'negligible' or that its use does not have 'unacceptable acute or chronic effects on colony survival and development, taking into account effects on honeybee larvae and honeybee behavior'.[24]

The need to adopt a specific EU action on pollinators has brought the EC to adopt in 2018 the above-mentioned 'EU Pollinators Initiative'.[25] In this communication, the EC has tried to set long-term and short-term actions aiming at improving knowledge of pollinator decline, its causes and consequences; tackling the causes of pollinator decline; and raising awareness, engaging society-at-large and promoting collaboration.

---

18. *Ibid.*
19. F. Sánchez-Bayo & K.A.G. Wyckhuys, Worldwide Decline of the Entomofauna: A Review of Its Drivers, in *Biological Conservation*, Vol. 232, April 2019, pp. 8-27.
20. Council Directive 92/43/EEC of 21 May 1992 on the conservation of natural habitats and of wild fauna and flora, in *OJ* L 206, 22.7.1992, pp. 7-50.
21. Directive 2009/147/EC of the European Parliament and of the Council of 30 November 2009 on the conservation of wild birds, in OJ L 20, 26.1.2010, p. 7-25.
22. For further information on the Natura 2000 Network *see* the dedicated webpage of the EC website: https://ec.europa.eu/environment/nature/natura2000/index_en.htm.
23. Communication from the Commission – Halting the loss of biodiversity by 2010 – and beyond – Sustaining ecosystem services for human well-being, Brussels, 22.5.2006, COM(2006)0216 final; EU Communication from the Commission to the European Parliament, the Council, the Economic and Social Committee and the Committee of the Regions, Our life insurance, our natural capital: an EU biodiversity strategy to 2020, Brussels, 3.5.2011, COM(2011)244 final; Communication from the Commission to the European Parliament, the Council, the European Economic and Social Committee and the Committee of the Eegions, EU Biodiversity Strategy for 2030 Bringing nature back into our lives, Brussels 20.5.2020, COM(2020)380 final.
24. On that point, *see infra* note 39, Joined Cases T-429/13 and T-451/13, *Bayer CropScience AG and Others v. Commission*, para. 135.
25. *See supra* note 16.

All the policy measures envisaged by the EC so far, though, have not proven to be very effective. In the Special Report[26] dedicated to the EU actions to protect wild pollinators, the European Court of Auditors (ECA) found that the EU had not taken a consistent approach and its initiatives lack specific effective measures to attain the objective. Among other things, the report highlights as the emergency authorizations granted by some MS for banned neonicotinoids - clothianidin, thiamexotham and imidacloprid - have undermined the EU effort to reduce the use of those substances which have been found to be harmful to pollinators.

The next sections will focus on the analysis of the restrictions adopted by the EC for the use of the above-mentioned substances and on the weaknesses of the process for granting national emergency authorizations.

§17.03 THE RESTRICTIONS ON THE USE OF NEONICOTINOIDS IN THE EU

As mentioned in the previous section, five neonicotinoids have been approved in the EU since 2005. To date, only one has been approved without any restriction (acetamiprid);[27] among the others, one has been approved with restrictions (imidacloprid),[28] for two the authorization has expired (clothianidin and thiamethoxam),[29] while the renewal of the authorization for the last one (thiacloprid) has not been granted as the EC found that the approval criteria provided for in Article 4 of the PPP Regulation were no longer satisfied.[30]

26. European Court of Auditors, 'Protection of wild pollinators in the EU - Commission initiatives have not borne fruit', 15, 2020.
27. Commission Implementing Regulation (EU) 2018/113 of 24 January 2018 renewing the approval of the active substance acetamiprid in accordance with Regulation (EC) No. 1107/2009 of the European Parliament and of the Council concerning the placing of plant protection products on the market, and amending the Annex to Commission Implementing Regulation (EU) No. 540/2011, in OJ L 20, 25.1.2018, pp. 7-10.
28. Commission Implementing Regulation (EU) 2017/195 of 3 February 2017 amending Implementing Regulation (EU) No. 540/2011 as regards the extension of the approval periods of several active substances listed in Part B of the Annex to Implementing Regulation (EU) No. 686/2012 (AIR IV renewal programme), in OJ L L 31, 4.2.2017, pp. 21-24.
29. Commission Implementing Regulation (EU) 2018/84 of 19 January 2018 amending Implementing Regulation (EU) No. 540/2011 as regards the extension of the approval periods of the active substances chlorpyrifos, chlorpyrifos-methyl, clothianidin, copper compounds, dimoxystrobin, mancozeb, mecoprop-p, metiram, oxamyl, pethoxamid, propiconazole, propineb, propyzamide, pyraclostrobin and zoxamide in OJ L 16, 20.1.2018, pp. 8-10; Commission Implementing Regulation (EU) 2018/524 of 28 March 2018 amending Implementing Regulation (EU) No. 540/2011 as regards the extension of the approval periods of the active substances Bacillus subtilis (Cohn 1872) Strain QST 713, identical with strain AQ 713, clodinafop, clopyralid, cyprodinil, dichlorprop-P, fosetyl, mepanipyrim, metconazole, metrafenone, pirimicarb, Pseudomonas chlororaphis strain: MA 342, pyrimethanil, quinoxyfen, rimsulfuron, spinosad, thiacloprid, thiamethoxam, thiram, tolclofos-methyl, triclopyr, trinexapac, triticonazole and ziram, in OJ L 88, 4.4.2018, pp. 4-6.
30. Commission Implementing Regulation (EU) 2020/23 of 13 January 2020 concerning the non-renewal of the approval of the active substance thiacloprid, in accordance with Regulation (EC) No. 1107/2009 of the European Parliament and of the Council concerning the placing of plant protection products on the market, and amending the Annex to Commission Implementing Regulation (EU) No. 540/2011, in OJ L 8, 14.1.2020, pp. 8-11.

Table 17.1 EU Regulation of Neonicotinoids

Name of the Active Substance	*Approval*	*Restrictions*	*Status*
Thiacloprid	EC Directive 2004/99/EC	/	NOT APPROVED (Regulation (EU) 2020/23)
Acetamiprid	EC Directive 2004/99/EC	/	APPROVED until 28/02/2033 (Regulation (EU) 2018/113)
Clothianidin	EC Directive 2006/41/EC	EC Directive 2010/21/EU EC Regulation 485/2013 EC Regulation 2018/784	Authorization EXPIRED 31/1/2019
Thiamethoxam	EC Directive 2007/6/EC	EC Directive 2010/21/EU EC Regulation 485/2013 EC Regulation 2018/785	Authorization EXPIRED 30/4/2019
Imidacloprid	EC Directive 2008/116/EC	EC Directive 2010/21/EU EC Regulation 485/2013 EC Regulation 2018/783	APPROVED until 31/7/2022 (Regulation (EU) 2017/195)

The restrictions that have been adopted by the EC since 2010 have regarded the use of three active substances: clothianidin, thiamethoxam and imidacloprid.

The EC Directive 2010/21/EU provided for some restriction on the use of such substances as seed treatment and obliged MS to adopt mitigation measures to protect honeybees as well as to initiate monitoring programmes in order to verify their real exposure to such substances in areas extensively used by bees for foraging or by beekeepers.[31]

In 2012 new scientific information on the potential harmful effects of neonicotinoids on bees was published. As a consequence, according to Article 21 of the PPP Regulation, the EC decided to review the authorization approval of the three active substances.[32] It asked the European Food Safety Authority (hereinafter, 'EFSA') to assess this new information and to review the risk assessment as regards their impact on bees. The opinion of the authority was clear: for certain crops there are high acute risks for bees from pesticides containing the three substances under analysis. As a

31. Commission Directive 2010/21/EU of 12 March 2010 amending Annex I to Council Directive 91/414/EEC as regards the specific provisions relating to clothianidin, thiamethoxam, fipronil and imidacloprid, in OJ L 65, 13.3.2010, pp. 27-30.
32. *See supra* note 10.

consequence, the EC considered that the authorizations granted no longer satisfied the approval criteria provided for in Article 4 of the PPP Regulation;[33] thus, it proposed to further restrict the use of the three active substances by banning their use in bee-attractive crops (including maize, oilseed rape and sunflower) with the exception of uses in greenhouses, of treatment of some crops after flowering and of winter cereals, of any non-professional use, indoors or outdoors. The proposal of the EC was then submitted to the Standing Committee on the Food Chain and Animal Health in accordance with Article 78(2) of the PPP Regulation. The Committee, which is composed of representatives of the MS, did not deliver an opinion (thirteen MS voted in favour of the EC proposal, nine voted against and five abstained),[34] nor did it the Appeal Committee (fifteen MS voted in favour, eight against and four abstained).[35] The EC decided nonetheless to maintain its proposal, in the light of the urgency to protect the bees from the use of the three neonicotinoids; in May 2013, the Commission Implementing Regulation 485/2013 was thus adopted.[36]

The use of the three neonicotinoids has been further restricted in 2018, when the EC decided to adopt measures to completely ban their outdoor uses.[37] In this case the EC proposals were supported by a qualified majority of MS in the competent committee meeting.[38] As a result, only the use in permanent greenhouses has remained possible. In the light of these restrictions, Bayer and Syngenta who were the applicants for the renewal of approvals of, respectively, clothianidin and thiamethoxam withdrew their applications.

The restrictions to the use of the three neonicotinoids provided in Regulation 485/2013 are still the object of a case in front of the European Court of Justice. Indeed, in August 2013, the Bayer group, which produced and marketed imidacloprid and clothianidin in the EU, and Syngenta, which produced and marketed thiamethoxam, brought proceedings before the General Court seeking the annulment of the regulation.[39] Both actions were dismissed by the General Court in May 2018; now an appeal brought by the Bayer Group is pending before the Court of Justice.[40]

33. For an overview of the approval criteria laid down in Article 4 of the PPP Regulation, *see* D. Corona, 'The EU Regulatory Framework on Pesticides', in 'Contaminants and Restricted Substances', in: B. van der Meulen, B. Wernaart (eds), *EU Food Law Handbook*, 2020, Wageningen Academic Publishing, pp. 253-262.
34. SCFCAH Phytomharmaceuticals Plant Protection Products Legislation, meeting of 15 March 2013, CMTD(2013)236.
35. Appeal Committee Plant Protection Products Legislation, meeting of 29 April 2013, CMTD(2013)400.
36. Commission Implementing Regulation (EU) No. 485/2013 of 24 May 2013 amending Implementing Regulation (EU) No. 540/2011, as regards the conditions of approval of the active substances clothianidin, thiamethoxam and imidacloprid, and prohibiting the use and sale of seeds treated with plant protection products containing those active substances, in OJ L 139, 25.5.2013, pp. 12-26.
37. Commission Implementing Regulations (EU) 2018/783-784-785 of 29 May 2018, in OJ L 132, 30.5.2018, pp. 31 ss.
38. PAFF Committee – Pesticides Legislation, meeting of 27 April 2018, CMTD(2018)385.
39. Joined Cases T-429/13, *Bayer CropScience AG and Others v. Commission* and T-451/13, *Syngenta Crop Protection AG and Others v. Commission*, judgment of 17 May 2018, EU:T:2018:280.
40. Case C-499/18P, *Bayer CropScience AG and Others v. Commission*, case pending.

§17.04 THE EMERGENCY AUTHORIZATIONS GRANTED BY MS

Despite the ban, between 2013 and 2019, MS have adopted 206 emergency authorizations that have, de facto, almost quashed the effects of the EU ban (*see* Figure 17.1). Indeed, according to Article 53 of the PPP Regulation, in special circumstances and for a period not exceeding 120 days, MS are allowed to authorize the placing on the market of pesticides which are not authorized or are authorized for different uses than those initially granted where such measure appears necessary because of a danger which cannot be contained otherwise. Such national measures are not subject to any previous authorizations by the EC. The MS are only required to inform the other MS and the EC of the decisions taken by sending a notification template including information about research activities undertaken by the MS for all categories of dangers justifying the emergency. In particular, in the template they shall describe if there are alternative control measures to the use of the unauthorized substances and the research efforts undertaken and/or in progress, their aims, their funding, and their expected date of results, especially in cases of repeated notifications.

Figure 17.1 Emergency Authorizations Granted for Using Neonicotinoids Between 2013 and 2019

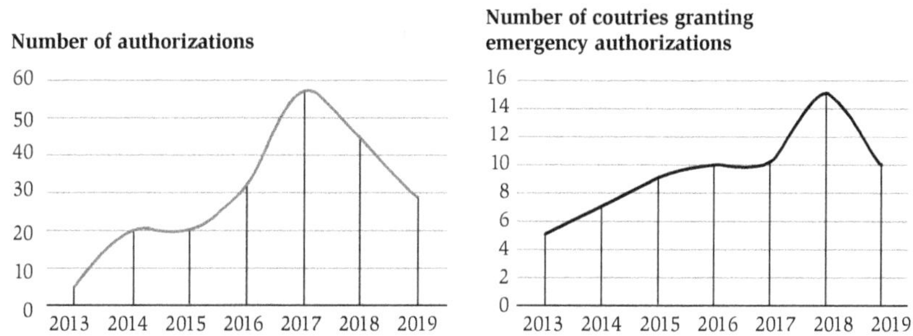

Source: ECA Special Report based on Commission information extracted from PPPAMS system on 24 January 2020.

According to the data collected by ECA related to 2018-2019, forty-three out of the seventy-nine notifications sent to the EC did not include any information on research activities conducted to find alternatives. Moreover, in 2018, when the complete ban for all outdoor uses was in place for the three neonicotinoids, fifteen MS allowed their use. In 2020 (despite the fact that the approval of clothianidin already expired and that of thiamethoxam has expired in April), ten MS have notified the EC of nineteen emergency authorizations involving their use applicable in the first half of the year.[41]

In consideration of the significant number of emergency authorizations granted by MS, according to Article 53(2) of the PPP Regulation, the EC asked EFSA to assess

41. Data available in the EU Commission database dedicated to MS emergency authorizations: https://ec.europa.eu/food/plant/pesticides/eu-pesticides-database/ppp/pppeas/screen/home.

the use of neonicotinoids repeatedly authorized in 2017 by Bulgaria, Estonia, Finland, Hungary, Lithuania and Romania. The authority published the related reports in 2018 and concluded that three MS, namely Hungary, Lithuania and Romania could have used either alternative active substances or even non-chemical alternatives (such as crop rotation or soil tillage); in the case of Bulgaria, EFSA said that the evaluation could not be finalized as the information provided by the country was not in line with what was requested by the related legislation.[42]

As a consequence of the EFSA reports, the EC requested these four MS to stop granting emergency authorizations for the three neonicotinoids; nonetheless, also in 2018 and 2019 Lithuania and Romania continued to grant such authorizations on the basis of Article 53 of the PPP Regulation. At this point, the EC, also in order to give a strong signal to all MS as regards the improper use of the emergency authorization tool, proposed two decisions requiring Romania and Lithuania to stop granting such derogations for future seasons in accordance with Article 53(3)(a) of the PPP Regulation. As previously seen as regards the adoption of Regulation 485/2013, the Standing Committee on Plants, Animals, Food and Feed did not deliver an opinion (the proposed decision concerning Romania obtained ten votes in favour, three against and fifteen abstentions; the decision concerning Lithuania obtained ten votes in favour, four against and fourteen abstentions),[43] nor did it the Appeal Committee (as for the proposed decision on Romania, eleven MS voted in favour, three against and fourteen abstained; as for the proposed decision on Lithuania, eleven MS voted in favour, four against and thirteen abstained).[44] Hence, considering it necessary to decide that both Romania[45] and Lithuania[46] may not repeat the granting of emergency authorizations for pesticides containing the three neonicotinoids, the EC decided nonetheless to adopt its decisions.

As we have seen before, the emergency authorizations involving the use of imidacloprid, clothianidin and thiamethoxam have also continued in 2020. In particular, as regards Romania, the latter has granted four emergency authorizations involving the use of the three neonicotinoids for corn and sugar beet seeds in the annual farming season.[47]

42. EFSA, Technical Reports published on 21 June 2018, Supporting publication 2018:EN-1416-1417-1418-1419-1420-1421-1422, available at: https://www.efsa.europa.eu/en/press/news/180621.
43. PAFF Committee, section Phytopharmaceuticals – Legislation, meeting on 21-22 October 2019, CMTD(2019)1189.
44. Appeal Committee – Phytopharmaceuticals-Legislation, meeting on 25 November 2019, CMTD(2019)1384.
45. Commission Implementing Decision (EU) 2020/152 of 3 February 2020 prohibiting Romania to repeat granting authorisations under Article 53(1) of Regulation (EC) No. 1107/2009 for the plant protection products containing the active substance clothianidin or imidacloprid for use on Brassica napus against Phyllotreta spp. or Psylliodes spp., in OJ L 33 of 5.2.2020, p. 16.
46. Commission Implementing Decision (EU) 2020/153 of 3 February 2020 prohibiting Lithuania to repeat granting authorisations under Article 53(1) of Regulation (EC) No. 1107/2009 for the plant protection products containing the active substance thiamethoxam for use on spring rape against Phyllotreta spp. and/or Psylliodes spp., in OJ L 33 of 5.2.2020, p. 19.
47. *See supra* note 41.

§17.05 CONCLUDING REMARKS

Notwithstanding the constant efforts of the EU to put in place effective strategy to protect bees and, ultimately, biodiversity, its actions have been weakened by a series of factors basically attributable to the non-compliance of MS.

Starting from the Sustainable Use Directive, as of today, MS have not yet set clear targets and reviewed their national plans necessary to ensure that the general principles of IPM are implemented by all professional users, despite the obligation to do so provided in by Article 14(4) thereof. This was the picture of the situation showed in the EC Report on the implementation of the Directive in 2017;[48] unfortunately, not much progress has been made according to the new Report of 2020, which says: 'the assessment of the implementation of IPM continues to be the most widespread weakness in the application of the Sustainable Use Directive. Consequently, Member States have failed to exploit the significant potential for greater adoption of IPM, including the more widespread adoption of non-chemical pest control techniques',[49] such as crop rotation and soil tillage.

Indeed, looking at the assessment made by EFSA on the emergency authorizations for the use of neonicotinoids granted by, in particular, Romania and Lithuania, the latter keep granting emergency authorizations according to Article 53 of the PPP Regulation without even exploring the possibility to use alternative non-chemical methods. The use of chemical pesticides is certainly effective and rapid, but in order to comply with the Sustainable Use Directive and, more in general, with the EU policy on pesticides, it should be left to those circumstances where no alternative methods or less impacting pesticides are available. To this aim, from one side, each MS should put in place a serious long-term strategy to reduce the use of chemical compounds in agriculture and, from the other, the EC should more strictly monitor the actual implementation of the Directive across the years. In 2012, indeed, the EC opened infringement proceedings against seventeen MS for not having communicated the transposition measures of the Directive.[50] All proceedings were subsequently closed, but without a proper check of the completeness or correctness of MS's transposition.[51]

The repeated use of the emergency authorizations is another signal of non-compliance of MS with the scope of PPP Regulation – that is, reducing the use of chemical compounds and protecting human and animal health and the environment – and, in particular, with Article 53 thereof. Such provision, indeed, has been conceived

48. Report from the Commission to the European Parliament and the Council on Member State National Action Plans and on progress in the implementation of Directive 2009/128/EC on the sustainable use of pesticides, Brussels, 10.10.2017, COM(2017) 587 final.
49. Report from the Commission to the European Parliament and the Council on the experience gained by Member States on the implementation of national targets established in their National Action Plans and on progress in the implementation of Directive 2009/128/EC on the sustainable use of pesticides, Brussels, 20.5.2020, COM(2020) 204 final.
50. Data available in the EU Commission database dedicated to infringement decisions: https://ec.europa.eu/atwork/applying-eu-law/infringements-proceedings/infringement_decisions/?lang_code=en.
51. ECA Special Report, Sustainable use of plant protection products: limited progress in measuring and reducing risks, 05/2020.

as an extrema ratio solution and not as a normal practice of MS, as the steady increase in the number of emergency authorizations notifications sent to the EC has been showing.[52] A number of reasons have been put forward to explain this trend, such as the emergence of new pests, the loss of a number of pesticides with widespread use which have to be replaced by other products containing different active substances etc.;[53] however, as the cases of the emergency authorizations granted by Romania and Lithuania show, MS often simply find easier to make use of Article 53 of the PPP Regulation than undertake research activities involving the use of less impacting substances or non-chemical alternatives to them.

Indeed, the EC has been granted the power to review the approval of active substances at any time in accordance with Article 21 of the PPP Regulation; by contrast, the possibility to adopt emergency authorizations has been left by the same regulation to the sole competence of MS. Moreover, the EC seems not equipped to perform a review of each single notification received in accordance with Article 53 of the PPP Regulation. At the same time, however, it is worth to note that the EC does not frequently trigger the mechanisms provided in by Article 53(2) and (3) of the Regulation, namely the possibility to ask EFSA for an opinion on the emergency authorizations and to take a formal decision imposing MS to stop granting them. The case of the use of neonicotinoids by some MS described in the previous section, indeed, has been the first example of this kind. Even though it seems quite unlikely that the EC will eventually decide to open infringement procedures against MS in case of misuse of Article 53 of the PPP Regulation, the adoption of a decision imposing to stop making use of such provision - such as those addressed to Romania and Lithuania - would mark a significant sign of the EC's determination to effectively pursue the objective of significantly reducing the use of pesticides in the EU as envisaged in the Farm to Fork Strategy.[54]

In its recent Communication on Chemicals Strategy, the EC stressed that 'EU must ensure full enforcement of its rules on chemicals both internally and at its borders, and promote them as a gold standard worldwide, in line with our international commitments'.[55] The challenge ahead for the EC is to find a way to reconcile this long-term vision on chemicals with the actual implementation of the legislative framework governing the use of pesticides by MS. In this scenario, the EC could find an important ally in EU citizens who are increasingly concerned about the impact of pesticides on human and animal health and the environment. In response to the European citizens' initiatives 'Ban glyphosate' the EC committed itself to improve its control over a correct and effective implementation of the Sustainable Use Directive

52. Commission Staff Working Group accompanying the Report from the Commission to the European Parliament and the Council on the Evaluation of Regulation (EC) No. 1107/2009 on the placing of plant protection products on the market and of regulation (EC) No. 396/2005 in maximum residue levels of pesticides, Brussels, 20.5.2020, SWD(2020) 87 final.
53. *Ibid.*
54. *See supra* note 12.
55. Communication on Chemicals Strategy for Sustainability Towards a Toxic-Free Environment, Brussels, 14 October 2020, COM(2020) 667 final.

and the PPP Regulation;[56] at the same time, however, an introduction of more strict targets, as regards the former legislative instrument, or an amendment making more difficult for MS to grant emergency authorizations, as regards the latter, are not in the pipeline. In 2019 a specific citizens' initiative on the protection of bees has been launched.[57] It aims, among alia, at: phasing out synthetic pesticides in EU agriculture by 80% by 2030, supporting a rapid increase in agro-ecological and organic practice, enabling farmer-based training and research into pesticide free farming. Looking at these proposals, they are similar to those contained in the Farm to Fork Strategy[58] proposed by the EC. Thus, an EU long-term strategy to protect bees and, more in general, biodiversity could be more successfully undertaken by closely involving citizens and making MS responsible in front of them for the non-compliance with the relevant EU policies.

56. For more information on this initiative, *see* the dedicated webpage on the EC website: https://europa.eu/citizens-initiative/initiatives/details/2017/000002_en.
57. For more information on this initiative, *see* the dedicated webpage on the EC website: https://europa.eu/citizens-initiative/initiatives/details/2019/000016_en.
58. *See supra* note 12.

CHAPTER 18

Biotechnology and Food and Feed Safety Assessment

Gijs A. Kleter & Harry A. Kuiper

Genetically modified (GM) crops have been grown at a large scale since the mid-1990s, particularly large commodity crops with herbicide tolerance and insect resistance as main traits. Before these crops can be brought onto the market, a thorough safety assessment has to be carried out as part of regulatory approval/consultation procedures in many countries around the world. Part of this assessment will consist of an evaluation of the safety of GM crop-derived foods and feeds for human and animal health, which is carried out according to internationally harmonized principles of the comparative assessment comparing the GM crop with a non-GM counterpart with a history of safe use. Recent developments in biotechnology, such as RNA interference and gene editing, may pose new challenges to the current safety paradigm with regard to proportionality to risks and the difficulty to distinguish new varieties from those that have been bred through conventional breeding and mutagenesis.

§18.01 INTRODUCTION

[A] Background

Since the introduction of the first genetically modified (GM) commodity crops grown at a large scale in Northern and Southern America in the mid-1990s, they have become increasingly adopted by farmers worldwide. The global acreage of farmland covered with GM crops amounted to 192 million hectares in 2018. Most of these are accounted for by the major commodity crops maize, soy, cotton and canola. The major traits with which these have been modified include herbicide tolerance and insect resistance.[1]

In case of herbicide tolerance, the crops have been modified so as to sustain otherwise lethal applications of broad-spectrum herbicides, such as those containing glyphosate. The mechanisms behind this resistance are the introduction of insensitive variants of the target enzymes that are otherwise inhibited by the active herbicide ingredient (e.g., enoylpyruvyl-shikimate-phosphate synthase, which is inhibited by glyphosate) or enzymes that metabolize the active ingredient to less or non-toxic forms (e.g., glyphosate oxidase). This way, these herbicides can be sprayed over the top of the tolerant crops to control the weeds growing in between the crop rows. This obviates the need to spray in a more directed fashion while also affording more flexibility in the timing of herbicide application.[2]

In the case of GM insect-resistant crops, a great part of these crops have been modified with genes coding for the expression of insecticidal Cry proteins from *Bacillus thuringiensis*. This is a soil bacterium that has also been used commercially as a natural pesticide in agriculture and forestry for decades. The Cry proteins occur within crystal inclusions, exhibiting toxicity against specific insect genera, such as lepidopterans (moths) or coleopterans (beetles), but not in humans or livestock animals. While both herbicide tolerance and insect resistance have dominated the market so far, newer traits that have emerged in the past few years include:

- increased quality (such as oilseeds producing oils that are more stable towards frying);
- enhanced nutritional value (such as oilseed producing omega-3-rich oils);
- increased yield;
- heightened resilience towards drought and other stressors.

Besides the relatively straightforward modifications with low-level expression of enzymes and insecticidal proteins, more recent modifications also straddle the engineering of metabolic pathways, and the introduction of transcription factors turning on or off multiple genes at once. In addition, the newest developments also show a trend towards other methods of genetic modification at the interface between the more 'traditional' methods of recombinant DNA methods and conventional and mutagenesis breeding, such as gene editing, oligonucleotide-directed mutagenesis, and RNA interference.[3]

It is conceivable that these new technologies raise questions as regards their safety not only for the crop itself but also for the humans and livestock animals that will ultimately consume these crops. Food and feed safety is a policy priority and has been enshrined in national laws and internationally agreed safety standards and protocols.

---

1. ISAAA, *Brief 54: Global Status of Commercialized Biotech/GM Crops: 2018* (Ithaca NY: International Service for the Acquisition of Agbiotech Applications, 2019), https://www.isaaa.org/resources/publications/briefs/54/default.asp.
2. ISAAA (Ithaca NY: International Service for the Acquisition of Agbiotech Applications, 2017), https://www.isaaa.org/resources/publications/pocketk/2/default.asp.
3. *Ibid.*

In many countries, potential risks of GM crops have to be assessed before they can be allowed onto the market. The new developments therefore raise the question as to whether the current paradigms still suffice to protect consumer and animal health and maintain the high level of quality and safety standards achieved over the past decades. Below we will highlight in further detail the food safety practices for human foods and animal feeds derived from GM crops that are currently pursued globally and explore to what extent they need to be adapted to accommodate two of these advanced biotechnological techniques, namely gene editing and RNAi.

§18.02 SAFETY ASSESSMENT

[A] Food and Feed Safety in General

Intoxication through food has been an issue since ages, such as those caused massively in the Middle Ages by consumption of cereals containing toxic natural compounds, the ergot alkaloids. These had been formed by moulds growing on these crops in structures known as 'mother corn' on cereals. It was only centuries later that the true cause was identified. In a broader sense, food safety science historically received an impetus in the nineteenth century with the introduction of procedures such as pasteurization and it has since evolved. Currently, internationally harmonized practices and standards are promulgated worldwide through the Codex Alimentarius, which is Latin for 'food law', a joint collaboration between the United Nations' Food and Agriculture Organization and the World Health Organization. Most countries of the world are Codex members and while it is not an authoritative organization, its outputs (standards, protocols, guidelines, codes of practice) are to be implemented at the national level by these members. This is because they will serve as primary reference for the World Trade Organization in case of disputes over the safety of internationally traded foods, such as when one nation bars the import of a given food from another nation for safety reasons.[4] This means that the foods should comply with Codex standards, while countries are still allowed to impose stricter measures as long as they are able to scientifically back them.

In its general principles, Codex Alimentarius distinguishes between risk assessment, risk management and risk communication, the combination of which is referred to as 'risk analysis'. Risk assessment is considered as being an objective, scientific process, through which risk professionals are able to provide expert advice to policymakers and other risk managers who have to reach decisions on whether and how to prevent, contain, and mitigate risks, weighing the pros and cons of the various options at hand. The latter may involve not only the actual risk but also other

4. World Trade Organization, *The WTO and the FAO/WHO Codex Alimentarius* (World Trade Organization, Geneva), https://www.wto.org/english/thewto_e/coher_e/wto_codex_e.htm.

socio-economic and policy considerations, such as costs, benefits, and policy priorities.[5]

Codex also provides a detailed description of a tiered approach towards risk assessment, with four distinct actions. According to Codex principles, risk assessment is composed of the following items:[6]

(1) hazard identification, with the hazard being an agent such as a chemical substance, microorganism or physical object, that has the capacity to cause harm to the consumer of a food product containing it;
(2) hazard characterization, which includes the exploration of the types of effects that can be caused by the hazard (e.g., toxicity symptoms), its kinetics and metabolism after uptake (for chemicals), dose-response relationships, etc.;
(3) exposure assessment, in which the actual intake of a particular hazard (substance, pathogen, etc.) is estimated. This usually entails the combination of data on the level of the hazard in the food consumed, and the amounts of the hazardous food ingested. A distinction is also to be made between chronic exposure and acute exposure, as well as the various subpopulations of consumers, particularly those at risk, such as infants and the elderly;
(4) risk characterization, in which the data from the previous steps are brought together to arrive at a weighed conclusion on the actual risk.

Food safety agencies around the world increasingly publish the outcomes of their risk assessments as well as the underlying data, which fits well with the recent trend towards increased transparency of public and other organizations.

[B] Safety Assessment of Biotechnology

Specifically for biotechnology, Codex Alimentarius has also published internationally harmonized guidelines for the risk analysis and the safety assessment of foods derived from crops obtained through modern biotechnology with the use of recombinant DNA in plants, microorganisms and animals.[7] The publication of the first guidelines in 2003 actually followed upon a long-standing activity of various international organizations such as the Organisation for Economic Cooperation and Development (OECD), Food and Agricultural Organization, and World Health Organization, which convened experts on the various subtopics to pursue consensus on risk assessment strategies. These organizations were forward looking in that they initiated these activities already

5. Codex Alimentarius Commission, *Procedural Manual* (Rome: Joint FAO/WHO Food Standards Programme, c/o Food and Agriculture Organization, 26th ed., 2018), http://www.fao.org/3/i8608en/I8608EN.pdf.
6. Codex Alimentarius, *supra* note 5.
7. Codex Alimentarius Commission, *Guideline for the Conduct of Food Safety Assessment of Foods Derived from Recombinant-DNA Plants* (Rome: Joint FAO/WHO Food Standards Programme, c/o Food and Agriculture Organization, 2003), http://www.fao.org/fileadmin/user_upload/gmfp/docs/CAC.GL_45_2003.pdf.

years before the first large-scale commercialization of GM commodity crops in the mid-1990s of the last century.[8]

The main principle of these guidelines is the comparative safety assessment. Central to this is the comparison of a GM product with its non-GM counterpart, with the latter having a history of safe use. The reason behind this approach is that foods are complex mixtures with a great variety of compounds that may have opposite effects, adverse or beneficial, depending on the dose in which they are ingested. Moreover, the safety of these foods has usually become established through a long history of use, in which the choice of food species, selection criteria by breeders, food processing methods, and record of safe consumption, for example, have helped to select those foods that on balance have positive impacts in terms of nutrition, taste and other features, without adverse health impacts. Given issues with bulkiness, palatability, and nutrient balance, it is also very difficult to test for the safety of food in animals. Unlike for purified chemical compounds, this can only be done with a limited dose range for whole foods for these reasons.[9] Figure 18.1 schematically summarizes this comparative, stepwise approach and the various aspects considered.

8. H.A. Kuiper et al., *Assessment of the food safety issues related to genetically modified foods*, 503-528 Plant J. 27 (2001), doi: 10.1046/j.1365-313X.2001.01119.x.
9. E.J. Kok et al., *Comparative safety assessment of plant-derived foods*, 98-113 Reg. Toxicol. Pharmacol. 50 (2008), doi: 10.1016/j.yrtph.2007.09.007.

Figure 18.1 Comparative Safety Assessment Approach for GM Crops

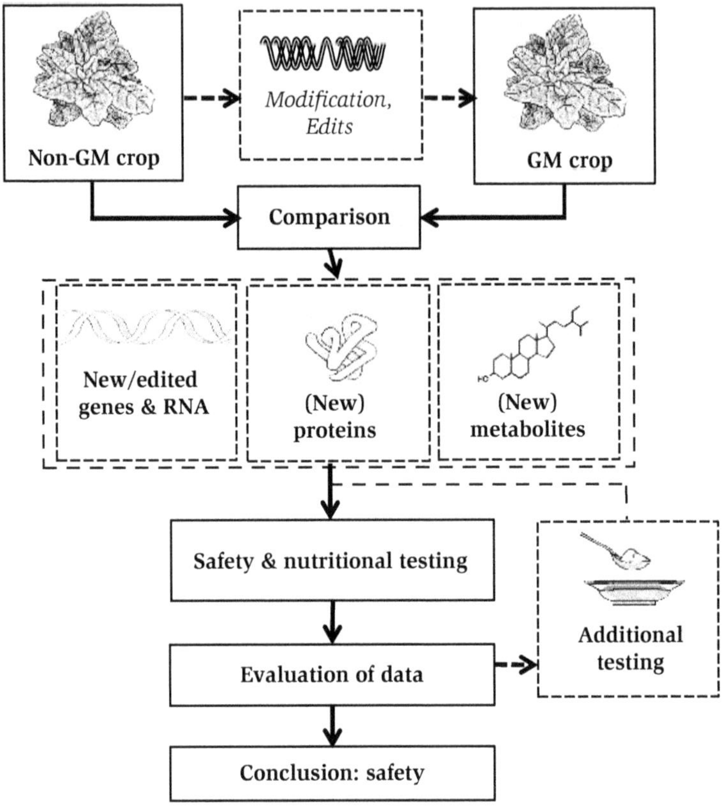

One of the initial steps in the safety assessment of genetically modified organisms (GMOs) is the so-called molecular characterization, for which there needs to be data on the genetic materials used to modify the host organism. This should include a description of the 'vector' used to transfer the DNA of interest into the host. For the genetic modification of crops, this may, for example, be a plasmid of circular DNA with the DNA sequences of interest. Such plasmids, if used in pure form have previously been produced in substantial amounts in recombinant bacteria for instance, and could be introduced into the host cells using methods such as the 'particle gun' or 'biolistics' in which cells or tissues are exposed to accelerated particles coated with DNA, be it plasmid DNA or linear DNA molecules prepared in vitro before the actual modification event. Another method would be to exploit the plasmid-transferring capabilities of *Agrobacterium tumefaciens*, the natural cause of crown gall tumours in a wide range of plants. These bacteria have the unique propensity to transfer DNA (the T-DNA from plasmids) to their host's genomes, tweaking them into producing compounds (such as octopine, nopaline) that can be utilized by the *A. tumefaciens* cells infecting them. Genetic engineers nowadays employ *A. tumefaciens* transformed with recombinant, disarmed plasmids, in which the T-DNA has been replaced with sequences of interest, so that the *A. tumefaciens* is not pathogenic anymore but will still transfer the T-DNA.[10]

The vectors used for these transformations can be prepared from the DNA from various different sources, including promoters, intervening sequences, coding sequences and terminators. For plants, for example, the 35S promoter of the Cauliflower Mosaic Virus is a constitutive promoter, that is, it is active across different plant tissues and development stages. This could then be combined with coding sequences from a gene from a completely different source, which also holds true for the translation termination signal. For the safety assessment, applicants need to provide an overview of the various elements brought together in the vector.

Besides the vector, the process and conditions used for modification of the host with DNA from the vector and the characterization of the inserted DNA also need to be described. Depending on the method used, the modification may have led to the insertion of one or more copies of the genes of interest, which may also have become rearranged or altered, such as insertion of multiple copies, rearranged orientation, truncation, point mutations, etc. This means that the inserted sequence may actually differ from the corresponding parts in the transformation vector. Various methods can be used to characterize the insert and its flanks. Information on the flanking sequences can be used to verify the actual location with a genome, provided enough annotated genome data for the particular host is available as from thousands of organisms whose DNA has already been sequenced. Methods commonly used for characterization of an inserted DNA sequence include Southern blotting, sequencing and Southern-by-Sequencing. In addition, Southern blots with probes specific for vector parts that are not intended to be introduced could give additional reassurance that these parts have indeed not been incorporated into the genomic DNA of the GM host.

Besides the characterization of the inserted DNA, its stability of inheritance over multiple generations also has to be confirmed in the case of crops. This will also help to check if inheritance follows patterns as expected according to Mendelian laws, another strong indication of stable integration and normal behaviour.

An important initial comparative analysis is that of the composition of the food and feed-producing organism. In these comparisons, the GMO is compared to a genetically close non-GM counterpart with a history of safety use, so that the alterations identified can more securely be attributed to the genetic modification and not to other confounding factors. In the case of GM insect-resistant maize producing an insecticidal protein from *B. thuringiensis*, the comparator would be near-isogenic, conventional, non-GM maize. Such compositional analysis is done in a targeted fashion, focusing on a wide, comprehensive range of compounds, straddling macronutrients (protein, fat, moisture, ash, carbohydrates, fibre), fatty and amino acids,

10. L.B.T. Matsaunyane, I.A. Dubery, Molecular Approaches to Address Intended and Unintended Effects and Substantial Equivalence of Genetically Modified Crops, in: M.S. Khan, K.A. Malik (Eds), *Transgenic Crops, Emerging Trends and Future Perspectives* (London & Rijeka: IntechOpen, 2019), doi: 10.5772/intechopen.80339, https://www.intechopen.com/books/transgenic-crops-emerging-trends-and-future-perspectives/molecular-approaches-to-address-intended-and-unintended-effects-and-substantial-equivalence-of-genet.

micronutrients (vitamins, minerals), secondary metabolites (e.g., phenolics), antinutrients (e.g., phytic acid, trypsin inhibitor), and toxins (e.g., potato alkaloids). Conceivably, given the great variety among crops and their roles in the human and animal diets, the key parameters to be analysed for each of these crops will vary from one crop to another.[11] The OECD Working Group on the Safety of Novel Foods and Feeds has developed a range of consensus documents in which key parameters for new crop varieties are recommended. These are used as authoritative documents by product developers and risk assessors across the globe. It is recognized that these are lists of suggested key parameters. These usually have to be done in samples of edible tissues from crops, such as grains, fruits and tubers for both humans and animals, and forage/vines for livestock animals.[12] These crops preferably have been grown in different locations, representing the breadth of conditions that will be encountered during commercial production. The data thus obtained will help to identify changes brought about both intendedly and unintendedly.[13]

Any changes observed then need to be explained in terms of relevance. One could compare these observed difference with the bandwidth of levels that commonly occur in crops consumed by humans and animals, indicative of what has been consumed safely over the past era. Such data could be derived from literature. The OECD consensus documents cited above, for example, provide ranges of such values (minimum-maximum) indicative of what the variability will be. Field trials performed for dossier applications usually also include commercial 'reference' varieties that are commonly grown in the test location region and adapted to the local conditions. The inclusion of these references allows for straightforward comparisons as other confounding factors are lacking since they are grown in the same locations, preferably in multiple, replicated plots following a randomized design. While difference testing is commonly performed, say using a Student's t-test or ANOVA with $p < 0.05$, this controls the error of finding false positives but still runs the risk of a high likelihood of false negatives. The statistical answer to this, as recommended by the European Food Safety Authority (EFSA) GMO Panel and EU legislation, is to perform an additional equivalence test, which controls the error of falsely concluding that something is equivalent when it is actually not. Towards this end the EFSA GMO panel recommended a statistical approach with details on how to design field trials, for example, as well as the number of reference varieties to be included. Different categories of outcomes can be discerned, depending upon whether the median of the distribution of the test item is within the confidence interval of reference varieties and whether the distribution curves overlap. These categories are: equivalent, equivalence more likely than not, non-equivalence more likely than equivalence, and non-equivalence, as well

11. Kok et al., *supra* note 9.
12. OECD, *Consensus Documents: Work on the Safety of Novel Foods and Feeds: Plants* (Paris: Organization for Economic Cooperation and Development), https://www.oecd.org/chemicalsafety/biotrack/consensus-document-for-work-on-safety-novel-and-foods-feeds-plants.htm.
13. Codex alimentarius, *supra* note 7.

as cases that are not amenable to equivalence testing due to too little variability or many values below the limit of quantification.[14]

Similar to the compositional analysis, a comparative approach can be followed to measure and compare the agronomic and phenotypic characteristics of the crop, which usually entails an analysis of crop physiology, development, performance and response to biotic and abiotic stressors. Among others, these usually include the number of plants that emerge in a field after sowing, the height, appearance, days until flowering/anthesis, lodging of the plants, maturity, grain weight, insect and pathogen infestation, among many others. The same statistical procedures can be applied as for the compositional analysis, albeit that for some semi-quantitative and qualitative measures, methods may need to be adapted. The food and feed safety implications of differences in agronomic and phenotypic characteristics may not be as obvious as for composition, but they still could provide indications of unexpected or unwanted changes caused by the genetic modification, which would then warrant further exploration into the underlying mechanisms

Based on the outcomes, it can be decided to carry out further testing. These tests usually comprise the following elements:[15]

(1) Potential toxicity: this entails a combination of methods, such as:
   - In silico: Bioinformatics-supported searches for homology between the amino acid sequence of a newly expressed protein and those of known toxic proteins.
   - In vitro: For newly expressed proteins, usually the digestibility by proteolytic enzymes (particularly pepsin) is tested. The underlying rationale is that resistant proteins might be more likely to be available for uptake and exertion of toxic action. For non-protein compounds, other types of in vitro tests might also be relevant such as cytotoxicity and genotoxicity, although these are not done routinely given that the safety of such compounds is either confirmed based on existing data or in vivo testing is done.
   - In vivo: with a review on responsible use of laboratory animals, this should only be done if there is a true necessity, For newly expressed proteins without a known safety profile, for example, the EFSA GMO panel recommended repeated subchronic oral toxicity studies. Commonly, 28-day studies are performed towards this end. Testing with the whole foods is considered to be too insensitive given the limitations

14. EU, *Commission Implementing Regulation (EU) No 503/2013 of 3 April 2013 on applications for authorisation of genetically modified food and feed in accordance with Regulation (EC) No 1829/2003 of the European Parliament and of the Council and amending Commission Regulations (EC) No 641/2004 and (EC) No 1981/2006*, 1-48 Off. J. L157 (2013), https://eur-lex.europa.eu/LexUriServ/LexUriServ.do?uri=OJ:L:2013:157:0001:0048:EN:PDF.
15. G.A. Kleter, M.Y. Noordam, Safety Assessment of Genetically Modified Foods (Chapter 3), in: R. Rai Vittal (Ed.), *Advances in Food Biotechnology* (Chichester: Wiley, 2016), 27-36, doi:10.1002/9781118864463.fmatter.

already indicated above, such as limited dose range, nutritional imbalance, palatability, etc.

(2) Potential allergenicity: as there are no single tests with a definitive yes-or-no answer to the question if something could become an allergen, the current assessment is based on a weight-of-evidence approach, taking into account various aspects that together give an impression of the likelihood of a newly expressed protein becoming an allergen or not. The focus is mainly on potential cross-reactivity with known allergens (e.g., proteins from nuts, milk, apple, crustaceans) while de novo allergies against the new protein will be much harder to predict. Similar to toxicity, these tests include:
   - Information on the allergenic nature of the gene donors.
   - In silico comparisons of protein sequences to those of known allergens.
   - In vitro digestibility.
   - In vivo testing, namely sera testing with sera from patients allergic to an allergen with which potential cross-reactivity has been identified.
   - In addition, the allergen repertoire and possible changes therein if allergenic hosts will be analysed, while it is realized that patients already allergic to the host will have to keep avoiding exposure to it, whether GM or not.

(3) Nutritional assessment may be needed in case of modifications affecting the nutrient profile, nutritional tests in target animals such as rapidly growing broilers, calves and swine.

(4) Potential for horizontal transfer is a common part of the environmental risk assessment, and mainly focuses on the likelihood of transfer of antibiotic resistance marker genes, if present. So far, no spontaneous transfer has been observed to occur between plant DNA and microbial DNA unless there is already some degree of homology between fragments of both, allowing for replacement of the microbial with plant DNA through homologous recombination. Yet arises the question of whether there is any increased risk over the current background of antibiotic resistance, which can already be pervasive, caused by such a hypothetical transfer, and whether the acquired resistance may interfere with antibiotic therapies. For genes that were previously widely used in genetic engineering, particularly kanamycin resistance genes, these have not been considered to pose any such risks. In addition, the selective advantages that other types of genetic material than antibiotic resistance genes may afford to new recipients will also have to be considered.

(5) Whole-product testing: In case there are still outstanding issues that cannot be resolved by the various tests described above for purified compound testing, testing of the whole food/feed product through animal feeding trials may provide additional reassurance of the absence of adverse effects of consumption of the new product. These may entail the repeated-dose oral toxicity type of testing in laboratory rodents, for example, and also nutritional performance studies in model livestock species such as the rapidly growing broiler chicken (reaching maturity within forty-two days), swine and bovine. Yet Codex Alimentarius and others caution that there are several drawbacks inherent to

whole-product testing. Part of this relates to the fact that whole foods are complex mixtures of a wide range of compounds, each with a particular risk profile of positive and negative impacts on the health of the animal, depending on their level within the food and the dosage provided to the animal. Unlike for purified chemical testing, administering the test compounds in a wide dose range to the animals will not be possible due to nutrient imbalance but also limited intake by the animals, bulkiness, and palatability. Moreover, such trials can only be justified by a clear hypothesis of specific adverse effects as pointed out by various documents from experts consulted by EFSA and from European research projects (GRACE, G-TwYST, GMO90+) that have the added value of animal feeding trials and possible alternatives.

§18.03 IMPLICATIONS OF NEW DEVELOPMENTS FOR THE SAFETY ASSESSMENT

[A] Specific Safety Features of RNA Interference

There has actually been already a long-standing record of application of 'gene silencing' in crop biotechnology, with virus-resistant papaya, cucurbits, and potatoes being among the first commercialized GM crops in the 1990s. Virus resistance had been achieved in these cases by introducing analogues of partial viral sequences coding for coat proteins, helicases, and other targets in viruses. This effectively interferes with the replication and further proliferation of these viruses when they infect the particular crop. A notable, more recent development is that of RNAi built into crops in order to afford protection against external insect pests, e.g., corn rootworm-resistant maize expressing dsRNA that targets the *Snf7* gene encoding an intracellular protein tracking pathway protein. Besides virus resistance, also modified fatty acid and starch compositions have been achieved in oilseed crops (soybean, canola) and potato, respectively.[16]

While the effect of 'gene silencing' was already known and exploited, the finer mechanisms of it, called 'RNA interference', have become increasingly elucidated over time. In the case of RNA interference (RNAi), the first step entails the formation or introduction of double-stranded RNA (dsRNA) molecules into a eukaryotic cell. These can have the form of, for example, hairpin-shaped RNA molecules that fold unto themselves, forming double-stranded segments. Alternatively, single-stranded RNA molecules can be introduced (e.g., from introduced transgenes) that bind to complementary native messenger RNA (mRNA). These dsRNA molecules will be processed by biochemical machinery that recognizes, binds and degrades dsRNA, as a kind of immune system. This can be ascribed to the fact that in nature, dsRNA molecules are also formed as large molecules in, for example, cells infected by certain viruses. Also

16. A. Younis et al., *RNA interference (RNAi) induced gene silencing: a promising approach of hi-tech plant breeding*, 1150-1158 Int J. Biol Sci. 10(10) (2014), doi:10.7150/ijbs.10452.

smaller dsRNA complexes occur but then between native cell-encoded mRNA and microRNA molecules, which modulate endogenous gene activity by triggering the same control system. This system can also be exploited by genetic engineers to silence genes of interest within a host crop but also to express dsRNA molecules that will act on essential genes of pathogens (fungi) or pests (insects) attacking the host, provided these are sensitive towards uptake and processing of the exogenous RNA, such as is the case in certain species of beetles and moulds.[17]

This recent re-surge of RNAi applications in GM crops raises the question as to whether these to be assessed differently from the mainstream of those expressing transgenes, given that there is no expression of newly expressed proteins but suppression in some cases. An important aspect when considering the action of the dsRNA introduced into the GM recipient is that of possible off-target silencing of other genes besides the ones targeted. To this end, prediction of off-target effects can be achieved using bioinformatics, searching for nucleotide sequence homologies between the introduced RNA molecule and counterparts from the transcriptome of the recipient host.[18] This also has to take into account the stringency of the conditions under which alignment has to occur in order to be processed by the cellular machinery (including components known as Dicer and Argonaut). While generic search algorithms and databases can be helpful, various specialized resources do exist, particularly to help scientist design RNA molecules for silencing genes for experimental purposes (not GM crops). Any off-target effects of relevance would also conceivably become evident during comparative analysis for effects in the crop, including an extensive analysis of compositional parameters as usually carried out for the pre-market risk assessment of GM crops.

While the primary stage for off-target effects is the plant host, there has been a substantive discussion around possible targets in the consumer based on some yet unconfirmed reports on uptake into serum and off-target effects of plant RNA (not from GM plants). Arguably, for this to attain relevant levels at the target and for gene inhibition to happen, many physiological and other barriers would have to be overcome,[19] as discussed to a great extent in a review commissioned by the EFSA GMO Panel.[20]

---

17. *Ibid.*
18. EPA SAP, *A Set of Scientific Issues Being Considered by the Environmental Protection Agency Regarding: RNAi Technology: Program Formulation for Human Health and Ecological Risk Assessment, FIFRA Scientific Advisory Panel Meeting, January 28, 2014 (SAP Minutes No. 2014-02)* (Washington D.C.: United States Environmental Protection Agency, Office of Pesticide Programs, 2015), https://www.epa.gov/sites/production/files/2015-06/documents/012814minutes.pdf.
19. J.S. Petrick et al., *Safety assessment of food and feed from biotechnology-derived crops employing RNA-mediated gene regulation to achieve desired traits: a scientific review,* 167-176 Regul. Toxicol. Pharmacol. 66(2) (2013), doi: 10.1016/j.yrtph.2013.03.008.
20. A. Dávalos et al., *Literature Review of Baseline Information on Non-coding RNA (ncRNA) to Support the Risk Assessment of ncRNA-Based Genetically Modified Plants for Food and Feed, EFSA Supporting Publication EN-1688* (Parma: European Food Safety Authority), doi: 10.2903/sp.efsa.2019.EN-1688, https://efsa.onlinelibrary.wiley.com/doi/10.2903/sp.efsa.2019.EN-1688.

[B] Specific Safety Features of Gene Editing

Gene-editing technologies frequently rely on so-called site-directed nucleases (SDNs), such as CRISPR Cas9 (clusters of regularly interspaced short palindromic repeats – CRISPR associated protein #9), which can cause small edits. In the case of SDN-1 enzymes, these edits are formed upon repair of double-strand breaks through non-homologous end-joining, resulting in small insertions and/or deletions ('indels') of DNA at the breakage site. This repair can also be done in a more controlled fashion by adding a oligonucleotide template containing sequences complementary to those bordering the breakage point, referred to as SDN-2. The template thus guides the repair system into introducing specific mutations (e.g., base replacements). In case of SDN-3, an added, exogenous DNA fragment is inserted at the breakage site, similar to transgenesis although with greater precision than for other recombinant DNA procedures.[21]

Rapid developments in gene editing have been taking place since 2012 owing to the appearance of the so-called CRISPR Cas9, besides the incumbent transcription activator-like effector nuclease and zinc finger nuclease enzymes that had already been in use for some time but that were more cumbersome to use. This system actually has its origin in a bacterial defence system against bacteriophages, much in the way of RNAi. CRISPR actually refers to fragments complementary to DNA from previously invading bacteriophages that have been stored in the bacterial host's genome and allows the host to recognize it upon repeated infection. The Cas (CRISPR-associated) enzyme then will bind the targeted sequence complexed to the CRISPR RNA and create double-strand DNA breaks. By tweaking this system, genetic engineers employ a Cas enzyme complexed with an artificial RNA molecule that acts as bait for a target sequence of interest. This CRISPR-Cas complex can then be used as SDN-1, 2 or 3 modalities.[22]

In the case of oligonucleotide-directed mutagenesis, a template is also used and introduced into the plant cells. This oligonucleotide template molecule (~20-100 bp) is complementary to the endogenous target sequence, except for one or a few bases. Upon binding and aligning of the template to the endogenous DNA, the mismatches between the non-complementary bases will be recognized by the intrinsic DNA repair system, and the mismatches replaced. This will result in point mutations, which will be passed onto subsequent generations after cell division. Herbicide-resistant canola developed through oligonucleotide-directed mutagenesis, for example, is currently being marketed in Norther America.[23]

There has been a discussion in various countries on how to assess and regulate gene-edited organisms. Particularly, such discussion focus on a question such as whether or not there is a similarity with natural mutations and/or mutations that could

21. T. Sprink et al., *Regulatory hurdles for genome editing: process- vs. product-based approaches in different regulatory contexts*, 1493-1506 Plant Cell Rep. 35(7) (2016), doi: 10.1007/s00299-016-1990-2.
22. *Ibid.*
23. *Ibid.*

have been achieved through traditional mutagenesis.[24] The studies performed so far are heterogeneous and few have indeed detected off-target mutations of gene editing performed in plants, indicating the necessity to further explore this in more depth.[25] This is crucial in the discussions on whether these gene-edited organisms need to be assigned the same regulatory status as GM organisms obtained with recombinant DNA or not. Important in this regard is also that a higher precision is expected in some cases, given that specific sequences are targeted, such as that concluded for SDN-3-mediated modifications by the EFSA GMO Panel.[26] Similar to what is written for RNAi above, possible off-target effects of editors can be predicted by bioinformatics, while also improved editors of CRISPR Cas with higher specificity have been created. It is conceivable that mutations may target changes in, e.g., composition, both intended and unintended. The comparative assessment would then still be valid to assess the extent and possible consequences of these changes. Yet the fact that many of the mutations cannot be unequivocally discerned from those caused by natural processes or conventional breeding bears its implications for detectability and traceability.[27]

§18.04 CONCLUDING REMARKS

In conclusion, a robust harmonized approach is applied to the safety assessment of GM crops, most of which currently have been obtained through recombinant DNA techniques involving the introduction of transgenic elements. Notwithstanding the differences in regulations between nations, this safety approach, as enshrined in Codex Alimentarius guidelines, has been successfully and satisfactorily applied over an extended period. These may be challenged, though, by new developments at the interface between conventional and transgenic breeding, such as the use of dsRNA and gene editors, which may call for adjustments to ensure that a risk-proportionate safety regime that is future-proof can still be applied to novel foods entering the market without unnecessarily stifling innovation.

24. M.F. Eckerstorfer et al., *Plants developed by new genetic modification techniques-comparison of existing regulatory frameworks in the EU and non-EU countries*, 26 Front. Bioeng. Biotechnol. 7 (2019), doi: 10.3389/fbioe.2019.00026.
25. D. Modrzejewski et al., *What is the available evidence for the range of applications of genome-editing as a new tool for plant trait modification and the potential occurrence of associated off-target effects: a systematic map*, 27 Envir. Evidence 8 (2019), doi: 10.1186/s13750-019-0171-5.
26. EFSA GMO Panel, *Scientific opinion addressing the safety assessment of plants developed using zinc finger nuclease 3 and other site-directed nucleases with similar function*, 2943 EFSA J. 10(10) (2012), doi: 10.2903/j.efsa.2012.2943.
27. L. Grohmann et al., *Detection and identification of genome editing in plants: challenges and opportunities*, 236 Front. Plant Sci. 10 (2019), doi: 10.3389/fpls.2019.00236.

Index

A

Action Plan, 315–317
Active substances, 341. *See also* Neonicotinoids
Adequate food, 171
  indirect recognition of right to, 179–180
  right to, 172–173, 176, 177, 179, 182, 184
Agenda 2030, 58, 69, 173–174
  nutrition
    climate change and, 75
    education and, 76
    equity, gender equality and inclusion, 72–73
    infrastructure, 72
    peace and stability, 74
    poverty and economy, 74–75
Agreement on agriculture (AoA), 12
Agreement on the application of sanitary and phytosanitary measures (SPS), 103
Agricultural law. *See* EU agricultural law
Agricultural market information system (AMIS), 14
Agriculture. *See also* Common Agricultural Policy; EU Agricultural Law
  activity, 270
  defined, 269–270
  products, 269–270
Agrobacterium tumefaciens, 358–359
Agro-food production, 335
Animal feed safety, 354–356
Animal Protection Index, 152
Animal protein
  empowering consumers on health and environmental costs, 250
  equalize consumption through feed carbon-pricing, 249–250
Animal welfare, 147–150
  animal protection and legal gap
    Animal Protection Index, 152
    Brambell Report, 150–151
    ethical debate, 151
  COVID-19 pandemic, 149
  current legal framework
    anti-cruelty laws, 153
    AWA, 153
    CAK, 156
    EU animal welfare law, 154
    Humane Methods of Livestock Slaughter Act, 155
  defined, 160
  international standards
    intensive farming, 157
    international environmental law, 156–157
    IPCC Report on climate change and land, 157
    livestock production, 157
    OIE (*see* World Organization for Animal Health (OIE))
Anti-cruelty laws, 153
Appropriate level of sanitary or

phytosanitary protection (ALOP), 122
Australia and New Zealand
AUST L products, 206
complementary medicines, 207
complementary medicines (CM), 204–206
FSANZ, 202
general level health claims, 202–203
market failure, 206–207
self-substantiated general level claims (Australia), 203
self-substantiated general level food-health relationship claim, 203–204

B

Bali Package, 13
Ban glyphosate, 350–351
Bees
emergency authorizations granted by MS, 347–348
EU actions to combat loss of honeybee populations
bee colony collapse disorder, 342–343
Habitats Directive, 343
neonicotinoids, 342
pollinators, 343
use of pesticides and protection of bees, 345
wild pollinators, 343
restrictions to use of neonicotinoids in EU, 344–346
Best available techniques (BAT)
food waste and, 330–331
Best Environmental Management Practices for the food and beverage manufacturing sector (BEMPs food and beverage), 319
Bilateral investment treaties (BITs), 23–25
Biodiversity, 85–86
bees protection (*see* Bees)
loss in livestock production, 238–239
loss of, 341, 343
Biological role claims, 196–197
Biowaste, 311, 313
Birds Directive, 343
Body mass index (BMI), 61
Brambell Report, The, 150–151
By-product, 312

C

Canada
disease risk reduction claims, 196
functional food, 195–196
general health claims, 196
nutrient function claims, 196–197
Carcinogenic impact
livestock production, 239–240
CESCR General Comment No. 12: The Right to Adequate Food (Article 11) (GC 12), 19–20, 20, 27, 38–39
Chemicals in meat production, 240–241
Circular economy package
Directive 2018/851, 324–325
food waste definition
Directive 2018/851, by, 324–325
Report 2017, by, 323–324
Report 2017, 323–324
SDG and, 315–317
Climate change policy, 75
environmental and health targets, integration of, 248–249
empowering consumers on health and environmental costs of animal protein, 250
feed carbon-pricing, equalize animal protein consumption through, 249–250
food waste on, 309
greenhouse gas emissions on food losses, 309
international trade law, and GATT/WTO law, 246–247

labelling and other consumer information measures, 247–248
Codex Alimentarius, 91, 121, 178, 355
achievements
expectations requiring continued work, 98–99
HACCP, 99
score card, 98
challenges, 105
committee structure, 95–96
consensus
adopted by, 97–98
challenges to, 107–108
cooperation, achievement through, 95
food labelling system, 104
food safety, 104
fraud, opportunities for, 108
general principles, 355–356
issues, overcoming, 105
kava *(piper mythesticum),* 106
makgeolli and alcoholic beverages, 106–107
mandate, 94
never-ending task, 108–109
nutrition and labelling standards, 104
prehistory to Greek, from, 93
risk-analysis system, 104
risk assessment, 355–356
safety assessment of biotechnology, 356–357
SDGs and, 100–101
decent work and economic growth: SDG8, 100–101
food waste and management of chemicals: SDG12, 101
good health and well-being: SDG3, 100
no poverty: SDG1, 100
partnerships for SDGs: SDG17, 101
zero hunger: SDG2, 100
status of standards, 94–95
strategic plan 2020-2025, 101–102
work process and scientific basis, 96–97
Codex Austriacus, 93
Codex Food labelling system, 104
CoExtra project, 245
Committee on Economic, Social and Cultural Rights (CESCR), 19–20, 38–39, 42
Committee on World Food Security (CWFS), 5, 9, 10, 20, 21, 26, 27
Common agricultural policy (CAP), 261
non-exclusive areas of union competence, and, 263–264
on objectives of, 265–266
price policy, 280–281
direct payments, 282–283
institutional prices, 282
price regulation, 281
SPS, 282
structure policy
aid to agriculture, 286
anti-productive purposes and rural development, 286–287
Communication in November 2017, 289–290
Conference of Member States, 283–284
cross compliance, 289
Directive 159/1972, 284
economic reasons, 283
political reasons, 283
social reasons, 283
two-pillar CAP, 287–288
Competition law
agricultural derogation
Regulation 26/62, 275
Regulation 1308/2013, 276–277
general rules, 273–275
Compliance
with food law (*see* Control, inspection and approval procedures)
SPS, 132
Concentrated animal feeding operations (CAFOs), 148, 150
Conformity assessment. *See* Control, inspection and approval procedures
Consensus

challenges to, 107
Codex Alimentarius, 97–98
Control, inspection and approval procedures, 125–128
de facto barrier to entry to food supply chains, 127
legal framework for, 128–129
rules on, 130
equitable fees, 139–140
non-discrimination, 133–139
prior approval systems, 140–145
undue delay, 131–133
scope of application, 129–130
Controlled atmosphere killing (CAK), 156
Convention on Biological Diversity (CBD), 85–86
Convention on the Elimination of All Forms of Discrimination Against Women (1979), 18
Convention on the Rights of Persons with Disabilities (2006), 18
Convention on the Rights of the Child (1989), 18
COVID-19 pandemic, 6, 52–55
Animal welfare, 149
dual challenge of malnutrition and, 78–79
EU agricultural law, 292–293
EU food law, 259–261
food waste production and management, effect on, 334–336
micronutrient deficiency, 61
nutrition and, 63–64
demand-side impacts, 65
supply-side impacts, 64–65
overweight, 61
Crop biotechnology
safety assessment of
Agrobacterium tumefaciens, 358–359
biolistics, 358
Codex Alimentarius, 356–357
comparative approach for GM crops, 358
GM product *vs.* non-GM, 357, 359–360
inserted DNA, 359
molecular characterization, 358–359
nutritional assessment, 362
particle gun, 358
potential allergenicity, 362
potential for horizontal transfer, 362
potential toxicity, 361–362
whole-product testing, 362–363

D

Decade of action on nutrition, 57–58
Agenda 2030 (*see* Agenda 2030)
COVID-19, 63–64
demand-side impacts, 65
supply-side impacts, 64–65
deterioration of world nutrition status, 61–63
dual challenge of malnutrition and COVID-19, 78–79
food systems, 66–68
global priority, 58–59
governance and accountability systems, 71
health systems, 68
international trade, 69–71
key players, 59–60
malnutrition
micronutrient deficiency, 61
overweight, 61
undernutrition, 60–61
social protection, 69
stocktaking of implementation of, 76–78
supportive environment, 71
Decision on the Special Safeguard Mechanism (SSM) for Developing Countries (Decision on SSM), 13
Declaration of Nyéléni (2007), 32
Declaration of the World Food Summit: five years later (2002), 7

Declaration of the World Summit on Food Security (2009), 7
Deterrence, 215, 223, 224
Dietary Supplement Health and Education Act (DSHEA), 193, 201
Dietary supplements, 193–195
Direct Regulation
agencies and legislation, 216–223
food-borne illness, challenges, 218–220
international trade, challenges, 220–221
new legislation to address challenges, 222–223
state and local agencies, 223
Discrimination, 122–123
Doha Round of multilateral trade negotiations (Doha Development Agenda or Doha Round), 12
Domestication, 82

E

Economy, 74–75
Education, 76
Emergency authorisations
granted by MS, 347–348
Empiric breeding, 82–83
End of waste (EoW), 312
Environment. *See also* Climate change policy; Health and environment
animal protein diet, 236–239
feedstuffs trade
delocalization of environmental costs, 243
international transport costs, 243
supportive, 71
Equitable fees, 139–140
Equity, 72–73
EU agricultural law
agricultural activity, 270
agricultural products, 269–270
agriculture defined, 269–270
Annex I of TFEU, 270–272
common agricultural policy and non-exclusive areas, 263–264
COVID-19, 292–293
shared competence
CMOs, 266
food law, 268–269
Lisbon Treaty, 267, 268
meaning, 266–267
national rights, 266
single regulatory framework, 266–267
special features, 272–273
competition law, 273–277
prohibition of public aid, 277–279
trends in
CAP, 291–292
Communication of November 2017, 291
COVID-19 outbreak, 292–293
liberalism, 290–291
promotional function, 290
withdrawal agreement, 291
EU food law
COVID-19, 259–261
Farm to Fork strategy, 260–261
GFL, 259–260
Green Deal, 260
revival of food security, 261
cross-cutting sector, 255
defined, 253–254
essence of, search for, 257–259
EU regulatory capacity, 254–255
General Food Law (GFL) Regulation, 254
historical perspective, 254
sources and coverage
GFL, 255–256
Member States, 257
SPS Agreement, 255–256
EU guidelines on food donations (Notice). *See* Notice
European Centre for Diseases Prevention and Control (ECDC), 336

European Food Safety Authority (EFSA), 297
European Green Deal, 262, 341
FFTF strategy, 329–330
food quality, 330
food value chain, 328–329
labelling, 330
Target 12.3 SGDs, 330
'use by' and 'best before' food labels, 330
European Platform for Food Loss and Food Waste (FLW Platform), 316
European Union (EU)
agricultural law (*see* EU agricultural law)
food defined, 198
food law (*see* EU food law)
function health claims, 199
health claims pertaining to children, 199
risk reduction claims, 199
supplements defined, 198–199

F

FAO Code of Conduct for Responsible Fisheries (1995), 27
FAO Food Price Index (FFPI), 335
FAO/IBP Technical Conference, 83–84
FAO Sugar Price Index, 335
FAO technical meeting of 1961, 83
FAO Voluntary Guidelines for the Responsible Management of Planted Forests (2006), 27
Farmed animals
OIE standards analysis on, 160–161
terrestrial code and welfare of
broiler chicken production systems, 163–164
limits of OIE standards, 164
slaughter of animals, 162
transportation of animals, 163
violent acts, 163
welfare at slaughter of birds, 163
welfare of beef cattle, 163
Farm to fork strategy, 260–261, 341, 351
Fat and obesity
livestock production, 241
Federal Food, Drug, and Cosmetic Act (FD&C Act), 218
Feed carbon-pricing, 249–250
Feedstuffs trade
environment, on
delocalization of environmental costs, 243
international transport costs, 243
health, on
consumers and foreign farmers, impact on, 244–245
herbicides and pesticides, lack on, 244–245
no traceability of imported foodstuffs, 245–246
protein deficit, 242–243
Food
defined, 198, 295, 310
fragile commodity, 92
need for, 92
Food and agricultural organization (FAO), 5, 58, 148, 306, 340
Food and drug administration (FDA), 191–192
Foodborne illness, 223–225
Food business operators obligations, 298
Food donations, 320–321
Food for specified health uses (FOSHU), 200–201
Food insecurity, 5–6
COVID-19 pandemic, 6
global food security (*see* Global food security)
hunger, 5
Food law, 295–296. *See also* EU food law
European Commission, by, 178
1997 Green Paper on the general principles, 178
Food loss, 306
Food safety, 92, 353–355
European Union

declination of food safety, 300–301
defectiveness of food product, 300–301
food chain, 300
food defined, 295
hygiene package, 298
hygiene requirements, 298–299
label, 301
liability for food product defects, 300
microbiological criterion, 299
RASFF, 302–303
risk, 297
traceability, 300
unsafe foods, 296
voluntary indications, 301
HACCP, 99
Joint FAO/WHO Food Standards Programme, 94
standards, 103
US, 213–232
WTO law, under
Brazil, 115–116
discrimination, 122–123
food-borne hazards, 113–114
international standards, 120–121
scientific basis, 118–120
SPS Agreement (*see* Sanitary and phytosanitary (SPS) Agreement)
TBT Agreement, 114
Food Safety Modernization Act (FSMA), 222, 227, 229, 230, 232
Food security, 296
2050, 82
domestication, 82
empiric breeding, 82–83
genetic resources movement, 83–84
Green Revolution, 83
Mendel's Laws, 83
components of, 62–63
right to food and (*see* Right to food)
system, 47
Food sovereignty, 42, 51–52
Food stamp programme, 183
Food storage, 328
Food supply chain
food loss, 306
Food systems, 66–68
COVID-19 pandemic, 52–55
Food trade
Codex standards facilitating trade, 103
harmonization and challenges to implementation, 102–103
sardines, 103–104
Food use for social innovation by optimising waste prevention strategies (FUSIONS), 317–318
Food waste in EU food law, 305–307, 336–337
BAT conclusions and, 330–331
circular economy package (*see* Circular economy package)
2018/851 Directive, measures taken after
Action Plan, 326
Circular Economy Package, 325
food donations, 326–328
food storage, 328
refrigerating appliances, 328
SDGs Target 12.3, 326
sustainable bioeconomy, 325–326
zero waste, 326
European Green Deal (*see* European Green Deal)
first (soft) regulatory actions in Europe
food defined, 310
Food Safety Regulation, 311
Landfill Directive, 310
food loss, 306
food waste legal definition, 317–321
Member States, legal developments in, 331–334
quantitative estimates
annual food waste, 307–308
climate change, 309
greenhouse gas emissions, 309
population growth, 308–309
Fragmentation
lack of coordination, and, 35–36

normative and institutional, 37
Framework law, 176–179
Fraud, 108
From farm to fork strategy, 329–330
Functional food
nutrient function claims, 196–197
probiotic claims, 197

G

Gadda Law, 333
Gender equality, 72–73
Gene editing
CRISPR Cas, 365
mutations, 365–366
oligonucleotide-directed mutagenesis, 365
site-directed nucleases (SDNs), 365
General agreement on tariff and trade (GATT), 11–14, 134–135
General Food Law (GFL) Regulation, 254
EU food law, 255–257
Generic health claims, 188, 208
Genetically modified (GM), 353–354. *See also* Crop biotechnology
herbicide tolerance, 354
insect-resistant crops, 354
Genetically modified organisms (GMOs), 89–90
Genetic resources movement, 83–84
Genome editing techniques, 90
Global food security
food insecurity and international trade law
institutional developments, 13–15
normative developments, 11–13
progress and challenges, 15–17
ICESCR, 7–8
institutional developments, 8–10
international human rights law
institutional developments, 20–21
normative developments, 17–20
progress and challenges, 21
international investment law
institutional developments, 27–28
normative developments, 23–27
principles of responsible investments, 25–27
private sector investment in agriculture, 21–23
problems and challenges, 28–29
international legal instruments, 7–8
normative developments, 6–8
progress and challenges, 10–11
world food conferences, 6–7
Global food system, 4–5
international law, and, 29
challenges, 32–36
debates, 30–31
democratic deficit, 33–34
fragmentation and lack of coordination, 35–36
legal landscape, 30
monitoring/enforcement challenges, 34–35
sovereignty concerns, 32–33
Global governance, 3, 29, 35–37
food security, 35–36
normative and institutional fragmentation, 37
Globalization of food and agricultural systems, 38
Global Report of Food Crisis 2020, 6
Global value chains (GVCs), 130–131
Governance and accountability systems, 71
Green chemistry, 90
Green Deal, 262
Greenhouse gas (GHG) emissions
food losses, 309
livestock production, 235, 237
Green Paper, 313–314
Green Revolution, 83

H

Habitats Directive, 343
Hazard Analysis and Critical Control Point (HACCP) system, 99
Hazard analysis critical control points

(Haccp), 298
Health and environment, 336
empowering consumers on health and environmental costs of animal protein, 250
feed carbon-pricing, equalize animal protein consumption through, 249–250
Health Canada, 195
Health claims
classification, 188
nature of, 188–189
regulation
Australia and New Zealand, 202–207
Canada, 195–198
European Union, 198–200
Japan, 200–202
United States, 191–195
regulatory objectives and pitfalls
market failure, 189–190
negative externalities, 190–191
non-market failure sources, 189–190
policymakers, 191
positive spillover effects, 191
structure/function, 188–189
Health foods, 188
Canada, 195–198
consumption-related market failures
information asymmetry, 190
negative externalities, 190–191
Japan, 200–202
Health infrastructure, 72
Health systems, 68
High-Level Panel of Experts on Food Security and Nutrition (HLPE), 36
Horizon 2020, 331
Humane Methods of Livestock Slaughter Act, 155
Human rights. *See* International human rights to food
Human Rights Council (HRC), 20
Hygiene package, 155, 298

I

Inclusion, 72–73
Industrial Emission Directive (IED), 330–331
Industrial livestock production, 148–149
Infrastructure, 72
Integrated pest management, 339–342
Intergovernmental panel on climate change (IPCC), 62
Interim Commission, 8
International Board for Plant Genetic Resources (IBPGR), 84
International Conference on Nutrition, 6
International Covenant on Economic, Social and Cultural Right (ICESCR), 7–8, 18, 42, 171
International Finance Corporation (IFC), 22
International food law, 4–5
global food security (*see* Global food security)
global food system, 29–36
International food standards
Codex, 121
SPS Agreement, 120–121
International Fund for Agricultural Development (IFAD), 9
International human rights to food, 171–174
International Panel on Climate Change (IPCC), 309
International Seed Treaty, 34–35
International trade, 69–71
law
GATT/WTO law, process and production methods and likeness under, 246–247
labelling and other consumer information measures, 247–248
International Treaty on Plant Genetic Resources for Food and Agriculture (IT-PGRFA), 86–89
multilateral system of access and benefit-sharing, 87

Nagoya Protocol, 88–89
SMTA, 87–88
International working group (IWG), 172–173

J

Japan
food for specified health uses (FOSHU), 200–201
foods with function claims (FFC), 201
food with nutrient function claims (FNFC), 201
FOSHU, 200–201
Joint Expert Committee on Contaminants and Food Additives (JECFA), 93–94
Joint FAO/WHO Food Standards Programme, 94
Judiciary, 179–180
defensor del pueblo de la nación, 181–182
Donald Trump's Executive Order on immigration, 182–183
food stamp programme, 183
human rights crisis, 181
Nepalese Court, 182
quasi-judicial appeals, 183–184
reasonableness, 180–181
right to food, 181
Toba community, 181–182

K

Kava *(piper mythesticum),* 106
Kitchen waste, 313–314

L

Land
livestock production, 238
Legal history, 3–39
Legal liability, 223–225
Life.Food-.Waste.StandUp, 333
Lisbon Treaty, 267, 268
Livestock production
animal protein diet, 235–236
carcinogenic impact, 239–240
chemicals in meat production, 240–241
environment, on, 236–239
fat and obesity, 241
GHG emissions, 237
health, on, 239–242
land and water, use of, 238
waste and biodiversity loss, 238–239
zoonotic infections, 241–242

M

Makgeolli, 106–107
Malnutrition
dual challenge and COVID-19, 78–79
micronutrient deficiencies, 61
overweight, 61
undernutrition, 60–61
Manhattan Principles, 149
Market failure
concept of, 189
consumption-related, 190
information asymmetry, due to, 190
Marrakesh Agreement, 14
Meat production
chemicals in, 240–241
Mendel's Laws, 83
Micronutrient deficiencies, 61
Millennium development goals (MDGs), 57
Ministerial Decision on Export Competition, 13

N

Nagoya Protocol, 88–89
Nairobi Ministerial Conference, 13
Nairobi Package, 13
Nationally determined contributions (NDC), 234
National ownership, 59
Neonicotinoids, 342

described, 342
emergency authorizations granted by MS, 347–348
restrictions to use in EU, 344–346
New governance, 214–216
New Zealand. *See* Australia and New Zealand
Non-communicable diseases (NCDs), 58
Non-discrimination
GATT, 134–135
less favourable treatment, 138
likeness, 135–136
like product analysis, 136–137
SPS Agreement, 137
TBT Agreement, 138–139
violation of provision, 134
Non-strain-specific probiotic claims, 197
Notice
surplus food defined, 320
Nutrient function claims, 196–197
Nutrition. *See also* Agenda 2030
COVID-19 and, 63–64
demand-side impacts, 65
supply-side impacts, 64–65
deterioration of world nutrition status, 61–63
food systems and, 66–68
global priority, 58–59
governance and, 71
health systems and, 68
international trade and, 69–71
key players, 59–60
multi-sectorial nature, 66–71
social protection and, 69
supportive environment and, 71
Nyéléni meeting, 31

O

Obesity. *See* Fat and obesity
Oligonucleotide-directed mutagenesis, 365
One Welfare concept, 165
One World, One Health (2008), 149
Optional Protocol to the ICESCR (Optional Protocol), 20, 21
Orange Fiber project, 332
Organic waste, 313
Overweight, 61

P

Paris Agreements, 234
Peace, 74
Peasants' Charter, 47–48
Pesticides, 340–342
active substance, 341
neonicotinoids (*see* Neonicotinoids)
Plant genetic resources (PGR), 86–87
Poultry scalding, 164
Poverty, 74–75
Precautionary principle, 118–119, 123
Pre-marketing approval. *See* Prior-approval systems
Principles for Responsible Agricultural Investment that respects rights, livelihoods and resources (PRAI)
principles, 25–26
Principles for Responsible Investment, 26
Prior-approval systems, 140–141
conformity assessment procedures, 141
disciplines, 143–144
risk assessment and review, 144–145
situations distinguished, 141–142
SPS Agreement, 143
tolerance determination and, 142–143
Probiotic claims, 197
Process and production methods (PPMs), 246
Product-specific health claims, 188
Prohibition of public aid
agricultural derogation, 279–280
aid defined, 278
General European Legislation
ban on public aid, 277
block exemption regulations, 279
public provenance of aid, 278

restitution, 279
Protection of health
health claims (*see* Health claims)
right to food (*see* Right to food)
Protein deficit, 242–243
Pure Food and Drug Act, 218

Q

Quality infrastructure, 72

R

Rapid alert system for food and feed (RASFF), 302–303
ReFED, 335
Report 2017
food waste defined, 323–324
Right to food, 41–42, 169–171, 184–185
challenges for, 52–55
COVID-19 pandemic, 52–55
expansion of, 50–52
food and health in international law, link between, 48–50
framework laws and monitoring mechanisms, 176–179
international human rights to food, 171–174
judiciary, 179–184
sectorial, regional and constitutional, 174–176
successive interpretation of, 46–48
travaux preparatoires, 42–46
UN General Assembly Declaration, 50–52
Voluntary Guidelines, 50–51
RNA interference (RNAi)
applications in GM crops, 364
double-stranded RNA (dsRNA) molecules, 363–364
gene silencing, 363
off-target effects, 364
virus resistance, 363
Rome Declaration on World Food Security (1996), 7, 18, 31
Rome Treaty, 273

S

Safe food, 49, 50, 98, 185
Sanitary and phytosanitary (SPS) agreement, 114–118, 127
ALOP, 122
control, inspection and approval procedures (*see* Control, inspection and approval procedures)
measures, 117–118, 123, 255
prior-approval systems, 143
risk assessment, 121–122
scope of, 116–118
Scientific basis, 118–120
Scientific discoveries, 208
SDGs of Agenda 2030
Target 12.3, 306, 315, 331
Social protection, 69
Soft law instruments, 8
Stability, 74
Standard material transfer agreement (SMTA), 87–88
State of Food Security in the World 2020, 5
Stockpiling Decision, 13
Strain specific probiotic claim, 197
Student's t-test, 360
Supermarketization, 35
Supplements
defined, 198–199
dietary, 193–195
Supportive environment, 71
Surplus food
defined, 320
Sustainable development goals (SDGs), 8
circular economy package and, 315–317
Action Plan, 317–319
FLW Platform, 316
SDGs Target 12.3, 315
Codex Alimentarius Commission and,

100–101
decent work and economic growth: SDG8, 100–101
food waste and management of chemicals: SDG12, 101
good health and well-being: SDG3, 101
no poverty: SDG1, 100
partnerships for SDGs: SDG17, 101
zero hunger: SDG2, 100

T

Technical barriers to trade (TBT), 103, 138–139
Terrestrial Animal Health Code, 160
The Jungle, 218
Travaux preparatoires, 42–46
Treaty on the Functioning of the European Union (TFEU)
Annex I, 270–272
Tripartite's Commitment, 159

U

UK's Animal Welfare Act (AWA), 153
Undernutrition, 60–61
Undue delay
conformity assessment procedure, 132
GVCs, 130–131
precautionary approach, 132–133
UN General Assembly Declaration, 50–52
UN Human Rights Council. *See* Human Rights Council (HRC)
United Nations (UN) Conference on Food and Agriculture in Hot Springs, Virginia, United States (1943 Conference), 6, 8
United Nations Declaration on the Rights of Peasants and Other People Working in Rural Areas (UNDROP), 32–33
United States (US), 213–214
dietary supplements, 193–195
FDA, 191–192
food safety
challenges, 231–232
Direct Regulation, 216–223
legal liability, 223–225
new governance approach, 214–216
private regulation, 225–231
nutrient content claims, 193
qualified health claims, 192–193
risk reduction health claims, 192
structure/function claims, 193
Universal Declaration of Human Rights (UDHR), 6, 17–18, 42–43, 171
Universal Declaration on Hunger, 7, 9
Paragraph 1, 18
Unsafe foods, 296
Uruguay Round, 12
goal, 15

V

Vegea, 332
Vision: 2020 UK Roadmap to Zero Food Waste to Landfill, 332–333
Voluntary Guidelines, 50–51

W

Waste
food (*see* Food waste in EU food law)
livestock production, 238–239
Waste Framework Directive (WFD), 306, 336
2008/98/EC, 311–312
biowaste, 313
by-product, 312
Green Paper and, 313–314
organic waste, 313
recycling society, 312
Water
livestock production, 238
White Paper on Food Safety, 254
World Bank Group, 22
World Declaration on Nutrition and Plan of Action for Nutrition, 7, 35

World Food Conference of 1974, 6
World Food Council, 9
World Food Program (WFP), 36
World Food Summit (WFS), 58
World Food Summit Action Plan (1996), 7, 18
World Food Summit Declaration (2002), 18
World Food Summit of 1996, 6
World Food Summit Plan of Action, 8, 18
World Health Organization (WHO)
  Global Burden of Disease Project, 240
  risk assessment (2007), 106
World Organization for Animal Health (OIE), 158–159
  analysis on farmed animals, 160–161
  Global Animal Welfare Strategy (2017), 159–160
  international standards, 160
  Strategic Plan for 2001-2005, 159
  Terrestrial Animal Health Code, 160
  Tripartite's Commitment, 159
World Summit on Food Security of 2009, 6
World Trade Organization (WTO), 12, 15–17
  control, inspection and approval procedures (*see* Control, inspection and approval procedures)
  law under food safety, 113–123
  Tenth Ministerial Conference in Nairobi, 13
WTO Agreement, 12

Z

Zoonotic infections
  livestock production, 241–242

ENERGY AND ENVIRONMENTAL LAW & POLICY SERIES

1. Stephen J. Turner, *A Substantive Environmental Right: An Examination of the Legal Obligations of Decision-makers towards the Environment*, 2009 (ISBN 978-90-411-2815-7).
2. Helle Tegner Anker, Birgitte Egelund Olsen & Anita Rønne (eds), *Legal Systems and Wind Energy: A Comparative Perspective*, 2009 (ISBN 978-90-411-2831-7).
3. David Langlet, *Prior Informed Consent and Hazardous Trade: Regulating Trade in Hazardous Goods at the Intersection of Sovereignty, Free Trade and Environmental Protection*, 2009 (ISBN 978-90-411-2821-8).
4. Louis J. Kotzé and Alexander R. Paterson (eds), *The Role of the Judiciary in Environmental Governance: Comparative Perspectives*, 2009 (ISBN 978-90-411-2708-2).
5. Tuula Honkonen, *The Common but Differentiated Responsibility Principle in Multilateral Environmental Agreement's: Regulatory and Policy Aspects*, 2009 (ISBN 978-90-411-3153-9).
6. Barbara Pozzo (ed.), *The Implementation of the Seveso Directives in an Enlarged Europe: A Look into the Past and a challenge for the Future*, 2009 (ISBN 978-90-411-2854-6).
7. Henrik M. Inadomi, *Independent Power Projects in Developing Countries: Legal Investment Protection and Consequences for Development*, 2010 (ISBN 978-90-411-3178-2).
8. Nahid Islam, *The Law of Non-Navigational Uses of International Watercourses: Options for Regional Regime-Building in Asia*, 2010 (ISBN 978-90-411-3196-6).
9. Yasuhiro Shigeta, *International Judicial Control of Environmental Protection: Standard Setting, Compliance Control and the Development of International Environmental Law by the International Judiciary*, 2010 (ISBN 978-90-411-3151-5).
10. Katleen Janssen, *The Availability of Spatial and Environmental Data in the European Union: At the Crossroads between Public and Economic Interests*, 2010 (ISBN 978-90-411-3287-1).
11. Henrik Bjørnebye, *Investing in EU Energy Security: Exploring the Regulatory Approach to Tomorrow's Electricity Production*, 2010 (ISBN 978-90-411-3118-8).
12. Véronique Bruggeman, *Compensating catastrophe victims: A Comparative Law and Economics Approach*, 2010 (ISBN 978-90-411-3263-5).
13. Michael G. Faure, Han Lixin & Shan Hongjun, *Maritime Pollution Liability and Policy: China, Europe and the US*, 2010 (ISBN 978-90-411-2869-0).

14. Anton Ming-Zhi Gao, *Regulating Gas Liberalization: A Comparative Study on Unbundling and Open Access Regimes in the US, Europe, Japan, South Korea and Taiwan*, 2010 (ISBN 978-90-411-3347-2).
15. Mustafa Erkan, *International Energy Investment Law: Stability through Contractual Clauses*, 2011 (ISBN 978-90-411-3411-0).
16. Levente Borzsa´k, *The Impact of Environmental Concerns on the Public Enforcement Mechanism under EU law: Environmental protection in the 25th hour*, 2011 (ISBN 978-90-411-3408-0).
17. Tarcísio Hardman Reis, *Compensation for Environmental Damages under International Law: The Role of the International Judge*, 2011 (ISBN 978-90-411-3437-0).
18. Kim Talus, *Vertical Natural Gas Transportation Capacity, Upstream Commodity Contracts and EU Competition Law*, 2011 (ISBN 978-90-411-3407-3).
19. WangHui, *Civil Liability for Marine Oil Pollution Damage: A Comparative and Economic Study of the International, US and Chinese Compensation Regime*, 2011 (ISBN 978-90-411-3672-5).
20. Chowdhury Ishrak Ahmed Siddiky, *Cross-Border Pipeline Arrangements: What Would a Single Regulatory Framework Look Like?*, 2012 (ISBN 978-90-411-3844-6).
21. Rozeta Karova, *Liberalization of Electricity Markets and Public Service Obligations in the Energy Community*, 2012 (ISBN 978-90-411-3849-1).
22. Sandra Cassotta, *Environmental Damage and Liability Problems in a Multilevel Context: The Case of the Environmental Liability Directive*, 2012 (ISBN 978-90-411-3830-9).
23. Mark Wilde, *Civil Liability for Environmental Damage: Comparative Analysis of Law and Policy in Europe and US*, 2013 (ISBN 978-90-411-3233-8).
24. Bernard Taverne, *Petroleum, Industry and Governments: A Study of the Involvement of Industry and Governments in Exploring for and Producing Petroleum*, 2013 (ISBN 978-90-411-4563-5).
25. Anton Ming-Zhi Gao & Chien Te Fan (eds), *Legal Issues of Renewable Energy in the Asia Region: Recent Developments in a Post-Fukushima and Post-Kyoto Protocol Era*, 2014 (ISBN 978-90-411-4856-8).
26. Sabina Manea, *The Instrumentalization of Property: Legal Interests in the EU Emissions Trading System*, 2014 (ISBN 978-90-411-5420-0).
27. Joseph A. Tolorunse, *Protection of Property Rights in Discovered Petroleum Reservoirs*, 2014 (ISBN 978-90-411-5604-4).
28. Katelijn Van Hende, *Offshore Wind in the European Union: Towards Integrated Management of Our Marine Waters*, 2015 (ISBN 978-90-411-5613-6).
29. Ken'ichi Matsumoto & Anton Ming-Zhi Gao (eds), *Economic Instruments to Combat Climate Change in Asian Countries*, 2015 (ISBN 978-90-411-5408-8).

30. Eduardo G. Pereira & Damilola S. Olawuyi (eds), *Practical Considerations to Negotiate an Enforceable Joint Operating Agreement under Civil Law Jurisdictions*, Second Edition, 2020 (ISBN 978-94-035-0664-7).
31. Ying Shen, *China's Way to Carbon Emissions Reduction: The Choice of Regulatory Instruments and Its Legal Challenges*, 2015 (ISBN 978-90-411-6049-2).
32. Roy Andrew Partain, *Environmental Hazards from Offshore Methane Hydrate Operations: Civil Liability and Regulations for Efficient Governance*, 2017 (ISBN 978-90-411-8730-7).
33. Anton Ming-Zhi Gao & Chien-Te Fan (eds), *The Development of a Comprehensive Legal Framework for the Promotion of Offshore Wind Power: The Lessons from Europe and Pacific Asia*, 2017 (ISBN 978-90-411-8397-2).
34. Tade Oyewunmi, *Regulating Gas Supply to Power Markets: Transnational Approaches to Competitiveness and Security of Supply*, 2018 (ISBN 978-90-411-9869-3).
35. Huseyin Cagri Corlu, *Application of Anti-manipulation Law to EU Wholesale Energy Markets and Its Interplay with EU Competition Law*, 2018 (ISBN 978-90-411-9603-3).
36. Kaisa Huhta, *Capacity Mechanisms in EU Energy Law: Ensuring Security of Supply in the Energy Transition*, 2019 (ISBN 978-94-035-1451-2).
37. Maria João C. Pereira Rolim, *Reconciling Energy, the Environment and Sustainable Development: The Role of Law and Regulation*, 2019 (ISBN 978-94-035-1461-1).
38. Eduardo G. Pereira, Alexandra Wawryk, Heike Trischmann, Catherine Banet & Keith B. Hall (eds), *The Regulation of Decommissioning, Abandonment and Reuse Initiatives in the Oil and Gas Industry: From Obligation to Opportunities*, 2020 (ISBN 978-94-035-0693-7).
39. Rasa Engstedt, *Handbook on European Nuclear Law: Competences of the Euratom Community under the Euratom Treaty*, 2021 (ISBN 978-94-035-2830-4).
40. Cinzia Caporale, Ilja Richard Pavone & Maria Pia Ragionieri (eds), *International Food Law: How Food Law can Balance Health, Environment and Animal Welfare*, 2021 (978-94-035-1761-2).

www.ingramcontent.com/pod-product-compliance
Lightning Source LLC
Chambersburg PA
CBHW071237230926
51849CB00001B/134
* 9 7 8 9 4 0 3 5 1 7 6 1 2 *